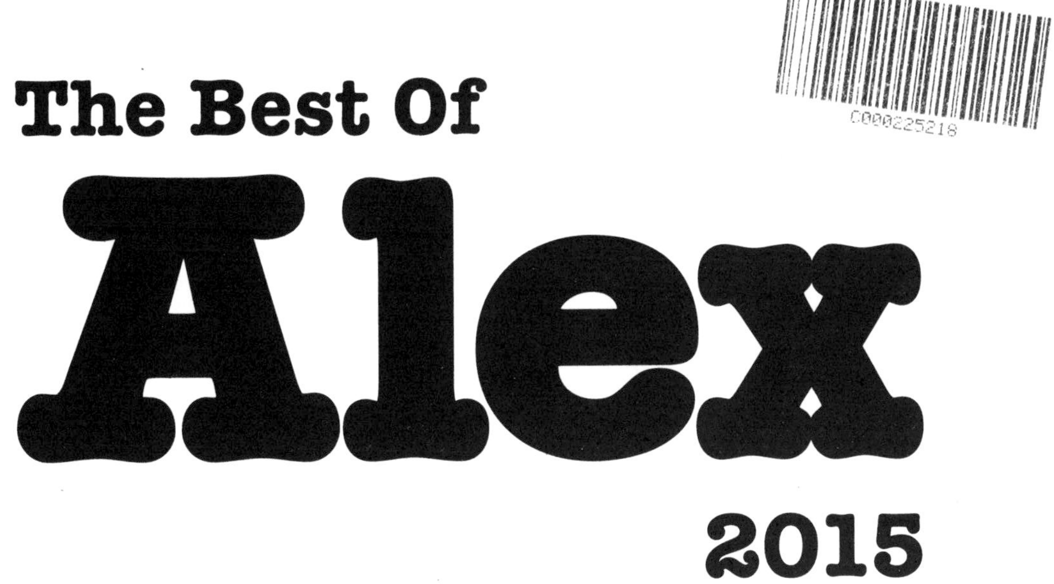

Charles Peattie & Russell Taylor

Masterley Publishing

The Best Of

Alex

2015

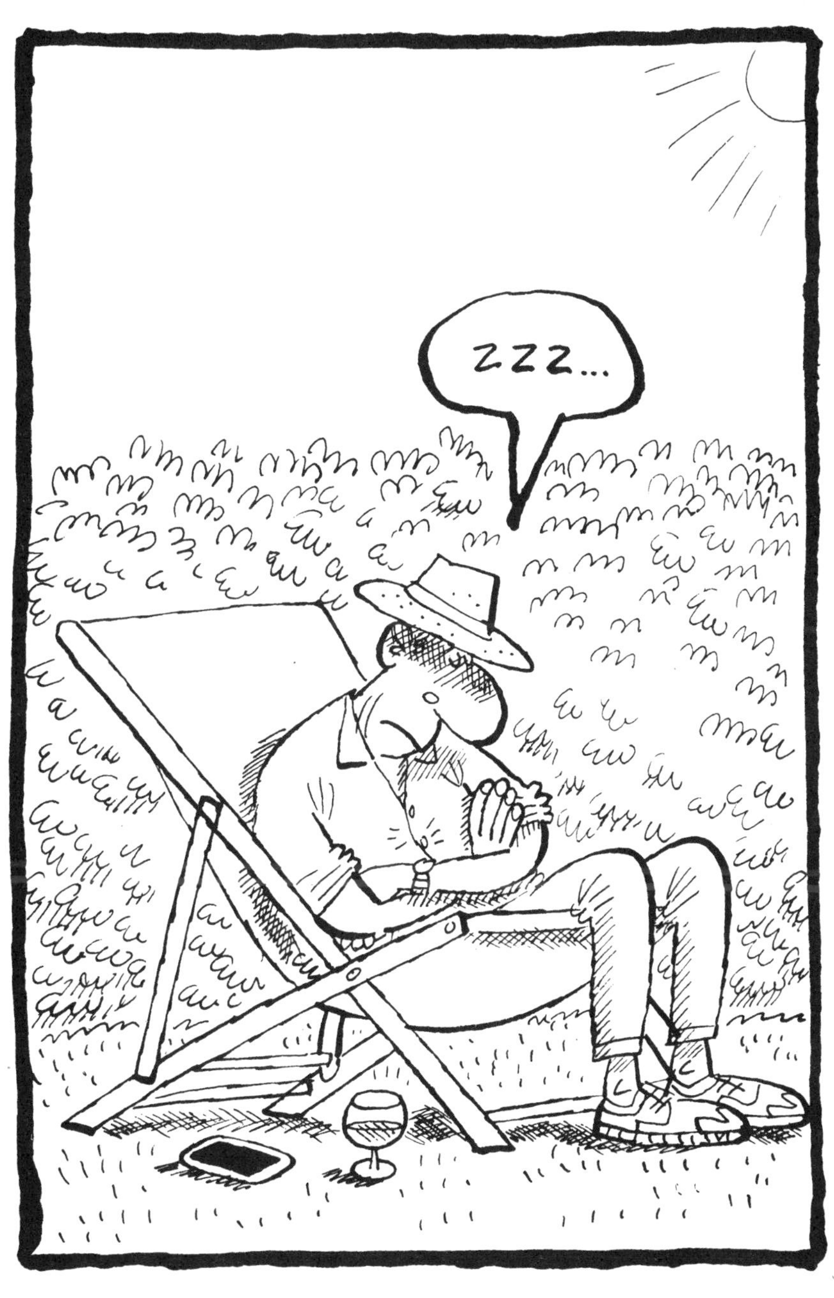

First Published in 2015 by MASTERLEY PUBLISHING

Layout and Artwork: Suzette Field and Louise Newton

ISBN: 978-1853759352
Printed and bound by CPI Group (UK) Ltd, Croydon, CR0 4YY

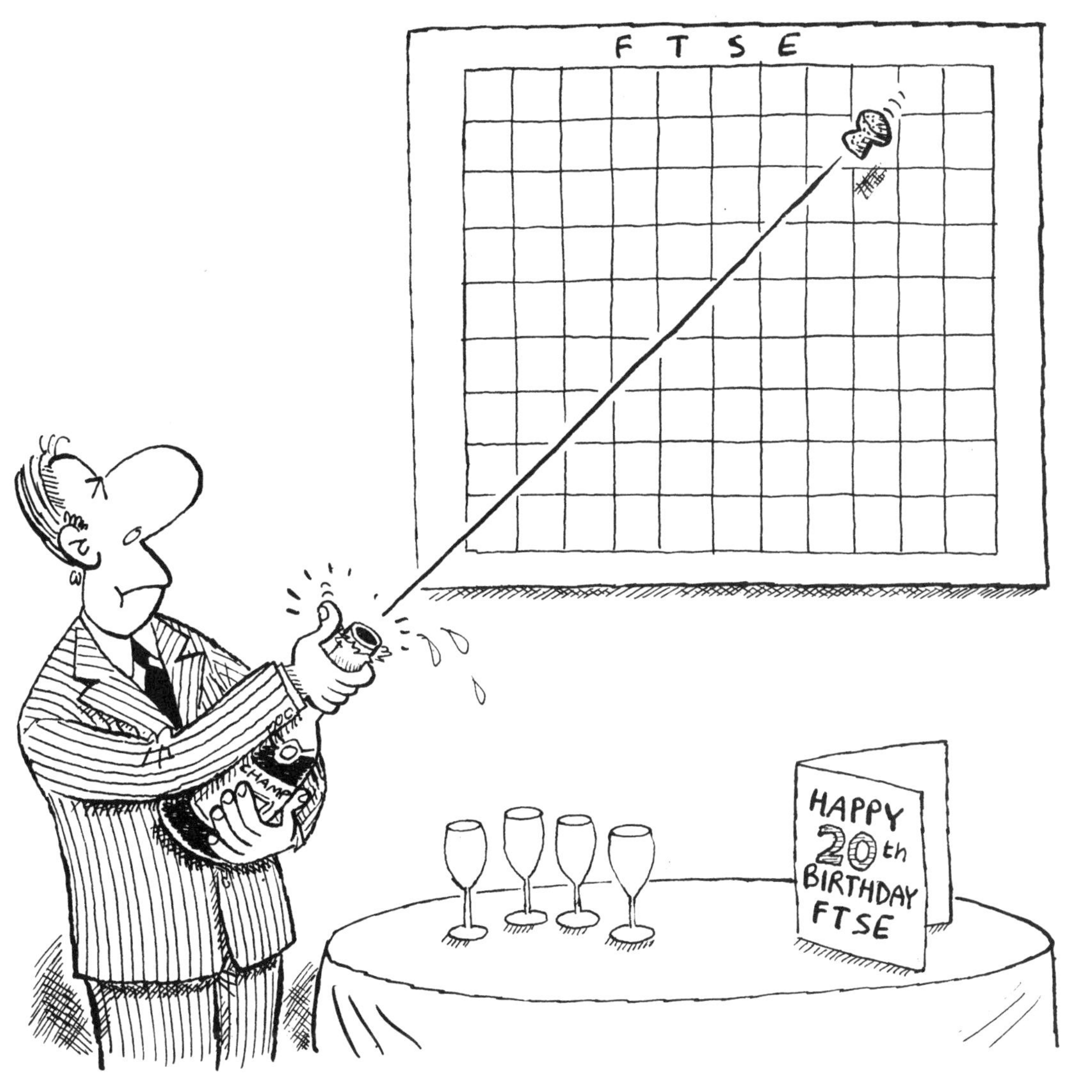

Our usual gratitude goes to our generous sponsors.

FTSE Group (FTSE) is the world-leader in the creation and management of index solutions.

Mondo Visione provides vital knowledge about the world's exchanges and trading venues.

ALEX IN WONDERLAND

November 2015 marks the 150th anniversary of the first publication of "Alice in Wonderland" and the financial world has been paying tribute by devising its own topsy-turvy version of Wonderland: a financial reality known as the "New Normal".

In this bizarre back-to-front world, economic models that were once straightforward have become baffling. Here are 'six impossible things' that Alex now has to believe before sending his graduate trainee out to get breakfast.

1. "Bad news is good news". Once upon a time bad news made markets go down, because it was, well, bad. But now bad news makes markets go up, because it means the central bankers whose stimulus packages are propping up the global economy will have to keep the money tap switched on a bit longer.

2. "Bonds can pay negative interest". Traditionally if you lent money to someone, they paid you interest for the privilege of borrowing it. Now it's the other way round: they borrow your money off you and you have to pay the interest to them.

3. "Interest rates can go below zero". This is bad news for savers, who will be charged to keep their money in the bank, but if you have a mortgage then theoretically the bank will pay you for it. Good news too for burglars once everyone starts stashing their savings in cash under the mattress.

4. "Money printing can save the global economy". In the past money printing (or QE) has led to hyperinflation (Weimar Germany, post WW2 Hungary, Zimbabwe), but we've printed $15 trillion of the stuff worldwide since the financial crisis and we've got deflation. So let's not worry about it and print some more.

5. "Chinese economic data is genuine". This is the one we need to keep believing and not allow any doubt to creep into our minds that the figures might all just be made up by Chinese Communist Party officials, otherwise the global economy is in deep doo-doo.

6. "Greece is now fixed". Close your eyes and try really hard..

This increasingly bizarre economic environment has made our jobs as satirists of the City of London paradoxically both easier and harder. On the one hand the financial news (once relegated to the end of the evening bulletin) has, for the last eight years or so, been making the headlines. But on the other hand financial and economic reality is becoming so surreal that it is very difficult to parody it. Oh well. Maybe, like Alice, we'll wake up and find it's all been a dream.

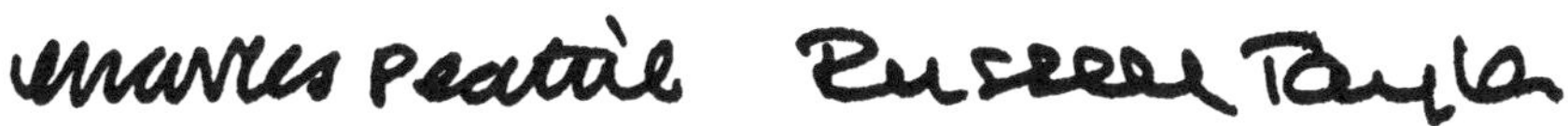

Charles Peattie and Russell Taylor

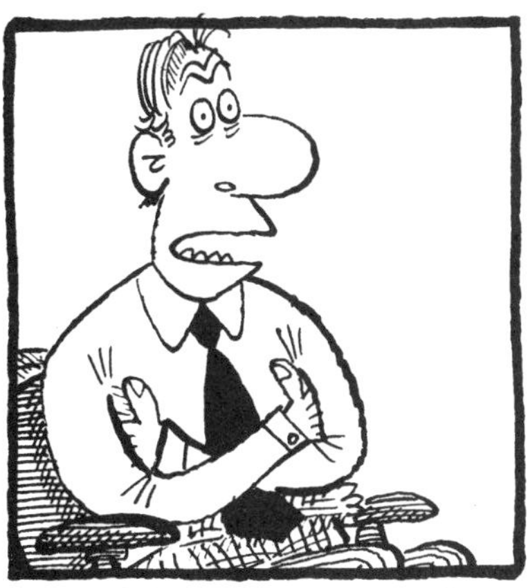

Alex - investment banker

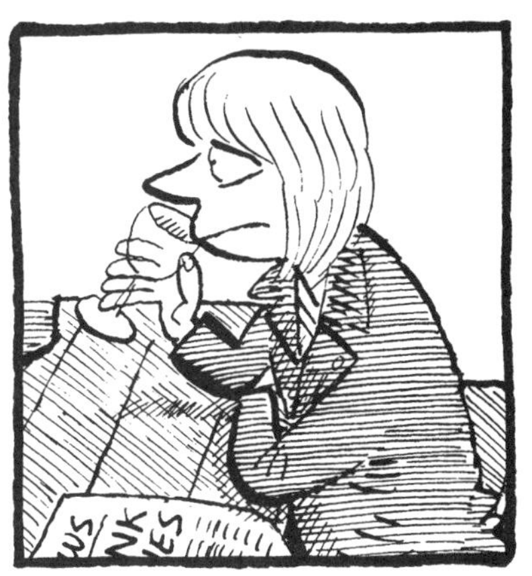

Penny - Alex's wife

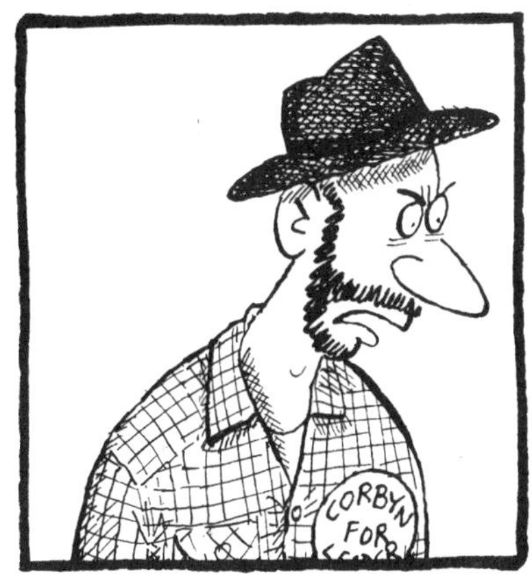

Christopher - Alex's son

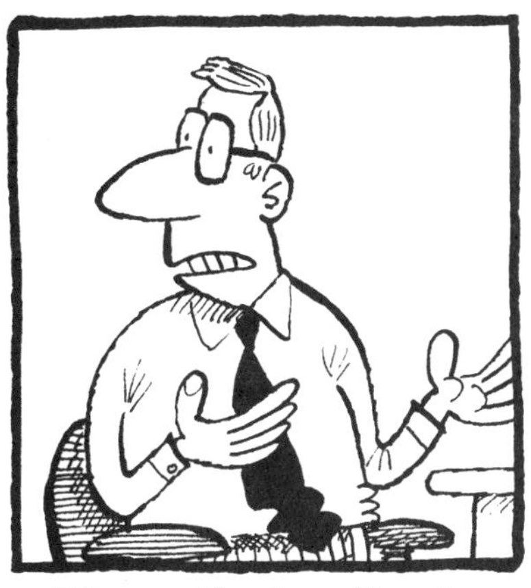

Clive - Alex's colleague

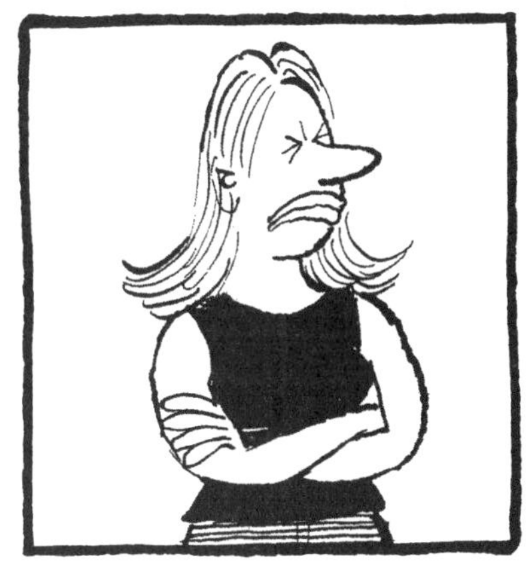

Bridget - Clive's wife

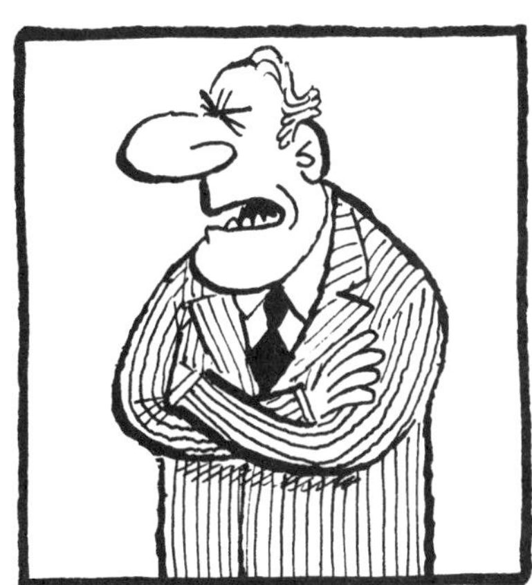

Rupert - senior banker

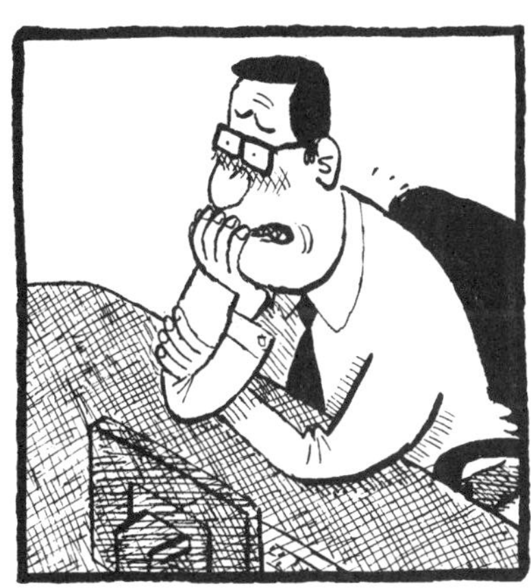

Cyrus - Alex's boss

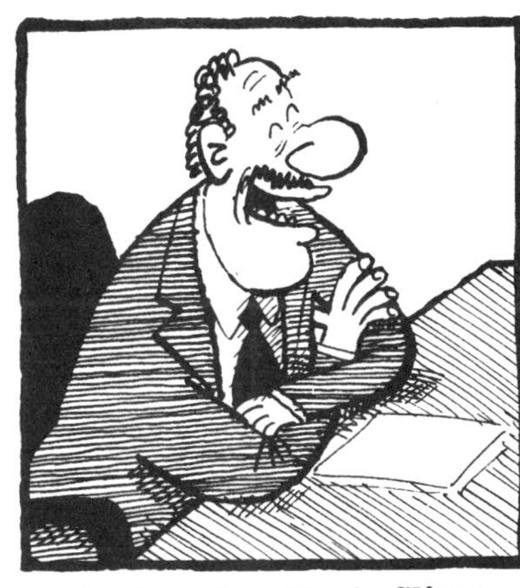

Hardcastle - Alex's Client

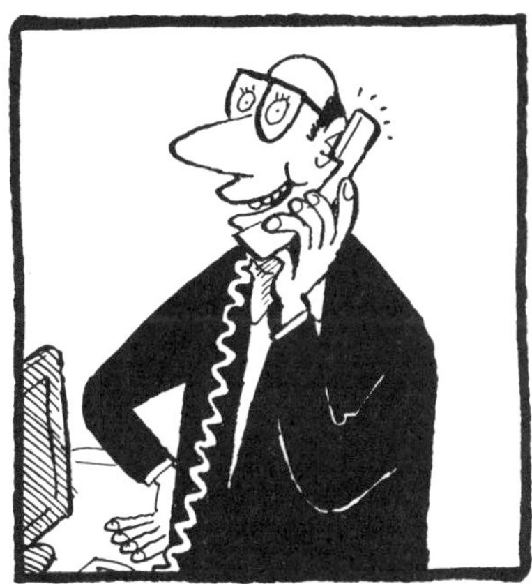

David - regulator

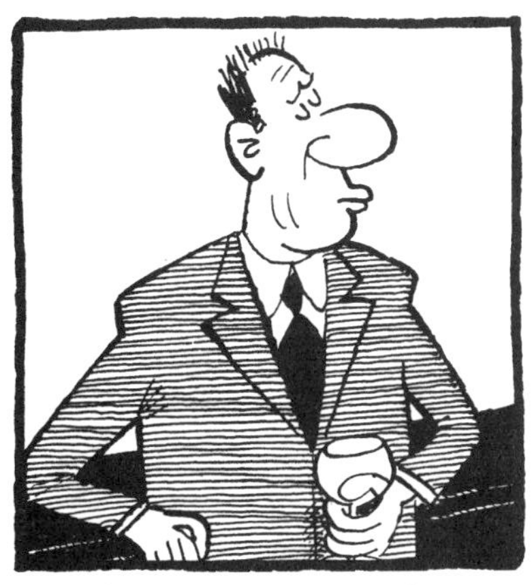

Vince - Essex trader

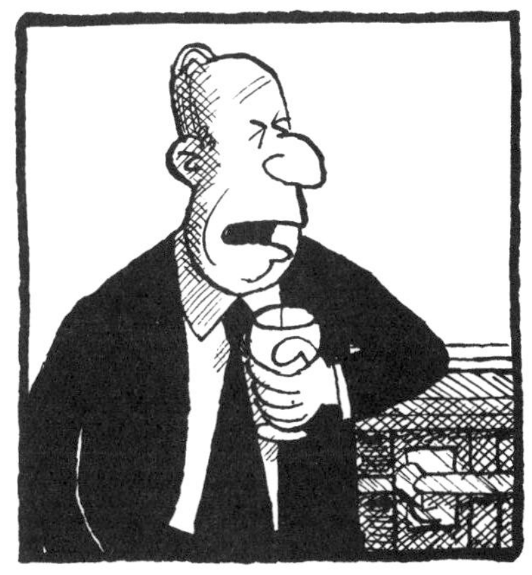

Justin - Tory MP

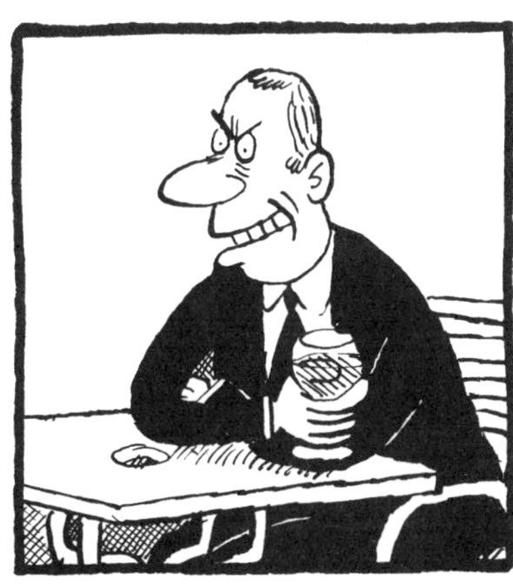

William - wealth manager

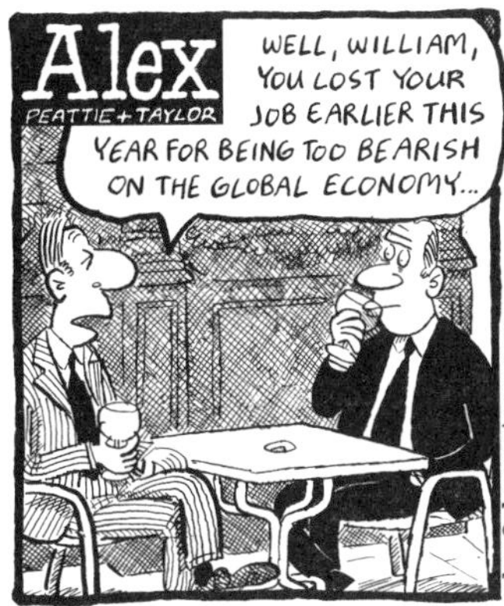
Alex
PEATTIE + TAYLOR
WELL, WILLIAM, YOU LOST YOUR JOB EARLIER THIS YEAR FOR BEING TOO BEARISH ON THE GLOBAL ECONOMY...

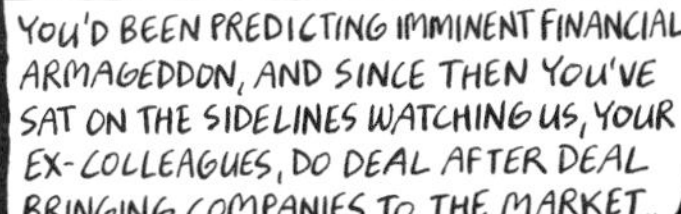
YOU'D BEEN PREDICTING IMMINENT FINANCIAL ARMAGEDDON, AND SINCE THEN YOU'VE SAT ON THE SIDELINES WATCHING US, YOUR EX-COLLEAGUES, DO DEAL AFTER DEAL BRINGING COMPANIES TO THE MARKET...

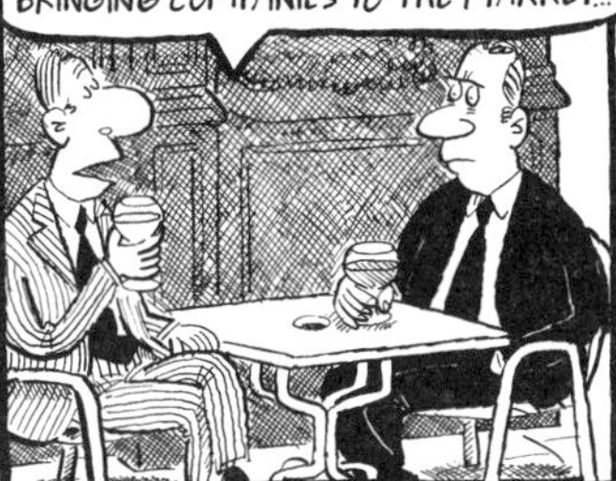
alex@alexcartoon.com

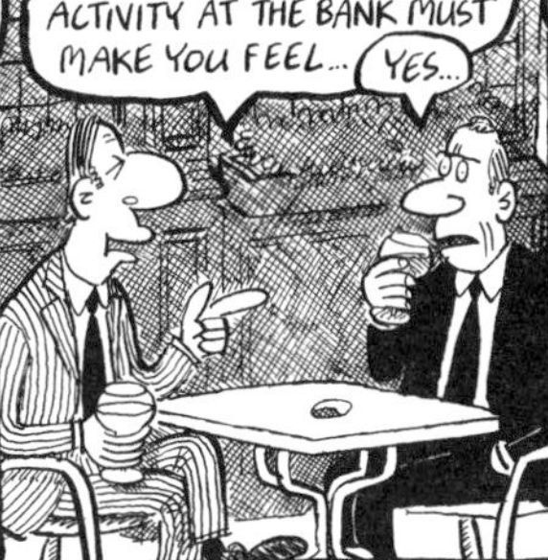
I CAN COMPLETELY UNDERSTAND HOW SEEING THE CURRENT RECORD LEVEL OF CORPORATE ACTIVITY AT THE BANK MUST MAKE YOU FEEL...
YES...

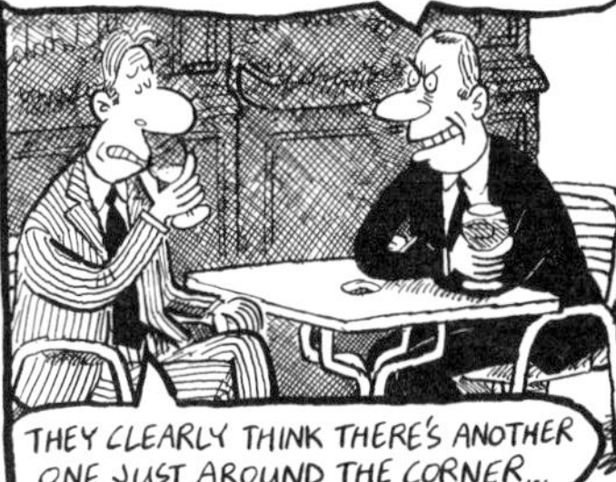
TOTALLY VINDICATED... THE PRIVATE EQUITY BOYS ARE DESPERATELY GETTING SHOT OF EVERY COMPANY THEY'VE HAD STUCK ON THEIR BOOKS SINCE BEFORE THE LAST CRASH...
THEY CLEARLY THINK THERE'S ANOTHER ONE JUST AROUND THE CORNER...

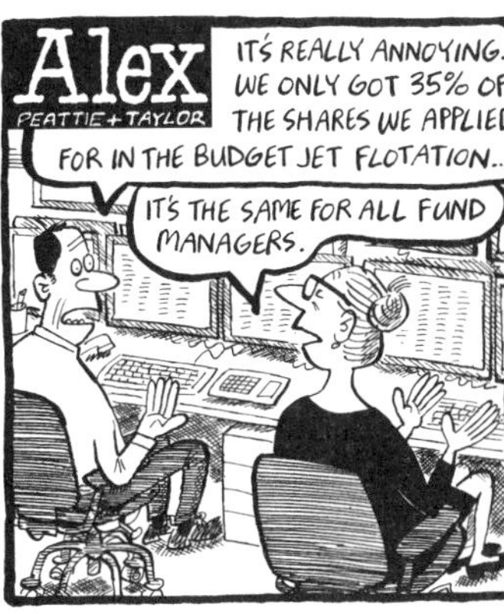
Alex
PEATTIE + TAYLOR
IT'S REALLY ANNOYING. WE ONLY GOT 35% OF THE SHARES WE APPLIED FOR IN THE BUDGET JET FLOTATION...
IT'S THE SAME FOR ALL FUND MANAGERS.

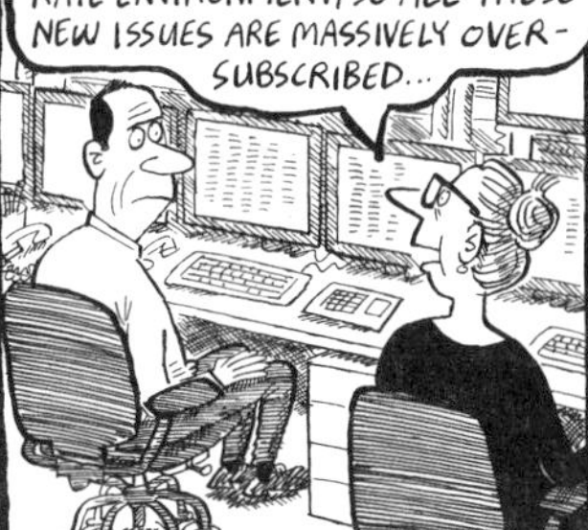
INVESTORS HAVE GOT SURPLUS CASH THAT THEY'RE DESPERATE TO GET A RETURN ON IN THIS ZERO INTEREST RATE ENVIRONMENT, SO ALL THESE NEW ISSUES ARE MASSIVELY OVER-SUBSCRIBED...
alex@alexcartoon.com
STILL, LOOK ON THE BRIGHT SIDE. GETTING 35% ISN'T SO BAD. THINGS COULD HAVE BEEN A WHOLE LOT WORSE...
YOU'RE RIGHT...

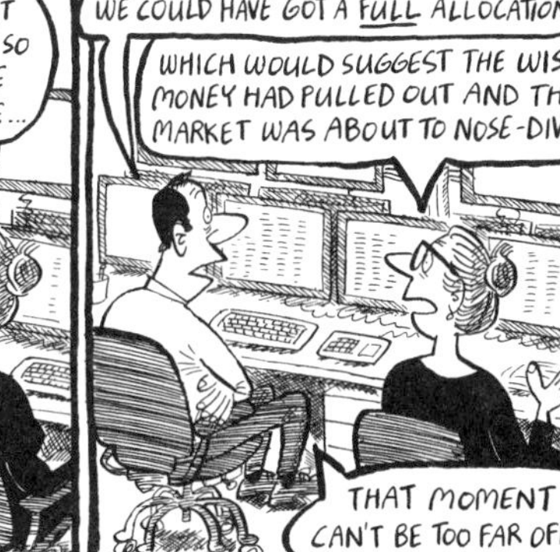
WE COULD HAVE GOT A FULL ALLOCATION...
WHICH WOULD SUGGEST THE WISE MONEY HAD PULLED OUT AND THE MARKET WAS ABOUT TO NOSE-DIVE...
THAT MOMENT CAN'T BE TOO FAR OFF...

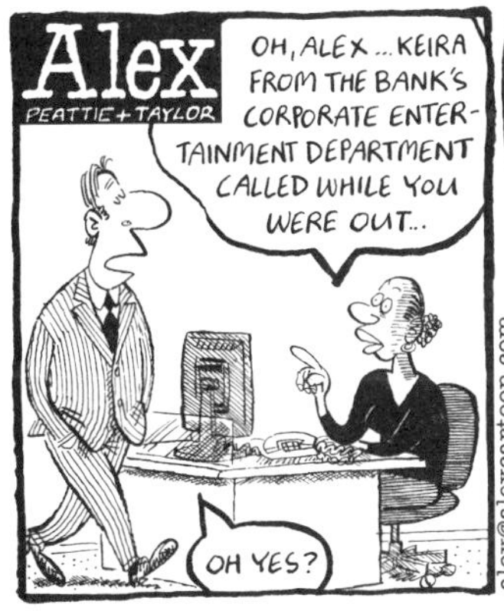
Alex
PEATTIE + TAYLOR
OH, ALEX... KEIRA FROM THE BANK'S CORPORATE ENTERTAINMENT DEPARTMENT CALLED WHILE YOU WERE OUT...
OH YES?

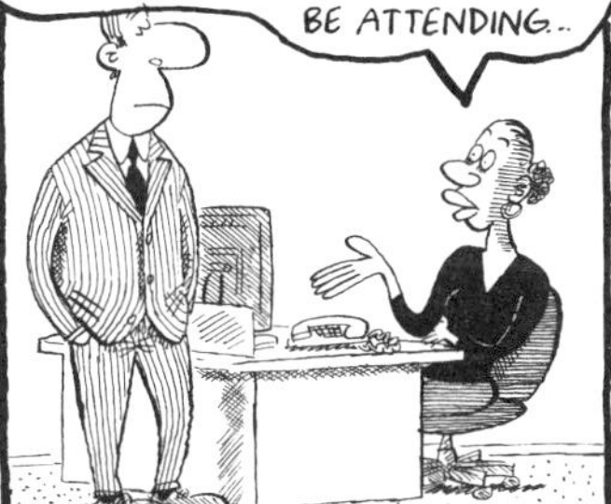
SHE SAYS YOU'VE RESERVED THE BANK'S BOX AT THE O2 FOR THE KYLIE MINOGUE CONCERT THIS WEEK BUT YOU'VE FAILED TO GIVE HER THE NAMES OF ANY CLIENTS WHO'LL BE ATTENDING...
alex@alexcartoon.com

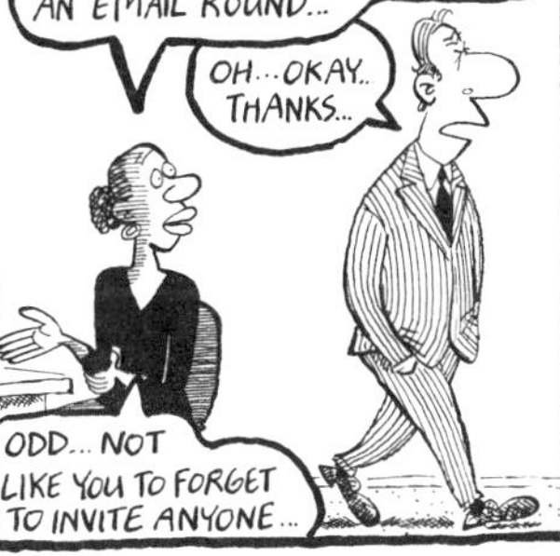
SO SHE'S RELEASING THE BOX AND OFFERING THE EVENING AS A FREE EVENT FOR BANK STAFF. SHE'S SENDING AN EMAIL ROUND...
OH... OKAY.. THANKS...
ODD... NOT LIKE YOU TO FORGET TO INVITE ANYONE...

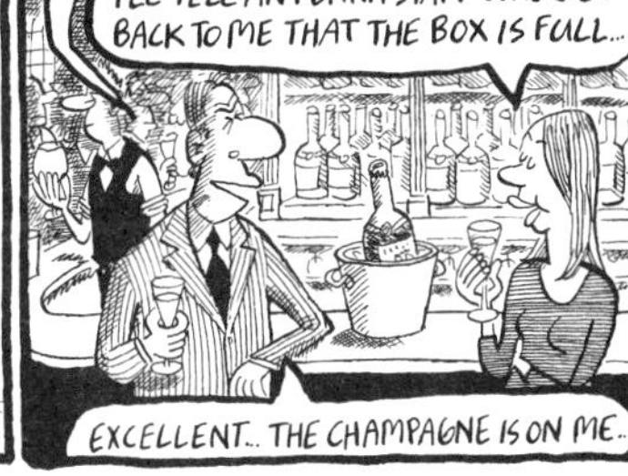
THANKS, KEIRA. I'VE HAD MY CLIENTS ON STAND-BY, AND NOW IT'S A FREE EVENT THEY'LL HAVE NO PROBLEMS WITH COMPLIANCE ABOUT ACCEPTING.
AND I'LL TELL ANY BANK STAFF WHO GET BACK TO ME THAT THE BOX IS FULL...
EXCELLENT... THE CHAMPAGNE IS ON ME..

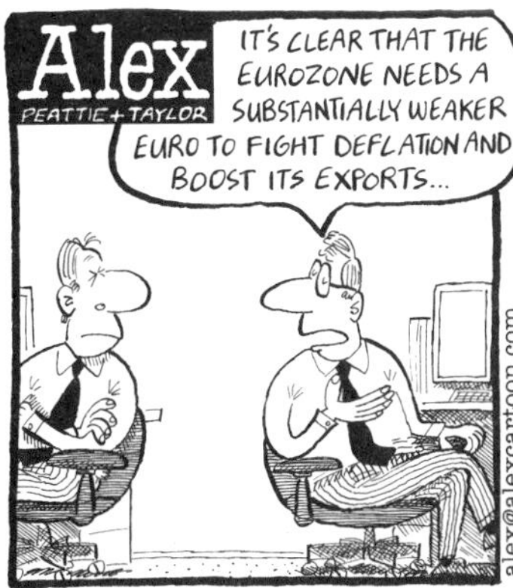
Alex
PEATTIE + TAYLOR
IT'S CLEAR THAT THE EUROZONE NEEDS A SUBSTANTIALLY WEAKER EURO TO FIGHT DEFLATION AND BOOST ITS EXPORTS...

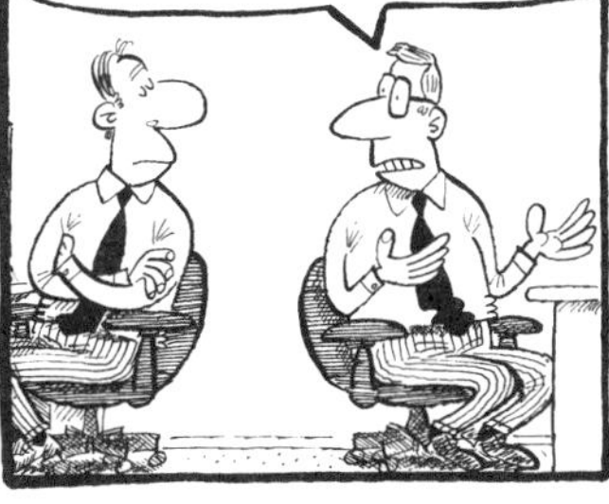
SO WHAT ON EARTH IS MARIO DRAGHI DOING? NOTHING BUT POSTURING AND MACHO TALK AND FAFFING AROUND WITH HALF-HEARTED, ILL-DEFINED MONETARY POLICIES THAT ACHIEVE PRECISELY NOTHING
alex@alexcartoon.com

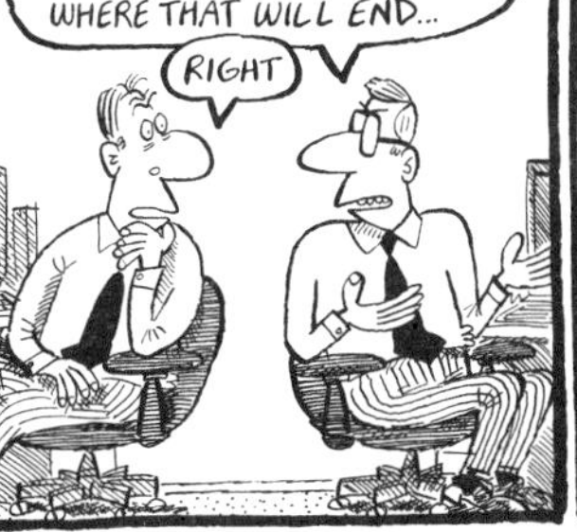
INVESTORS ARE ALREADY STARTING TO LOSE ALL CONFIDENCE IN HIM AND THE EUROPEAN CENTRAL BANK AND IT'S NOT HARD TO SEE WHERE THAT WILL END...
RIGHT
EVERYONE WILL PULL THEIR MONEY OUT OF EUROPE...
ER, WHICH WILL HAVE THE EFFECT OF CAUSING THE EURO TO WEAKEN...
YOU KNOW, IT'S QUITE POSSIBLE THAT THE MAN IS A GENIUS...

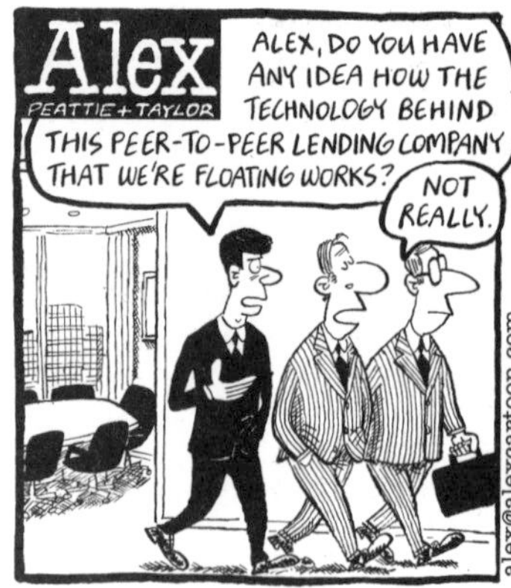
Alex
PEATTIE + TAYLOR
ALEX, DO YOU HAVE ANY IDEA HOW THE TECHNOLOGY BEHIND THIS PEER-TO-PEER LENDING COMPANY THAT WE'RE FLOATING WORKS?
NOT REALLY.

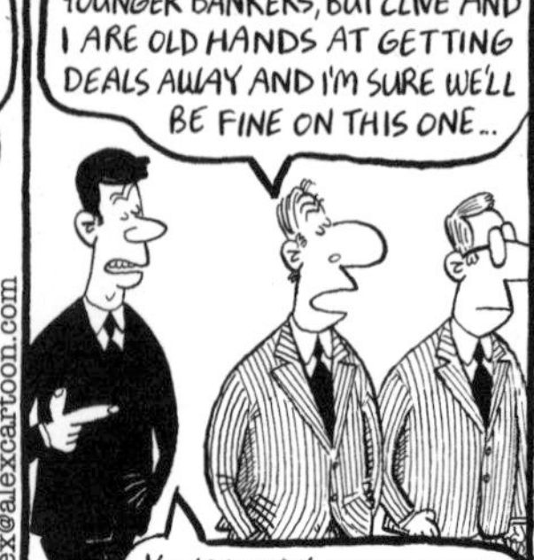
I LEAVE ALL THAT STUFF UP TO YOU YOUNGER BANKERS, BUT CLIVE AND I ARE OLD HANDS AT GETTING DEALS AWAY AND I'M SURE WE'LL BE FINE ON THIS ONE...
YOU'RE VERY COMPLACENT...

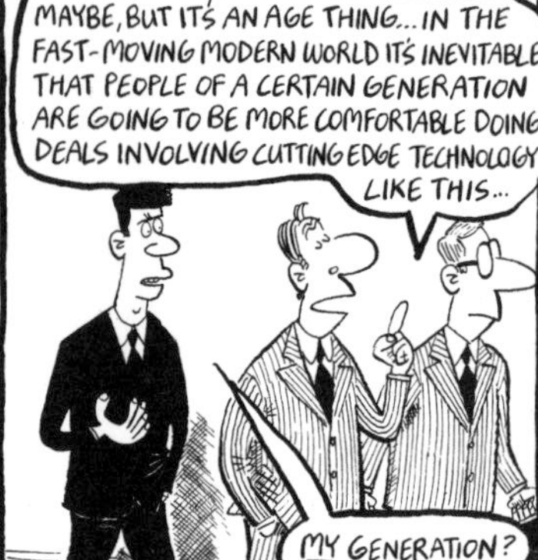
MAYBE, BUT IT'S AN AGE THING... IN THE FAST-MOVING MODERN WORLD IT'S INEVITABLE THAT PEOPLE OF A CERTAIN GENERATION ARE GOING TO BE MORE COMFORTABLE DOING DEALS INVOLVING CUTTING EDGE TECHNOLOGY LIKE THIS...
MY GENERATION?

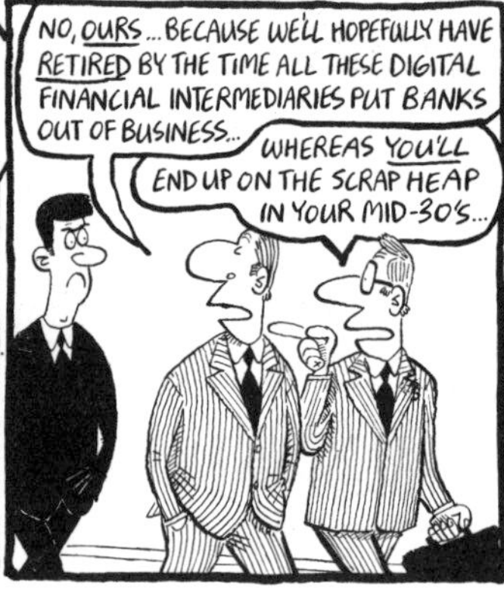
NO, OURS... BECAUSE WE'LL HOPEFULLY HAVE RETIRED BY THE TIME ALL THESE DIGITAL FINANCIAL INTERMEDIARIES PUT BANKS OUT OF BUSINESS...
WHEREAS YOU'LL END UP ON THE SCRAP HEAP IN YOUR MID-30'S...

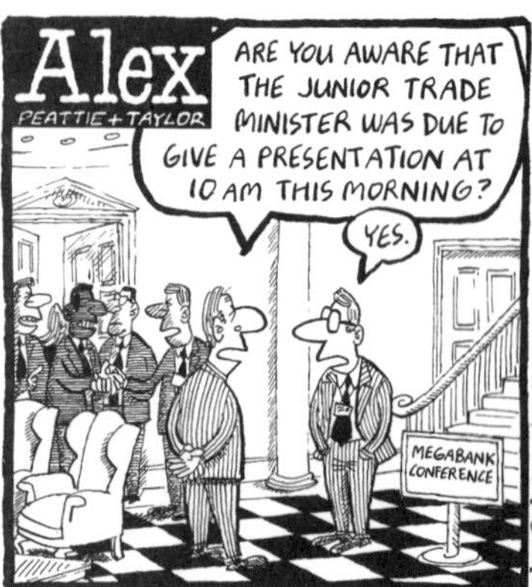
Alex
PEATTIE + TAYLOR
ARE YOU AWARE THAT THE JUNIOR TRADE MINISTER WAS DUE TO GIVE A PRESENTATION AT 10 AM THIS MORNING?
YES.
MEGABANK CONFERENCE

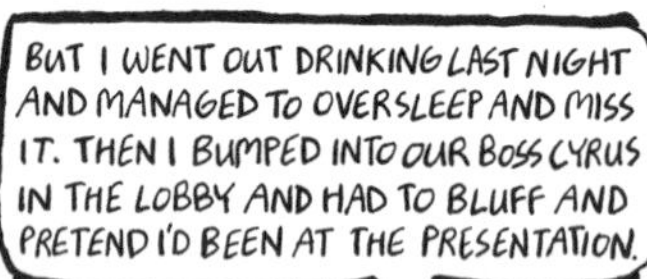
BUT I WENT OUT DRINKING LAST NIGHT AND MANAGED TO OVERSLEEP AND MISS IT. THEN I BUMPED INTO OUR BOSS CYRUS IN THE LOBBY AND HAD TO BLUFF AND PRETEND I'D BEEN AT THE PRESENTATION.

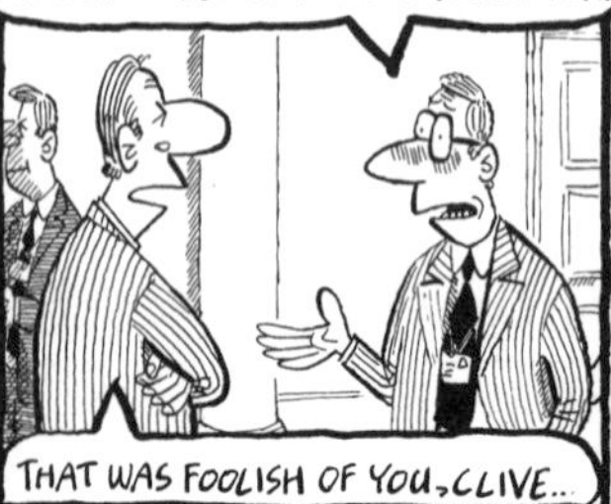
THAT WAS FOOLISH OF YOU, CLIVE...

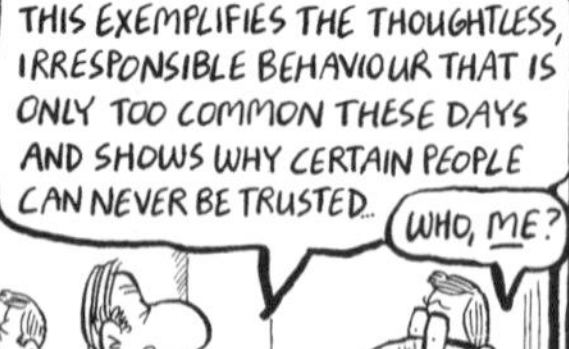
THIS EXEMPLIFIES THE THOUGHTLESS, IRRESPONSIBLE BEHAVIOUR THAT IS ONLY TOO COMMON THESE DAYS AND SHOWS WHY CERTAIN PEOPLE CAN NEVER BE TRUSTED...
WHO, ME?

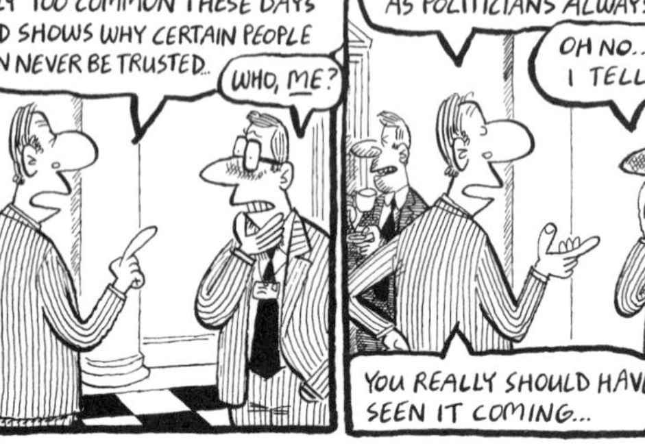
NO, MEMBERS OF PARLIAMENT... THE MINISTER CANCELLED AT THE LAST MINUTE AS POLITICIANS ALWAYS DO...
OH NO... WHAT DO I TELL CYRUS...?
YOU REALLY SHOULD HAVE SEEN IT COMING...

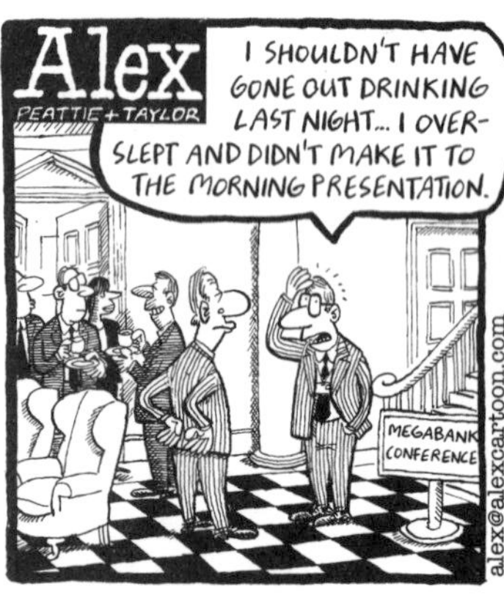
Alex
PEATTIE + TAYLOR
I SHOULDN'T HAVE GONE OUT DRINKING LAST NIGHT... I OVER-SLEPT AND DIDN'T MAKE IT TO THE MORNING PRESENTATION.
MEGABANK CONFERENCE

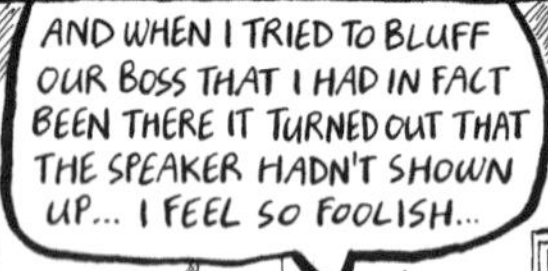
AND WHEN I TRIED TO BLUFF OUR BOSS THAT I HAD IN FACT BEEN THERE IT TURNED OUT THAT THE SPEAKER HADN'T SHOWN UP... I FEEL SO FOOLISH...

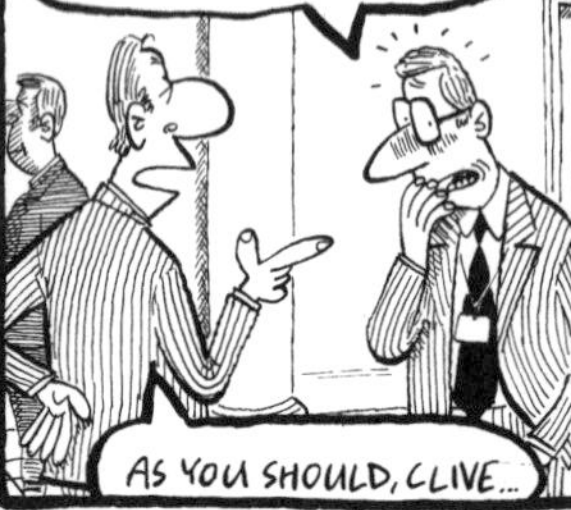
AS YOU SHOULD, CLIVE...

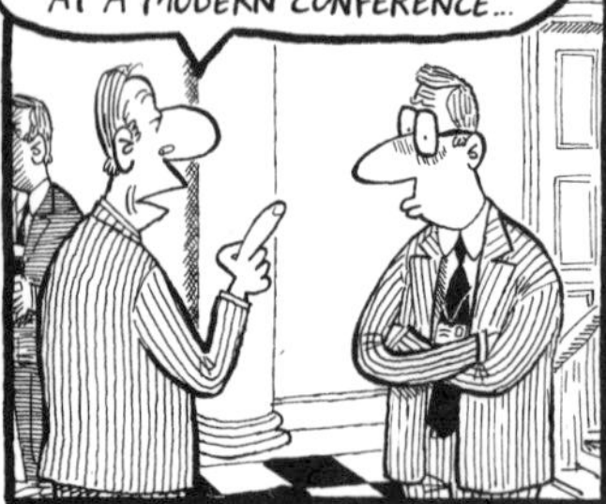
YOUR BEHAVIOUR BELONGS TO A BYGONE AGE... LYING IN BED HUNGOVER AND MISSING KEY PRESENTATIONS...? THERE'S NO EXCUSE FOR THAT SORT OF THING AT A MODERN CONFERENCE...

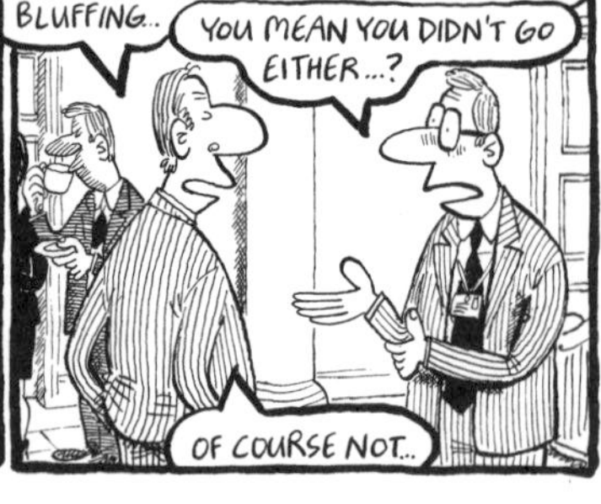
THESE DAYS ALL THE PROCEEDINGS ARE BROADCAST AS LIVE "WEBINARS" ON THE INTERNET, SO YOU CAN KEEP TABS ON THEM FROM YOUR BED FOR THE PURPOSES OF LATER BLUFFING...
YOU MEAN YOU DIDN'T GO EITHER...?
OF COURSE NOT...

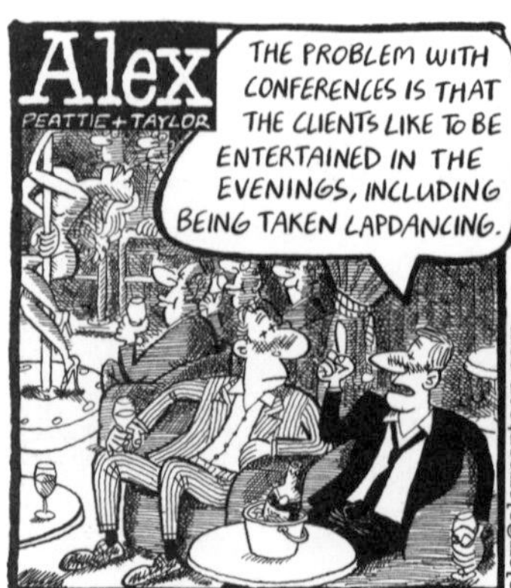
Alex
PEATTIE + TAYLOR
THE PROBLEM WITH CONFERENCES IS THAT THE CLIENTS LIKE TO BE ENTERTAINED IN THE EVENINGS, INCLUDING BEING TAKEN LAPDANCING.

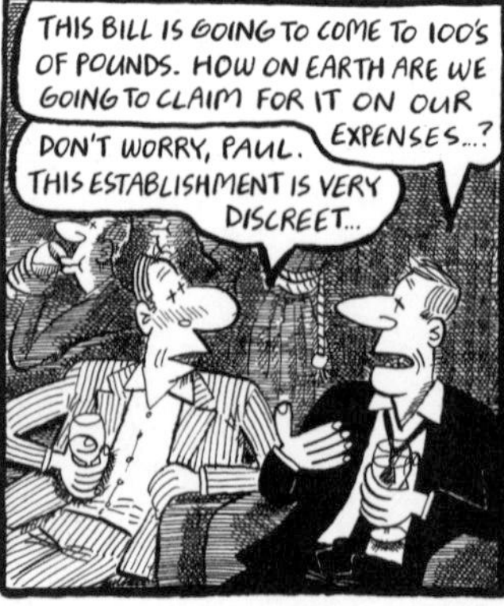
THIS BILL IS GOING TO COME TO 100'S OF POUNDS. HOW ON EARTH ARE WE GOING TO CLAIM FOR IT ON OUR EXPENSES...?
DON'T WORRY, PAUL. THIS ESTABLISHMENT IS VERY DISCREET...

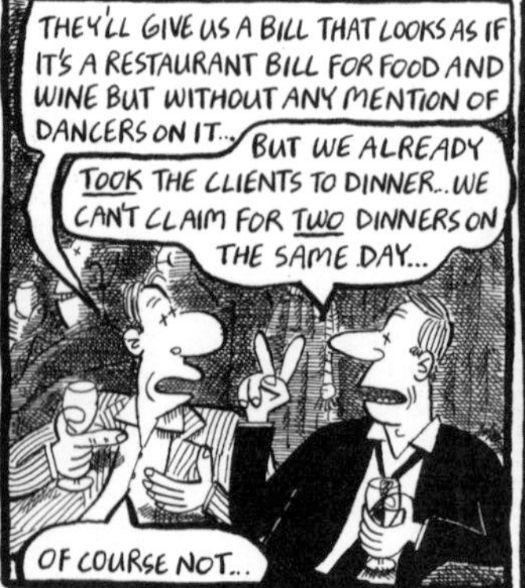
THEY'LL GIVE US A BILL THAT LOOKS AS IF IT'S A RESTAURANT BILL FOR FOOD AND WINE BUT WITHOUT ANY MENTION OF DANCERS ON IT...
BUT WE ALREADY TOOK THE CLIENTS TO DINNER... WE CAN'T CLAIM FOR TWO DINNERS ON THE SAME DAY...
OF COURSE NOT...

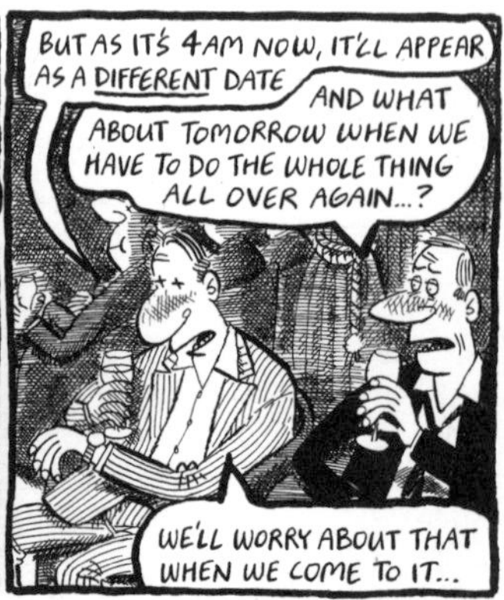
BUT AS IT'S 4AM NOW, IT'LL APPEAR AS A DIFFERENT DATE
AND WHAT ABOUT TOMORROW WHEN WE HAVE TO DO THE WHOLE THING ALL OVER AGAIN...?
WE'LL WORRY ABOUT THAT WHEN WE COME TO IT...

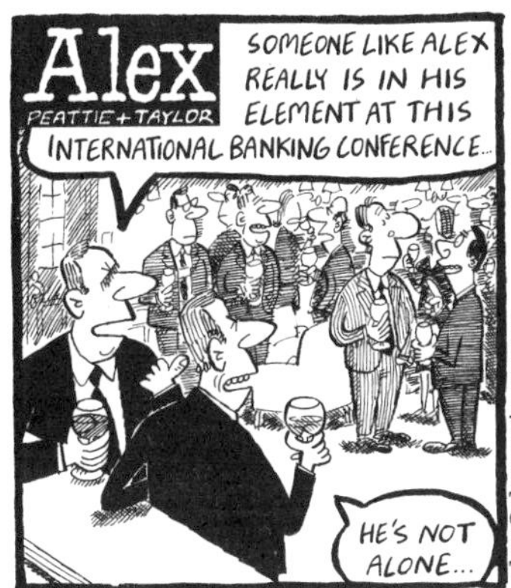
Alex
PEATTIE + TAYLOR
SOMEONE LIKE ALEX REALLY IS IN HIS ELEMENT AT THIS INTERNATIONAL BANKING CONFERENCE..
HE'S NOT ALONE...

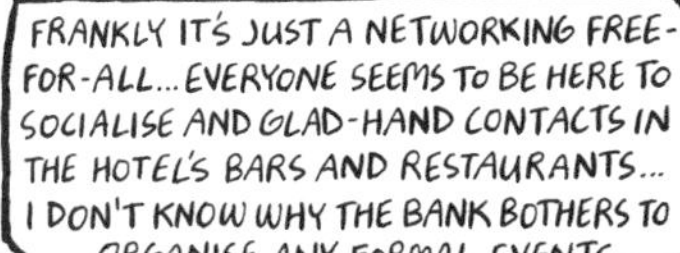
FRANKLY IT'S JUST A NETWORKING FREE-FOR-ALL... EVERYONE SEEMS TO BE HERE TO SOCIALISE AND GLAD-HAND CONTACTS IN THE HOTEL'S BARS AND RESTAURANTS... I DON'T KNOW WHY THE BANK BOTHERS TO ORGANISE ANY FORMAL EVENTS...

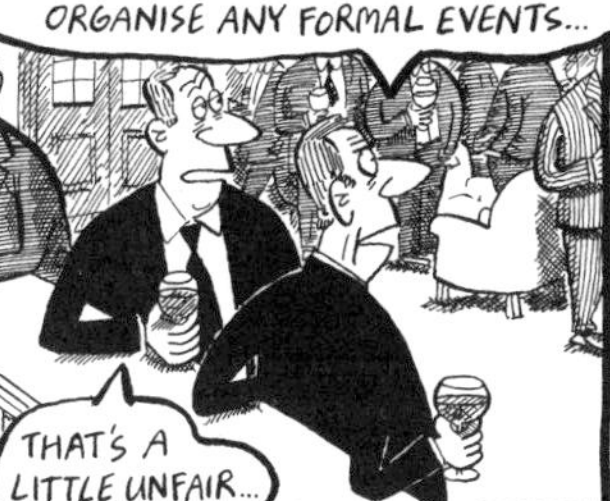
THAT'S A LITTLE UNFAIR...
alex@alexcartoon.com

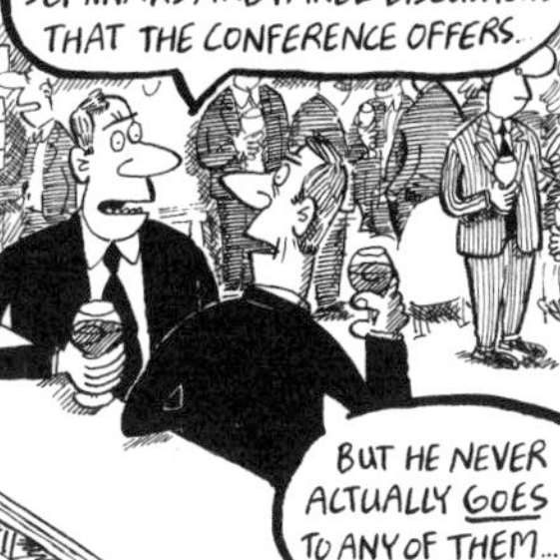
I KNOW ALEX ALWAYS TALKS ABOUT THE IMPORTANCE OF A FULL DAILY PROGRAMME OF LECTURES, SEMINARS AND PANEL DISCUSSIONS THAT THE CONFERENCE OFFERS..
BUT HE NEVER ACTUALLY GOES TO ANY OF THEM...

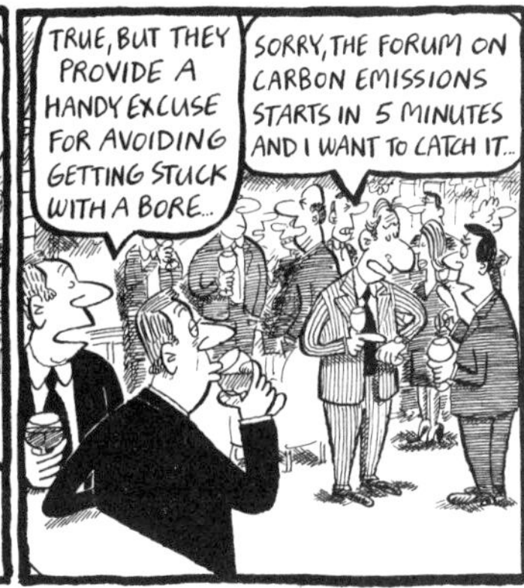
TRUE, BUT THEY PROVIDE A HANDY EXCUSE FOR AVOIDING GETTING STUCK WITH A BORE..
SORRY, THE FORUM ON CARBON EMISSIONS STARTS IN 5 MINUTES AND I WANT TO CATCH IT..

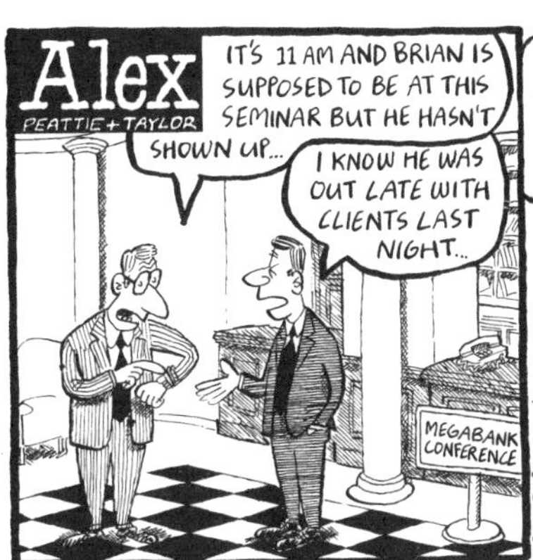
Alex
PEATTIE + TAYLOR
IT'S 11 AM AND BRIAN IS SUPPOSED TO BE AT THIS SEMINAR BUT HE HASN'T SHOWN UP...
I KNOW HE WAS OUT LATE WITH CLIENTS LAST NIGHT...
MEGABANK CONFERENCE

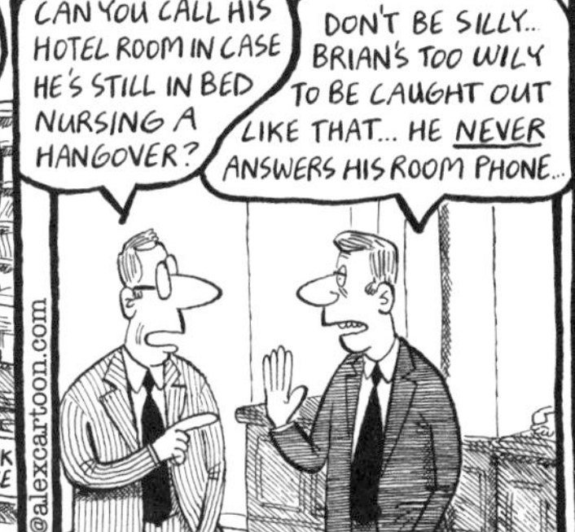
CAN YOU CALL HIS HOTEL ROOM IN CASE HE'S STILL IN BED NURSING A HANGOVER?
DON'T BE SILLY.. BRIAN'S TOO WILY TO BE CAUGHT OUT LIKE THAT... HE NEVER ANSWERS HIS ROOM PHONE...
alex@alexcartoon.com

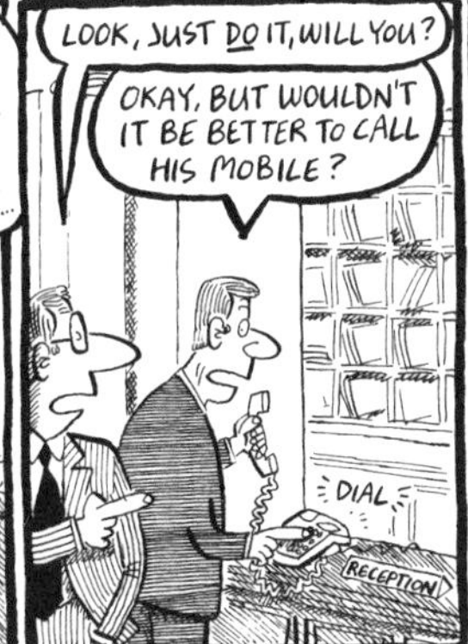
LOOK, JUST DO IT, WILL YOU?
OKAY, BUT WOULDN'T IT BE BETTER TO CALL HIS MOBILE?
DIAL
RECEPTION

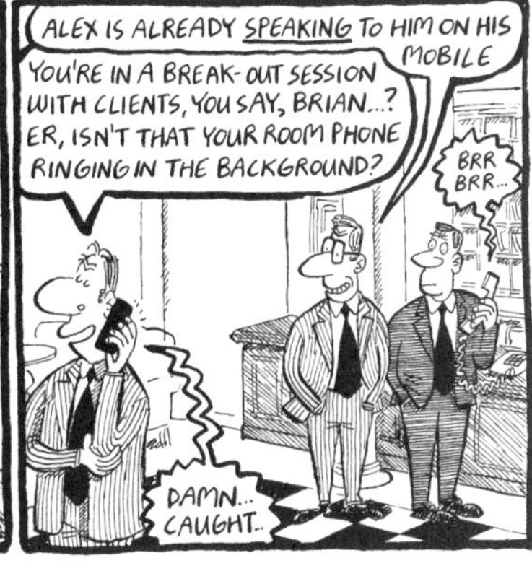
ALEX IS ALREADY SPEAKING TO HIM ON HIS MOBILE
YOU'RE IN A BREAK-OUT SESSION WITH CLIENTS, YOU SAY, BRIAN...? ER, ISN'T THAT YOUR ROOM PHONE RINGING IN THE BACKGROUND?
BRR BRR...
DAMN... CAUGHT..

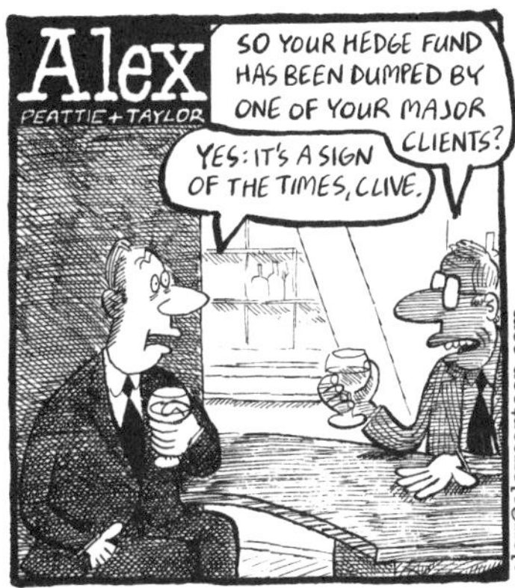
Alex
PEATTIE + TAYLOR
SO YOUR HEDGE FUND HAS BEEN DUMPED BY ONE OF YOUR MAJOR CLIENTS?
YES: IT'S A SIGN OF THE TIMES, CLIVE.

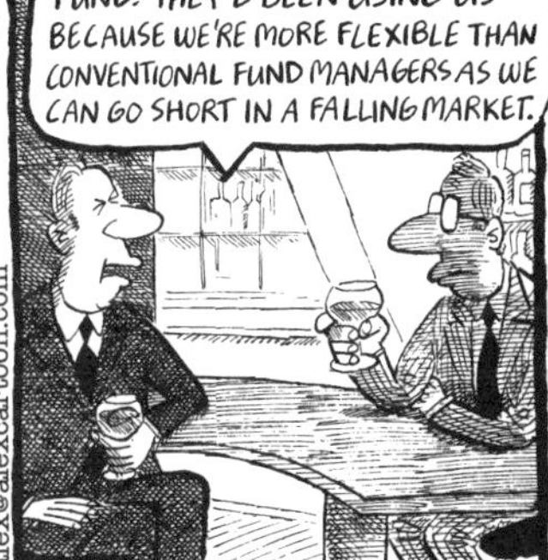
IT WAS A LOCAL AUTHORITY PENSION FUND. THEY'D BEEN USING US BECAUSE WE'RE MORE FLEXIBLE THAN CONVENTIONAL FUND MANAGERS AS WE CAN GO SHORT IN A FALLING MARKET.
alex@alexcartoon.com

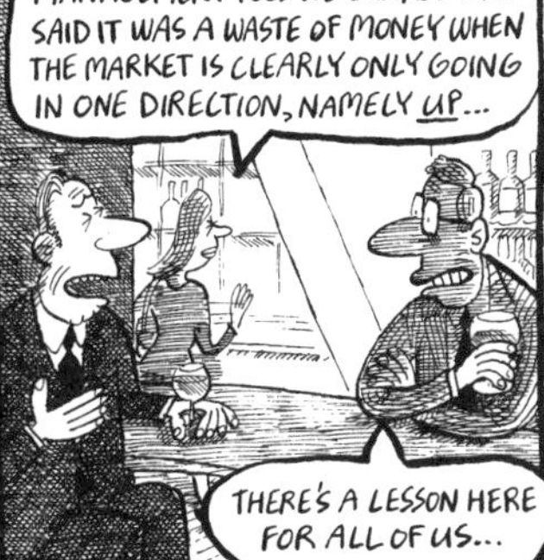
BUT THEY BALKED AT THE HIGHER MANAGEMENT FEES WE CHARGE AND SAID IT WAS A WASTE OF MONEY WHEN THE MARKET IS CLEARLY ONLY GOING IN ONE DIRECTION, NAMELY UP...
THERE'S A LESSON HERE FOR ALL OF US...

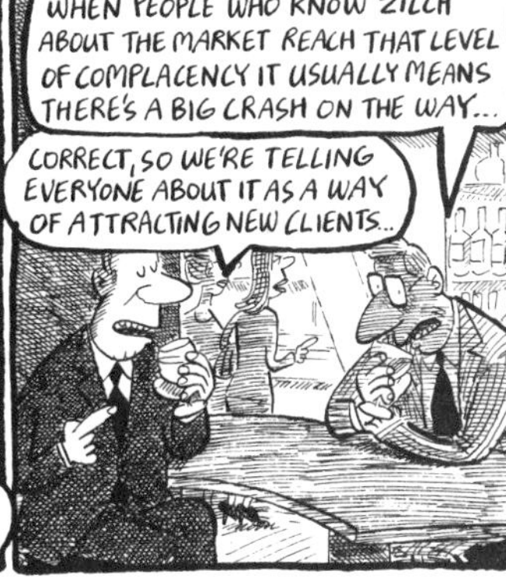
WHEN PEOPLE WHO KNOW ZILCH ABOUT THE MARKET REACH THAT LEVEL OF COMPLACENCY IT USUALLY MEANS THERE'S A BIG CRASH ON THE WAY...
CORRECT, SO WE'RE TELLING EVERYONE ABOUT IT AS A WAY OF ATTRACTING NEW CLIENTS..

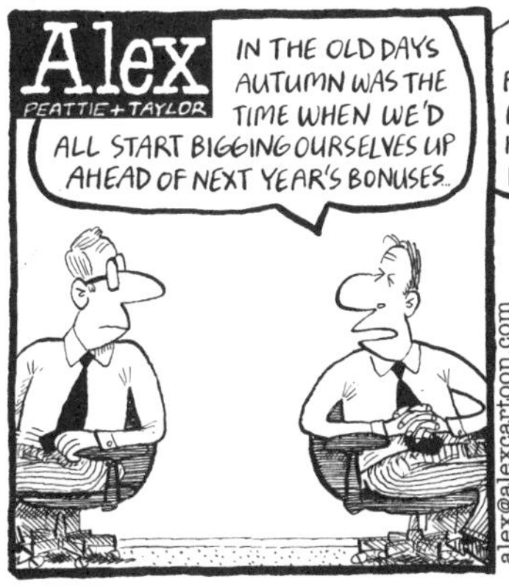
Alex
PEATTIE + TAYLOR
IN THE OLD DAYS AUTUMN WAS THE TIME WHEN WE'D ALL START BIGGING OURSELVES UP AHEAD OF NEXT YEAR'S BONUSES..

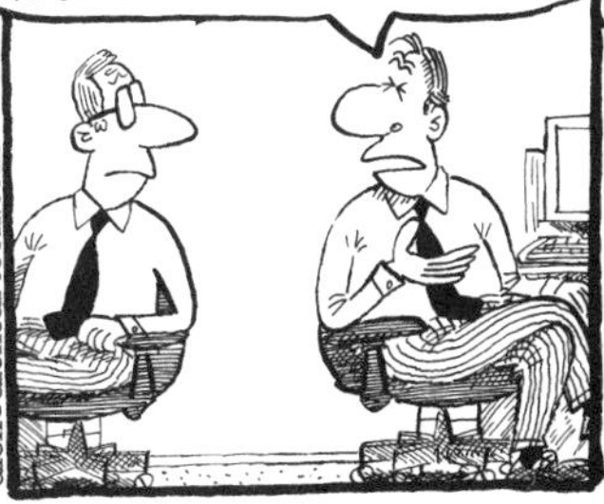
BUT IT'S ALL VERY DIFFERENT IN THE POST CRISIS "NEW NORMAL". PEOPLE ARE MORE CONCERNED WITH TOEING THE LINE, KEEPING THEIR HEADS DOWN AND NOT DRAWING ATTENTION TO THEMSELVES..
alex@alexcartoon.com
SOMEHOW I CAN'T SEE MYSELF TODAY WALKING INTO THE BOSS'S OFFICE AND BANGING ON ABOUT HOW MUCH MONEY I'VE MADE FOR THE BANK...
NO..

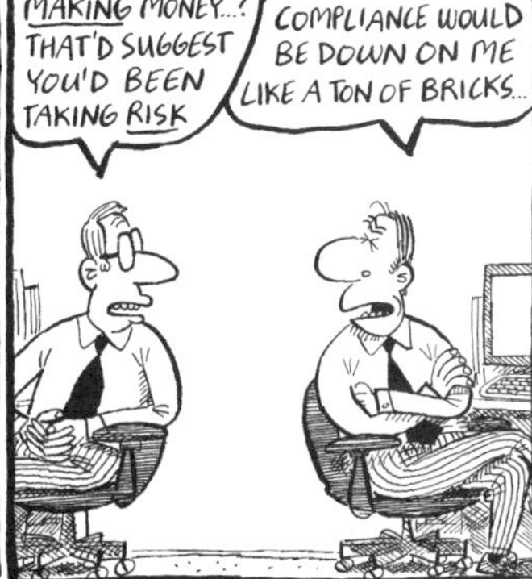
MAKING MONEY...? THAT'D SUGGEST YOU'D BEEN TAKING RISK
COMPLIANCE WOULD BE DOWN ON ME LIKE A TON OF BRICKS..

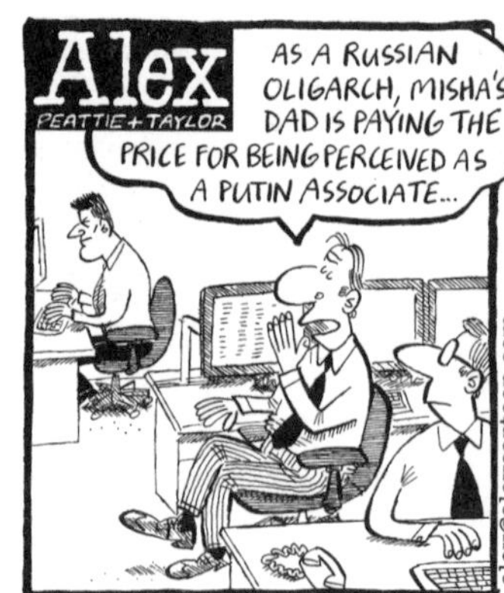
Alex
PEATTIE+TAYLOR
AS A RUSSIAN OLIGARCH, MISHA'S DAD IS PAYING THE PRICE FOR BEING PERCEIVED AS A PUTIN ASSOCIATE...
alex@alexcartoon.com

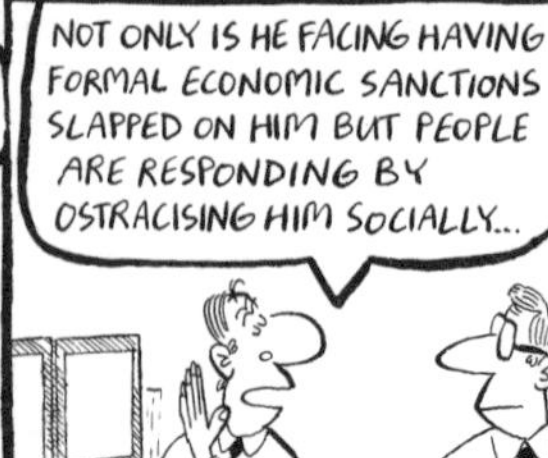
NOT ONLY IS HE FACING HAVING FORMAL ECONOMIC SANCTIONS SLAPPED ON HIM BUT PEOPLE ARE RESPONDING BY OSTRACISING HIM SOCIALLY...

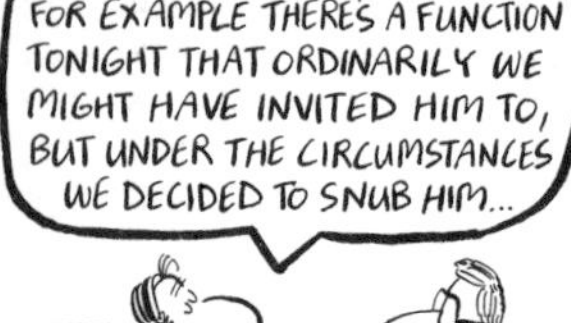
FOR EXAMPLE THERE'S A FUNCTION TONIGHT THAT ORDINARILY WE MIGHT HAVE INVITED HIM TO, BUT UNDER THE CIRCUMSTANCES WE DECIDED TO SNUB HIM...

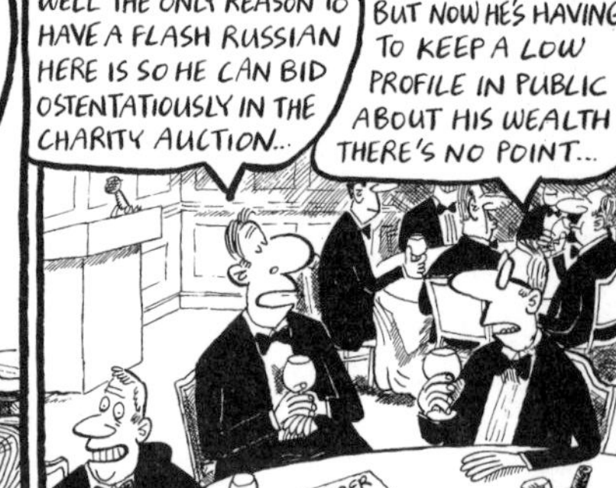
WELL THE ONLY REASON TO HAVE A FLASH RUSSIAN HERE IS SO HE CAN BID OSTENTATIOUSLY IN THE CHARITY AUCTION...
BUT NOW HE'S HAVING TO KEEP A LOW PROFILE IN PUBLIC ABOUT HIS WEALTH THERE'S NO POINT...
OCTOBER CLUB CHARITY DINNER

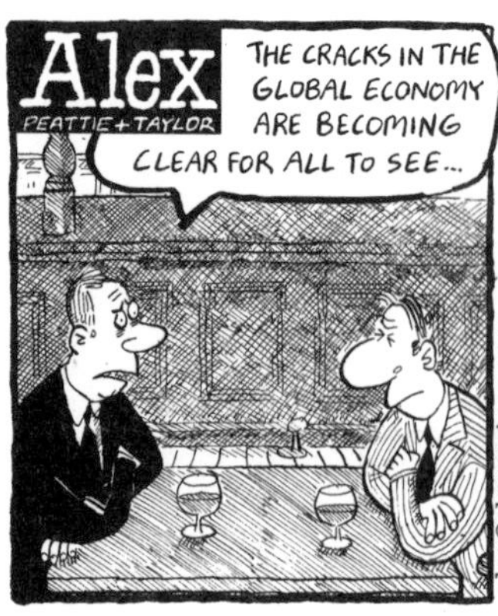
Alex
PEATTIE+TAYLOR
THE CRACKS IN THE GLOBAL ECONOMY ARE BECOMING CLEAR FOR ALL TO SEE...
alex@alexcartoon.com

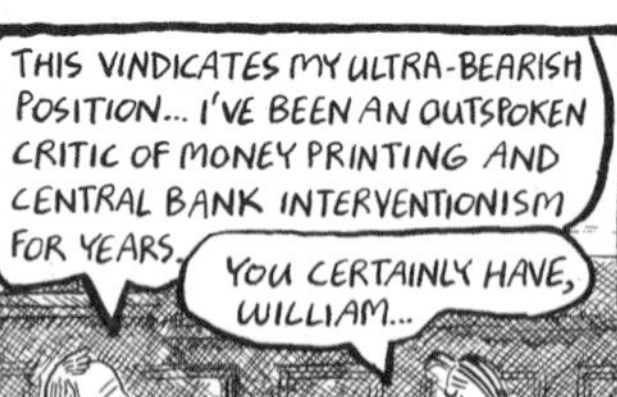
THIS VINDICATES MY ULTRA-BEARISH POSITION... I'VE BEEN AN OUTSPOKEN CRITIC OF MONEY PRINTING AND CENTRAL BANK INTERVENTIONISM FOR YEARS.
YOU CERTAINLY HAVE, WILLIAM...

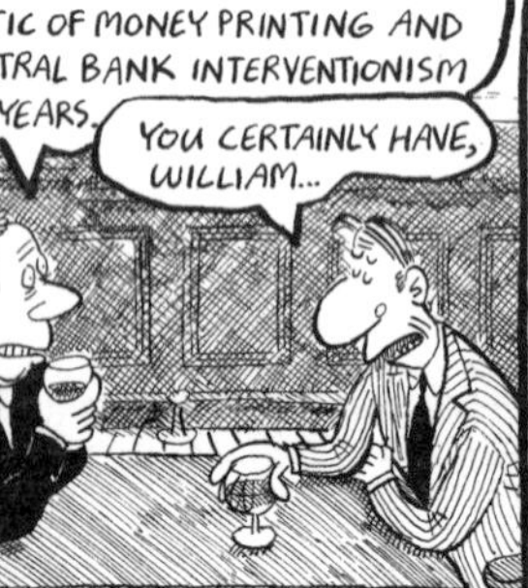

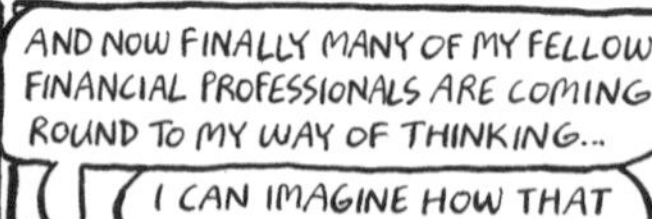
AND NOW FINALLY MANY OF MY FELLOW FINANCIAL PROFESSIONALS ARE COMING ROUND TO MY WAY OF THINKING...
I CAN IMAGINE HOW THAT MUST MAKE YOU FEEL...

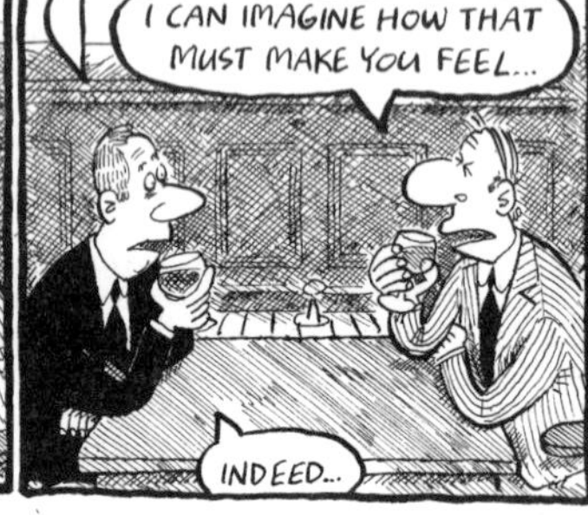
INDEED...

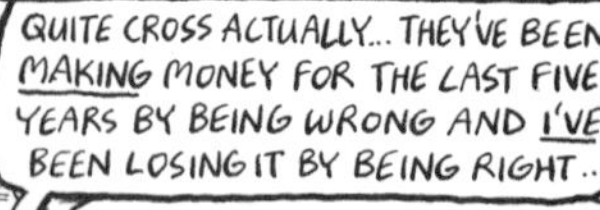
QUITE CROSS ACTUALLY... THEY'VE BEEN MAKING MONEY FOR THE LAST FIVE YEARS BY BEING WRONG AND I'VE BEEN LOSING IT BY BEING RIGHT...
AND CLIENTS ONLY REMEMBER THE BIT ABOUT THE MONEY...

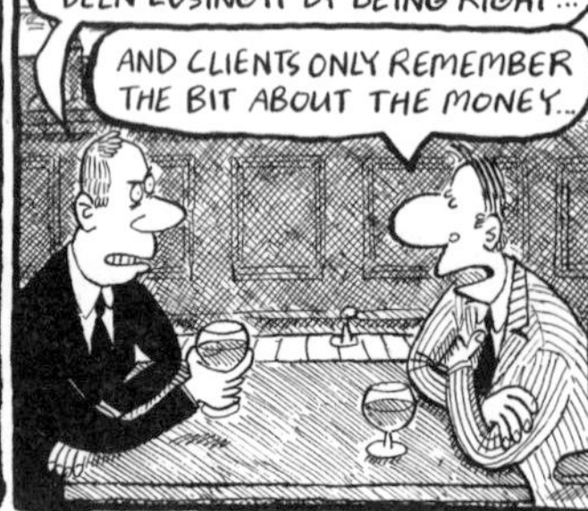

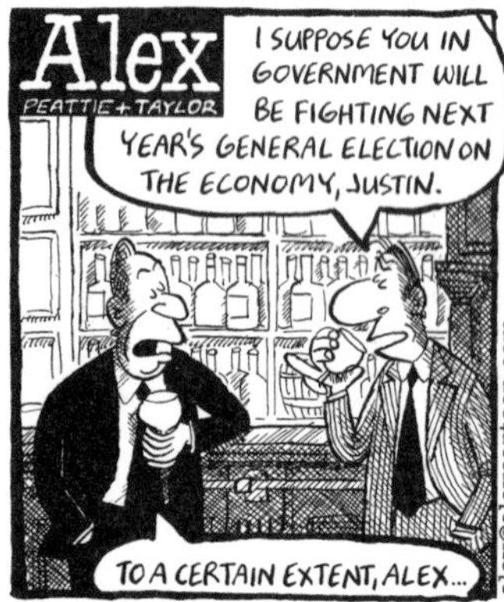
Alex
PEATTIE+TAYLOR
I SUPPOSE YOU IN GOVERNMENT WILL BE FIGHTING NEXT YEAR'S GENERAL ELECTION ON THE ECONOMY, JUSTIN.
TO A CERTAIN EXTENT, ALEX...
alex@alexcartoon.com

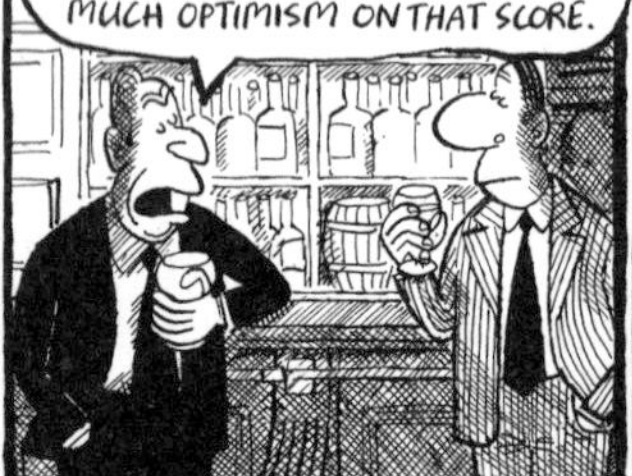
OBVIOUSLY WE FEEL THAT ONE OF OUR GREATEST LEGACIES TO THE COUNTRY IS THE STRONG ECONOMIC RECOVERY OUR POLICIES HAVE BROUGHT ABOUT, BUT IT'S IMPORTANT NOT TO CREATE TOO MUCH OPTIMISM ON THAT SCORE.

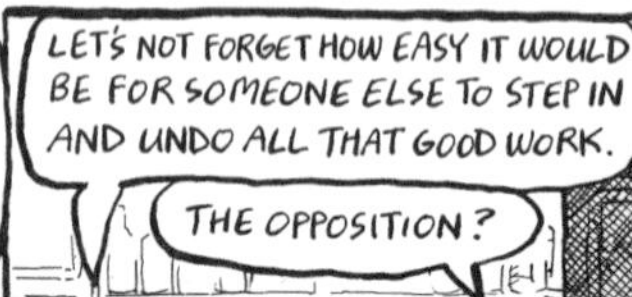
LET'S NOT FORGET HOW EASY IT WOULD BE FOR SOMEONE ELSE TO STEP IN AND UNDO ALL THAT GOOD WORK.
THE OPPOSITION?

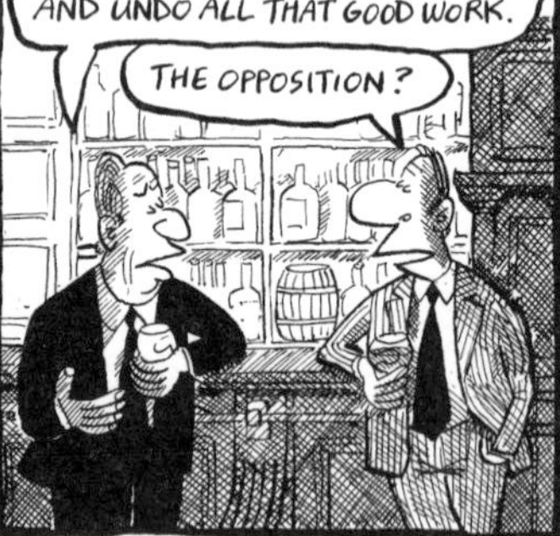

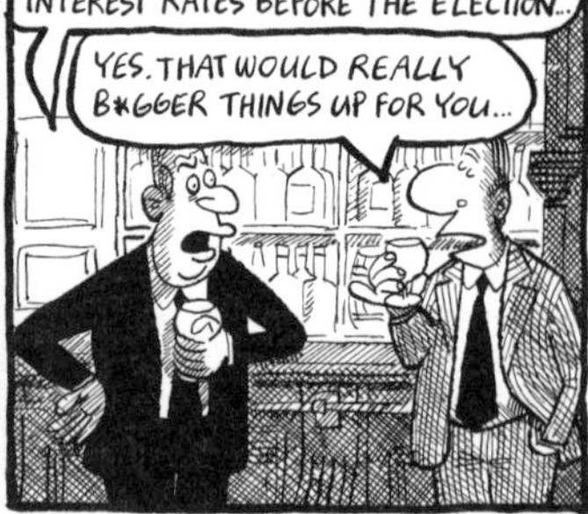
NO, THE BANK OF ENGLAND... THE LAST THING WE WANT IS THEM GETTING ALL BULLISH AND HIKING INTEREST RATES BEFORE THE ELECTION...
YES. THAT WOULD REALLY B*GGER THINGS UP FOR YOU...

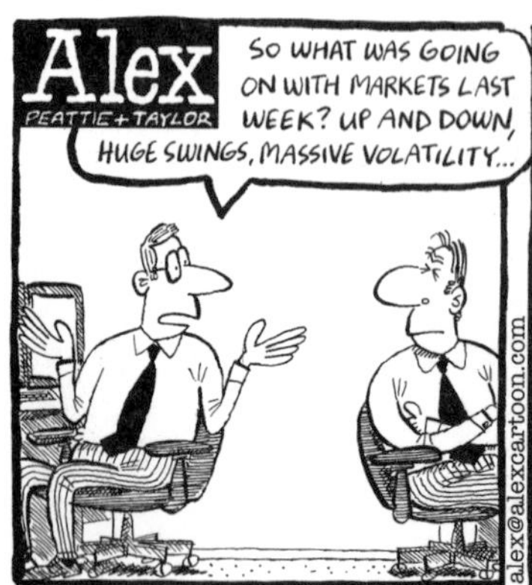
Alex
PEATTIE+TAYLOR
SO WHAT WAS GOING ON WITH MARKETS LAST WEEK? UP AND DOWN, HUGE SWINGS, MASSIVE VOLATILITY...
alex@alexcartoon.com

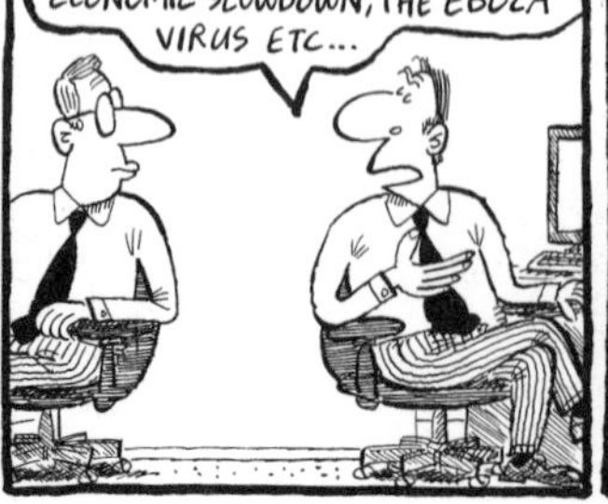
I THINK A LOT OF PEOPLE GOT COLD FEET AND STARTED SELLING THE MARKET BECAUSE OF FEARS OF DEFLATION, A RENEWED EUROZONE CRISIS, GLOBAL ECONOMIC SLOWDOWN, THE EBOLA VIRUS ETC...

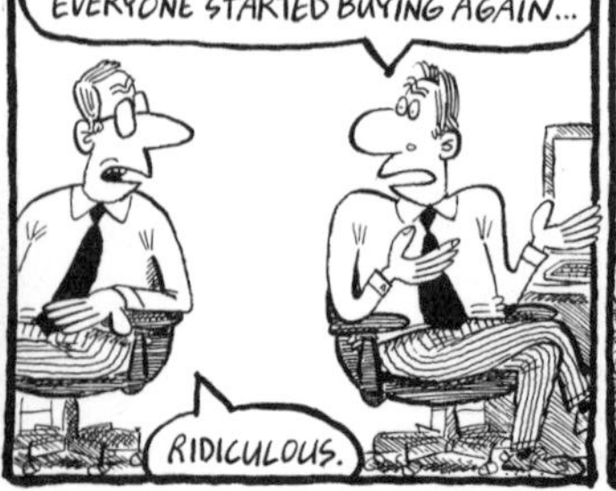
BUT THEN THEY REALISED THAT ALL THE MARKET UNCERTAINTY WOULD SPOOK THE CENTRAL BANKS AND MAKE AN INTEREST RATE RISE LESS LIKELY, SO EVERYONE STARTED BUYING AGAIN...
RIDICULOUS.

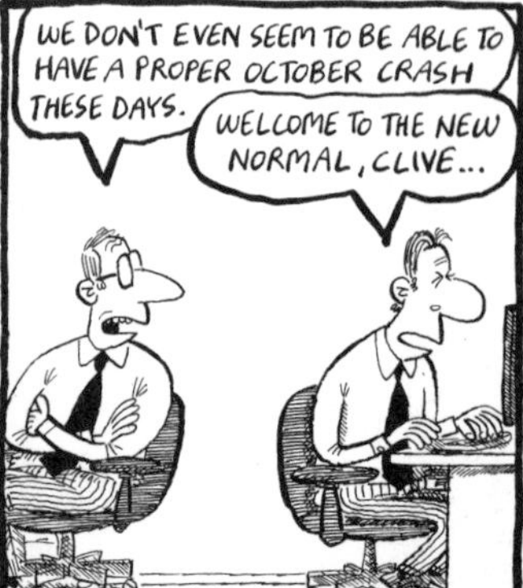
WE DON'T EVEN SEEM TO BE ABLE TO HAVE A PROPER OCTOBER CRASH THESE DAYS.
WELCOME TO THE NEW NORMAL, CLIVE...

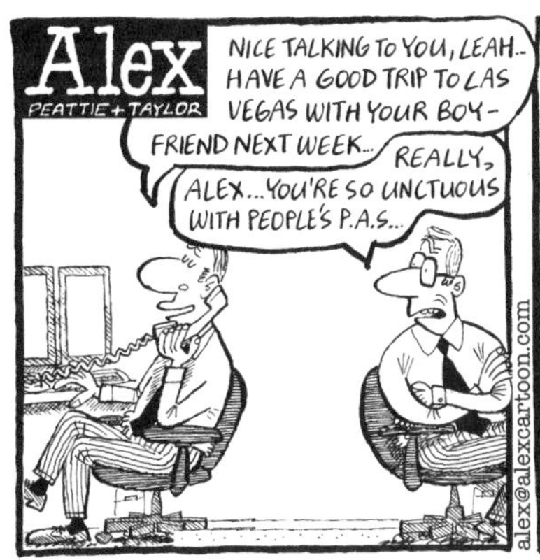
Alex
PEATTIE + TAYLOR
NICE TALKING TO YOU, LEAH.. HAVE A GOOD TRIP TO LAS VEGAS WITH YOUR BOY-FRIEND NEXT WEEK...
REALLY, ALEX... YOU'RE SO UNCTUOUS WITH PEOPLE'S P.A.S...

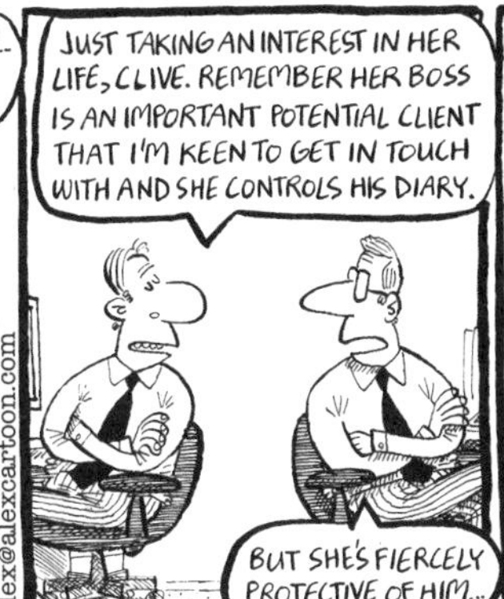
JUST TAKING AN INTEREST IN HER LIFE, CLIVE. REMEMBER HER BOSS IS AN IMPORTANT POTENTIAL CLIENT THAT I'M KEEN TO GET IN TOUCH WITH AND SHE CONTROLS HIS DIARY.
BUT SHE'S FIERCELY PROTECTIVE OF HIM...
alex@alexcartoon.com

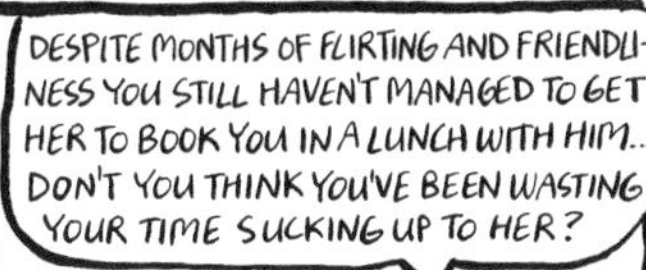
DESPITE MONTHS OF FLIRTING AND FRIENDLI-NESS YOU STILL HAVEN'T MANAGED TO GET HER TO BOOK YOU IN A LUNCH WITH HIM... DON'T YOU THINK YOU'VE BEEN WASTING YOUR TIME SUCKING UP TO HER?

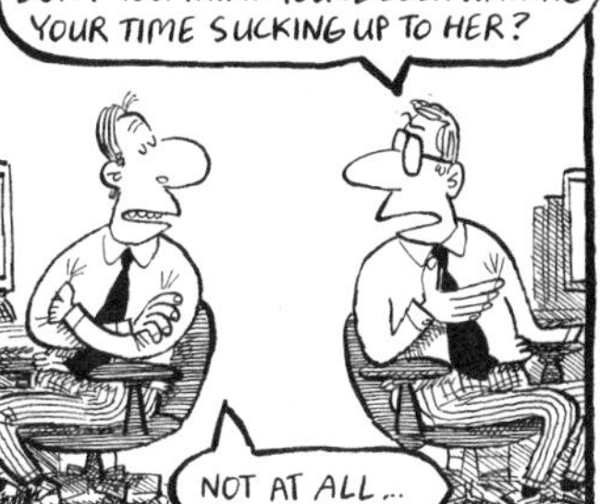
NOT AT ALL...

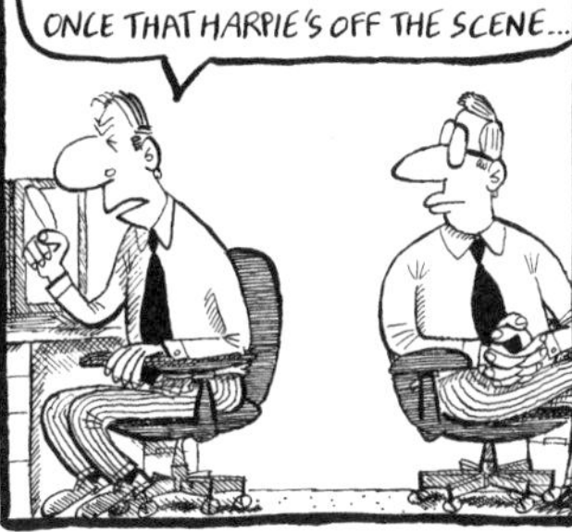
NOT NOW I KNOW SHE'S AWAY NEXT WEEK AND THERE'LL BE A TEMP DOING HER JOB WHO I SHOULD HAVE NO TROUBLE WHEEDLING MY WAY PAST ONCE THAT HARPIE'S OFF THE SCENE...

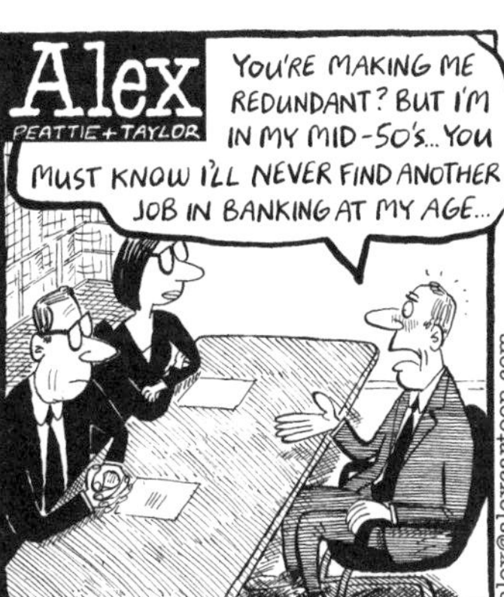
Alex
PEATTIE + TAYLOR
YOU'RE MAKING ME REDUNDANT? BUT I'M IN MY MID-50'S... YOU MUST KNOW I'LL NEVER FIND ANOTHER JOB IN BANKING AT MY AGE...

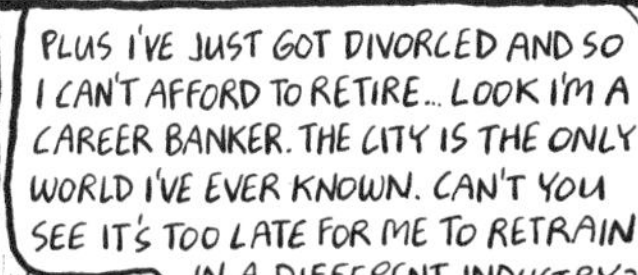
PLUS I'VE JUST GOT DIVORCED AND SO I CAN'T AFFORD TO RETIRE... LOOK I'M A CAREER BANKER. THE CITY IS THE ONLY WORLD I'VE EVER KNOWN. CAN'T YOU SEE IT'S TOO LATE FOR ME TO RETRAIN IN A DIFFERENT INDUSTRY?

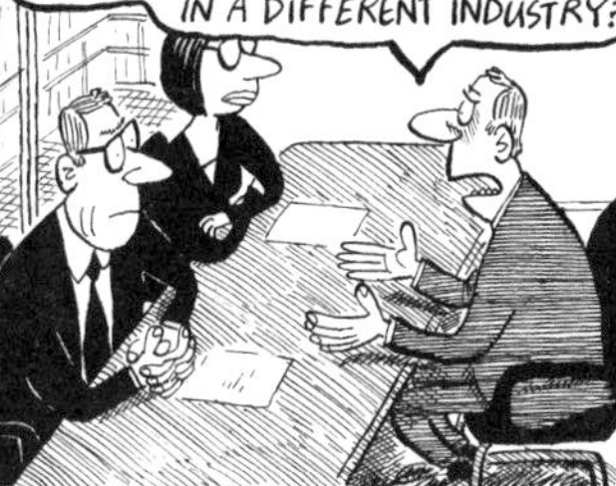
alex@alexcartoon.com

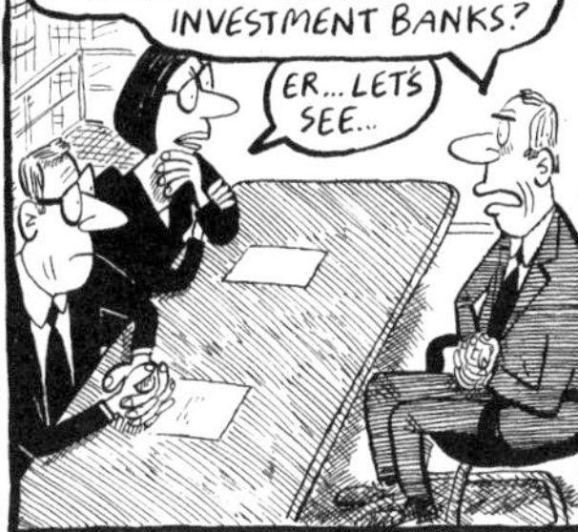
DON'T YOU GIVE ANY THOUGHT TO WHAT HAPPENS TO PEOPLE LIKE ME WHEN WE GET TOSSED CALLOUSLY ASIDE BY BIG INVESTMENT BANKS?
ER... LET'S SEE...
YOU GET RECRUITED BY THE REGULATORS?
EXACTLY... THE F.C.A. HAS PLENTY OF JOBS FOR PEOPLE LIKE ME WHO KNOW ALL THE BIG BANKS' SCAMS... AND GOD KNOWS I KNOW ALL ABOUT THE ONES HERE...
ER, MAYBE WE SHOULD RECONSIDER...

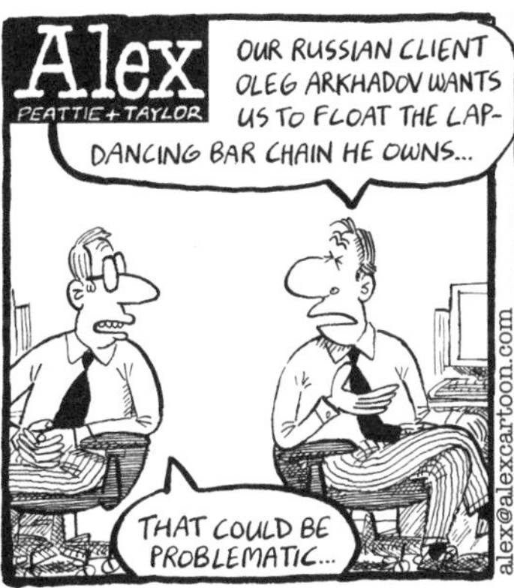
Alex
PEATTIE + TAYLOR
OUR RUSSIAN CLIENT OLEG ARKHADOV WANTS US TO FLOAT THE LAP-DANCING BAR CHAIN HE OWNS...
THAT COULD BE PROBLEMATIC...

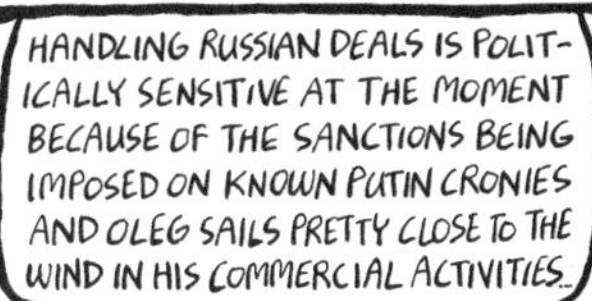
HANDLING RUSSIAN DEALS IS POLIT-ICALLY SENSITIVE AT THE MOMENT BECAUSE OF THE SANCTIONS BEING IMPOSED ON KNOWN PUTIN CRONIES AND OLEG SAILS PRETTY CLOSE TO THE WIND IN HIS COMMERCIAL ACTIVITIES...

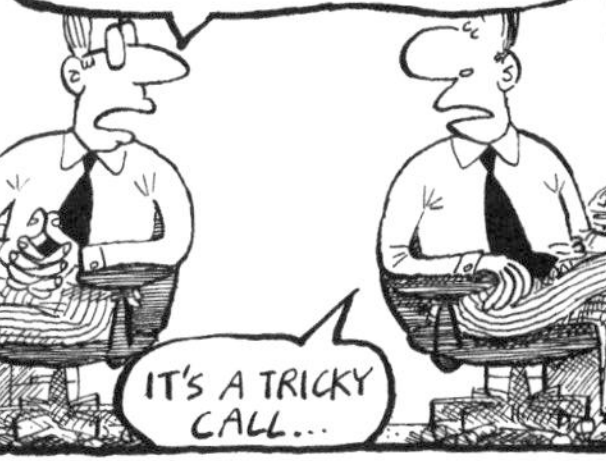
IT'S A TRICKY CALL...
alex@alexcartoon.com

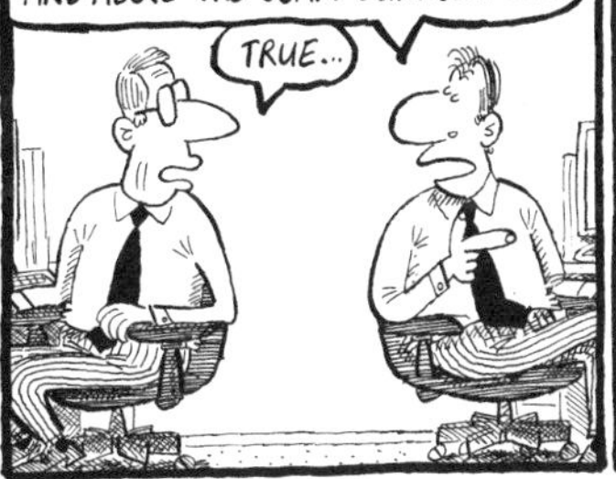
BUT ONE HAS TO REMEMBER THAT THERE'S A LOT OF PRESSURE ON HIM THESE DAYS TO ESTABLISH A REPUTAT-ION FOR BEING AN HONEST, RESPECTABLE AND ABOVE-THE-BOARD BUSINESSMAN.
TRUE...

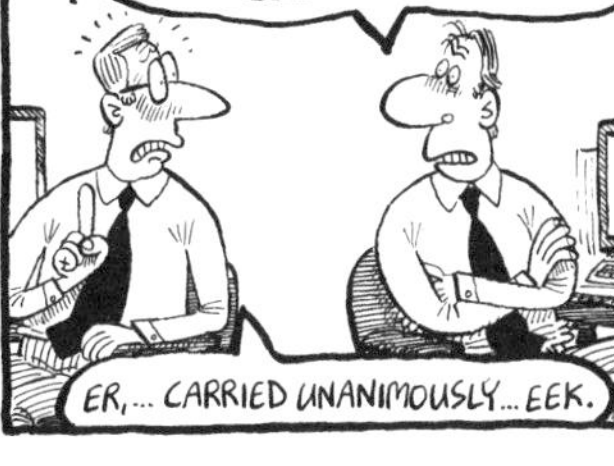
WHICH MEANS NOW HE'S EVEN MORE LIKELY TO SEND ROUND HIS HENCHMEN TO SORT OUT ANYONE WHO HAS THE TEMERITY TO SUGGEST OTHERWISE...
QUITE. SO I VOTE WE AGREE TO WORK WITH HIM. IT'S SAFER...
ER,... CARRIED UNANIMOUSLY... EEK.

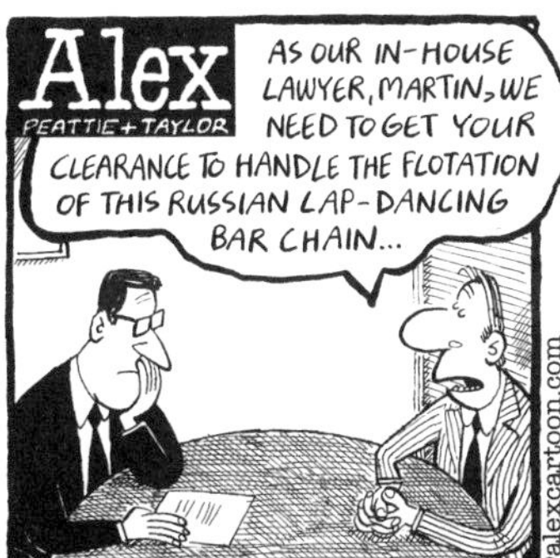
Alex
PEATTIE + TAYLOR
AS OUR IN-HOUSE LAWYER, MARTIN, WE NEED TO GET YOUR CLEARANCE TO HANDLE THE FLOTATION OF THIS RUSSIAN LAP-DANCING BAR CHAIN...

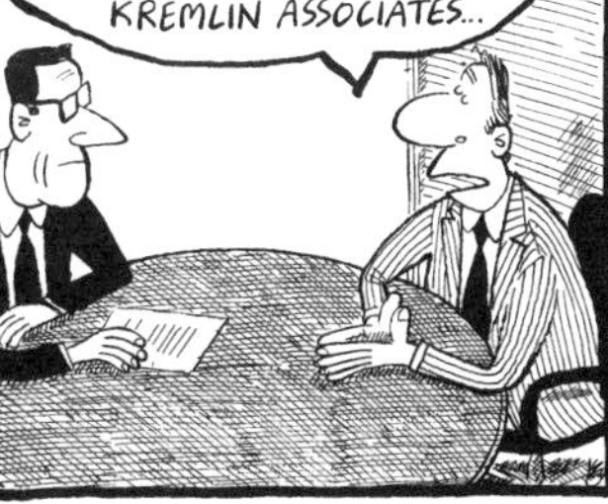
OBVIOUSLY ONE HAS TO BE AWARE OF THE RISKS OF DOING DEALS WITH RUSSIAN-OWNED BUSINESSES IN VIEW OF THE INTERNATIONAL SANCTIONS BEING IMPOSED ON KREMLIN ASSOCIATES...
alex@alexcartoon.com

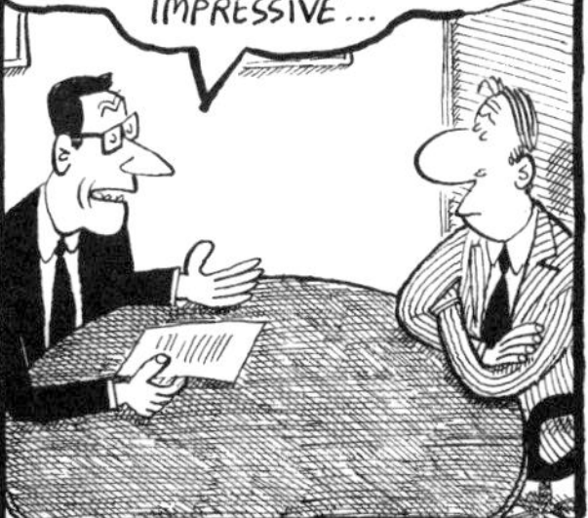
I THINK YOU'RE FINE TO GO AHEAD, ALEX. I'VE CHECKED OUT THE COMPANY IN QUESTION VERY THOROUGHLY AND PROFESSIONALLY I FIND IT VERY IMPRESSIVE...
IT'S HELD BY A BEWILDERINGLY COMPLEX CHAIN OF OFFSHORE TRUSTS REGISTERED IN THE CAYMAN ISLES AND LIECHTENSTEIN.. I'VE NO IDEA WHO ACTUALLY OWNS IT...
EXCELLENT. IF YOU CAN'T FIGURE IT OUT, WHO ELSE WILL?
I MIGHT USE IT AS AN EXAMPLE IN MY NEXT TAX EVASION SEMINAR.

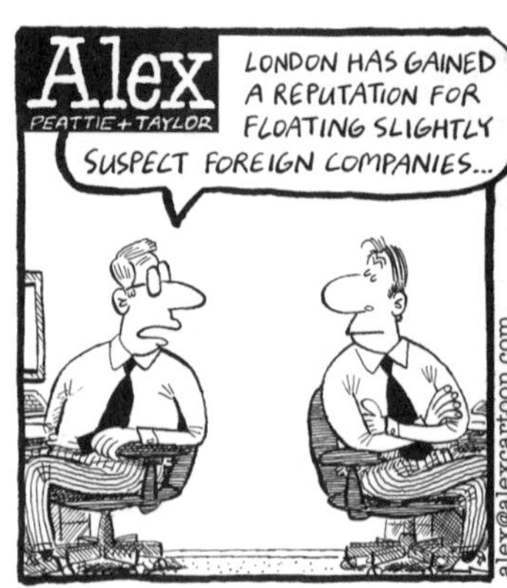
Alex
PEATTIE+TAYLOR
LONDON HAS GAINED A REPUTATION FOR FLOATING SLIGHTLY SUSPECT FOREIGN COMPANIES...

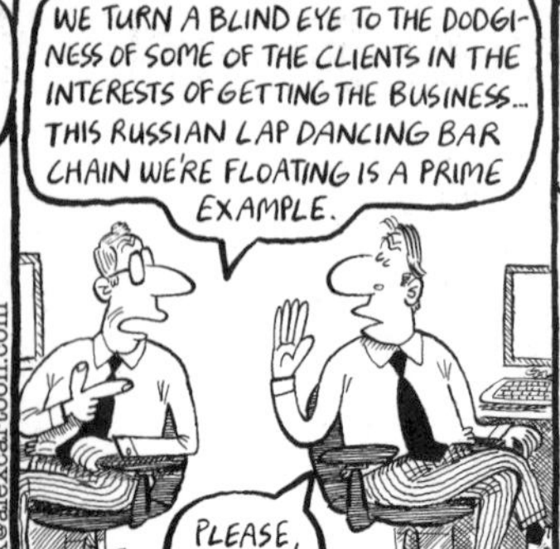
WE TURN A BLIND EYE TO THE DODGINESS OF SOME OF THE CLIENTS IN THE INTERESTS OF GETTING THE BUSINESS... THIS RUSSIAN LAP DANCING BAR CHAIN WE'RE FLOATING IS A PRIME EXAMPLE.
PLEASE, CLIVE...
alex@alexcartoon.com

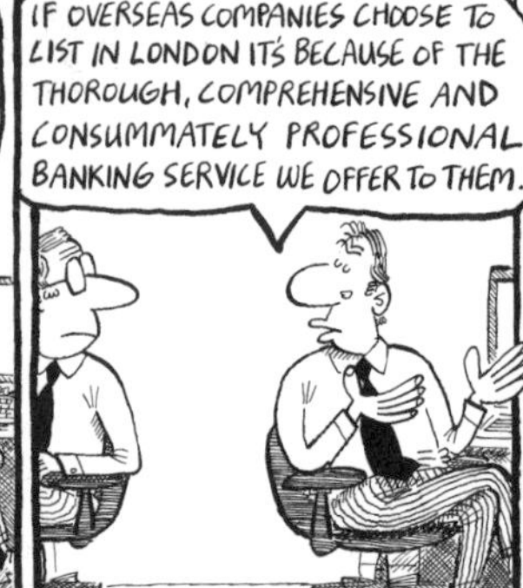
IF OVERSEAS COMPANIES CHOOSE TO LIST IN LONDON IT'S BECAUSE OF THE THOROUGH, COMPREHENSIVE AND CONSUMMATELY PROFESSIONAL BANKING SERVICE WE OFFER TO THEM.

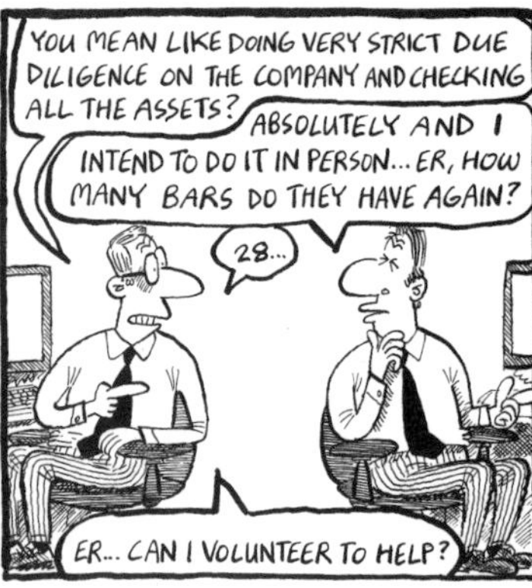
YOU MEAN LIKE DOING VERY STRICT DUE DILIGENCE ON THE COMPANY AND CHECKING ALL THE ASSETS?
ABSOLUTELY AND I INTEND TO DO IT IN PERSON... ER, HOW MANY BARS DO THEY HAVE AGAIN?
28...
ER... CAN I VOLUNTEER TO HELP?

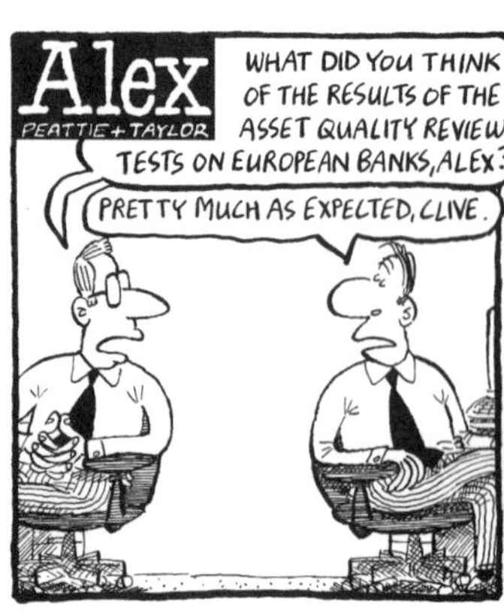
Alex
PEATTIE+TAYLOR
WHAT DID YOU THINK OF THE RESULTS OF THE ASSET QUALITY REVIEW TESTS ON EUROPEAN BANKS, ALEX?
PRETTY MUCH AS EXPECTED, CLIVE.
alex@alexcartoon.com

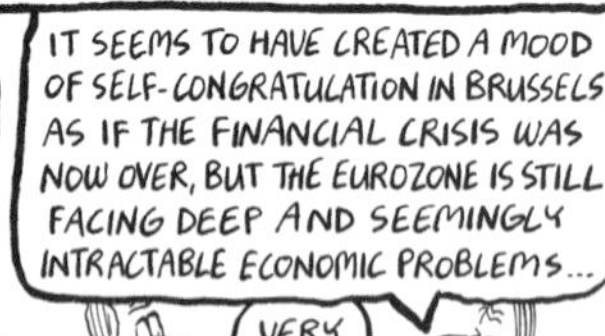
IT SEEMS TO HAVE CREATED A MOOD OF SELF-CONGRATULATION IN BRUSSELS AS IF THE FINANCIAL CRISIS WAS NOW OVER, BUT THE EUROZONE IS STILL FACING DEEP AND SEEMINGLY INTRACTABLE ECONOMIC PROBLEMS...

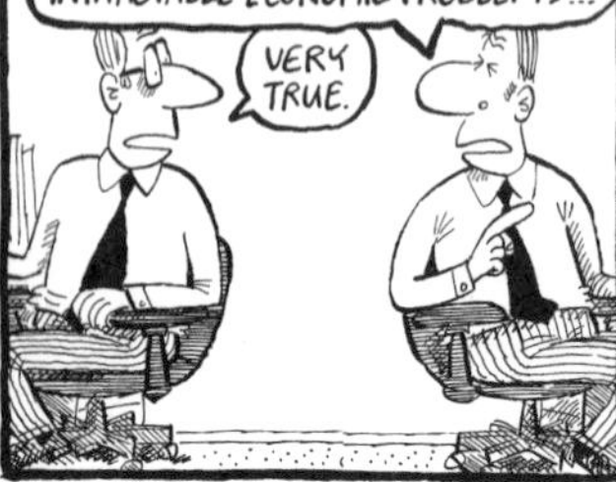
VERY TRUE.

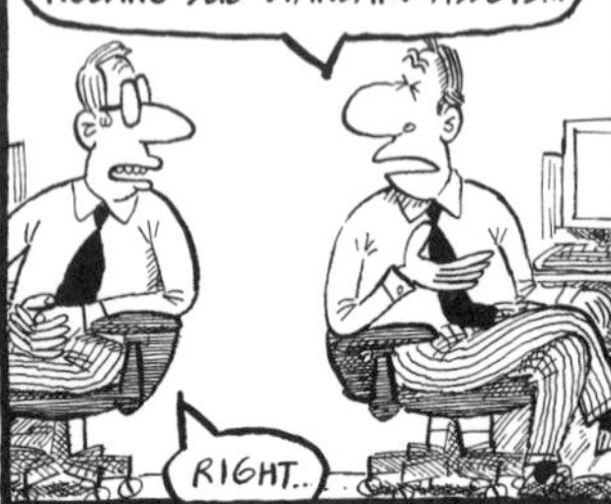
STILL, I SUPPOSE IT'S GOOD TO HAVE THESE BOXES TICKED. THE MAJORITY OF BANKS PASSED THE TEST, WHILE A FEW WERE FOUND TO STILL BE HOLDING SUB-STANDARD ASSETS...
RIGHT...

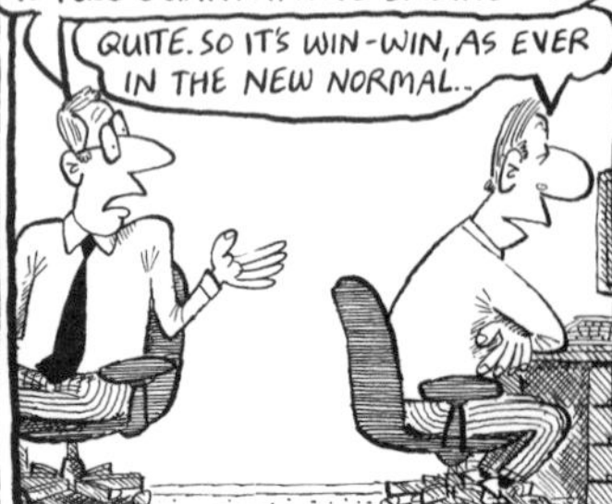
I.E.: JUST THE SORT OF TOXIC JUNK THE EUROPEAN CENTRAL BANK WILL BE PURCHASING OFF THEM WHEN IT INEVITABLY RESORTS TO FULL QUANTITATIVE EASING....
QUITE. SO IT'S WIN-WIN, AS EVER IN THE NEW NORMAL...

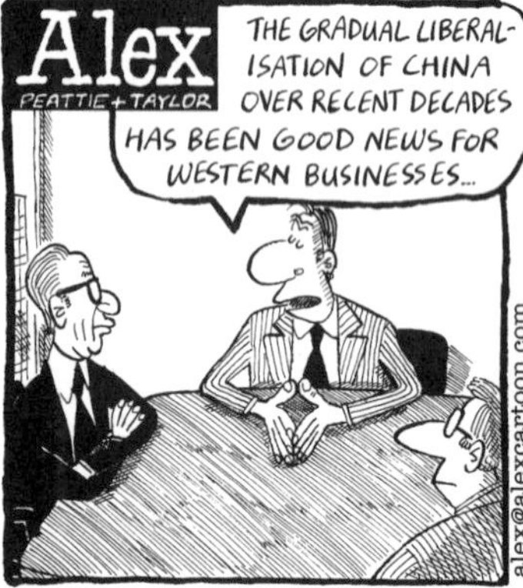
Alex
PEATTIE+TAYLOR
THE GRADUAL LIBERALISATION OF CHINA OVER RECENT DECADES HAS BEEN GOOD NEWS FOR WESTERN BUSINESSES...
alex@alexcartoon.com

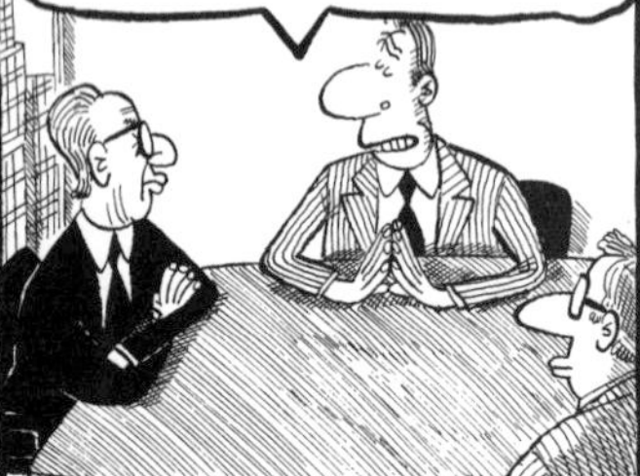
LUXURY GOODS COMPANIES LIKE YOURS HAVE MADE A FORTUNE FROM THE DEMAND OF THE HUGE NEW CHINESE MIDDLE CLASS FOR UPMARKET EUROPEAN BRANDS AND LABELS...

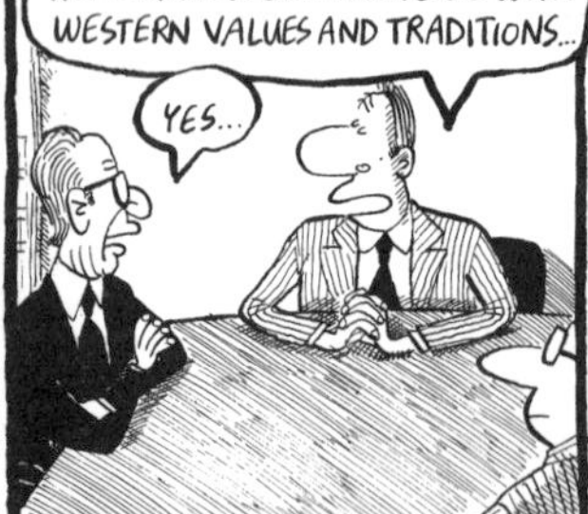
AND NOW THE CHINESE GOVERNMENT HAS INTRODUCED FRESH INITIATIVES WHICH WILL BRING THE COUNTRY FURTHER IN LINE WITH WESTERN VALUES AND TRADITIONS...
YES...

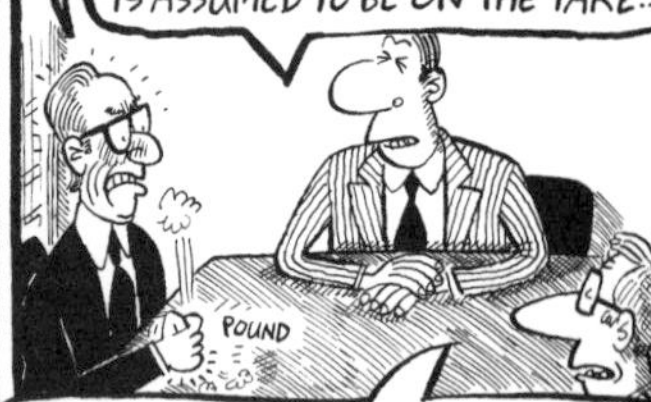
THIS BLASTED ANTI-CORRUPTION DRIVE. IT'S MOST ANNOYING...
NOWADAYS ANYONE SEEN FLAUNTING DESIGNER CLOTHES OR ACCESSORIES IS ASSUMED TO BE ON THE TAKE...
POUND
I'M AFRAID YOUR COMPANY WILL HAVE TO ANNOUNCE ANOTHER PROFIT WARNING...

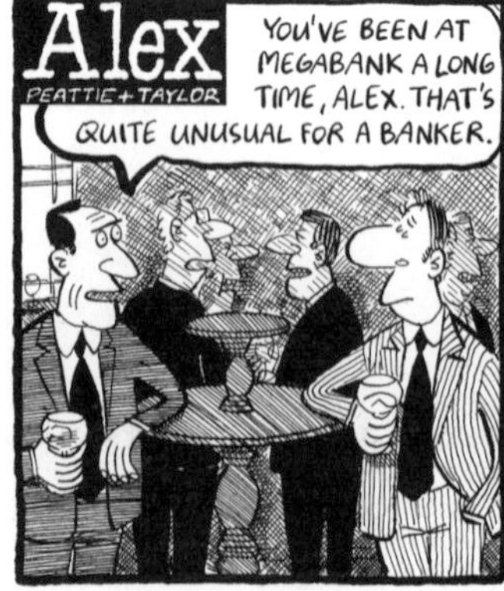
Alex
PEATTIE+TAYLOR
YOU'VE BEEN AT MEGABANK A LONG TIME, ALEX. THAT'S QUITE UNUSUAL FOR A BANKER.
alex@alexcartoon.com

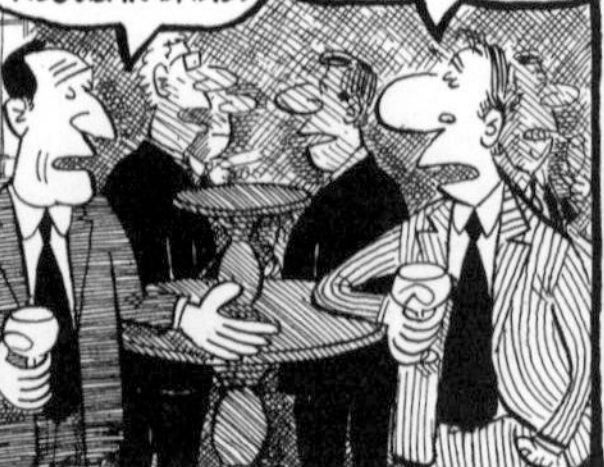
AFTER ALL, IN OUR INDUSTRY THE BEST WAY TO BOOST ONE'S EARNINGS IS TO MOVE JOBS ON A REGULAR BASIS.
TRUE. BUT THERE'S THE RISK THAT THINGS MIGHT NOT WORK OUT WITH A NEW EMPLOYER...

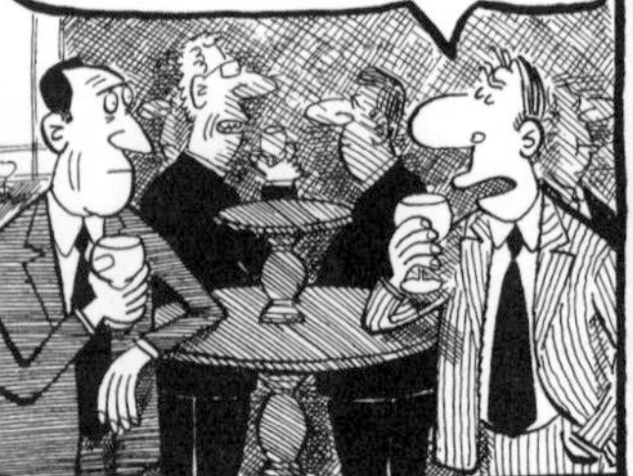
FRANKLY WITH ALL THE INSECURITY ENGENDERED BY THE FINANCIAL CRISIS OVER THE LAST SEVEN YEARS I THINK I'VE DONE THE RIGHT THING AND MY LOYALTY IS NOW BEING REWARDED...

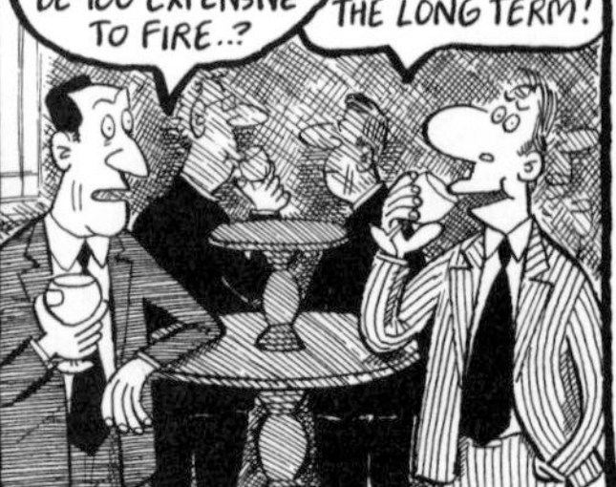
WHAT, BECAUSE YOU'RE NOW ENTITLED TO SO MANY LONG-SERVICE BENEFITS THAT YOU'D BE TOO EXPENSIVE TO FIRE..?
QUITE... AND PEOPLE SAY WE BANKERS DON'T THINK IN THE LONG TERM!

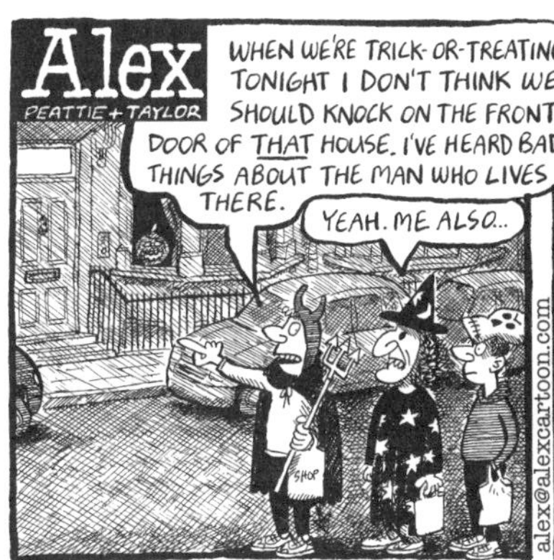
Alex
PEATTIE + TAYLOR
WHEN WE'RE TRICK-OR-TREATING TONIGHT I DON'T THINK WE SHOULD KNOCK ON THE FRONT DOOR OF THAT HOUSE. I'VE HEARD BAD THINGS ABOUT THE MAN WHO LIVES THERE.
YEAH. ME ALSO...
SHOP

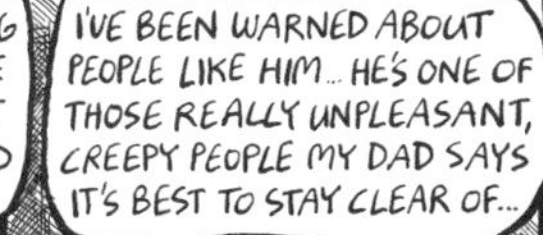
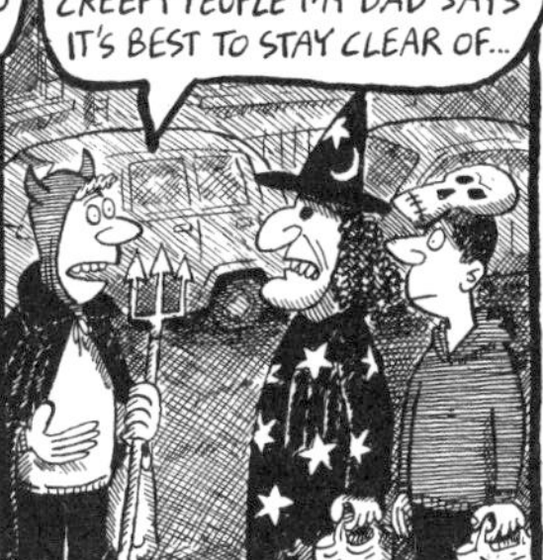
I'VE BEEN WARNED ABOUT PEOPLE LIKE HIM... HE'S ONE OF THOSE REALLY UNPLEASANT, CREEPY PEOPLE MY DAD SAYS IT'S BEST TO STAY CLEAR OF...
alex@alexcartoon.com

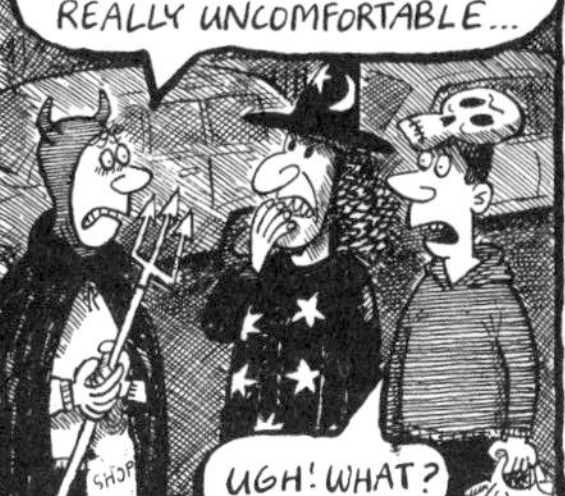
THERE'S A STORY THAT LAST YEAR ON HALLOWEEN HE CAME TO THE DOOR AND GAVE SWEETS AND CANDY TO TWO KIDS AND THEN DID SOMETHING THAT MADE THEM BOTH FEEL REALLY UNCOMFORTABLE...
UGH! WHAT?

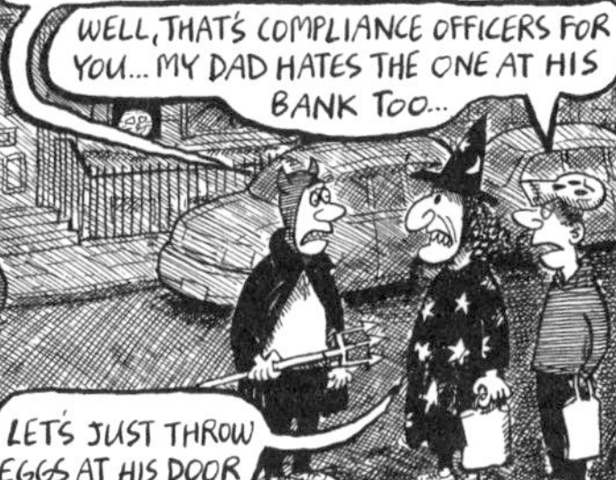
HE MADE THEM READ AND SIGN THESE REALLY LONG ANTI-BRIBERY FORMS DETAILING THE VALUE OF HIS HOSPITALITY. THEY WERE STANDING IN THE RAIN FOR 45 MINUTES...
WELL, THAT'S COMPLIANCE OFFICERS FOR YOU... MY DAD HATES THE ONE AT HIS BANK TOO...
LET'S JUST THROW EGGS AT HIS DOOR

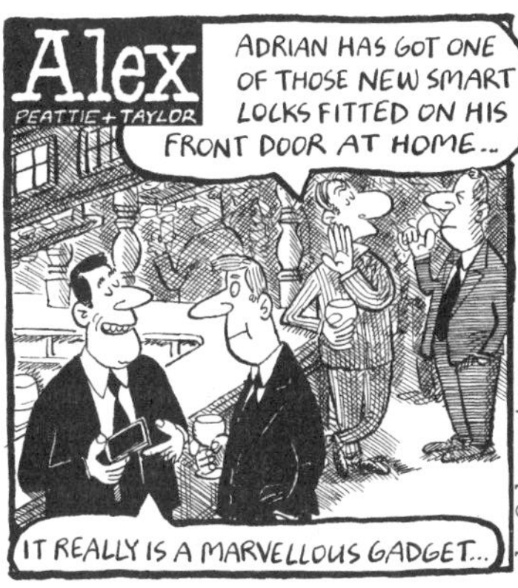
Alex
PEATTIE + TAYLOR
ADRIAN HAS GOT ONE OF THOSE NEW SMART LOCKS FITTED ON HIS FRONT DOOR AT HOME...
IT REALLY IS A MARVELLOUS GADGET...
alex@alexcartoon.com

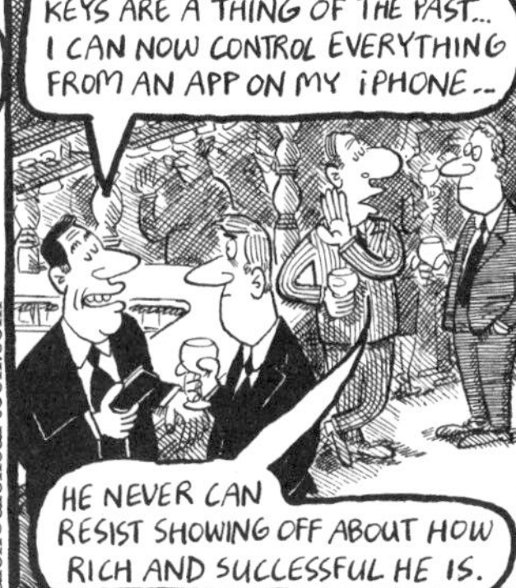
KEYS ARE A THING OF THE PAST... I CAN NOW CONTROL EVERYTHING FROM AN APP ON MY iPHONE...
HE NEVER CAN RESIST SHOWING OFF ABOUT HOW RICH AND SUCCESSFUL HE IS.

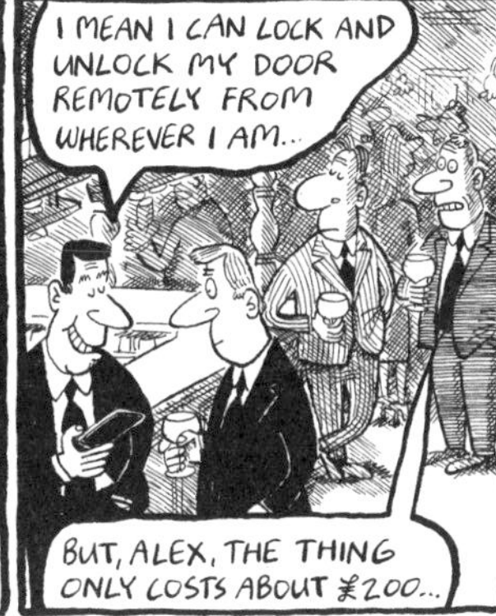
I MEAN I CAN LOCK AND UNLOCK MY DOOR REMOTELY FROM WHEREVER I AM...
BUT, ALEX, THE THING ONLY COSTS ABOUT £200...

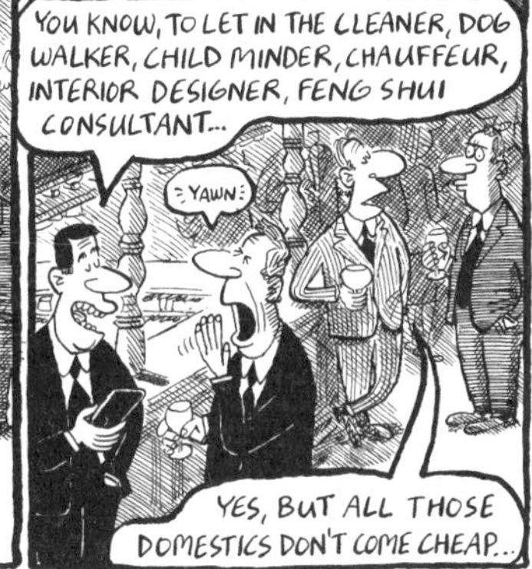
YOU KNOW, TO LET IN THE CLEANER, DOG WALKER, CHILD MINDER, CHAUFFEUR, INTERIOR DESIGNER, FENG SHUI CONSULTANT...
YAWN
YES, BUT ALL THOSE DOMESTICS DON'T COME CHEAP...

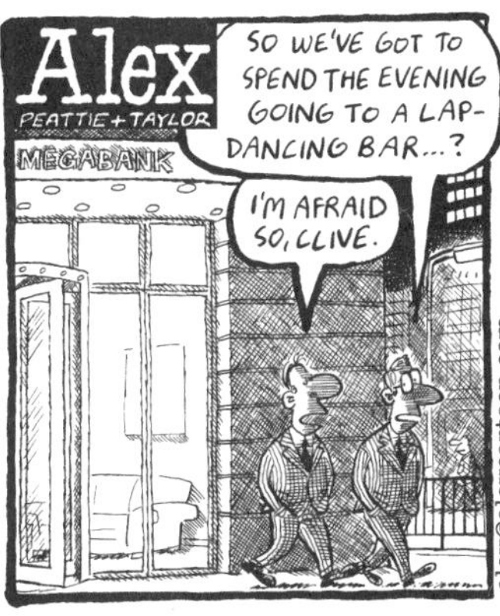
Alex
PEATTIE + TAYLOR
SO WE'VE GOT TO SPEND THE EVENING GOING TO A LAP-DANCING BAR...?
MEGABANK
I'M AFRAID SO, CLIVE.
alex@alexcartoon.com

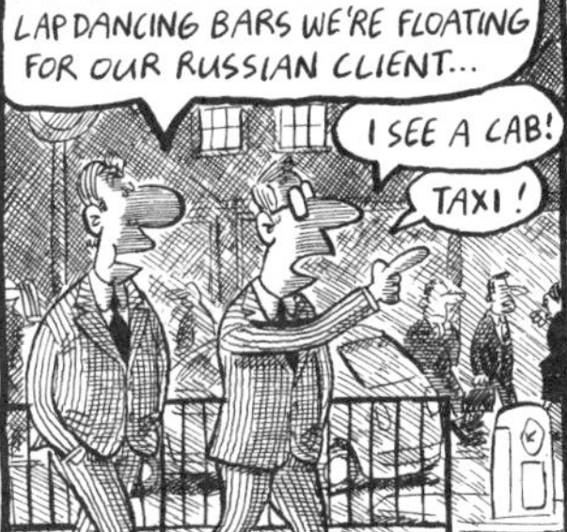
IT'S PART OF OUR DUE DILIGENCE OBLIGATIONS FOR THIS CHAIN OF LAP DANCING BARS WE'RE FLOATING FOR OUR RUSSIAN CLIENT...
I SEE A CAB!
TAXI!

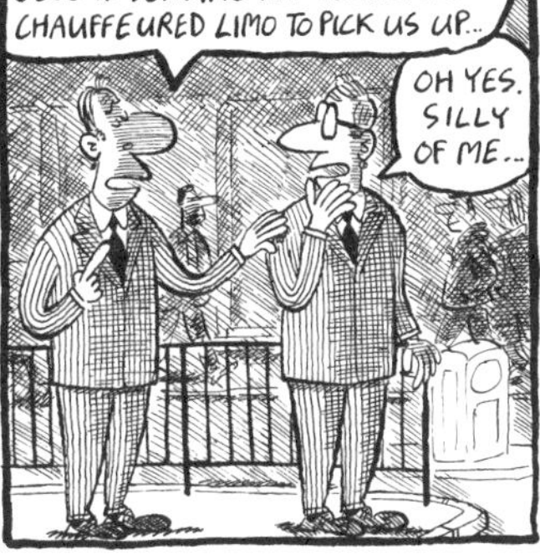
HOLD ON, CLIVE... NO NEED FOR THAT. OLEG IS SENDING HIS PERSONAL CHAUFFEURED LIMO TO PICK US UP...
OH YES. SILLY OF ME...

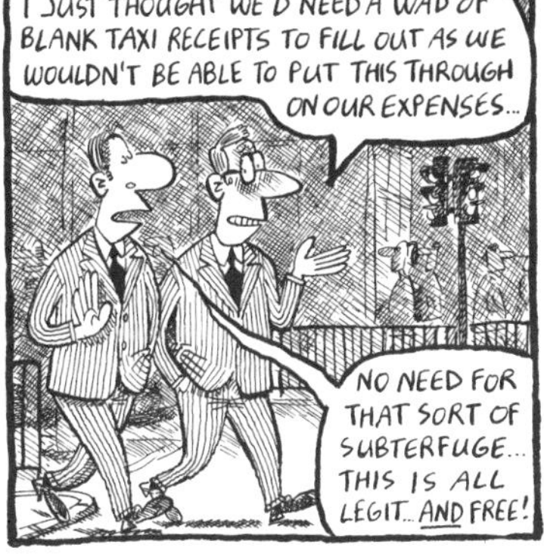
I JUST THOUGHT WE'D NEED A WAD OF BLANK TAXI RECEIPTS TO FILL OUT AS WE WOULDN'T BE ABLE TO PUT THIS THROUGH ON OUR EXPENSES...
NO NEED FOR THAT SORT OF SUBTERFUGE... THIS IS ALL LEGIT... AND FREE!

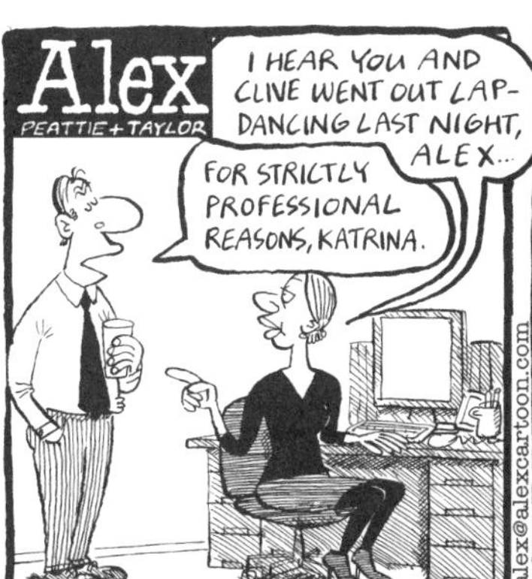
Alex
PEATTIE + TAYLOR
I HEAR YOU AND CLIVE WENT OUT LAP-DANCING LAST NIGHT, ALEX...
FOR STRICTLY PROFESSIONAL REASONS, KATRINA.
alex@alexcartoon.com

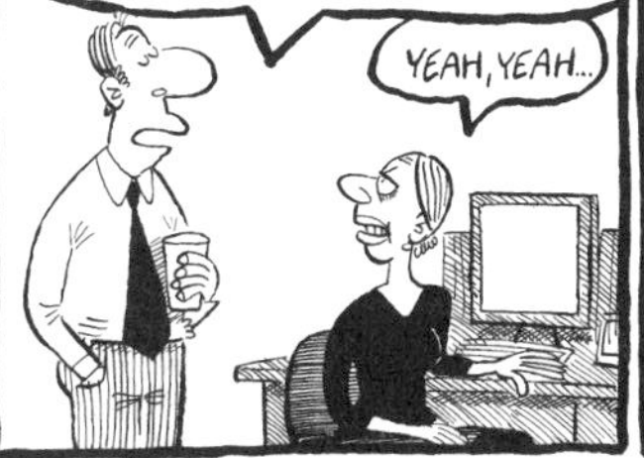
WE'RE FLOATING A CHAIN OF LAP-DANCING BARS AND OBVIOUSLY WE HAD TO DO THE DUE DILIGENCE: CHECKING THAT THE BARS ACTUALLY EXIST AND ARE ADEQUATELY STOCKED WITH DANCERS, DRINKS ETC...
YEAH, YEAH...

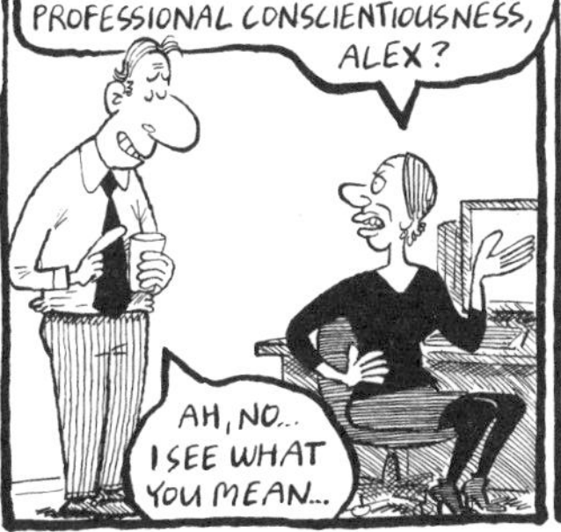
ARE YOU REALLY TRYING TO KID ME THAT YOU'VE JUST BEEN VISITING THESE BARS OUT OF A SPIRIT OF PROFESSIONAL CONSCIENTIOUSNESS, ALEX?
AH, NO... I SEE WHAT YOU MEAN...

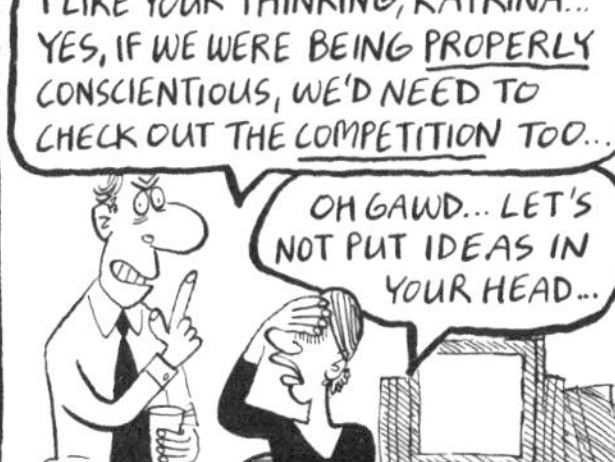
I LIKE YOUR THINKING, KATRINA... YES, IF WE WERE BEING PROPERLY CONSCIENTIOUS, WE'D NEED TO CHECK OUT THE COMPETITION TOO...
OH GAWD... LET'S NOT PUT IDEAS IN YOUR HEAD...

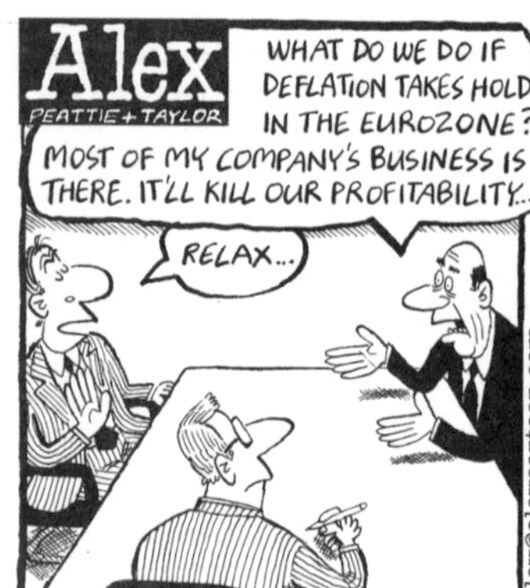
Alex
PEATTIE+TAYLOR
WHAT DO WE DO IF DEFLATION TAKES HOLD IN THE EUROZONE?
MOST OF MY COMPANY'S BUSINESS IS THERE. IT'LL KILL OUR PROFITABILITY...
RELAX...
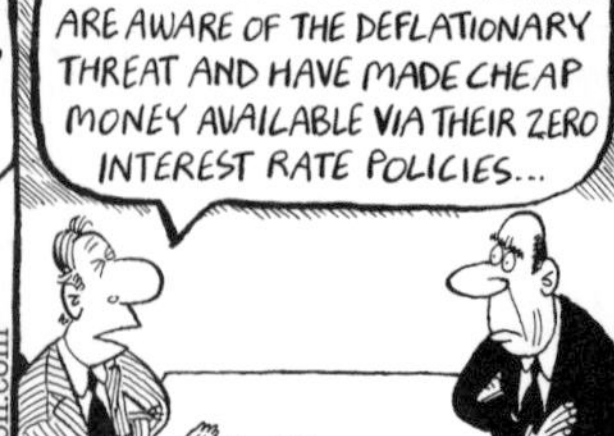
DON'T FORGET THAT CENTRAL BANKS ARE AWARE OF THE DEFLATIONARY THREAT AND HAVE MADE CHEAP MONEY AVAILABLE VIA THEIR ZERO INTEREST RATE POLICIES...
alex@alexcartoon.com
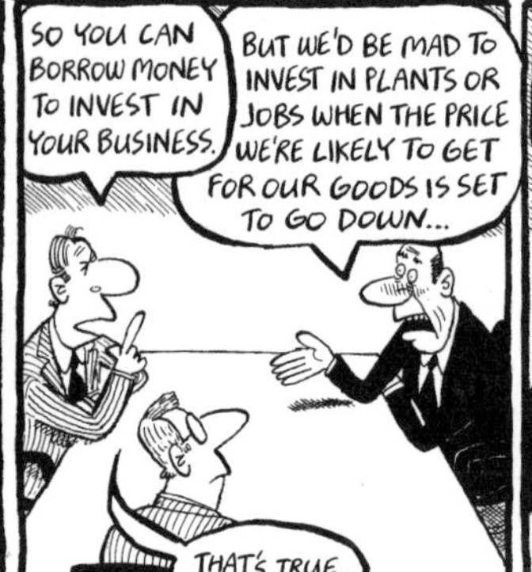
SO YOU CAN BORROW MONEY TO INVEST IN YOUR BUSINESS.
BUT WE'D BE MAD TO INVEST IN PLANTS OR JOBS WHEN THE PRICE WE'RE LIKELY TO GET FOR OUR GOODS IS SET TO GO DOWN...
THAT'S TRUE...
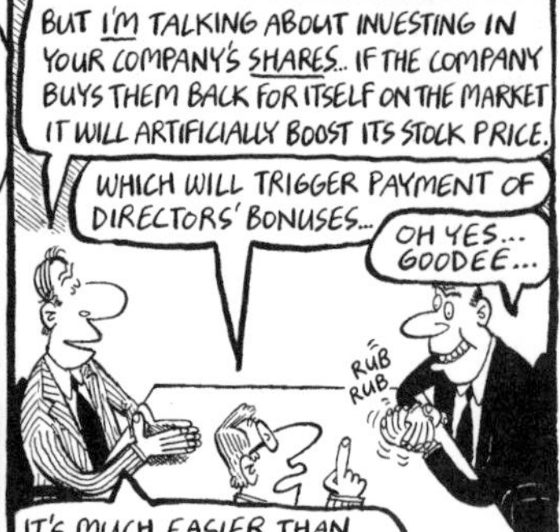
BUT I'M TALKING ABOUT INVESTING IN YOUR COMPANY'S SHARES.. IF THE COMPANY BUYS THEM BACK FOR ITSELF ON THE MARKET IT WILL ARTIFICIALLY BOOST ITS STOCK PRICE.
WHICH WILL TRIGGER PAYMENT OF DIRECTORS' BONUSES...
OH YES... GOODEE...
RUB RUB
IT'S MUCH EASIER THAN HAVING TO MAKE PROFITS...
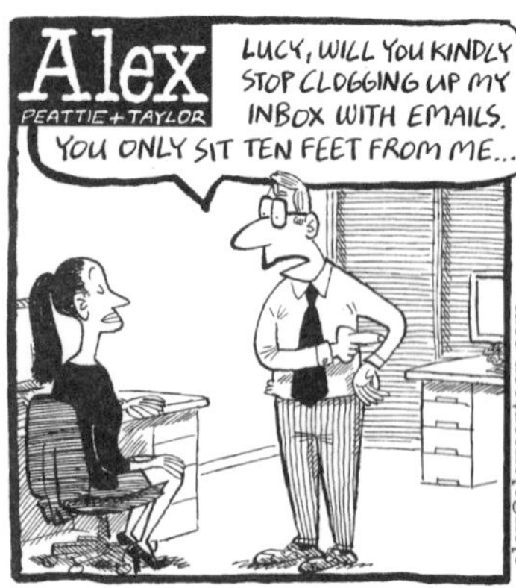
Alex
PEATTIE+TAYLOR
LUCY, WILL YOU KINDLY STOP CLOGGING UP MY INBOX WITH EMAILS.
YOU ONLY SIT TEN FEET FROM ME...
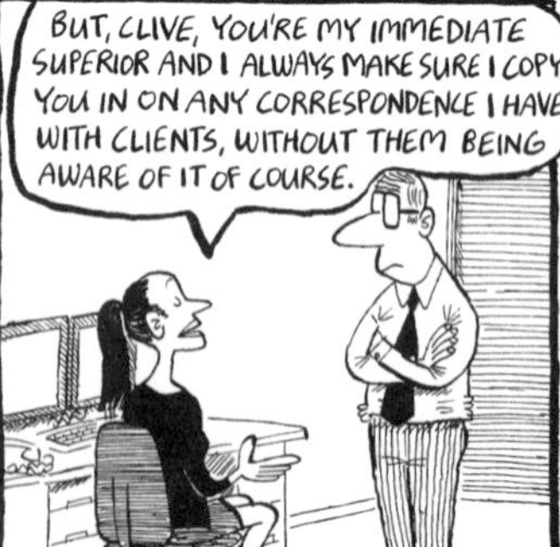
BUT, CLIVE, YOU'RE MY IMMEDIATE SUPERIOR AND I ALWAYS MAKE SURE I COPY YOU IN ON ANY CORRESPONDENCE I HAVE WITH CLIENTS, WITHOUT THEM BEING AWARE OF IT OF COURSE.
alex@alexcartoon.com
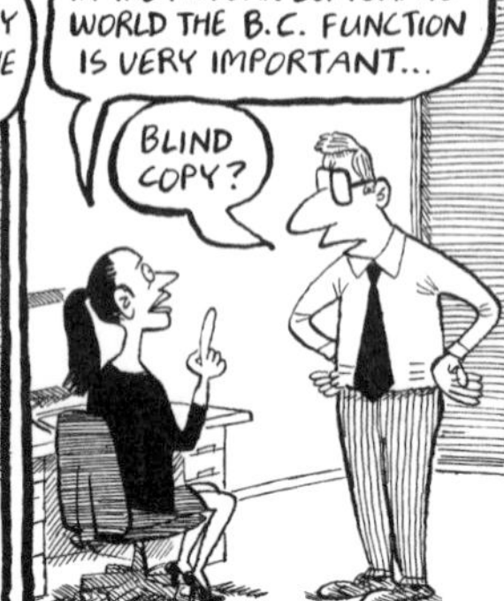
IN THE MODERN CORPORATE WORLD THE B.C. FUNCTION IS VERY IMPORTANT...
BLIND COPY?
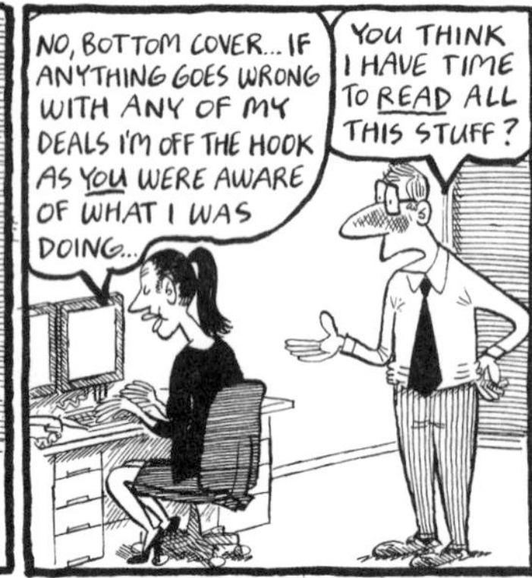
NO, BOTTOM COVER... IF ANYTHING GOES WRONG WITH ANY OF MY DEALS I'M OFF THE HOOK AS YOU WERE AWARE OF WHAT I WAS DOING...
YOU THINK I HAVE TIME TO READ ALL THIS STUFF?
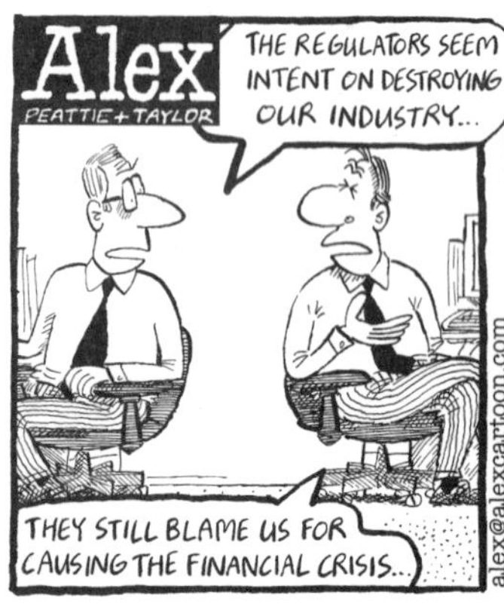
Alex
PEATTIE+TAYLOR
THE REGULATORS SEEM INTENT ON DESTROYING OUR INDUSTRY...
THEY STILL BLAME US FOR CAUSING THE FINANCIAL CRISIS...
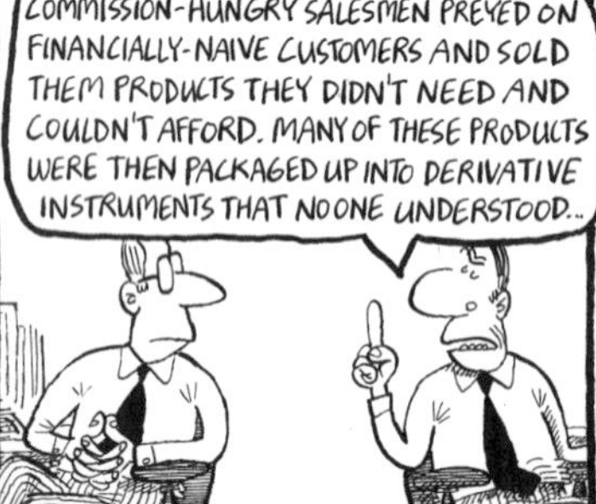
COMMISSION-HUNGRY SALESMEN PREYED ON FINANCIALLY-NAIVE CUSTOMERS AND SOLD THEM PRODUCTS THEY DIDN'T NEED AND COULDN'T AFFORD. MANY OF THESE PRODUCTS WERE THEN PACKAGED UP INTO DERIVATIVE INSTRUMENTS THAT NO ONE UNDERSTOOD...
alex@alexcartoon.com
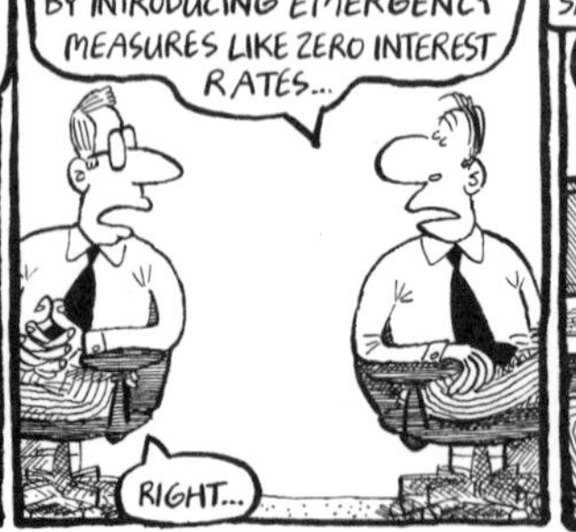
THIS CRASHED THE MARKETS AND THE CENTRAL BANKS HAD TO BAIL OUT THE FINANCIAL SYSTEM BY INTRODUCING EMERGENCY MEASURES LIKE ZERO INTEREST RATES...
RIGHT...
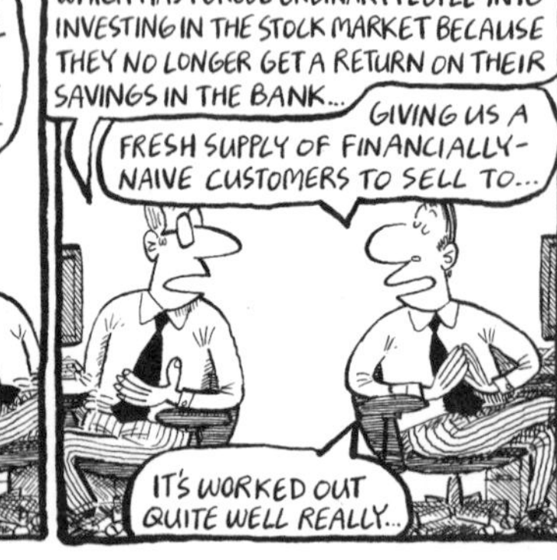
WHICH HAS FORCED ORDINARY PEOPLE INTO INVESTING IN THE STOCK MARKET BECAUSE THEY NO LONGER GET A RETURN ON THEIR SAVINGS IN THE BANK...
GIVING US A FRESH SUPPLY OF FINANCIALLY-NAIVE CUSTOMERS TO SELL TO...
IT'S WORKED OUT QUITE WELL REALLY...
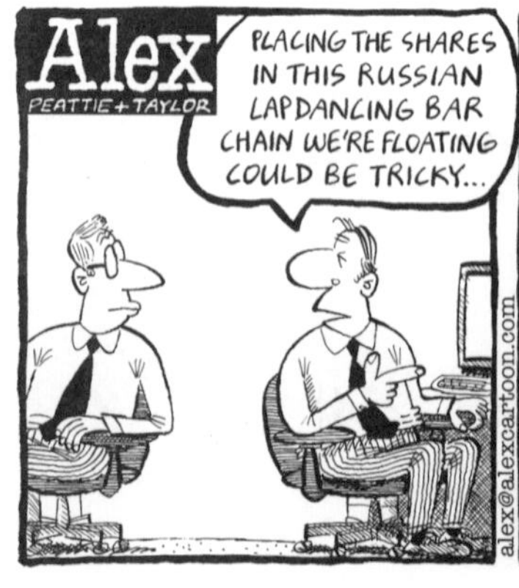
Alex
PEATTIE+TAYLOR
PLACING THE SHARES IN THIS RUSSIAN LAPDANCING BAR CHAIN WE'RE FLOATING COULD BE TRICKY...
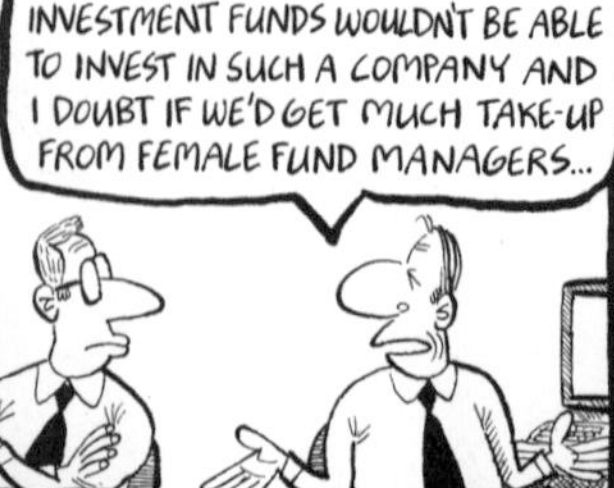
OBVIOUSLY MANAGERS OF ETHICAL INVESTMENT FUNDS WOULDN'T BE ABLE TO INVEST IN SUCH A COMPANY AND I DOUBT IF WE'D GET MUCH TAKE-UP FROM FEMALE FUND MANAGERS...
alex@alexcartoon.com
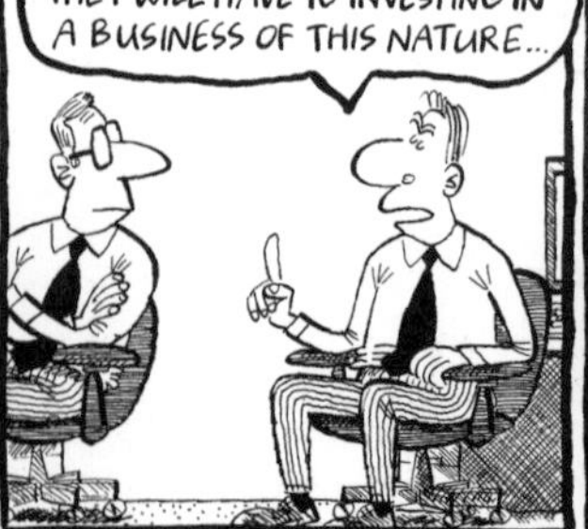
AS FOR THE OTHERS, WE MAY HAVE TO WORK HARD TO OVERCOME THE OBVIOUS PROFESSIONAL OBJECTIONS THEY WILL HAVE TO INVESTING IN A BUSINESS OF THIS NATURE...
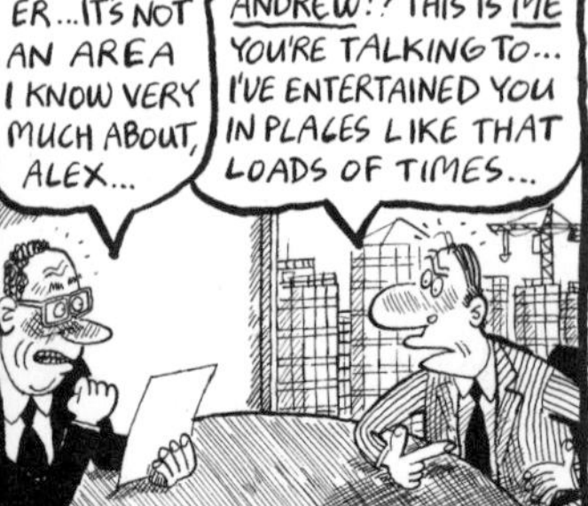
ER...IT'S NOT AN AREA I KNOW VERY MUCH ABOUT, ALEX...
ANDREW!? THIS IS ME YOU'RE TALKING TO... I'VE ENTERTAINED YOU IN PLACES LIKE THAT LOADS OF TIMES...
AHEM...

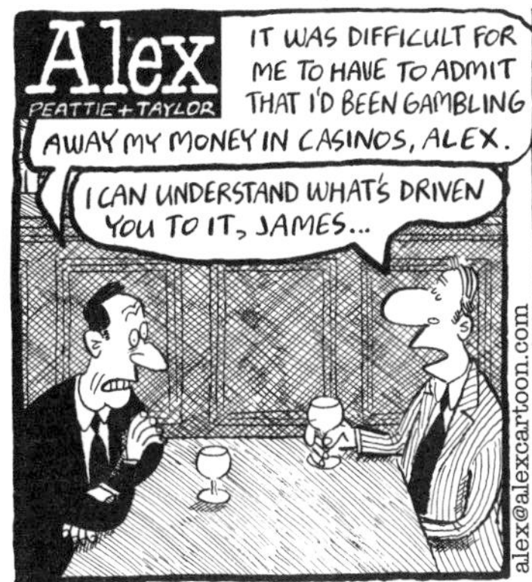
Alex
PEATTIE + TAYLOR
IT WAS DIFFICULT FOR ME TO HAVE TO ADMIT THAT I'D BEEN GAMBLING AWAY MY MONEY IN CASINOS, ALEX.
I CAN UNDERSTAND WHAT'S DRIVEN YOU TO IT, JAMES...
alex@alexcartoon.com

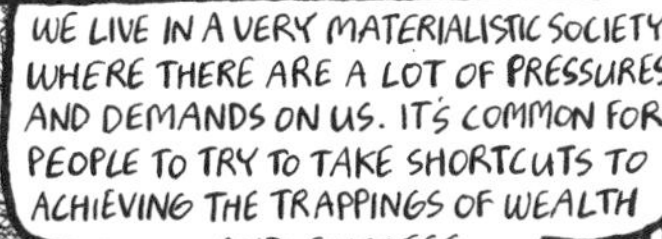
WE LIVE IN A VERY MATERIALISTIC SOCIETY WHERE THERE ARE A LOT OF PRESSURES AND DEMANDS ON US. IT'S COMMON FOR PEOPLE TO TRY TO TAKE SHORTCUTS TO ACHIEVING THE TRAPPINGS OF WEALTH AND SUCCESS...

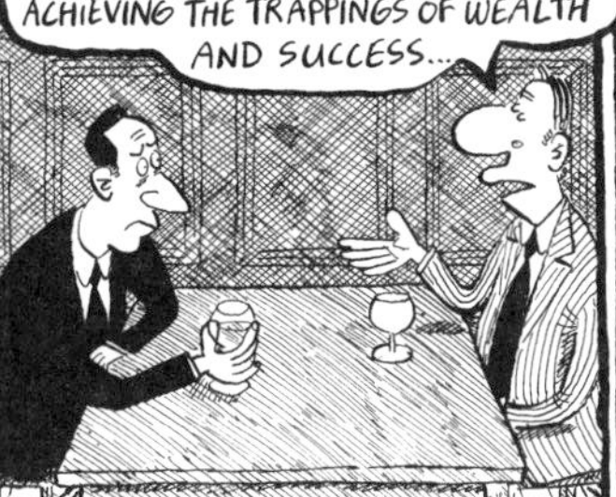

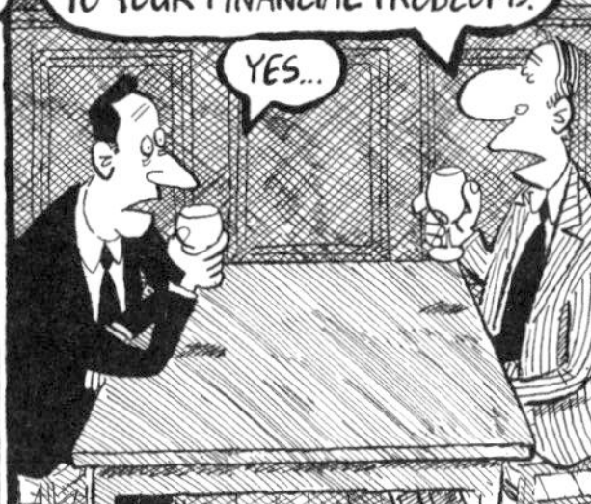
YOU WOULDN'T BE THE FIRST PERSON WHO'S TURNED TO GAMBLING IN THE HOPE THAT IT MIGHT PROVIDE A SOLUTION TO YOUR FINANCIAL PROBLEMS.
YES...

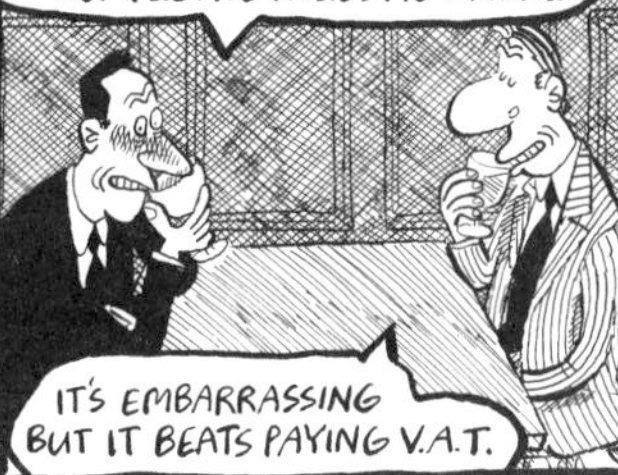
I NEED TO PAY MY BUILDER £50,000 IN CASH TO CONVERT MY STABLE BLOCK, BUT THE ONLY LEGITIMATE WAY I COULD WITHDRAW SUMS LIKE THAT FROM THE BANK WAS TO TELL THEM I HAVE A COMPULSIVE ROULETTE HABIT...
IT'S EMBARRASSING BUT IT BEATS PAYING V.A.T.

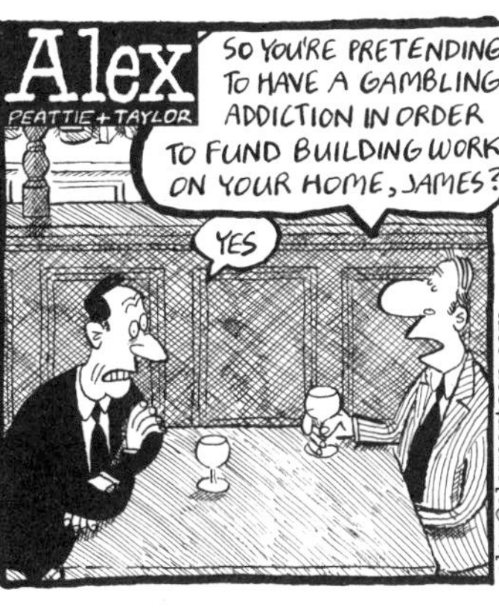
Alex
PEATTIE + TAYLOR
SO YOU'RE PRETENDING TO HAVE A GAMBLING ADDICTION IN ORDER TO FUND BUILDING WORK ON YOUR HOME, JAMES?
YES
alex@alexcartoon.com

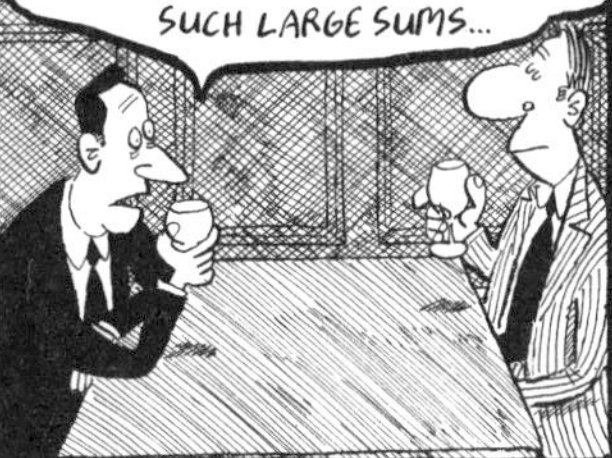
I NEED TO PAY MY BUILDER £50,000 IN CASH, SO I'VE BEEN WITHDRAWING £5,000 A WEEK FROM MY BANK. UNFORTUNATELY UNDER MONEY LAUNDERING RULES THEY ARE OBLIGED TO ASK ME WHAT I INTEND TO DO WITH SUCH LARGE SUMS...

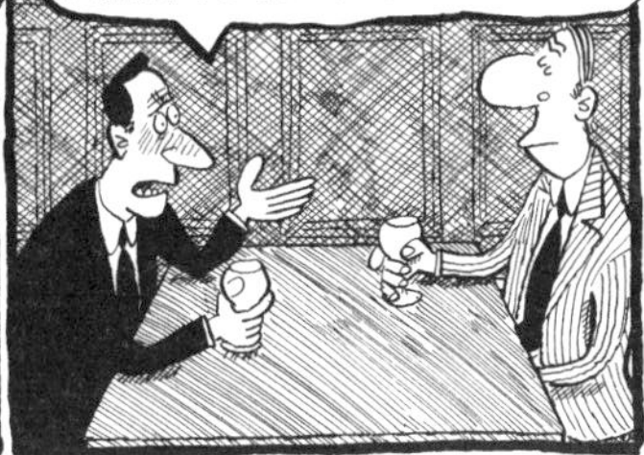
OBVIOUSLY IT'S PROFESSIONALLY EMBARRASSING FOR ME TO HAVE TO GO BACK TO THE BANK WEEK AFTER WEEK TELLING THE CASHIER THAT I NEED THE MONEY TO FUND MY ROULETTE HABIT... WITH EVERYTHING THAT IMPLIES ABOUT ME.

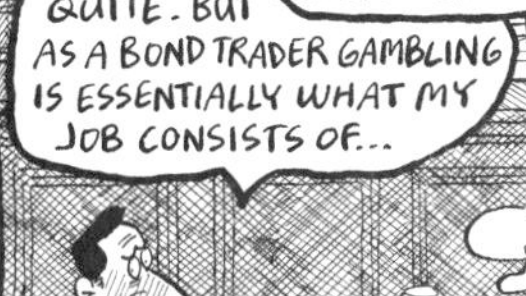
WHAT, THAT WITH REGULAR BIG LOSSES LIKE THAT YOU MUST BE A USELESS GAMBLER?
QUITE. BUT AS A BOND TRADER GAMBLING IS ESSENTIALLY WHAT MY JOB CONSISTS OF...

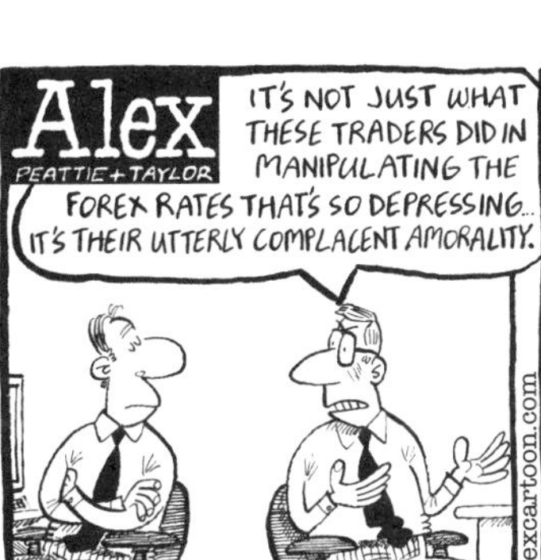
Alex
PEATTIE + TAYLOR
IT'S NOT JUST WHAT THESE TRADERS DID IN MANIPULATING THE FOREX RATES THAT'S SO DEPRESSING... IT'S THEIR UTTERLY COMPLACENT AMORALITY.
alex@alexcartoon.com

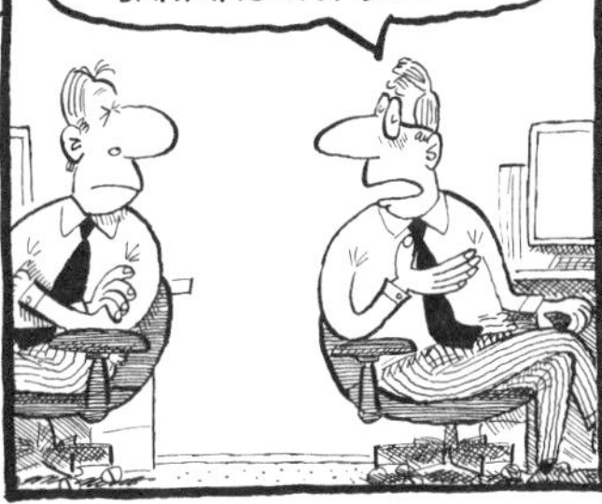
FRANKLY THE TRANSCRIPTS OF THOSE BRAGGING CHAT ROOM CONVERSATIONS ABOUT THEIR COLLUSION ON FIXING PRICES BESMIRCHES THE ENTIRE BANKING WORLD...

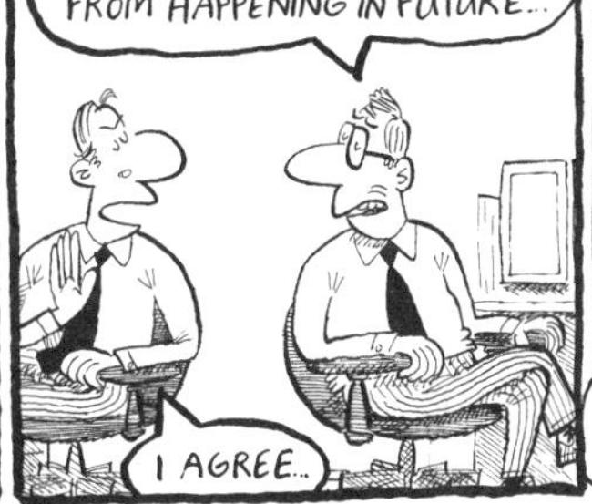
IT'S THE SORT OF BEHAVIOUR THAT'S TOTALLY UNACCEPTABLE IN THE MODERN CITY.. THERE NEEDS TO BE A PROPER CODE TO PREVENT THIS FROM HAPPENING IN FUTURE...
I AGREE..

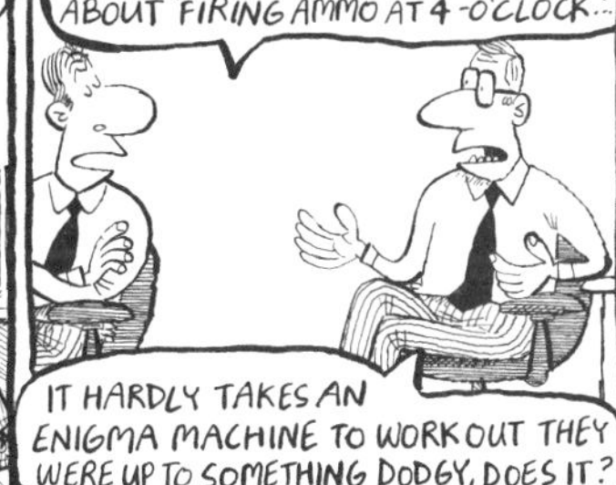
IF YOU DON'T WANT COMPLIANCE TO DECIPHER YOUR MESSAGES, YOU NEED TO DO BETTER THAN CALLING YOURSELF "THE A-TEAM" AND TALKING ABOUT "FIRING AMMO AT 4-O'CLOCK."
IT HARDLY TAKES AN ENIGMA MACHINE TO WORK OUT THEY WERE UP TO SOMETHING DODGY, DOES IT?

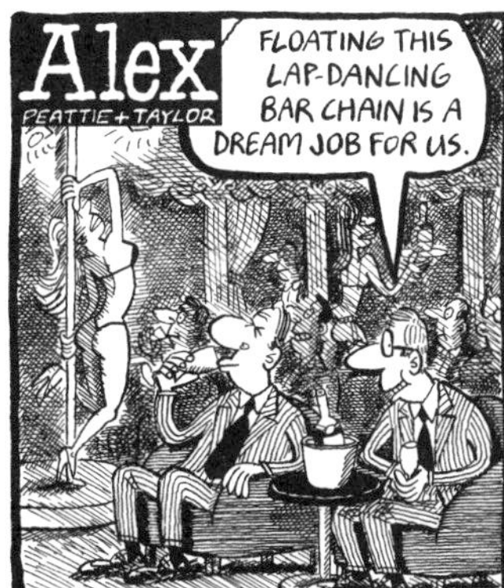
Alex
PEATTIE + TAYLOR
FLOATING THIS LAP-DANCING BAR CHAIN IS A DREAM JOB FOR US.
alex@alexcartoon.com

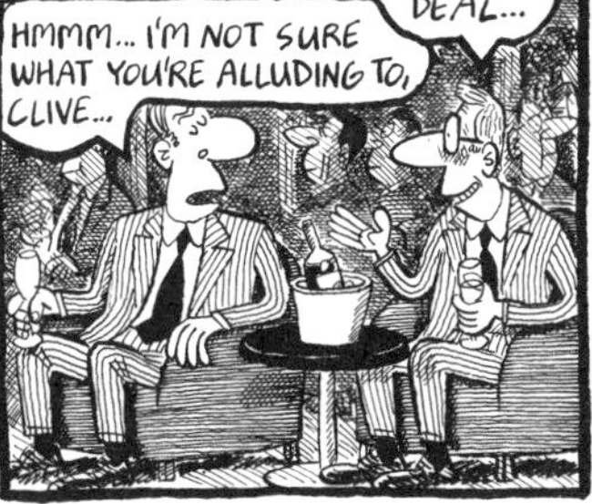
AFTER ALL IT GIVES US THE EXCUSE TO VISIT LAP-DANCING ESTABLISHMENTS ON THE VALID PRETEXT OF DOING DUE DILIGENCE AND PREPARATION FOR THE DEAL...
HMMM... I'M NOT SURE WHAT YOU'RE ALLUDING TO, CLIVE...

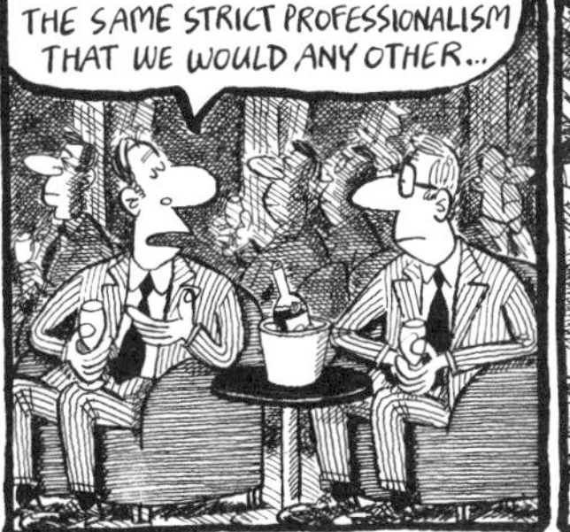
BUT MAY I REMIND YOU THAT WE HAVE AN OBLIGATION TO APPROACH THIS TRANSACTION WITH THE SAME STRICT PROFESSIONALISM THAT WE WOULD ANY OTHER...

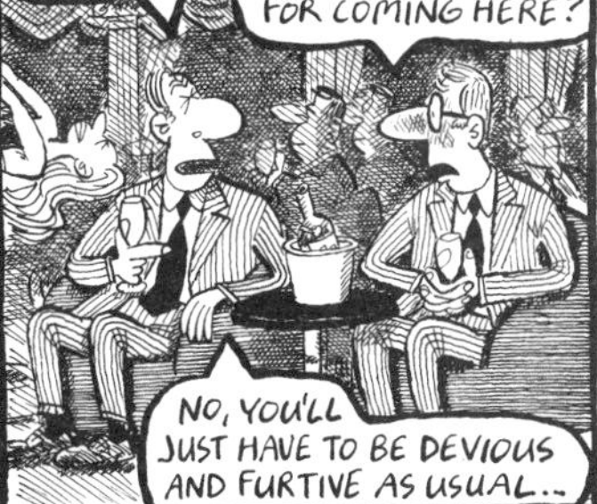
IN OTHER WORDS TO KEEP IT ALL TOTALLY SECRET.
YOU MEAN I CAN'T TELL MY WIFE MY BONA FIDE REASON FOR COMING HERE?
NO, YOU'LL JUST HAVE TO BE DEVIOUS AND FURTIVE AS USUAL...

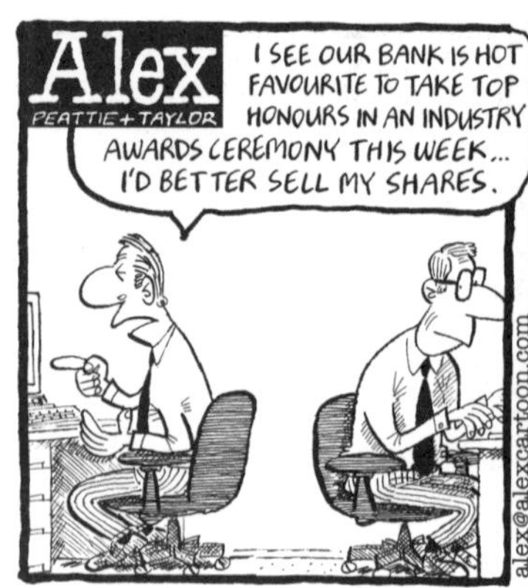

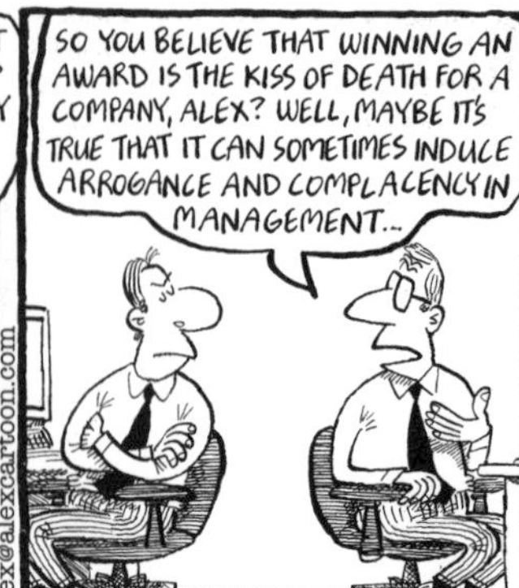

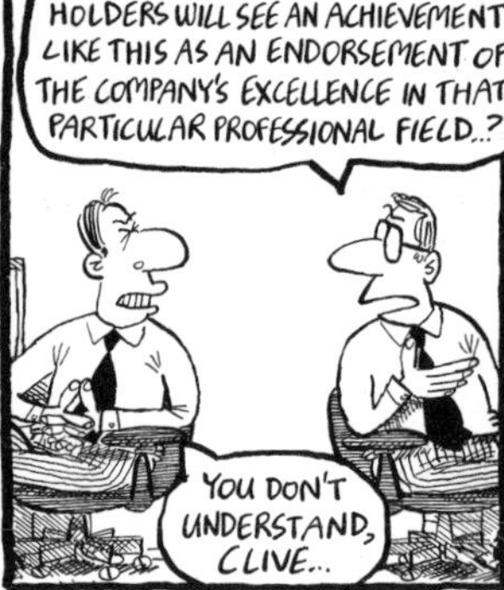

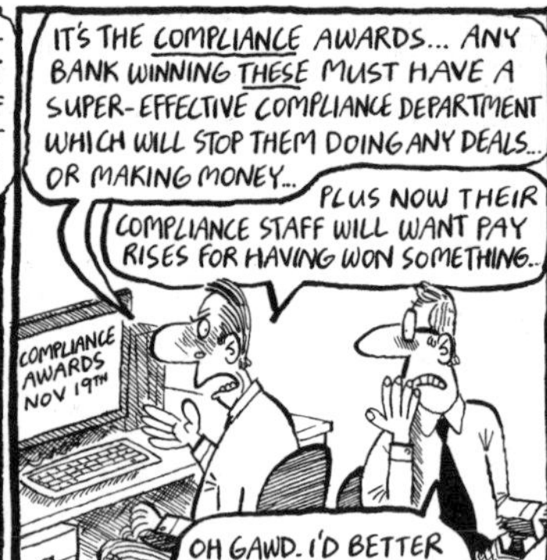

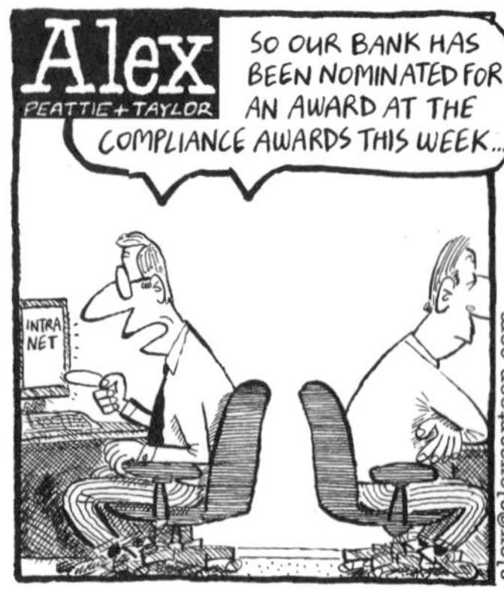

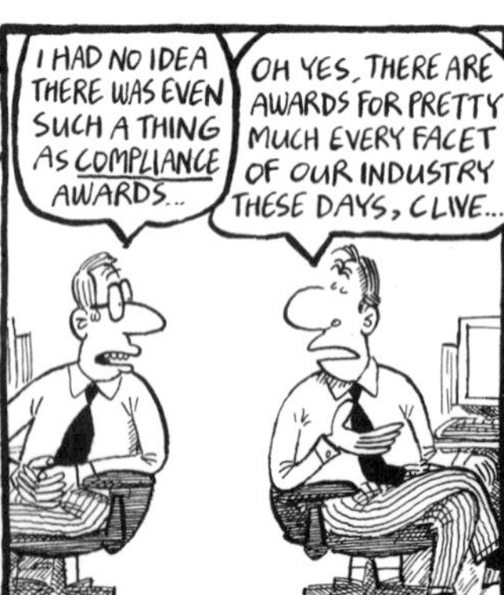

THESE EVENTS ARE REAL MONEY-SPINNERS FOR THE COMPANIES THAT ORGANISE THEM. BANKS LIKE OURS PAY FOR TABLES AT THE EVENT, PAY TO SPONSOR INDIVIDUAL AWARDS AND TAKE OUT ADS IN THE PROGRAMME...

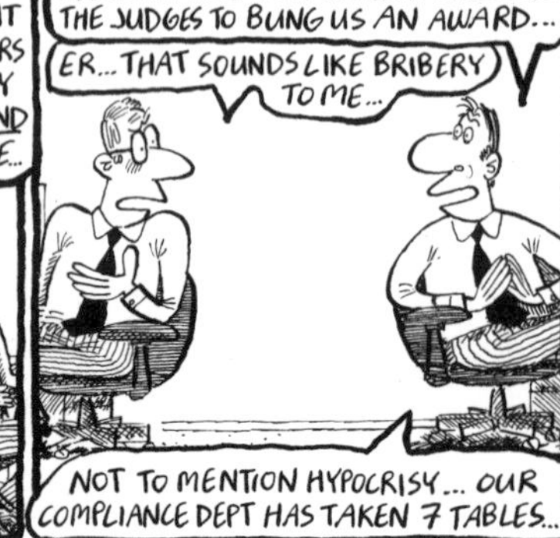

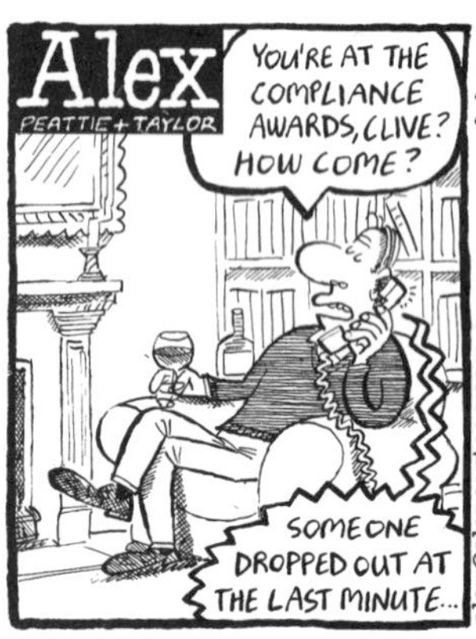

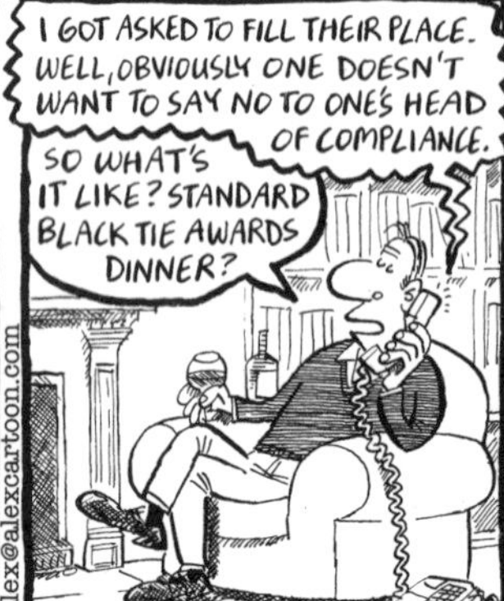

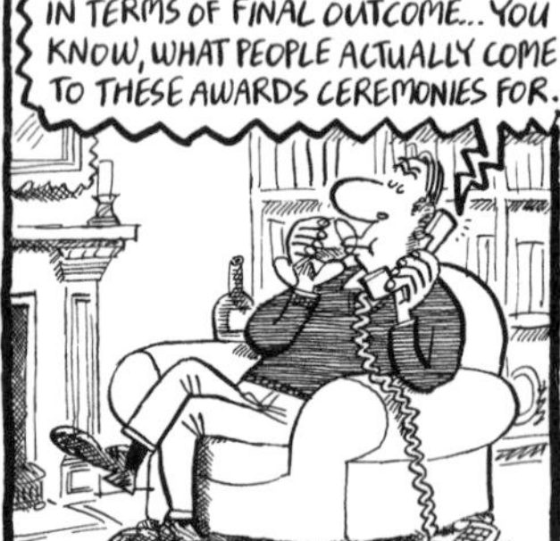

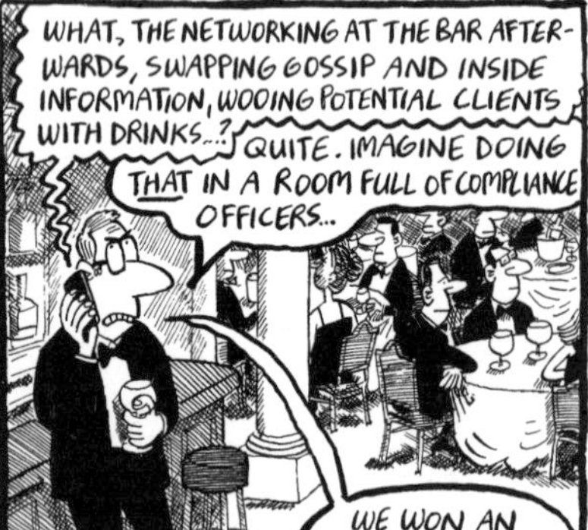

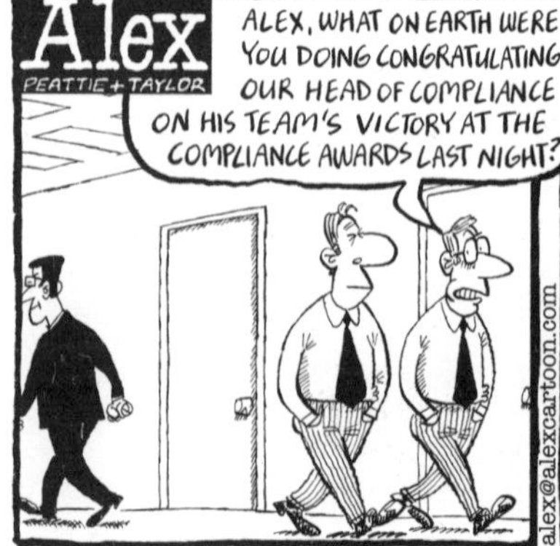

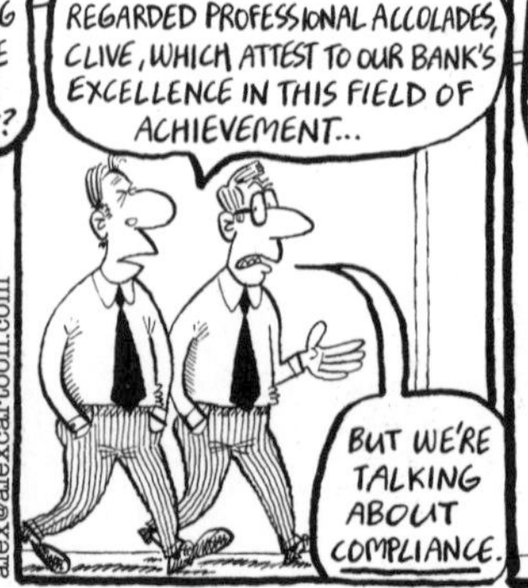

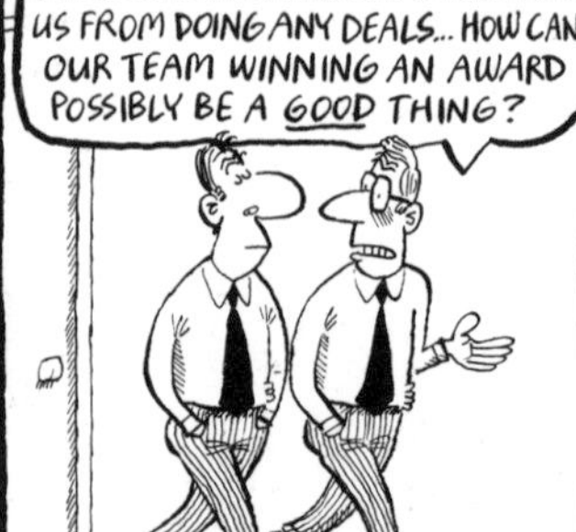

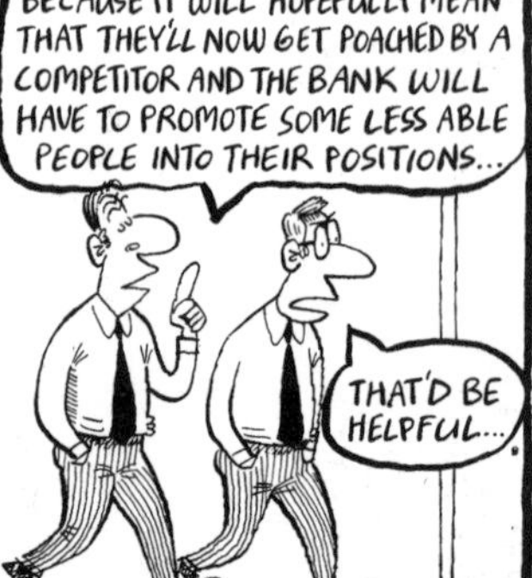

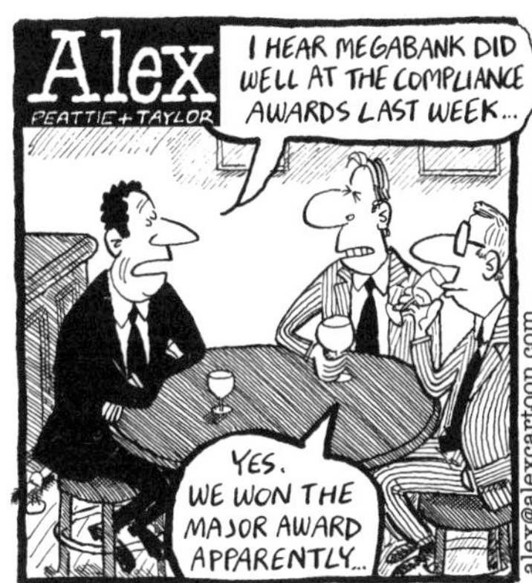
Alex
PEATTIE + TAYLOR
I HEAR MEGABANK DID WELL AT THE COMPLIANCE AWARDS LAST WEEK...
YES. WE WON THE MAJOR AWARD APPARENTLY...
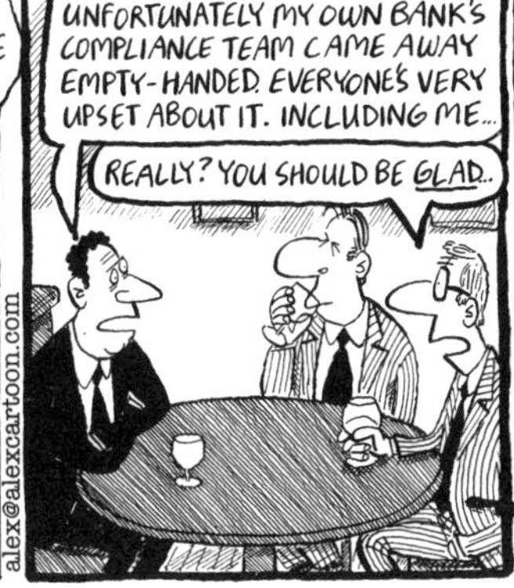
UNFORTUNATELY MY OWN BANK'S COMPLIANCE TEAM CAME AWAY EMPTY-HANDED. EVERYONE'S VERY UPSET ABOUT IT. INCLUDING ME...
REALLY? YOU SHOULD BE GLAD...
alex@alexcartoon.com
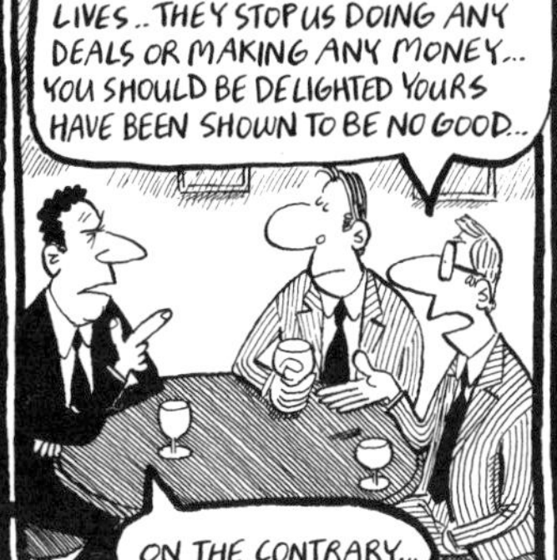
COMPLIANCE IS THE BANE OF BANKERS' LIVES.. THEY STOP US DOING ANY DEALS OR MAKING ANY MONEY... YOU SHOULD BE DELIGHTED YOURS HAVE BEEN SHOWN TO BE NO GOOD...
ON THE CONTRARY...
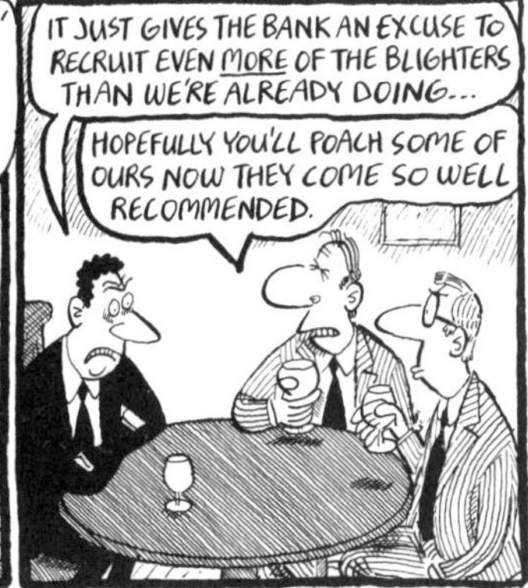
IT JUST GIVES THE BANK AN EXCUSE TO RECRUIT EVEN MORE OF THE BLIGHTERS THAN WE'RE ALREADY DOING...
HOPEFULLY YOU'LL POACH SOME OF OURS NOW THEY COME SO WELL RECOMMENDED.
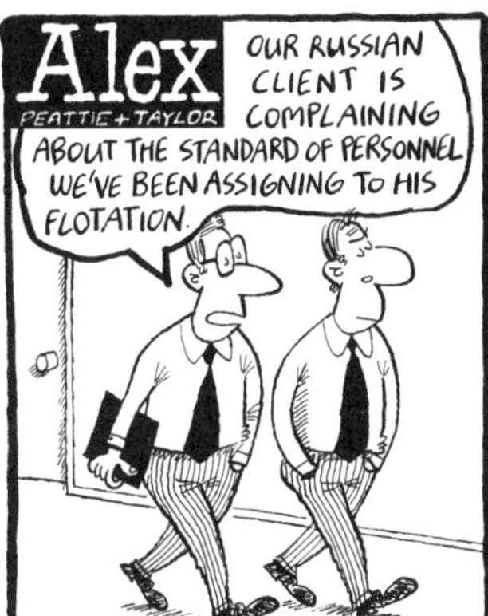
Alex
PEATTIE + TAYLOR
OUR RUSSIAN CLIENT IS COMPLAINING ABOUT THE STANDARD OF PERSONNEL WE'VE BEEN ASSIGNING TO HIS FLOTATION.
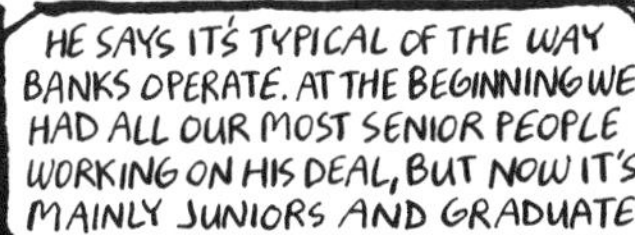
HE SAYS IT'S TYPICAL OF THE WAY BANKS OPERATE. AT THE BEGINNING WE HAD ALL OUR MOST SENIOR PEOPLE WORKING ON HIS DEAL, BUT NOW IT'S MAINLY JUNIORS AND GRADUATE TRAINEES...
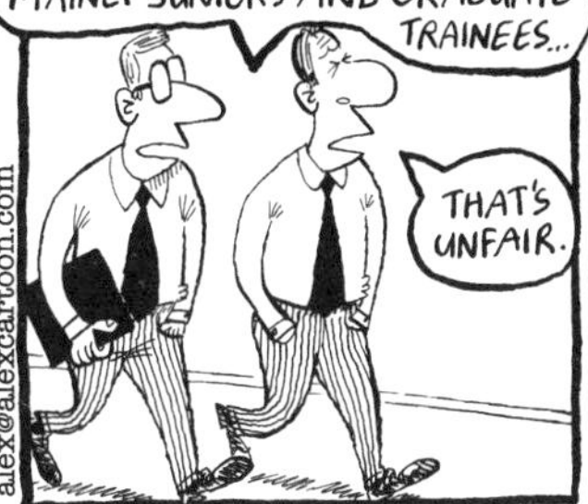
THAT'S UNFAIR.
alex@alexcartoon.com
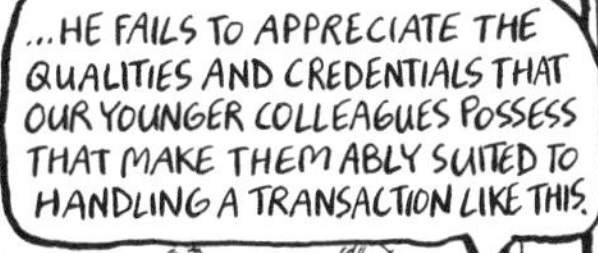
...HE FAILS TO APPRECIATE THE QUALITIES AND CREDENTIALS THAT OUR YOUNGER COLLEAGUES POSSESS THAT MAKE THEM ABLY SUITED TO HANDLING A TRANSACTION LIKE THIS.
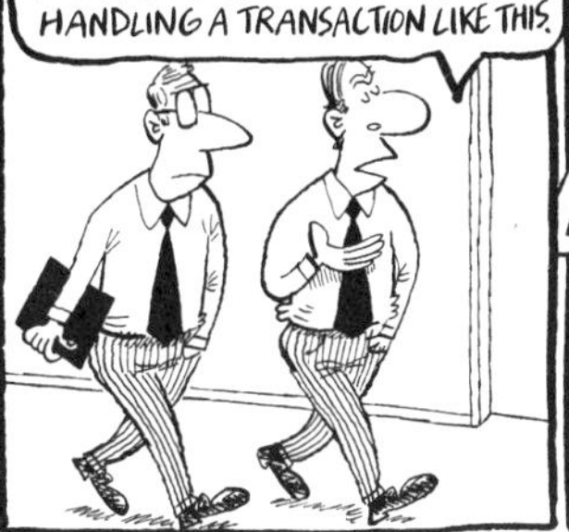
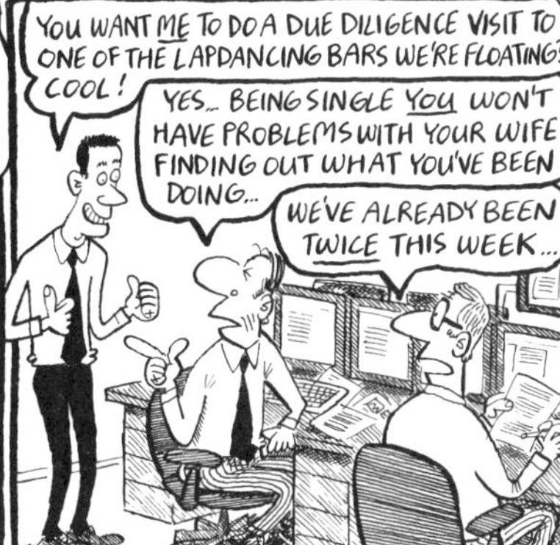
YOU WANT ME TO DO A DUE DILIGENCE VISIT TO ONE OF THE LAPDANCING BARS WE'RE FLOATING? COOL!
YES... BEING SINGLE YOU WON'T HAVE PROBLEMS WITH YOUR WIFE FINDING OUT WHAT YOU'VE BEEN DOING...
WE'VE ALREADY BEEN TWICE THIS WEEK...
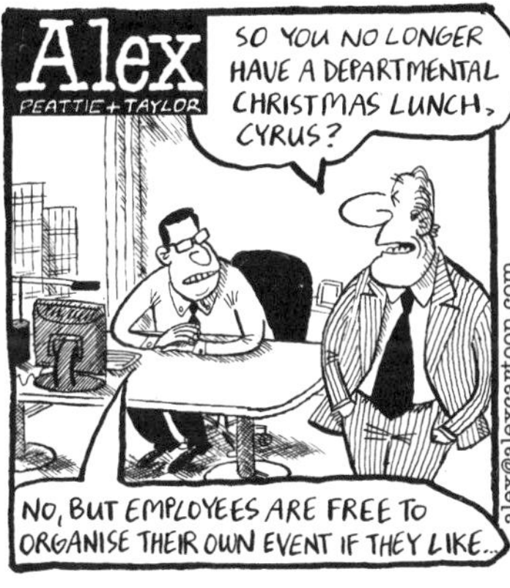
Alex
PEATTIE + TAYLOR
SO YOU NO LONGER HAVE A DEPARTMENTAL CHRISTMAS LUNCH, CYRUS?
NO, BUT EMPLOYEES ARE FREE TO ORGANISE THEIR OWN EVENT IF THEY LIKE...
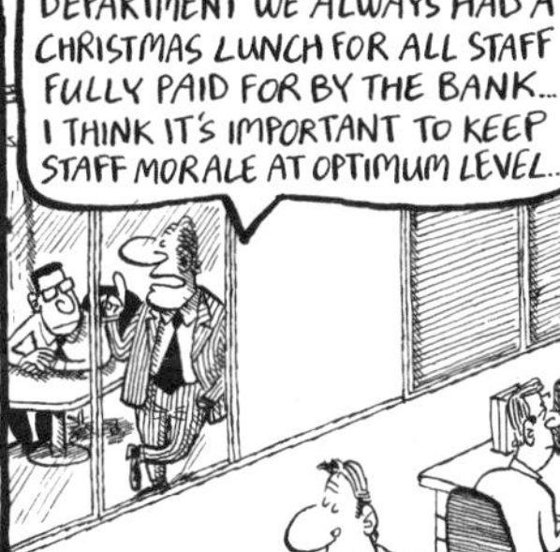
WELL, WHEN I WAS RUNNING THIS DEPARTMENT WE ALWAYS HAD A CHRISTMAS LUNCH FOR ALL STAFF FULLY PAID FOR BY THE BANK... I THINK IT'S IMPORTANT TO KEEP STAFF MORALE AT OPTIMUM LEVEL...
alex@alexcartoon.com
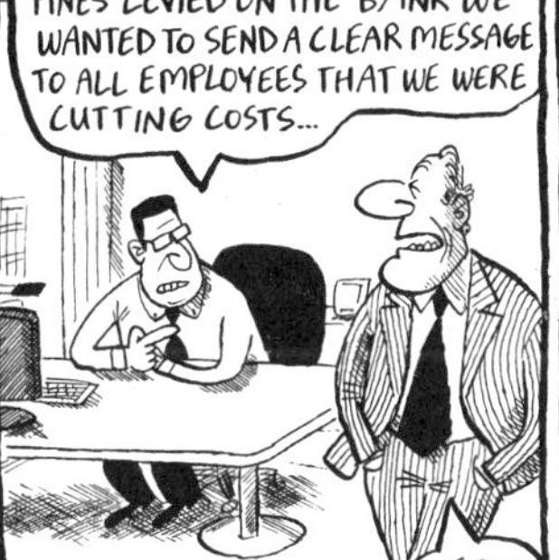
I THOUGHT WITH ALL THE RECENT FINES LEVIED ON THE BANK WE WANTED TO SEND A CLEAR MESSAGE TO ALL EMPLOYEES THAT WE WERE CUTTING COSTS...
WE DO..
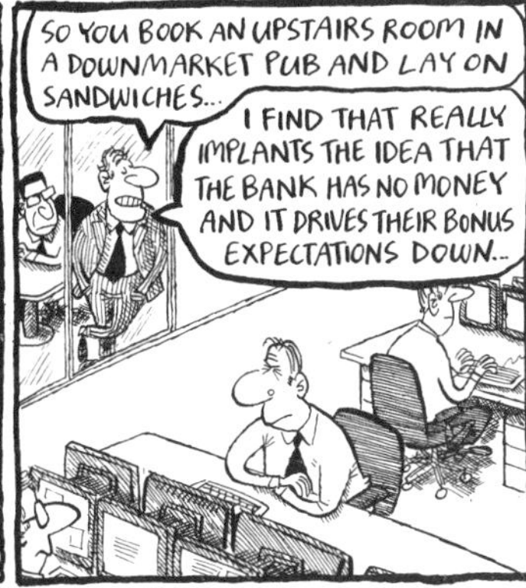
SO YOU BOOK AN UPSTAIRS ROOM IN A DOWNMARKET PUB AND LAY ON SANDWICHES...
I FIND THAT REALLY IMPLANTS THE IDEA THAT THE BANK HAS NO MONEY AND IT DRIVES THEIR BONUS EXPECTATIONS DOWN...
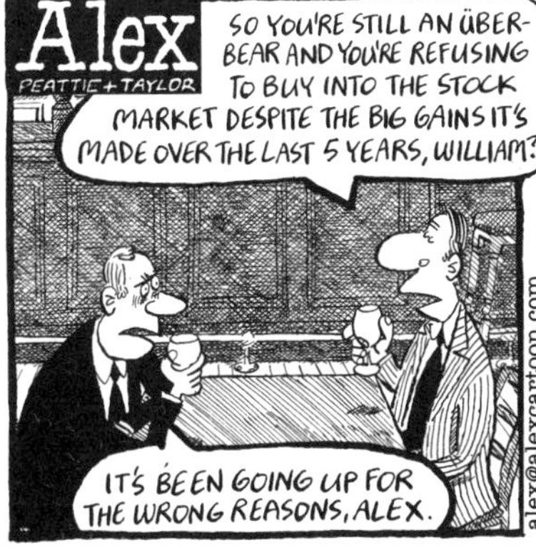
Alex
PEATTIE + TAYLOR
SO YOU'RE STILL AN ÜBER-BEAR AND YOU'RE REFUSING TO BUY INTO THE STOCK MARKET DESPITE THE BIG GAINS IT'S MADE OVER THE LAST 5 YEARS, WILLIAM?
IT'S BEEN GOING UP FOR THE WRONG REASONS, ALEX.
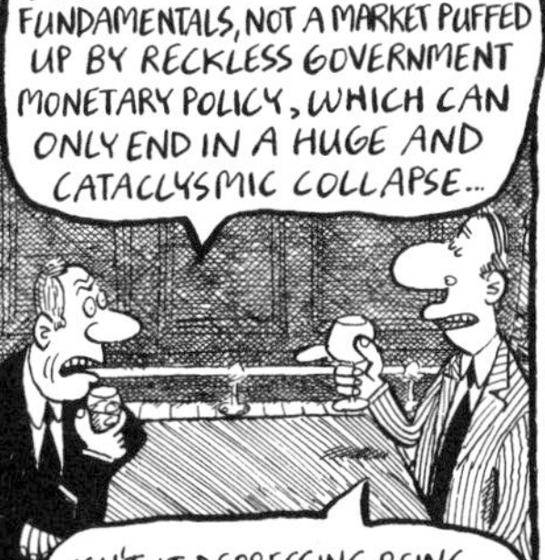
I WANT TO INVEST IN LONG-TERM FUNDAMENTALS, NOT A MARKET PUFFED UP BY RECKLESS GOVERNMENT MONETARY POLICY, WHICH CAN ONLY END IN A HUGE AND CATACLYSMIC COLLAPSE...
ISN'T IT DEPRESSING BEING SO GLOOMY ABOUT EVERYTHING?
alex@alexcartoon.com
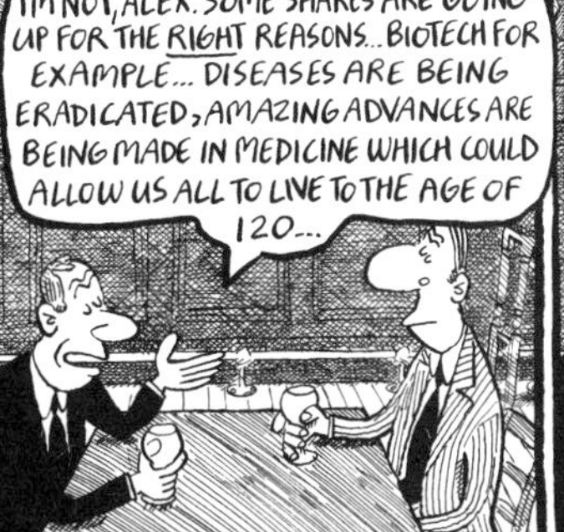
I'M NOT, ALEX. SOME SHARES ARE GOING UP FOR THE RIGHT REASONS... BIOTECH FOR EXAMPLE... DISEASES ARE BEING ERADICATED, AMAZING ADVANCES ARE BEING MADE IN MEDICINE WHICH COULD ALLOW US ALL TO LIVE TO THE AGE OF 120...
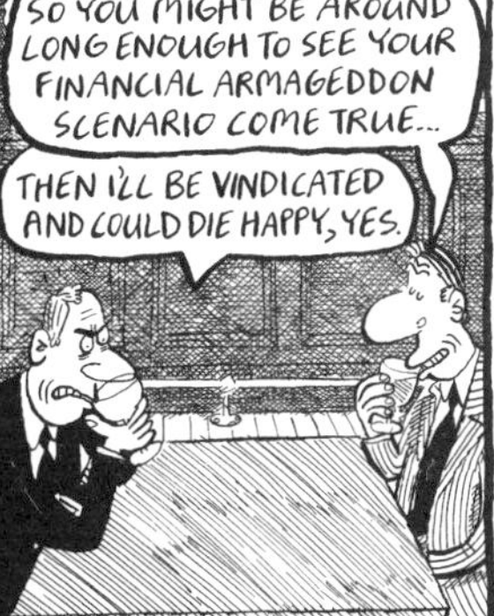
SO YOU MIGHT BE AROUND LONG ENOUGH TO SEE YOUR FINANCIAL ARMAGEDDON SCENARIO COME TRUE...
THEN I'LL BE VINDICATED AND COULD DIE HAPPY, YES.

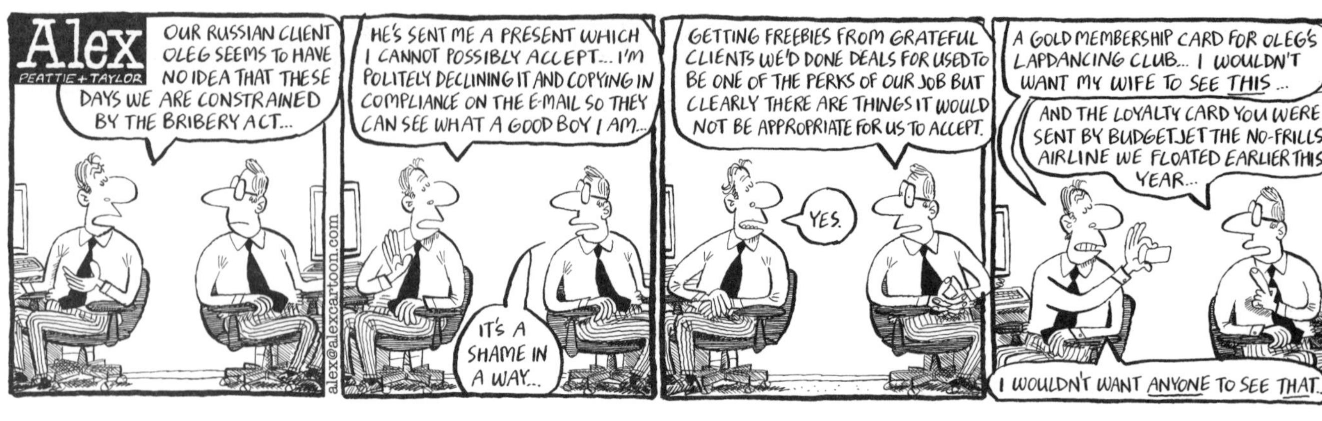
Alex
PEATTIE + TAYLOR
OUR RUSSIAN CLIENT OLEG SEEMS TO HAVE NO IDEA THAT THESE DAYS WE ARE CONSTRAINED BY THE BRIBERY ACT...
HE'S SENT ME A PRESENT WHICH I CANNOT POSSIBLY ACCEPT... I'M POLITELY DECLINING IT AND COPYING IN COMPLIANCE ON THE E-MAIL SO THEY CAN SEE WHAT A GOOD BOY I AM...
IT'S A SHAME IN A WAY...
alex@alexcartoon.com
GETTING FREEBIES FROM GRATEFUL CLIENTS WE'D DONE DEALS FOR USED TO BE ONE OF THE PERKS OF OUR JOB BUT CLEARLY THERE ARE THINGS IT WOULD NOT BE APPROPRIATE FOR US TO ACCEPT.
YES.
A GOLD MEMBERSHIP CARD FOR OLEG'S LAPDANCING CLUB... I WOULDN'T WANT MY WIFE TO SEE THIS...
AND THE LOYALTY CARD YOU WERE SENT BY BUDGETJET THE NO-FRILLS AIRLINE WE FLOATED EARLIER THIS YEAR...
I WOULDN'T WANT ANYONE TO SEE THAT...

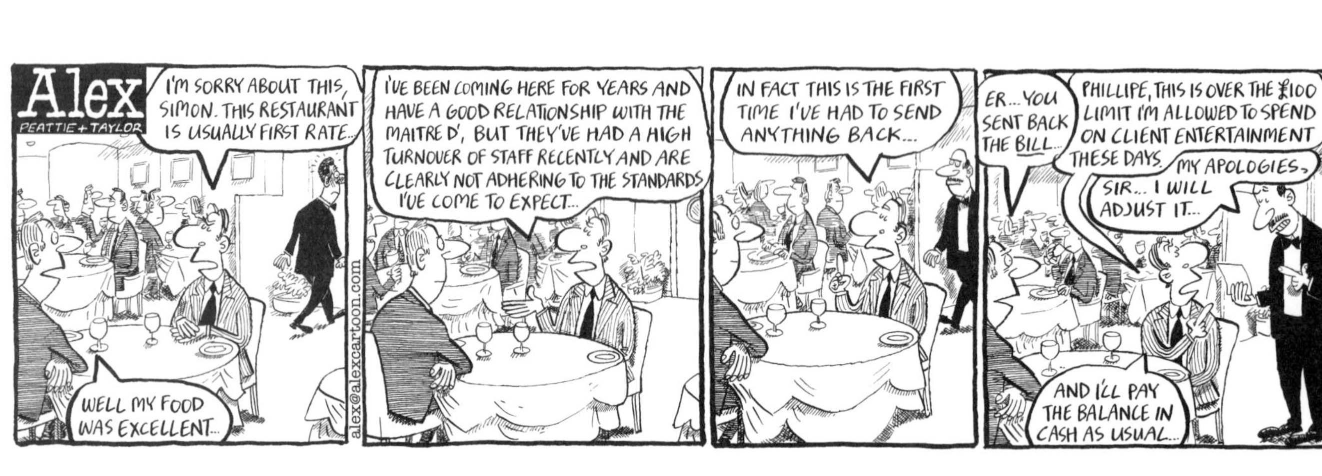
Alex
PEATTIE + TAYLOR
I'M SORRY ABOUT THIS, SIMON. THIS RESTAURANT IS USUALLY FIRST RATE...
WELL MY FOOD WAS EXCELLENT...
alex@alexcartoon.com
I'VE BEEN COMING HERE FOR YEARS AND HAVE A GOOD RELATIONSHIP WITH THE MAITRE D', BUT THEY'VE HAD A HIGH TURNOVER OF STAFF RECENTLY AND ARE CLEARLY NOT ADHERING TO THE STANDARDS I'VE COME TO EXPECT...
IN FACT THIS IS THE FIRST TIME I'VE HAD TO SEND ANYTHING BACK...
ER... YOU SENT BACK THE BILL...
PHILLIPE, THIS IS OVER THE £100 LIMIT I'M ALLOWED TO SPEND ON CLIENT ENTERTAINMENT THESE DAYS.
MY APOLOGIES, SIR... I WILL ADJUST IT...
AND I'LL PAY THE BALANCE IN CASH AS USUAL...

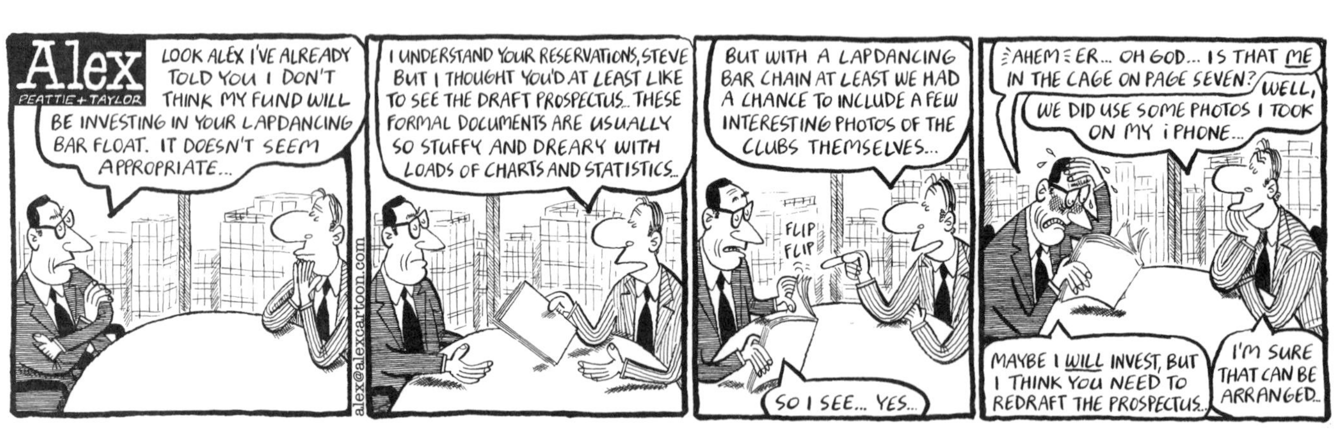
Alex
PEATTIE + TAYLOR
LOOK ALEX I'VE ALREADY TOLD YOU I DON'T THINK MY FUND WILL BE INVESTING IN YOUR LAPDANCING BAR FLOAT. IT DOESN'T SEEM APPROPRIATE...
alex@alexcartoon.com
I UNDERSTAND YOUR RESERVATIONS, STEVE BUT I THOUGHT YOU'D AT LEAST LIKE TO SEE THE DRAFT PROSPECTUS.. THESE FORMAL DOCUMENTS ARE USUALLY SO STUFFY AND DREARY WITH LOADS OF CHARTS AND STATISTICS...
BUT WITH A LAPDANCING BAR CHAIN AT LEAST WE HAD A CHANCE TO INCLUDE A FEW INTERESTING PHOTOS OF THE CLUBS THEMSELVES...
FLIP FLIP
SO I SEE... YES...
AHEM ER... OH GOD... IS THAT ME IN THE CAGE ON PAGE SEVEN?
WELL, WE DID USE SOME PHOTOS I TOOK ON MY iPHONE...
MAYBE I WILL INVEST, BUT I THINK YOU NEED TO REDRAFT THE PROSPECTUS...
I'M SURE THAT CAN BE ARRANGED...

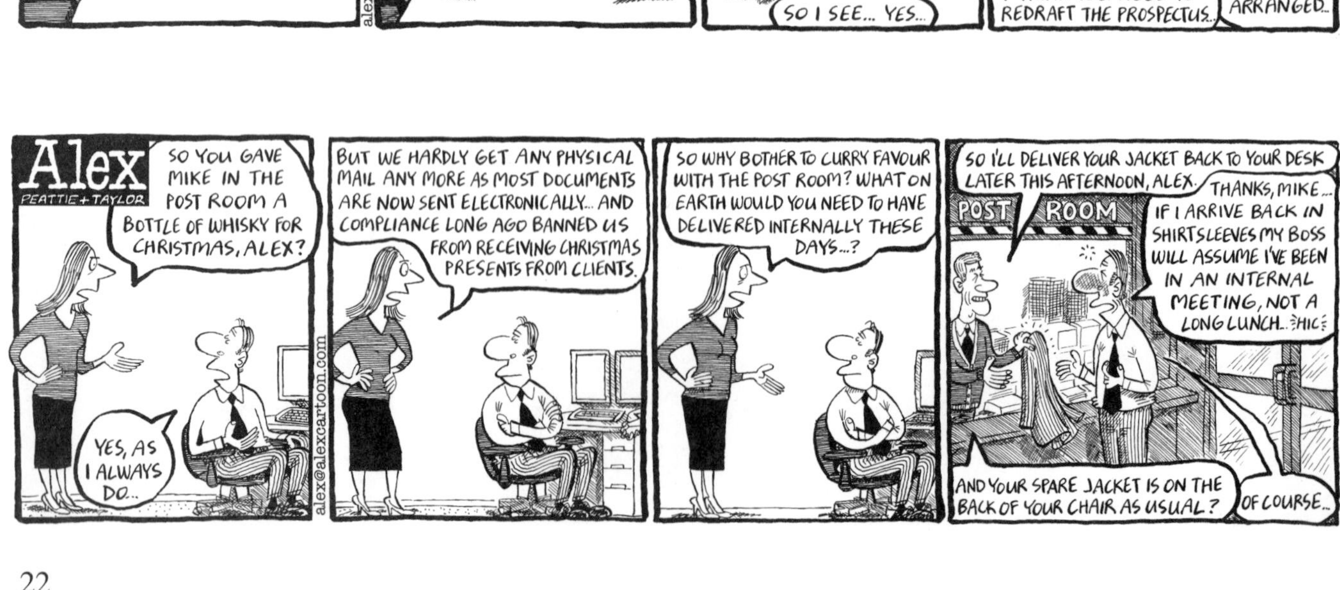
Alex
PEATTIE + TAYLOR
SO YOU GAVE MIKE IN THE POST ROOM A BOTTLE OF WHISKY FOR CHRISTMAS, ALEX?
YES, AS I ALWAYS DO...
alex@alexcartoon.com
BUT WE HARDLY GET ANY PHYSICAL MAIL ANY MORE AS MOST DOCUMENTS ARE NOW SENT ELECTRONICALLY... AND COMPLIANCE LONG AGO BANNED US FROM RECEIVING CHRISTMAS PRESENTS FROM CLIENTS.
SO WHY BOTHER TO CURRY FAVOUR WITH THE POST ROOM? WHAT ON EARTH WOULD YOU NEED TO HAVE DELIVERED INTERNALLY THESE DAYS...?
SO I'LL DELIVER YOUR JACKET BACK TO YOUR DESK LATER THIS AFTERNOON, ALEX.
POST ROOM
THANKS, MIKE... IF I ARRIVE BACK IN SHIRTSLEEVES MY BOSS WILL ASSUME I'VE BEEN IN AN INTERNAL MEETING, NOT A LONG LUNCH... HIC
AND YOUR SPARE JACKET IS ON THE BACK OF YOUR CHAIR AS USUAL?
OF COURSE...

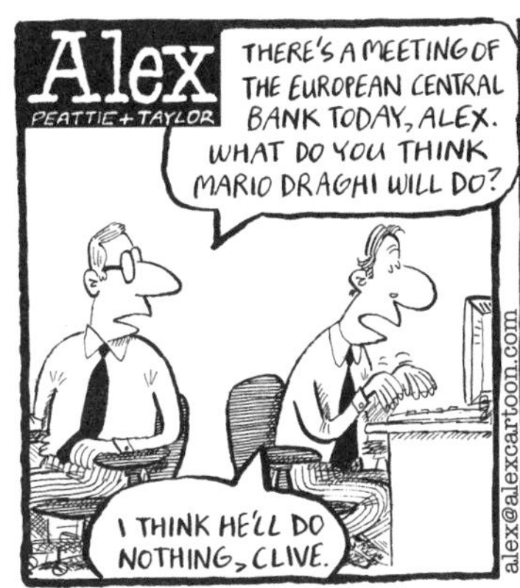
Alex
PEATTIE + TAYLOR
THERE'S A MEETING OF THE EUROPEAN CENTRAL BANK TODAY, ALEX. WHAT DO YOU THINK MARIO DRAGHI WILL DO?
I THINK HE'LL DO NOTHING, CLIVE.
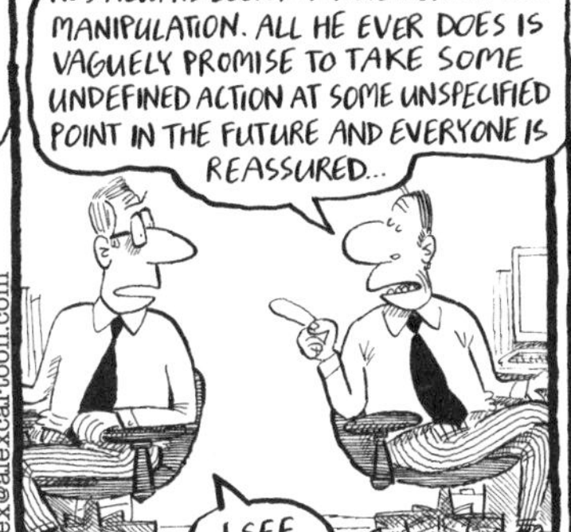
HE'S ALWAYS BEEN A MASTER OF MARKET MANIPULATION. ALL HE EVER DOES IS VAGUELY PROMISE TO TAKE SOME UNDEFINED ACTION AT SOME UNSPECIFIED POINT IN THE FUTURE AND EVERYONE IS REASSURED...
I SEE...
alex@alexcartoon.com
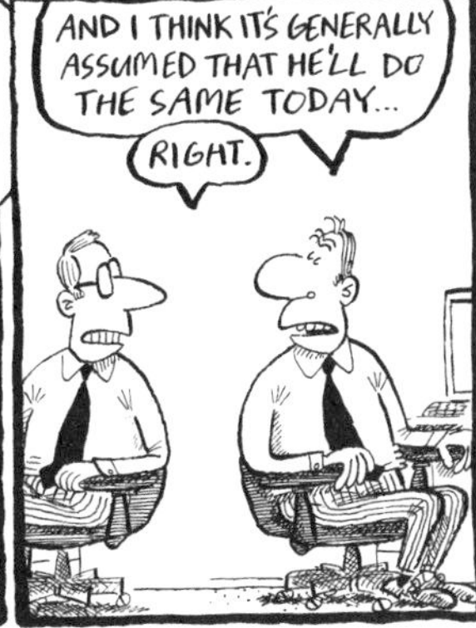
AND I THINK IT'S GENERALLY ASSUMED THAT HE'LL DO THE SAME TODAY...
RIGHT.
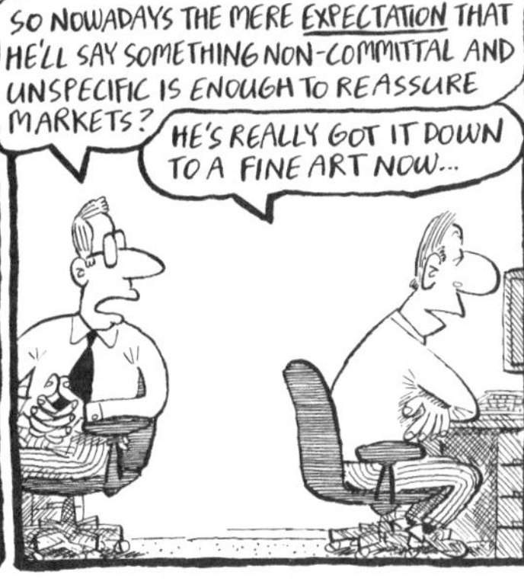
SO NOWADAYS THE MERE EXPECTATION THAT HE'LL SAY SOMETHING NON-COMMITTAL AND UNSPECIFIC IS ENOUGH TO REASSURE MARKETS?
HE'S REALLY GOT IT DOWN TO A FINE ART NOW...

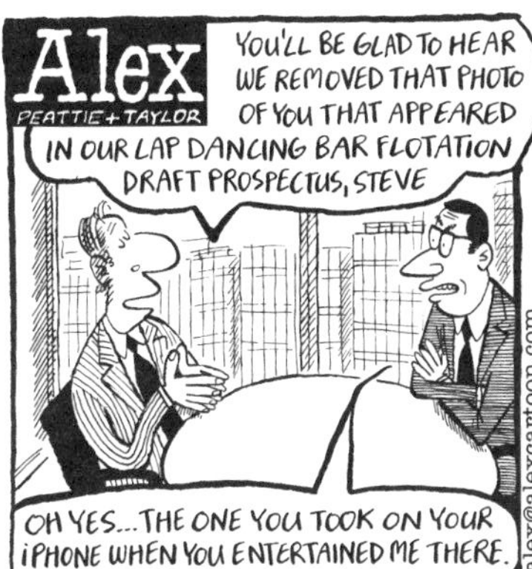
Alex
PEATTIE + TAYLOR
YOU'LL BE GLAD TO HEAR WE REMOVED THAT PHOTO OF YOU THAT APPEARED IN OUR LAP DANCING BAR FLOTATION DRAFT PROSPECTUS, STEVE
OH YES... THE ONE YOU TOOK ON YOUR iPHONE WHEN YOU ENTERTAINED ME THERE.
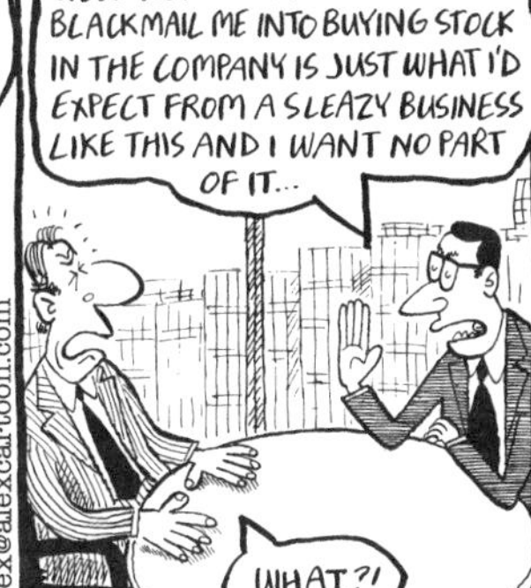
WELL YOUR TAWDRY ATTEMPT TO BLACKMAIL ME INTO BUYING STOCK IN THE COMPANY IS JUST WHAT I'D EXPECT FROM A SLEAZY BUSINESS LIKE THIS AND I WANT NO PART OF IT...
WHAT?!
alex@alexcartoon.com
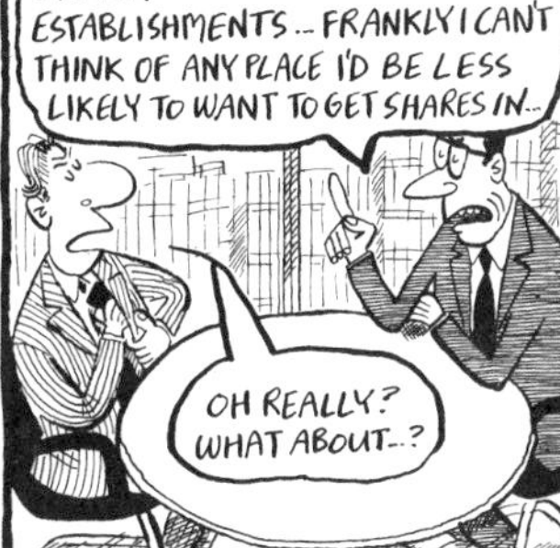
I RUN AN ETHICAL FUND, ALEX... I WANT NOTHING TO DO WITH SUCH ESTABLISHMENTS... FRANKLY I CAN'T THINK OF ANY PLACE I'D BE LESS LIKELY TO WANT TO GET SHARES IN...
OH REALLY? WHAT ABOUT...?
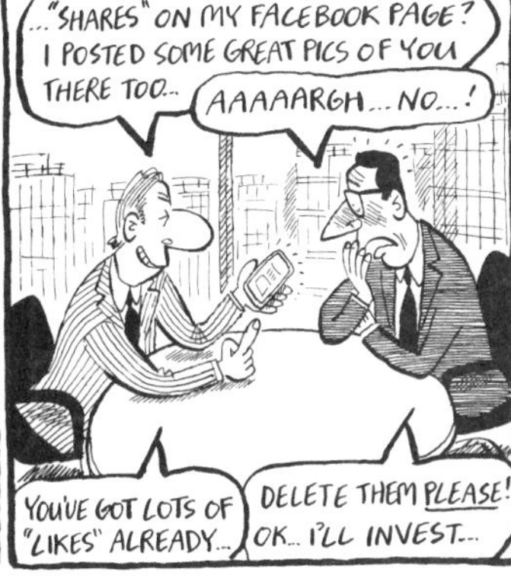
..."SHARES" ON MY FACEBOOK PAGE? I POSTED SOME GREAT PICS OF YOU THERE TOO...
AAAAARGH... NO...!
YOU'VE GOT LOTS OF "LIKES" ALREADY...
DELETE THEM PLEASE! OK... I'LL INVEST...

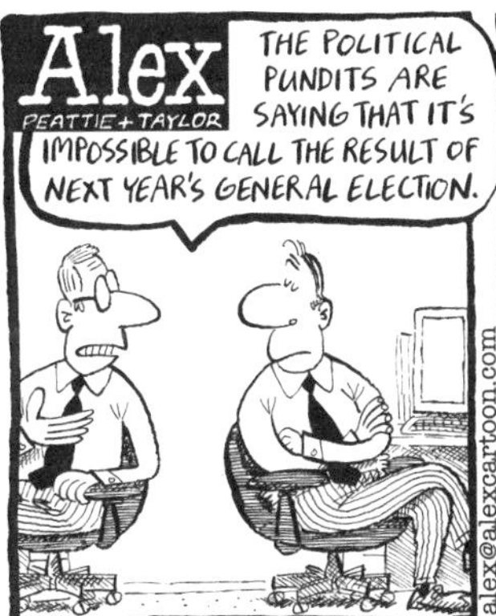
Alex
PEATTIE + TAYLOR
THE POLITICAL PUNDITS ARE SAYING THAT IT'S IMPOSSIBLE TO CALL THE RESULT OF NEXT YEAR'S GENERAL ELECTION.
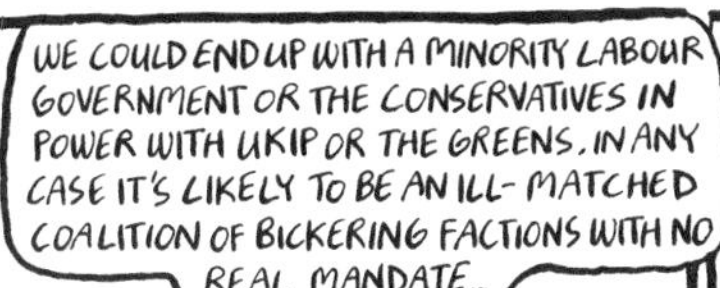
WE COULD END UP WITH A MINORITY LABOUR GOVERNMENT OR THE CONSERVATIVES IN POWER WITH UKIP OR THE GREENS. IN ANY CASE IT'S LIKELY TO BE AN ILL-MATCHED COALITION OF BICKERING FACTIONS WITH NO REAL MANDATE...
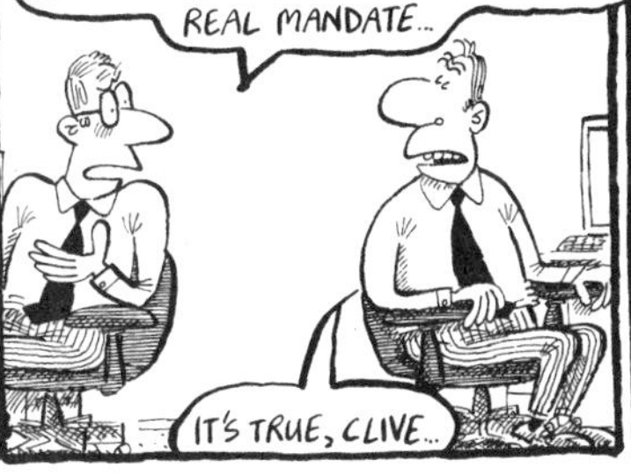
IT'S TRUE, CLIVE...
alex@alexcartoon.com
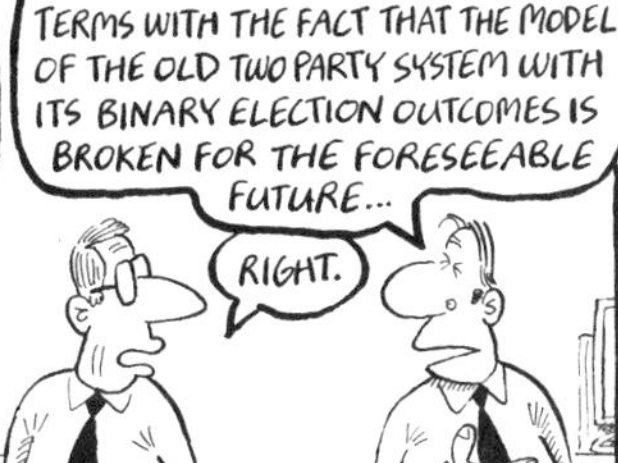
WE'RE GOING TO HAVE TO COME TO TERMS WITH THE FACT THAT THE MODEL OF THE OLD TWO PARTY SYSTEM WITH ITS BINARY ELECTION OUTCOMES IS BROKEN FOR THE FORESEEABLE FUTURE...
RIGHT.
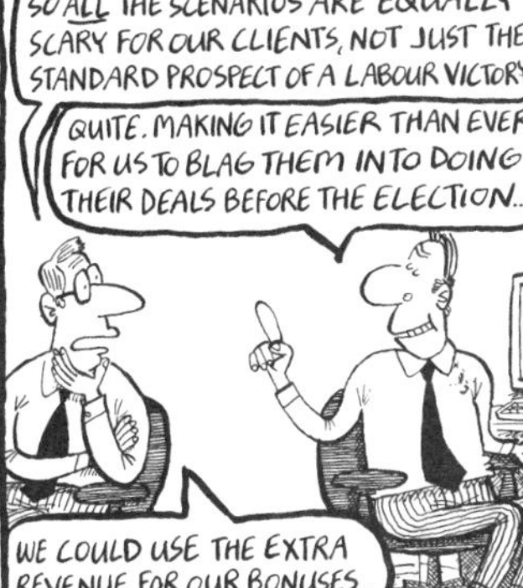
SO ALL THE SCENARIOS ARE EQUALLY SCARY FOR OUR CLIENTS, NOT JUST THE STANDARD PROSPECT OF A LABOUR VICTORY?
QUITE. MAKING IT EASIER THAN EVER FOR US TO BLAG THEM INTO DOING THEIR DEALS BEFORE THE ELECTION...
WE COULD USE THE EXTRA REVENUE FOR OUR BONUSES...

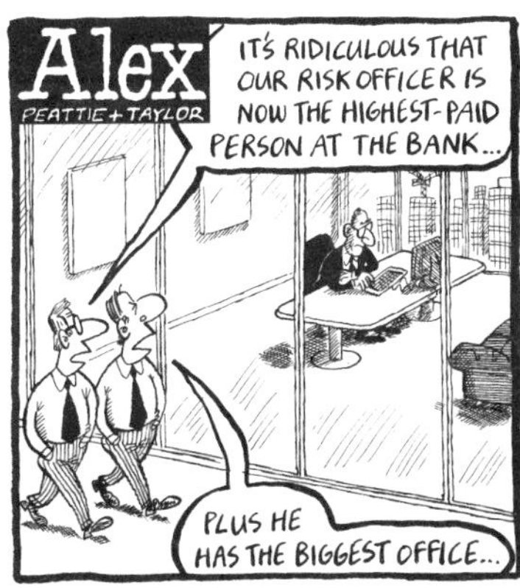
Alex
PEATTIE + TAYLOR
IT'S RIDICULOUS THAT OUR RISK OFFICER IS NOW THE HIGHEST-PAID PERSON AT THE BANK...
PLUS HE HAS THE BIGGEST OFFICE...
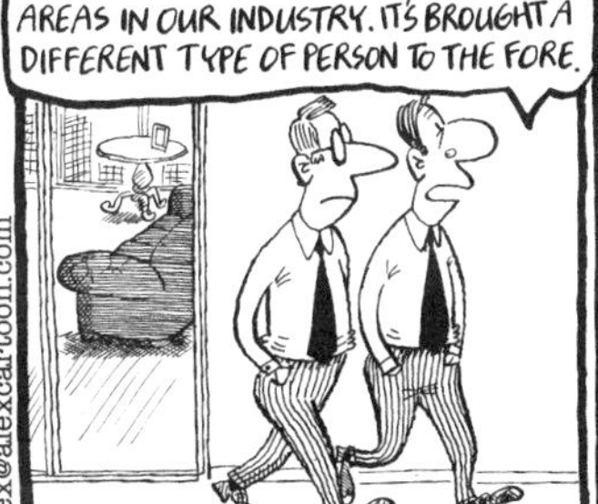
IT'S A REFLECTION OF HOW THE CITY HAS CHANGED, CLIVE. COMPLIANCE AND RISK MANAGEMENT ARE NOW THE GROWTH AREAS IN OUR INDUSTRY. IT'S BROUGHT A DIFFERENT TYPE OF PERSON TO THE FORE.
alex@alexcartoon.com
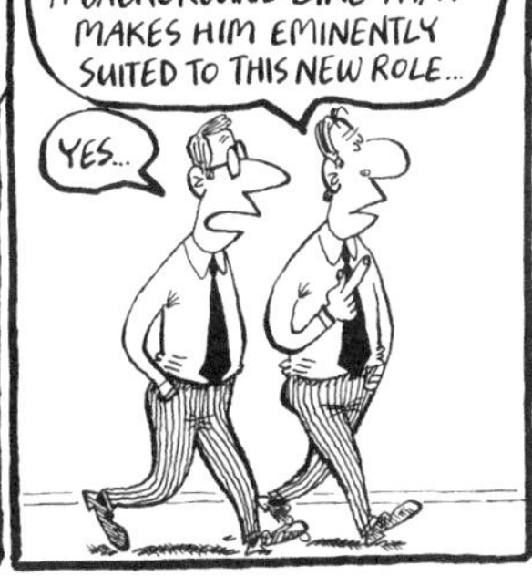
APPARENTLY OUR MAN IS A CAREER ACCOUNTANT. OBVIOUSLY A BACKGROUND LIKE THAT MAKES HIM EMINENTLY SUITED TO THIS NEW ROLE...
YES...
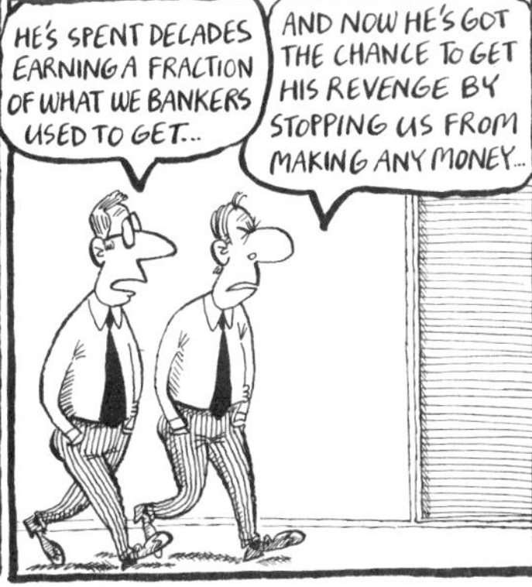
HE'S SPENT DECADES EARNING A FRACTION OF WHAT WE BANKERS USED TO GET...
AND NOW HE'S GOT THE CHANCE TO GET HIS REVENGE BY STOPPING US FROM MAKING ANY MONEY...

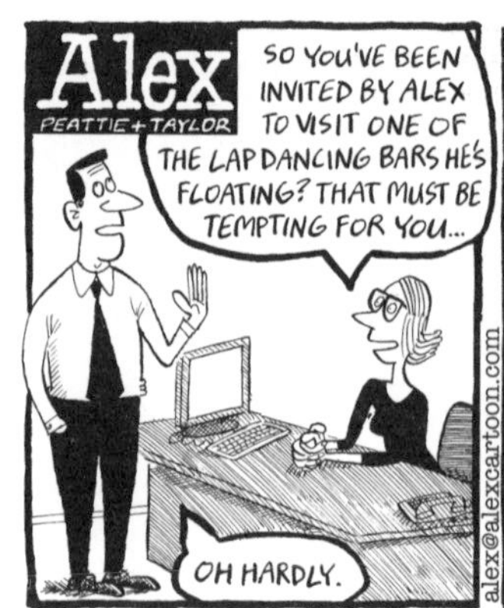
Alex
PEATTIE + TAYLOR
SO YOU'VE BEEN INVITED BY ALEX TO VISIT ONE OF THE LAP DANCING BARS HE'S FLOATING? THAT MUST BE TEMPTING FOR YOU...
OH HARDLY.
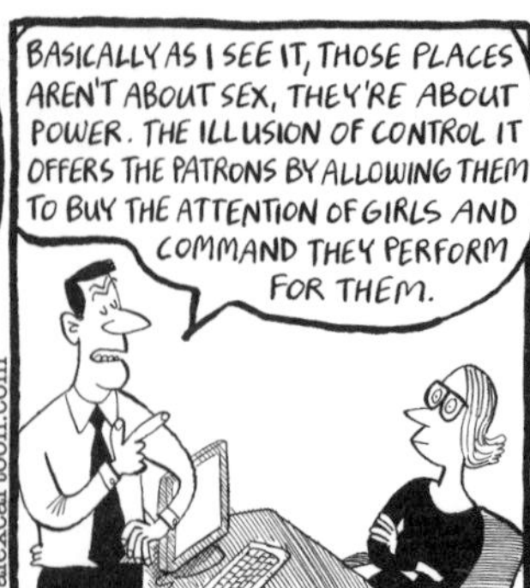
BASICALLY AS I SEE IT, THOSE PLACES AREN'T ABOUT SEX, THEY'RE ABOUT POWER. THE ILLUSION OF CONTROL IT OFFERS THE PATRONS BY ALLOWING THEM TO BUY THE ATTENTION OF GIRLS AND COMMAND THEY PERFORM FOR THEM.
alex@alexcartoon.com
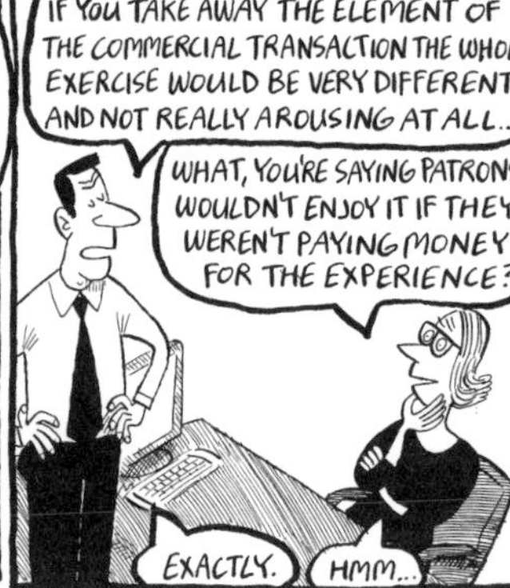
IF YOU TAKE AWAY THE ELEMENT OF THE COMMERCIAL TRANSACTION THE WHOLE EXERCISE WOULD BE VERY DIFFERENT AND NOT REALLY AROUSING AT ALL...
WHAT, YOU'RE SAYING PATRONS WOULDN'T ENJOY IT IF THEY WEREN'T PAYING MONEY FOR THE EXPERIENCE?
EXACTLY.
HMM...
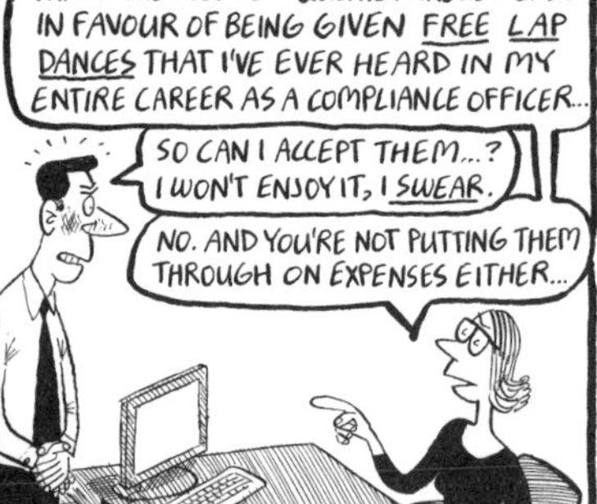
THAT'S THE MOST ELOQUENTLY ARGUED CASE IN FAVOUR OF BEING GIVEN FREE LAP DANCES THAT I'VE EVER HEARD IN MY ENTIRE CAREER AS A COMPLIANCE OFFICER...
SO CAN I ACCEPT THEM...? I WON'T ENJOY IT, I SWEAR.
NO. AND YOU'RE NOT PUTTING THEM THROUGH ON EXPENSES EITHER...
DAMN.

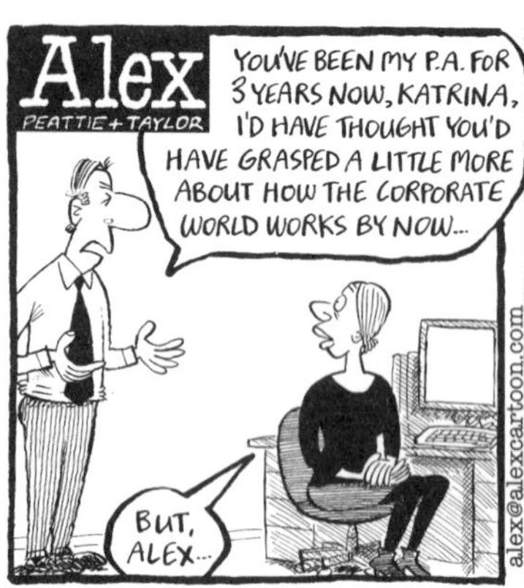
Alex
PEATTIE + TAYLOR
YOU'VE BEEN MY P.A. FOR 3 YEARS NOW, KATRINA, I'D HAVE THOUGHT YOU'D HAVE GRASPED A LITTLE MORE ABOUT HOW THE CORPORATE WORLD WORKS BY NOW...
BUT, ALEX...
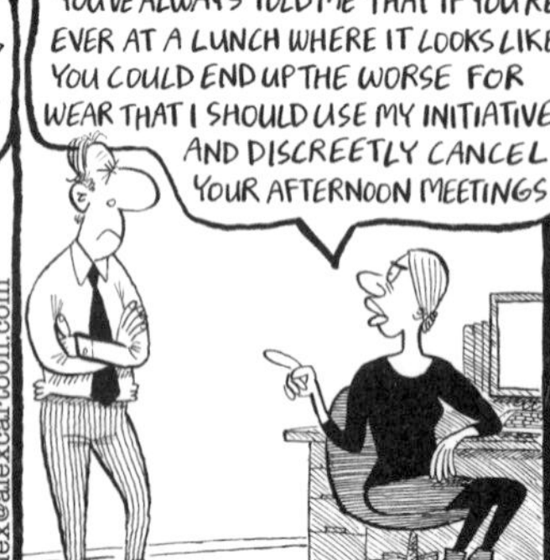
YOU'VE ALWAYS TOLD ME THAT IF YOU'RE EVER AT A LUNCH WHERE IT LOOKS LIKE YOU COULD END UP THE WORSE FOR WEAR THAT I SHOULD USE MY INITIATIVE AND DISCREETLY CANCEL YOUR AFTERNOON MEETINGS.
alex@alexcartoon.com
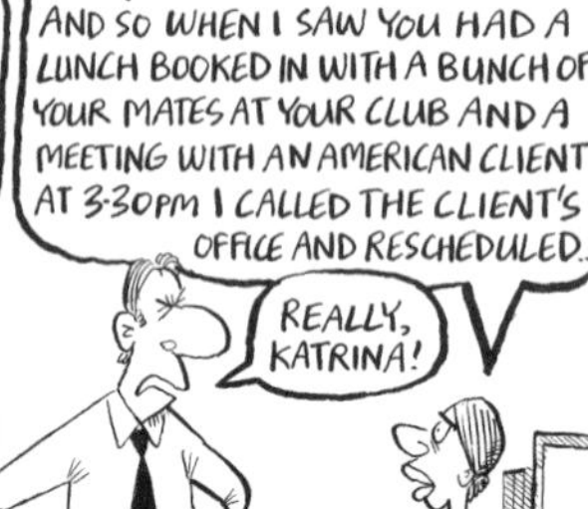
WELL, IT'S 2 WEEKS BEFORE XMAS AND SO WHEN I SAW YOU HAD A LUNCH BOOKED IN WITH A BUNCH OF YOUR MATES AT YOUR CLUB AND A MEETING WITH AN AMERICAN CLIENT AT 3:30PM I CALLED THE CLIENT'S OFFICE AND RESCHEDULED...
REALLY, KATRINA!
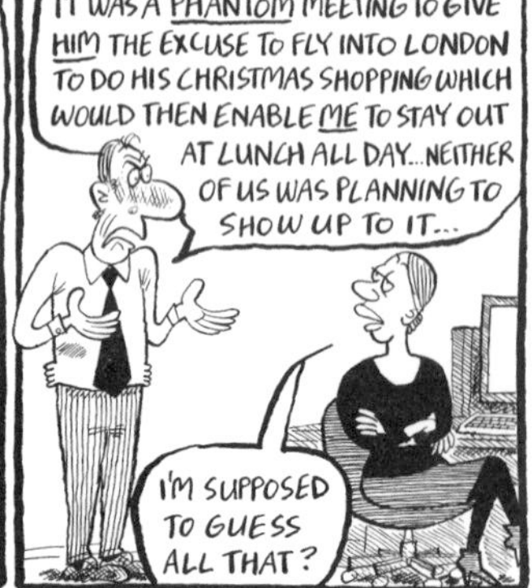
IT WAS A PHANTOM MEETING TO GIVE HIM THE EXCUSE TO FLY INTO LONDON TO DO HIS CHRISTMAS SHOPPING WHICH WOULD THEN ENABLE ME TO STAY OUT AT LUNCH ALL DAY... NEITHER OF US WAS PLANNING TO SHOW UP TO IT...
I'M SUPPOSED TO GUESS ALL THAT?

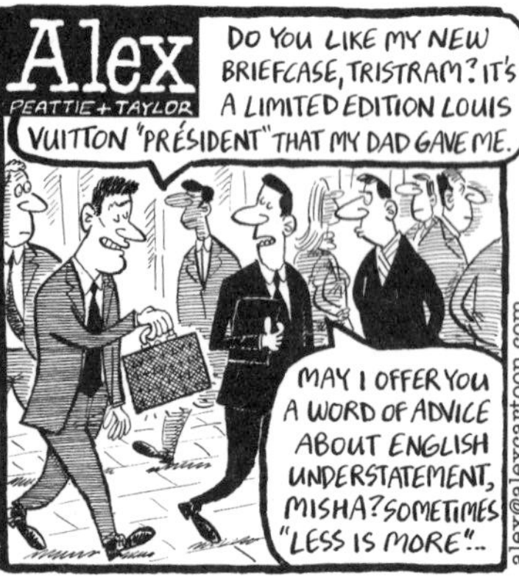
Alex
PEATTIE + TAYLOR
DO YOU LIKE MY NEW BRIEFCASE, TRISTRAM? IT'S A LIMITED EDITION LOUIS VUITTON "PRÉSIDENT" THAT MY DAD GAVE ME.
MAY I OFFER YOU A WORD OF ADVICE ABOUT ENGLISH UNDERSTATEMENT, MISHA? SOMETIMES "LESS IS MORE"...
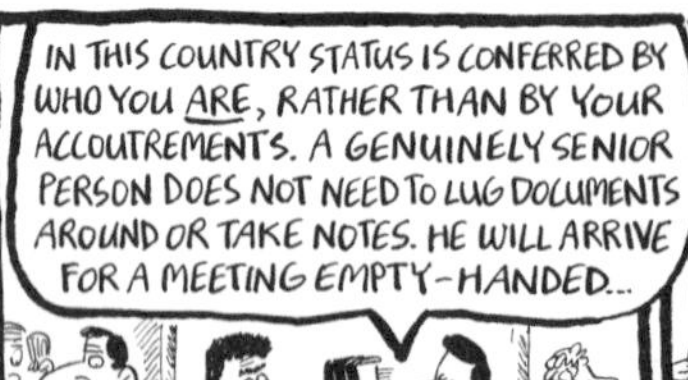
IN THIS COUNTRY STATUS IS CONFERRED BY WHO YOU ARE, RATHER THAN BY YOUR ACCOUTREMENTS. A GENUINELY SENIOR PERSON DOES NOT NEED TO LUG DOCUMENTS AROUND OR TAKE NOTES. HE WILL ARRIVE FOR A MEETING EMPTY-HANDED...
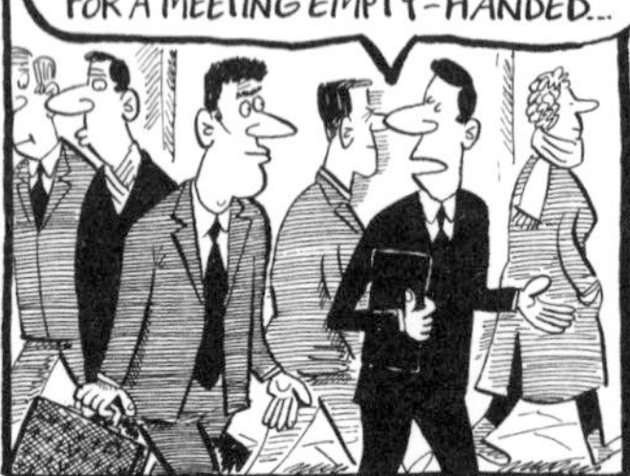
alex@alexcartoon.com
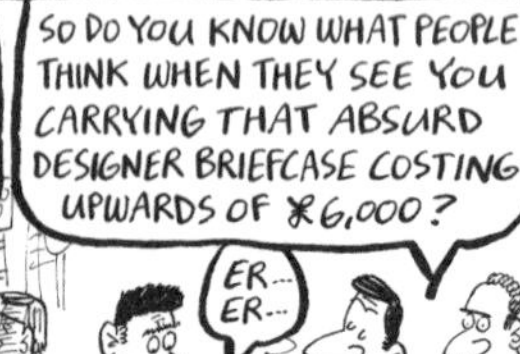
SO DO YOU KNOW WHAT PEOPLE THINK WHEN THEY SEE YOU CARRYING THAT ABSURD DESIGNER BRIEFCASE COSTING UPWARDS OF ¥6,000?
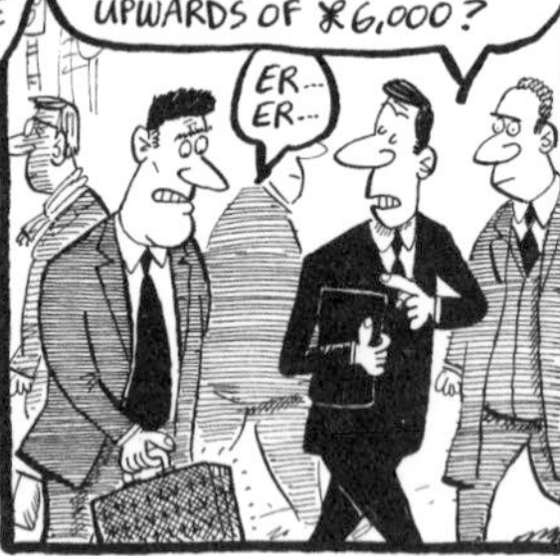
ER... ER...
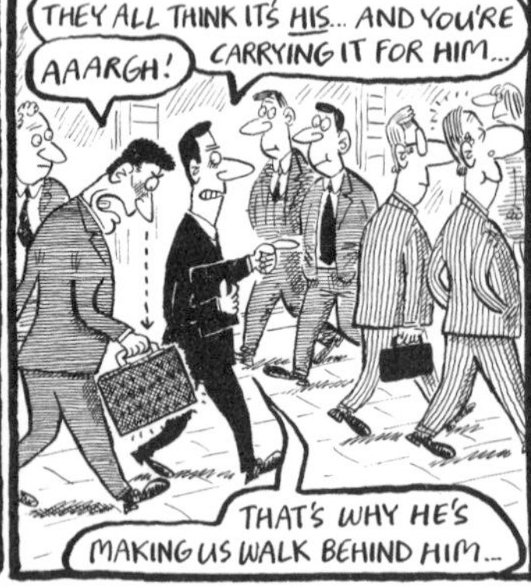
THEY ALL THINK IT'S HIS... AND YOU'RE CARRYING IT FOR HIM...
AAARGH!
THAT'S WHY HE'S MAKING US WALK BEHIND HIM...

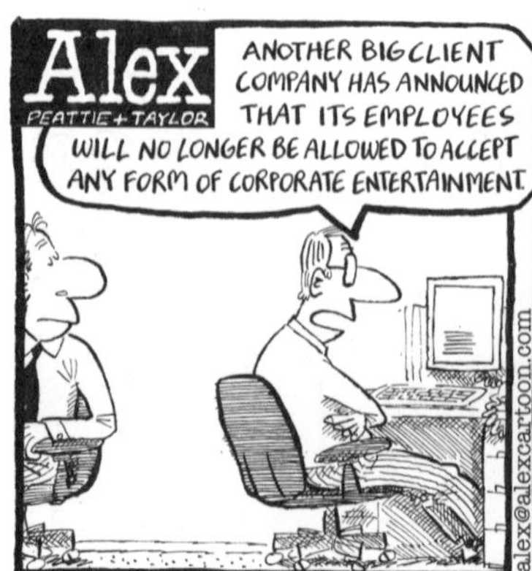
Alex
PEATTIE + TAYLOR
ANOTHER BIG CLIENT COMPANY HAS ANNOUNCED THAT ITS EMPLOYEES WILL NO LONGER BE ALLOWED TO ACCEPT ANY FORM OF CORPORATE ENTERTAINMENT.
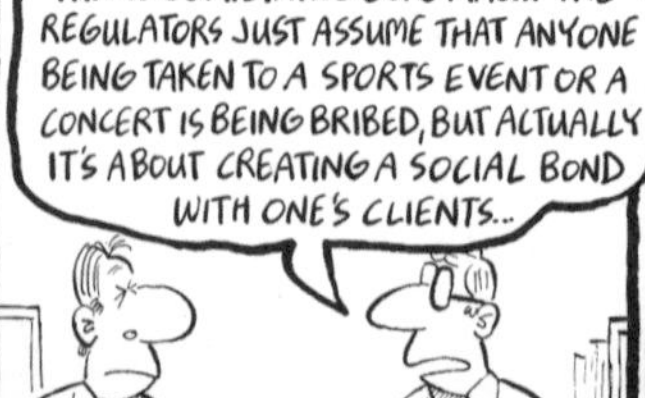
THIS IS COMPLIANCE GONE MAD... THE REGULATORS JUST ASSUME THAT ANYONE BEING TAKEN TO A SPORTS EVENT OR A CONCERT IS BEING BRIBED, BUT ACTUALLY IT'S ABOUT CREATING A SOCIAL BOND WITH ONE'S CLIENTS...
alex@alexcartoon.com
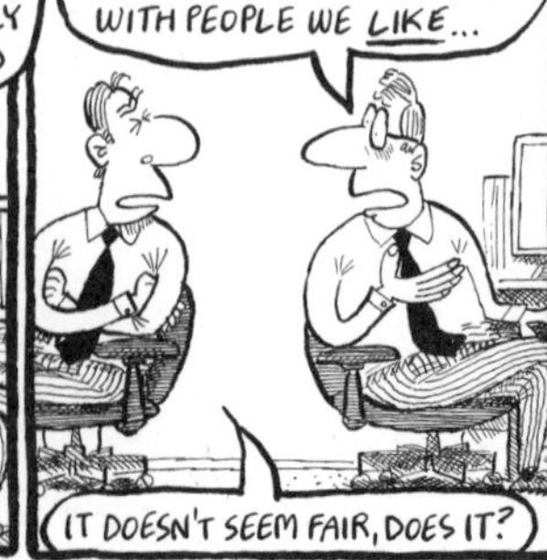
AFTER ALL WE'RE ONLY HUMAN BEINGS AND AT THE END OF THE DAY WE TEND TO DO BUSINESS WITH PEOPLE WE LIKE...
IT DOESN'T SEEM FAIR, DOES IT?
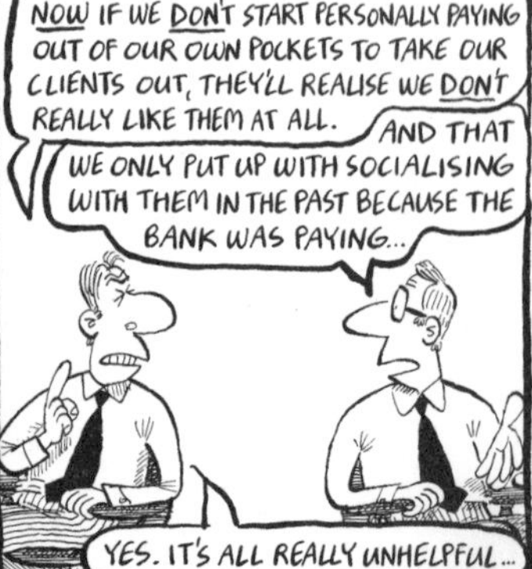
NOW IF WE DON'T START PERSONALLY PAYING OUT OF OUR OWN POCKETS TO TAKE OUR CLIENTS OUT, THEY'LL REALISE WE DON'T REALLY LIKE THEM AT ALL.
AND THAT WE ONLY PUT UP WITH SOCIALISING WITH THEM IN THE PAST BECAUSE THE BANK WAS PAYING...
YES. IT'S ALL REALLY UNHELPFUL...

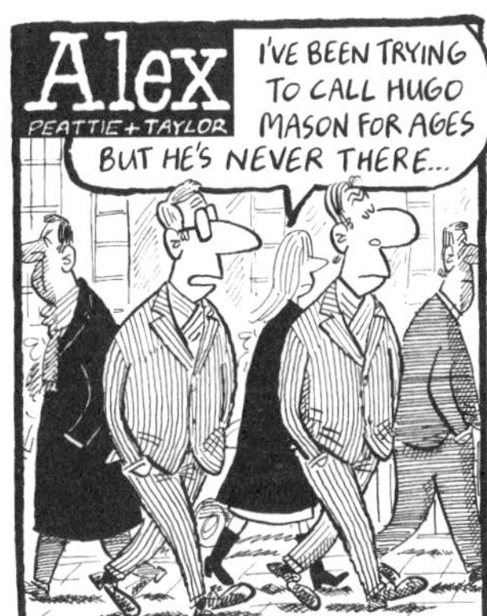
Alex
PEATTIE + TAYLOR
I'VE BEEN TRYING TO CALL HUGO MASON FOR AGES BUT HE'S NEVER THERE...

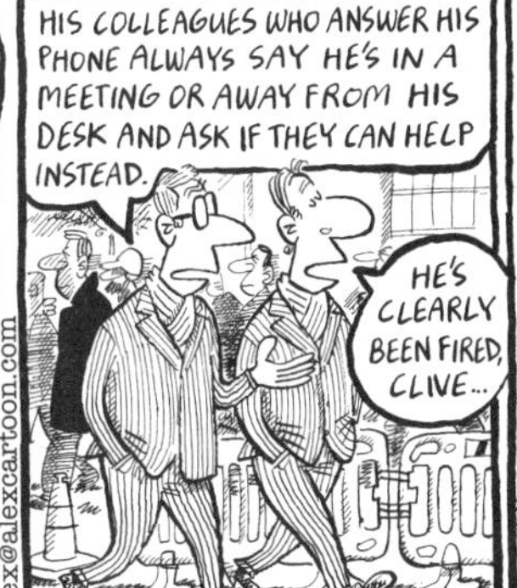
HIS COLLEAGUES WHO ANSWER HIS PHONE ALWAYS SAY HE'S IN A MEETING OR AWAY FROM HIS DESK AND ASK IF THEY CAN HELP INSTEAD.
HE'S CLEARLY BEEN FIRED, CLIVE...
alex@alexcartoon.com

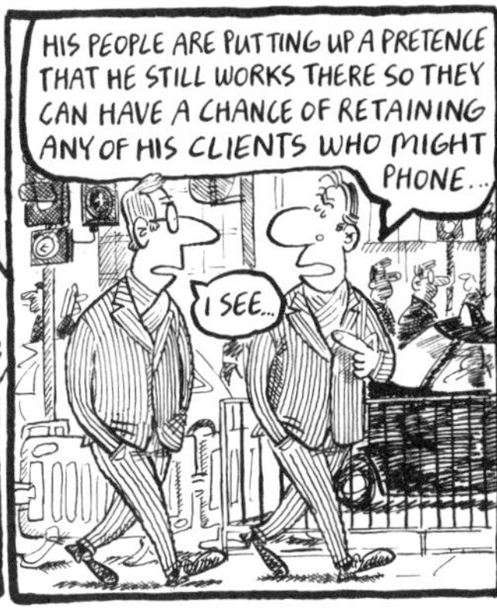
HIS PEOPLE ARE PUTTING UP A PRETENCE THAT HE STILL WORKS THERE SO THEY CAN HAVE A CHANCE OF RETAINING ANY OF HIS CLIENTS WHO MIGHT PHONE...
I SEE...

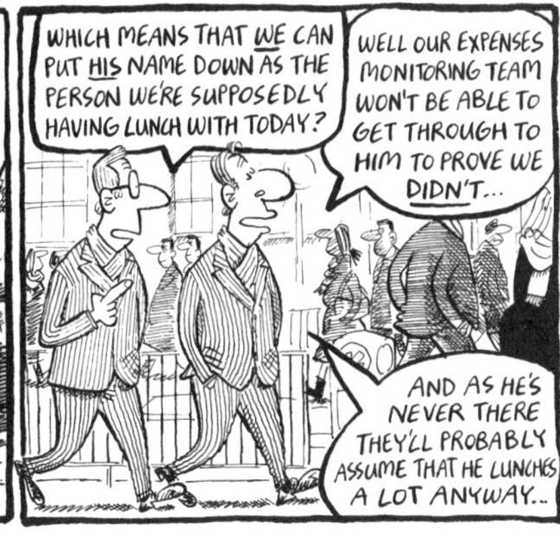
WHICH MEANS THAT WE CAN PUT HIS NAME DOWN AS THE PERSON WE'RE SUPPOSEDLY HAVING LUNCH WITH TODAY?
WELL OUR EXPENSES MONITORING TEAM WON'T BE ABLE TO GET THROUGH TO HIM TO PROVE WE DIDN'T...
AND AS HE'S NEVER THERE THEY'LL PROBABLY ASSUME THAT HE LUNCHES A LOT ANYWAY...

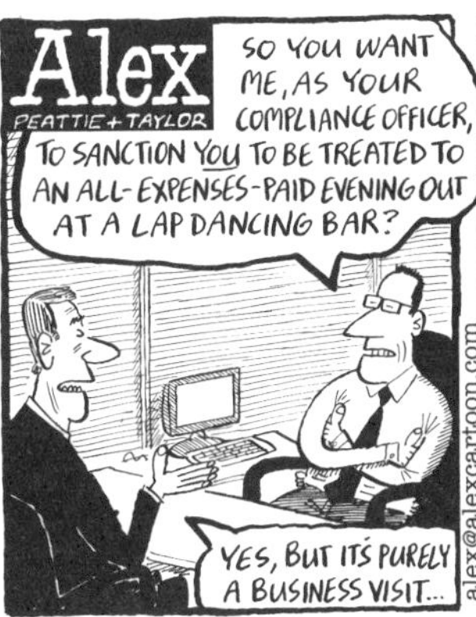
Alex
PEATTIE + TAYLOR
SO YOU WANT ME, AS YOUR COMPLIANCE OFFICER, TO SANCTION YOU TO BE TREATED TO AN ALL-EXPENSES-PAID EVENING OUT AT A LAP DANCING BAR?
YES, BUT IT'S PURELY A BUSINESS VISIT...

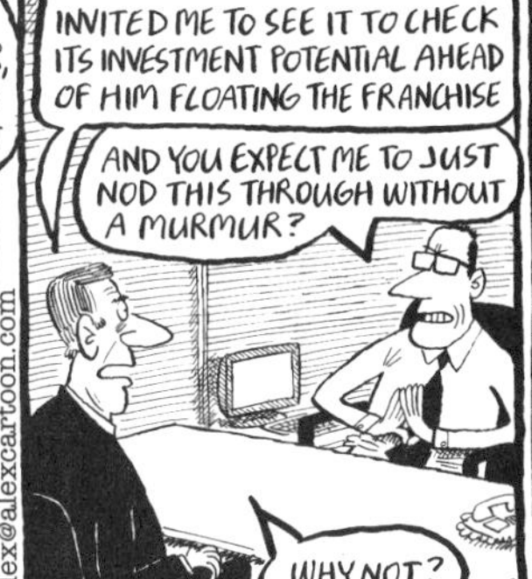
ALEX MASTERLEY OF MEGABANK INVITED ME TO SEE IT TO CHECK ITS INVESTMENT POTENTIAL AHEAD OF HIM FLOATING THE FRANCHISE
AND YOU EXPECT ME TO JUST NOD THIS THROUGH WITHOUT A MURMUR?
WHY NOT?
alex@alexcartoon.com

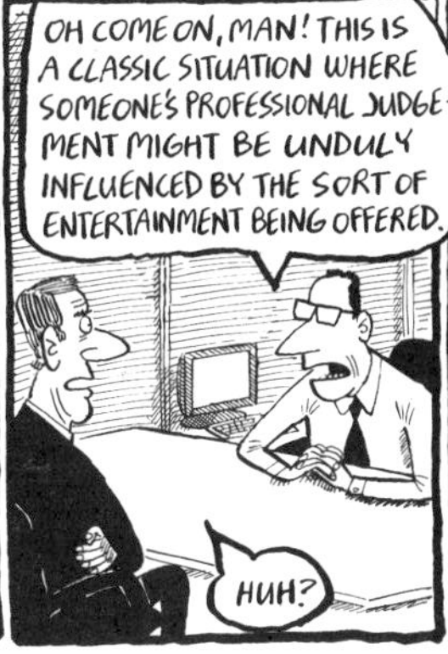
OH COME ON, MAN! THIS IS A CLASSIC SITUATION WHERE SOMEONE'S PROFESSIONAL JUDGEMENT MIGHT BE UNDULY INFLUENCED BY THE SORT OF ENTERTAINMENT BEING OFFERED.
HUH?

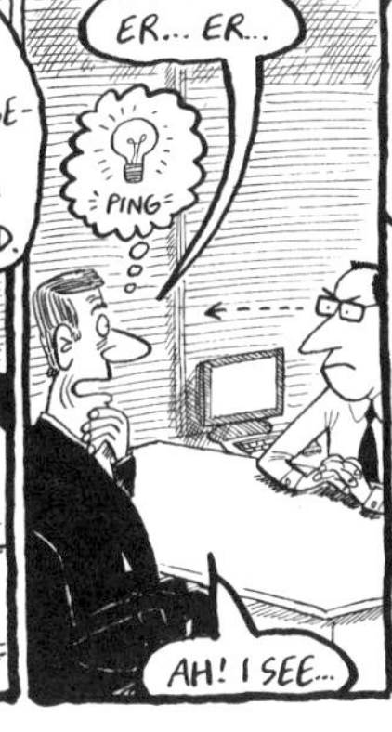
ER... ER...
PING
AH! I SEE...

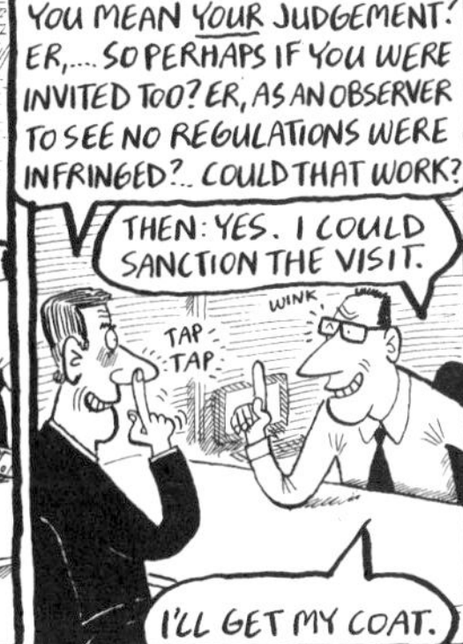
YOU MEAN YOUR JUDGEMENT? ER,... SO PERHAPS IF YOU WERE INVITED TOO? ER, AS AN OBSERVER TO SEE NO REGULATIONS WERE INFRINGED?.. COULD THAT WORK?
THEN: YES. I COULD SANCTION THE VISIT.
WINK
TAP TAP
I'LL GET MY COAT.

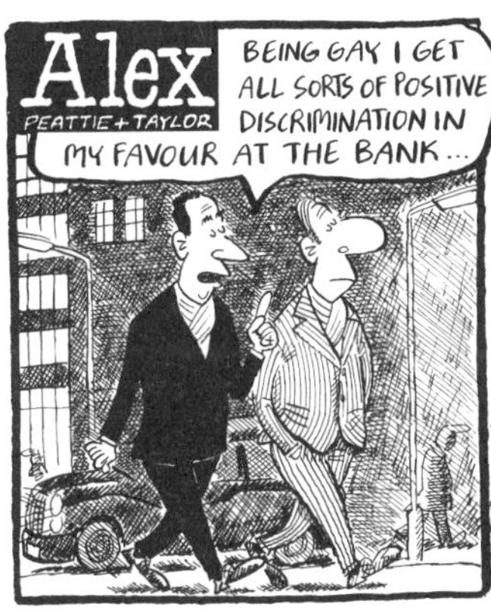
Alex
PEATTIE + TAYLOR
BEING GAY I GET ALL SORTS OF POSITIVE DISCRIMINATION IN MY FAVOUR AT THE BANK...

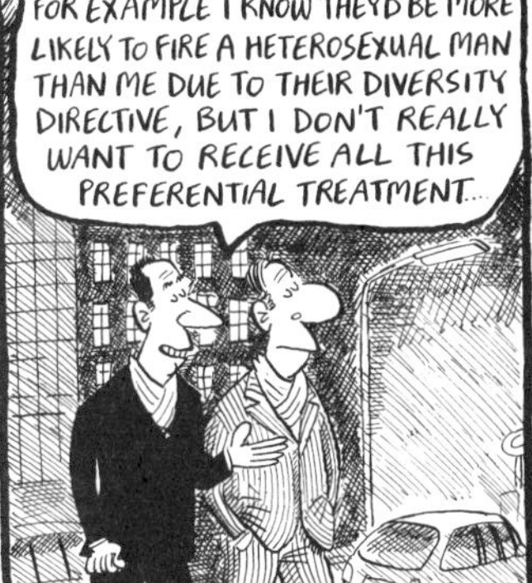
FOR EXAMPLE I KNOW THEY'D BE MORE LIKELY TO FIRE A HETEROSEXUAL MAN THAN ME DUE TO THEIR DIVERSITY DIRECTIVE, BUT I DON'T REALLY WANT TO RECEIVE ALL THIS PREFERENTIAL TREATMENT...
alex@alexcartoon.com

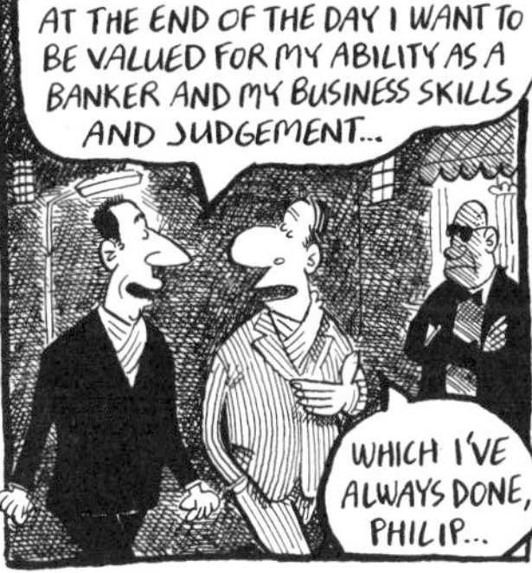
I'M HAPPY FOR MY SEXUALITY TO BE RECOGNISED AND RESPECTED, BUT AT THE END OF THE DAY I WANT TO BE VALUED FOR MY ABILITY AS A BANKER AND MY BUSINESS SKILLS AND JUDGEMENT...
WHICH I'VE ALWAYS DONE, PHILIP...

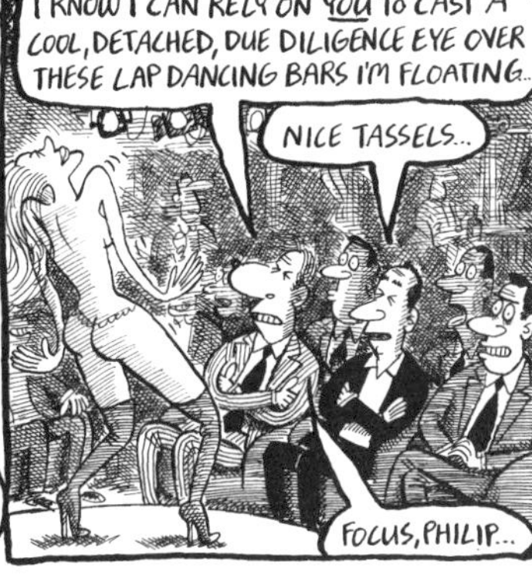
I KNOW I CAN RELY ON YOU TO CAST A COOL, DETACHED, DUE DILIGENCE EYE OVER THESE LAP DANCING BARS I'M FLOATING...
NICE TASSELS...
FOCUS, PHILIP...

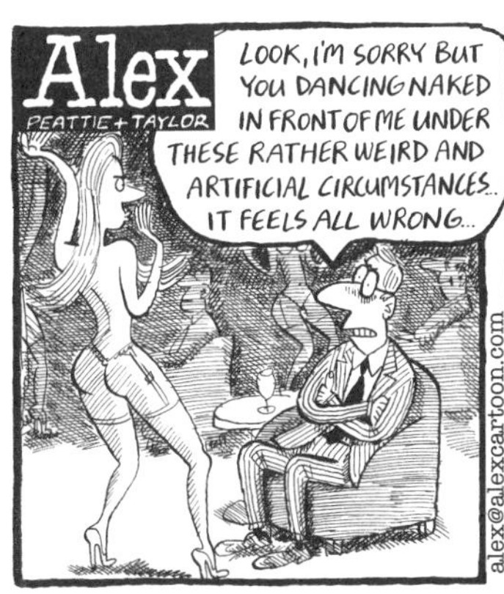
Alex
PEATTIE + TAYLOR
LOOK, I'M SORRY BUT YOU DANCING NAKED IN FRONT OF ME UNDER THESE RATHER WEIRD AND ARTIFICIAL CIRCUMSTANCES... IT FEELS ALL WRONG...

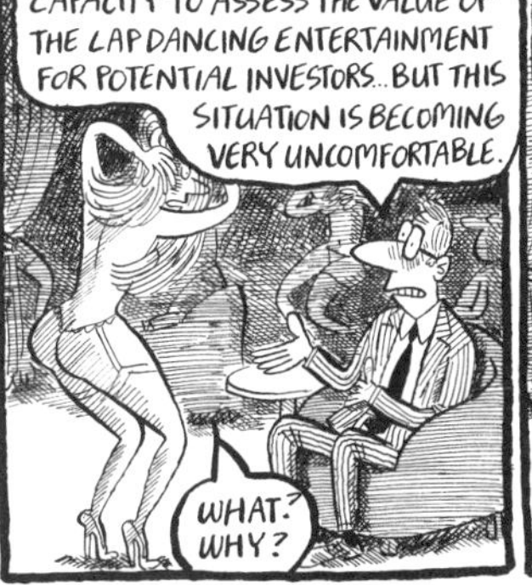
AS YOU KNOW, I'M HERE IN A BUSINESS CAPACITY TO ASSESS THE VALUE OF THE LAP DANCING ENTERTAINMENT FOR POTENTIAL INVESTORS... BUT THIS SITUATION IS BECOMING VERY UNCOMFORTABLE.
WHAT? WHY?
alex@alexcartoon.com

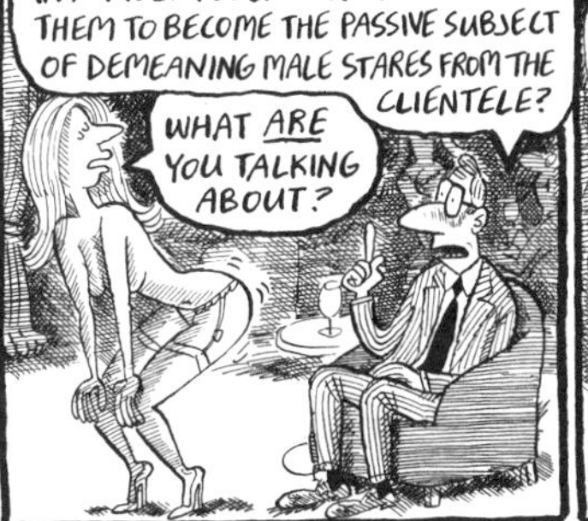
OH COME ON. YOU MUST BE ABLE TO SEE IT'S A SITUATION THAT PLACES ONE PERSON IN A DISEMPOWERED POSITION BY CAUSING THEM TO BECOME THE PASSIVE SUBJECT OF DEMEANING MALE STARES FROM THE CLIENTELE?
WHAT ARE YOU TALKING ABOUT?

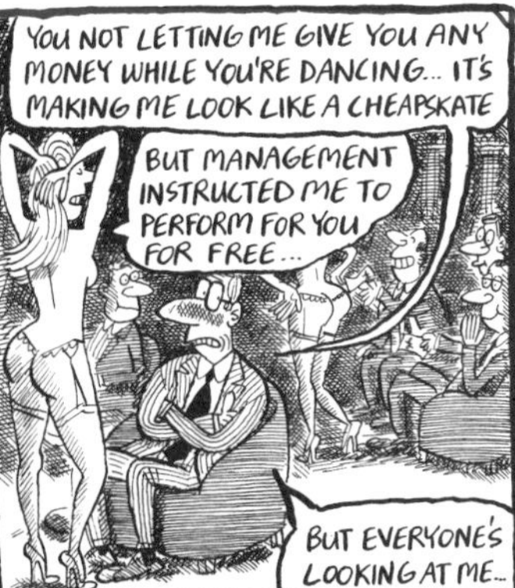
YOU NOT LETTING ME GIVE YOU ANY MONEY WHILE YOU'RE DANCING... IT'S MAKING ME LOOK LIKE A CHEAPSKATE
BUT MANAGEMENT INSTRUCTED ME TO PERFORM FOR YOU FOR FREE...
BUT EVERYONE'S LOOKING AT ME...

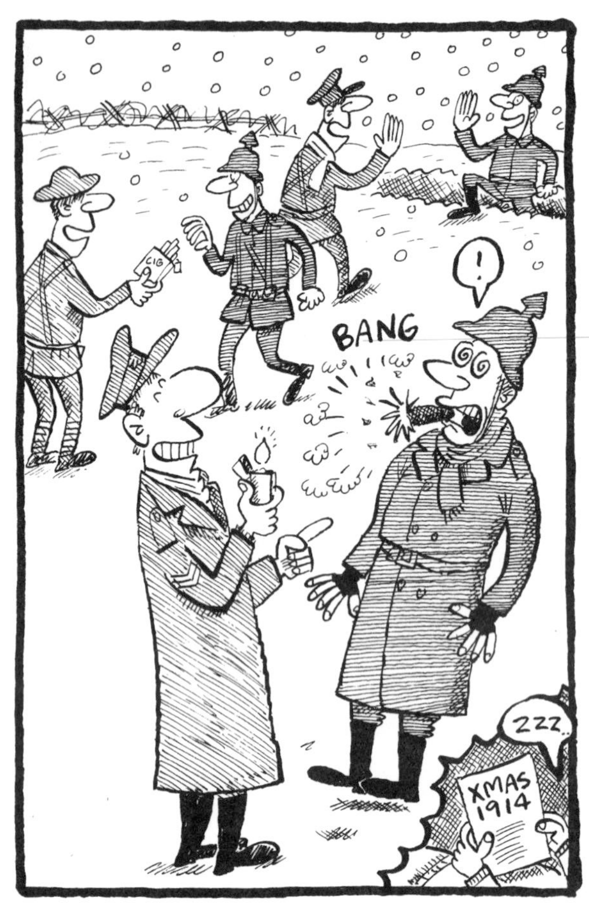
CIG
!
BANG
ZZZ...
XMAS 1914

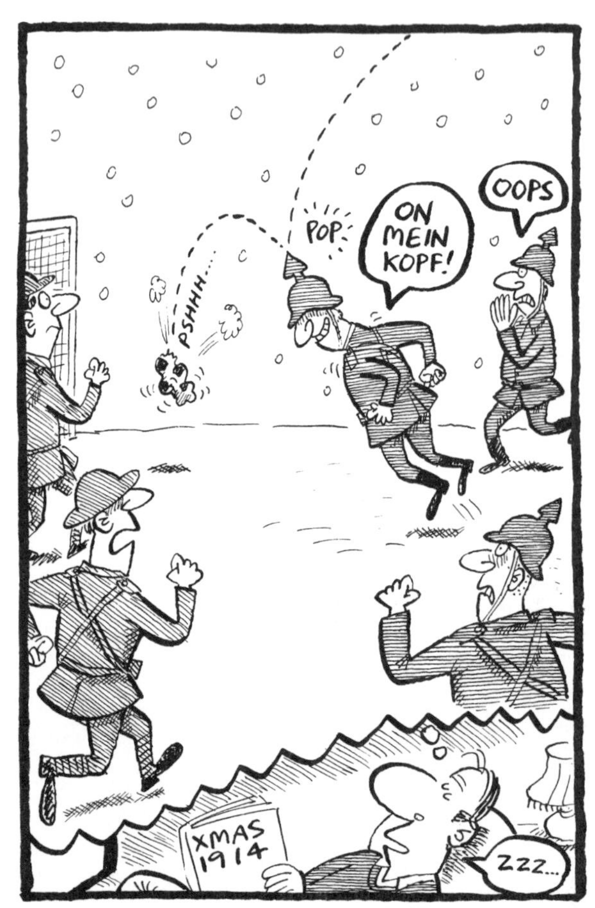
PSHHH...
POP
ON MEIN KOPF!
OOPS
XMAS 1914
ZZZ...

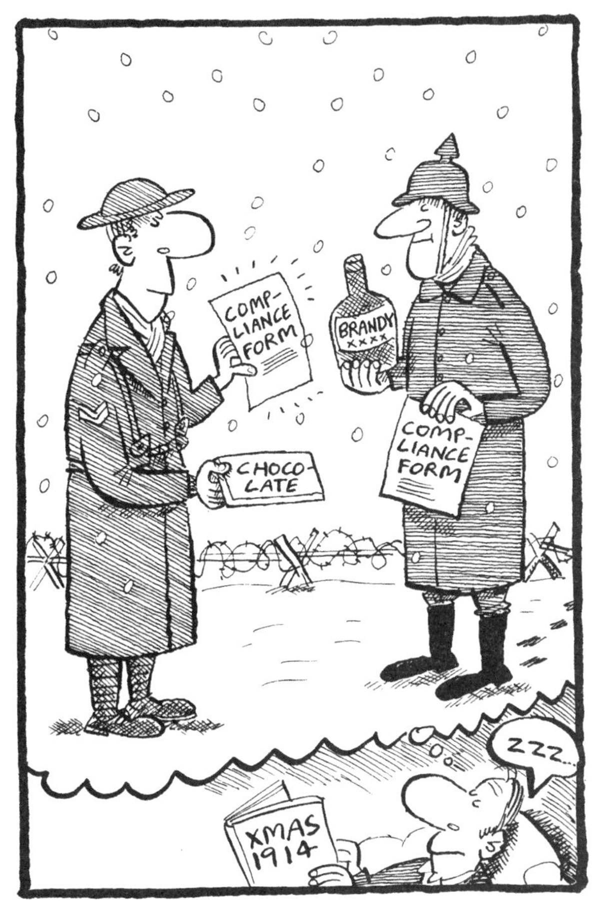
COMP-
LIANCE
FORM
BRANDY
XXXX
CHOCO-
LATE
COMP-
LIANCE
FORM
ZZZ...
XMAS
1914

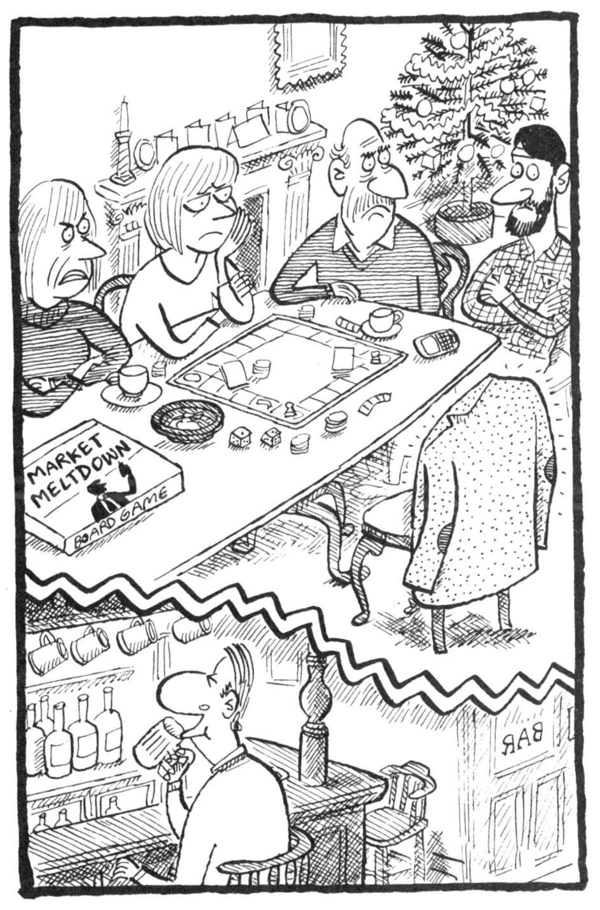
MARKET
MELTDOWN
BOARD GAME
BAR

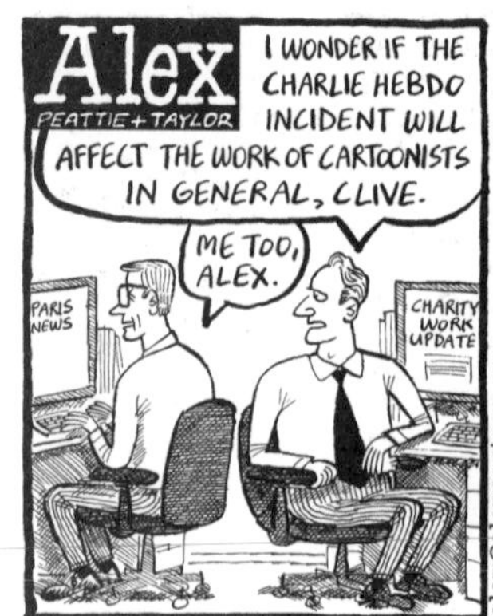
Alex
PEATTIE + TAYLOR
I WONDER IF THE CHARLIE HEBDO INCIDENT WILL AFFECT THE WORK OF CARTOONISTS IN GENERAL, CLIVE.
ME TOO, ALEX.
PARIS NEWS
CHARITY WORK UPDATE
alex@alexcartoon.com

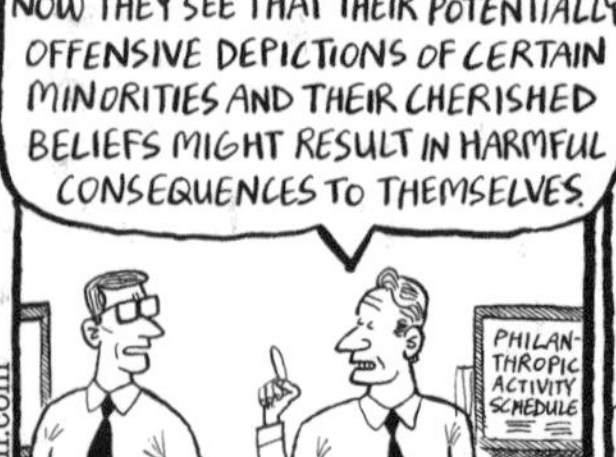
NOW THEY SEE THAT THEIR POTENTIALLY OFFENSIVE DEPICTIONS OF CERTAIN MINORITIES AND THEIR CHERISHED BELIEFS MIGHT RESULT IN HARMFUL CONSEQUENCES TO THEMSELVES.
PHILAN-THROPIC ACTIVITY SCHEDULE
INDEED.

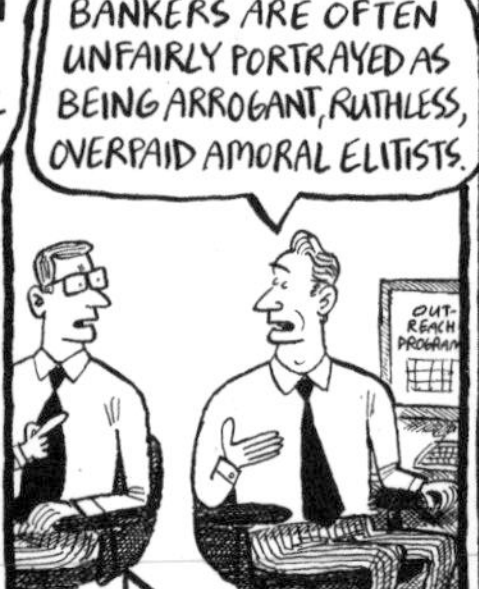
LIKE FOR EXAMPLE: WE BANKERS ARE OFTEN UNFAIRLY PORTRAYED AS BEING ARROGANT, RUTHLESS, OVERPAID AMORAL ELITISTS.
OUT-REACH PROGRAM
ER... BUT, ALEX...

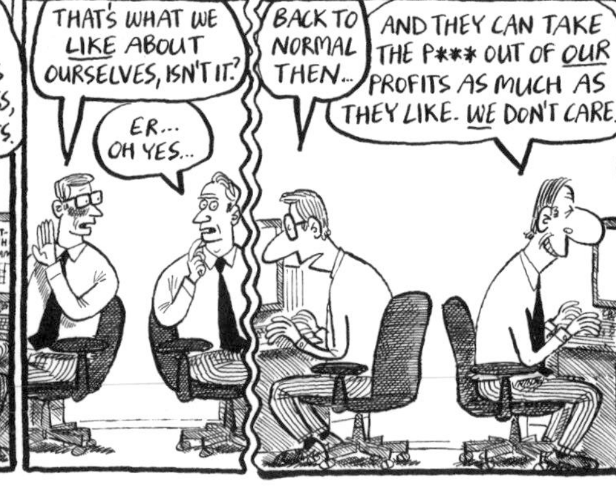
THAT'S WHAT WE LIKE ABOUT OURSELVES, ISN'T IT?
ER... OH YES...
BACK TO NORMAL THEN...
AND THEY CAN TAKE THE P*** OUT OF OUR PROFITS AS MUCH AS THEY LIKE. WE DON'T CARE.

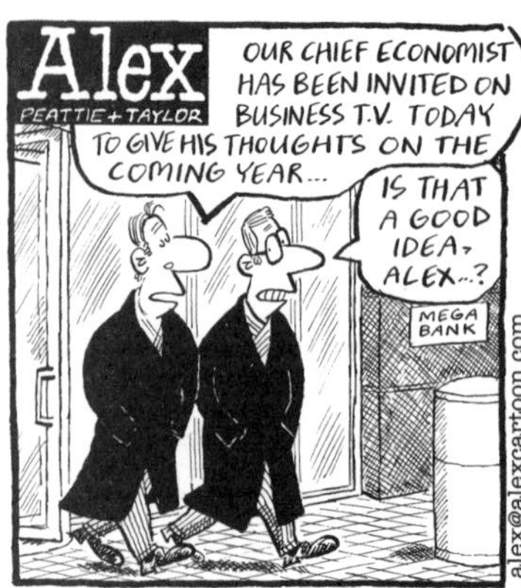
Alex
PEATTIE + TAYLOR
OUR CHIEF ECONOMIST HAS BEEN INVITED ON BUSINESS T.V. TODAY TO GIVE HIS THOUGHTS ON THE COMING YEAR...
IS THAT A GOOD IDEA, ALEX...?
MEGA BANK
alex@alexcartoon.com

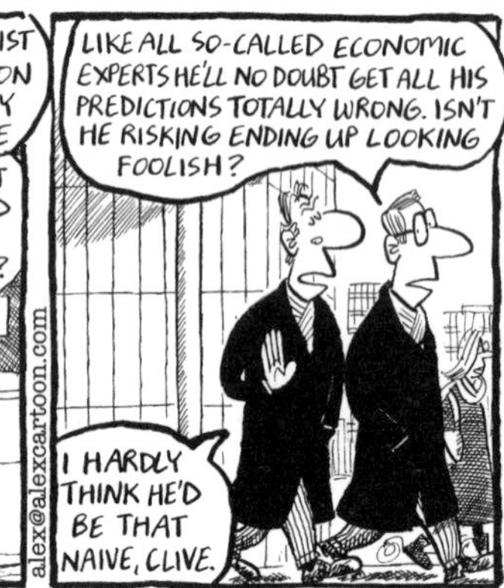
LIKE ALL SO-CALLED ECONOMIC EXPERTS HE'LL NO DOUBT GET ALL HIS PREDICTIONS TOTALLY WRONG. ISN'T HE RISKING ENDING UP LOOKING FOOLISH?
I HARDLY THINK HE'D BE THAT NAIVE, CLIVE.

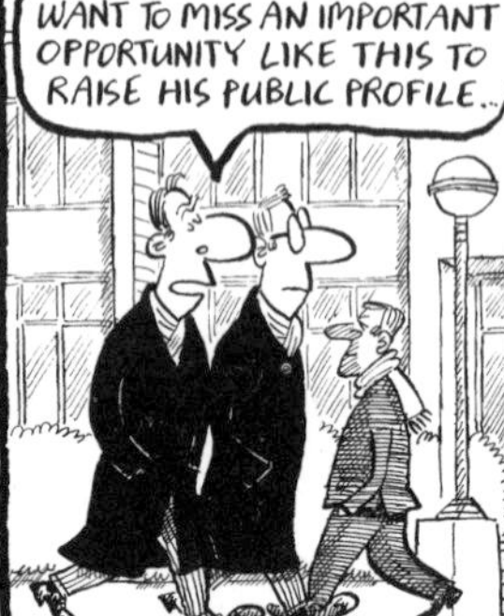
IN ANY CASE HE WOULDN'T WANT TO MISS AN IMPORTANT OPPORTUNITY LIKE THIS TO RAISE HIS PUBLIC PROFILE...

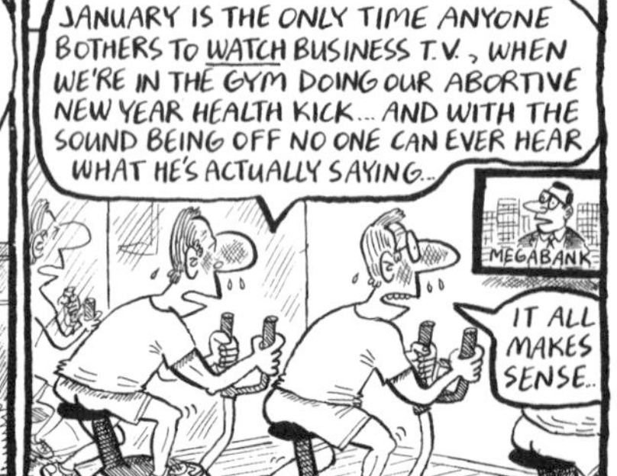
JANUARY IS THE ONLY TIME ANYONE BOTHERS TO WATCH BUSINESS T.V., WHEN WE'RE IN THE GYM DOING OUR ABORTIVE NEW YEAR HEALTH KICK... AND WITH THE SOUND BEING OFF NO ONE CAN EVER HEAR WHAT HE'S ACTUALLY SAYING...
MEGABANK
IT ALL MAKES SENSE...

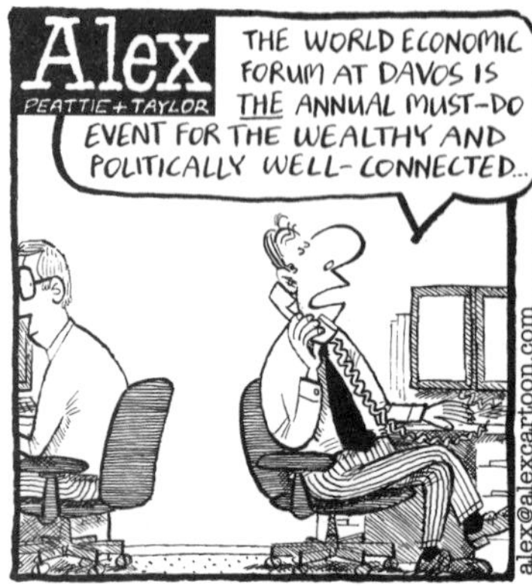
Alex
PEATTIE + TAYLOR
THE WORLD ECONOMIC FORUM AT DAVOS IS THE ANNUAL MUST-DO EVENT FOR THE WEALTHY AND POLITICALLY WELL-CONNECTED...
alex@alexcartoon.com

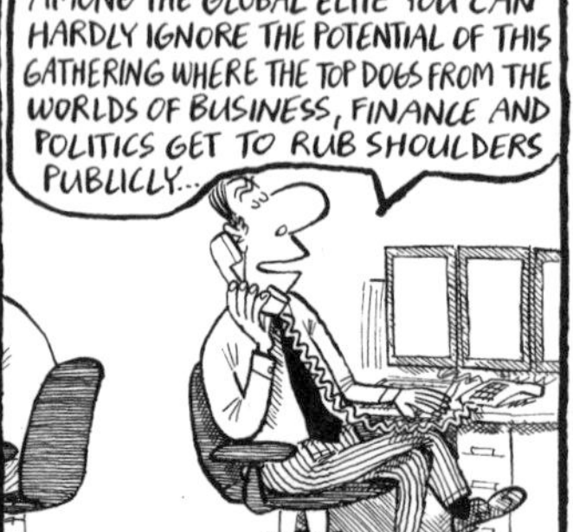
IF YOU WANT TO RETAIN YOUR PLACE AMONG THE GLOBAL ELITE YOU CAN HARDLY IGNORE THE POTENTIAL OF THIS GATHERING WHERE THE TOP DOGS FROM THE WORLDS OF BUSINESS, FINANCE AND POLITICS GET TO RUB SHOULDERS PUBLICLY...

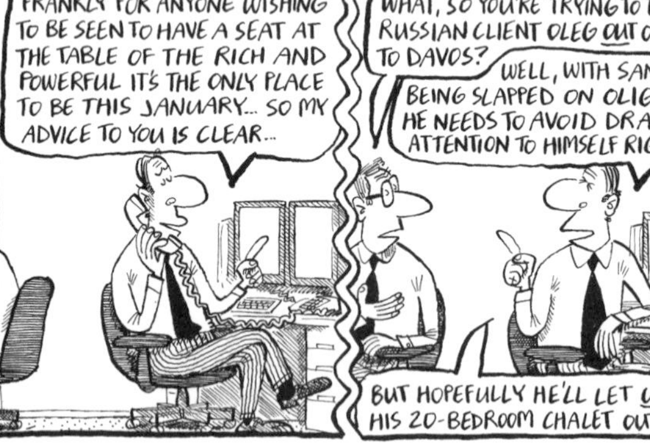
FRANKLY FOR ANYONE WISHING TO BE SEEN TO HAVE A SEAT AT THE TABLE OF THE RICH AND POWERFUL IT'S THE ONLY PLACE TO BE THIS JANUARY... SO MY ADVICE TO YOU IS CLEAR...
WHAT, SO YOU'RE TRYING TO TALK OUR RUSSIAN CLIENT OLEG OUT OF GOING TO DAVOS?
WELL, WITH SANCTIONS BEING SLAPPED ON OLIGARCHS HE NEEDS TO AVOID DRAWING ATTENTION TO HIMSELF RIGHT NOW...
BUT HOPEFULLY HE'LL LET US USE HIS 20-BEDROOM CHALET OUT THERE.

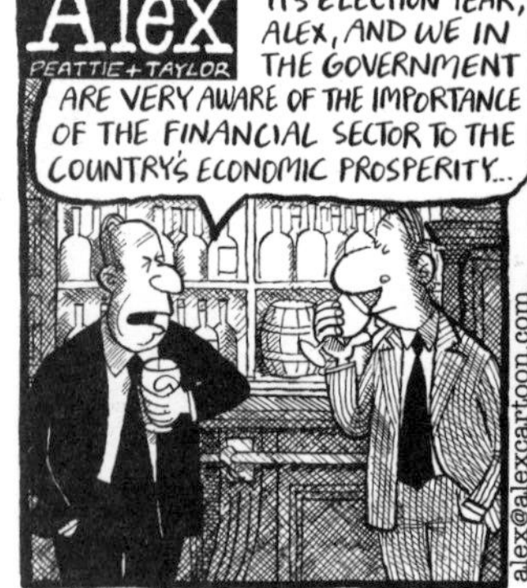
Alex
PEATTIE + TAYLOR
IT'S ELECTION YEAR, ALEX, AND WE IN THE GOVERNMENT ARE VERY AWARE OF THE IMPORTANCE OF THE FINANCIAL SECTOR TO THE COUNTRY'S ECONOMIC PROSPERITY...
alex@alexcartoon.com

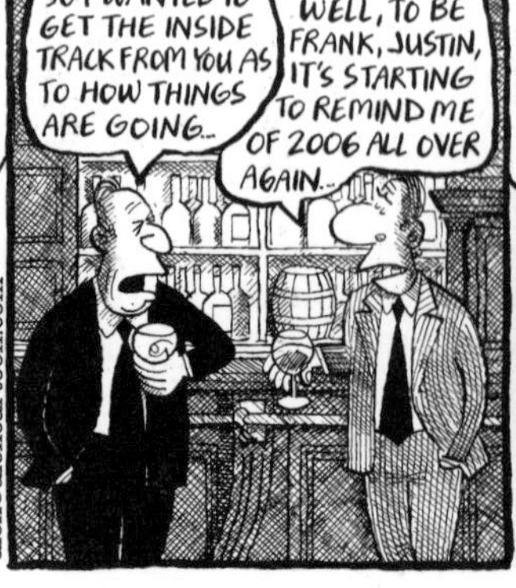
SO I WANTED TO GET THE INSIDE TRACK FROM YOU AS TO HOW THINGS ARE GOING...
WELL, TO BE FRANK, JUSTIN, IT'S STARTING TO REMIND ME OF 2006 ALL OVER AGAIN...

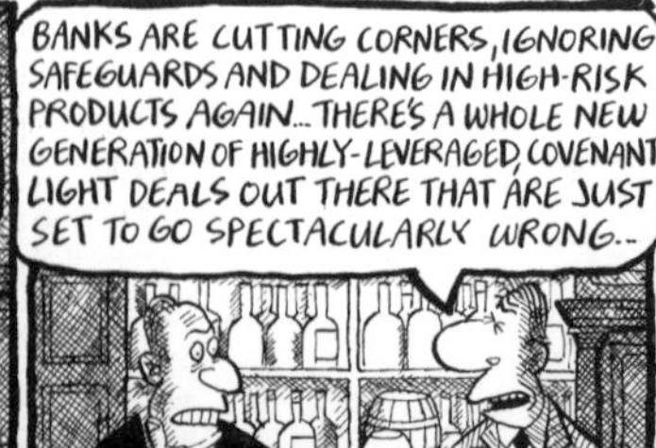
BANKS ARE CUTTING CORNERS, IGNORING SAFEGUARDS AND DEALING IN HIGH-RISK PRODUCTS AGAIN... THERE'S A WHOLE NEW GENERATION OF HIGHLY-LEVERAGED, COVENANT-LIGHT DEALS OUT THERE THAT ARE JUST SET TO GO SPECTACULARLY WRONG...
REALLY...?

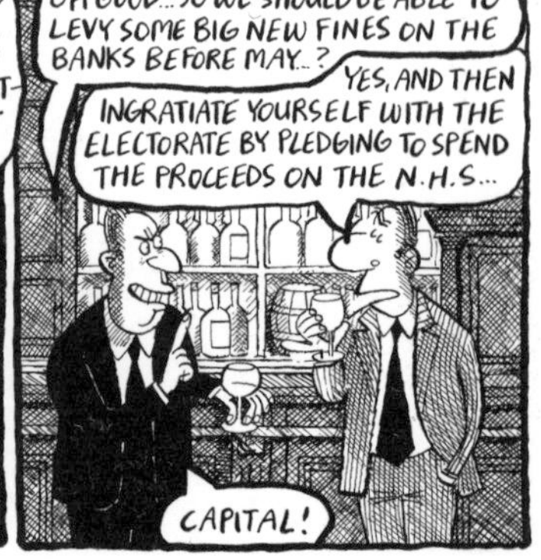
OH GOOD... SO WE SHOULD BE ABLE TO LEVY SOME BIG NEW FINES ON THE BANKS BEFORE MAY...?
YES, AND THEN INGRATIATE YOURSELF WITH THE ELECTORATE BY PLEDGING TO SPEND THE PROCEEDS ON THE N.H.S...
CAPITAL!

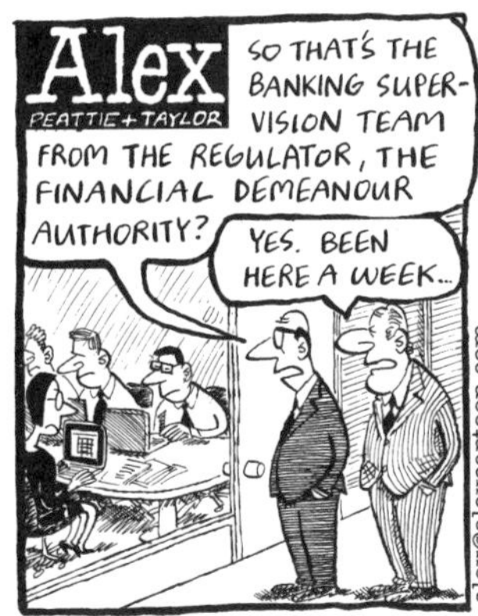
Alex
PEATTIE + TAYLOR
SO THAT'S THE BANKING SUPER-VISION TEAM FROM THE REGULATOR, THE FINANCIAL DEMEANOUR AUTHORITY?
YES. BEEN HERE A WEEK...
alex@alexcartoon.com

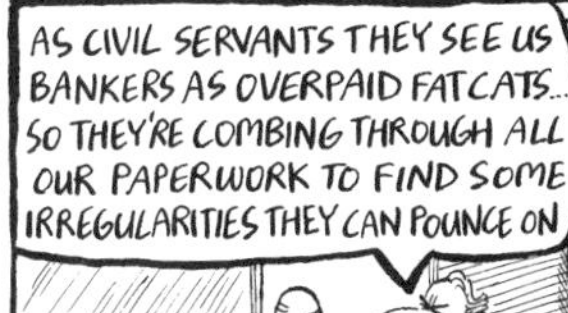
AS CIVIL SERVANTS THEY SEE US BANKERS AS OVERPAID FAT CATS... SO THEY'RE COMBING THROUGH ALL OUR PAPERWORK TO FIND SOME IRREGULARITIES THEY CAN POUNCE ON

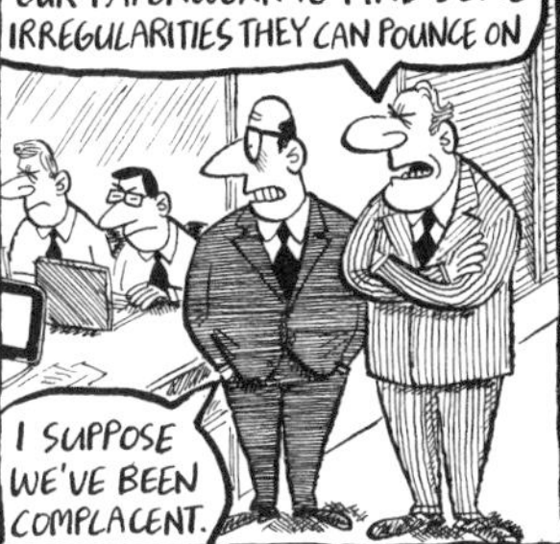
I SUPPOSE WE'VE BEEN COMPLACENT.

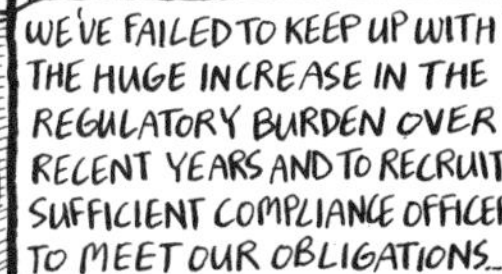
WE'VE FAILED TO KEEP UP WITH THE HUGE INCREASE IN THE REGULATORY BURDEN OVER RECENT YEARS AND TO RECRUIT SUFFICIENT COMPLIANCE OFFICERS TO MEET OUR OBLIGATIONS...

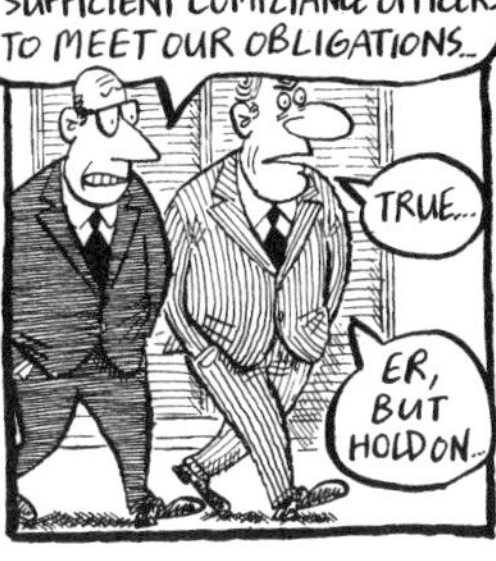
TRUE...
ER, BUT HOLD ON...

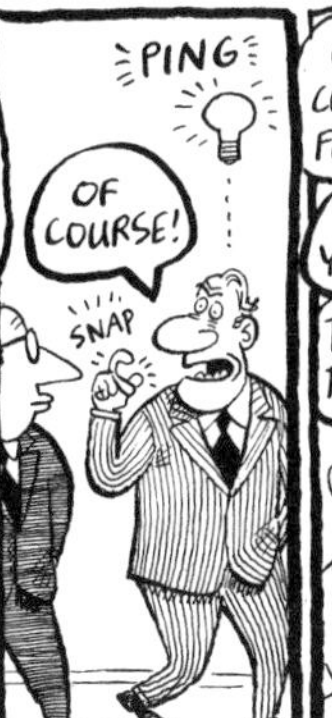
PING
OF COURSE!
SNAP

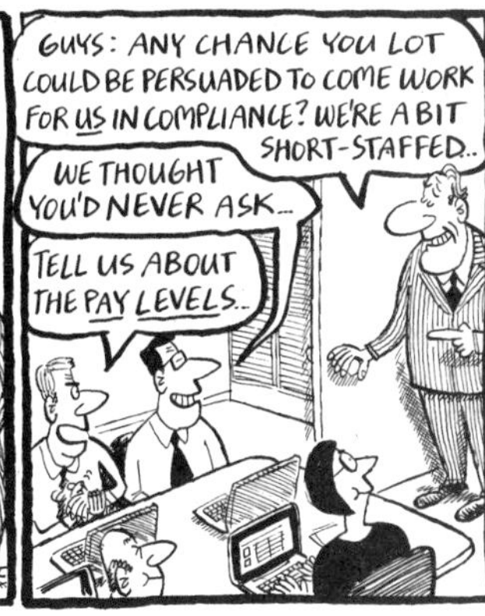
GUYS: ANY CHANCE YOU LOT COULD BE PERSUADED TO COME WORK FOR US IN COMPLIANCE? WE'RE A BIT SHORT-STAFFED...
WE THOUGHT YOU'D NEVER ASK...
TELL US ABOUT THE PAY LEVELS...

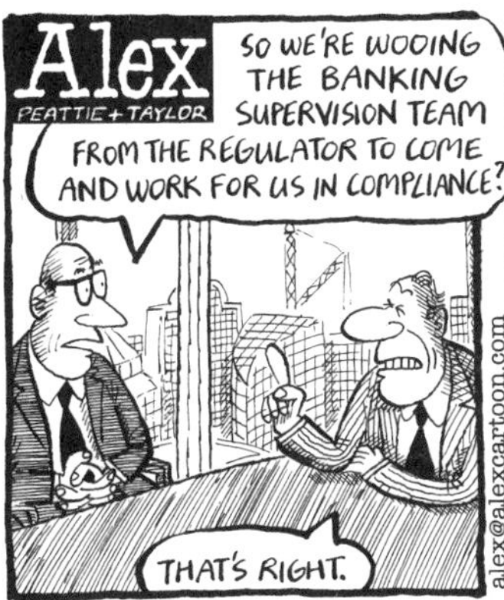
Alex
PEATTIE + TAYLOR
SO WE'RE WOOING THE BANKING SUPERVISION TEAM FROM THE REGULATOR TO COME AND WORK FOR US IN COMPLIANCE?
THAT'S RIGHT.
alex@alexcartoon.com

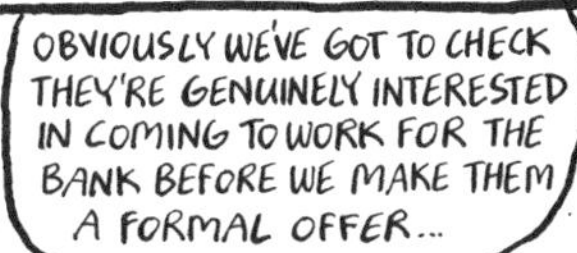
OBVIOUSLY WE'VE GOT TO CHECK THEY'RE GENUINELY INTERESTED IN COMING TO WORK FOR THE BANK BEFORE WE MAKE THEM A FORMAL OFFER...

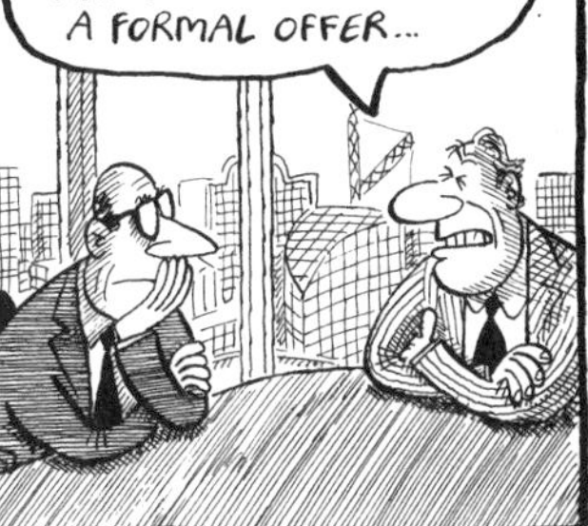

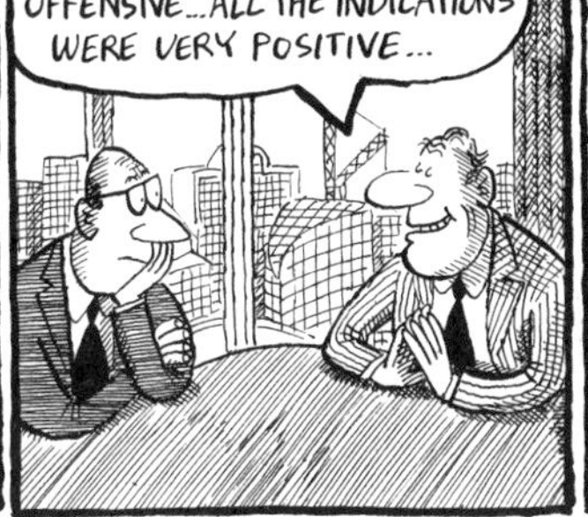
SO WE TOOK THEM TO A DISCREET DINNER AT MY CLUB LAST NIGHT AS PART OF OUR CHARM OFFENSIVE... ALL THE INDICATIONS WERE VERY POSITIVE...

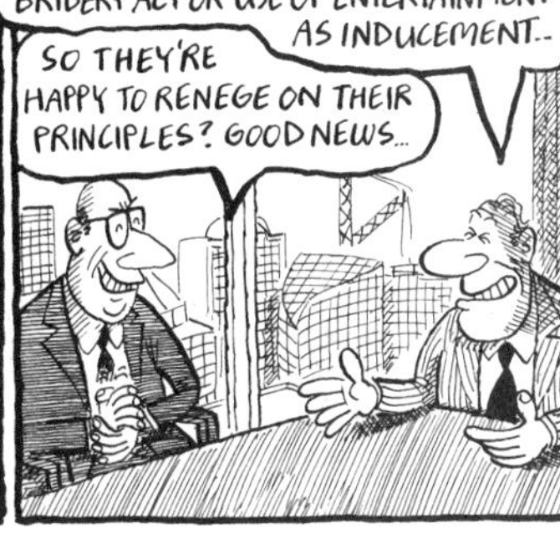
THERE WASN'T SO MUCH AS A MURMUR FROM ANY OF THEM ABOUT THE BRIBERY ACT OR USE OF ENTERTAINMENT AS INDUCEMENT...
SO THEY'RE HAPPY TO RENEGE ON THEIR PRINCIPLES? GOOD NEWS...

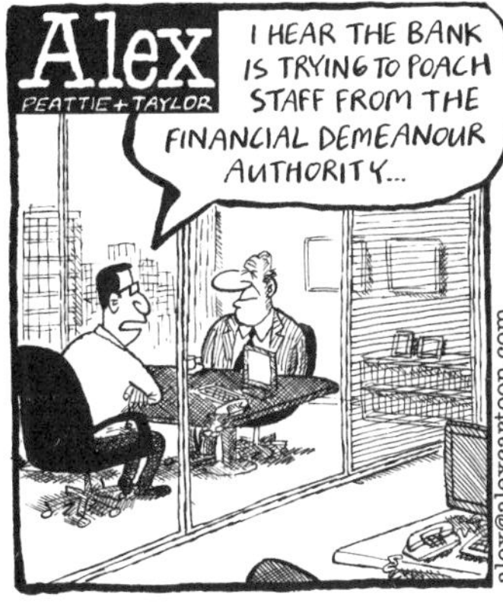
Alex
PEATTIE + TAYLOR
I HEAR THE BANK IS TRYING TO POACH STAFF FROM THE FINANCIAL DEMEANOUR AUTHORITY...
alex@alexcartoon.com

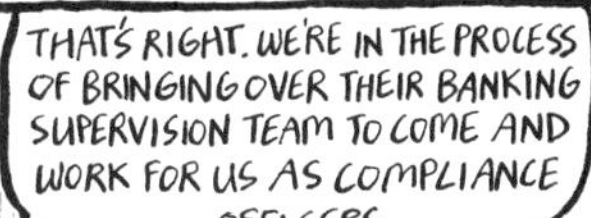
THAT'S RIGHT. WE'RE IN THE PROCESS OF BRINGING OVER THEIR BANKING SUPERVISION TEAM TO COME AND WORK FOR US AS COMPLIANCE OFFICERS...

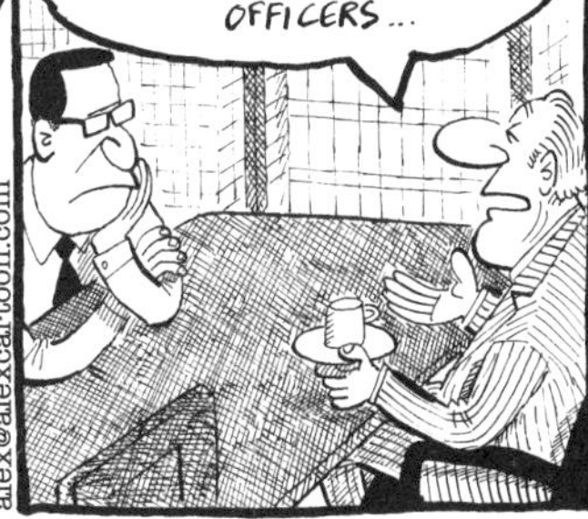

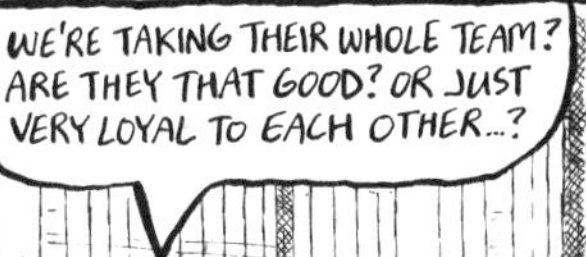
WE'RE TAKING THEIR WHOLE TEAM? ARE THEY THAT GOOD? OR JUST VERY LOYAL TO EACH OTHER...?

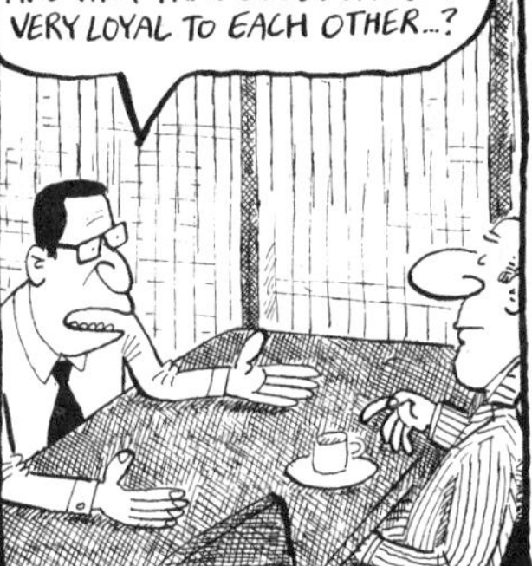

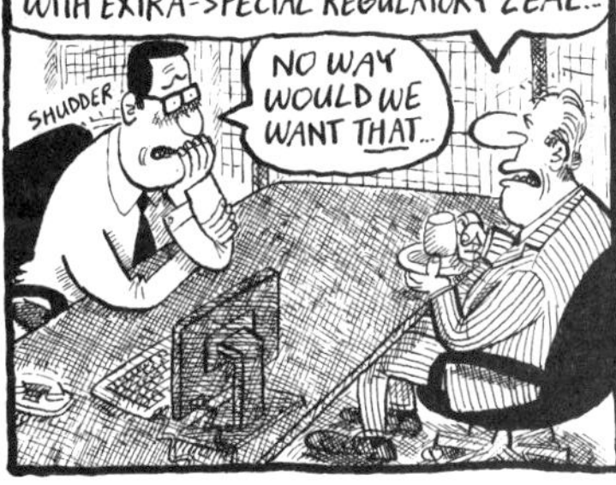
NEITHER... BUT ANYONE WE LEFT BEHIND WOULD BE SO P*SSED OFF AT MISSING OUT ON A BIG SALARY HERE THAT HE'D START TO SCRUTINISE THE BANK'S ACTIVITIES WITH EXTRA-SPECIAL REGULATORY ZEAL...
SHUDDER
NO WAY WOULD WE WANT THAT...

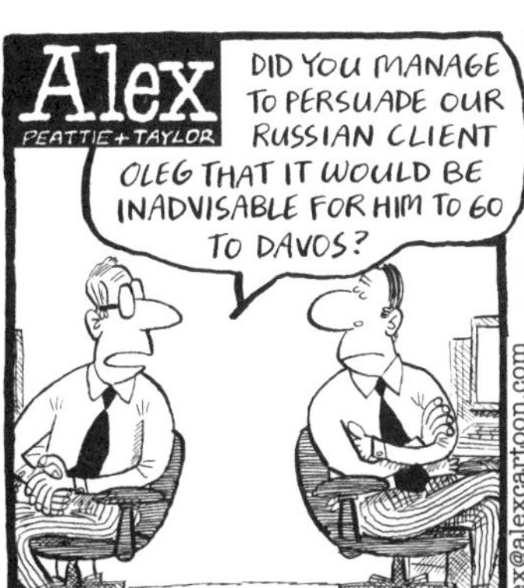
Alex
PEATTIE + TAYLOR
DID YOU MANAGE TO PERSUADE OUR RUSSIAN CLIENT OLEG THAT IT WOULD BE INADVISABLE FOR HIM TO GO TO DAVOS?
alex@alexcartoon.com

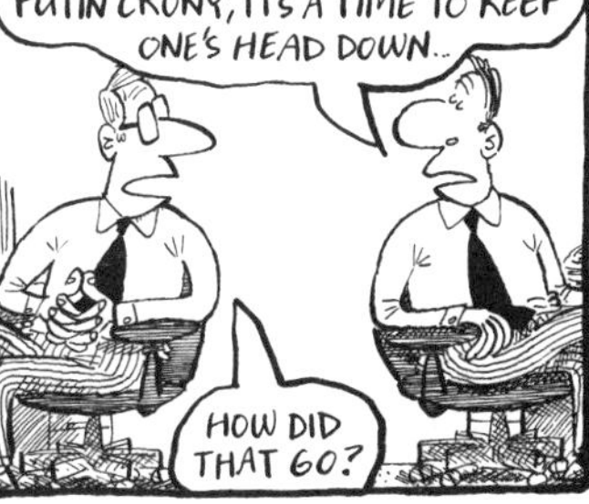
WELL, I REITERATED THAT WITH THE PUNISHING EFFECT OF THE ECONOMIC SANCTIONS BEING IMPOSED ON ANYONE VISIBLY BENEFITING FROM BEING A PUTIN CRONY, IT'S A TIME TO KEEP ONE'S HEAD DOWN...
HOW DID THAT GO?
I THINK HE UNDERSTANDS THE RISK ATTENDANT ON HAVING INCREASED PUBLIC ATTENTION FOCUSED ON HIM...
RIGHT...

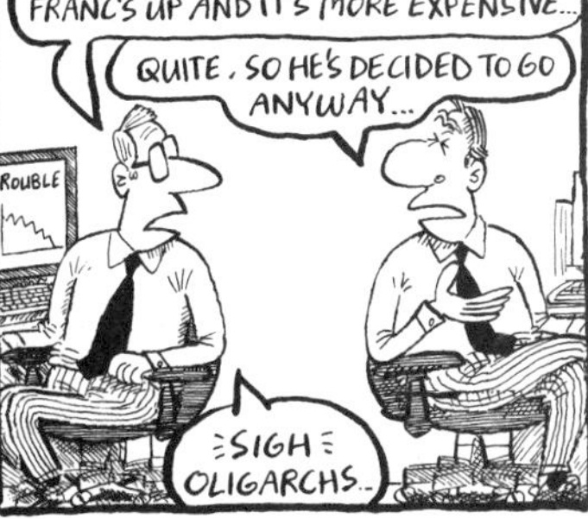
LIKE IF HE WASN'T AT DAVOS PEOPLE MIGHT ASSUME HE SIMPLY COULDN'T AFFORD IT, ESPECIALLY NOW THE SWISS FRANC'S UP AND IT'S MORE EXPENSIVE...
QUITE. SO HE'S DECIDED TO GO ANYWAY...
ROUBLE
SIGH
OLIGARCHS...

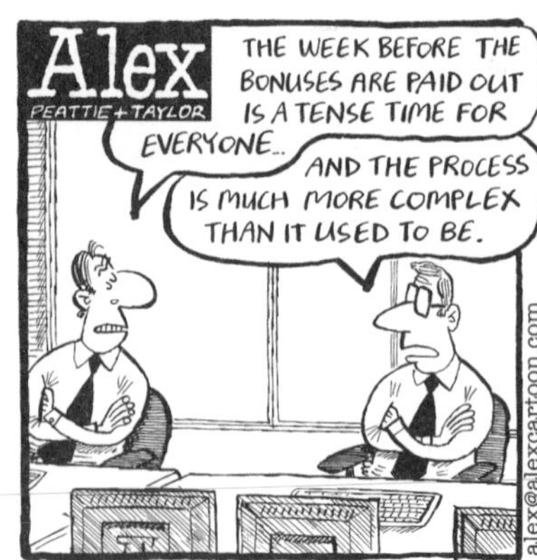
Alex
PEATTIE + TAYLOR
THE WEEK BEFORE THE BONUSES ARE PAID OUT IS A TENSE TIME FOR EVERYONE...
AND THE PROCESS IS MUCH MORE COMPLEX THAN IT USED TO BE.

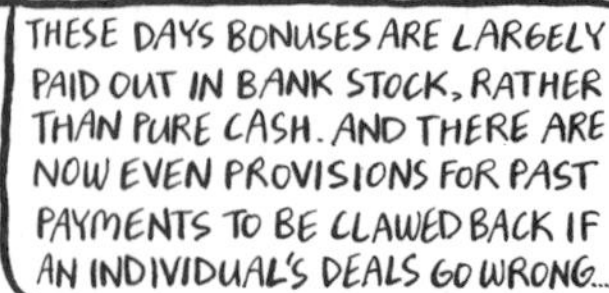
THESE DAYS BONUSES ARE LARGELY PAID OUT IN BANK STOCK, RATHER THAN PURE CASH. AND THERE ARE NOW EVEN PROVISIONS FOR PAST PAYMENTS TO BE CLAWED BACK IF AN INDIVIDUAL'S DEALS GO WRONG...

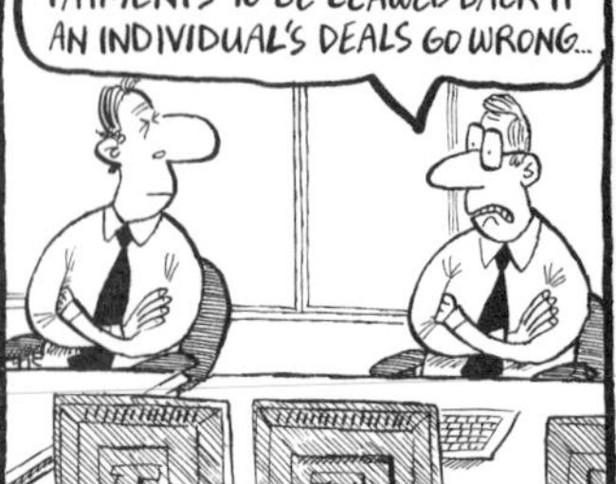
alex@alexcartoon.com

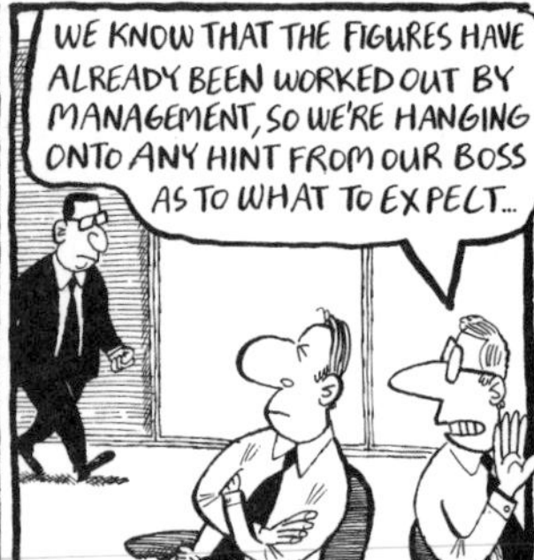
WE KNOW THAT THE FIGURES HAVE ALREADY BEEN WORKED OUT BY MANAGEMENT, SO WE'RE HANGING ONTO ANY HINT FROM OUR BOSS AS TO WHAT TO EXPECT...

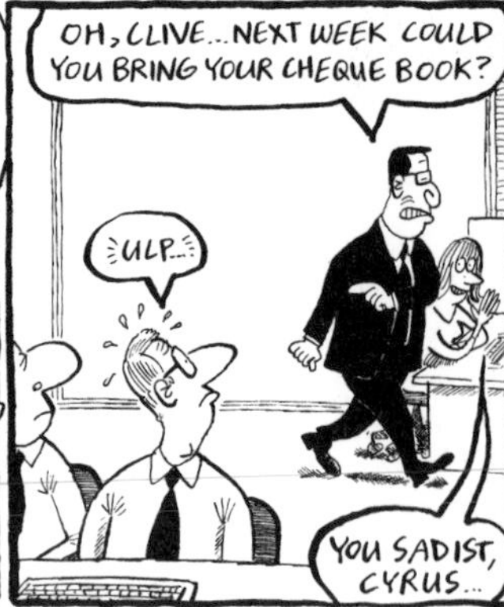
OH, CLIVE... NEXT WEEK COULD YOU BRING YOUR CHEQUE BOOK?
ULP...
YOU SADIST, CYRUS...

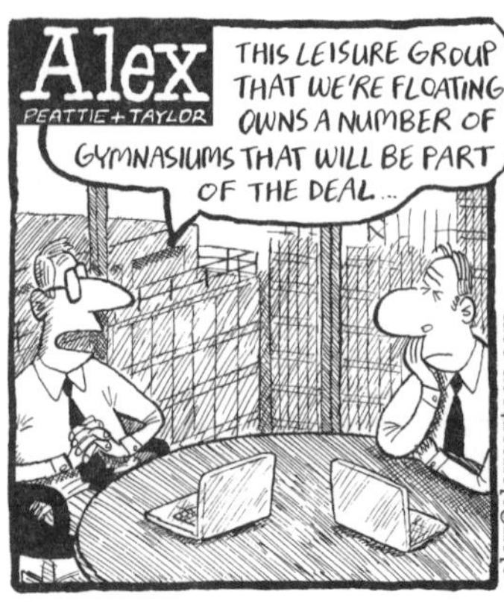
Alex
PEATTIE + TAYLOR
THIS LEISURE GROUP THAT WE'RE FLOATING OWNS A NUMBER OF GYMNASIUMS THAT WILL BE PART OF THE DEAL...
alex@alexcartoon.com

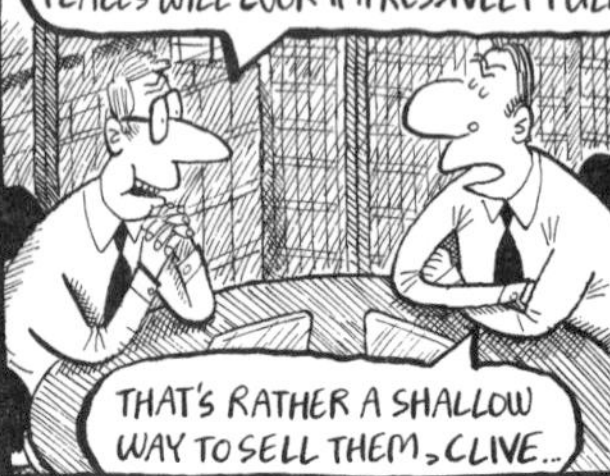
THIS MONTH WOULD BE A GOOD TIME TO TAKE INVESTORS ROUND AND SHOW THEM THE GYMS... JANUARY IS THE MOST POPULAR TIME FOR PEOPLE TO EMBARK ON FITNESS REGIMES, SO THE PLACES WILL LOOK IMPRESSIVELY FULL...
THAT'S RATHER A SHALLOW WAY TO SELL THEM, CLIVE...

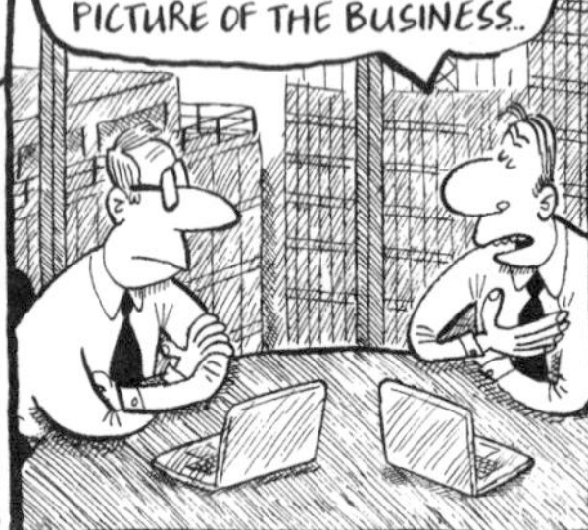
BEAR IN MIND THAT OUR CLIENTS ARE SERIOUS INVESTORS. I THINK WE NEED TO GIVE THEM A MORE REALISTIC PICTURE OF THE BUSINESS..

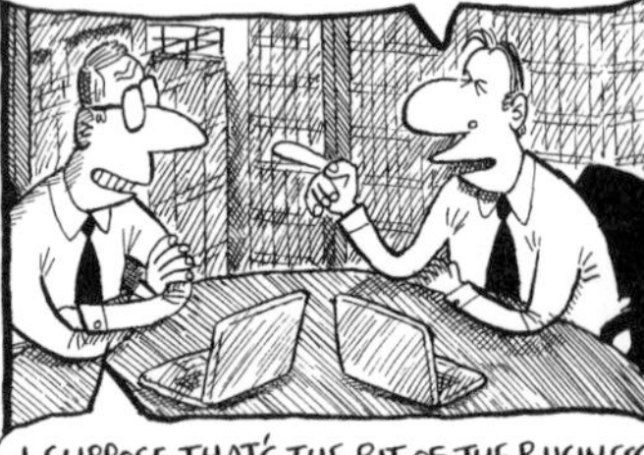
LET'S TAKE THEM ROUND IN MARCH WHEN THE PLACE IS EMPTY BECAUSE EVERYONE'S GIVEN UP GOING BUT ARE STILL PAYING SUBS VIA DIRECT DEBIT...
I SUPPOSE THAT'S THE BIT OF THE BUSINESS MODEL THAT MAKES THE REAL MONEY...

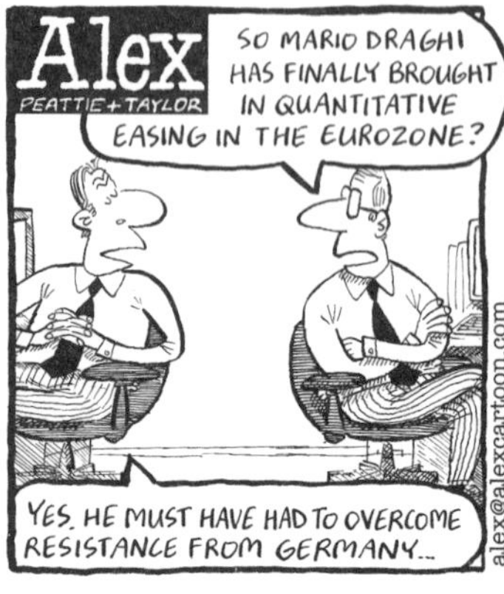
Alex
PEATTIE + TAYLOR
SO MARIO DRAGHI HAS FINALLY BROUGHT IN QUANTITATIVE EASING IN THE EUROZONE?
YES. HE MUST HAVE HAD TO OVERCOME RESISTANCE FROM GERMANY...
alex@alexcartoon.com

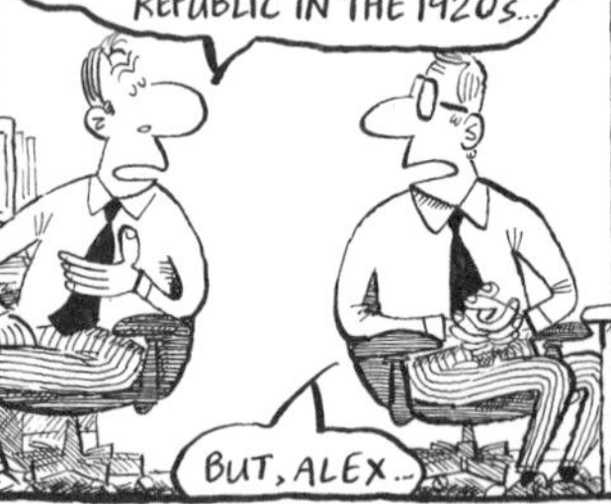
AFTER ALL Q.E. INVOLVES MONEY PRINTING AND THAT POLICY CLASSICALLY STOKES UP INFLATION, AS THE GERMANS REMEMBER ONLY TOO WELL FROM THE HYPERINFLATION OF THE WEIMAR REPUBLIC IN THE 1920s...
BUT, ALEX...

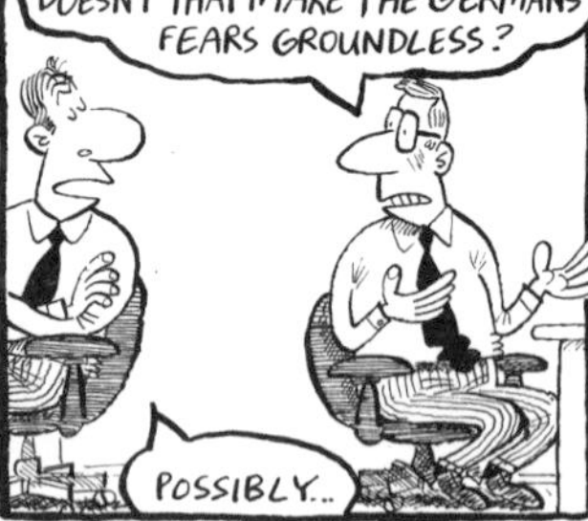
THE Q.E. INTRODUCED IN THE U.S.A., U.K. AND JAPAN RECENTLY HAS ACTUALLY LED TO LOW LEVELS OF INFLATION, BORDERING ON DEFLATION. DOESN'T THAT MAKE THE GERMANS' FEARS GROUNDLESS?
POSSIBLY...

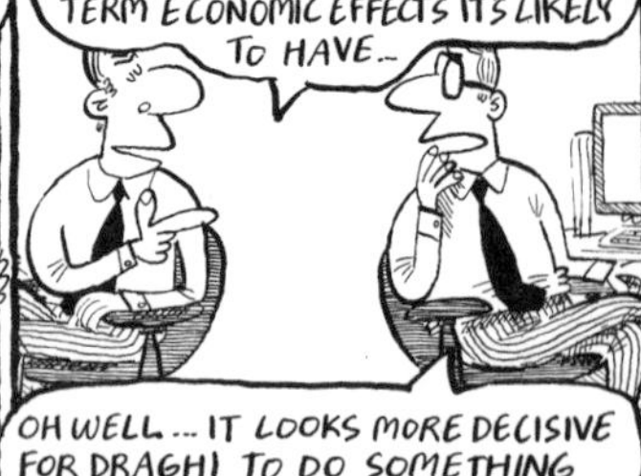
PERHAPS THEY SHOULD WORRY INSTEAD ABOUT HOW IT SHOWS THAT ABSOLUTELY NOBODY UNDERSTANDS HOW Q.E. WORKS OR WHAT LONG-TERM ECONOMIC EFFECTS IT'S LIKELY TO HAVE...
OH WELL... IT LOOKS MORE DECISIVE FOR DRAGHI TO DO SOMETHING RATHER THAN NOTHING, I SUPPOSE...

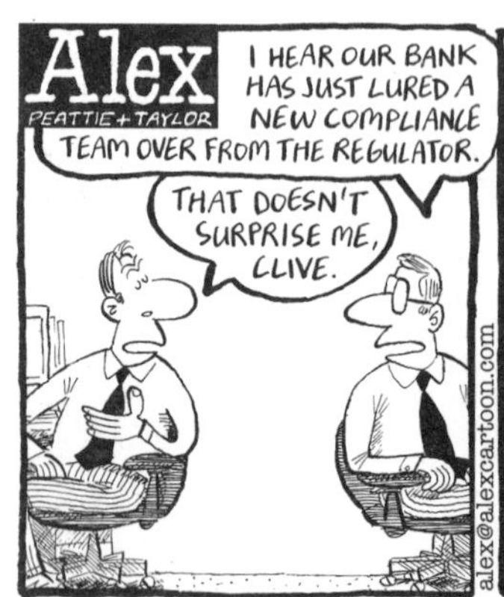
Alex
PEATTIE + TAYLOR
I HEAR OUR BANK HAS JUST LURED A NEW COMPLIANCE TEAM OVER FROM THE REGULATOR.
THAT DOESN'T SURPRISE ME, CLIVE.
alex@alexcartoon.com

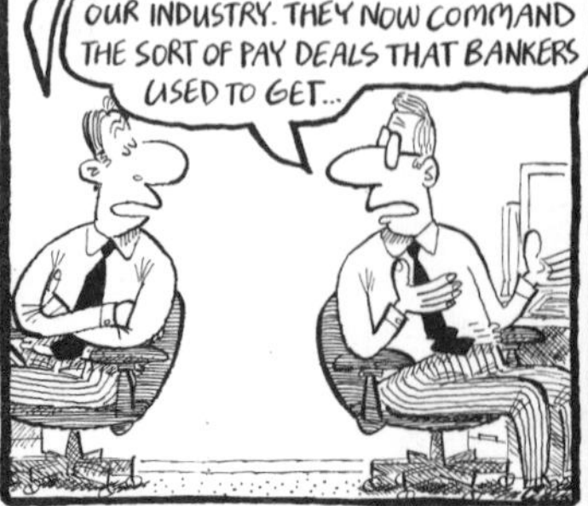
COMPLIANCE IS THE ONLY AREA THAT BANKS WANT TO RECRUIT ANYONE IN THESE DAYS...
THEY'RE THE NEW SUPERSTARS OF OUR INDUSTRY. THEY NOW COMMAND THE SORT OF PAY DEALS THAT BANKERS USED TO GET...

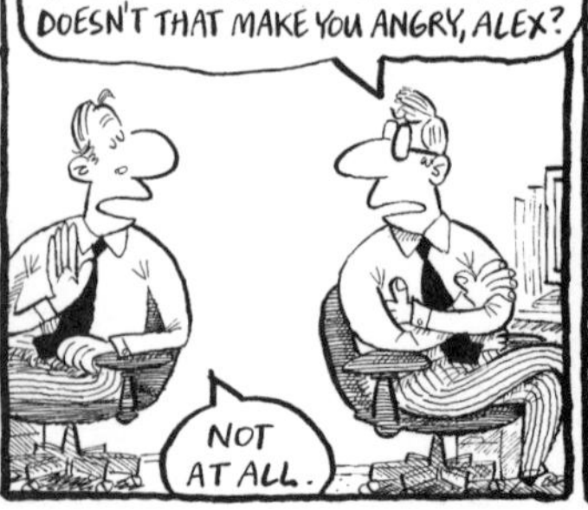
THEIR EGOS REALLY ARE OUT OF CONTROL. I HEAR THEY EVEN MANAGED TO NEGOTIATE THEMSELVES PACKAGES THAT INCLUDE A ONE-YEAR GUARANTEE... DOESN'T THAT MAKE YOU ANGRY, ALEX?
NOT AT ALL.

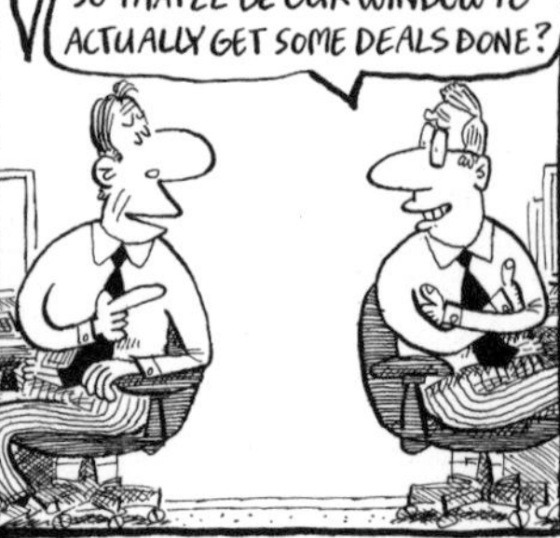
IT MEANS THEY'LL BE COMPLACENT FOR THE FIRST YEAR AND WON'T BOTHER TO DO ANY WORK...
SO THAT'LL BE OUR WINDOW TO ACTUALLY GET SOME DEALS DONE?

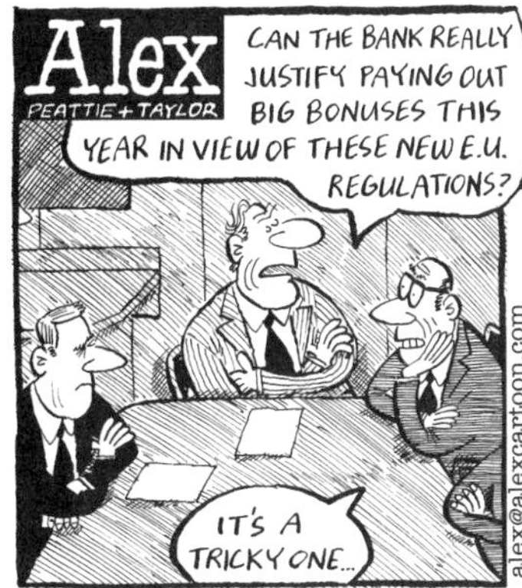
Alex
PEATTIE+TAYLOR
CAN THE BANK REALLY JUSTIFY PAYING OUT BIG BONUSES THIS YEAR IN VIEW OF THESE NEW E.U. REGULATIONS?
IT'S A TRICKY ONE...

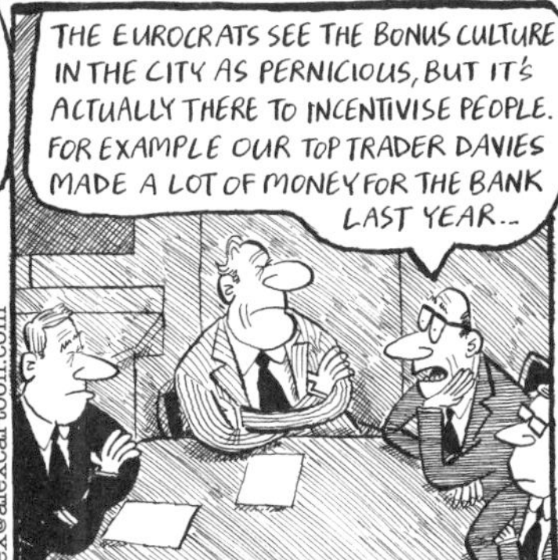
alex@alexcartoon.com
THE EUROCRATS SEE THE BONUS CULTURE IN THE CITY AS PERNICIOUS, BUT IT'S ACTUALLY THERE TO INCENTIVISE PEOPLE. FOR EXAMPLE OUR TOP TRADER DAVIES MADE A LOT OF MONEY FOR THE BANK LAST YEAR...

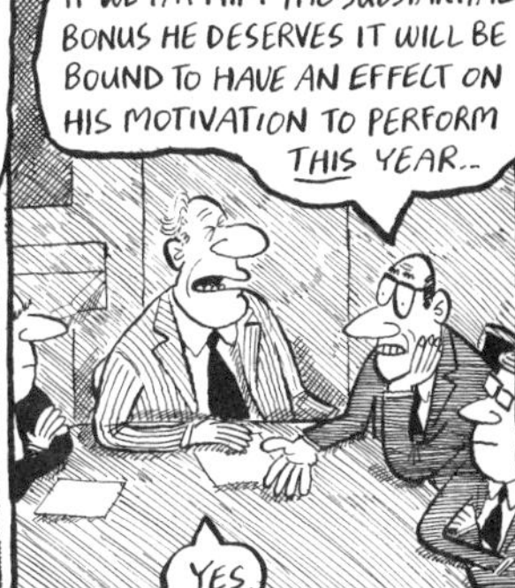
IF WE PAY HIM THE SUBSTANTIAL BONUS HE DESERVES IT WILL BE BOUND TO HAVE AN EFFECT ON HIS MOTIVATION TO PERFORM THIS YEAR...
YES.

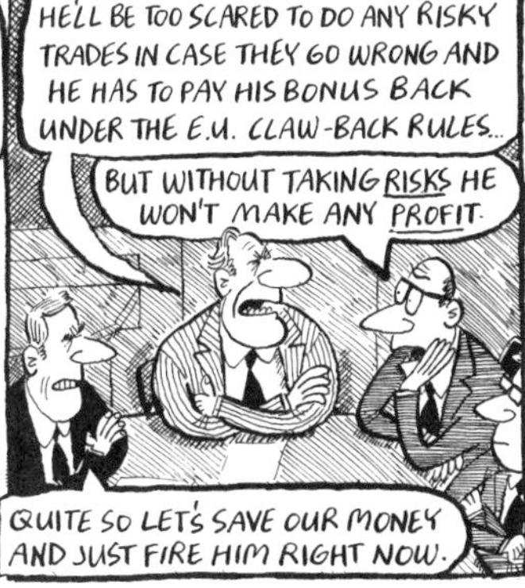
HE'LL BE TOO SCARED TO DO ANY RISKY TRADES IN CASE THEY GO WRONG AND HE HAS TO PAY HIS BONUS BACK UNDER THE E.U. CLAW-BACK RULES...
BUT WITHOUT TAKING RISKS HE WON'T MAKE ANY PROFIT.
QUITE SO LET'S SAVE OUR MONEY AND JUST FIRE HIM RIGHT NOW.

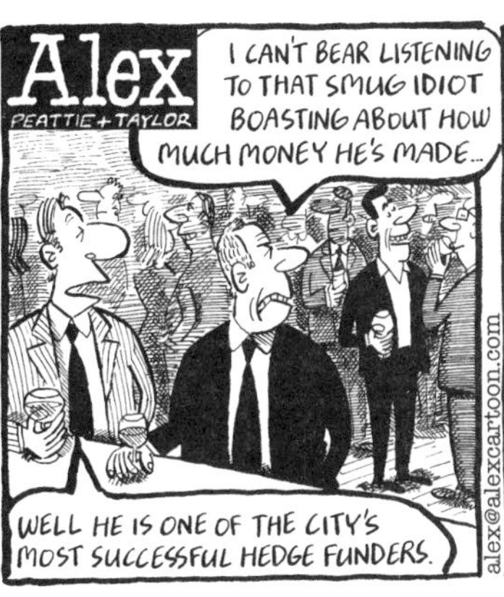
Alex
PEATTIE+TAYLOR
I CAN'T BEAR LISTENING TO THAT SMUG IDIOT BOASTING ABOUT HOW MUCH MONEY HE'S MADE...
WELL HE IS ONE OF THE CITY'S MOST SUCCESSFUL HEDGE FUNDERS.

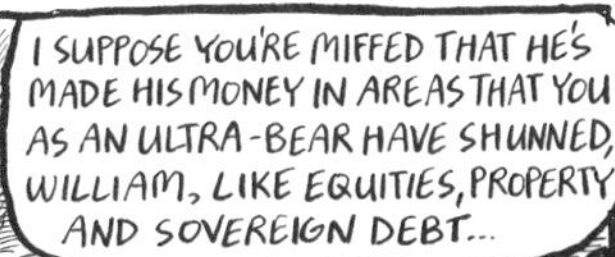
I SUPPOSE YOU'RE MIFFED THAT HE'S MADE HIS MONEY IN AREAS THAT YOU AS AN ULTRA-BEAR HAVE SHUNNED, WILLIAM, LIKE EQUITIES, PROPERTY AND SOVEREIGN DEBT...

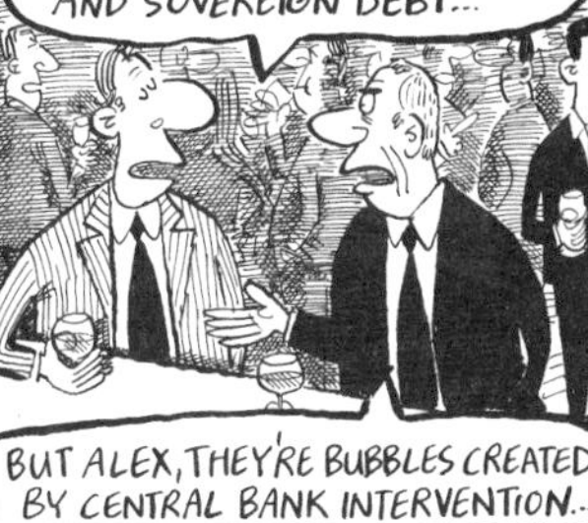
alex@alexcartoon.com
BUT ALEX, THEY'RE BUBBLES CREATED BY CENTRAL BANK INTERVENTION...

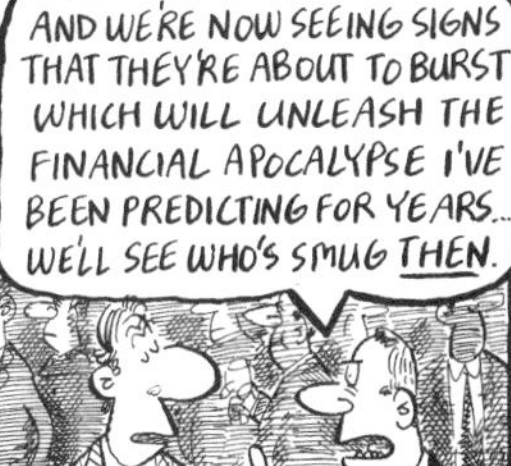
AND WE'RE NOW SEEING SIGNS THAT THEY'RE ABOUT TO BURST WHICH WILL UNLEASH THE FINANCIAL APOCALYPSE I'VE BEEN PREDICTING FOR YEARS... WE'LL SEE WHO'S SMUG THEN.
WE WILL...

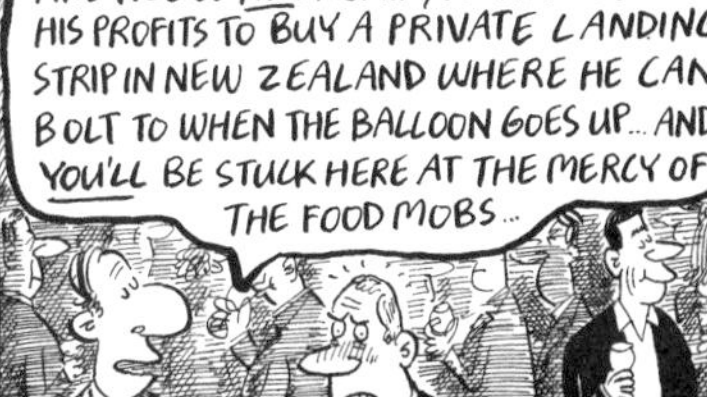
AND IT'LL BE HIM AGAIN, BECAUSE HE USED HIS PROFITS TO BUY A PRIVATE LANDING STRIP IN NEW ZEALAND WHERE HE CAN BOLT TO WHEN THE BALLOON GOES UP... AND YOU'LL BE STUCK HERE AT THE MERCY OF THE FOOD MOBS...

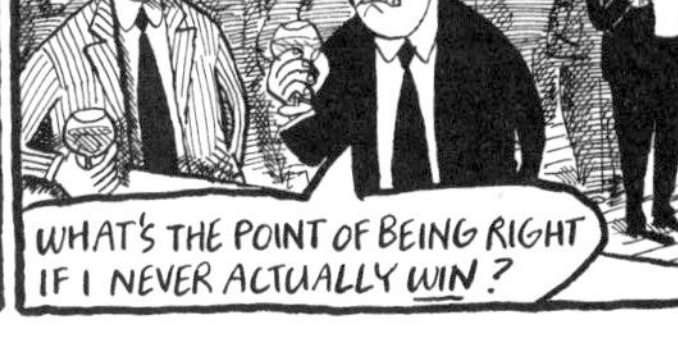
WHAT'S THE POINT OF BEING RIGHT IF I NEVER ACTUALLY WIN?

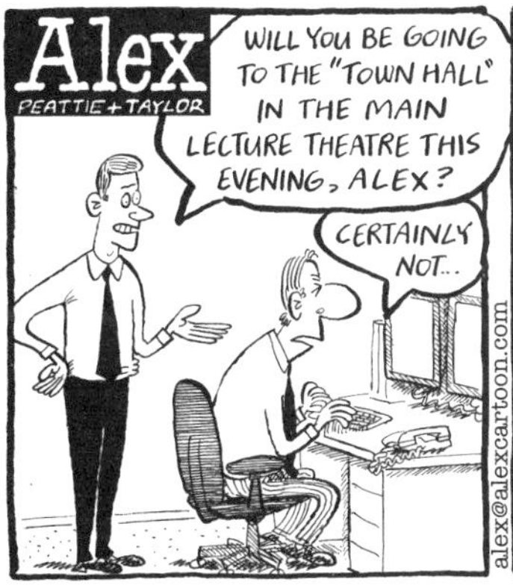
Alex
PEATTIE+TAYLOR
WILL YOU BE GOING TO THE "TOWN HALL" IN THE MAIN LECTURE THEATRE THIS EVENING, ALEX?
CERTAINLY NOT...

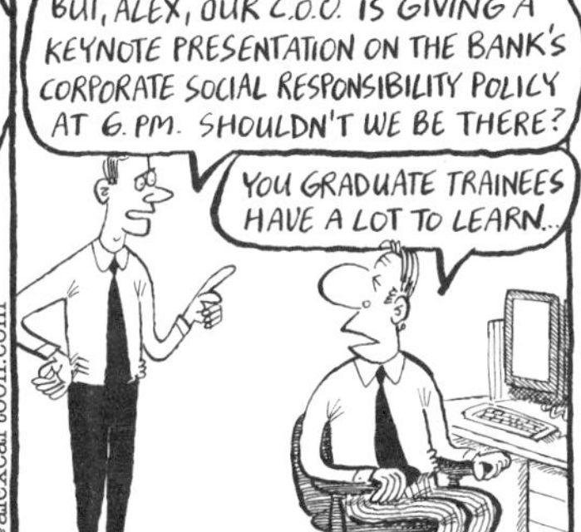
alex@alexcartoon.com
BUT, ALEX, OUR C.O.O. IS GIVING A KEYNOTE PRESENTATION ON THE BANK'S CORPORATE SOCIAL RESPONSIBILITY POLICY AT 6.PM. SHOULDN'T WE BE THERE?
YOU GRADUATE TRAINEES HAVE A LOT TO LEARN...

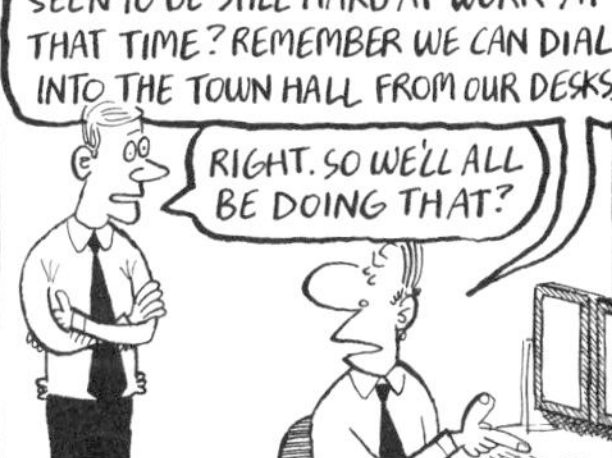
CAN'T YOU SEE IT LOOKS BETTER IF WE'RE SEEN TO BE STILL HARD AT WORK AT THAT TIME? REMEMBER WE CAN DIAL INTO THE TOWN HALL FROM OUR DESKS.
RIGHT. SO WE'LL ALL BE DOING THAT?

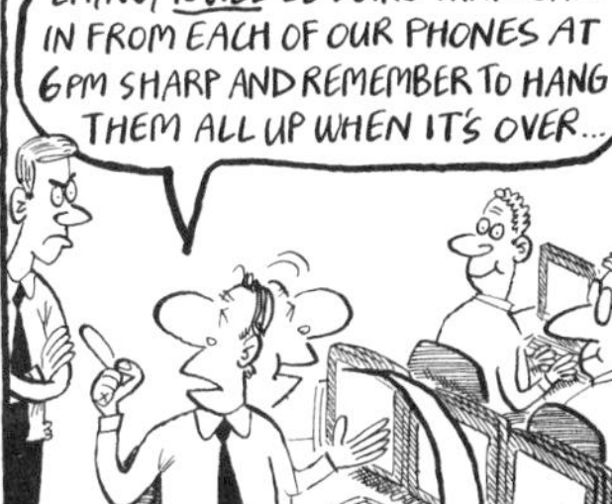
ER, NO, YOU'LL BE DOING THAT... CALL IN FROM EACH OF OUR PHONES AT 6PM SHARP AND REMEMBER TO HANG THEM ALL UP WHEN IT'S OVER...
NOW... WHO'S COMING TO THE WINE BAR?

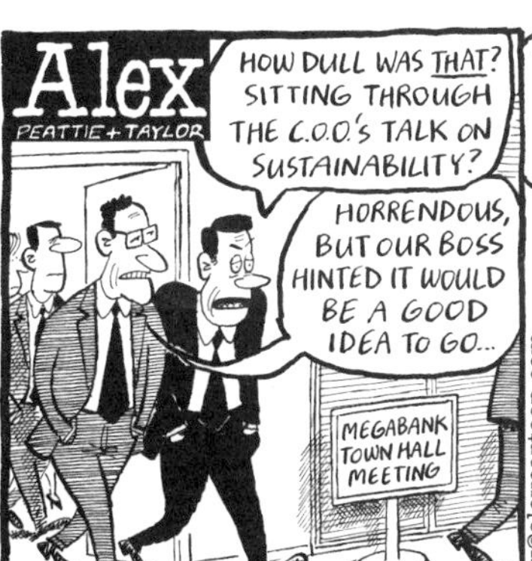
Alex
PEATTIE+TAYLOR
HOW DULL WAS THAT? SITTING THROUGH THE C.O.O.'S TALK ON SUSTAINABILITY?
HORRENDOUS, BUT OUR BOSS HINTED IT WOULD BE A GOOD IDEA TO GO...
MEGABANK TOWN HALL MEETING

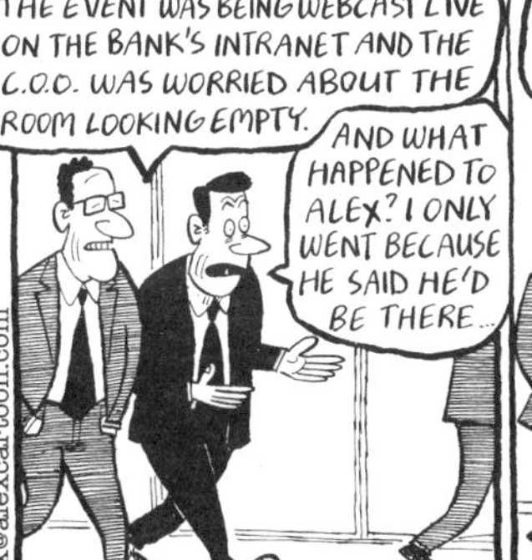
alex@alexcartoon.com
THE EVENT WAS BEING WEBCAST LIVE ON THE BANK'S INTRANET AND THE C.O.O. WAS WORRIED ABOUT THE ROOM LOOKING EMPTY.
AND WHAT HAPPENED TO ALEX? I ONLY WENT BECAUSE HE SAID HE'D BE THERE...

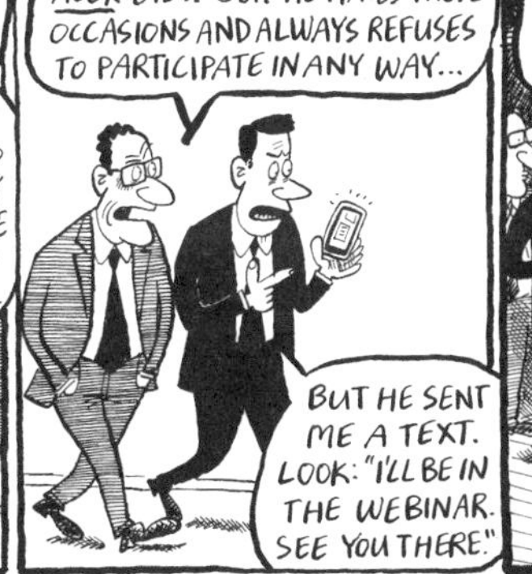
ALEX DID?! BUT HE HATES THOSE OCCASIONS AND ALWAYS REFUSES TO PARTICIPATE IN ANY WAY...
BUT HE SENT ME A TEXT. LOOK: "I'LL BE IN THE WEBINAR. SEE YOU THERE."

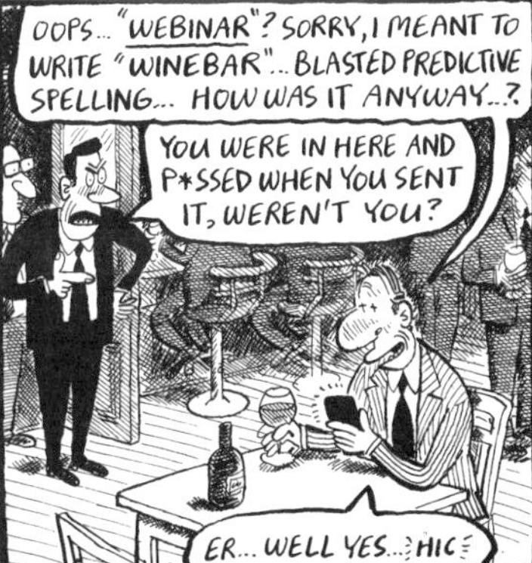
OOPS... "WEBINAR"? SORRY, I MEANT TO WRITE "WINEBAR"... BLASTED PREDICTIVE SPELLING... HOW WAS IT ANYWAY...?
YOU WERE IN HERE AND P*SSED WHEN YOU SENT IT, WEREN'T YOU?
ER... WELL YES... HIC

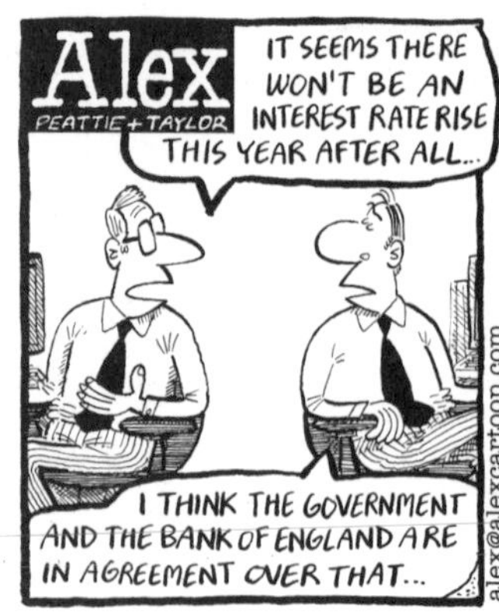
Alex
PEATTIE + TAYLOR
IT SEEMS THERE WON'T BE AN INTEREST RATE RISE THIS YEAR AFTER ALL...
I THINK THE GOVERNMENT AND THE BANK OF ENGLAND ARE IN AGREEMENT OVER THAT...
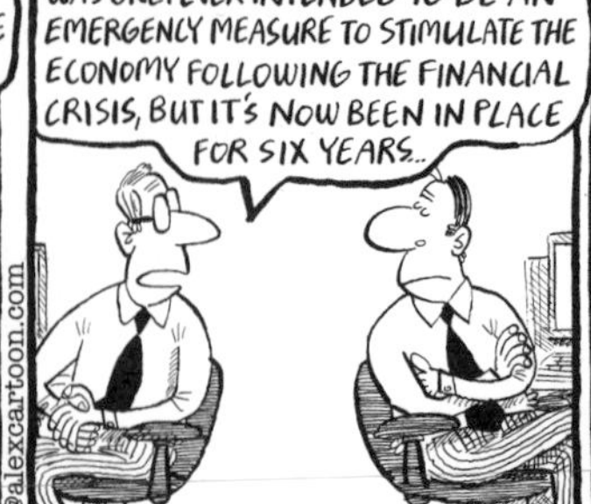
BUT THE ZERO INTEREST RATE POLICY WAS ONLY EVER INTENDED TO BE AN EMERGENCY MEASURE TO STIMULATE THE ECONOMY FOLLOWING THE FINANCIAL CRISIS, BUT IT'S NOW BEEN IN PLACE FOR SIX YEARS...
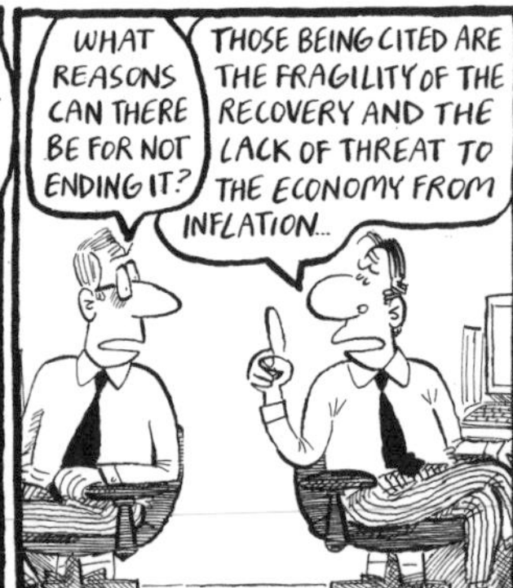
WHAT REASONS CAN THERE BE FOR NOT ENDING IT?
THOSE BEING CITED ARE THE FRAGILITY OF THE RECOVERY AND THE LACK OF THREAT TO THE ECONOMY FROM INFLATION...
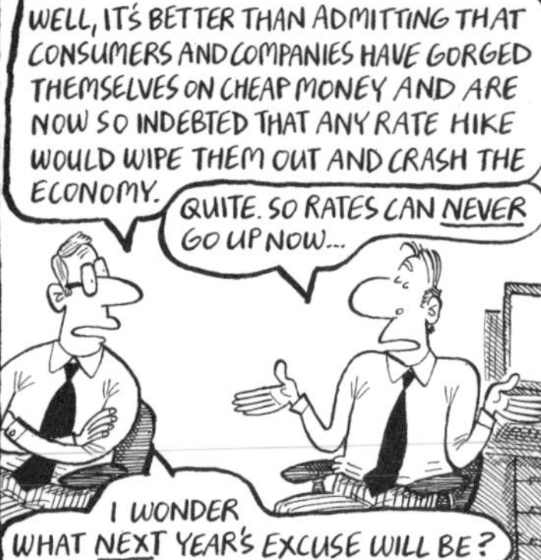
WELL, IT'S BETTER THAN ADMITTING THAT CONSUMERS AND COMPANIES HAVE GORGED THEMSELVES ON CHEAP MONEY AND ARE NOW SO INDEBTED THAT ANY RATE HIKE WOULD WIPE THEM OUT AND CRASH THE ECONOMY.
QUITE. SO RATES CAN NEVER GO UP NOW...
I WONDER WHAT NEXT YEAR'S EXCUSE WILL BE?

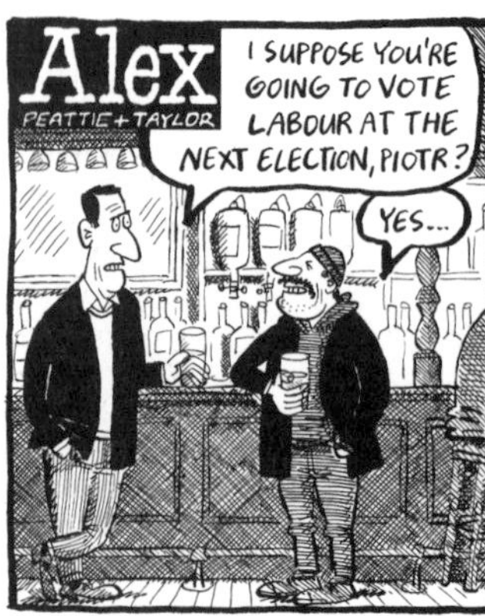
Alex
PEATTIE + TAYLOR
I SUPPOSE YOU'RE GOING TO VOTE LABOUR AT THE NEXT ELECTION, PIOTR?
YES...
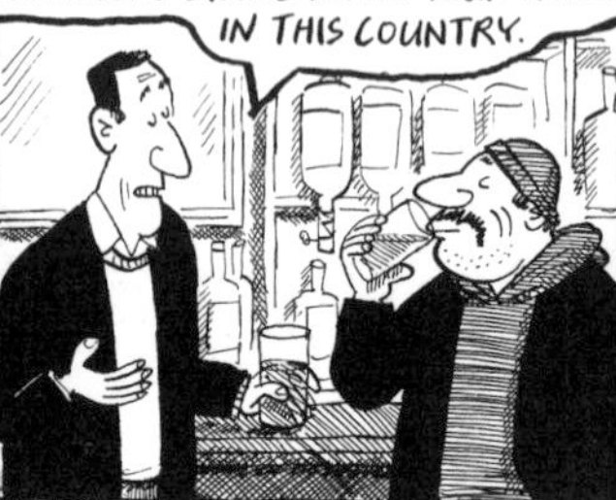
IT'S UNDERSTANDABLE. IT WAS THE PREVIOUS LABOUR GOVERNMENT THAT RELAXED BORDER CONTROLS FROM EUROPE ALLOWING POLISH BUILDERS LIKE YOU TO COME OVER AND MAKE A HANDSOME LIVING PLYING YOUR TRADE IN THIS COUNTRY.
NOW YOU'VE GOT YOUR CITIZENSHIP HERE, YOU'LL VOTE FOR THE PARTY WHOSE POLICIES YOU ASSOCIATE WITH BOOSTING YOUR EARNING POWER...
YES.
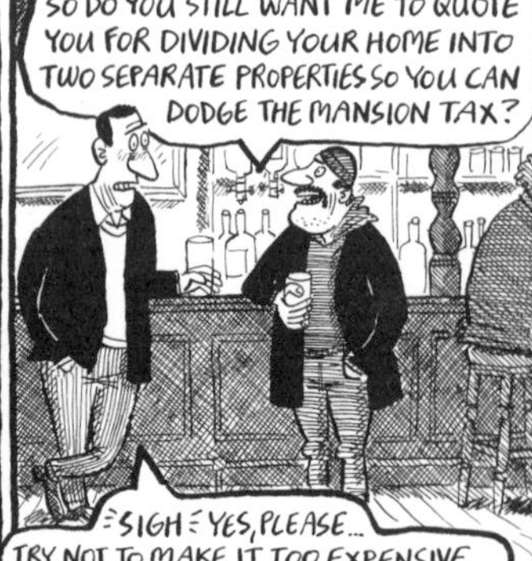
SO DO YOU STILL WANT ME TO QUOTE YOU FOR DIVIDING YOUR HOME INTO TWO SEPARATE PROPERTIES SO YOU CAN DODGE THE MANSION TAX?
SIGH YES, PLEASE... TRY NOT TO MAKE IT TOO EXPENSIVE...

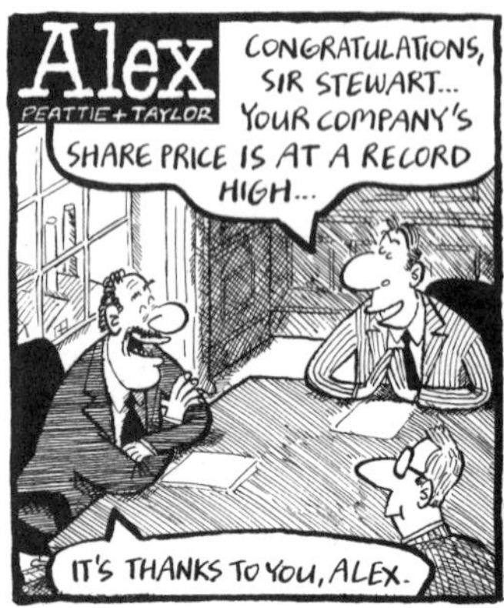
Alex
PEATTIE + TAYLOR
CONGRATULATIONS, SIR STEWART... YOUR COMPANY'S SHARE PRICE IS AT A RECORD HIGH...
IT'S THANKS TO YOU, ALEX.
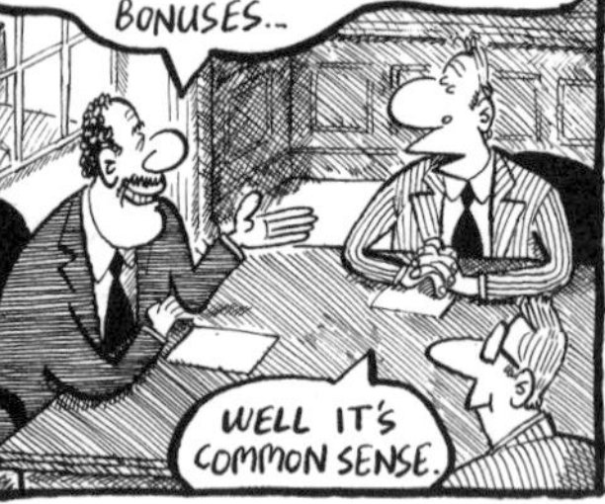
YOU ADVISED US TO TAKE ADVANTAGE OF ULTRA-LOW INTEREST RATES TO BORROW MONEY AND BUY BACK OUR COMPANY'S OWN SHARES, WHICH BOOSTED THEIR VALUE AND TRIGGERED OUR DIRECTORS' BONUSES...
WELL IT'S COMMON SENSE.
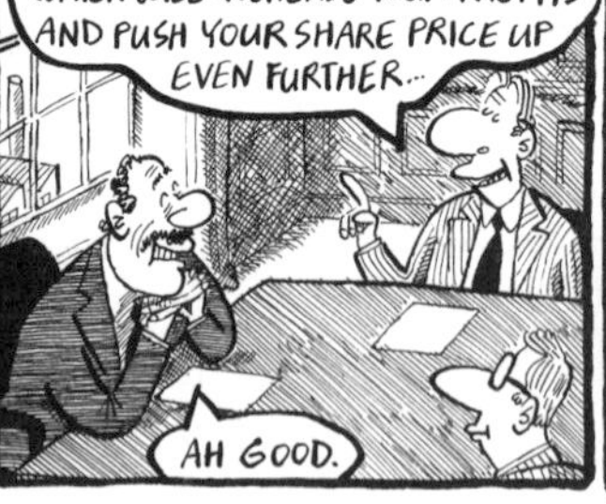
AND THIS YEAR LOOKS EVEN BETTER. YOUR OPERATING COSTS WILL BE SLASHED THANKS TO THE FALLING OIL PRICE, PLUS LACK OF EMPLOYEE WAGE GROWTH, WHICH WILL INCREASE YOUR PROFITS AND PUSH YOUR SHARE PRICE UP EVEN FURTHER...
AH GOOD.
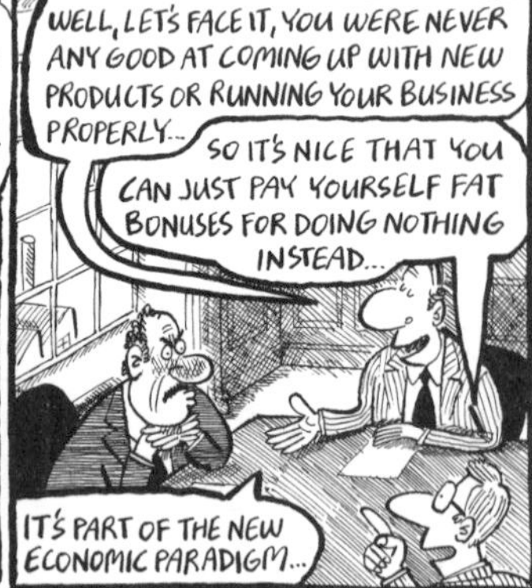
WELL, LET'S FACE IT, YOU WERE NEVER ANY GOOD AT COMING UP WITH NEW PRODUCTS OR RUNNING YOUR BUSINESS PROPERLY...
SO IT'S NICE THAT YOU CAN JUST PAY YOURSELF FAT BONUSES FOR DOING NOTHING INSTEAD...
IT'S PART OF THE NEW ECONOMIC PARADIGM...

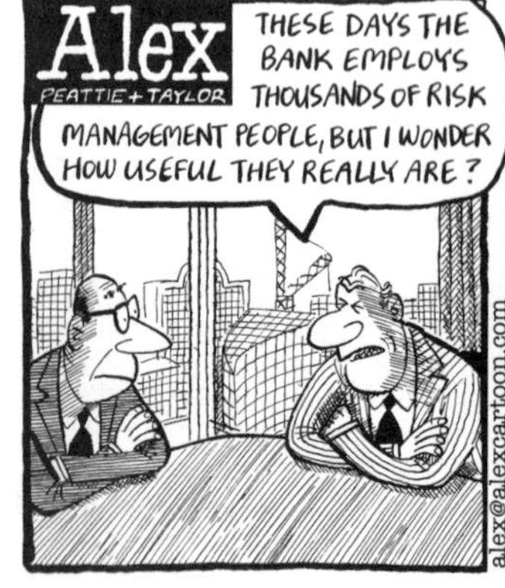
Alex
PEATTIE + TAYLOR
THESE DAYS THE BANK EMPLOYS THOUSANDS OF RISK MANAGEMENT PEOPLE, BUT I WONDER HOW USEFUL THEY REALLY ARE?
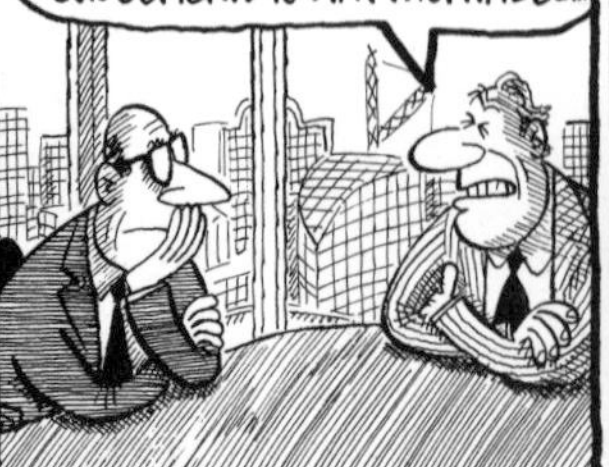
THEY SPEND THEIR WHOLE DAY PORING OVER OUR TRADING BOOKS MAKING SURE WE'RE NOT TOO EXPOSED IN ANY PARTICULAR AREA. BUT BANKS NEED TO MAKE RISKY JUDGEMENTS TO STAY PROFITABLE...
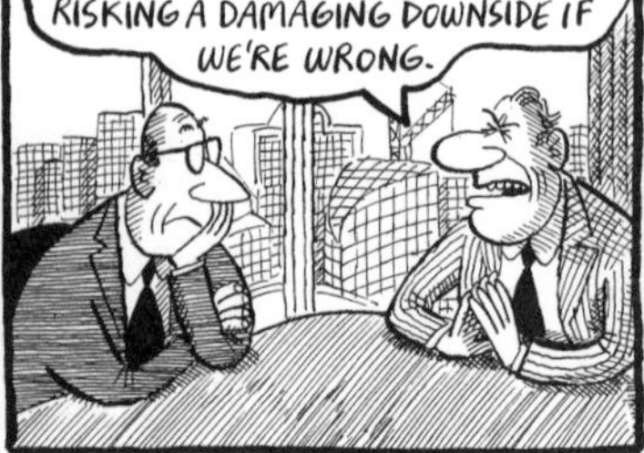
THERE ARE STILL PARTS OF OUR OPERATION WHERE WE PUNT HUGE AMOUNTS OF MONEY, BASED ON NOTHING MORE THAN A GUT FEELING WITH NO CERTAINTY OF HAVING MADE THE RIGHT CALL AND RISKING A DAMAGING DOWNSIDE IF WE'RE WRONG.
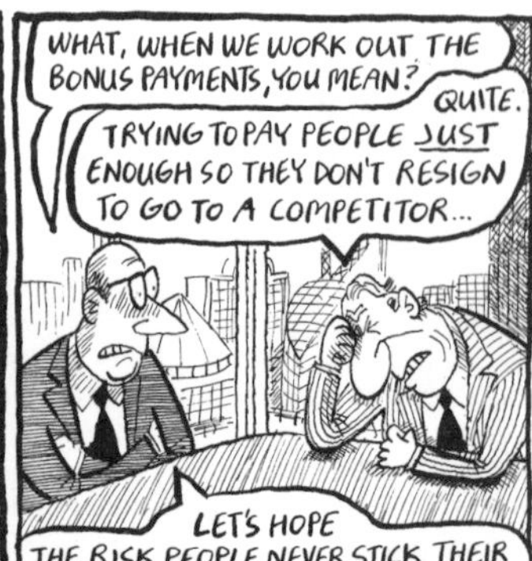
WHAT, WHEN WE WORK OUT THE BONUS PAYMENTS, YOU MEAN?
QUITE. TRYING TO PAY PEOPLE JUST ENOUGH SO THEY DON'T RESIGN TO GO TO A COMPETITOR...
LET'S HOPE THE RISK PEOPLE NEVER STICK THEIR NOSES IN THIS SIDE OF OUR BUSINESS...

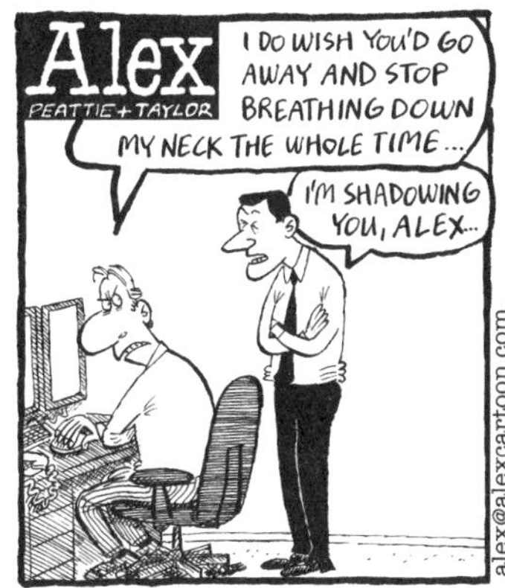
Alex
PEATTIE + TAYLOR
I DO WISH YOU'D GO AWAY AND STOP BREATHING DOWN MY NECK THE WHOLE TIME...
I'M SHADOWING YOU, ALEX...

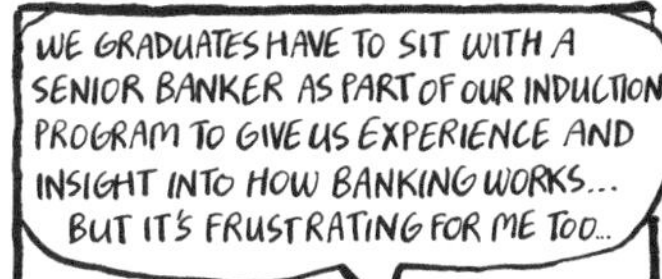
WE GRADUATES HAVE TO SIT WITH A SENIOR BANKER AS PART OF OUR INDUCTION PROGRAM TO GIVE US EXPERIENCE AND INSIGHT INTO HOW BANKING WORKS... BUT IT'S FRUSTRATING FOR ME TOO...

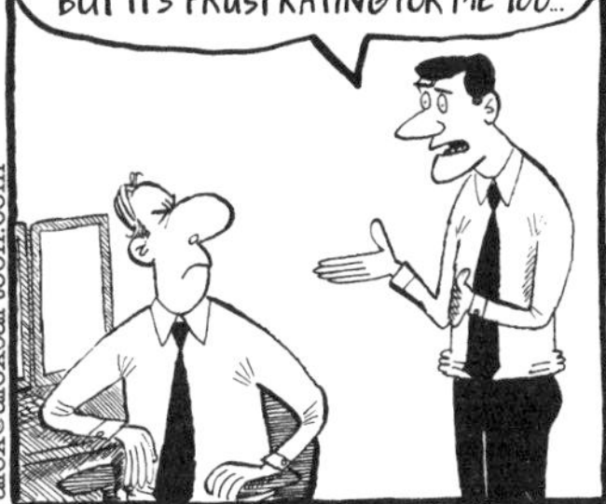

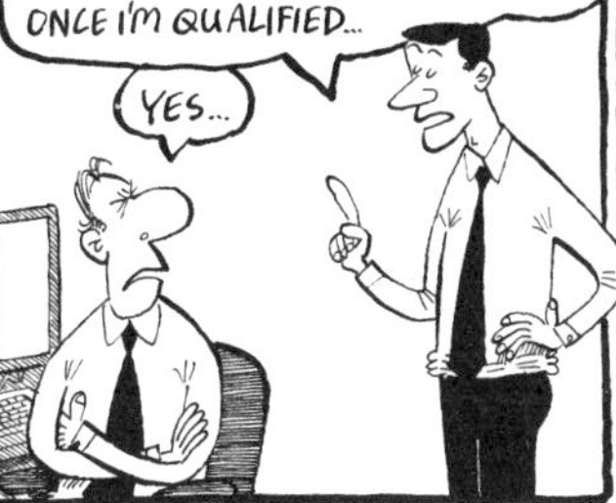
I'M JUST PASSIVELY WATCHING WHAT YOU DO, LISTENING TO YOUR CONVERSATIONS WITH CLIENTS AND TRYING TO ANALYSE WHAT IT ALL SIGNIFIES, BUT JUST IMAGINE WHAT I'LL BE DOING ONCE I'M QUALIFIED...
YES...

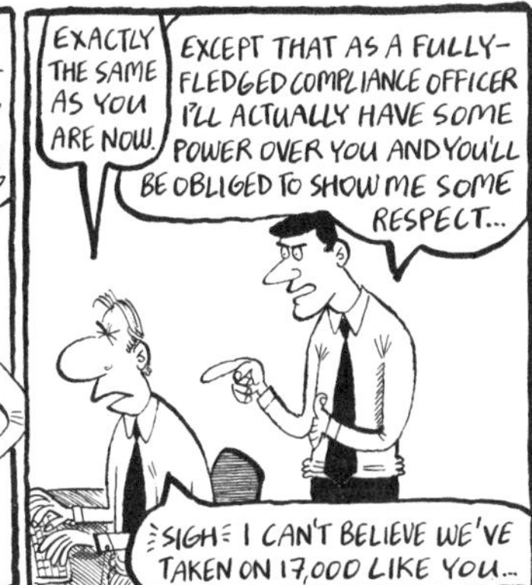
EXACTLY THE SAME AS YOU ARE NOW.
EXCEPT THAT AS A FULLY-FLEDGED COMPLIANCE OFFICER I'LL ACTUALLY HAVE SOME POWER OVER YOU AND YOU'LL BE OBLIGED TO SHOW ME SOME RESPECT...
SIGH I CAN'T BELIEVE WE'VE TAKEN ON 17,000 LIKE YOU...

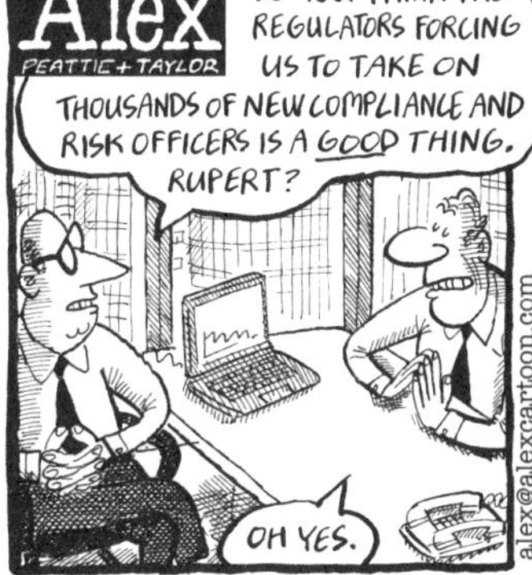
Alex
PEATTIE + TAYLOR
SO YOU THINK THE REGULATORS FORCING US TO TAKE ON THOUSANDS OF NEW COMPLIANCE AND RISK OFFICERS IS A GOOD THING, RUPERT?
OH YES.

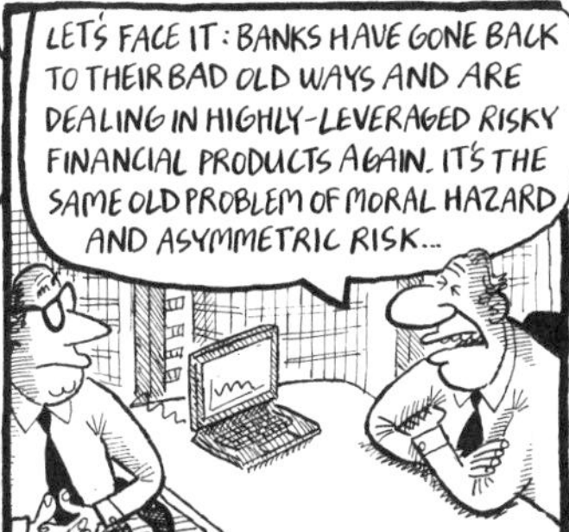
LET'S FACE IT: BANKS HAVE GONE BACK TO THEIR BAD OLD WAYS AND ARE DEALING IN HIGHLY-LEVERAGED RISKY FINANCIAL PRODUCTS AGAIN. IT'S THE SAME OLD PROBLEM OF MORAL HAZARD AND ASYMMETRIC RISK...

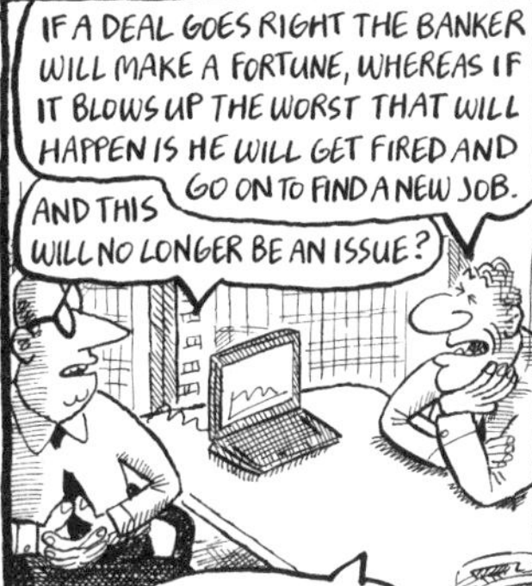
IF A DEAL GOES RIGHT THE BANKER WILL MAKE A FORTUNE, WHEREAS IF IT BLOWS UP THE WORST THAT WILL HAPPEN IS HE WILL GET FIRED AND GO ON TO FIND A NEW JOB.
AND THIS WILL NO LONGER BE AN ISSUE?
HOPEFULLY NOT.

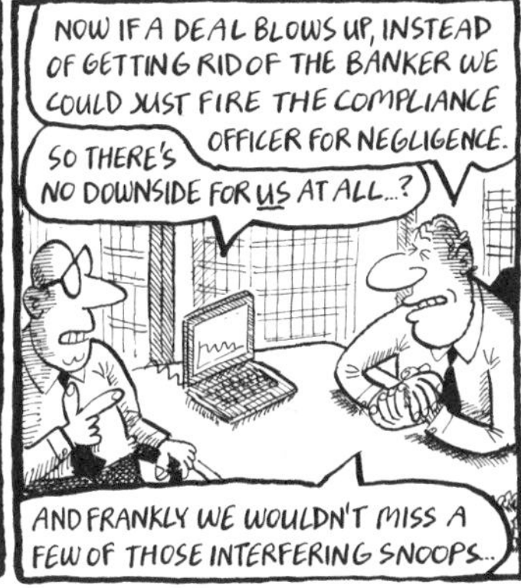
NOW IF A DEAL BLOWS UP, INSTEAD OF GETTING RID OF THE BANKER WE COULD JUST FIRE THE COMPLIANCE OFFICER FOR NEGLIGENCE.
SO THERE'S NO DOWNSIDE FOR US AT ALL...?
AND FRANKLY WE WOULDN'T MISS A FEW OF THOSE INTERFERING SNOOPS...

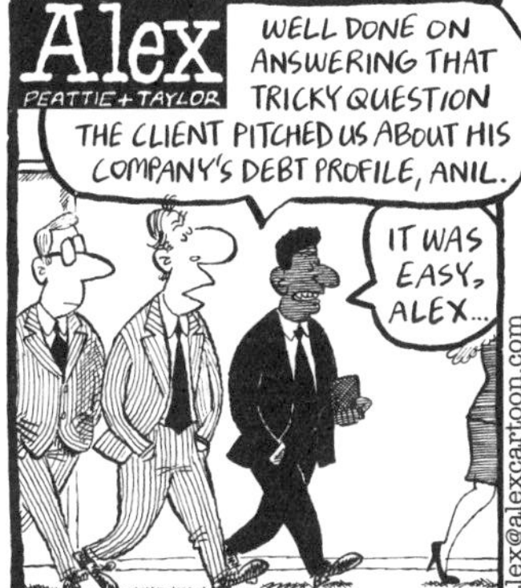
Alex
PEATTIE + TAYLOR
WELL DONE ON ANSWERING THAT TRICKY QUESTION THE CLIENT PITCHED US ABOUT HIS COMPANY'S DEBT PROFILE, ANIL.
IT WAS EASY, ALEX...

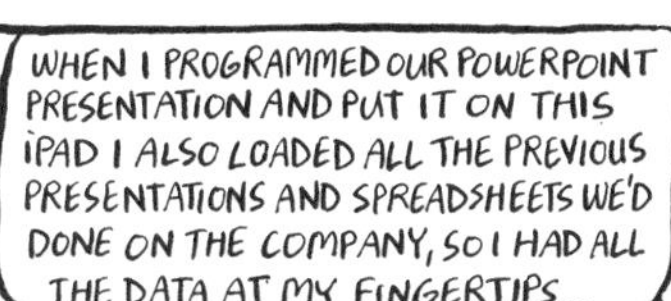
WHEN I PROGRAMMED OUR POWERPOINT PRESENTATION AND PUT IT ON THIS IPAD I ALSO LOADED ALL THE PREVIOUS PRESENTATIONS AND SPREADSHEETS WE'D DONE ON THE COMPANY, SO I HAD ALL THE DATA AT MY FINGERTIPS...

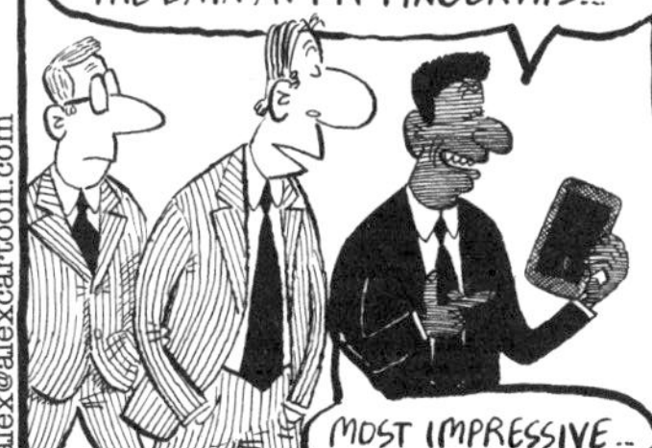
MOST IMPRESSIVE...

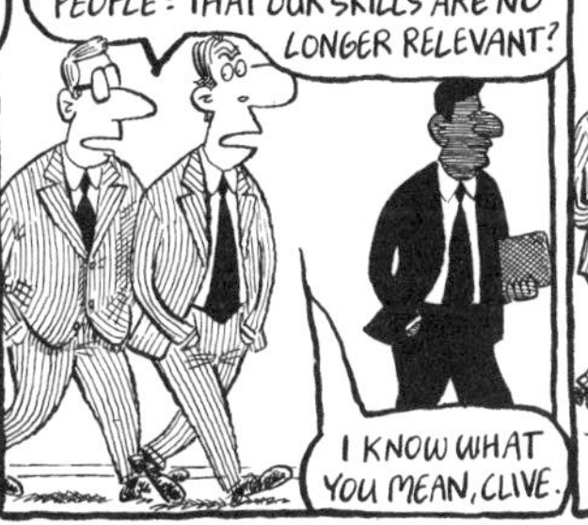
TECHNOLOGY REALLY IS MARVELLOUS THESE DAYS, ISN'T IT, ALEX? BUT DON'T YOU WORRY SOMETIMES THAT IT'S MARGINALISING US OLDER PEOPLE? THAT OUR SKILLS ARE NO LONGER RELEVANT?
I KNOW WHAT YOU MEAN, CLIVE.

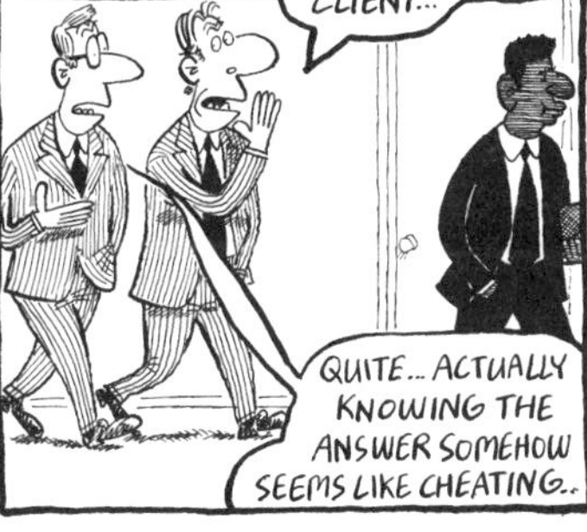
NORMALLY IN THAT SITUATION IT'D HAVE BEEN UP TO ONE OF US TO BLUFF, BLUSTER AND BULLSH*T CONVINCINGLY TO THE CLIENT...
QUITE... ACTUALLY KNOWING THE ANSWER SOMEHOW SEEMS LIKE CHEATING...

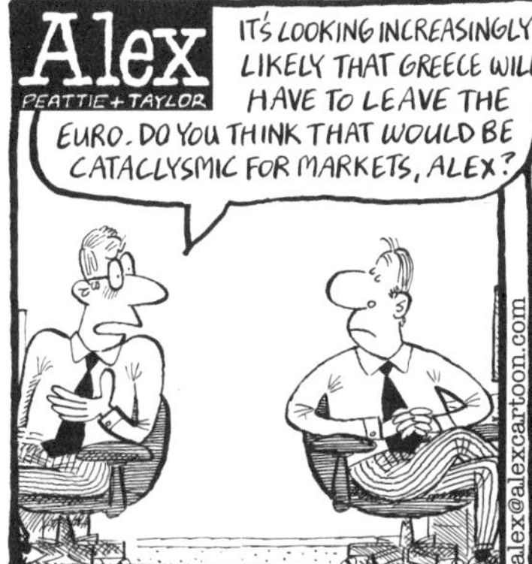
Alex
PEATTIE + TAYLOR
IT'S LOOKING INCREASINGLY LIKELY THAT GREECE WILL HAVE TO LEAVE THE EURO. DO YOU THINK THAT WOULD BE CATACLYSMIC FOR MARKETS, ALEX?

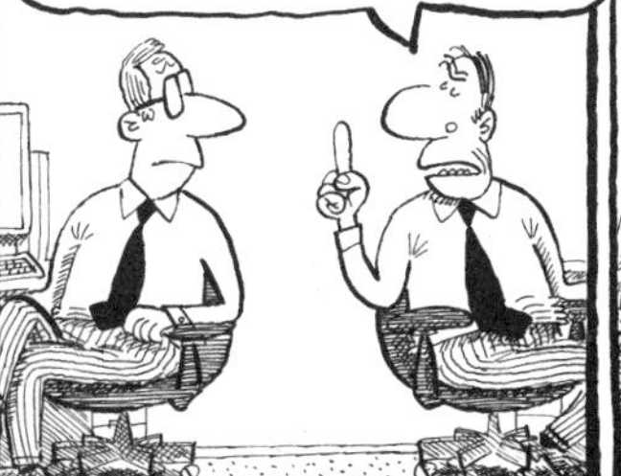
WHAT MARKETS DON'T LIKE, CLIVE, IS SHOCKS OR UNEXPECTED NEWS, BUT THE POSSIBILITY OF A GREEK DEFAULT OR EXIT FROM THE SINGLE CURRENCY HAS BEEN ON THE CARDS FOR YEARS.

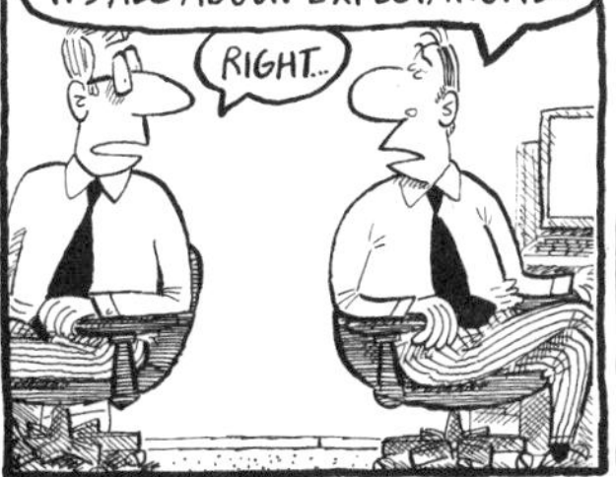
WE'VE ALL BEEN LIVING THROUGH THIS "NEW NORMAL" SINCE 2008 AND WE'VE HAD PLENTY OF TIME TO ANALYSE AND PLAN FOR WHAT WOULD TRANSPIRE IF THE GREECE CRISIS CAME TO A HEAD... IT'S ALL ABOUT EXPECTATIONS...
RIGHT...
AND THE EXPECTATION IS THAT THERE'D BE AN E.U. FUDGE, BAIL-OUT OR KICKING OF THE CAN FURTHER DOWN THE ROAD AS USUAL?
QUITE. SO IF WE DO GET AN ACTUAL GREXIT THIS TIME IT'S GOING TO TAKE EVERYONE BY SURPRISE...
IT'LL BE LEHMAN CUBED I RECKON...

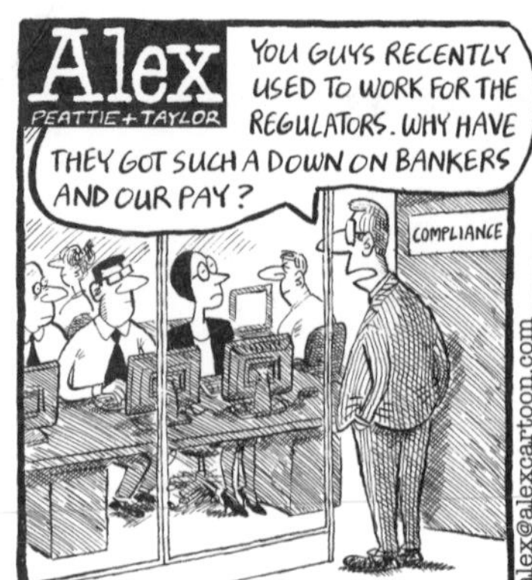
Alex
PEATTIE + TAYLOR
YOU GUYS RECENTLY USED TO WORK FOR THE REGULATORS. WHY HAVE THEY GOT SUCH A DOWN ON BANKERS AND OUR PAY?
COMPLIANCE

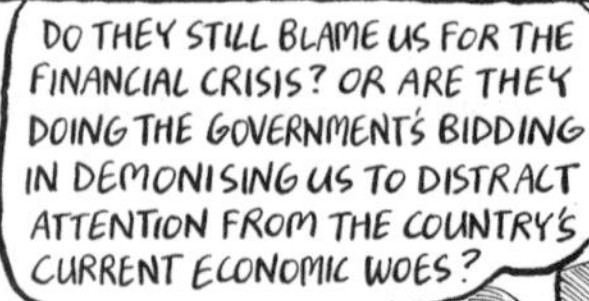
DO THEY STILL BLAME US FOR THE FINANCIAL CRISIS? OR ARE THEY DOING THE GOVERNMENT'S BIDDING IN DEMONISING US TO DISTRACT ATTENTION FROM THE COUNTRY'S CURRENT ECONOMIC WOES?

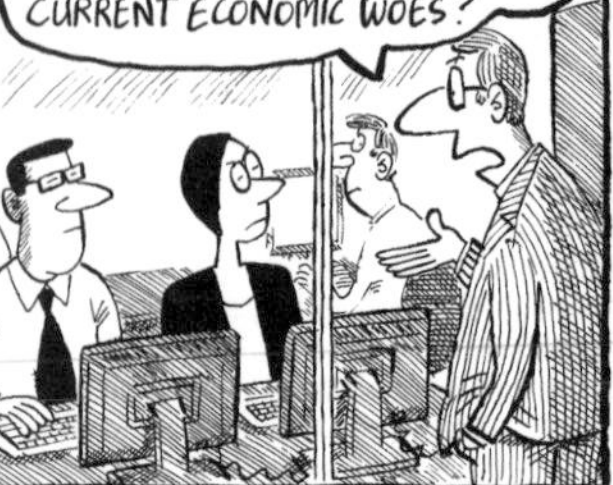
alex@alexcartoon.com

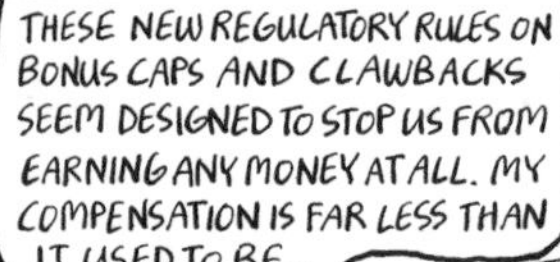
THESE NEW REGULATORY RULES ON BONUS CAPS AND CLAWBACKS SEEM DESIGNED TO STOP US FROM EARNING ANY MONEY AT ALL. MY COMPENSATION IS FAR LESS THAN IT USED TO BE...

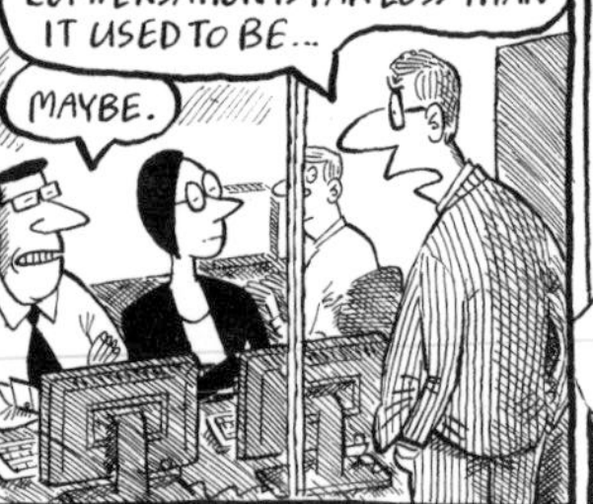
MAYBE.

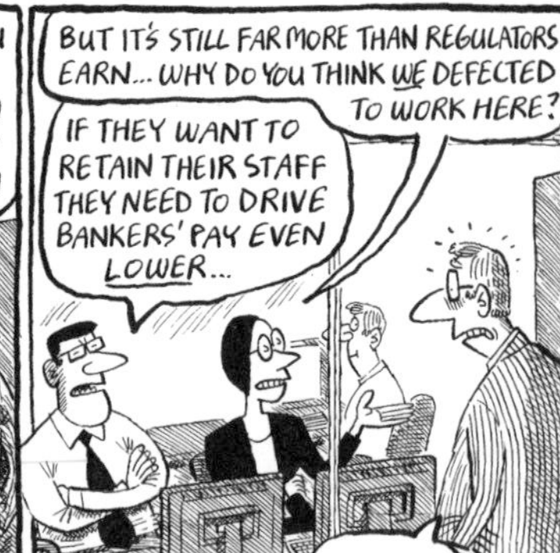
BUT IT'S STILL FAR MORE THAN REGULATORS EARN... WHY DO YOU THINK WE DEFECTED TO WORK HERE?
IF THEY WANT TO RETAIN THEIR STAFF THEY NEED TO DRIVE BANKERS' PAY EVEN LOWER...
OH GOD...

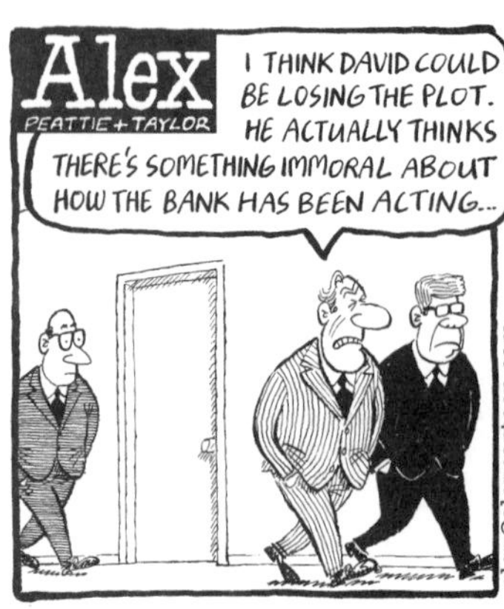
Alex
PEATTIE + TAYLOR
I THINK DAVID COULD BE LOSING THE PLOT. HE ACTUALLY THINKS THERE'S SOMETHING IMMORAL ABOUT HOW THE BANK HAS BEEN ACTING...

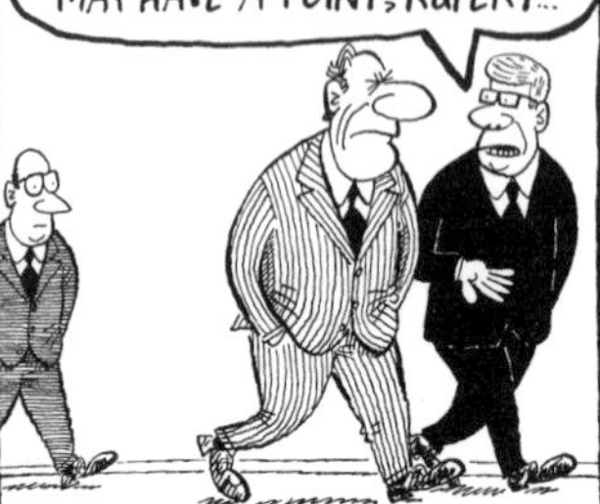
YOU MEAN US POACHING STAFF FROM THE FINANCIAL DEMEANOUR AUTHORITY TO COME AND WORK AS COMPLIANCE OFFICERS HERE AT MEGABANK? HE MAY HAVE A POINT, RUPERT...
alex@alexcartoon.com

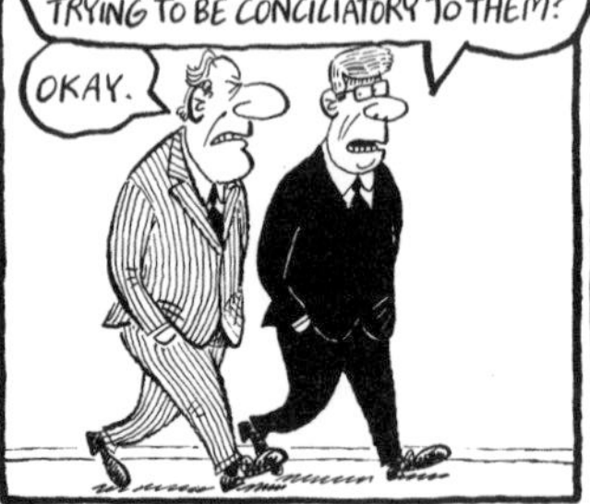
IS IT REALLY A GOOD IDEA FOR US TO ANTAGONISE THE ORGANISATION THAT'S RESPONSIBLE FOR REGULATING OUR BANK? SURELY WE SHOULD BE TRYING TO BE CONCILIATORY TO THEM?
OKAY.

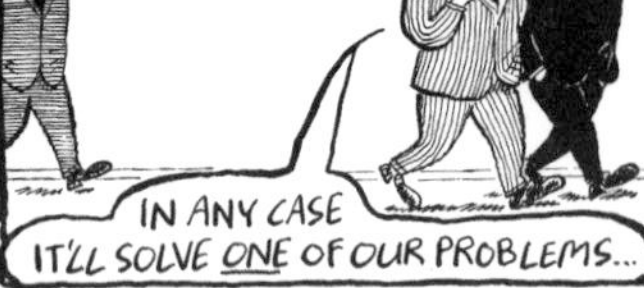
WHY DON'T WE SEND DAVID OVER TO WORK FOR THEM ON SECONDMENT?
GOOD IDEA. HOPEFULLY HE'LL SEE IT AS A BLATANT INSULT AND RESIGN, SAVING US HAVING TO GO TO THE EXPENSE OF FIRING HIM...
IN ANY CASE IT'LL SOLVE ONE OF OUR PROBLEMS...

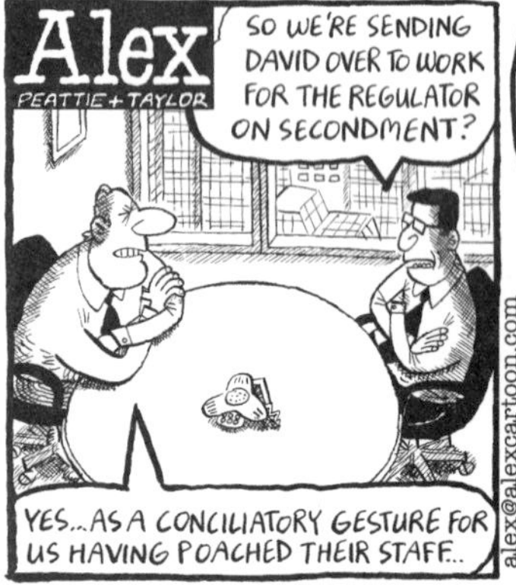
Alex
PEATTIE + TAYLOR
SO WE'RE SENDING DAVID OVER TO WORK FOR THE REGULATOR ON SECONDMENT?
YES... AS A CONCILIATORY GESTURE FOR US HAVING POACHED THEIR STAFF...

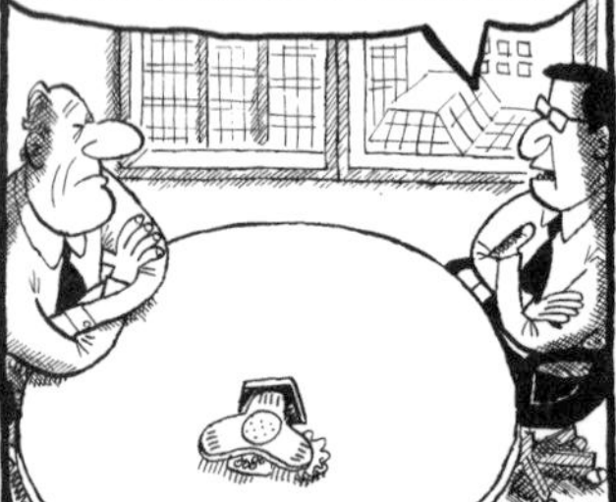
WILL WE NEED TO ENFORCE A PERIOD OF GARDENING LEAVE AND KEEP HIM OUT OF THE MARKET FOR 6 MONTHS? WE ALWAYS DO THAT WHEN A PERSON IS LEAVING TO WORK FOR A COMPETITOR...
alex@alexcartoon.com

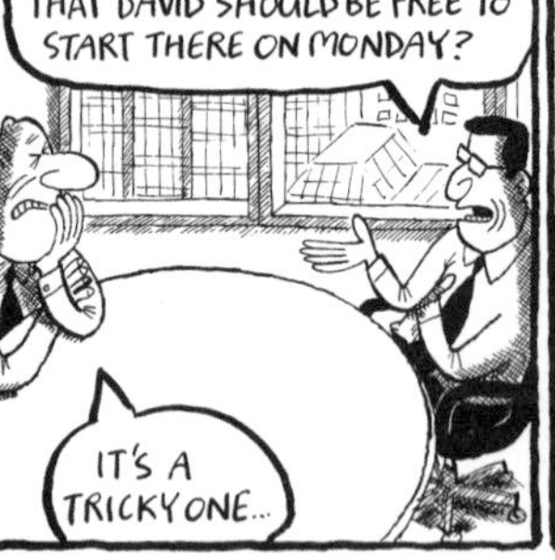
BUT THE FINANCIAL DEMEANOUR AUTHORITY IS NOT TECHNICALLY A COMPETITOR... SO DOES THAT MEAN THAT DAVID SHOULD BE FREE TO START THERE ON MONDAY?
IT'S A TRICKY ONE...

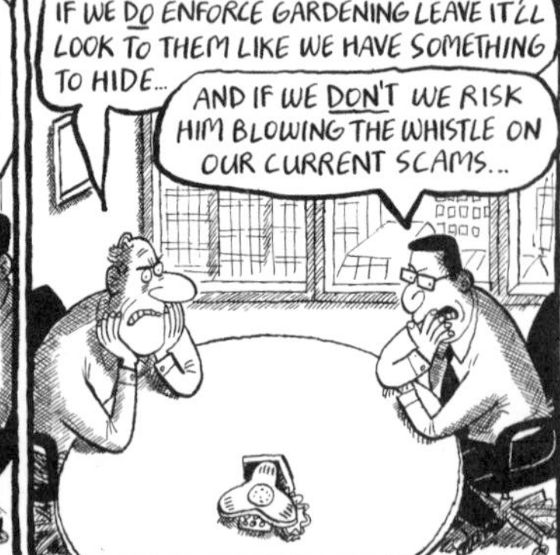
IF WE DO ENFORCE GARDENING LEAVE IT'LL LOOK TO THEM LIKE WE HAVE SOMETHING TO HIDE...
AND IF WE DON'T WE RISK HIM BLOWING THE WHISTLE ON OUR CURRENT SCAMS...

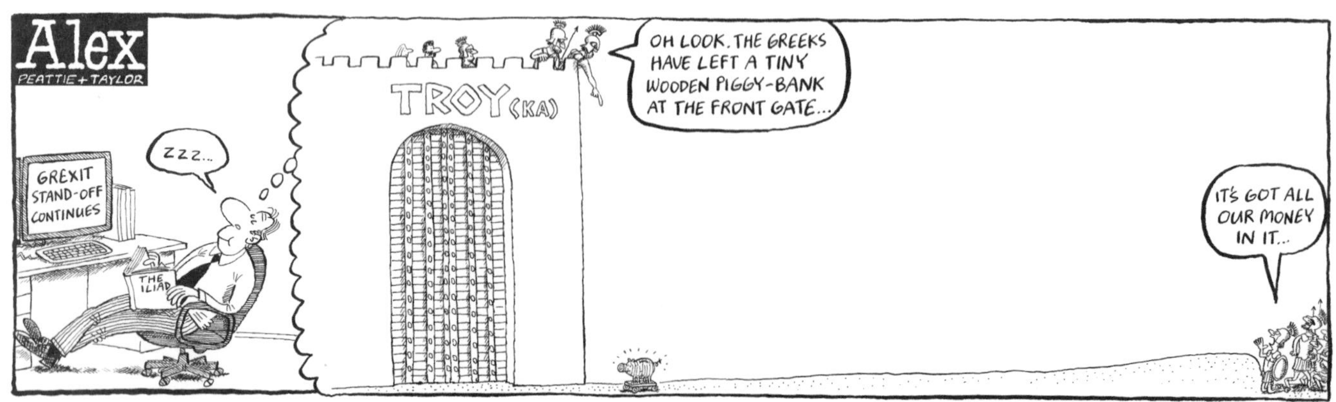
Alex
PEATTIE + TAYLOR
GREXIT STAND-OFF CONTINUES
ZZZ...
THE ILIAD
TROY(KA)
OH LOOK. THE GREEKS HAVE LEFT A TINY WOODEN PIGGY-BANK AT THE FRONT GATE...
IT'S GOT ALL OUR MONEY IN IT...

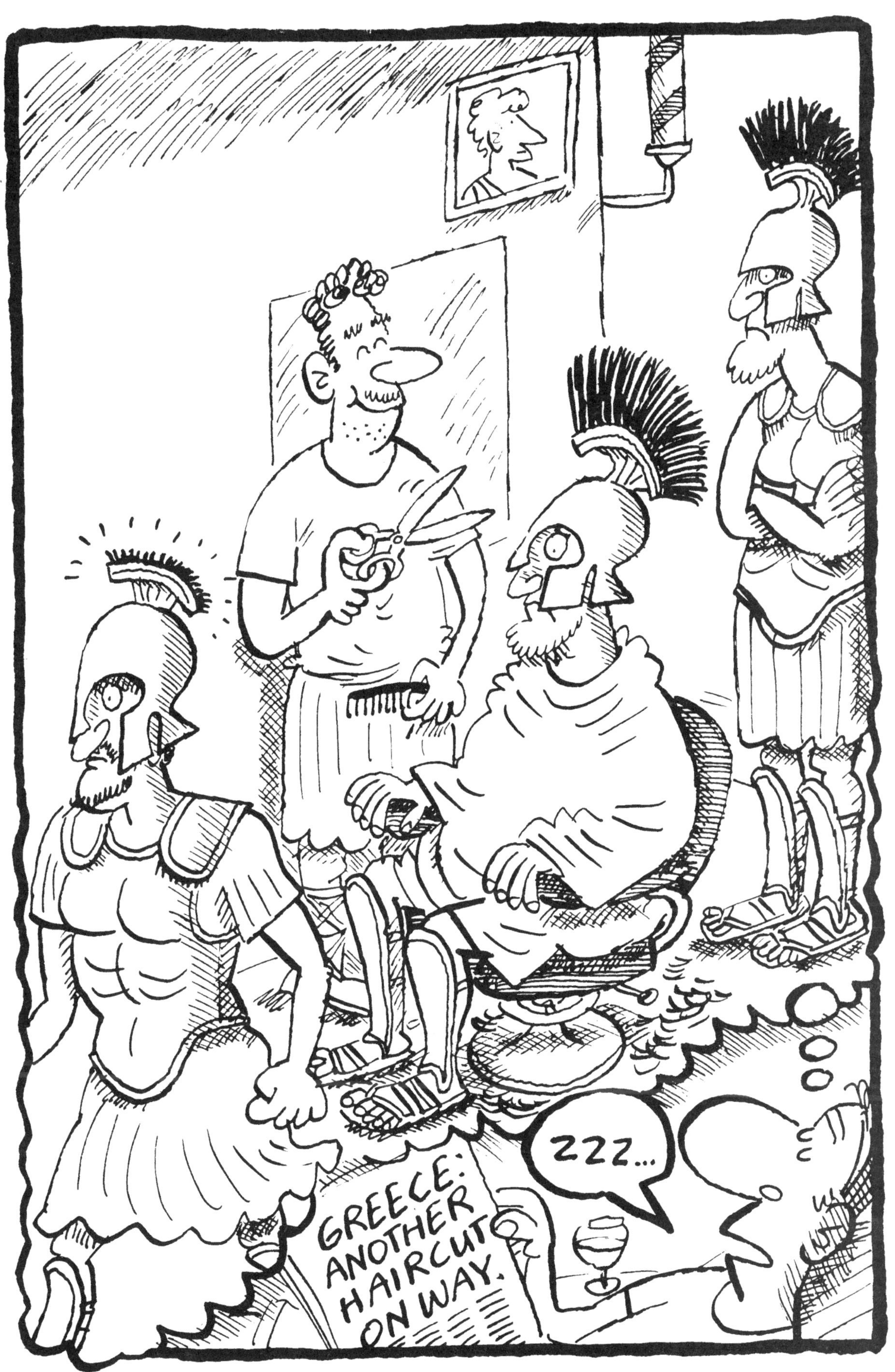
ZZZ...
GREECE: ANOTHER HAIRCUT ON WAY.

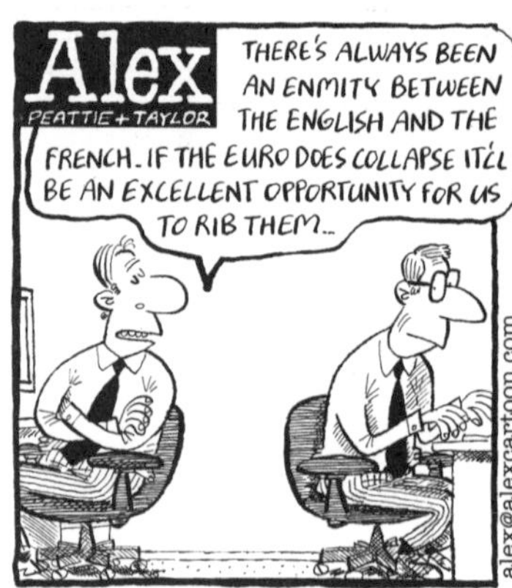
Alex
PEATTIE + TAYLOR
THERE'S ALWAYS BEEN AN ENMITY BETWEEN THE ENGLISH AND THE FRENCH. IF THE EURO DOES COLLAPSE IT'LL BE AN EXCELLENT OPPORTUNITY FOR US TO RIB THEM...
alex@alexcartoon.com

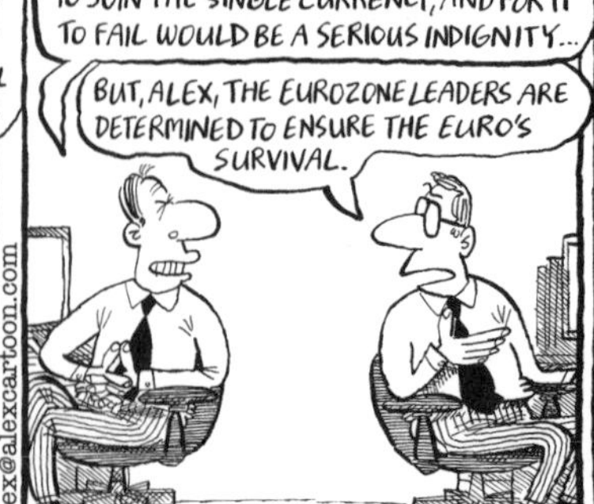
THEY WERE FURIOUS WHEN BRITAIN REFUSED TO JOIN THE SINGLE CURRENCY, AND FOR IT TO FAIL WOULD BE A SERIOUS INDIGNITY...
BUT, ALEX, THE EUROZONE LEADERS ARE DETERMINED TO ENSURE THE EURO'S SURVIVAL.

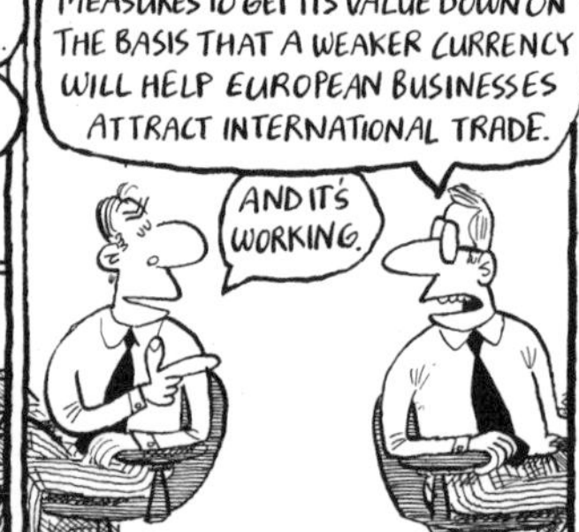
THEY'VE BEEN TAKING MONETARY MEASURES TO GET ITS VALUE DOWN ON THE BASIS THAT A WEAKER CURRENCY WILL HELP EUROPEAN BUSINESSES ATTRACT INTERNATIONAL TRADE.
AND IT'S WORKING.

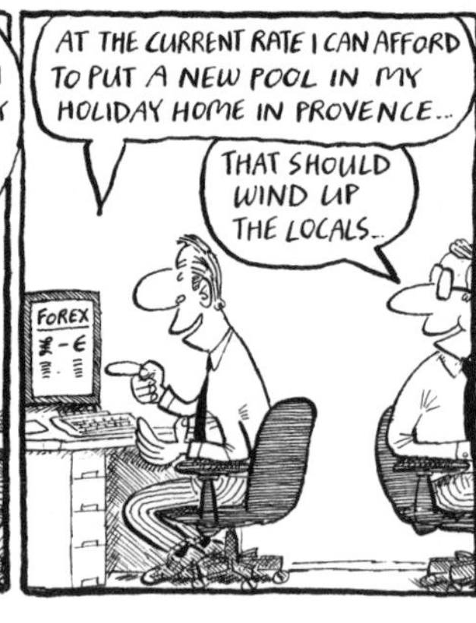
AT THE CURRENT RATE I CAN AFFORD TO PUT A NEW POOL IN MY HOLIDAY HOME IN PROVENCE...
THAT SHOULD WIND UP THE LOCALS...
FOREX
£ - €

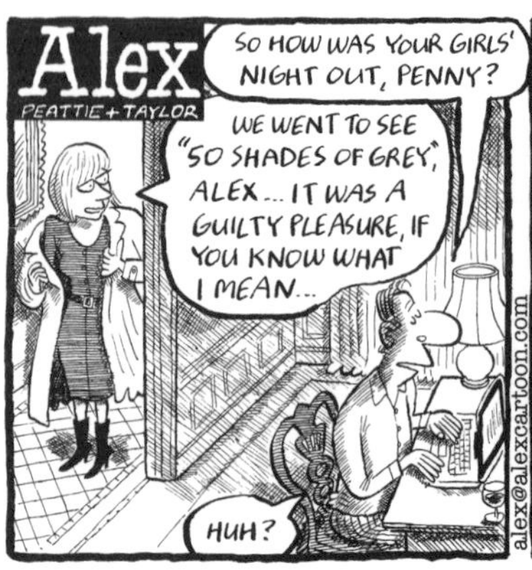
Alex
PEATTIE + TAYLOR
SO HOW WAS YOUR GIRLS' NIGHT OUT, PENNY?
WE WENT TO SEE "50 SHADES OF GREY," ALEX... IT WAS A GUILTY PLEASURE, IF YOU KNOW WHAT I MEAN...
HUH?
alex@alexcartoon.com

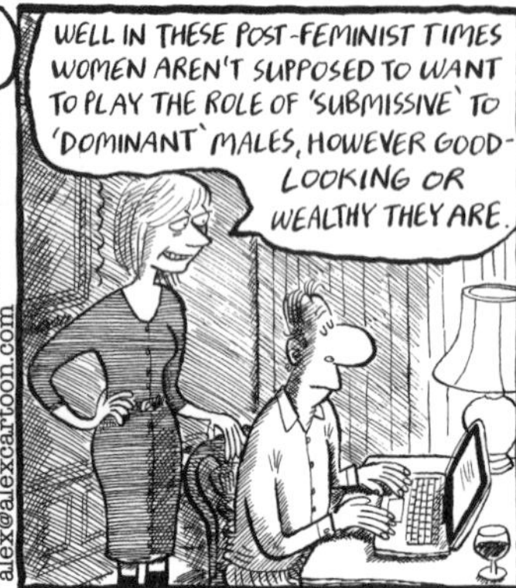
WELL IN THESE POST-FEMINIST TIMES WOMEN AREN'T SUPPOSED TO WANT TO PLAY THE ROLE OF 'SUBMISSIVE' TO 'DOMINANT' MALES, HOWEVER GOOD-LOOKING OR WEALTHY THEY ARE.

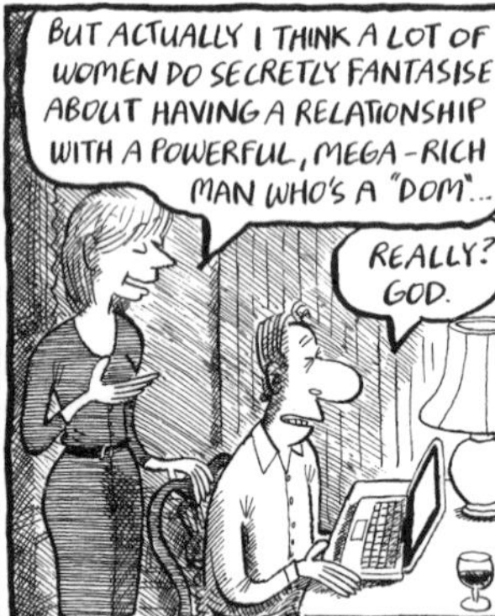
BUT ACTUALLY I THINK A LOT OF WOMEN DO SECRETLY FANTASISE ABOUT HAVING A RELATIONSHIP WITH A POWERFUL, MEGA-RICH MAN WHO'S A "DOM"...
REALLY? GOD.

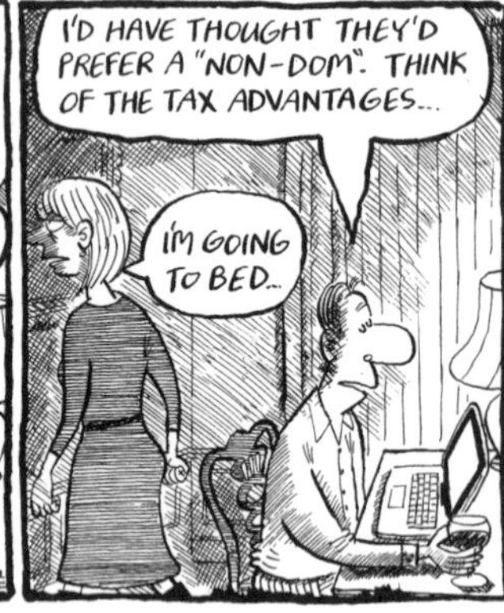
I'D HAVE THOUGHT THEY'D PREFER A "NON-DOM". THINK OF THE TAX ADVANTAGES...
I'M GOING TO BED...

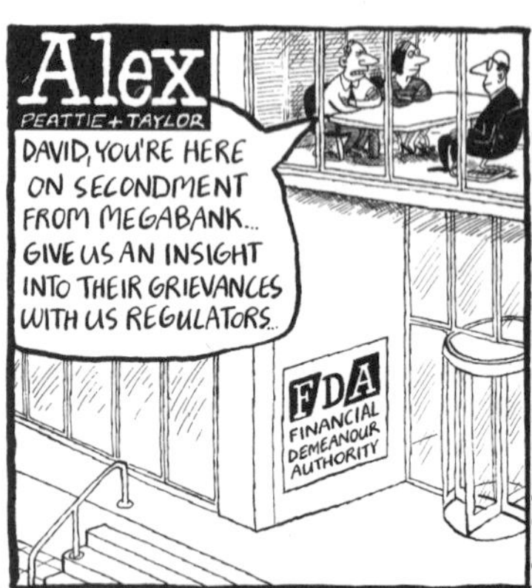
Alex
PEATTIE + TAYLOR
DAVID, YOU'RE HERE ON SECONDMENT FROM MEGABANK... GIVE US AN INSIGHT INTO THEIR GRIEVANCES WITH US REGULATORS...
FDA
FINANCIAL DEMEANOUR AUTHORITY
alex@alexcartoon.com

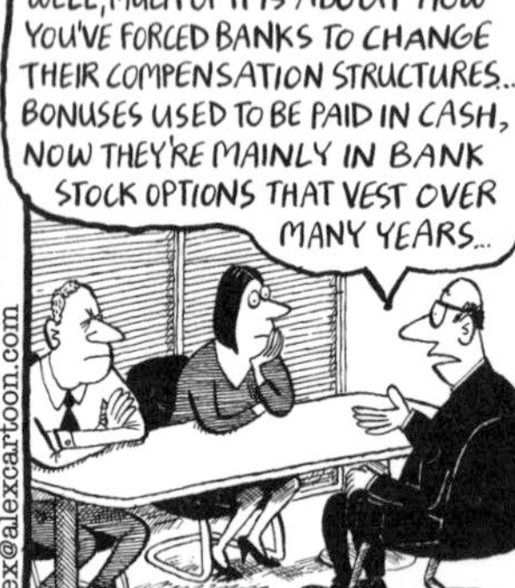
WELL, MUCH OF IT IS ABOUT HOW YOU'VE FORCED BANKS TO CHANGE THEIR COMPENSATION STRUCTURES... BONUSES USED TO BE PAID IN CASH, NOW THEY'RE MAINLY IN BANK STOCK OPTIONS THAT VEST OVER MANY YEARS...

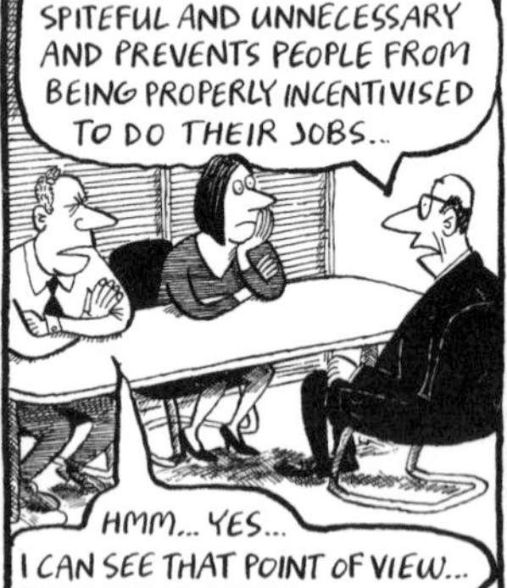
BANKERS THINK THIS SYSTEM IS SPITEFUL AND UNNECESSARY AND PREVENTS PEOPLE FROM BEING PROPERLY INCENTIVISED TO DO THEIR JOBS...
HMM... YES... I CAN SEE THAT POINT OF VIEW...

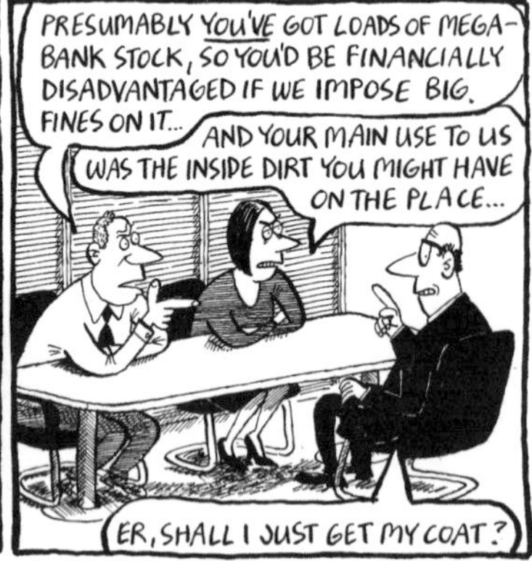
PRESUMABLY YOU'VE GOT LOADS OF MEGABANK STOCK, SO YOU'D BE FINANCIALLY DISADVANTAGED IF WE IMPOSE BIG FINES ON IT...
AND YOUR MAIN USE TO US WAS THE INSIDE DIRT YOU MIGHT HAVE ON THE PLACE...
ER, SHALL I JUST GET MY COAT?

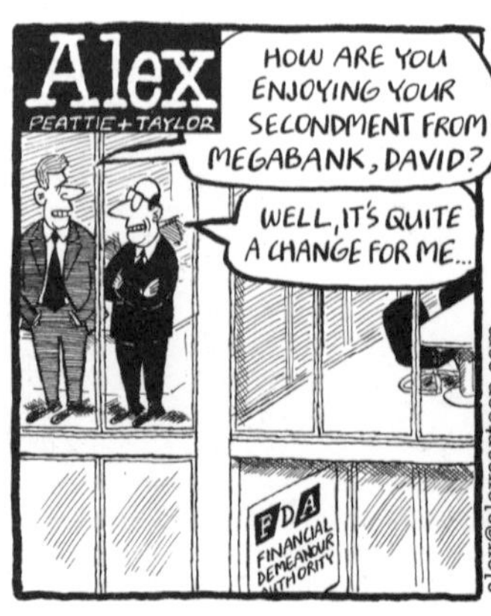
Alex
PEATTIE + TAYLOR
HOW ARE YOU ENJOYING YOUR SECONDMENT FROM MEGABANK, DAVID?
WELL, IT'S QUITE A CHANGE FOR ME...
FDA
FINANCIAL DEMEANOUR AUTHORITY
alex@alexcartoon.com

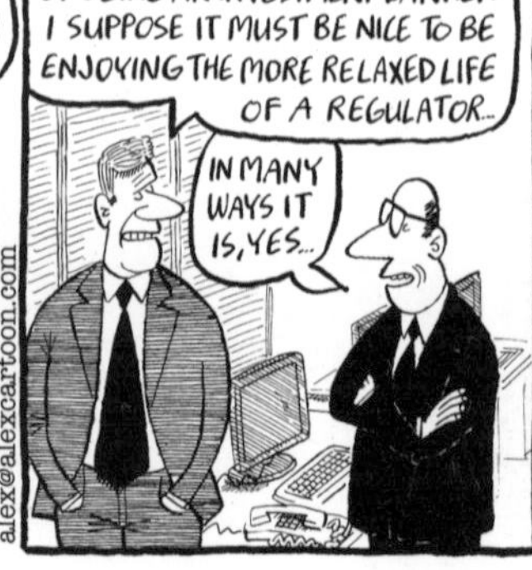
AFTER THE STRESSES AND STRAINS OF BEING AN INVESTMENT BANKER I SUPPOSE IT MUST BE NICE TO BE ENJOYING THE MORE RELAXED LIFE OF A REGULATOR...
IN MANY WAYS IT IS, YES...

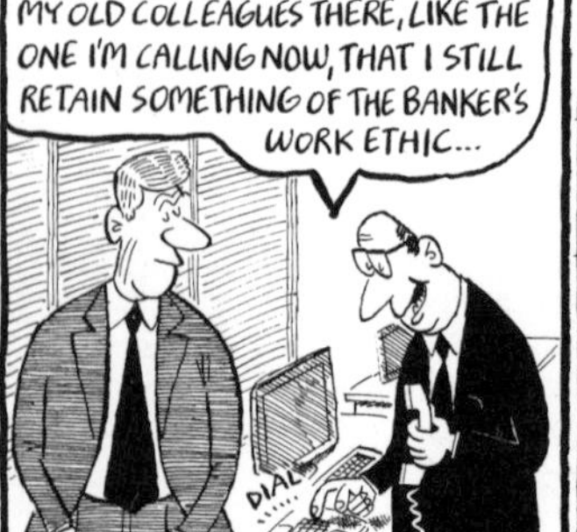
THOUGH, AS I'M RESPONSIBLE FOR OVERSEEING MEGABANK I LIKE TO SHOW MY OLD COLLEAGUES THERE, LIKE THE ONE I'M CALLING NOW, THAT I STILL RETAIN SOMETHING OF THE BANKER'S WORK ETHIC...
DIAL

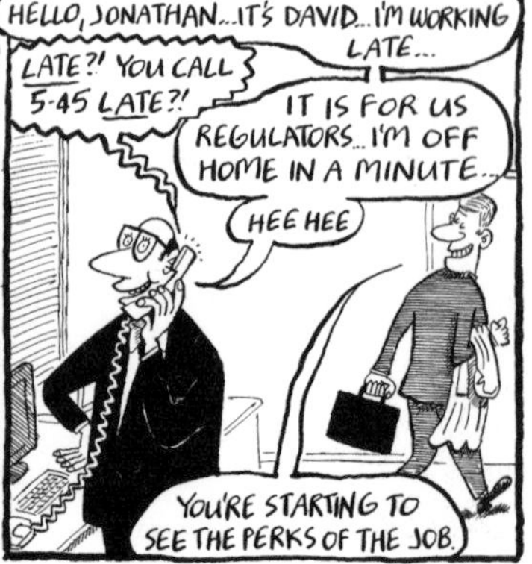
HELLO, JONATHAN... IT'S DAVID... I'M WORKING LATE...
LATE?! YOU CALL 5.45 LATE?!
IT IS FOR US REGULATORS... I'M OFF HOME IN A MINUTE...
HEE HEE
YOU'RE STARTING TO SEE THE PERKS OF THE JOB.

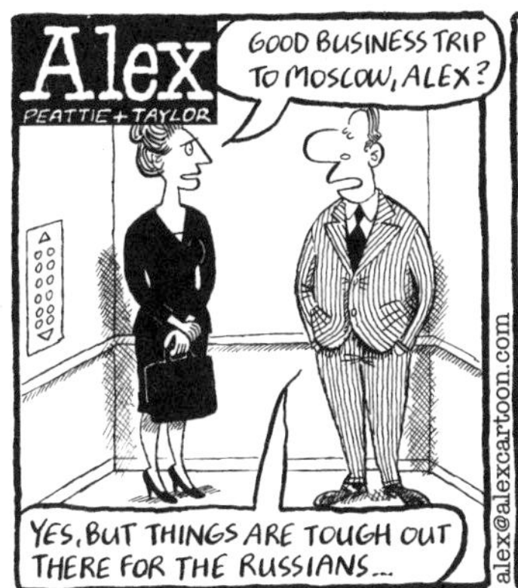

Alex
PEATTIE+TAYLOR
GOOD BUSINESS TRIP TO MOSCOW, ALEX?
YES, BUT THINGS ARE TOUGH OUT THERE FOR THE RUSSIANS...

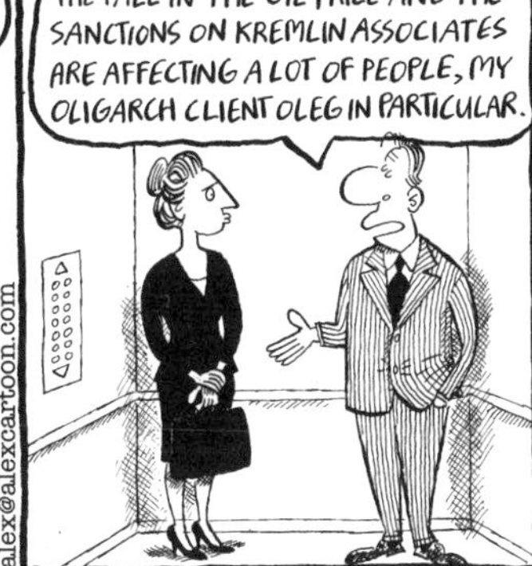

THE FALL IN THE OIL PRICE AND THE SANCTIONS ON KREMLIN ASSOCIATES ARE AFFECTING A LOT OF PEOPLE, MY OLIGARCH CLIENT OLEG IN PARTICULAR.

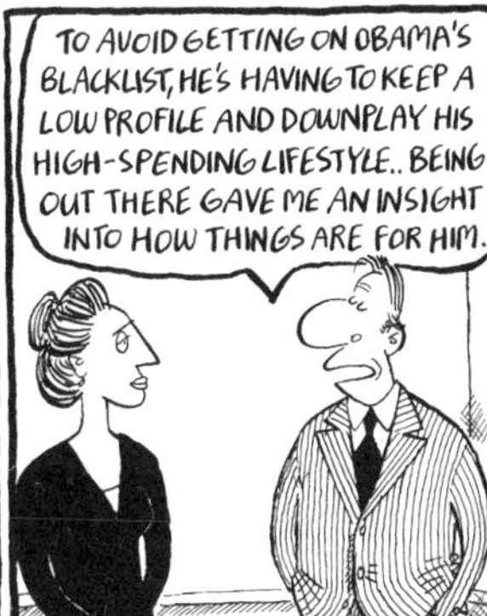

TO AVOID GETTING ON OBAMA'S BLACKLIST, HE'S HAVING TO KEEP A LOW PROFILE AND DOWNPLAY HIS HIGH-SPENDING LIFESTYLE.. BEING OUT THERE GAVE ME AN INSIGHT INTO HOW THINGS ARE FOR HIM.

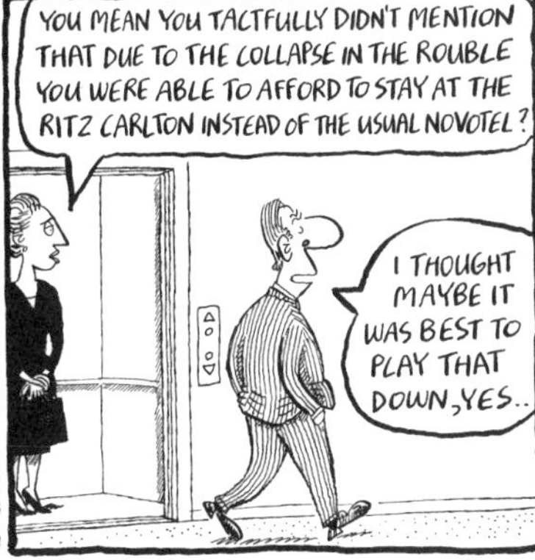

YOU MEAN YOU TACTFULLY DIDN'T MENTION THAT DUE TO THE COLLAPSE IN THE ROUBLE YOU WERE ABLE TO AFFORD TO STAY AT THE RITZ CARLTON INSTEAD OF THE USUAL NOVOTEL?
I THOUGHT MAYBE IT WAS BEST TO PLAY THAT DOWN, YES..

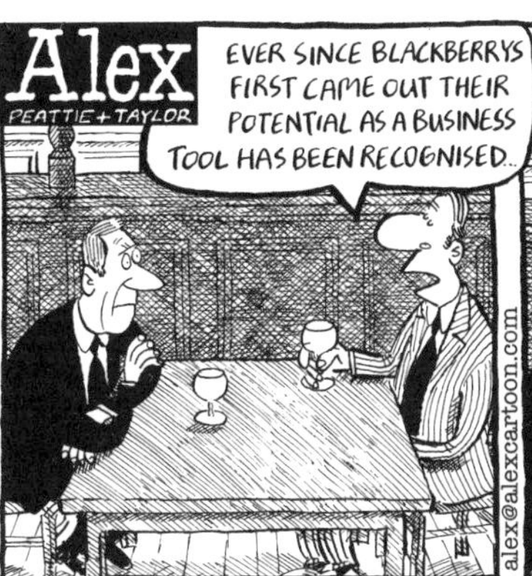

Alex
PEATTIE+TAYLOR
EVER SINCE BLACKBERRYS FIRST CAME OUT THEIR POTENTIAL AS A BUSINESS TOOL HAS BEEN RECOGNISED..

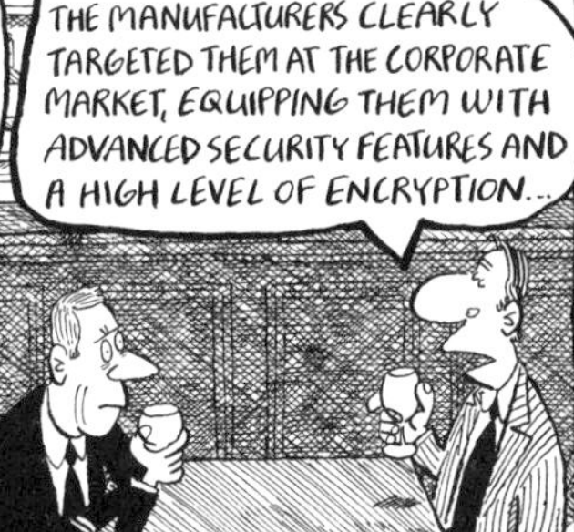

THE MANUFACTURERS CLEARLY TARGETED THEM AT THE CORPORATE MARKET, EQUIPPING THEM WITH ADVANCED SECURITY FEATURES AND A HIGH LEVEL OF ENCRYPTION...

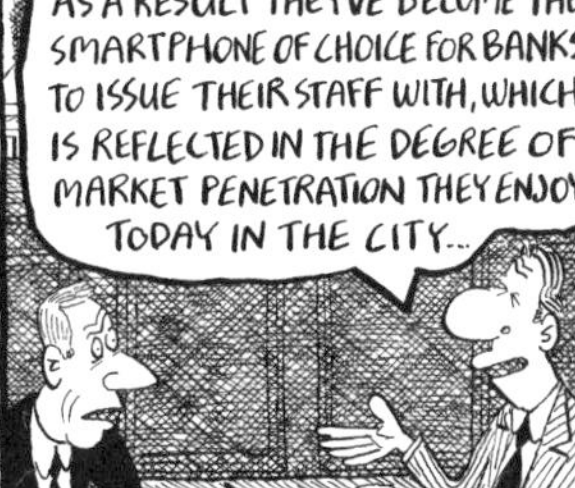

AS A RESULT THEY'VE BECOME THE SMARTPHONE OF CHOICE FOR BANKS TO ISSUE THEIR STAFF WITH, WHICH IS REFLECTED IN THE DEGREE OF MARKET PENETRATION THEY ENJOY TODAY IN THE CITY...
EH?... BUT ONE NEVER SEES THEM ANY MORE.

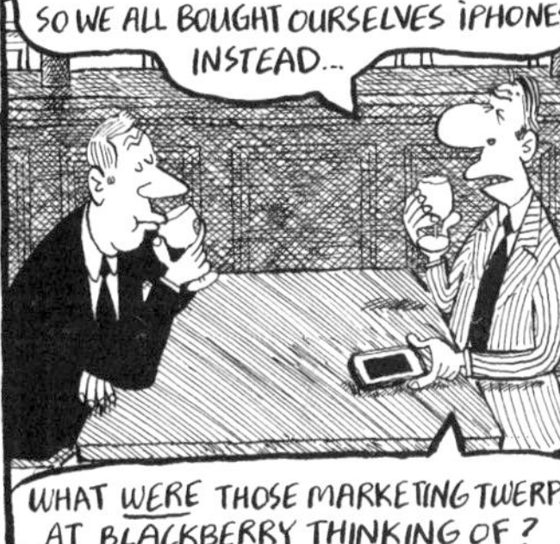

OF COURSE NOT.. EVERYTHING ONE DOES ON THEM IS MONITORED BY COMPLIANCE, SO WE ALL BOUGHT OURSELVES iPHONES INSTEAD...
WHAT WERE THOSE MARKETING TWERPS AT BLACKBERRY THINKING OF?

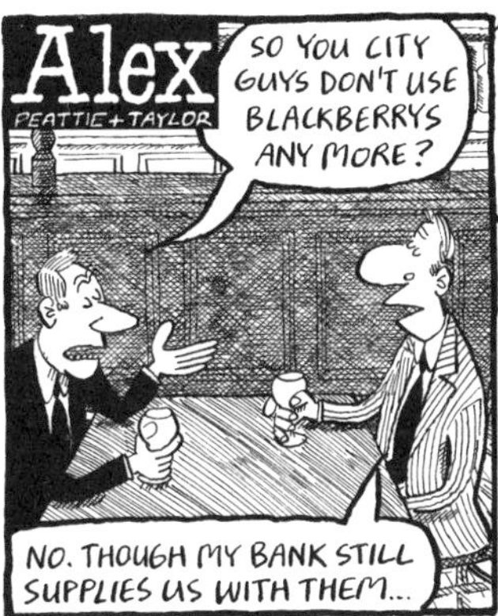

Alex
PEATTIE+TAYLOR
SO YOU CITY GUYS DON'T USE BLACKBERRYS ANY MORE?
NO. THOUGH MY BANK STILL SUPPLIES US WITH THEM...

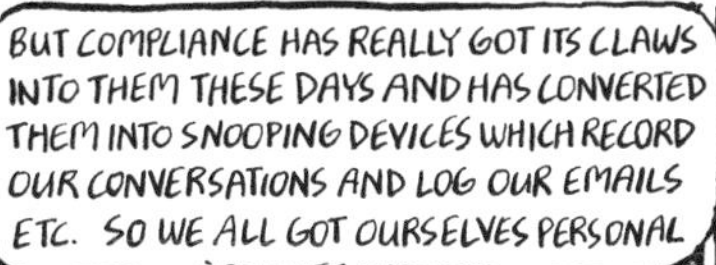

BUT COMPLIANCE HAS REALLY GOT ITS CLAWS INTO THEM THESE DAYS AND HAS CONVERTED THEM INTO SNOOPING DEVICES WHICH RECORD OUR CONVERSATIONS AND LOG OUR EMAILS ETC. SO WE ALL GOT OURSELVES PERSONAL iPHONES INSTEAD..

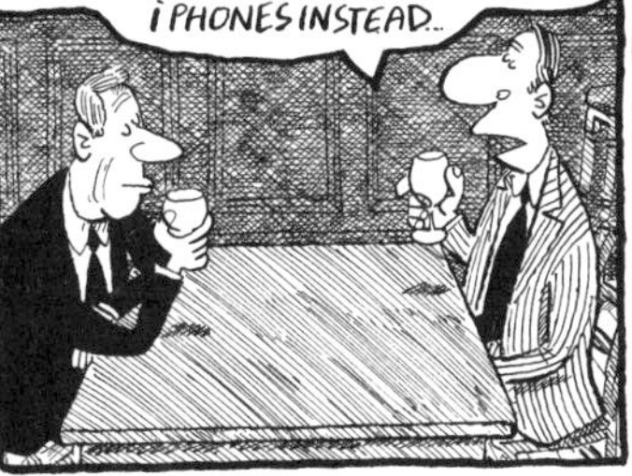

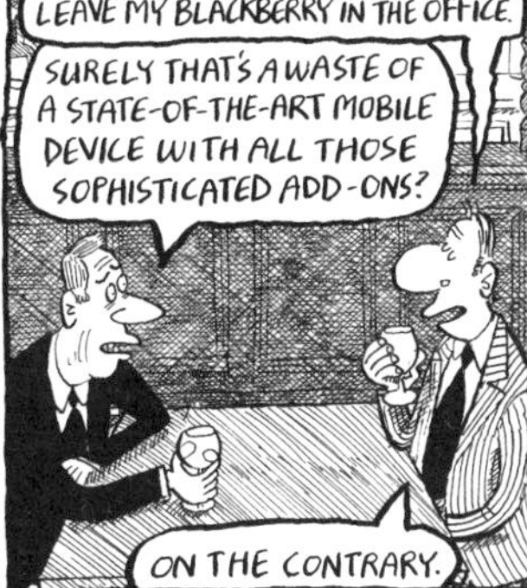

FRANKLY WHEN I GO OUT I JUST LEAVE MY BLACKBERRY IN THE OFFICE.
SURELY THAT'S A WASTE OF A STATE-OF-THE-ART MOBILE DEVICE WITH ALL THOSE SOPHISTICATED ADD-ONS?
ON THE CONTRARY.

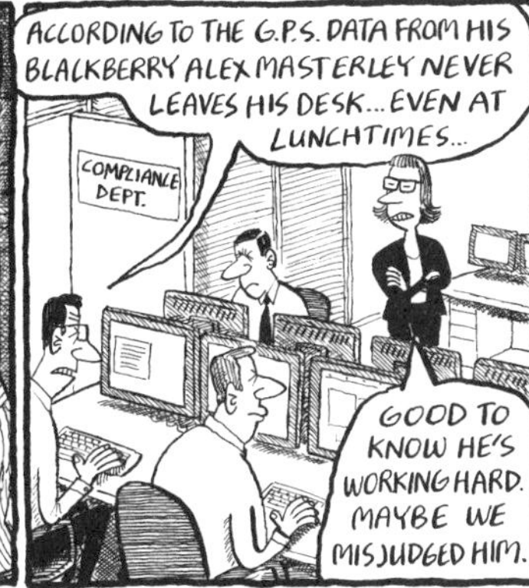

ACCORDING TO THE G.P.S. DATA FROM HIS BLACKBERRY ALEX MASTERLEY NEVER LEAVES HIS DESK... EVEN AT LUNCHTIMES...
COMPLIANCE DEPT.
GOOD TO KNOW HE'S WORKING HARD. MAYBE WE MISJUDGED HIM.

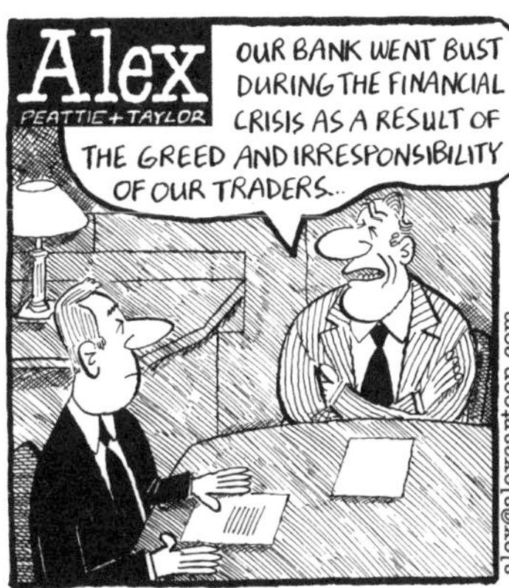

Alex
PEATTIE+TAYLOR
OUR BANK WENT BUST DURING THE FINANCIAL CRISIS AS A RESULT OF THE GREED AND IRRESPONSIBILITY OF OUR TRADERS...

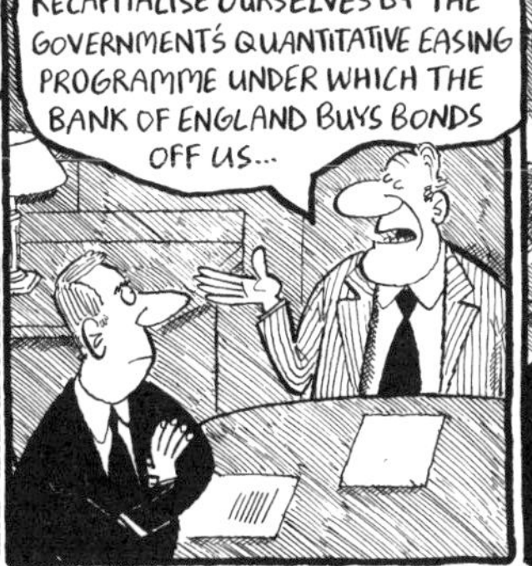

CLEARLY WE'VE BEEN ENABLED TO RECAPITALISE OURSELVES BY THE GOVERNMENT'S QUANTITATIVE EASING PROGRAMME UNDER WHICH THE BANK OF ENGLAND BUYS BONDS OFF US...

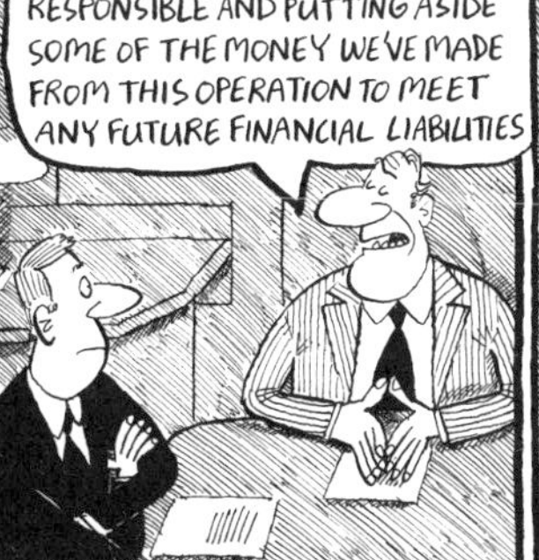

SO OBVIOUSLY WE'RE BEING RESPONSIBLE AND PUTTING ASIDE SOME OF THE MONEY WE'VE MADE FROM THIS OPERATION TO MEET ANY FUTURE FINANCIAL LIABILITIES

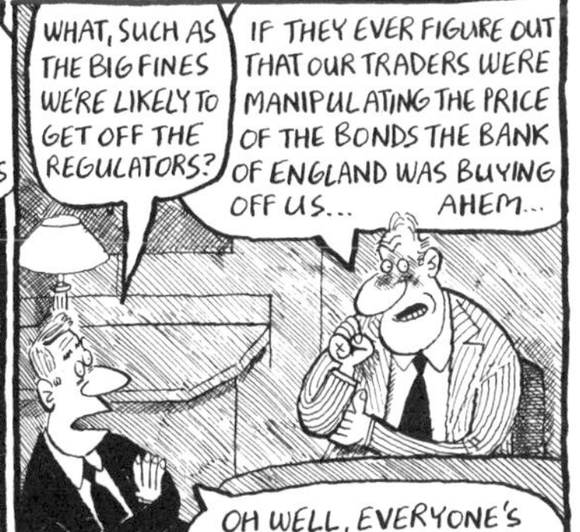

WHAT, SUCH AS THE BIG FINES WE'RE LIKELY TO GET OFF THE REGULATORS?
IF THEY EVER FIGURE OUT THAT OUR TRADERS WERE MANIPULATING THE PRICE OF THE BONDS THE BANK OF ENGLAND WAS BUYING OFF US... AHEM...
OH WELL, EVERYONE'S TRADERS WERE DOING THAT...

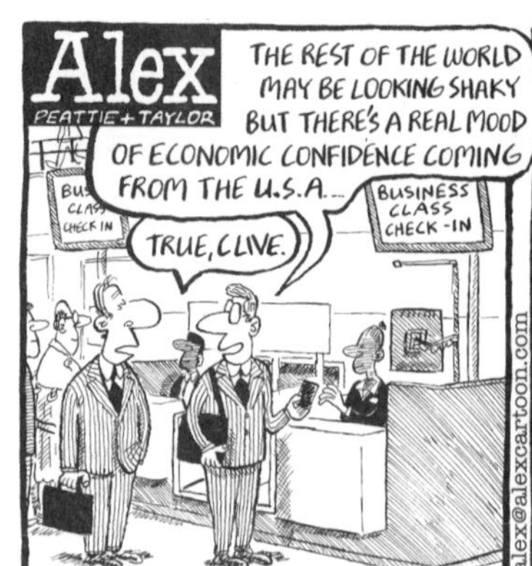
Alex
PEATTIE + TAYLOR
THE REST OF THE WORLD MAY BE LOOKING SHAKY BUT THERE'S A REAL MOOD OF ECONOMIC CONFIDENCE COMING FROM THE U.S.A...
BUSINESS CLASS CHECK-IN
TRUE, CLIVE.

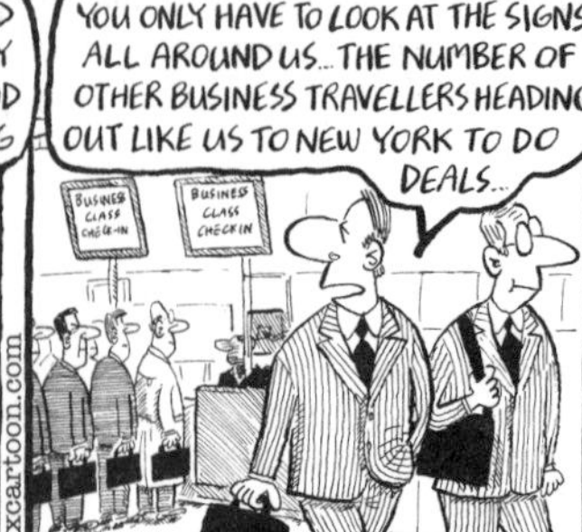
YOU ONLY HAVE TO LOOK AT THE SIGNS ALL AROUND US... THE NUMBER OF OTHER BUSINESS TRAVELLERS HEADING OUT LIKE US TO NEW YORK TO DO DEALS...
alex@alexcartoon.com

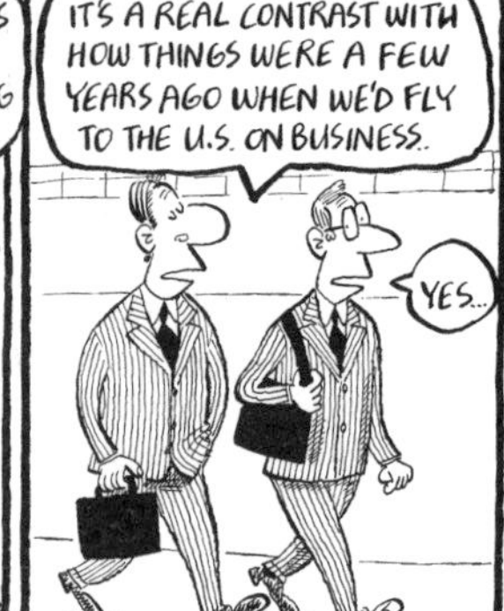
IT'S A REAL CONTRAST WITH HOW THINGS WERE A FEW YEARS AGO WHEN WE'D FLY TO THE U.S. ON BUSINESS...
YES...

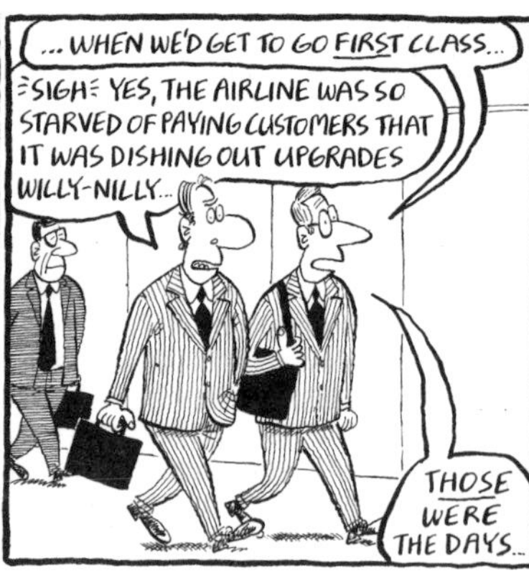
... WHEN WE'D GET TO GO FIRST CLASS...
SIGH YES, THE AIRLINE WAS SO STARVED OF PAYING CUSTOMERS THAT IT WAS DISHING OUT UPGRADES WILLY-NILLY...
THOSE WERE THE DAYS...

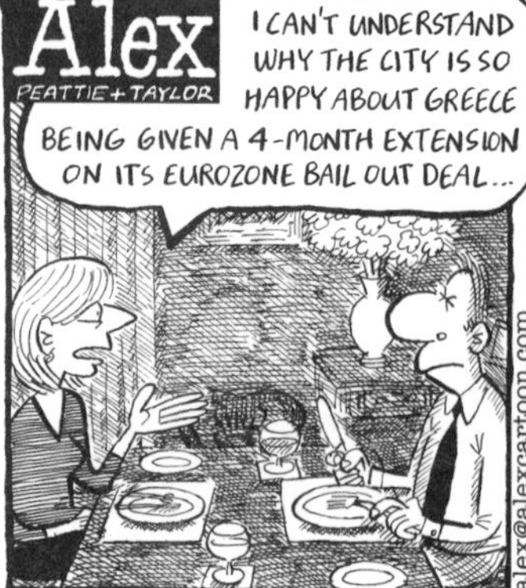
Alex
PEATTIE + TAYLOR
I CAN'T UNDERSTAND WHY THE CITY IS SO HAPPY ABOUT GREECE BEING GIVEN A 4-MONTH EXTENSION ON ITS EUROZONE BAIL OUT DEAL...

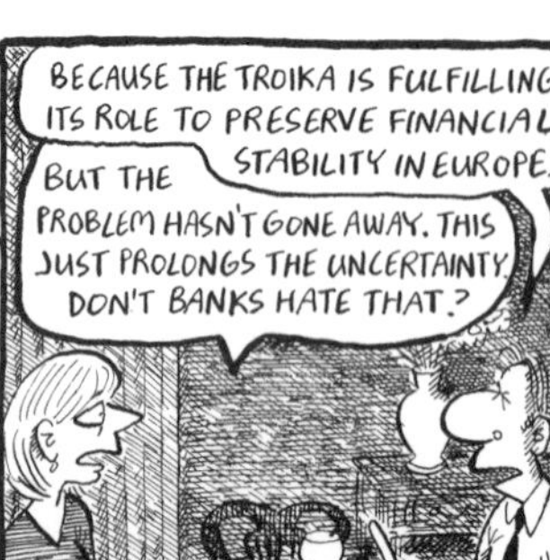
BECAUSE THE TROIKA IS FULFILLING ITS ROLE TO PRESERVE FINANCIAL STABILITY IN EUROPE...
BUT THE PROBLEM HASN'T GONE AWAY. THIS JUST PROLONGS THE UNCERTAINTY. DON'T BANKS HATE THAT?
alex@alexcartoon.com

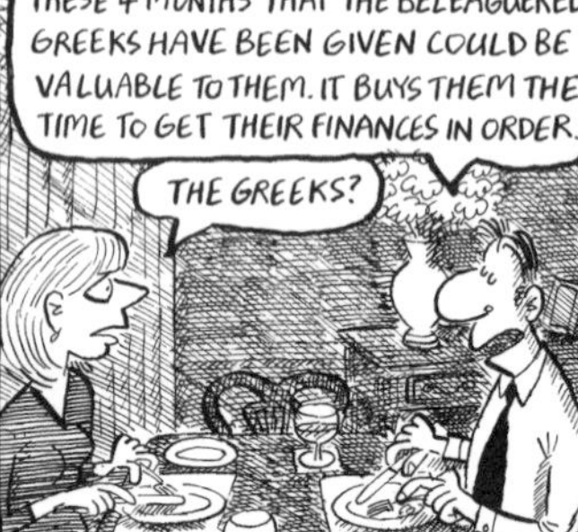
LOOK, PENNY. BANKS APPRECIATE THAT THESE 4 MONTHS THAT THE BELEAGUERED GREEKS HAVE BEEN GIVEN COULD BE VALUABLE TO THEM. IT BUYS THEM THE TIME TO GET THEIR FINANCES IN ORDER...
THE GREEKS?

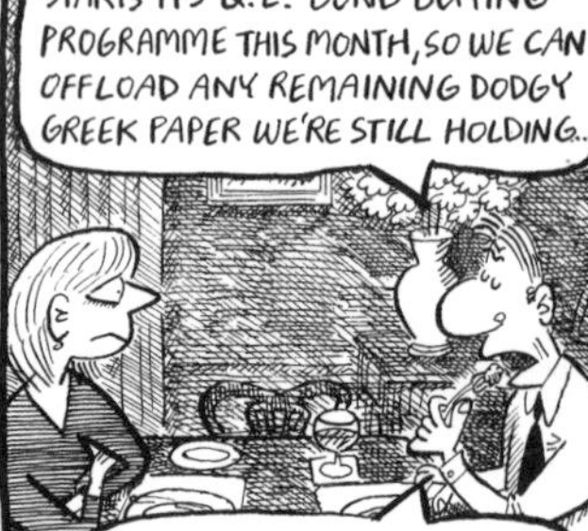
NO, THE BANKS... THE EUROZONE STARTS ITS Q.E. BOND BUYING PROGRAMME THIS MONTH, SO WE CAN OFFLOAD ANY REMAINING DODGY GREEK PAPER WE'RE STILL HOLDING...
AFTER THAT THE PLACE CAN GO BELLY-UP AS FAR AS WE CARE...

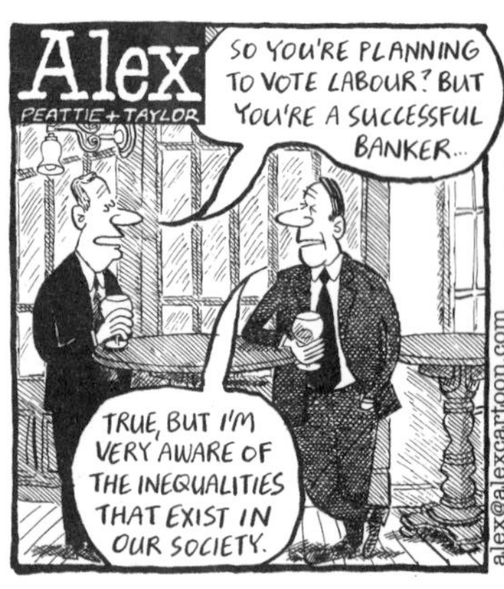
Alex
PEATTIE + TAYLOR
SO YOU'RE PLANNING TO VOTE LABOUR? BUT YOU'RE A SUCCESSFUL BANKER...
TRUE, BUT I'M VERY AWARE OF THE INEQUALITIES THAT EXIST IN OUR SOCIETY.

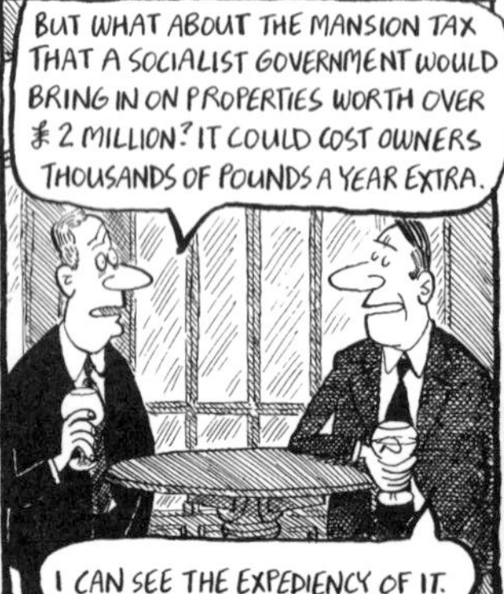
BUT WHAT ABOUT THE MANSION TAX THAT A SOCIALIST GOVERNMENT WOULD BRING IN ON PROPERTIES WORTH OVER £2 MILLION? IT COULD COST OWNERS THOUSANDS OF POUNDS A YEAR EXTRA.
I CAN SEE THE EXPEDIENCY OF IT.
alex@alexcartoon.com

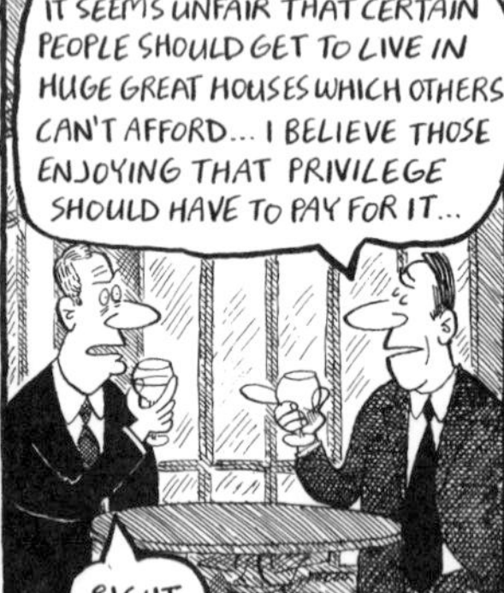
IT SEEMS UNFAIR THAT CERTAIN PEOPLE SHOULD GET TO LIVE IN HUGE GREAT HOUSES WHICH OTHERS CAN'T AFFORD... I BELIEVE THOSE ENJOYING THAT PRIVILEGE SHOULD HAVE TO PAY FOR IT...
RIGHT...

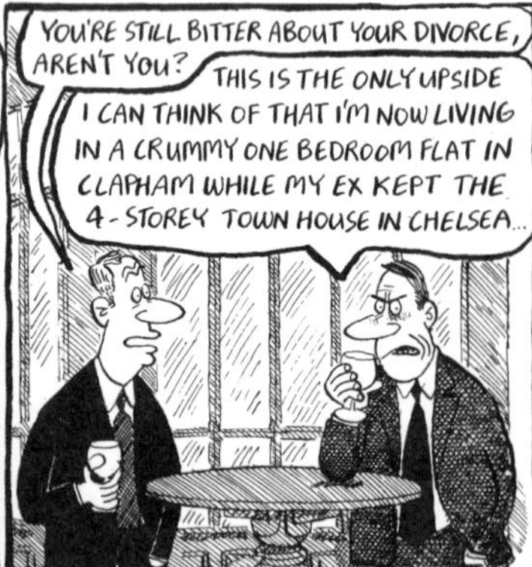
YOU'RE STILL BITTER ABOUT YOUR DIVORCE, AREN'T YOU?
THIS IS THE ONLY UPSIDE I CAN THINK OF THAT I'M NOW LIVING IN A CRUMMY ONE BEDROOM FLAT IN CLAPHAM WHILE MY EX KEPT THE 4-STOREY TOWN HOUSE IN CHELSEA...

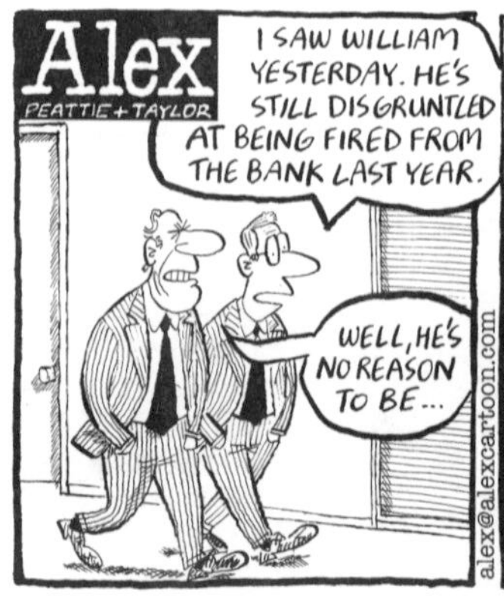
Alex
PEATTIE + TAYLOR
I SAW WILLIAM YESTERDAY. HE'S STILL DISGRUNTLED AT BEING FIRED FROM THE BANK LAST YEAR.
WELL, HE'S NO REASON TO BE...

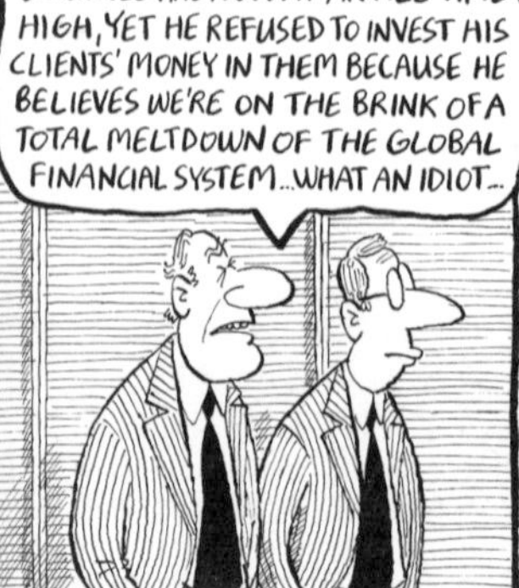
EQUITIES ARE NOW AT AN ALL-TIME HIGH, YET HE REFUSED TO INVEST HIS CLIENTS' MONEY IN THEM BECAUSE HE BELIEVES WE'RE ON THE BRINK OF A TOTAL MELTDOWN OF THE GLOBAL FINANCIAL SYSTEM... WHAT AN IDIOT...
alex@alexcartoon.com

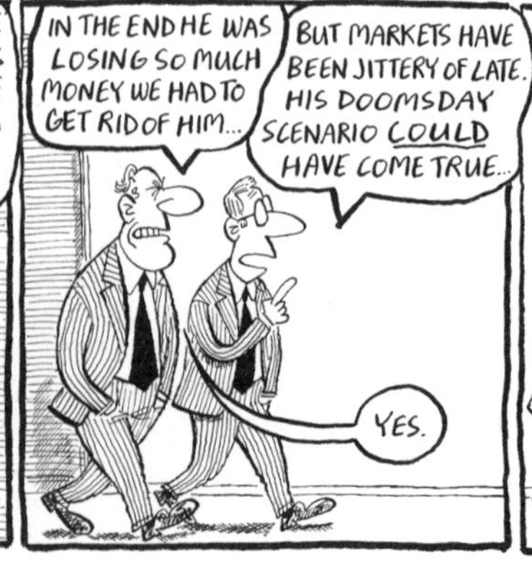
IN THE END HE WAS LOSING SO MUCH MONEY WE HAD TO GET RID OF HIM...
BUT MARKETS HAVE BEEN JITTERY OF LATE. HIS DOOMSDAY SCENARIO COULD HAVE COME TRUE...
YES.

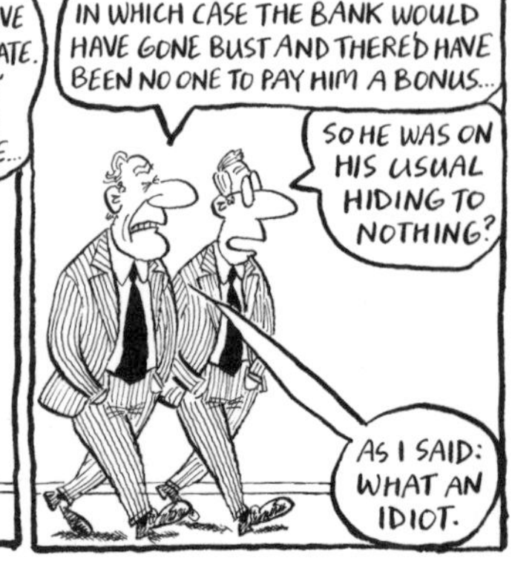
IN WHICH CASE THE BANK WOULD HAVE GONE BUST AND THERE'D HAVE BEEN NO ONE TO PAY HIM A BONUS...
SO HE WAS ON HIS USUAL HIDING TO NOTHING?
AS I SAID: WHAT AN IDIOT.

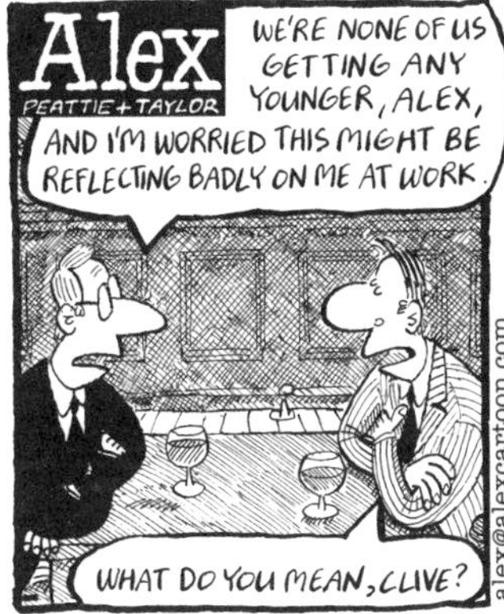
Alex
PEATTIE + TAYLOR
WE'RE NONE OF US GETTING ANY YOUNGER, ALEX, AND I'M WORRIED THIS MIGHT BE REFLECTING BADLY ON ME AT WORK.
WHAT DO YOU MEAN, CLIVE?

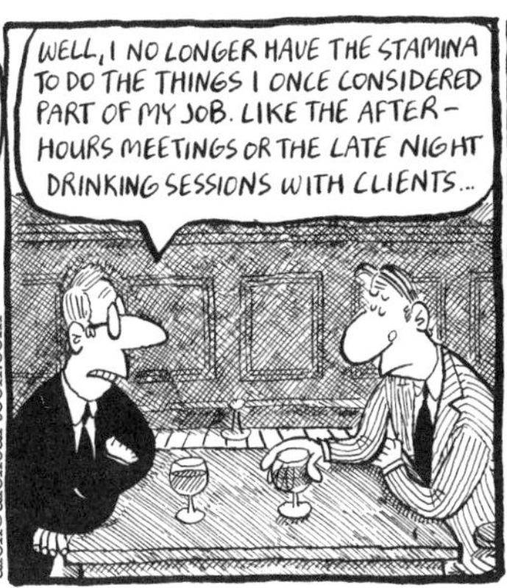
WELL, I NO LONGER HAVE THE STAMINA TO DO THE THINGS I ONCE CONSIDERED PART OF MY JOB. LIKE THE AFTER-HOURS MEETINGS OR THE LATE NIGHT DRINKING SESSIONS WITH CLIENTS...
alex@alexcartoon.com

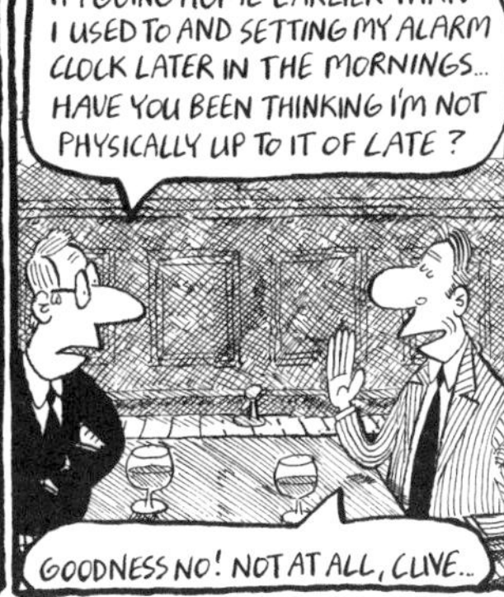
I'M GOING HOME EARLIER THAN I USED TO AND SETTING MY ALARM CLOCK LATER IN THE MORNINGS... HAVE YOU BEEN THINKING I'M NOT PHYSICALLY UP TO IT OF LATE?
GOODNESS NO! NOT AT ALL, CLIVE...

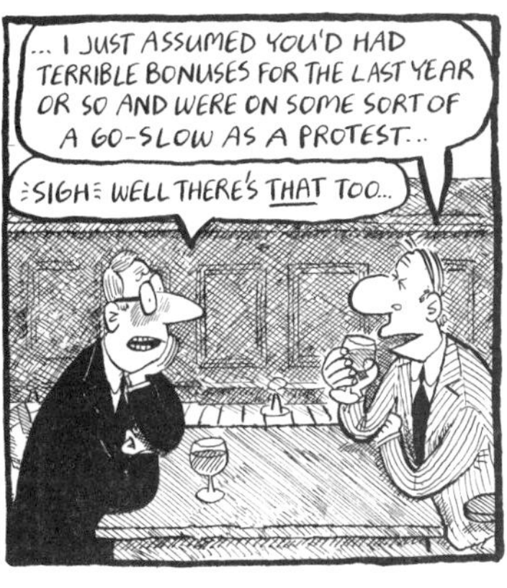
... I JUST ASSUMED YOU'D HAD TERRIBLE BONUSES FOR THE LAST YEAR OR SO AND WERE ON SOME SORT OF A GO-SLOW AS A PROTEST...
SIGH WELL THERE'S THAT TOO...

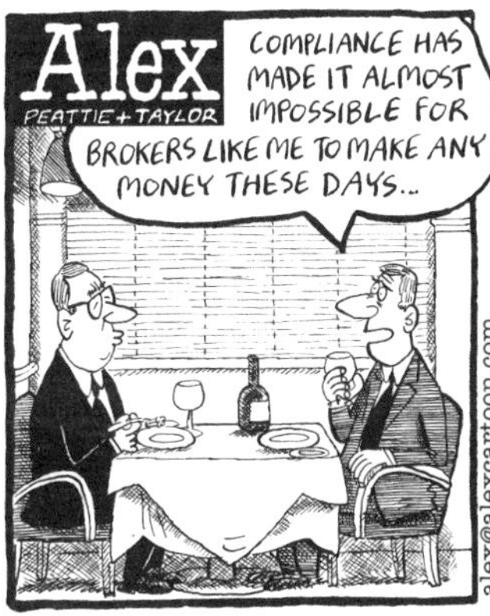
Alex
PEATTIE + TAYLOR
COMPLIANCE HAS MADE IT ALMOST IMPOSSIBLE FOR BROKERS LIKE ME TO MAKE ANY MONEY THESE DAYS...

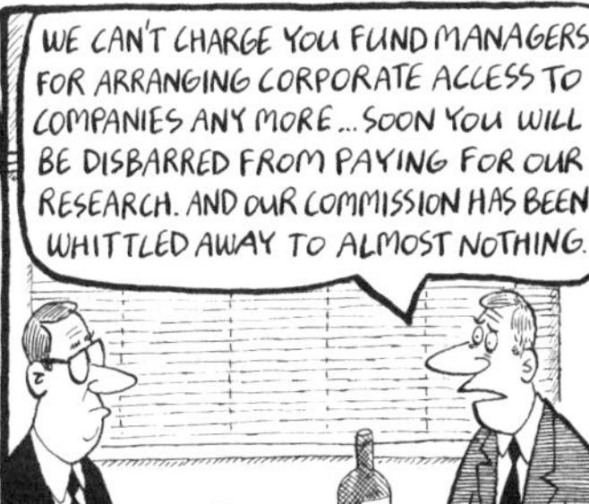
WE CAN'T CHARGE YOU FUND MANAGERS FOR ARRANGING CORPORATE ACCESS TO COMPANIES ANY MORE... SOON YOU WILL BE DISBARRED FROM PAYING FOR OUR RESEARCH. AND OUR COMMISSION HAS BEEN WHITTLED AWAY TO ALMOST NOTHING.
alex@alexcartoon.com

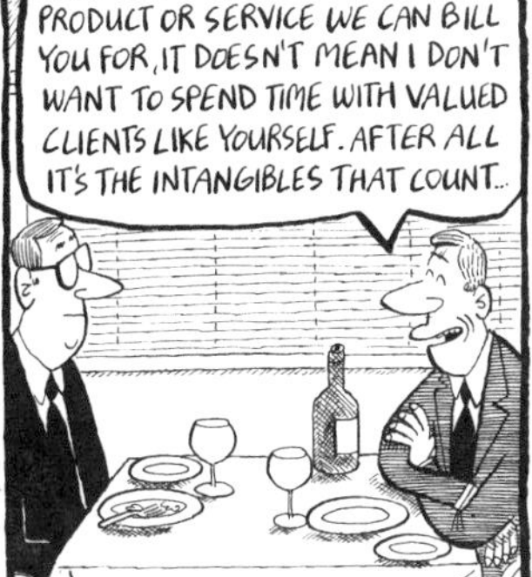
BUT JUST BECAUSE THERE'S NO PRODUCT OR SERVICE WE CAN BILL YOU FOR, IT DOESN'T MEAN I DON'T WANT TO SPEND TIME WITH VALUED CLIENTS LIKE YOURSELF. AFTER ALL IT'S THE INTANGIBLES THAT COUNT...

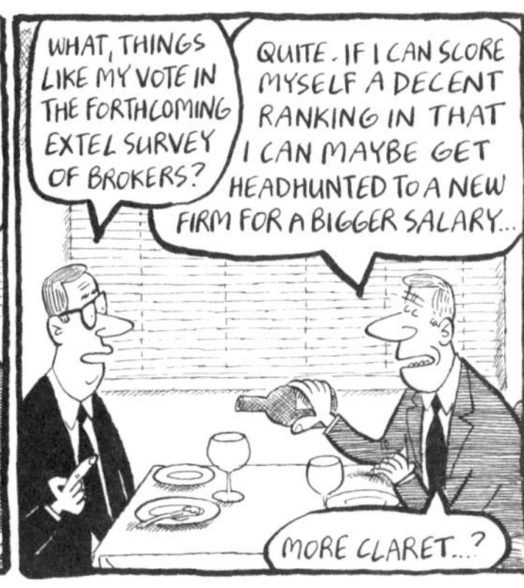
WHAT, THINGS LIKE MY VOTE IN THE FORTHCOMING EXTEL SURVEY OF BROKERS?
QUITE. IF I CAN SCORE MYSELF A DECENT RANKING IN THAT I CAN MAYBE GET HEADHUNTED TO A NEW FIRM FOR A BIGGER SALARY...
MORE CLARET...?

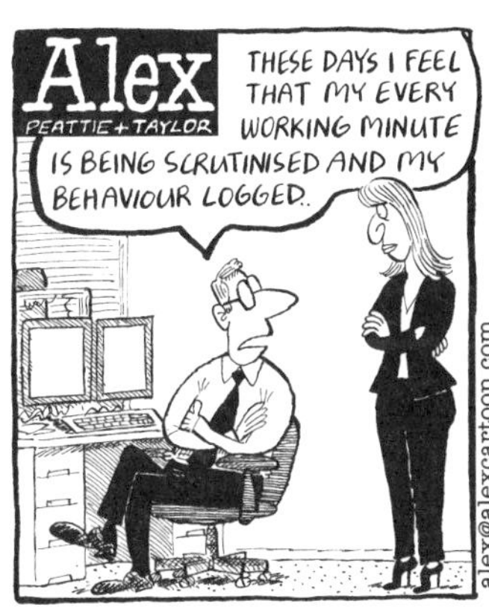
Alex
PEATTIE + TAYLOR
THESE DAYS I FEEL THAT MY EVERY WORKING MINUTE IS BEING SCRUTINISED AND MY BEHAVIOUR LOGGED.

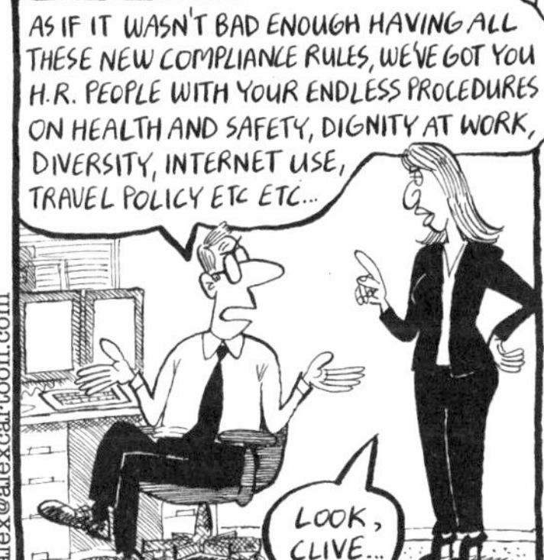
AS IF IT WASN'T BAD ENOUGH HAVING ALL THESE NEW COMPLIANCE RULES, WE'VE GOT YOU H.R. PEOPLE WITH YOUR ENDLESS PROCEDURES ON HEALTH AND SAFETY, DIGNITY AT WORK, DIVERSITY, INTERNET USE, TRAVEL POLICY ETC ETC...
LOOK, CLIVE...
alex@alexcartoon.com

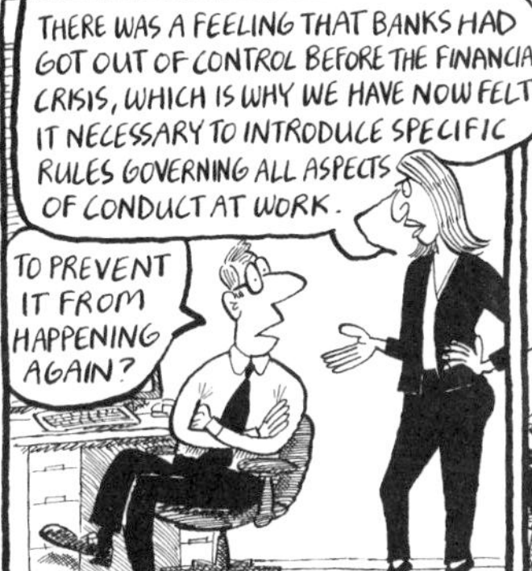
THERE WAS A FEELING THAT BANKS HAD GOT OUT OF CONTROL BEFORE THE FINANCIAL CRISIS, WHICH IS WHY WE HAVE NOW FELT IT NECESSARY TO INTRODUCE SPECIFIC RULES GOVERNING ALL ASPECTS OF CONDUCT AT WORK.
TO PREVENT IT FROM HAPPENING AGAIN?

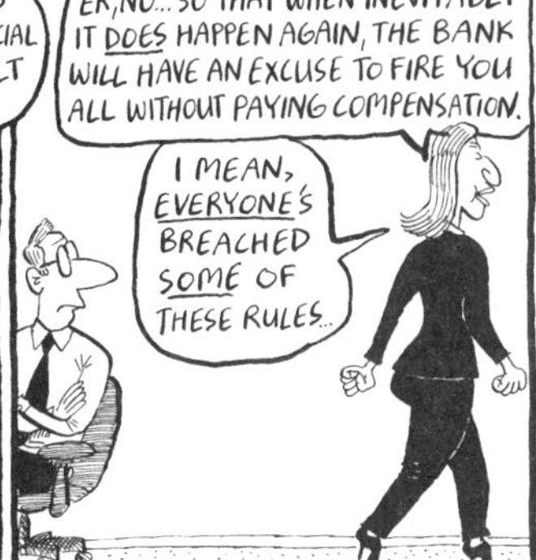
ER, NO... SO THAT WHEN INEVITABLY IT DOES HAPPEN AGAIN, THE BANK WILL HAVE AN EXCUSE TO FIRE YOU ALL WITHOUT PAYING COMPENSATION.
I MEAN, EVERYONE'S BREACHED SOME OF THESE RULES...

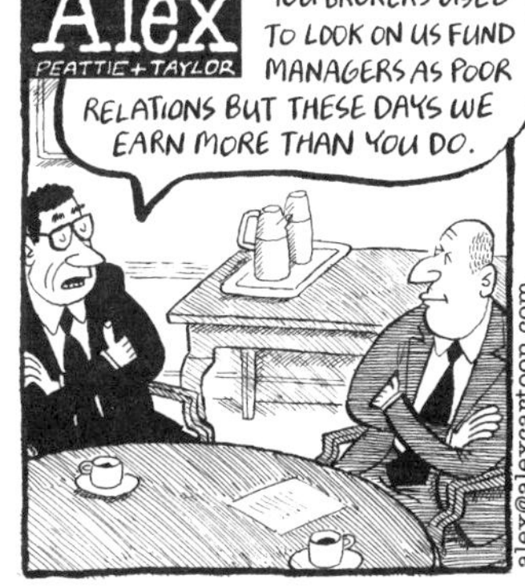
Alex
PEATTIE + TAYLOR
YOU BROKERS USED TO LOOK ON US FUND MANAGERS AS POOR RELATIONS BUT THESE DAYS WE EARN MORE THAN YOU DO.

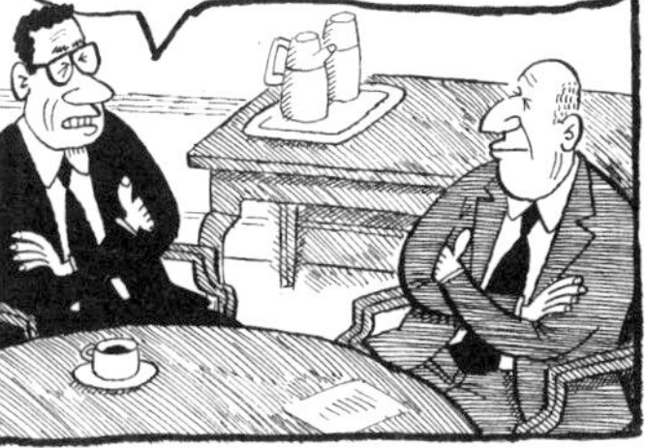
WITH INTEREST RATES AT ZERO PEOPLE CAN'T MAKE A RETURN ON THEIR MONEY BY LEAVING IT IN THE BANK, SO THEY NEED TO INVEST IT. HENCE OUR FUNDS ARE BIGGER AND WE CAN CREAM OFF MORE IN MANAGEMENT FEES...
alex@alexcartoon.com

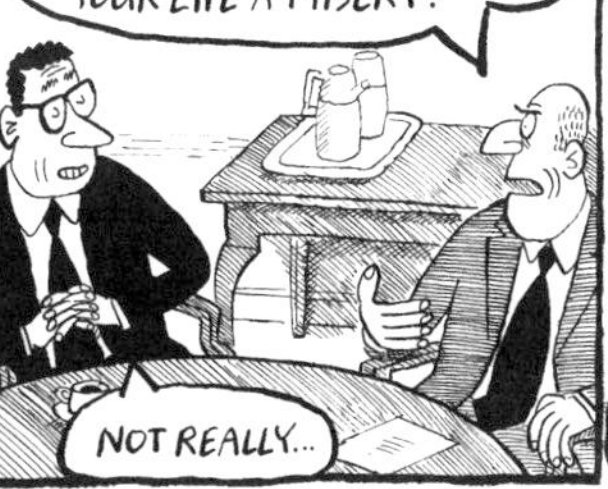
BUT SURELY THE MORE FINANCIAL RESPONSIBILITY YOU TAKE, THE MORE YOU HAVE COMPLIANCE ON YOUR BACK? DON'T YOU FIND THEIR ENDLESS NEW RULES ARE MAKING YOUR LIFE A MISERY?
NOT REALLY...

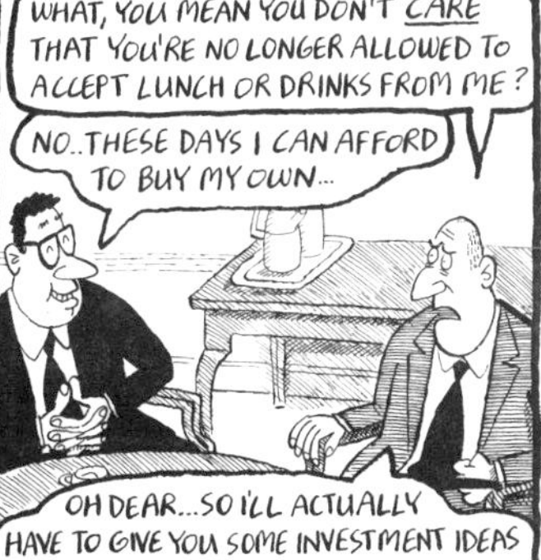
WHAT, YOU MEAN YOU DON'T CARE THAT YOU'RE NO LONGER ALLOWED TO ACCEPT LUNCH OR DRINKS FROM ME?
NO.. THESE DAYS I CAN AFFORD TO BUY MY OWN...
OH DEAR... SO I'LL ACTUALLY HAVE TO GIVE YOU SOME INVESTMENT IDEAS TO GET YOUR BUSINESS? DRAT...

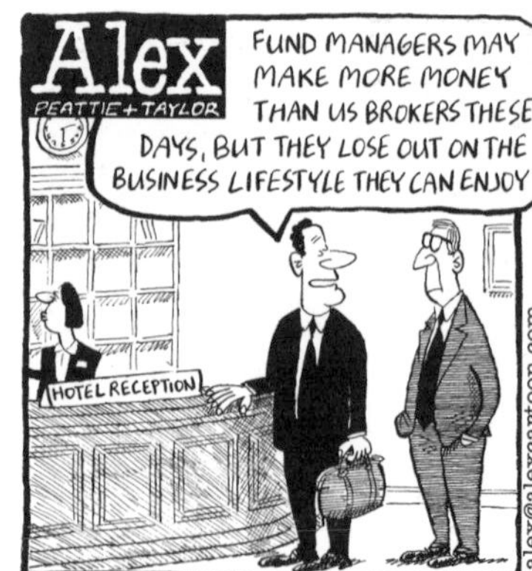
Alex
PEATTIE+TAYLOR
FUND MANAGERS MAY MAKE MORE MONEY THAN US BROKERS THESE DAYS, BUT THEY LOSE OUT ON THE BUSINESS LIFESTYLE THEY CAN ENJOY
HOTEL RECEPTION

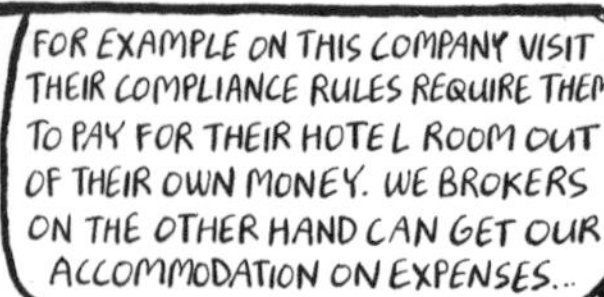
FOR EXAMPLE ON THIS COMPANY VISIT THEIR COMPLIANCE RULES REQUIRE THEM TO PAY FOR THEIR HOTEL ROOM OUT OF THEIR OWN MONEY. WE BROKERS ON THE OTHER HAND CAN GET OUR ACCOMMODATION ON EXPENSES...

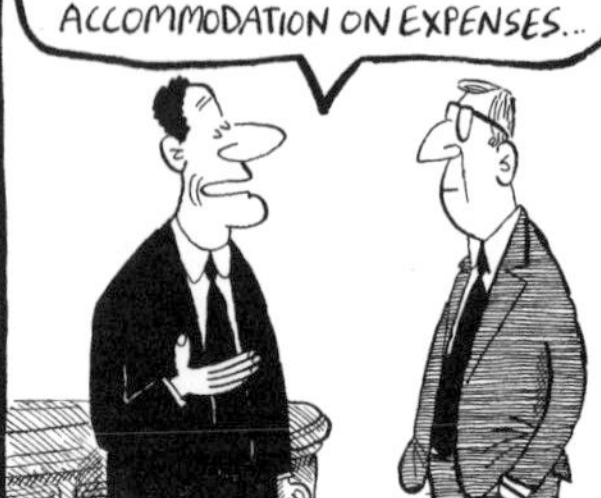
alex@alexcartoon.com

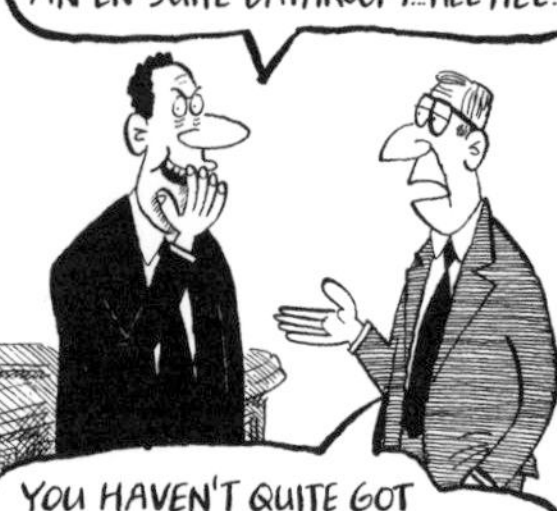
THE RESULT IS I'M STAYING IN A LUXURY SUITE WHILE MY CLIENT IS IN A TINY SINGLE ROOM WITHOUT EVEN AN EN-SUITE BATHROOM... HEE HEE...
YOU HAVEN'T QUITE GOT HOW IT WORKS YET, HAVE YOU?

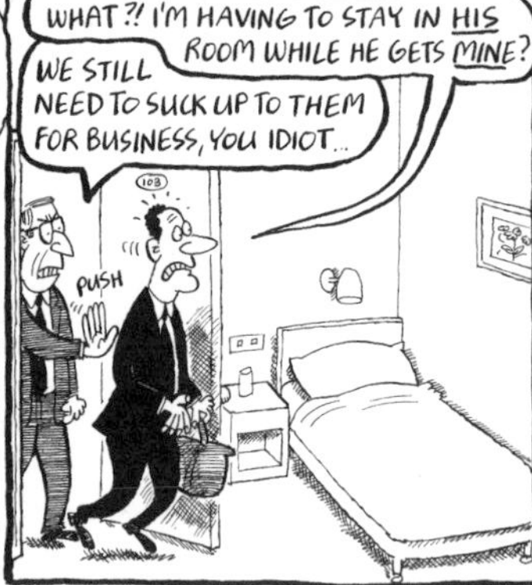
WHAT?! I'M HAVING TO STAY IN HIS ROOM WHILE HE GETS MINE?
WE STILL NEED TO SUCK UP TO THEM FOR BUSINESS, YOU IDIOT...
PUSH

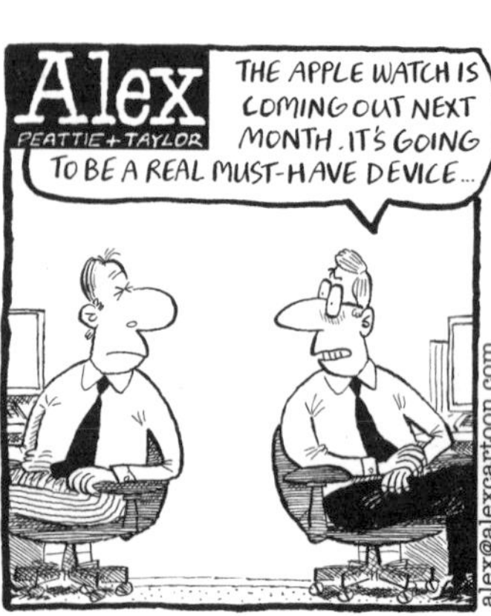
Alex
PEATTIE+TAYLOR
THE APPLE WATCH IS COMING OUT NEXT MONTH. IT'S GOING TO BE A REAL MUST-HAVE DEVICE...
alex@alexcartoon.com

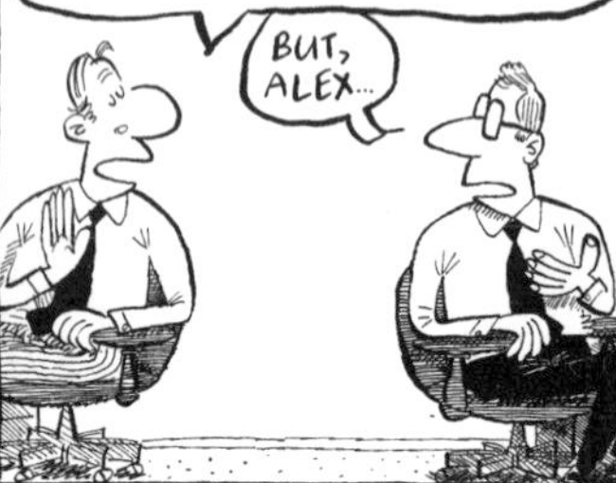
I'M SURE IT'S A STATE-OF-THE-ART PIECE OF KIT, CLIVE, BUT DON'T YOU SOMETIMES TIRE OF THE RELENTLESS PACE OF TECHNOLOGY TODAY? ITS CONSTANT STRIVING FOR PROGRESS AND INNOVATION?
BUT, ALEX...

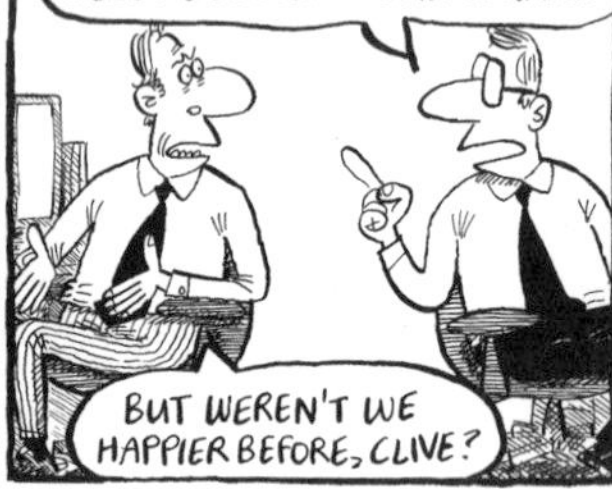
THIS GADGET CONTAINS THE MOST AMAZING FEATURES: IT'S A MOVIE PLAYER, A SOUND SYSTEM, A HEART RATE MONITOR, A PERSONAL ORGANISER AND A MOBILE PHONE, AS WELL AS BEING A PRECISION WATCH.
BUT WEREN'T WE HAPPIER BEFORE, CLIVE?
WHEN EACH ONE OF THOSE THINGS WAS A STATUS SYMBOL IN ITS OWN RIGHT?
IT CERTAINLY MEANT YOU COULD SPEND MORE MONEY ON THEM...
PEOPLE JUST DON'T UNDERSTAND CONSPICUOUS CONSUMPTION THESE DAYS...

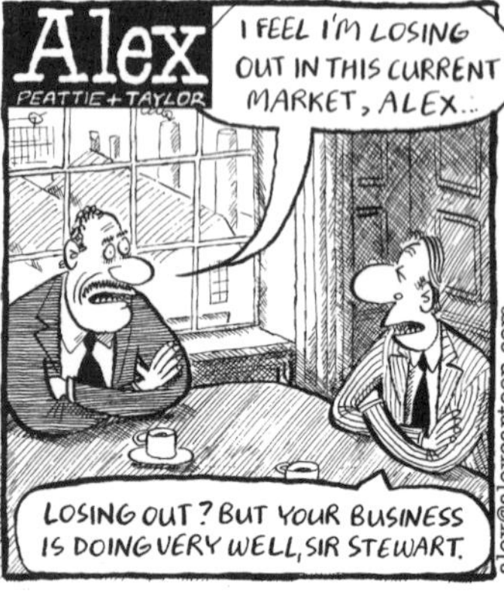
Alex
PEATTIE+TAYLOR
I FEEL I'M LOSING OUT IN THIS CURRENT MARKET, ALEX...
LOSING OUT? BUT YOUR BUSINESS IS DOING VERY WELL, SIR STEWART.
alex@alexcartoon.com

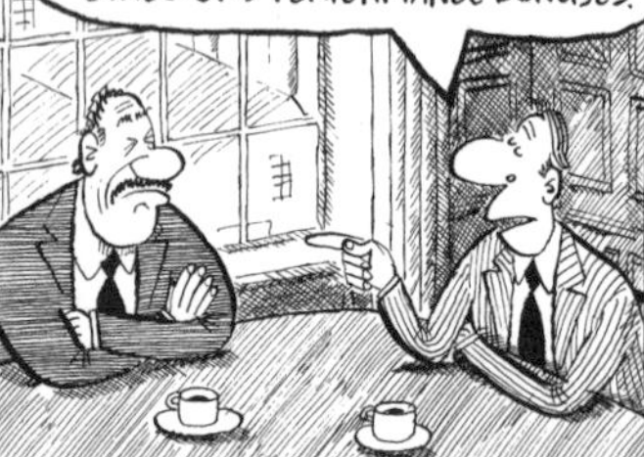
THANKS TO MY ADVICE YOUR COMPANY HAS TAKEN ADVANTAGE OF NEAR-ZERO INTEREST RATES TO BORROW MONEY AND BUY BACK ITS OWN SHARES, THUS BOOSTING THEIR PRICE AND TRIGGERING YOUR DIRECTORS' PERFORMANCE BONUSES.

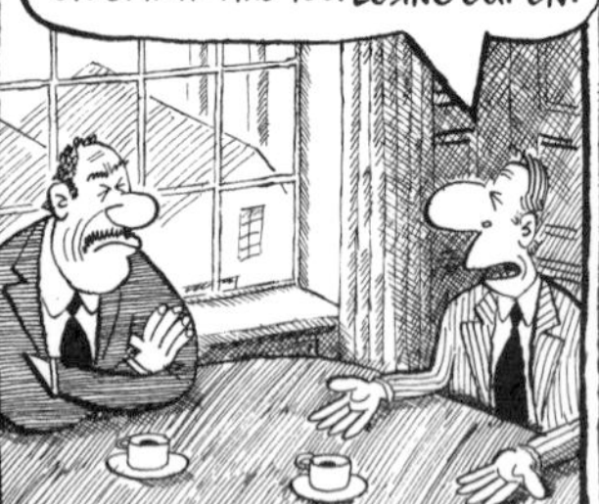
IN OTHER WORDS YOUR COMPANY'S VALUE IS SOARING AND YOU'RE MAKING SURE-FIRE MONEY WITHOUT HAVING TO DO ANY WORK... WHAT ON EARTH ARE YOU LOSING OUT ON?

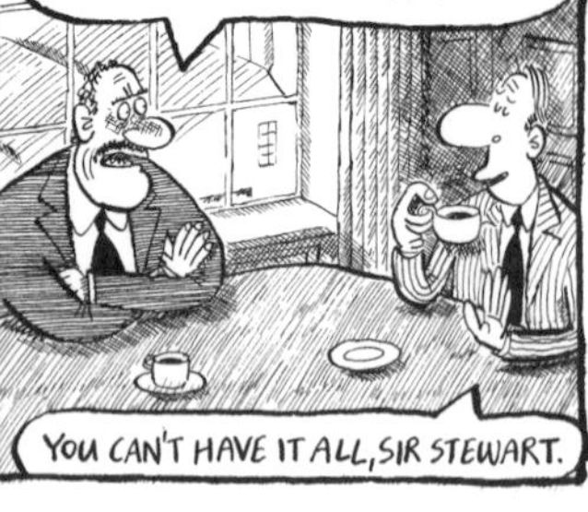
ER, THE VAGUE SENSE OF MORAL SUPERIORITY I USED TO FEEL OVER YOU BANKERS BACK IN THE DAY WHEN I ACTUALLY USED TO MAKE A PRODUCT AND THINK IN THE LONG TERM...
YOU CAN'T HAVE IT ALL, SIR STEWART.

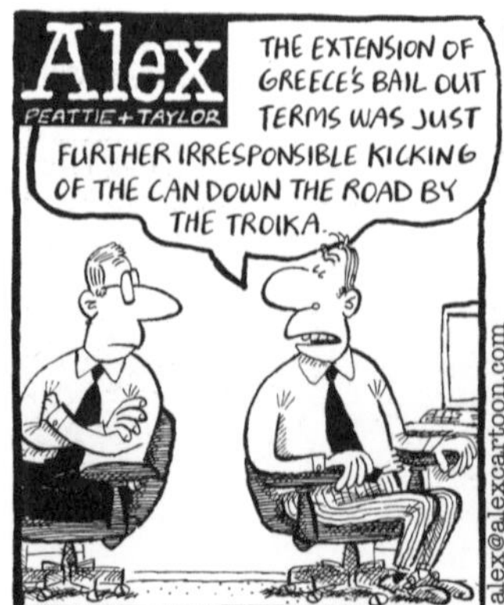
Alex
PEATTIE+TAYLOR
THE EXTENSION OF GREECE'S BAIL OUT TERMS WAS JUST FURTHER IRRESPONSIBLE KICKING OF THE CAN DOWN THE ROAD BY THE TROIKA...

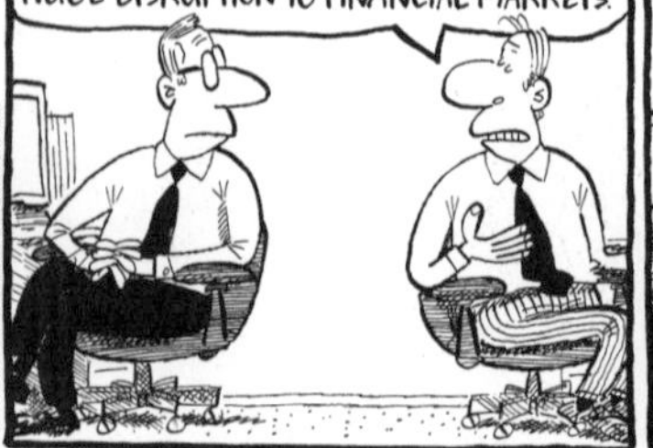
THE GREEKS AREN'T GOING TO SUDDENLY FIND THE MONEY TO PAY OFF THEIR LOANS, SO EITHER THE DEBT GETS WRITTEN OFF OR GREECE GETS KICKED OUT OF THE EURO... EITHER SCENARIO WILL BE SURE TO CAUSE HUGE DISRUPTION TO FINANCIAL MARKETS.
alex@alexcartoon.com

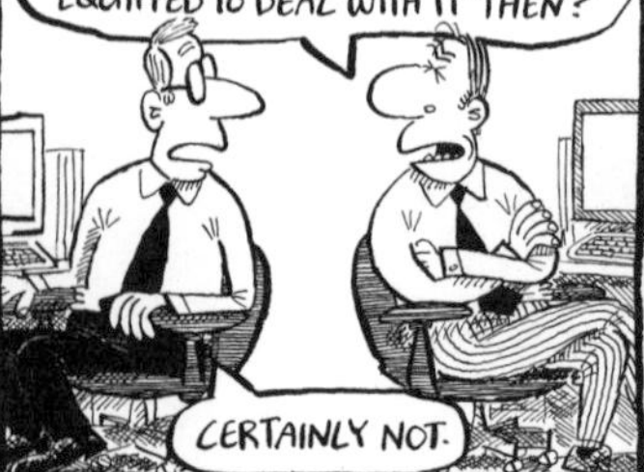
INSTEAD OF SORTING THE PROBLEM AT THE END OF FEBRUARY AND TAKING THE ECONOMIC PAIN THEN, WE'RE NOW GOING TO HAVE TO FACE IT ALL AGAIN 4 MONTHS LATER. DOES ANYONE REALLY THINK WE'LL BE BETTER EQUIPPED TO DEAL WITH IT THEN?
CERTAINLY NOT.

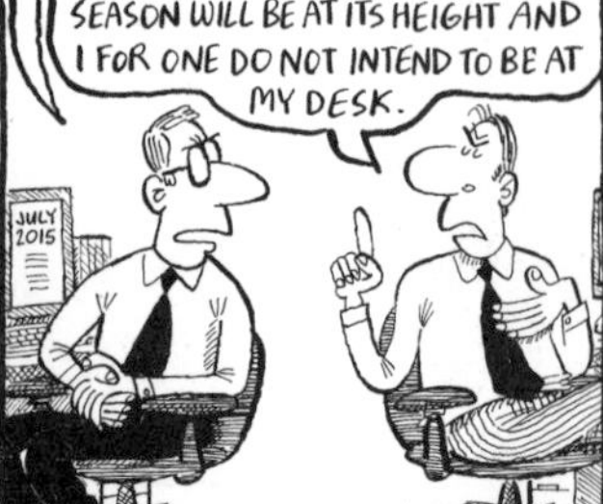
IT'S GOING TO CLASH WITH WIMBLEDON, HENLEY, THE OPEN AND THE ASHES...
EXACTLY. THE CORPORATE HOSPITALITY SEASON WILL BE AT ITS HEIGHT AND I FOR ONE DO NOT INTEND TO BE AT MY DESK.
JULY 2015

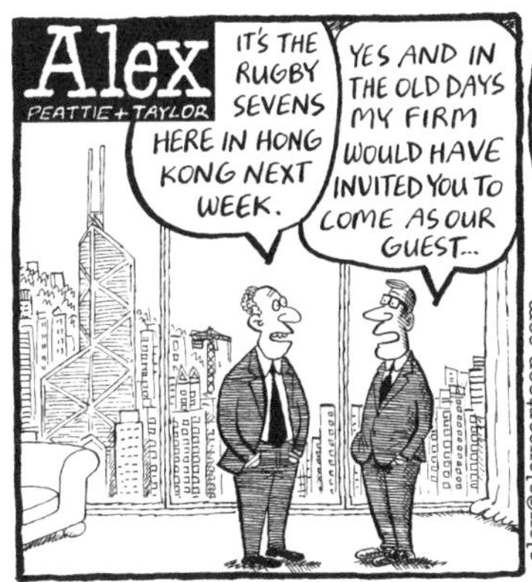
Alex
PEATTIE + TAYLOR
IT'S THE RUGBY SEVENS HERE IN HONG KONG NEXT WEEK.
YES AND IN THE OLD DAYS MY FIRM WOULD HAVE INVITED YOU TO COME AS OUR GUEST...
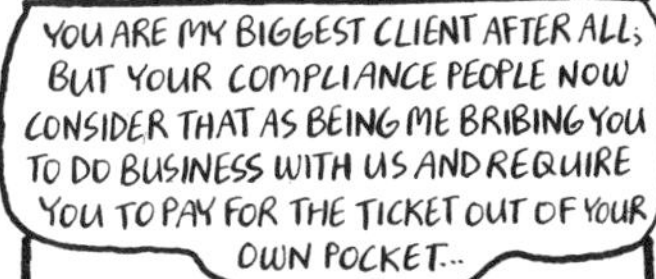
YOU ARE MY BIGGEST CLIENT AFTER ALL; BUT YOUR COMPLIANCE PEOPLE NOW CONSIDER THAT AS BEING ME BRIBING YOU TO DO BUSINESS WITH US AND REQUIRE YOU TO PAY FOR THE TICKET OUT OF YOUR OWN POCKET...
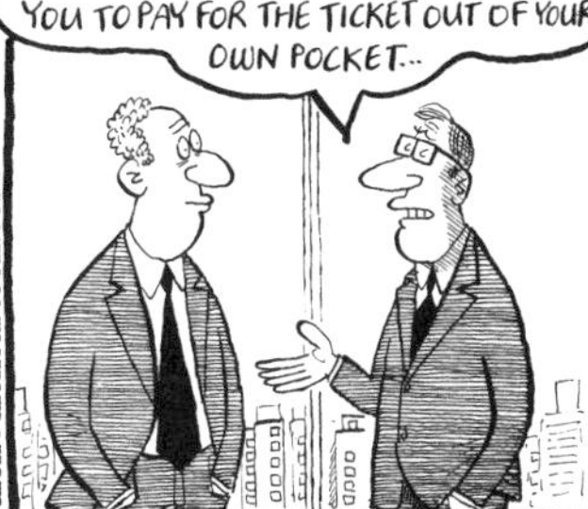
alex@alexcartoon.com
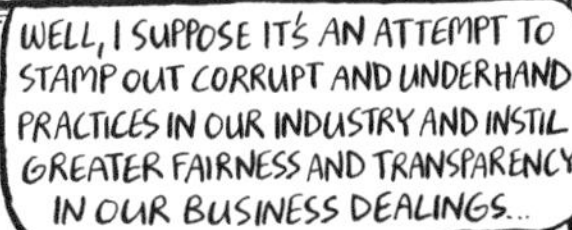
WELL, I SUPPOSE IT'S AN ATTEMPT TO STAMP OUT CORRUPT AND UNDERHAND PRACTICES IN OUR INDUSTRY AND INSTIL GREATER FAIRNESS AND TRANSPARENCY IN OUR BUSINESS DEALINGS...
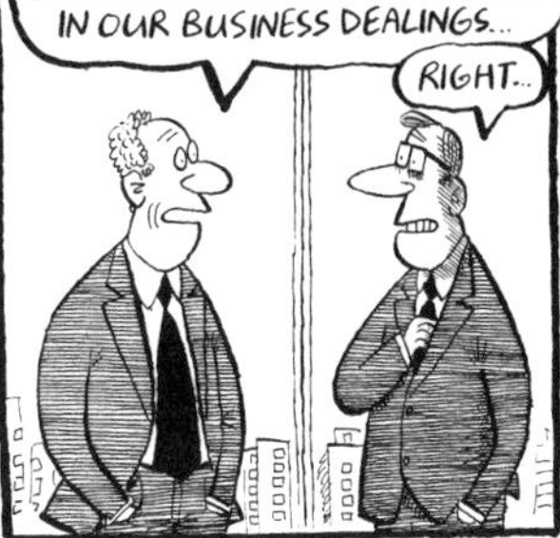
RIGHT...
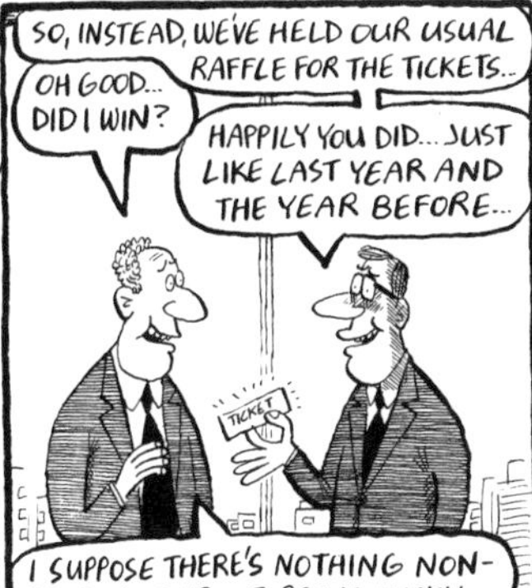
SO, INSTEAD, WE'VE HELD OUR USUAL RAFFLE FOR THE TICKETS...
OH GOOD... DID I WIN?
HAPPILY YOU DID... JUST LIKE LAST YEAR AND THE YEAR BEFORE...
TICKET
I SUPPOSE THERE'S NOTHING NON-COMPLIANT ABOUT BEING LUCKY...

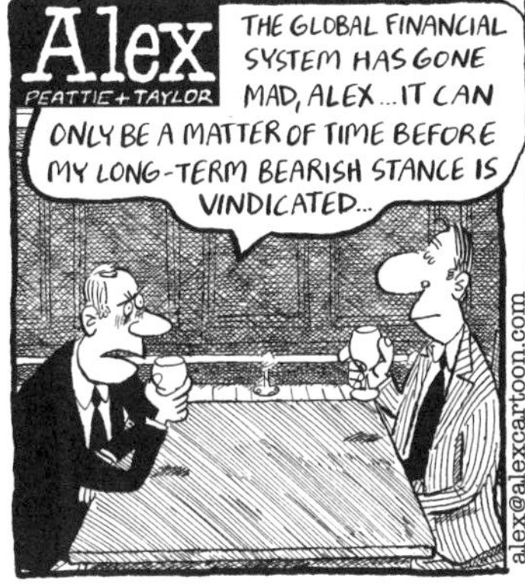
Alex
PEATTIE + TAYLOR
THE GLOBAL FINANCIAL SYSTEM HAS GONE MAD, ALEX... IT CAN ONLY BE A MATTER OF TIME BEFORE MY LONG-TERM BEARISH STANCE IS VINDICATED...
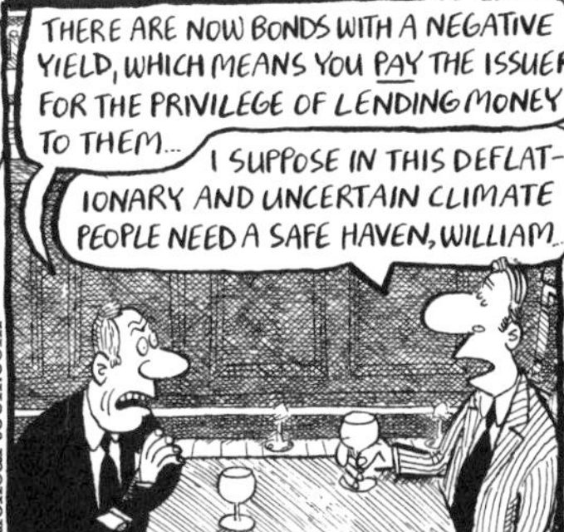
THERE ARE NOW BONDS WITH A NEGATIVE YIELD, WHICH MEANS YOU PAY THE ISSUER FOR THE PRIVILEGE OF LENDING MONEY TO THEM...
I SUPPOSE IN THIS DEFLATIONARY AND UNCERTAIN CLIMATE PEOPLE NEED A SAFE HAVEN, WILLIAM...
alex@alexcartoon.com
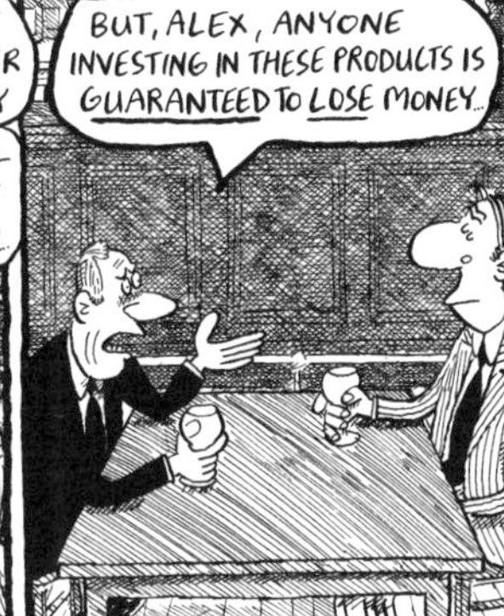
BUT, ALEX, ANYONE INVESTING IN THESE PRODUCTS IS GUARANTEED TO LOSE MONEY...
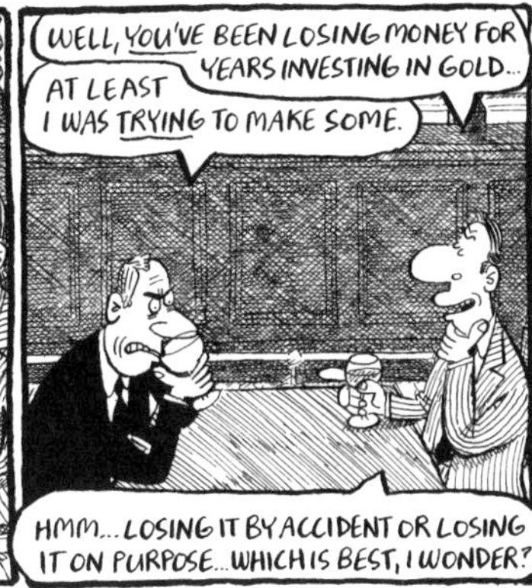
WELL, YOU'VE BEEN LOSING MONEY FOR YEARS INVESTING IN GOLD...
AT LEAST I WAS TRYING TO MAKE SOME.
HMM... LOSING IT BY ACCIDENT OR LOSING IT ON PURPOSE... WHICH IS BEST, I WONDER?

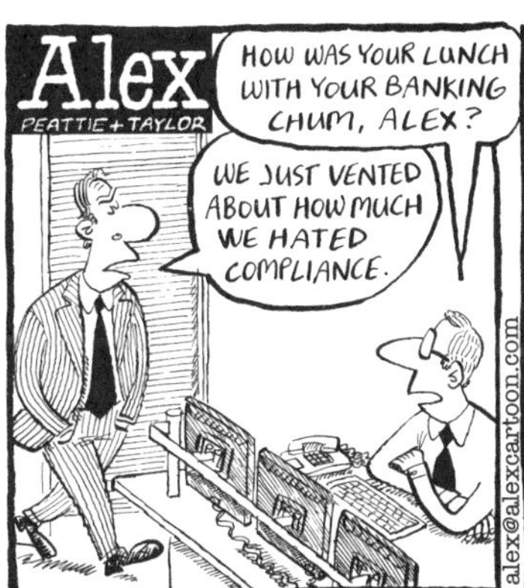
Alex
PEATTIE + TAYLOR
HOW WAS YOUR LUNCH WITH YOUR BANKING CHUM, ALEX?
WE JUST VENTED ABOUT HOW MUCH WE HATED COMPLIANCE.
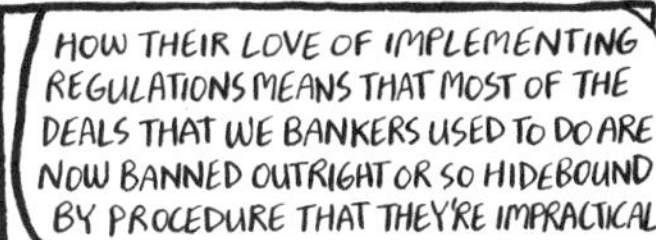
HOW THEIR LOVE OF IMPLEMENTING REGULATIONS MEANS THAT MOST OF THE DEALS THAT WE BANKERS USED TO DO ARE NOW BANNED OUTRIGHT OR SO HIDEBOUND BY PROCEDURE THAT THEY'RE IMPRACTICAL.
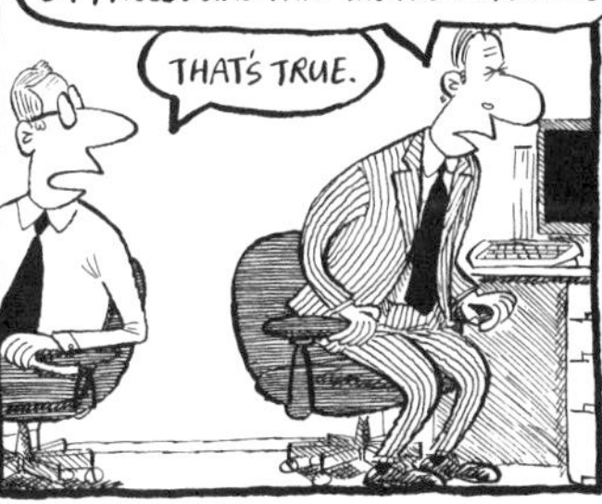
alex@alexcartoon.com
THAT'S TRUE.
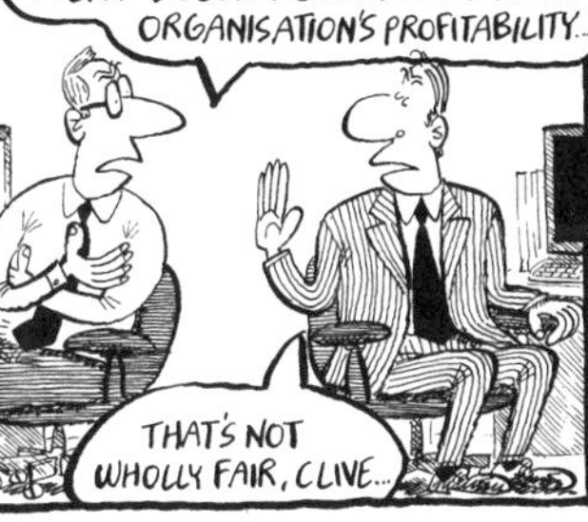
WHAT THOSE MIDDLE OFFICE MEDDLERS DON'T UNDERSTAND IS THAT IF WE DON'T DO ANY DEALS THE BANK DOESN'T MAKE ANY MONEY. AFTER ALL, THEIR DEPARTMENT DOESN'T CONTRIBUTE TO THE ORGANISATION'S PROFITABILITY...
THAT'S NOT WHOLLY FAIR, CLIVE...
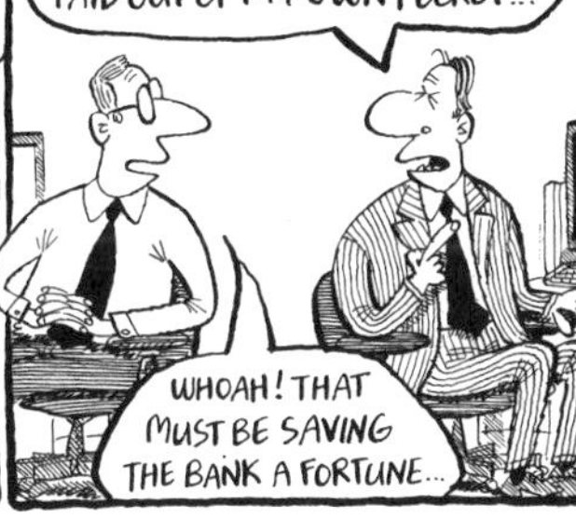
ONCE UPON A TIME I'D HAVE EXPENSED THE LUNCH, BUT THE PROCESS HAS BEEN MADE SO COMPLICATED THAT I COULDN'T BE BOTHERED AND JUST PAID OUT OF MY OWN POCKET...
WHOAH! THAT MUST BE SAVING THE BANK A FORTUNE...

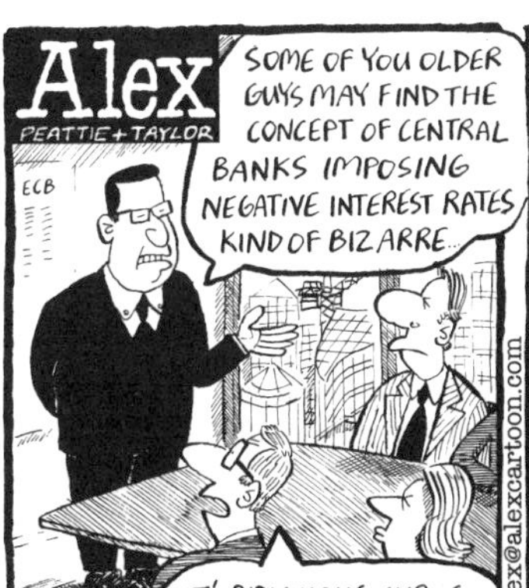
Alex
PEATTIE + TAYLOR
SOME OF YOU OLDER GUYS MAY FIND THE CONCEPT OF CENTRAL BANKS IMPOSING NEGATIVE INTEREST RATES KIND OF BIZARRE...
ECB
IT'S RIDICULOUS, CYRUS...
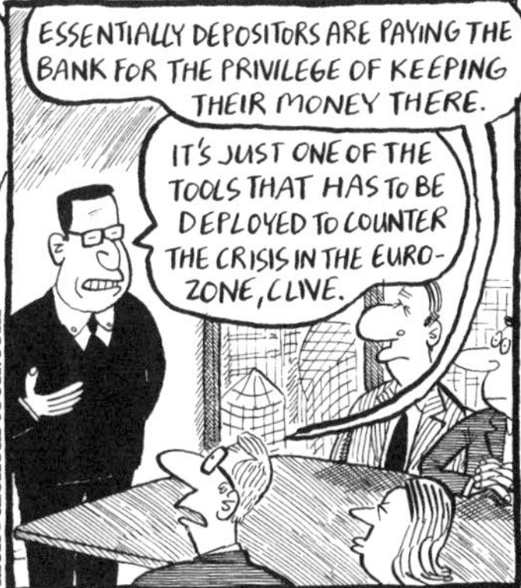
ESSENTIALLY DEPOSITORS ARE PAYING THE BANK FOR THE PRIVILEGE OF KEEPING THEIR MONEY THERE.
IT'S JUST ONE OF THE TOOLS THAT HAS TO BE DEPLOYED TO COUNTER THE CRISIS IN THE EURO-ZONE, CLIVE.
alex@alexcartoon.com
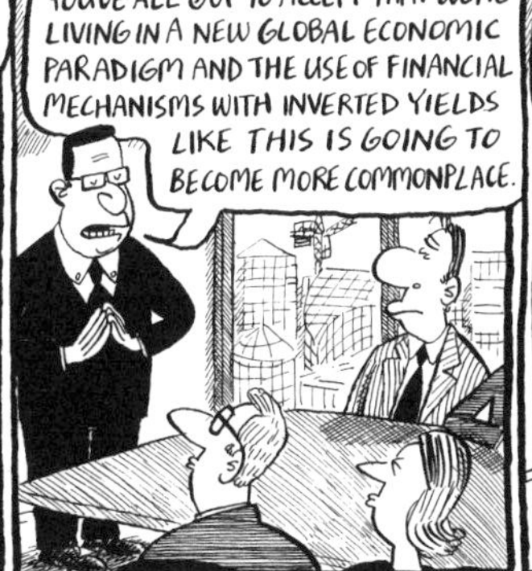
YOU'VE ALL GOT TO ACCEPT THAT WE'RE LIVING IN A NEW GLOBAL ECONOMIC PARADIGM AND THE USE OF FINANCIAL MECHANISMS WITH INVERTED YIELDS LIKE THIS IS GOING TO BECOME MORE COMMONPLACE.
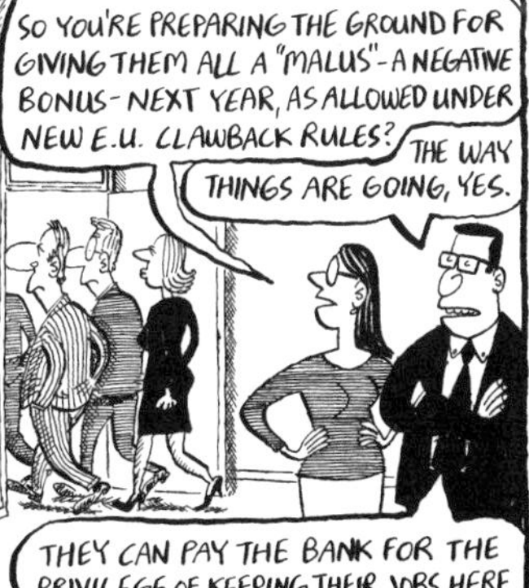
SO YOU'RE PREPARING THE GROUND FOR GIVING THEM ALL A "MALUS" - A NEGATIVE BONUS - NEXT YEAR, AS ALLOWED UNDER NEW E.U. CLAWBACK RULES?
THE WAY THINGS ARE GOING, YES.
THEY CAN PAY THE BANK FOR THE PRIVILEGE OF KEEPING THEIR JOBS HERE.

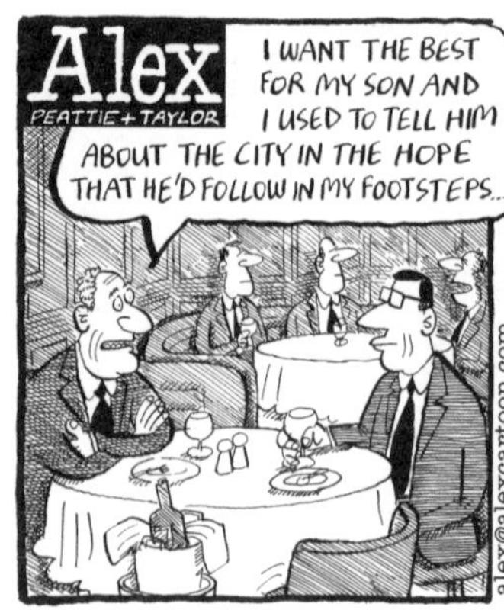
Alex
PEATTIE + TAYLOR
I WANT THE BEST FOR MY SON AND I USED TO TELL HIM ABOUT THE CITY IN THE HOPE THAT HE'D FOLLOW IN MY FOOTSTEPS...
alex@alexcartoon.com

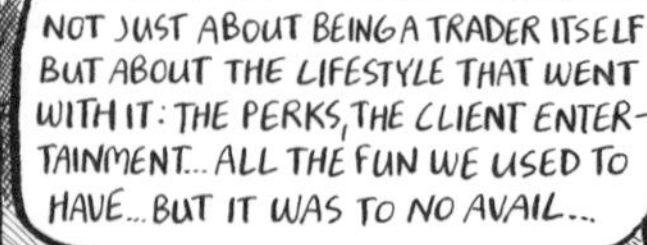
NOT JUST ABOUT BEING A TRADER ITSELF BUT ABOUT THE LIFESTYLE THAT WENT WITH IT: THE PERKS, THE CLIENT ENTERTAINMENT... ALL THE FUN WE USED TO HAVE... BUT IT WAS TO NO AVAIL...

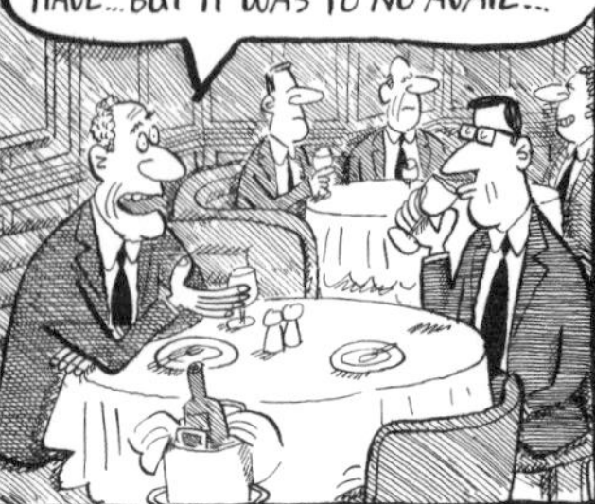

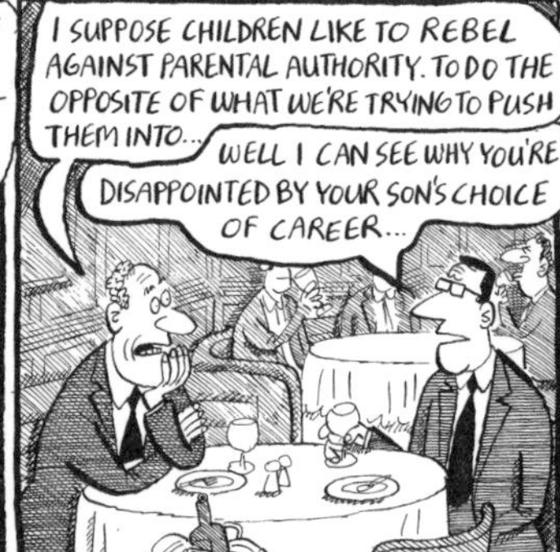
I SUPPOSE CHILDREN LIKE TO REBEL AGAINST PARENTAL AUTHORITY. TO DO THE OPPOSITE OF WHAT WE'RE TRYING TO PUSH THEM INTO...
WELL I CAN SEE WHY YOU'RE DISAPPOINTED BY YOUR SON'S CHOICE OF CAREER...

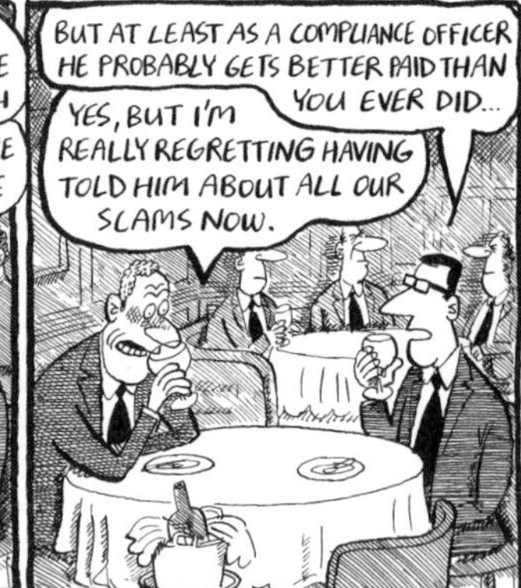
BUT AT LEAST AS A COMPLIANCE OFFICER HE PROBABLY GETS BETTER PAID THAN YOU EVER DID...
YES, BUT I'M REALLY REGRETTING HAVING TOLD HIM ABOUT ALL OUR SCAMS NOW.

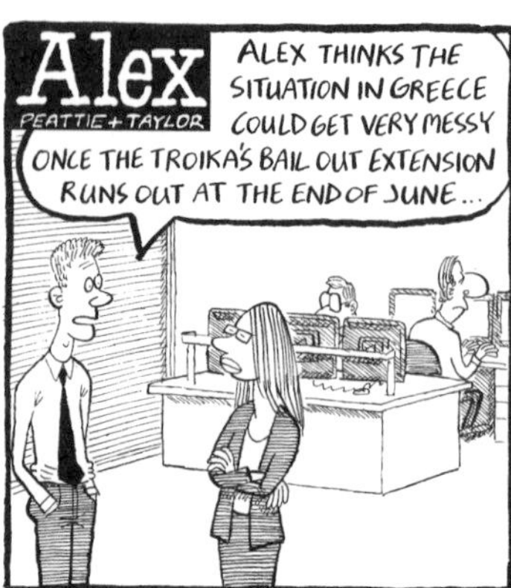
Alex
PEATTIE + TAYLOR
ALEX THINKS THE SITUATION IN GREECE COULD GET VERY MESSY ONCE THE TROIKA'S BAIL OUT EXTENSION RUNS OUT AT THE END OF JUNE...

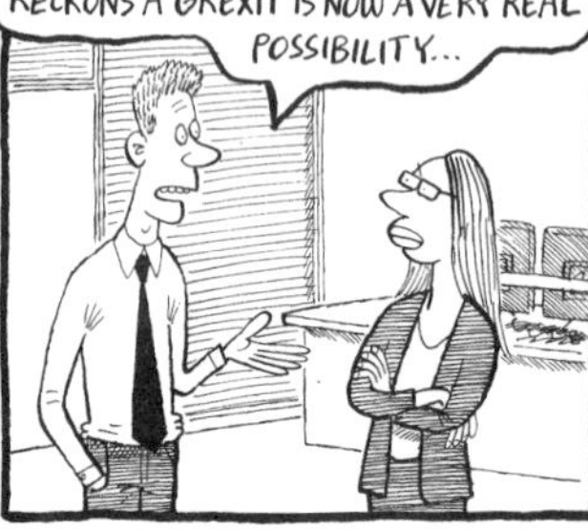
alex@alexcartoon.com
THE GREEKS ARE PLAYING HARDBALL AND IF THE GERMANS DON'T CALL THEIR BLUFF THE CONTAGION COULD SPREAD TO THE REST OF SOUTHERN EUROPE, SO ALEX RECKONS A GREXIT IS NOW A VERY REAL POSSIBILITY...
HE SAYS HIS ADVICE IS THAT IF WE HAVE ANY SUMMER HOLIDAY PLANS WE SHOULD CANCEL THEM...
HE MUST BE ANTICIPATING US ALL HAVING TO WORK FLAT OUT TO HANDLE THE MARKET CHAOS...
SO YOU THINK THERE'LL BE SOME NICE CHEAP HOLIDAYS GOING IN GREECE COME AUGUST?
ONCE THE NEW DRACHMA IS ISSUED AND THEN TANKS IMMEDIATELY, YES. I MIGHT BUY MYSELF AN ISLAND...
THAT'LL BE HANDY FOR WHEN THE BALLOON REALLY GOES UP...

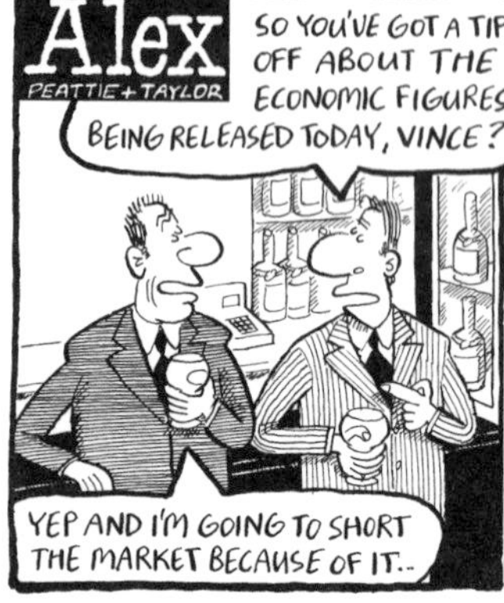
Alex
PEATTIE + TAYLOR
SO YOU'VE GOT A TIP OFF ABOUT THE ECONOMIC FIGURES BEING RELEASED TODAY, VINCE?
YEP AND I'M GOING TO SHORT THE MARKET BECAUSE OF IT...
alex@alexcartoon.com

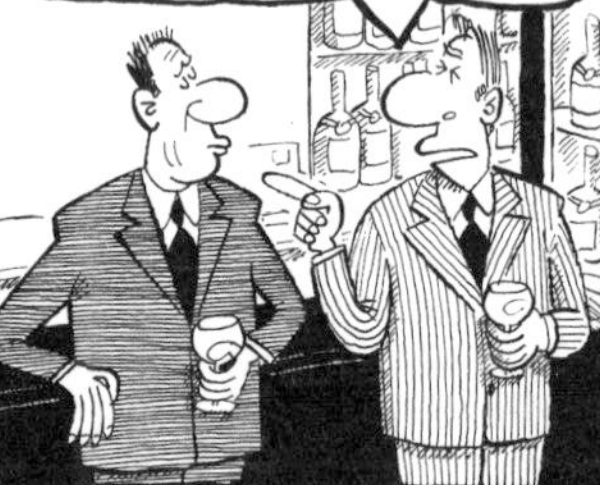
YOU SEE, THAT'S ONE OF THE REASONS THE PUBLIC HATES BANKERS: BECAUSE TRADERS LIKE YOU USE SHORT-SELLING AS A WAY OF MAKING MONEY OUT OF A STOCK MARKET COLLAPSE...

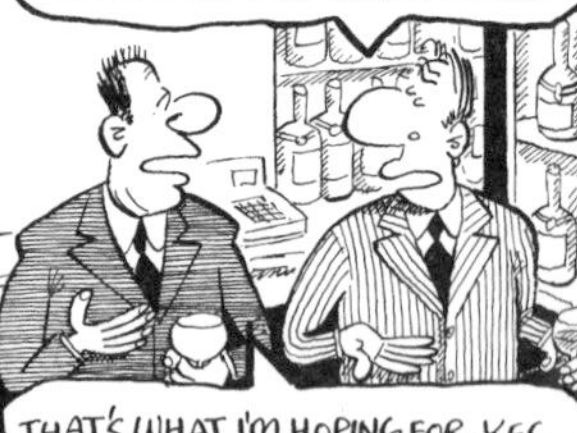
THEY PERCEIVE YOU AS CYNICALLY AND SELF-INTERESTEDLY WISHING FOR THE SORT OF ECONOMIC NEWS THAT WILL CAUSE A DROP IN BUSINESS CONFIDENCE AND A SUBSEQUENT FALL IN SHARE PRICES.
THAT'S WHAT I'M HOPING FOR, YES...

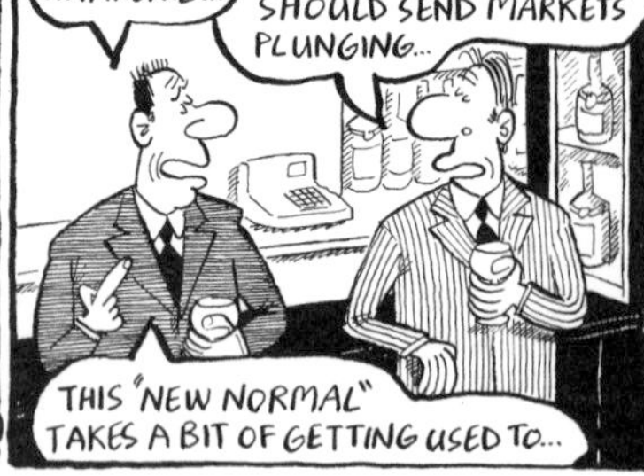
SOME GOOD NEWS... G.D.P. FIGURES ARE UP APPARENTLY...
AND THE FEAR THAT CENTRAL BANKS WILL RAISE INTEREST RATES AS A RESULT AND END THE CHEAP CREDIT BOOM SHOULD SEND MARKETS PLUNGING...
THIS "NEW NORMAL" TAKES A BIT OF GETTING USED TO...

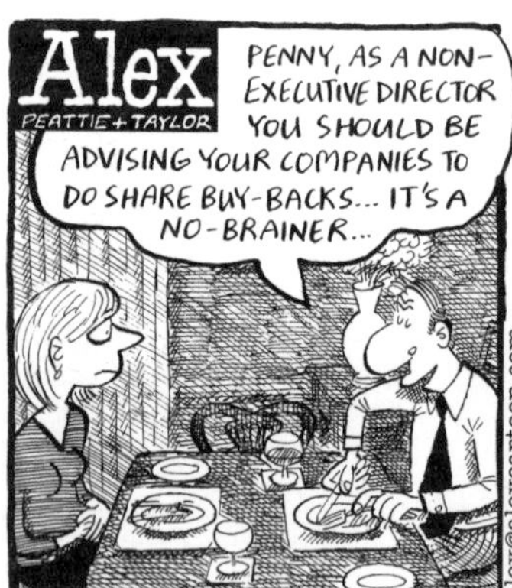
Alex
PEATTIE + TAYLOR
PENNY, AS A NON-EXECUTIVE DIRECTOR YOU SHOULD BE ADVISING YOUR COMPANIES TO DO SHARE BUY-BACKS... IT'S A NO-BRAINER...
alex@alexcartoon.com

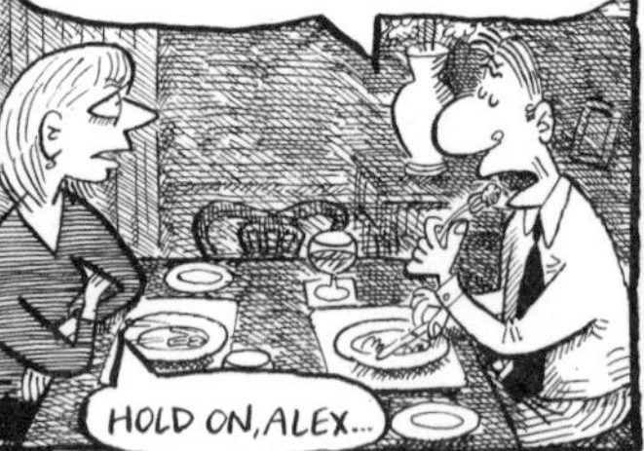
THE COMPANY BUYS ITS OWN SHARES WHICH BOOSTS THE PRICE. SO YOUR SHAREHOLDERS SEE THE VALUE OF THEIR INVESTMENT RISE AND THE DIRECTORS GET BONUSES FOR PRESIDING OVER A PROFITABLE FIRM... EVERYONE WINS!
HOLD ON, ALEX...

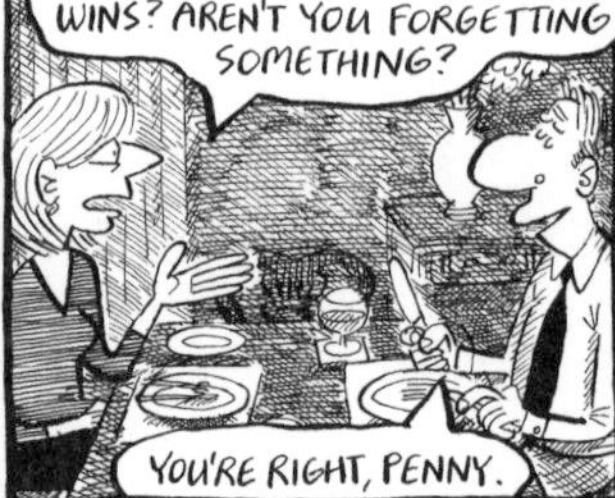
YOU'RE SUGGESTING A SCHEME THAT IGNORES THE COMPANY'S ACTUAL BUSINESS AND JUST ARTIFICIALLY INFLATES ITS VALUE BY FINANCIAL TRICKERY AND YOU SAY EVERYONE WINS? AREN'T YOU FORGETTING SOMETHING?
YOU'RE RIGHT, PENNY.

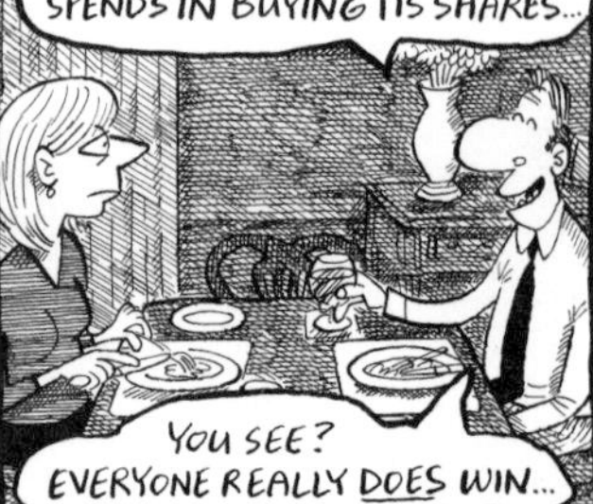
THERE'S US BANKERS TOO... WE MAKE 2% IN FEES FOR ORGANISING THE BOND ISSUE BY WHICH THE COMPANY BORROWS THE MONEY THAT IT THEN SPENDS IN BUYING ITS SHARES...
YOU SEE? EVERYONE REALLY DOES WIN...

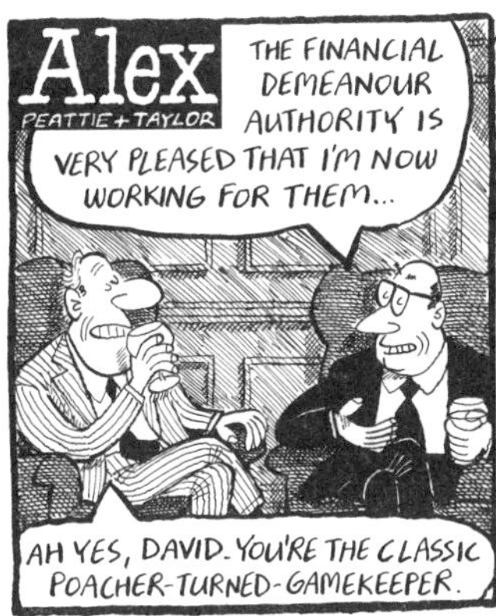
Alex
PEATTIE + TAYLOR
THE FINANCIAL DEMEANOUR AUTHORITY IS VERY PLEASED THAT I'M NOW WORKING FOR THEM...
AH YES, DAVID. YOU'RE THE CLASSIC POACHER-TURNED-GAMEKEEPER.

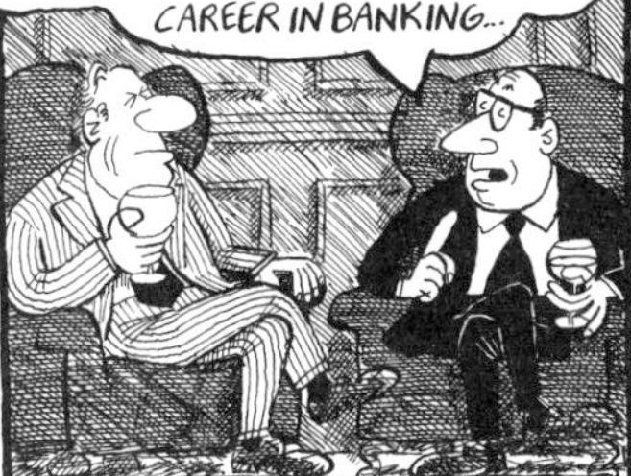
WELL, MOST REGULATORS ARE EX-LAWYERS OR BRAINY YOUNG GRADUATES WITH MBAs, BUT THEY TEND NOT TO HAVE ANY HANDS-ON EXPERIENCE OF HOW THE CITY ACTUALLY WORKS, WHEREAS I'VE HAD A 30-YEAR CAREER IN BANKING...
alex@alexcartoon.com

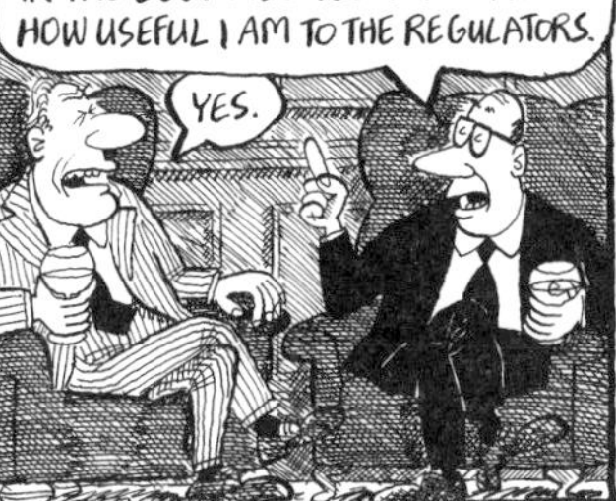
I'VE HAD FIRST-HAND EXPERIENCE WORKING IN VARIOUS BANKS IN THE CITY AND I RECKON I MUST KNOW ABOUT EVERY SCAM AND SUBTERFUGE IN THE BOOK... SO YOU CAN IMAGINE HOW USEFUL I AM TO THE REGULATORS.
YES.

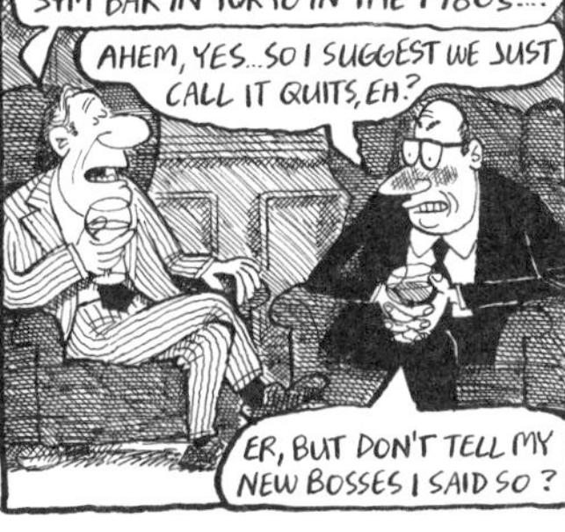
NOT VERY USEFUL AT ALL, GIVEN THAT SO MANY BANKS HAVE DIRT ON YOU... LIKE, DO YOU RECALL THE "BLACK ORCHID" S+M BAR IN TOKYO IN THE 1980's...?
AHEM, YES... SO I SUGGEST WE JUST CALL IT QUITS, EH?
ER, BUT DON'T TELL MY NEW BOSSES I SAID SO?

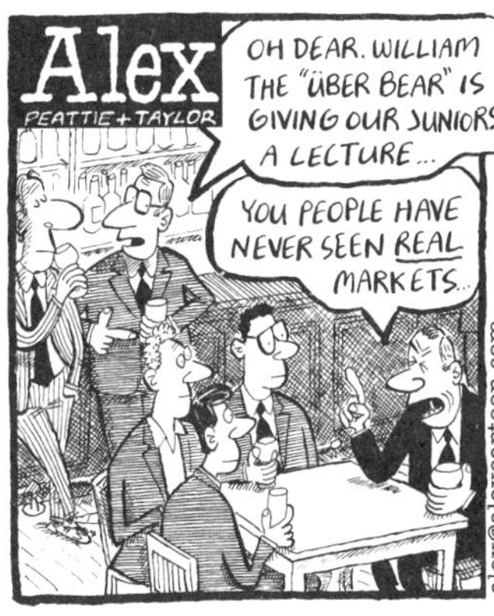
Alex
PEATTIE + TAYLOR
OH DEAR. WILLIAM THE "ÜBER BEAR" IS GIVING OUR JUNIORS A LECTURE...
YOU PEOPLE HAVE NEVER SEEN REAL MARKETS...

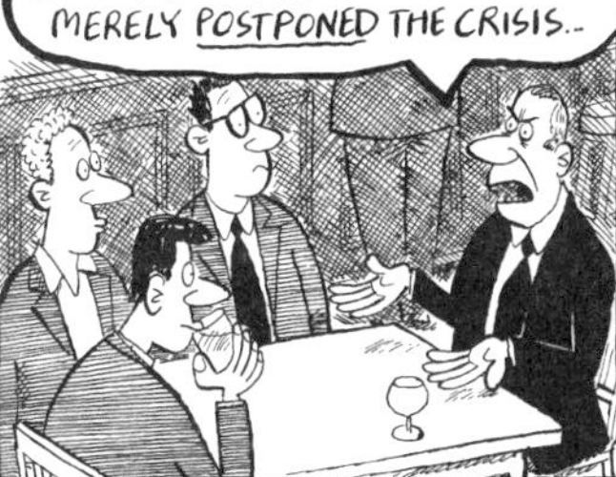
ALL YOU KNOW IS THE "NEW NORMAL" BUT THAT'S BEEN CREATED BY CENTRAL BANKS ARTIFICIALLY PROPPING UP THE ECONOMY WITH ZERO INTEREST RATES AND MONEY PRINTING... THEY'VE MERELY POSTPONED THE CRISIS...
alex@alexcartoon.com

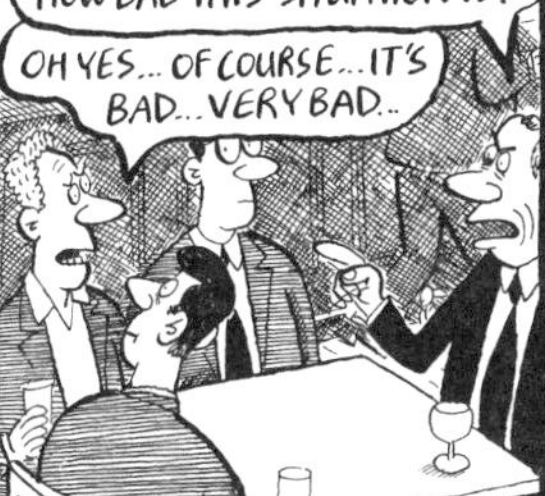
I'M TELLING YOU: WHEN THIS BUBBLE BURSTS IT'S GOING TO MAKE 2008 LOOK LIKE A PICNIC. DO YOU KIDS HAVE ANY IDEA HOW BAD THIS SITUATION IS?
OH YES... OF COURSE... IT'S BAD... VERY BAD...

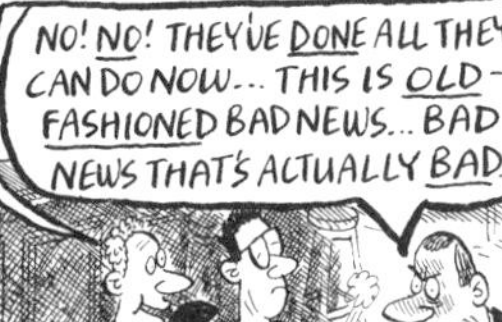
...WHICH MEANS IT'S ACTUALLY GOOD BECAUSE CENTRAL BANKS WILL HAVE TO INTERVENE AND THROW MONEY AT THE PROBLEM?
NO! NO! THEY'VE DONE ALL THEY CAN DO NOW... THIS IS OLD-FASHIONED BAD NEWS... BAD NEWS THAT'S ACTUALLY BAD.
POUND
IF HE PROVES TO BE RIGHT AT LEAST WE'LL HAVE GOT OUR SEMANTICS BACK...

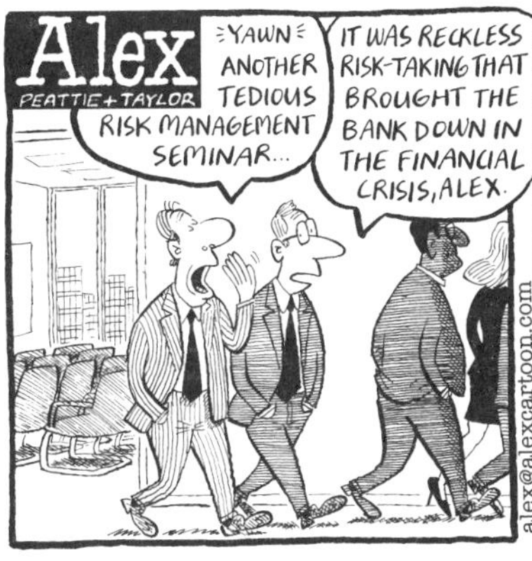
Alex
PEATTIE + TAYLOR
YAWN
ANOTHER TEDIOUS RISK MANAGEMENT SEMINAR...
IT WAS RECKLESS RISK-TAKING THAT BROUGHT THE BANK DOWN IN THE FINANCIAL CRISIS, ALEX.

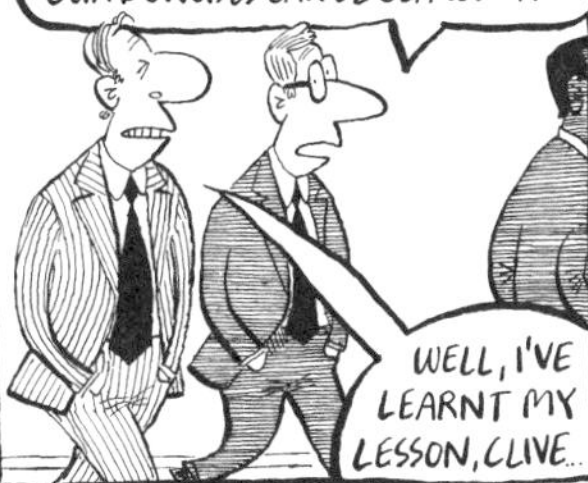
THAT'S WHY OUR BONUSES ARE NOW PAID IN STOCK OPTIONS THAT TAKE 3 YEARS TO VEST. NOT ONLY DOES IT ENCOURAGE LOYALTY TO THE BANK, BUT IF WE TAKE EXCESSIVE RISK OUR BONUSES CAN BE CLAWED BACK...
WELL, I'VE LEARNT MY LESSON, CLIVE...
alex@alexcartoon.com

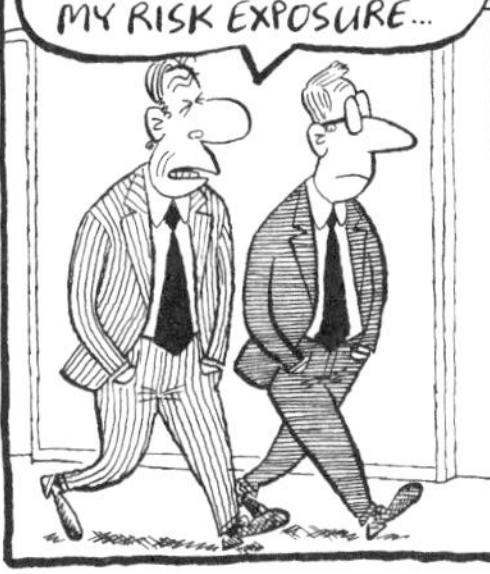
I'M FIRMLY ESCHEWING ANY RISKY BEHAVIOUR AND I'M ADOPTING A STRICT POLICY OF REDUCING AND DIVERSIFYING MY RISK EXPOSURE...

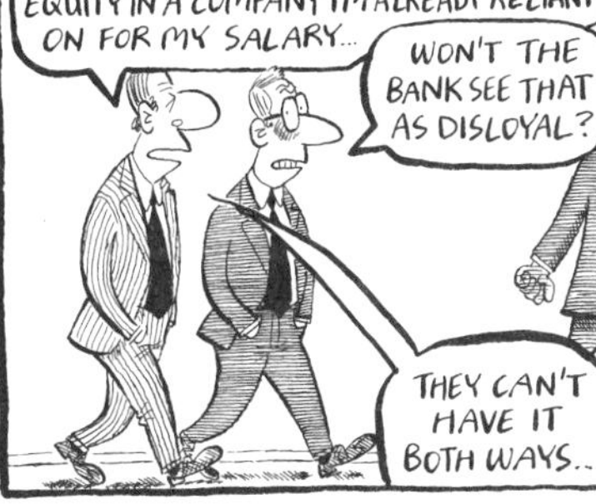
SO I'VE SOLD ALL THE MEGABANK STOCK THAT'S JUST VESTED FROM MY 2012 BONUS. WELL, IT'D BE DOUBLY RISKY FOR ME TO HOLD EQUITY IN A COMPANY I'M ALREADY RELIANT ON FOR MY SALARY...
WON'T THE BANK SEE THAT AS DISLOYAL?
THEY CAN'T HAVE IT BOTH WAYS...

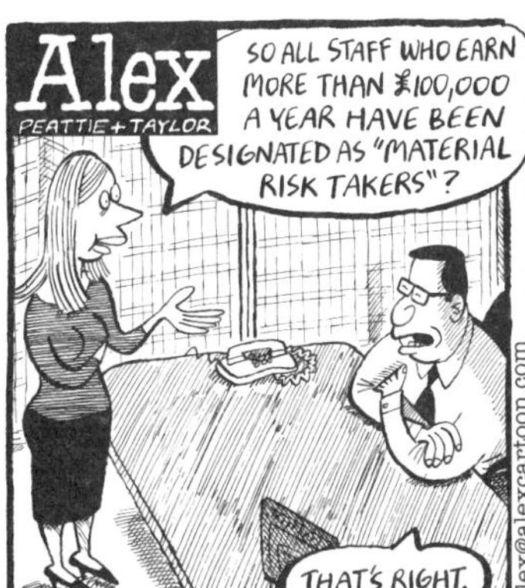
Alex
PEATTIE + TAYLOR
SO ALL STAFF WHO EARN MORE THAN £100,000 A YEAR HAVE BEEN DESIGNATED AS "MATERIAL RISK TAKERS"?
THAT'S RIGHT.
alex@alexcartoon.com
AND THIS MEANS THAT THEIR BONUSES CAN POTENTIALLY BE CLAWED BACK UP TO 7 YEARS AFTER THEY'VE BEEN AWARDED?
CORRECT. IT'S PART OF OUR DRIVE TO INSTIL A RESPONSIBLE EMPLOYEE MINDSET...

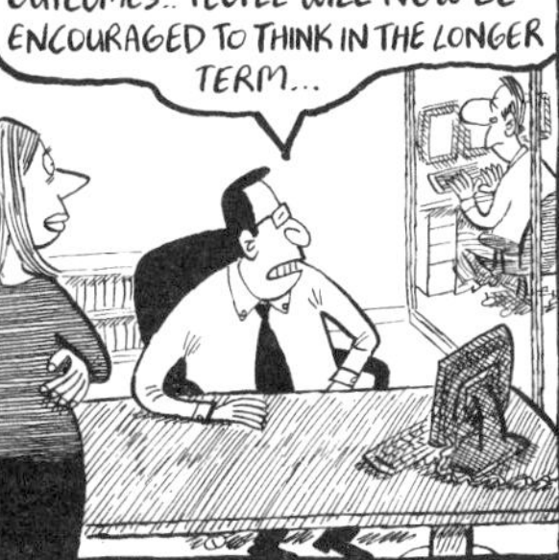
THE OLD-STYLE CASH BONUSES MAY HAVE INCENTIVIZED PEOPLE, BUT THEY INDUCED A FIXATION ON SHORT-TERM OUTCOMES... PEOPLE WILL NOW BE ENCOURAGED TO THINK IN THE LONGER TERM...
SO WHAT ARE THE CHANCES OF ME NOT SCREWING UP AT SOME POINT OVER THE NEXT 7 YEARS?
REALISTICALLY: NIL...
SO HOW INCENTIVISED DO I FEEL TO DO ANY WORK?

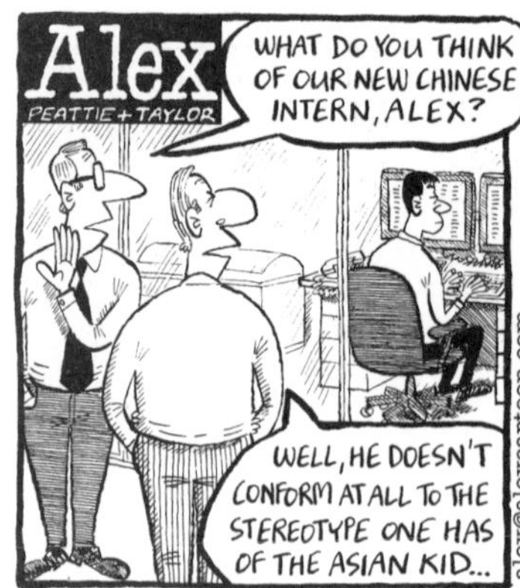
Alex
PEATTIE + TAYLOR
WHAT DO YOU THINK OF OUR NEW CHINESE INTERN, ALEX?
WELL, HE DOESN'T CONFORM AT ALL TO THE STEREOTYPE ONE HAS OF THE ASIAN KID...
alex@alexcartoon.com

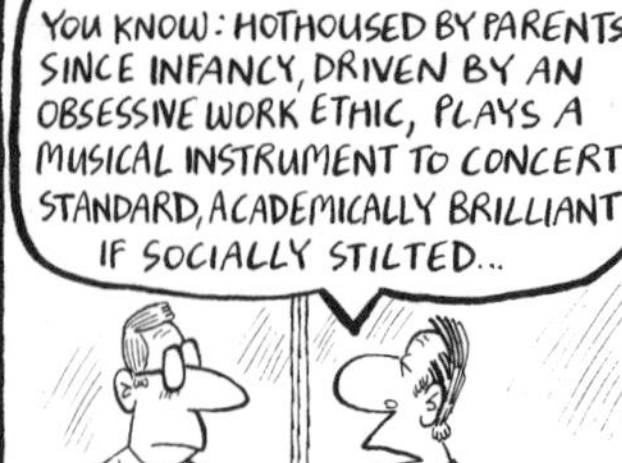
YOU KNOW: HOTHOUSED BY PARENTS SINCE INFANCY, DRIVEN BY AN OBSESSIVE WORK ETHIC, PLAYS A MUSICAL INSTRUMENT TO CONCERT STANDARD, ACADEMICALLY BRILLIANT IF SOCIALLY STILTED...

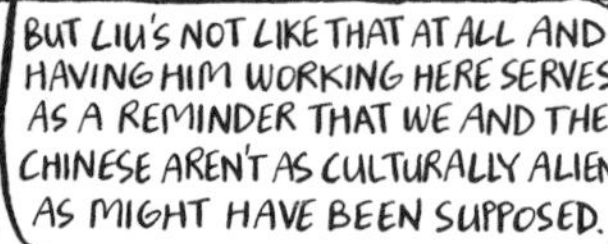
BUT LIU'S NOT LIKE THAT AT ALL AND HAVING HIM WORKING HERE SERVES AS A REMINDER THAT WE AND THE CHINESE AREN'T AS CULTURALLY ALIEN AS MIGHT HAVE BEEN SUPPOSED.

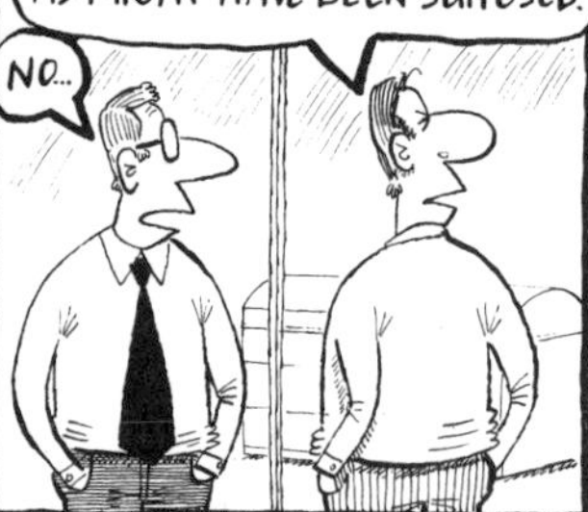
NO...

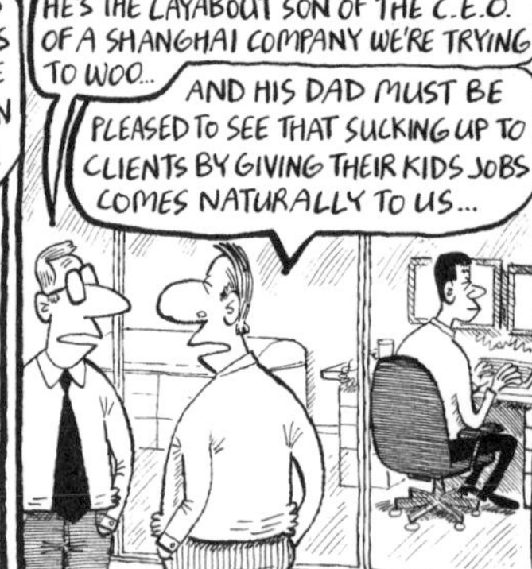
HE'S THE LAYABOUT SON OF THE C.E.O. OF A SHANGHAI COMPANY WE'RE TRYING TO WOO...
AND HIS DAD MUST BE PLEASED TO SEE THAT SUCKING UP TO CLIENTS BY GIVING THEIR KIDS JOBS COMES NATURALLY TO US...

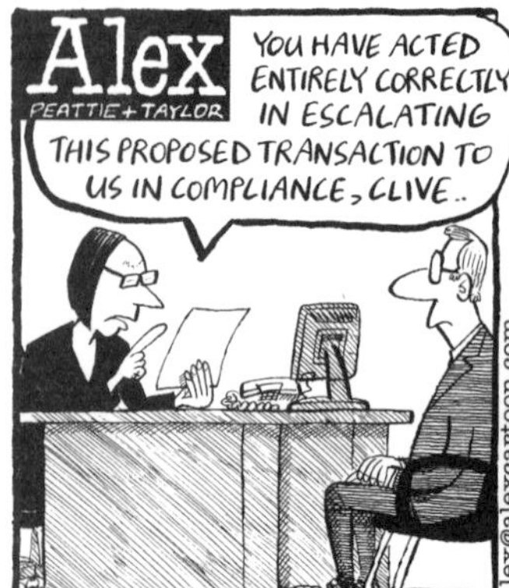
Alex
PEATTIE + TAYLOR
YOU HAVE ACTED ENTIRELY CORRECTLY IN ESCALATING THIS PROPOSED TRANSACTION TO US IN COMPLIANCE, CLIVE..
alex@alexcartoon.com

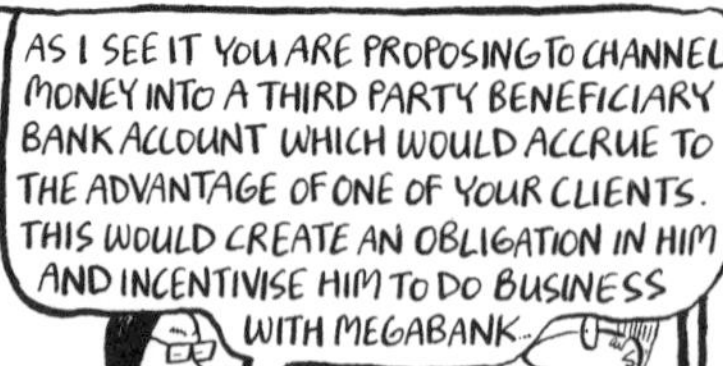
AS I SEE IT YOU ARE PROPOSING TO CHANNEL MONEY INTO A THIRD PARTY BENEFICIARY BANK ACCOUNT WHICH WOULD ACCRUE TO THE ADVANTAGE OF ONE OF YOUR CLIENTS. THIS WOULD CREATE AN OBLIGATION IN HIM AND INCENTIVISE HIM TO DO BUSINESS WITH MEGABANK...

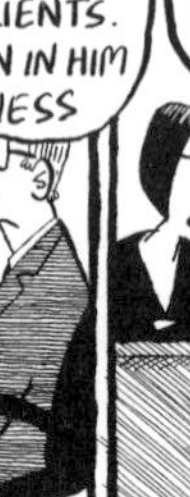

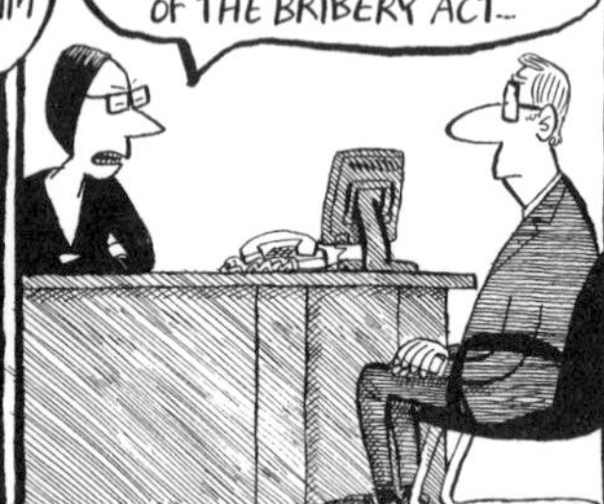
I'M AFRAID THAT NOT ONLY DOES THIS BREACH THE BANK'S GUIDE-LINES ON TRANSPARENCY, BUT IT IS ALSO IN DIRECT CONTRAVENTION OF THE BRIBERY ACT...

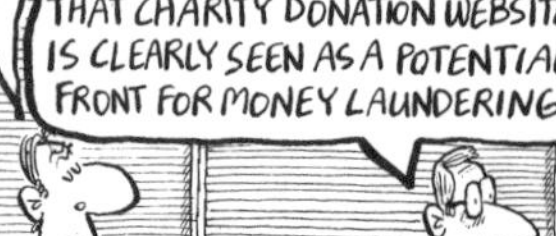
SO UNDER OUR NEW COMPLIANCE REGIME YOU CAN'T EVEN SPONSOR A CLIENT TO RUN THE LONDON MARATHON?

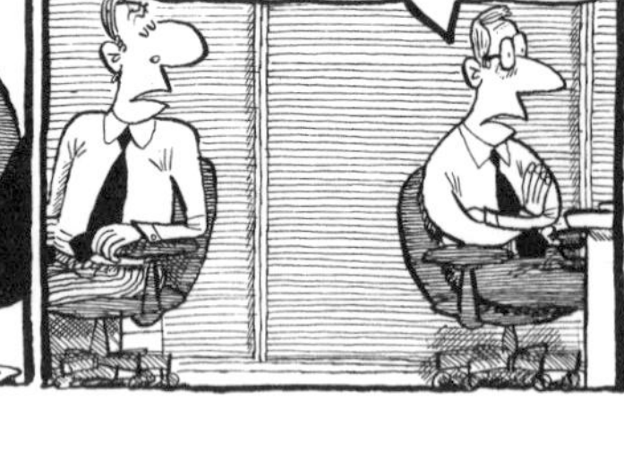
THAT CHARITY DONATION WEBSITE IS CLEARLY SEEN AS A POTENTIAL FRONT FOR MONEY LAUNDERING...

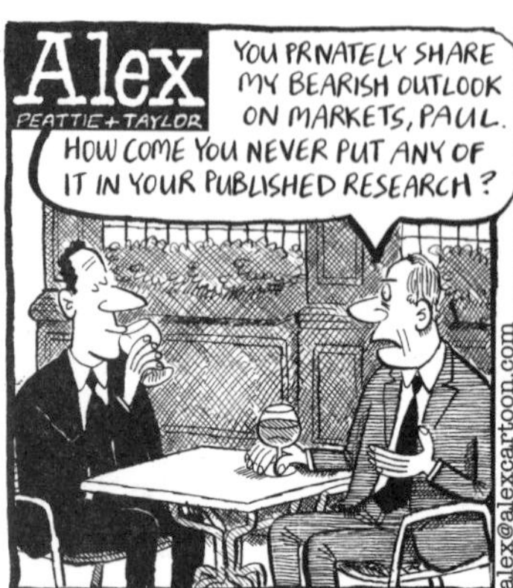
Alex
PEATTIE + TAYLOR
YOU PRIVATELY SHARE MY BEARISH OUTLOOK ON MARKETS, PAUL. HOW COME YOU NEVER PUT ANY OF IT IN YOUR PUBLISHED RESEARCH?
alex@alexcartoon.com

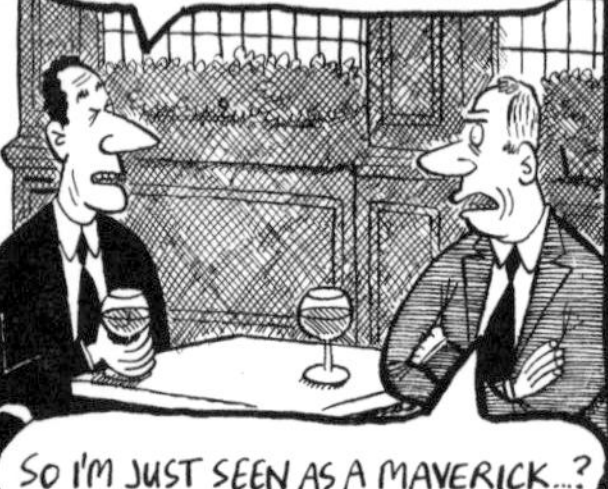
BECAUSE NO ONE WANTS TO HEAR BAD NEWS, WILLIAM. IT UNDERMINES BUSINESS CONFIDENCE. IN ANY CASE WE ANALYSTS LIKE TO CLUB TOGETHER AND HAVE THE SAME VIEW...
SO I'M JUST SEEN AS A MAVERICK...?
EXACTLY. PEOPLE ASSUME YOU'RE AN ATTENTION-SEEKER OR SOMEONE WITH AN AXE TO GRIND. INVESTORS CAN'T TAKE THE RISK OF FOLLOWING YOUR ADVICE...
JUST WAIT TILL MARKETS START TO UNWIND... THEN WE'LL SEE WHO GETS THE CREDIT...
YES

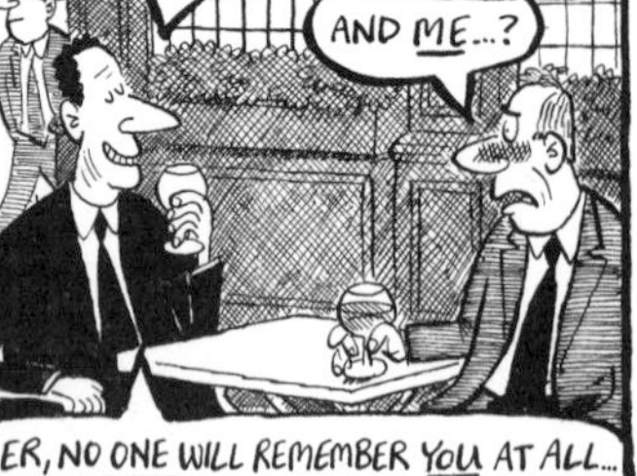
AND IT'LL BE ME ... BECAUSE WHEN I START SAYING THE SAME THING AS YOU I'LL BE SEEN AS HAVING "IDENTIFIED A TREND"... AND THEN ALL THE OTHER ANALYSTS WILL JUMP ON BOARD TOO...
AND ME...?
ER, NO ONE WILL REMEMBER YOU AT ALL...

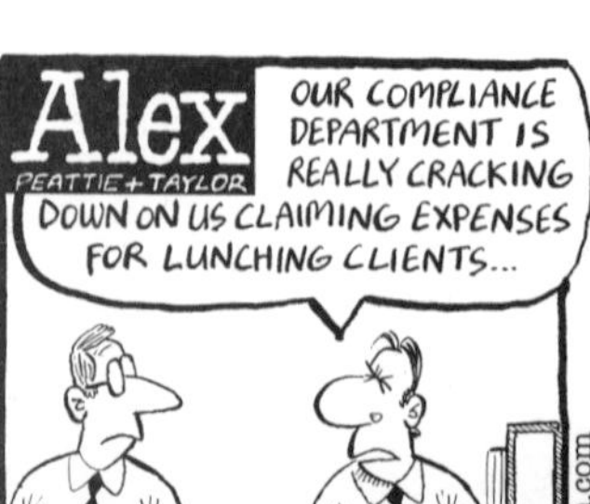
Alex
PEATTIE + TAYLOR
OUR COMPLIANCE DEPARTMENT IS REALLY CRACKING DOWN ON US CLAIMING EXPENSES FOR LUNCHING CLIENTS...
alex@alexcartoon.com

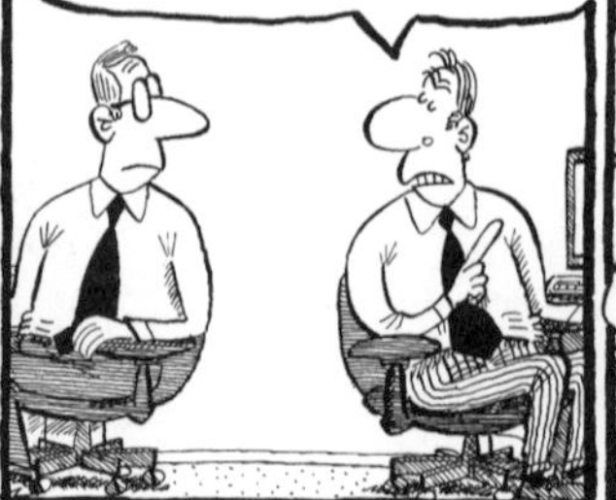
IT'S NOT JUST ABOUT COST-CUTTING. BUYING A MEAL FOR A CLIENT CAN APPARENTLY BE SEEN AS CREATING AN OBLIGATION AND THUS BRIBING THEM TO DO BUSINESS WITH US...

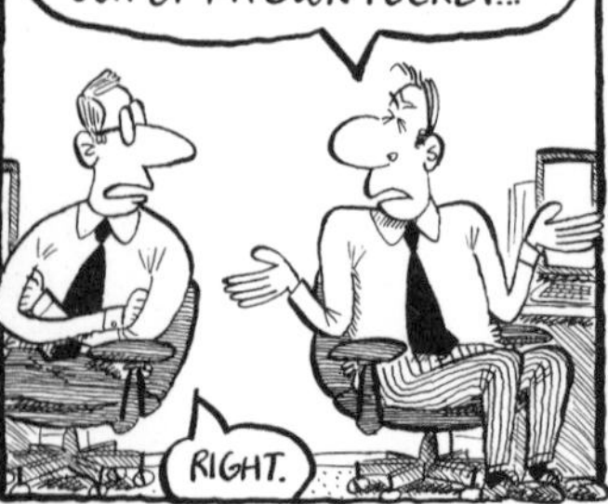
NOWADAYS IF I WANT TO HAVE A DECENT LUNCH WITH A FAVOURED CLIENT I HAVE TO TAKE A HALF DAY HOLIDAY AND PAY FOR THE MEAL OUT OF MY OWN POCKET...
RIGHT.

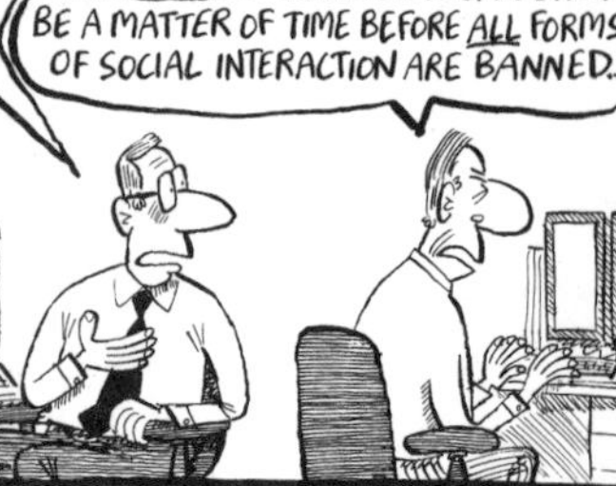
BUT DOESN'T THAT CREATE EVEN MORE OF AN OBLIGATION IN YOUR CLIENT IF HE KNOWS THAT YOU'RE GIVING UP YOUR OWN TIME AND LAVISHING YOUR OWN MONEY ON HIM?
EXACTLY. IT CAN ONLY BE A MATTER OF TIME BEFORE ALL FORMS OF SOCIAL INTERACTION ARE BANNED...

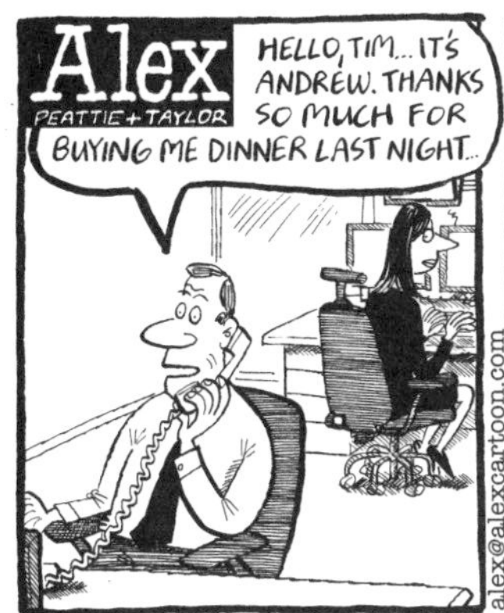
Alex
PEATTIE + TAYLOR
HELLO, TIM... IT'S ANDREW. THANKS SO MUCH FOR BUYING ME DINNER LAST NIGHT...
alex@alexcartoon.com

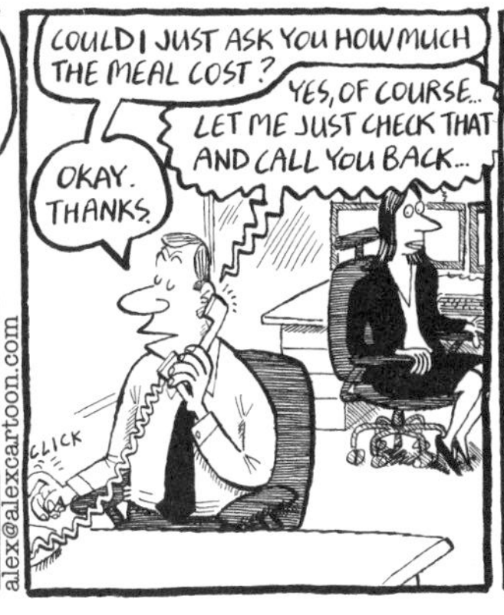
COULD I JUST ASK YOU HOW MUCH THE MEAL COST?
YES, OF COURSE... LET ME JUST CHECK THAT AND CALL YOU BACK...
OKAY. THANKS.
CLICK

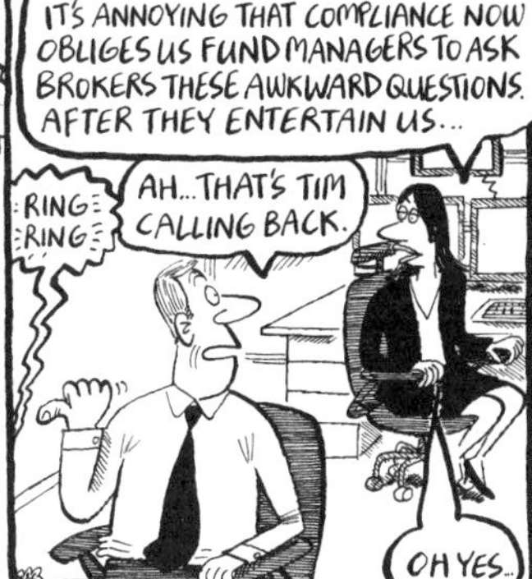
IT'S ANNOYING THAT COMPLIANCE NOW OBLIGES US FUND MANAGERS TO ASK BROKERS THESE AWKWARD QUESTIONS AFTER THEY ENTERTAIN US...
RING RING
AH... THAT'S TIM CALLING BACK.
OH YES...

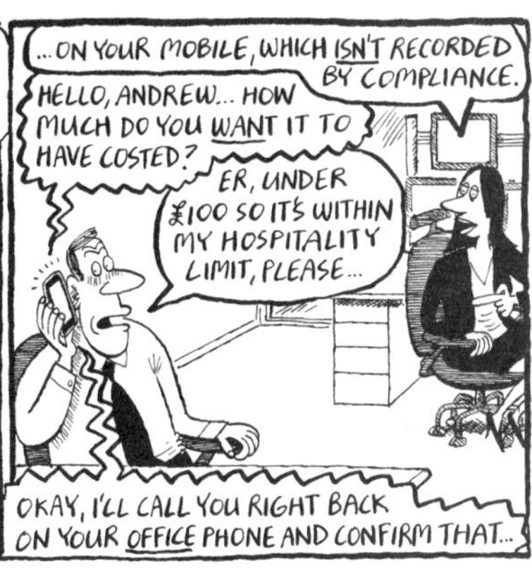
...ON YOUR MOBILE, WHICH ISN'T RECORDED BY COMPLIANCE.
HELLO, ANDREW... HOW MUCH DO YOU WANT IT TO HAVE COSTED?
ER, UNDER £100 SO IT'S WITHIN MY HOSPITALITY LIMIT, PLEASE...
OKAY, I'LL CALL YOU RIGHT BACK ON YOUR OFFICE PHONE AND CONFIRM THAT...

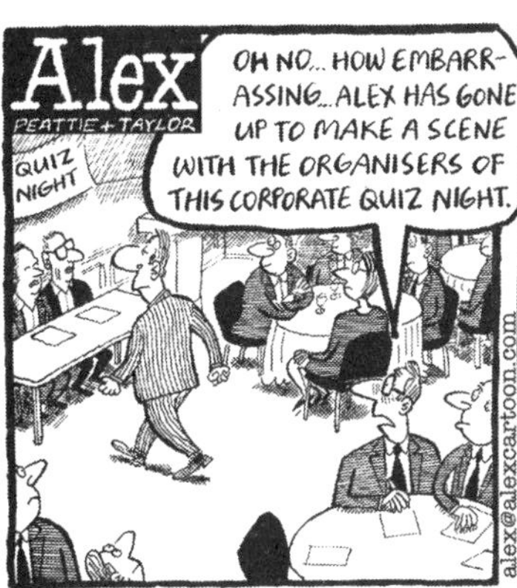
Alex
PEATTIE + TAYLOR
OH NO... HOW EMBARRASSING... ALEX HAS GONE UP TO MAKE A SCENE WITH THE ORGANISERS OF THIS CORPORATE QUIZ NIGHT.
QUIZ NIGHT
alex@alexcartoon.com

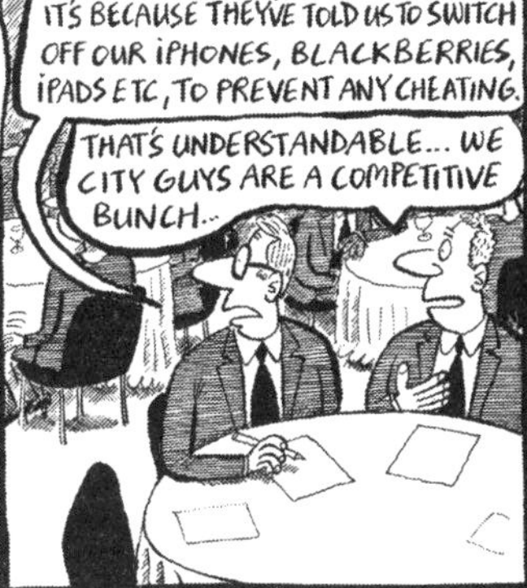
IT'S BECAUSE THEY'VE TOLD US TO SWITCH OFF OUR iPHONES, BLACKBERRIES, iPADS ETC, TO PREVENT ANY CHEATING.
THAT'S UNDERSTANDABLE... WE CITY GUYS ARE A COMPETITIVE BUNCH...

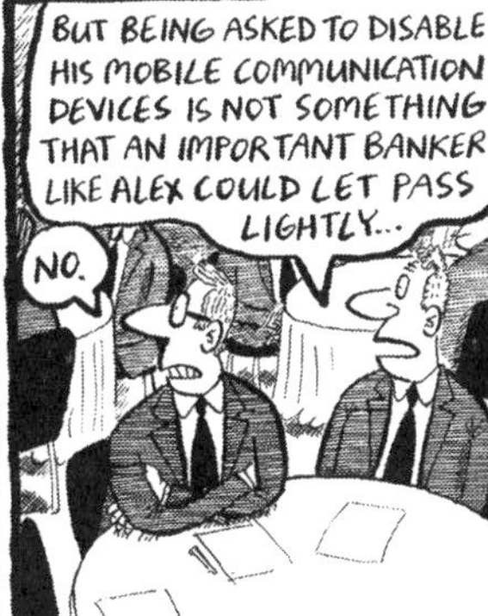
BUT BEING ASKED TO DISABLE HIS MOBILE COMMUNICATION DEVICES IS NOT SOMETHING THAT AN IMPORTANT BANKER LIKE ALEX COULD LET PASS LIGHTLY...
NO.

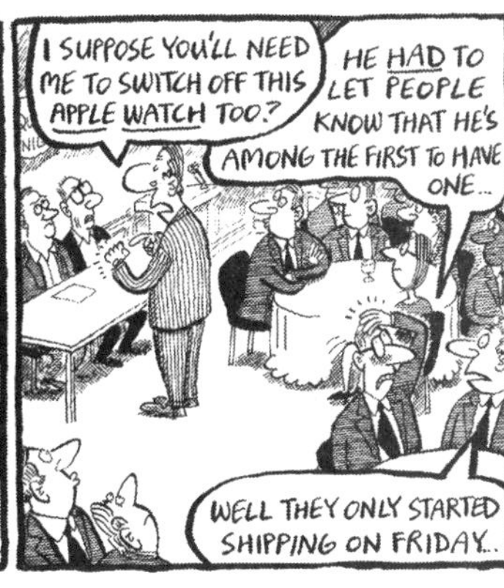
I SUPPOSE YOU'LL NEED ME TO SWITCH OFF THIS APPLE WATCH TOO?
HE HAD TO LET PEOPLE KNOW THAT HE'S AMONG THE FIRST TO HAVE ONE...
WELL THEY ONLY STARTED SHIPPING ON FRIDAY...

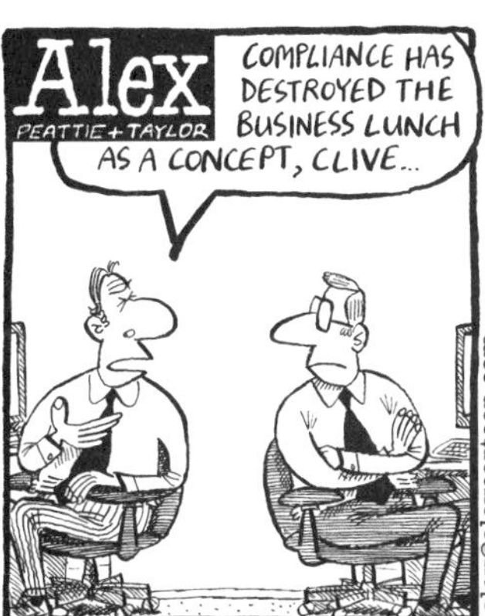
Alex
PEATTIE + TAYLOR
COMPLIANCE HAS DESTROYED THE BUSINESS LUNCH AS A CONCEPT, CLIVE...
alex@alexcartoon.com

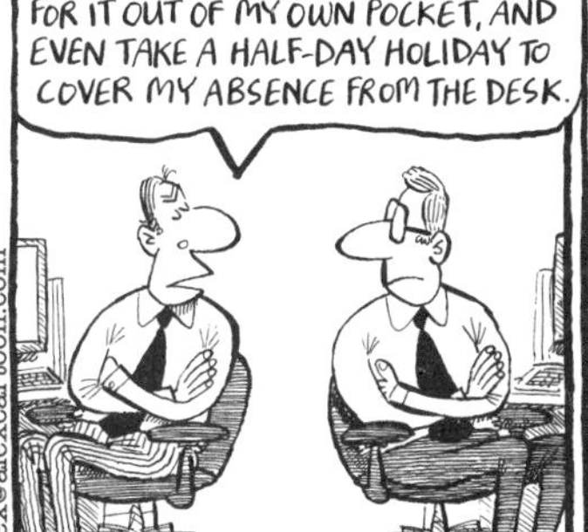
I HAD LUNCH WITH ONE OF MY CLIENTS YESTERDAY BUT I WAS OBLIGED TO PAY FOR IT OUT OF MY OWN POCKET, AND EVEN TAKE A HALF-DAY HOLIDAY TO COVER MY ABSENCE FROM THE DESK.

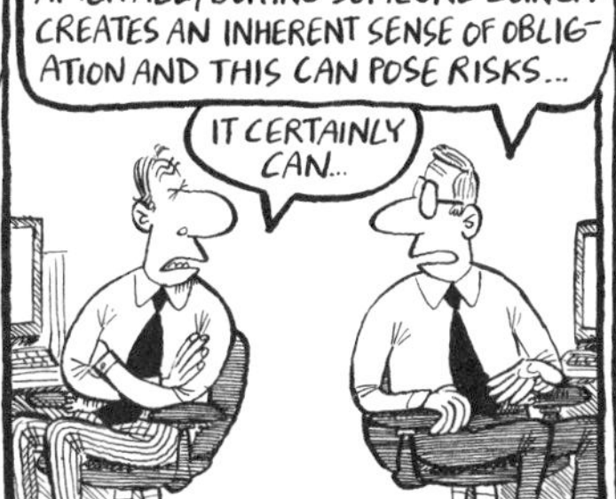
IT'S ALL TO DO WITH NOT BEING SEEN TO BE BRIBING CLIENTS TO DO BUSINESS WITH US. AFTER ALL, BUYING SOMEONE LUNCH CREATES AN INHERENT SENSE OF OBLIGATION AND THIS CAN POSE RISKS...
IT CERTAINLY CAN...

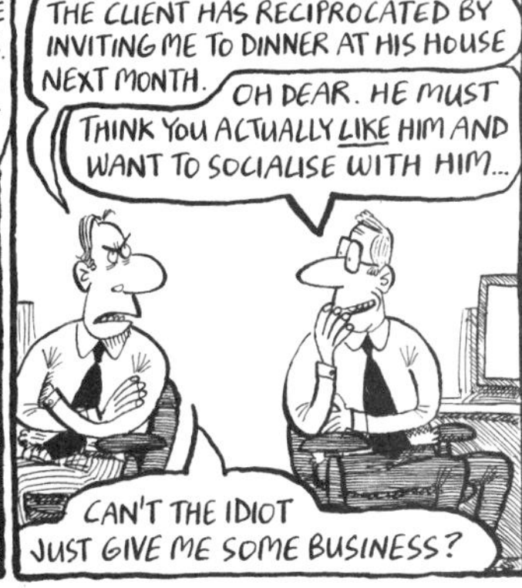
THE CLIENT HAS RECIPROCATED BY INVITING ME TO DINNER AT HIS HOUSE NEXT MONTH.
OH DEAR. HE MUST THINK YOU ACTUALLY LIKE HIM AND WANT TO SOCIALISE WITH HIM...
CAN'T THE IDIOT JUST GIVE ME SOME BUSINESS?

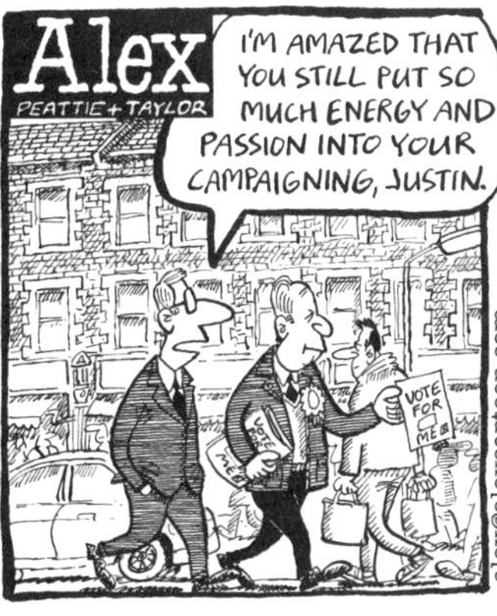
Alex
PEATTIE + TAYLOR
I'M AMAZED THAT YOU STILL PUT SO MUCH ENERGY AND PASSION INTO YOUR CAMPAIGNING, JUSTIN.
VOTE FOR ME!
alex@alexcartoon.com

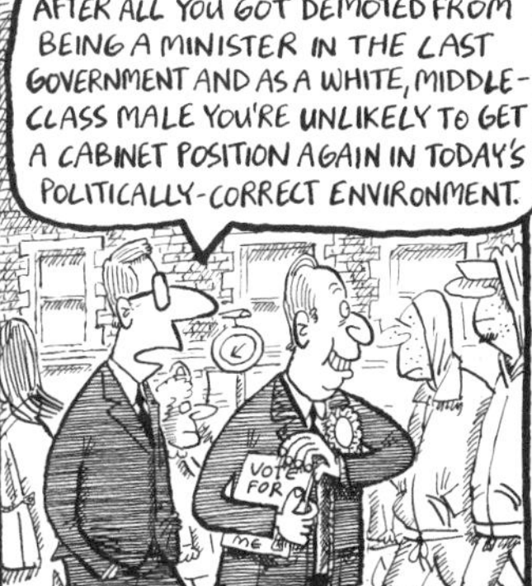
AFTER ALL YOU GOT DEMOTED FROM BEING A MINISTER IN THE LAST GOVERNMENT AND AS A WHITE, MIDDLE-CLASS MALE YOU'RE UNLIKELY TO GET A CABINET POSITION AGAIN IN TODAY'S POLITICALLY-CORRECT ENVIRONMENT.
VOTE FOR

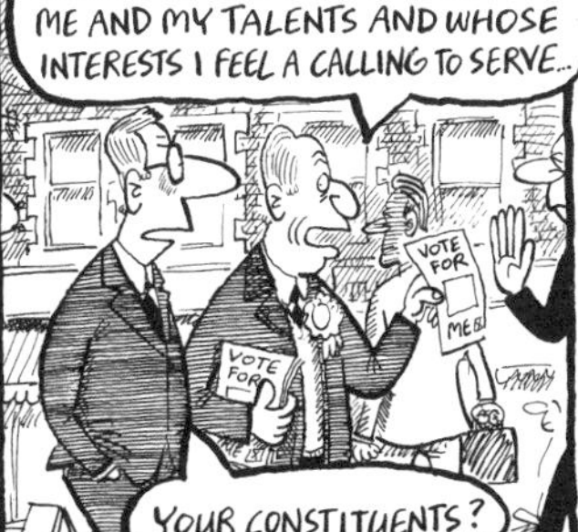
I MAY NOT BE DESTINED FOR HIGH OFFICE, CLIVE, BUT THERE ARE STILL PEOPLE OUT THERE WHO I BELIEVE NEED ME AND MY TALENTS AND WHOSE INTERESTS I FEEL A CALLING TO SERVE...
VOTE FOR ME!
YOUR CONSTITUENTS?

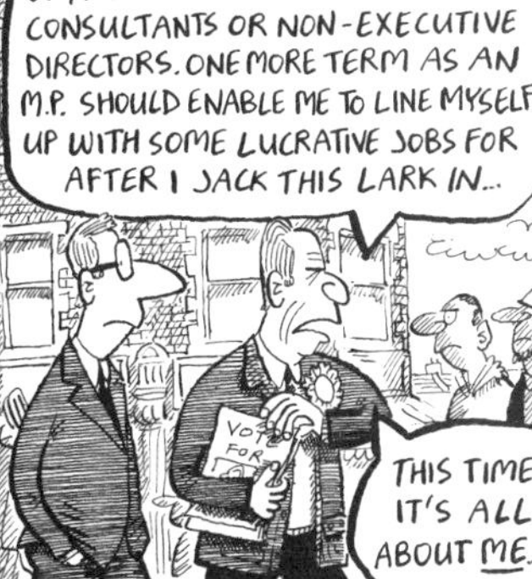
ER, NO... COMPANIES WHO REQUIRE CONSULTANTS OR NON-EXECUTIVE DIRECTORS. ONE MORE TERM AS AN M.P. SHOULD ENABLE ME TO LINE MYSELF UP WITH SOME LUCRATIVE JOBS FOR AFTER I JACK THIS LARK IN...
THIS TIME IT'S ALL ABOUT ME.

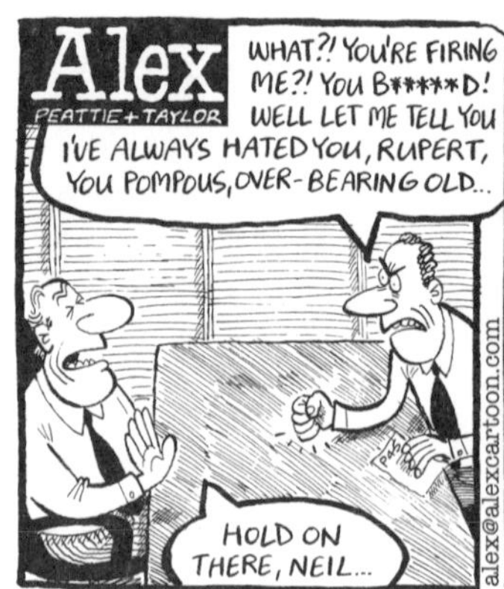
Alex
PEATTIE + TAYLOR
WHAT?! YOU'RE FIRING ME?! YOU B*****D! WELL LET ME TELL YOU I'VE ALWAYS HATED YOU, RUPERT, YOU POMPOUS, OVER-BEARING OLD...
HOLD ON THERE, NEIL...
alex@alexcartoon.com

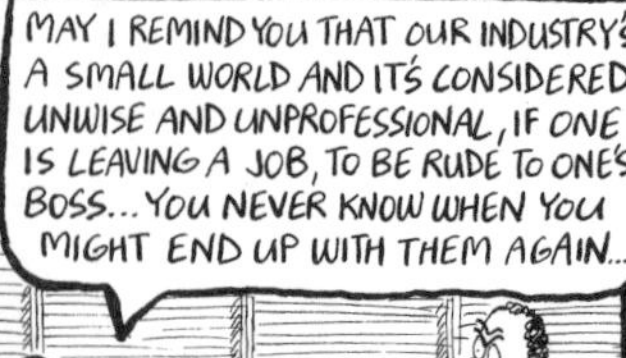
MAY I REMIND YOU THAT OUR INDUSTRY'S A SMALL WORLD AND IT'S CONSIDERED UNWISE AND UNPROFESSIONAL, IF ONE IS LEAVING A JOB, TO BE RUDE TO ONE'S BOSS... YOU NEVER KNOW WHEN YOU MIGHT END UP WITH THEM AGAIN...

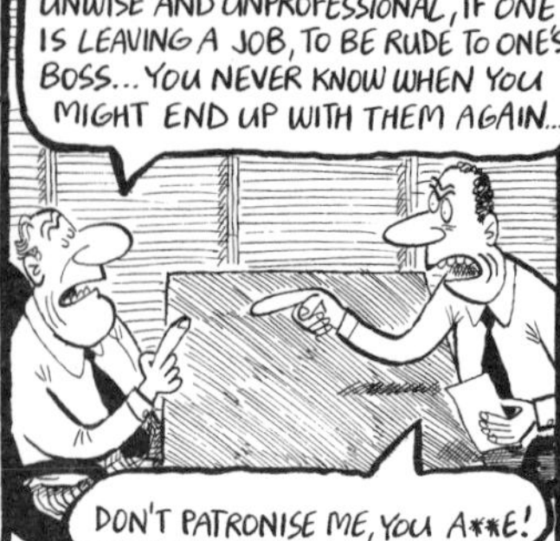
DON'T PATRONISE ME, YOU A**E!

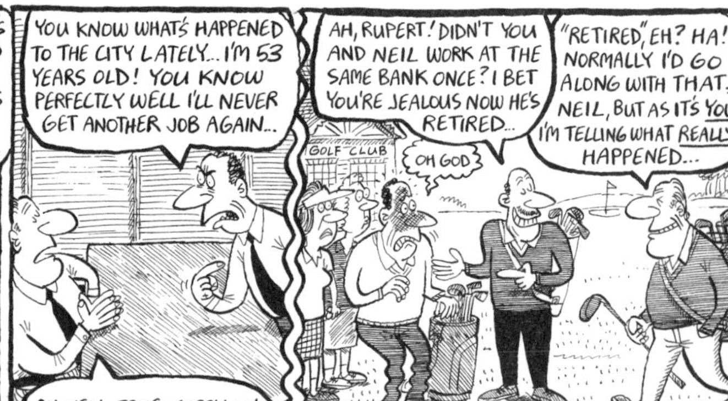
YOU KNOW WHAT'S HAPPENED TO THE CITY LATELY... I'M 53 YEARS OLD! YOU KNOW PERFECTLY WELL I'LL NEVER GET ANOTHER JOB AGAIN...
OH WELL, TRUE. CARRY ON...
AH, RUPERT! DIDN'T YOU AND NEIL WORK AT THE SAME BANK ONCE? I BET YOU'RE JEALOUS NOW HE'S RETIRED...
GOLF CLUB
OH GOD
"RETIRED", EH? HA! NORMALLY I'D GO ALONG WITH THAT, NEIL, BUT AS IT'S YOU I'M TELLING WHAT REALLY HAPPENED...

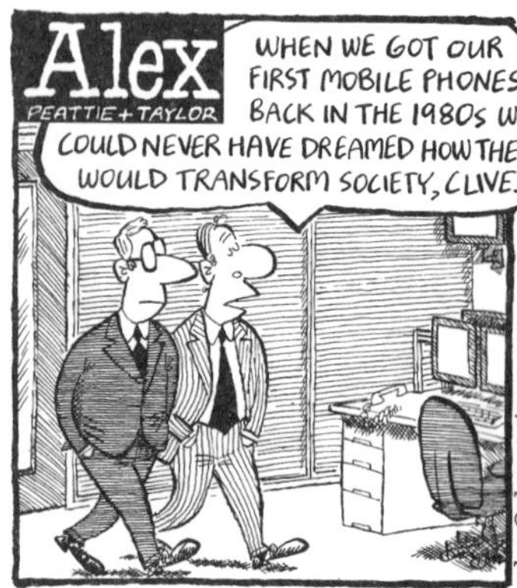
Alex
PEATTIE + TAYLOR
WHEN WE GOT OUR FIRST MOBILE PHONES BACK IN THE 1980s WE COULD NEVER HAVE DREAMED HOW THEY WOULD TRANSFORM SOCIETY, CLIVE.
alex@alexcartoon.com

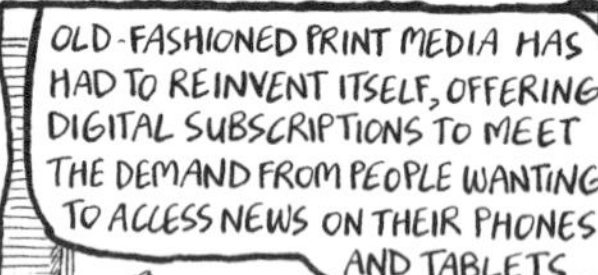
OLD-FASHIONED PRINT MEDIA HAS HAD TO REINVENT ITSELF, OFFERING DIGITAL SUBSCRIPTIONS TO MEET THE DEMAND FROM PEOPLE WANTING TO ACCESS NEWS ON THEIR PHONES AND TABLETS...

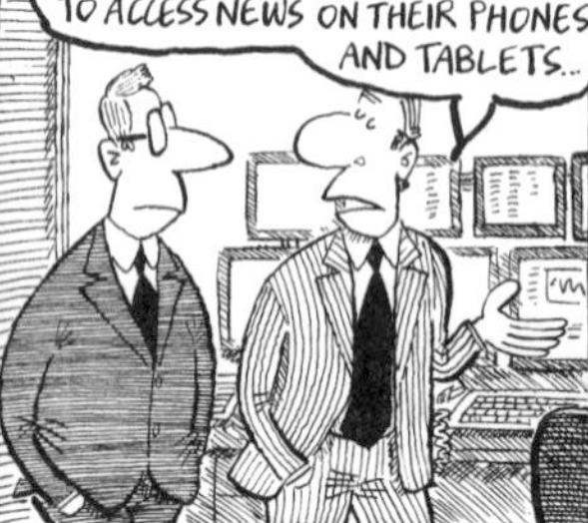

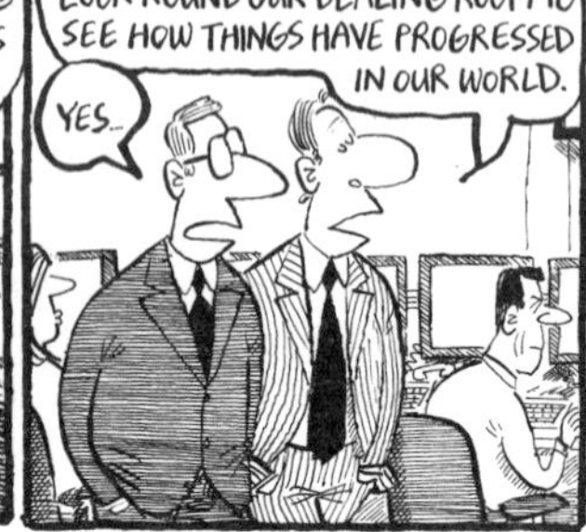
OF COURSE WE IN THE CITY HAVE ALWAYS BEEN EARLY ADOPTERS OF TECHNOLOGY. YOU ONLY HAVE TO LOOK ROUND OUR DEALING ROOM TO SEE HOW THINGS HAVE PROGRESSED IN OUR WORLD.
YES...

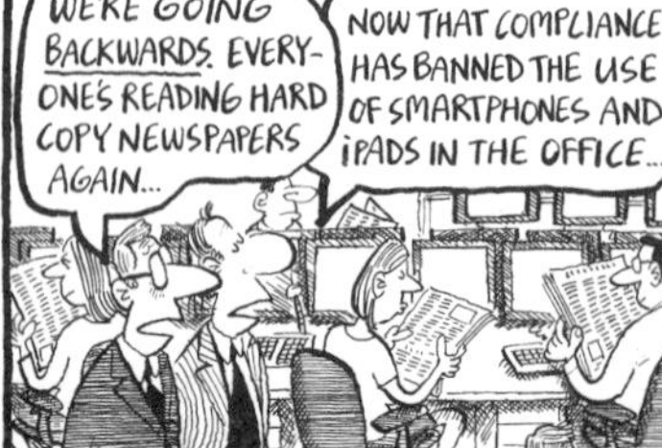
WE'RE GOING BACKWARDS. EVERY-ONE'S READING HARD COPY NEWSPAPERS AGAIN...
NOW THAT COMPLIANCE HAS BANNED THE USE OF SMARTPHONES AND iPADS IN THE OFFICE...

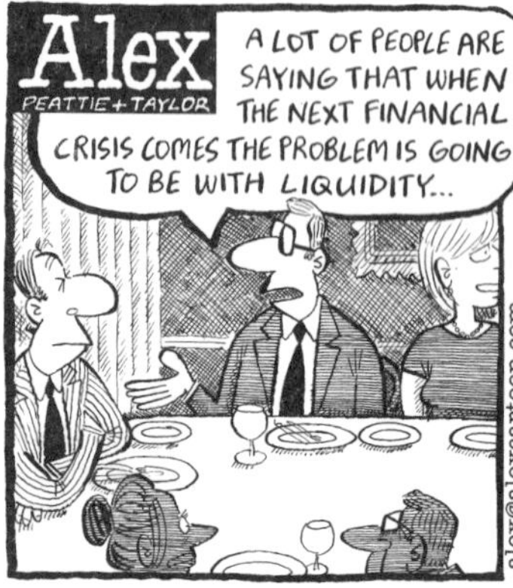
Alex
PEATTIE + TAYLOR
A LOT OF PEOPLE ARE SAYING THAT WHEN THE NEXT FINANCIAL CRISIS COMES THE PROBLEM IS GOING TO BE WITH LIQUIDITY...
alex@alexcartoon.com

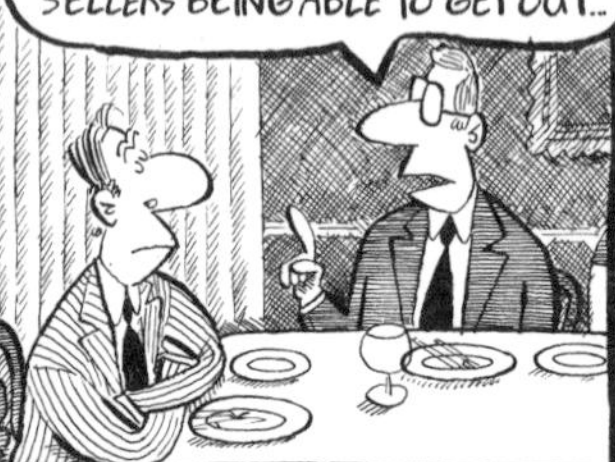
WITH CASH YIELDING NOTHING IN THE BANK, MANY INVESTORS HAVE PILED THEIR MONEY INTO PHYSICAL ASSETS, BUT SUCH MARKETS COULD EASILY SEIZE UP IN A CRISIS, PREVENTING SELLERS BEING ABLE TO GET OUT...

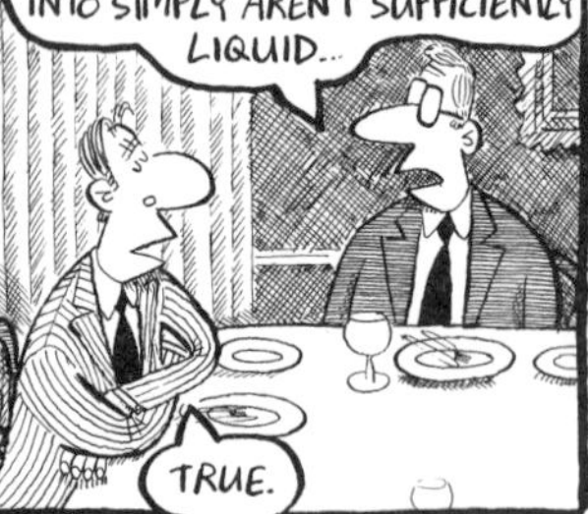
THE REALITY THAT MANY PEOPLE MAY HAVE TO FACE UP TO IS THAT THE PRODUCTS AND COMMODITIES WHICH THEY'VE PUT THEIR MONEY INTO SIMPLY AREN'T SUFFICIENTLY LIQUID...
TRUE.

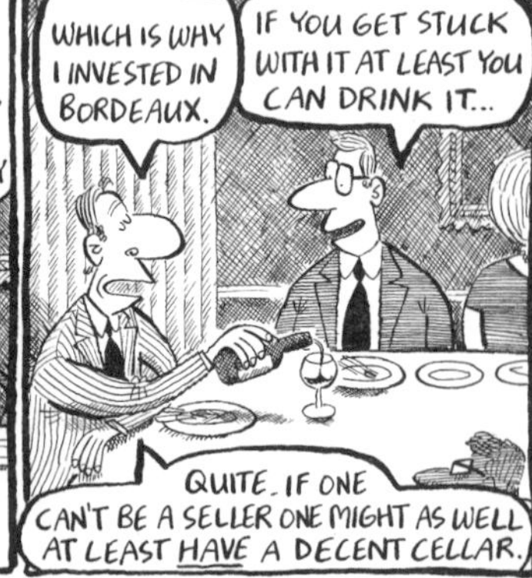
WHICH IS WHY I INVESTED IN BORDEAUX.
IF YOU GET STUCK WITH IT AT LEAST YOU CAN DRINK IT...
QUITE. IF ONE CAN'T BE A SELLER ONE MIGHT AS WELL AT LEAST HAVE A DECENT CELLAR.

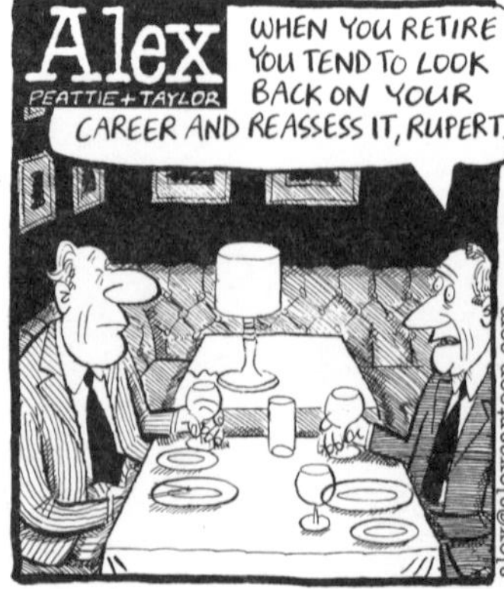
Alex
PEATTIE + TAYLOR
WHEN YOU RETIRE YOU TEND TO LOOK BACK ON YOUR CAREER AND REASSESS IT, RUPERT.
alex@alexcartoon.com

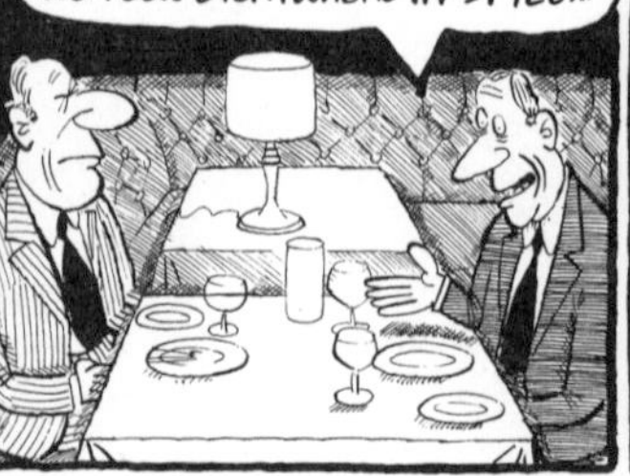
ON THE FACE OF IT I HAD ALL THE TRAPPINGS OF SUCCESS AND PRIVILEGE. I WAS A SENIOR EXECUTIVE AT A BIG AND PROSPEROUS COMPANY. WE EVEN HAD A CORPORATE JET WHICH MEANT WE FLEW EVERYWHERE IN STYLE...

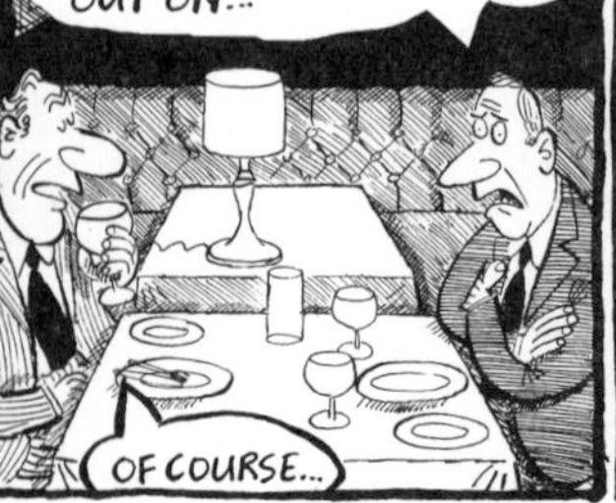
IT ALL FELT VERY GLAMOROUS... BUT NOW WHEN I LOOK BACK ON ALL THAT TIME I SPENT TRAVELLING ON BUSINESS, AWAY FROM HOME, I THINK OF WHAT I WAS MISSING OUT ON...
OF COURSE...

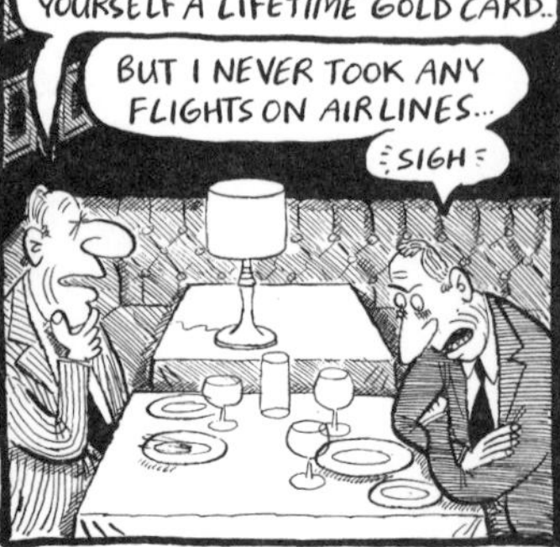
ALL THOSE AIRLINE TIER POINTS YOU'D HAVE AMASSED ENOUGH OF TO GET YOURSELF A LIFETIME GOLD CARD...
BUT I NEVER TOOK ANY FLIGHTS ON AIRLINES...
SIGH

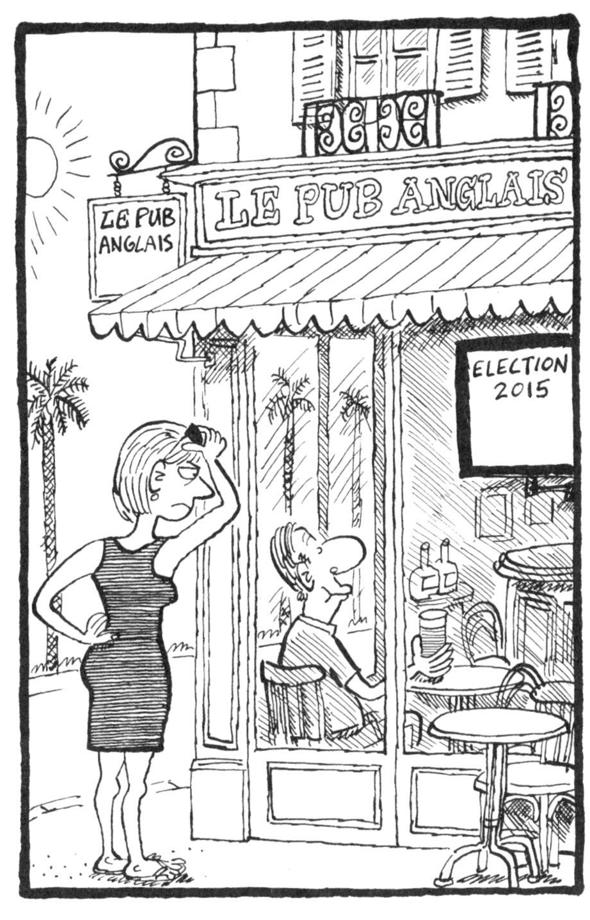
LE PUB ANGLAIS
LE PUB
ANGLAIS
ELECTION
2015

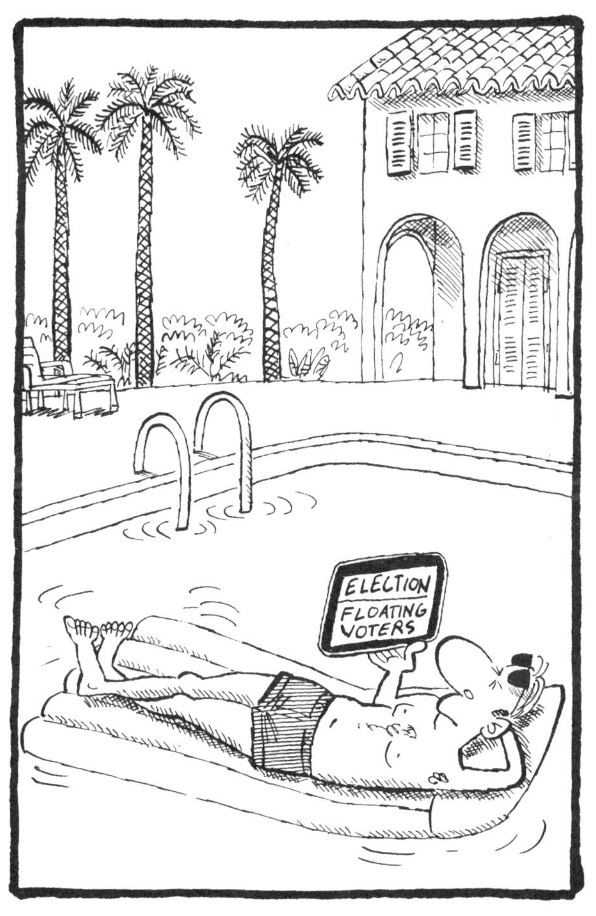
ELECTION
FLOATING
VOTERS

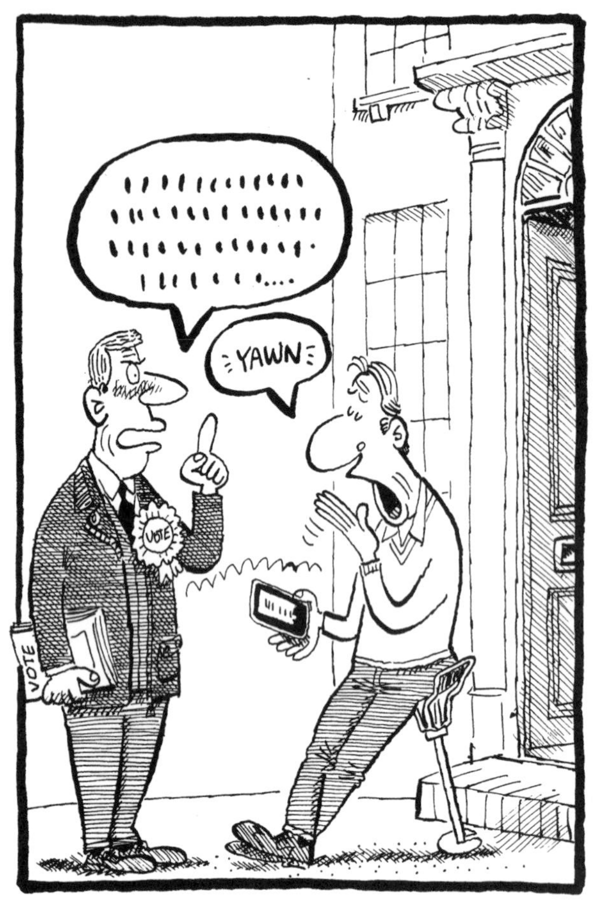
YAWN

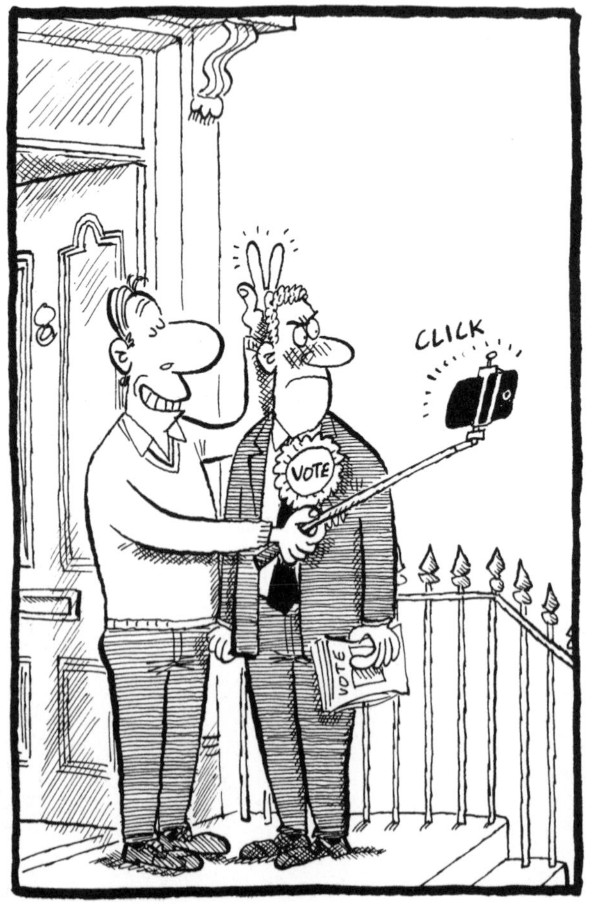
CLICK
VOTE
VOTE

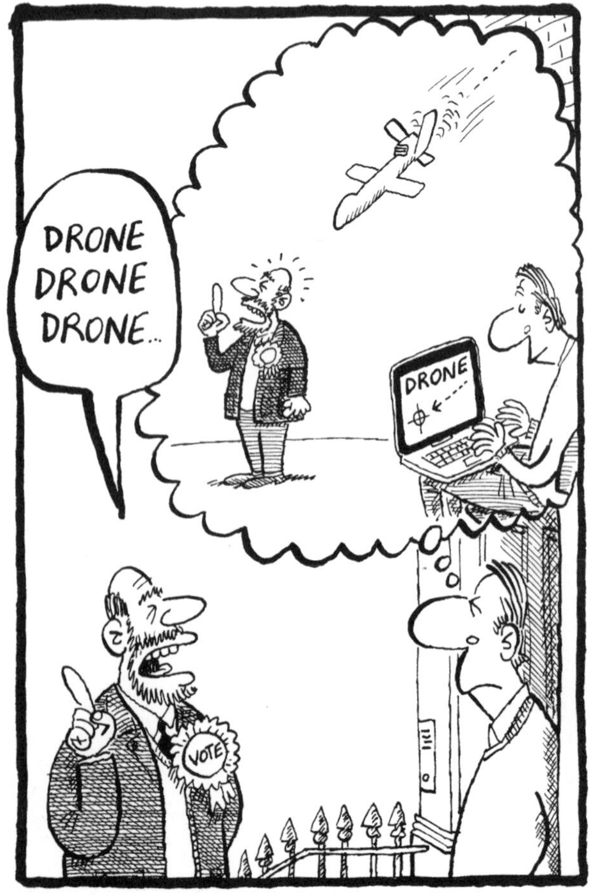
DRONE
DRONE
DRONE...
DRONE
VOTE

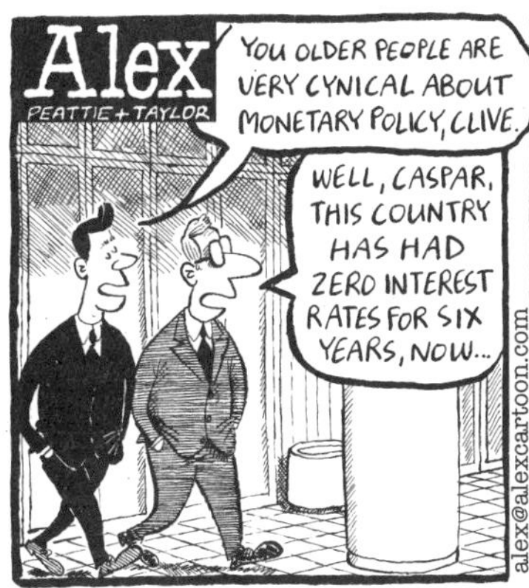
Alex
PEATTIE + TAYLOR
YOU OLDER PEOPLE ARE VERY CYNICAL ABOUT MONETARY POLICY, CLIVE.
WELL, CASPAR, THIS COUNTRY HAS HAD ZERO INTEREST RATES FOR SIX YEARS, NOW...
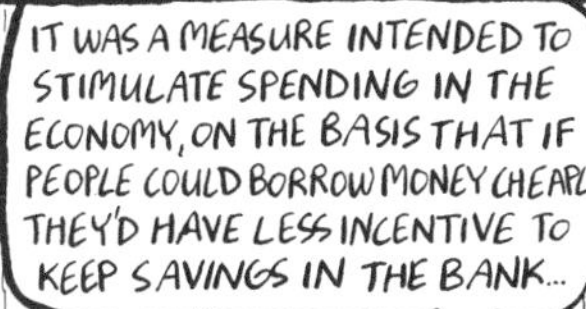
IT WAS A MEASURE INTENDED TO STIMULATE SPENDING IN THE ECONOMY, ON THE BASIS THAT IF PEOPLE COULD BORROW MONEY CHEAPLY THEY'D HAVE LESS INCENTIVE TO KEEP SAVINGS IN THE BANK...
alex@alexcartoon.com
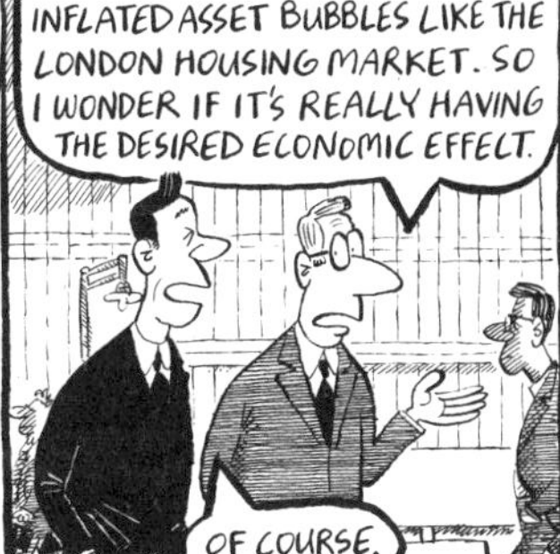
BUT THE MAIN CONSEQUENCE SEEMS TO HAVE BEEN THE CREATION OF OVER-INFLATED ASSET BUBBLES LIKE THE LONDON HOUSING MARKET. SO I WONDER IF IT'S REALLY HAVING THE DESIRED ECONOMIC EFFECT.
OF COURSE.
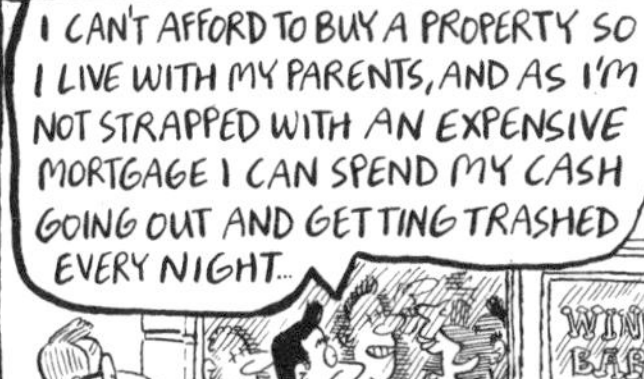
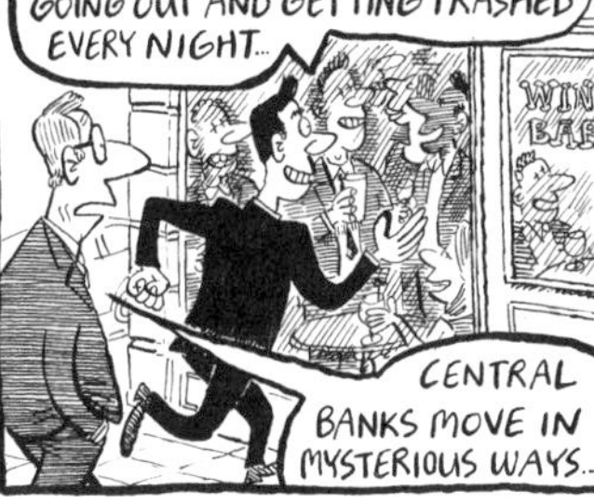
I CAN'T AFFORD TO BUY A PROPERTY SO I LIVE WITH MY PARENTS, AND AS I'M NOT STRAPPED WITH AN EXPENSIVE MORTGAGE I CAN SPEND MY CASH GOING OUT AND GETTING TRASHED EVERY NIGHT...
CENTRAL BANKS MOVE IN MYSTERIOUS WAYS...

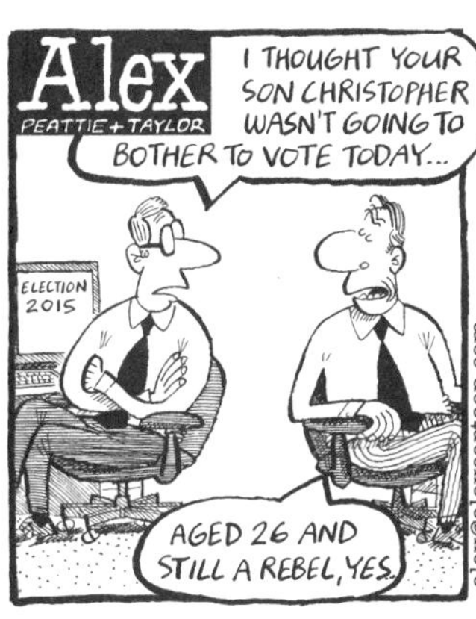
Alex
PEATTIE + TAYLOR
I THOUGHT YOUR SON CHRISTOPHER WASN'T GOING TO BOTHER TO VOTE TODAY...
ELECTION 2015
AGED 26 AND STILL A REBEL, YES.
alex@alexcartoon.com
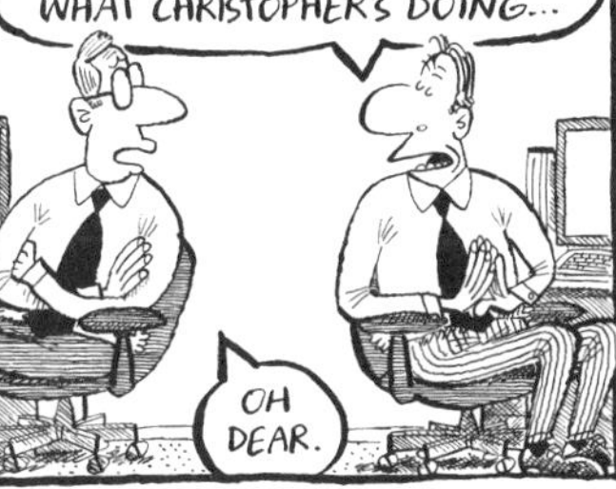
HE'S A DEVOTEE OF RUSSELL BRAND WHO USED TO TELL PEOPLE NOT TO VOTE BECAUSE IT WAS A WASTE OF TIME AND WON'T CHANGE ANYTHING, BUT NOW BRAND SAYS VOTE LABOUR SO THAT'S WHAT CHRISTOPHER'S DOING...
OH DEAR.
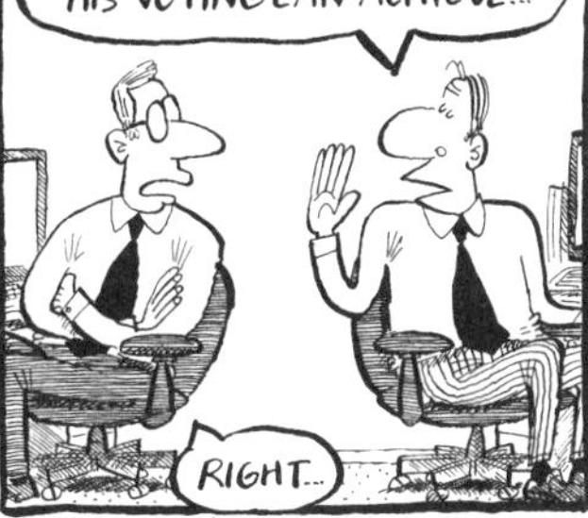
NO, NO, I'M QUITE HAPPY ABOUT IT... I'M GLAD TO SEE A YOUNG PERSON LIKE HIM EXERCISE HIS DEMOCRATIC RIGHT AND UNDERSTAND WHAT HIS VOTING CAN ACHIEVE...
RIGHT...
ABSOLUTELY NOTHING BECAUSE HE'S IN A ROCK SOLID CONSERVATIVE SEAT?
YUP. IT'S ONE OF THE FEW ADVANTAGES OF HAVING HIM STILL LIVING AT HOME WITH US.
HEH HEH

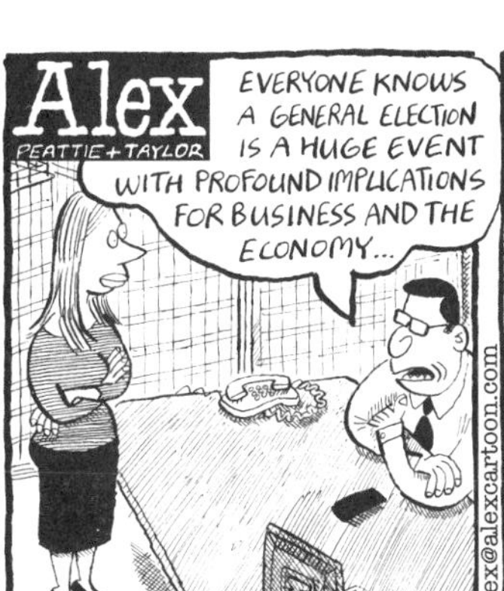
Alex
PEATTIE + TAYLOR
EVERYONE KNOWS A GENERAL ELECTION IS A HUGE EVENT WITH PROFOUND IMPLICATIONS FOR BUSINESS AND THE ECONOMY...
alex@alexcartoon.com
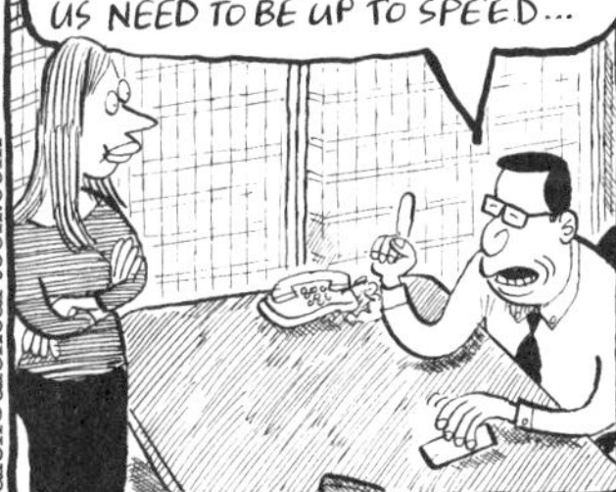
AND THE MORNING AFTER AN ELECTION IS WHEN THE BUSINESS TV CHANNELS CALL UP OUR GUYS ON THE BANK'S VIDEO LINK TO GET THEIR INSIGHTS ON THE AFTERMATH... AND ALL OF US NEED TO BE UP TO SPEED...
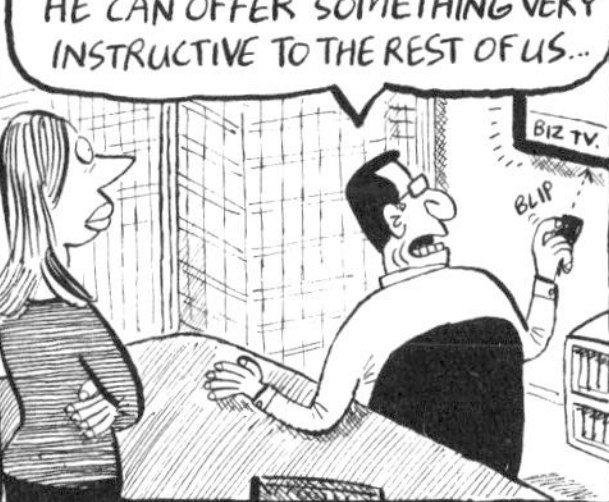
SO WHEN GUYS LIKE CLIVE MAKE IT THEIR TASK TO WATCH ALL THE BLOW-BY-BLOW COVERAGE OF THE RESULTS AS THEY UNFOLDED AND WERE DISCUSSED AT LENGTH BY THE PUNDITS HE CAN OFFER SOMETHING VERY INSTRUCTIVE TO THE REST OF US...
BIZ TV.
BLIP
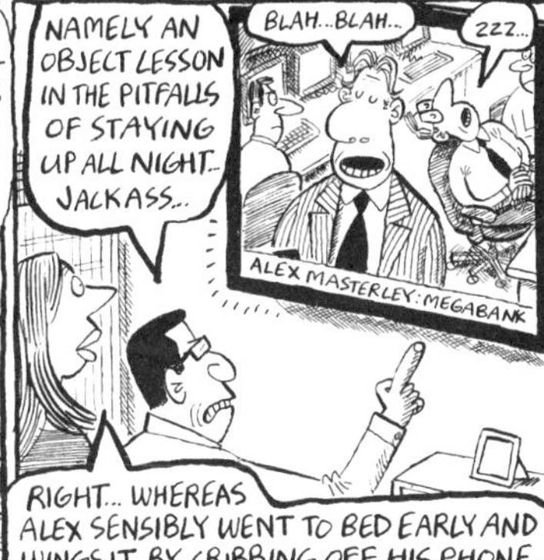
NAMELY AN OBJECT LESSON IN THE PITFALLS OF STAYING UP ALL NIGHT... JACKASS...
BLAH...BLAH...
ZZZ...
ALEX MASTERLEY: MEGABANK
RIGHT... WHEREAS ALEX SENSIBLY WENT TO BED EARLY AND WINGS IT BY CRIBBING OFF HIS PHONE...

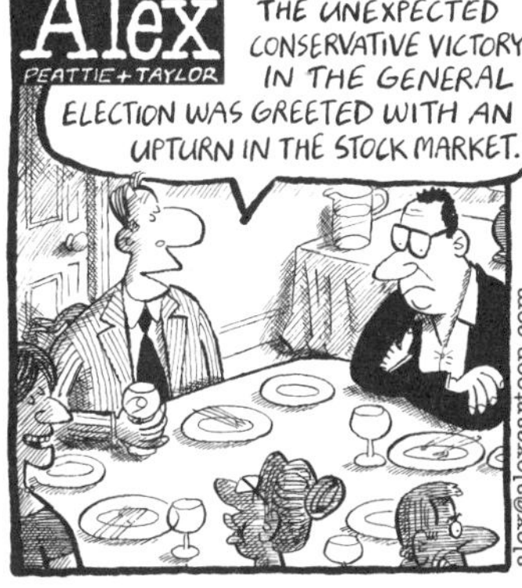
Alex
PEATTIE + TAYLOR
THE UNEXPECTED CONSERVATIVE VICTORY IN THE GENERAL ELECTION WAS GREETED WITH AN UPTURN IN THE STOCK MARKET.
alex@alexcartoon.com
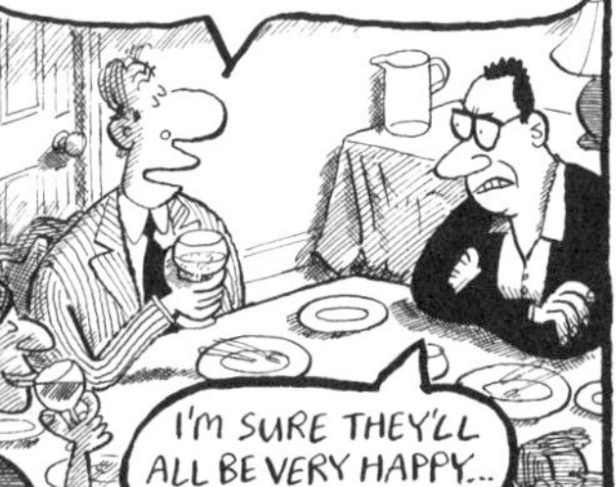
SECTORS THAT WOULD HAVE BEEN BADLY HIT BY LABOUR'S PUNITIVE TAXATION AND REGULATION POLICIES, SUCH AS ENERGY COMPANIES, BANKS AND ESTATE AGENTS POSTED BIG GAINS...
I'M SURE THEY'LL ALL BE VERY HAPPY...
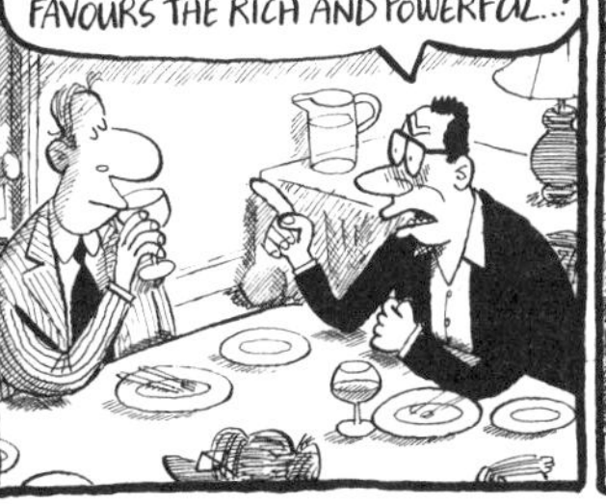
BUT WHAT ABOUT THOSE OF US WHO WORK IN AREAS OF SOCIETY THAT WILL SEE VERY REAL DAMAGE DONE TO THEIR FUTURES BY A TORY ECONOMIC REGIME WHICH BLATANTLY FAVOURS THE RICH AND POWERFUL...?
I DON'T THINK ANYONE'S GOING TO FEEL TOO SORRY FOR YOU TAX PLANNING LAWYERS, JASPER...
SIGH
WHEN I THINK OF THE FEES WE'D HAVE MADE UNDER A HARD-LEFT SOCIALIST GOVERNMENT...

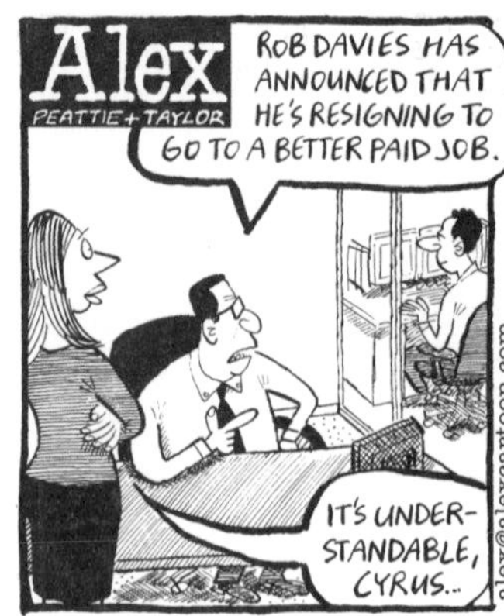
Alex
PEATTIE+TAYLOR
ROB DAVIES HAS ANNOUNCED THAT HE'S RESIGNING TO GO TO A BETTER PAID JOB.
IT'S UNDERSTANDABLE, CYRUS...
alex@alexcartoon.com

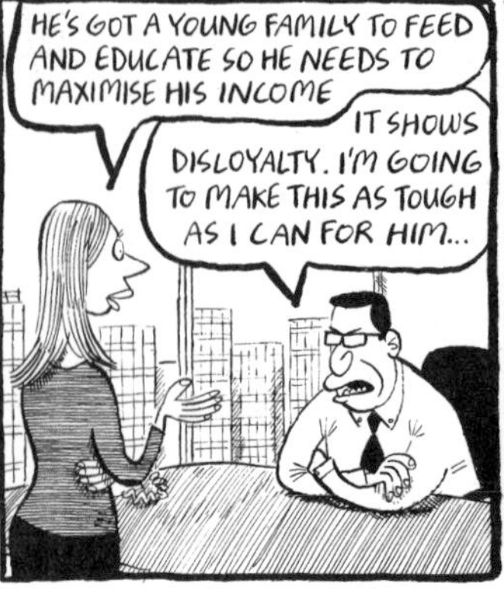
HE'S GOT A YOUNG FAMILY TO FEED AND EDUCATE SO HE NEEDS TO MAXIMISE HIS INCOME
IT SHOWS DISLOYALTY. I'M GOING TO MAKE THIS AS TOUGH AS I CAN FOR HIM...

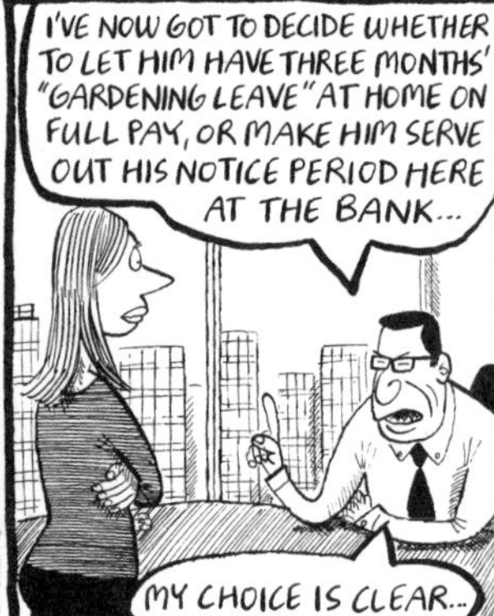
I'VE NOW GOT TO DECIDE WHETHER TO LET HIM HAVE THREE MONTHS' "GARDENING LEAVE" AT HOME ON FULL PAY, OR MAKE HIM SERVE OUT HIS NOTICE PERIOD HERE AT THE BANK...
MY CHOICE IS CLEAR...

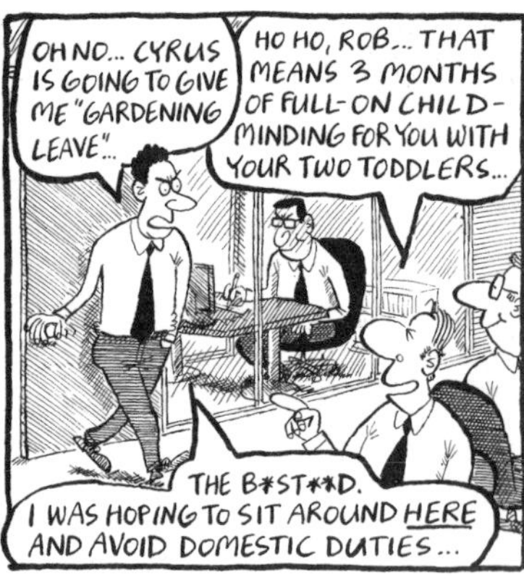
OH NO... CYRUS IS GOING TO GIVE ME "GARDENING LEAVE"...
HO HO, ROB... THAT MEANS 3 MONTHS OF FULL-ON CHILD-MINDING FOR YOU WITH YOUR TWO TODDLERS...
THE B*ST**D. I WAS HOPING TO SIT AROUND HERE AND AVOID DOMESTIC DUTIES...

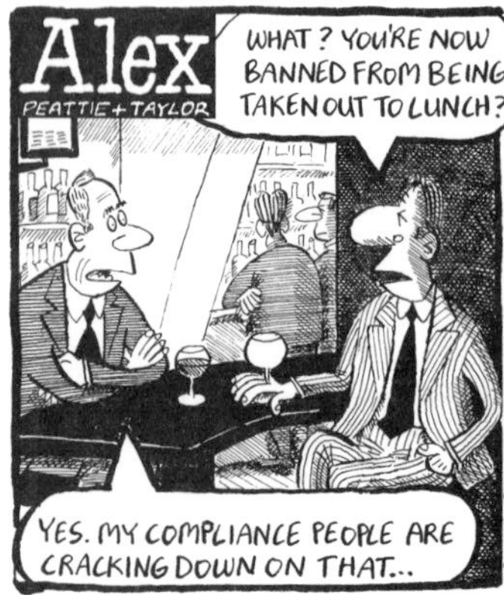
Alex
PEATTIE+TAYLOR
WHAT? YOU'RE NOW BANNED FROM BEING TAKEN OUT TO LUNCH?
YES. MY COMPLIANCE PEOPLE ARE CRACKING DOWN ON THAT...
alex@alexcartoon.com

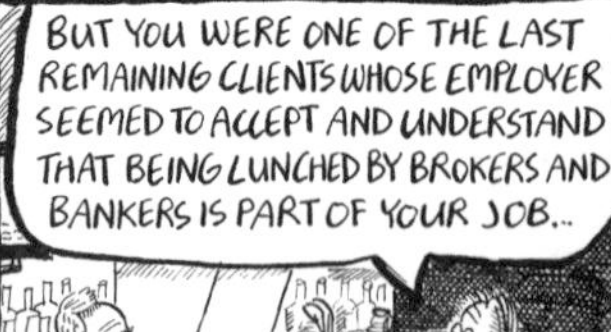
BUT YOU WERE ONE OF THE LAST REMAINING CLIENTS WHOSE EMPLOYER SEEMED TO ACCEPT AND UNDERSTAND THAT BEING LUNCHED BY BROKERS AND BANKERS IS PART OF YOUR JOB...

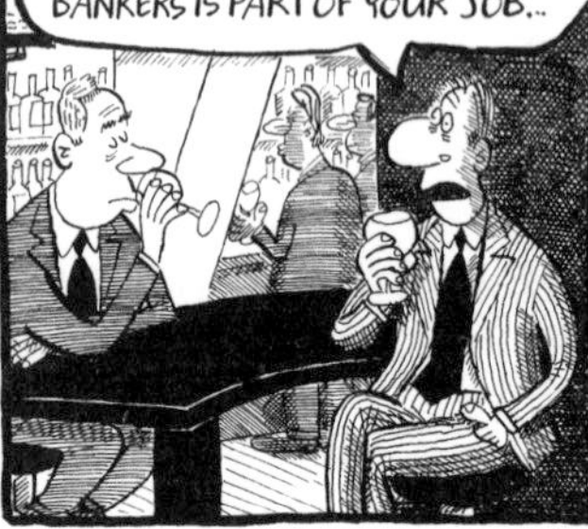

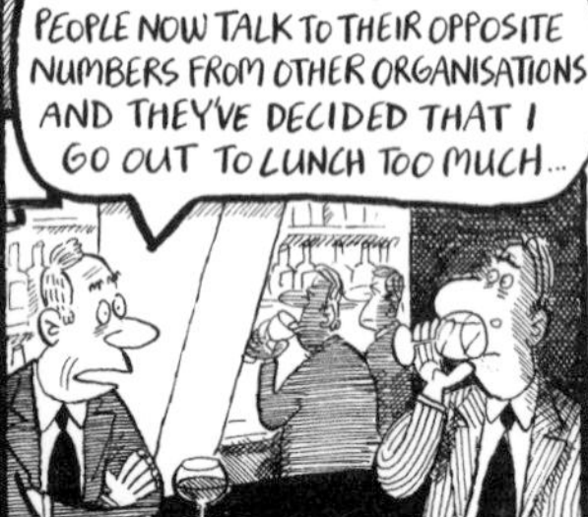
UNFORTUNATELY MY COMPLIANCE PEOPLE NOW TALK TO THEIR OPPOSITE NUMBERS FROM OTHER ORGANISATIONS AND THEY'VE DECIDED THAT I GO OUT TO LUNCH TOO MUCH...

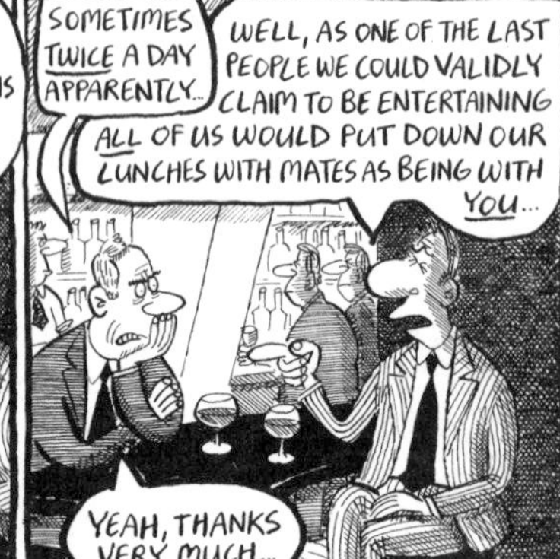
SOMETIMES TWICE A DAY APPARENTLY...
WELL, AS ONE OF THE LAST PEOPLE WE COULD VALIDLY CLAIM TO BE ENTERTAINING ALL OF US WOULD PUT DOWN OUR LUNCHES WITH MATES AS BEING WITH YOU...
YEAH, THANKS VERY MUCH...

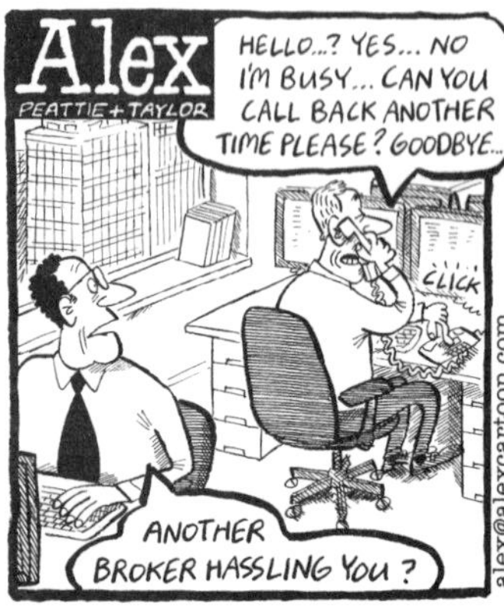
Alex
PEATTIE+TAYLOR
HELLO...? YES... NO I'M BUSY... CAN YOU CALL BACK ANOTHER TIME PLEASE? GOODBYE...
CLICK
ANOTHER BROKER HASSLING YOU?
alex@alexcartoon.com

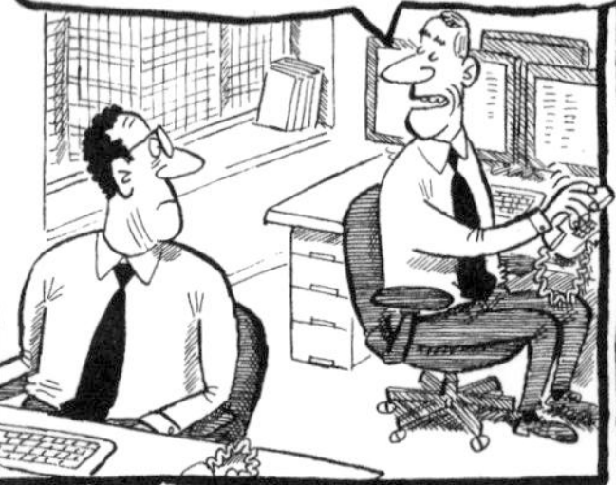
WELL, WE'RE THEIR CLIENTS AND THEY NEED TO SELL US INVESTMENT IDEAS. ALSO, THEY HAVE CLIENT RELATIONSHIP MANAGEMENT SYSTEMS WHICH LOG ALL THEIR CALLS TO ENSURE THEY'RE CONTACTING US REGULARLY.

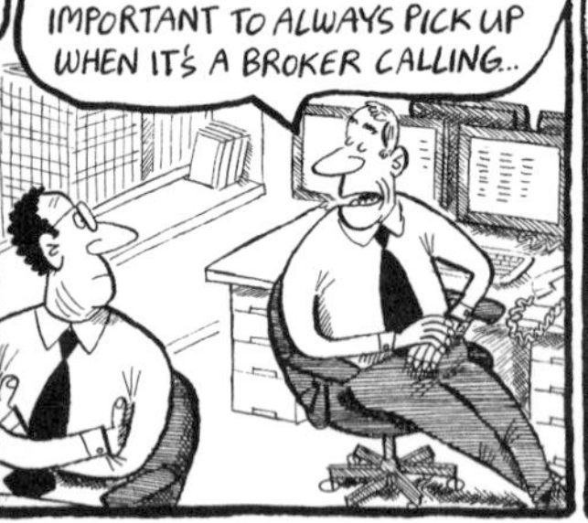
SOME OF US FUND MANAGERS NEVER ANSWER OUR PHONES AND LET CALLERS LEAVE LONG VOICEMAILS THAT NEVER GET LISTENED TO, BUT I THINK IT'S IMPORTANT TO ALWAYS PICK UP WHEN IT'S A BROKER CALLING...

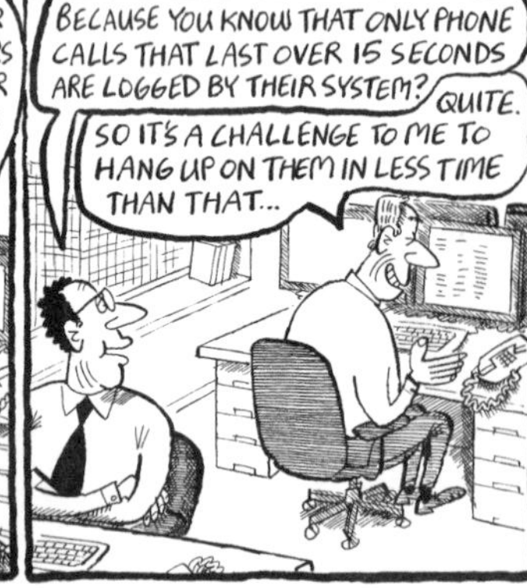
BECAUSE YOU KNOW THAT ONLY PHONE CALLS THAT LAST OVER 15 SECONDS ARE LOGGED BY THEIR SYSTEM?
QUITE.
SO IT'S A CHALLENGE TO ME TO HANG UP ON THEM IN LESS TIME THAN THAT...

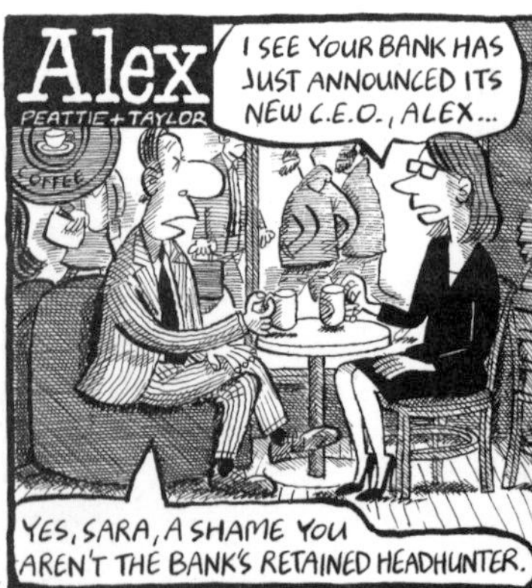
Alex
PEATTIE+TAYLOR
I SEE YOUR BANK HAS JUST ANNOUNCED ITS NEW C.E.O., ALEX...
COFFEE
YES, SARA, A SHAME YOU AREN'T THE BANK'S RETAINED HEADHUNTER.
alex@alexcartoon.com

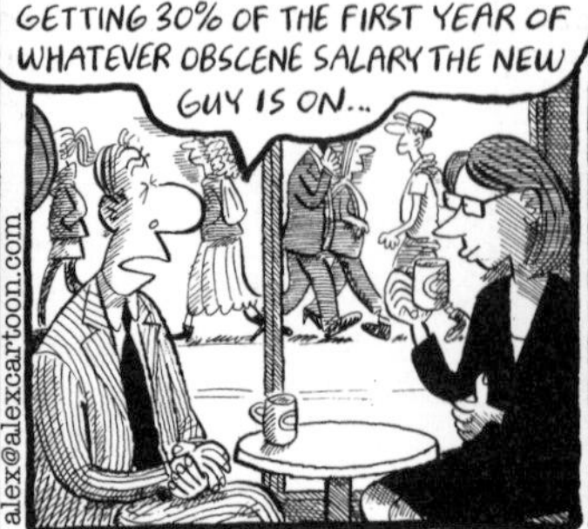
I IMAGINE THAT COULD HAVE BEEN A VERY LUCRATIVE COMMISSION FOR A RECRUITMENT CONSULTANT. A BIG SEARCH FEE, PLUS GETTING 30% OF THE FIRST YEAR OF WHATEVER OBSCENE SALARY THE NEW GUY IS ON...

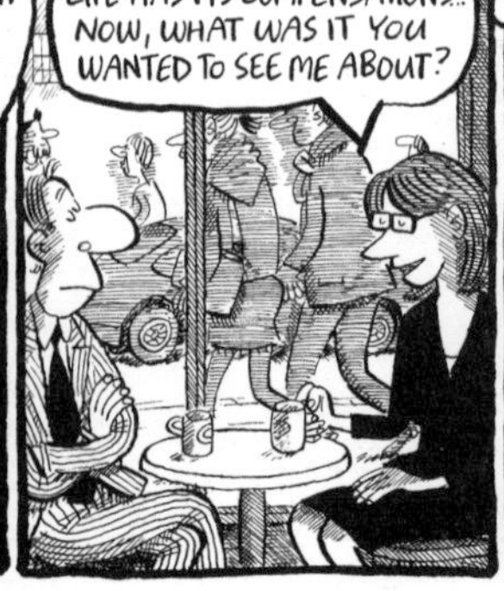
OH WELL... NEVER MIND... LIFE HAS ITS COMPENSATIONS... NOW, WHAT WAS IT YOU WANTED TO SEE ME ABOUT?

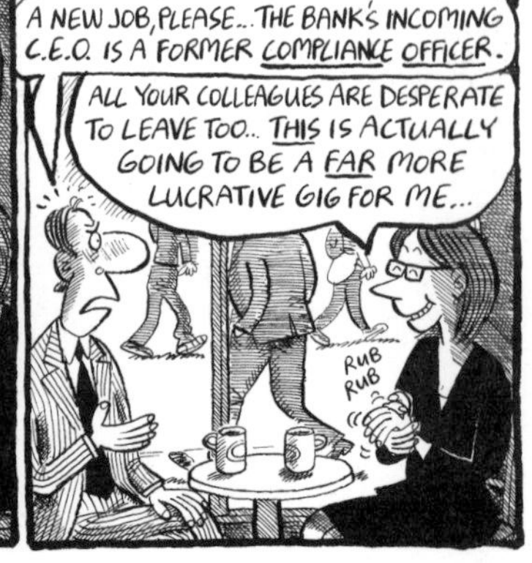
A NEW JOB, PLEASE... THE BANK'S INCOMING C.E.O. IS A FORMER COMPLIANCE OFFICER.
ALL YOUR COLLEAGUES ARE DESPERATE TO LEAVE TOO... THIS IS ACTUALLY GOING TO BE A FAR MORE LUCRATIVE GIG FOR ME...
RUB RUB

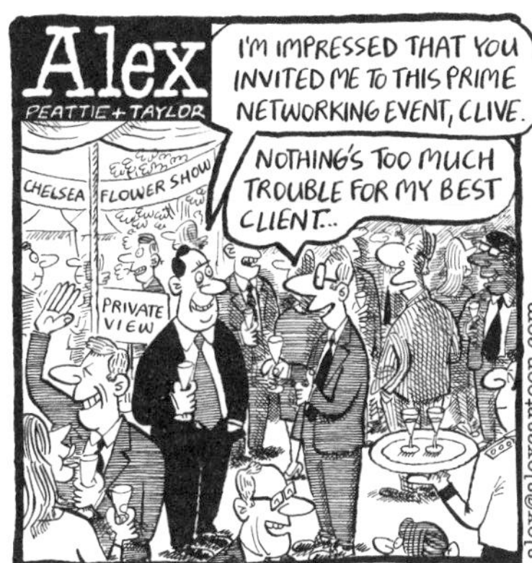
Alex
PEATTIE + TAYLOR
I'M IMPRESSED THAT YOU INVITED ME TO THIS PRIME NETWORKING EVENT, CLIVE.
NOTHING'S TOO MUCH TROUBLE FOR MY BEST CLIENT...
CHELSEA FLOWER SHOW
PRIVATE VIEW

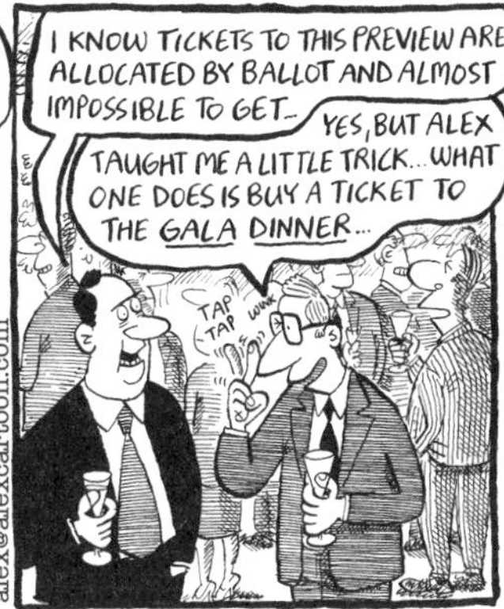
I KNOW TICKETS TO THIS PREVIEW ARE ALLOCATED BY BALLOT AND ALMOST IMPOSSIBLE TO GET...
YES, BUT ALEX TAUGHT ME A LITTLE TRICK... WHAT ONE DOES IS BUY A TICKET TO THE GALA DINNER...
TAP TAP
alex@alexcartoon.com

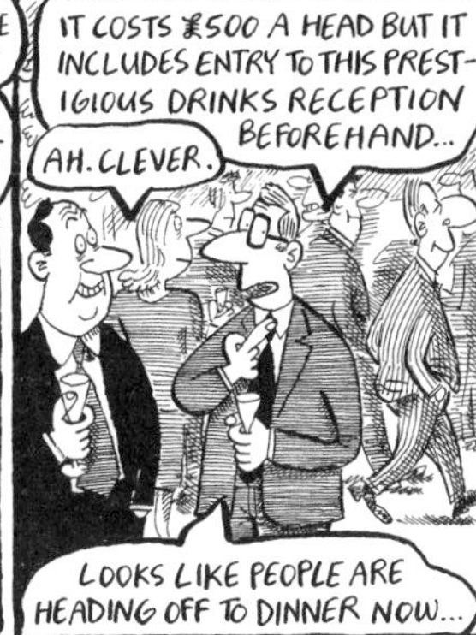
IT COSTS £500 A HEAD BUT IT INCLUDES ENTRY TO THIS PRESTIGIOUS DRINKS RECEPTION BEFOREHAND...
AH. CLEVER.
LOOKS LIKE PEOPLE ARE HEADING OFF TO DINNER NOW...

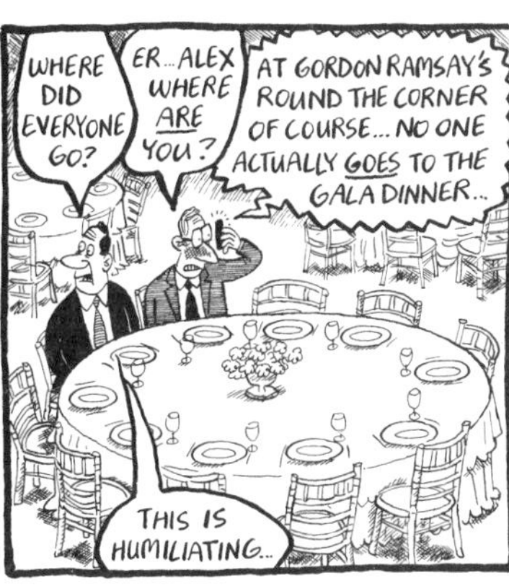
WHERE DID EVERYONE GO?
ER... ALEX WHERE ARE YOU?
AT GORDON RAMSAY'S ROUND THE CORNER OF COURSE... NO ONE ACTUALLY GOES TO THE GALA DINNER...
THIS IS HUMILIATING...

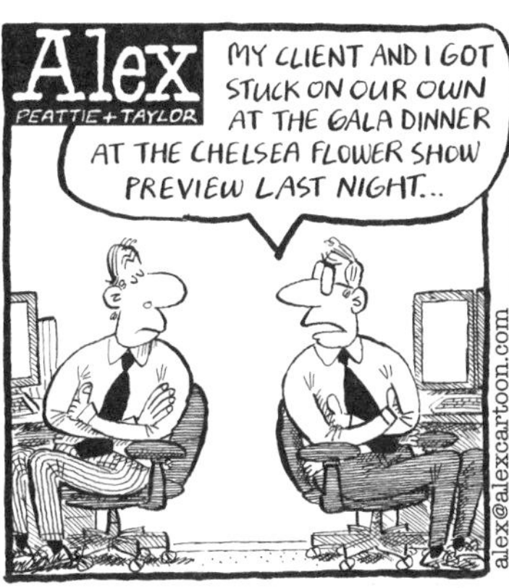
Alex
PEATTIE + TAYLOR
MY CLIENT AND I GOT STUCK ON OUR OWN AT THE GALA DINNER AT THE CHELSEA FLOWER SHOW PREVIEW LAST NIGHT...
alex@alexcartoon.com

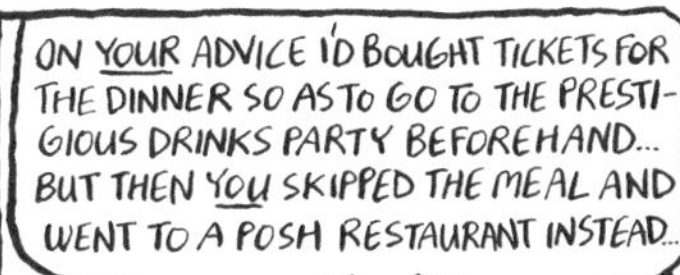
ON YOUR ADVICE I'D BOUGHT TICKETS FOR THE DINNER SO AS TO GO TO THE PRESTIGIOUS DRINKS PARTY BEFOREHAND... BUT THEN YOU SKIPPED THE MEAL AND WENT TO A POSH RESTAURANT INSTEAD...

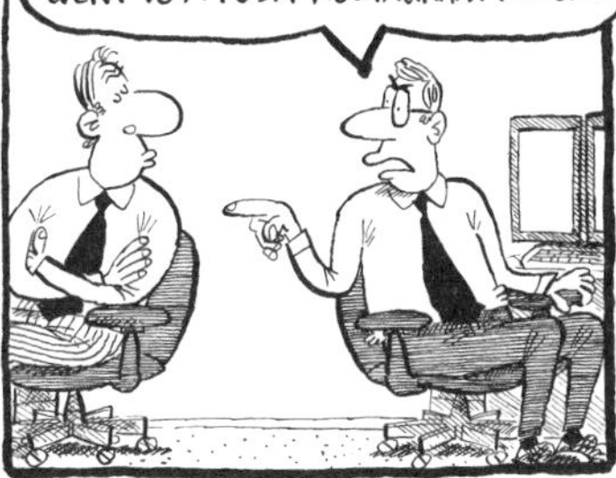

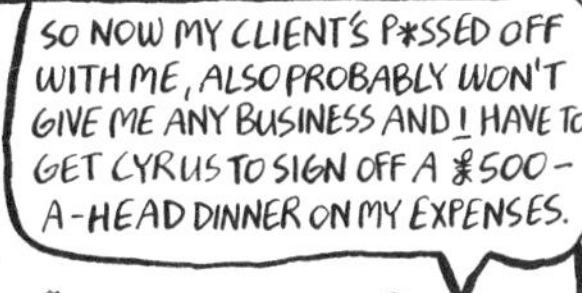
SO NOW MY CLIENT'S P*SSED OFF WITH ME, ALSO PROBABLY WON'T GIVE ME ANY BUSINESS AND I HAVE TO GET CYRUS TO SIGN OFF A £500-A-HEAD DINNER ON MY EXPENSES.

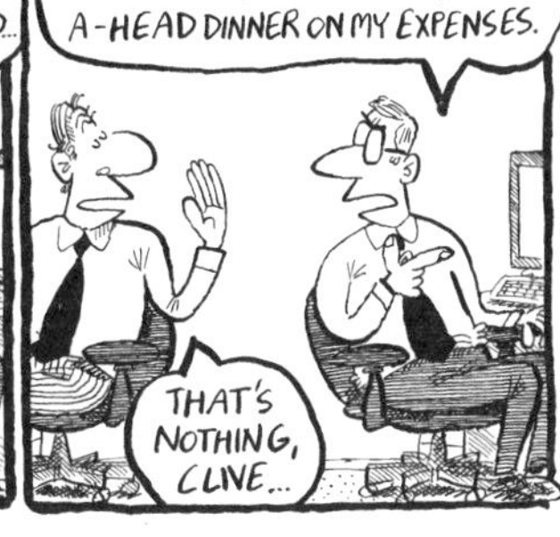
THAT'S NOTHING, CLIVE...

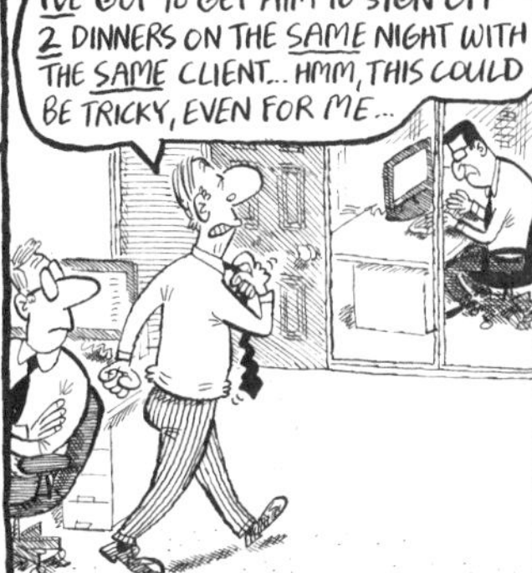
I'VE GOT TO GET HIM TO SIGN OFF 2 DINNERS ON THE SAME NIGHT WITH THE SAME CLIENT... HMM, THIS COULD BE TRICKY, EVEN FOR ME...

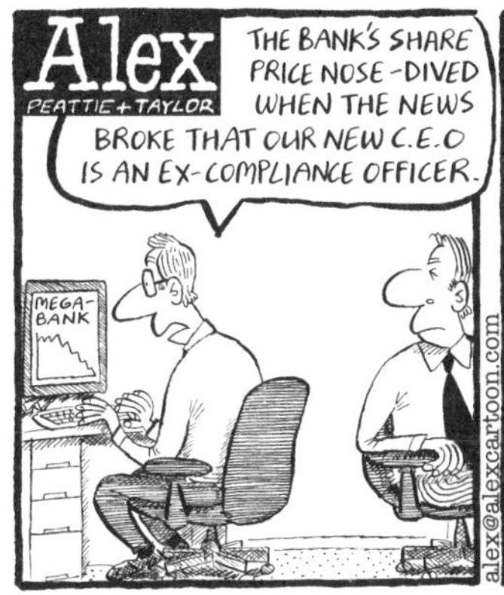
Alex
PEATTIE + TAYLOR
THE BANK'S SHARE PRICE NOSE-DIVED WHEN THE NEWS BROKE THAT OUR NEW C.E.O IS AN EX-COMPLIANCE OFFICER.
MEGA-BANK
alex@alexcartoon.com

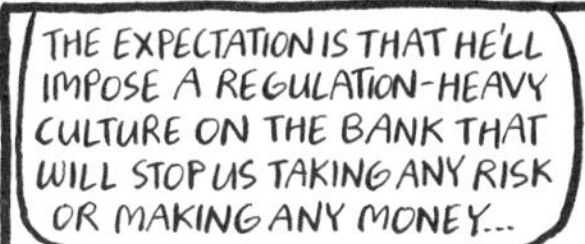
THE EXPECTATION IS THAT HE'LL IMPOSE A REGULATION-HEAVY CULTURE ON THE BANK THAT WILL STOP US TAKING ANY RISK OR MAKING ANY MONEY...

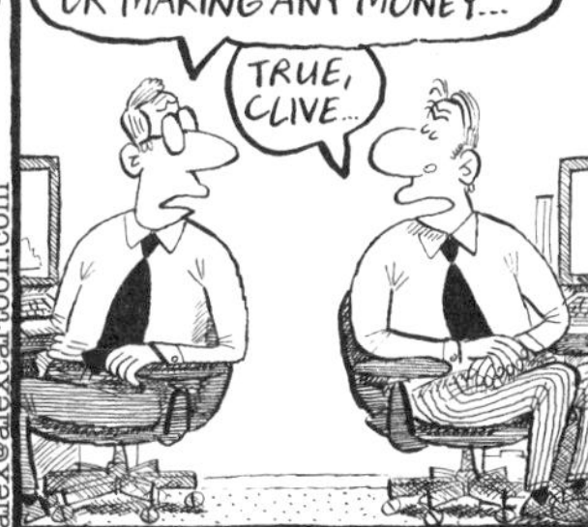
TRUE, CLIVE...

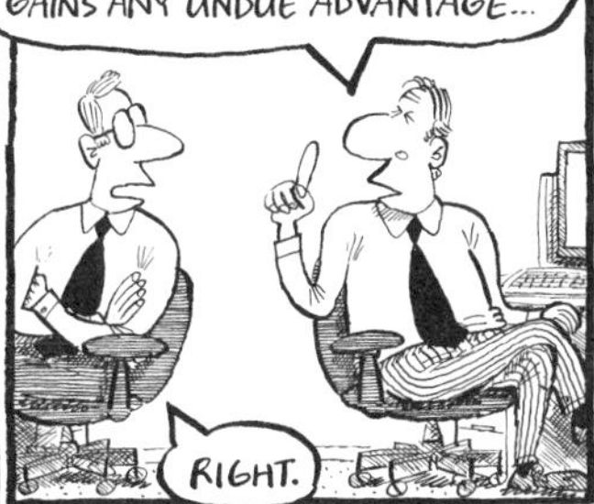
IT MAY BE BAD NEWS FOR OUR PAY, BUT AT LEAST THE BANK'S NEW BOSS IS SOMEONE WHO IS COMMITTED TO CREATING A LEVEL PLAYING FIELD WHERE NO ONE GAINS ANY UNDUE ADVANTAGE...
RIGHT.

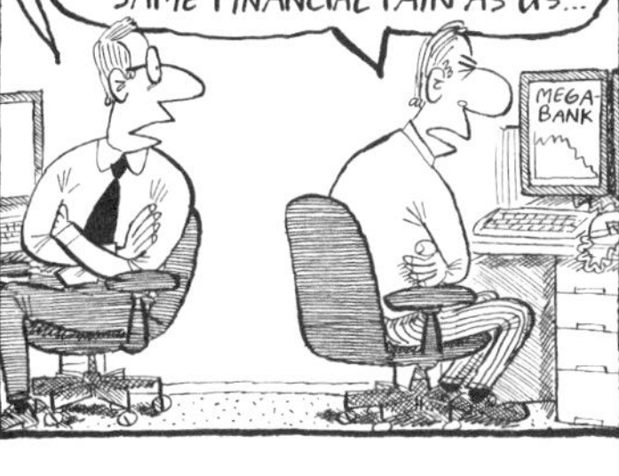
SO YOU THINK HE'LL HAVE AGREED TO HAVE A GOOD PART OF HIS COMPENSATION PAID IN BANK STOCK, LIKE THE REST OF US GET?
INCLUDING HIS SIGN-ON FEE, LET'S HOPE. I WANT HIM TO BE TAKING THE SAME FINANCIAL PAIN AS US...
MEGA-BANK

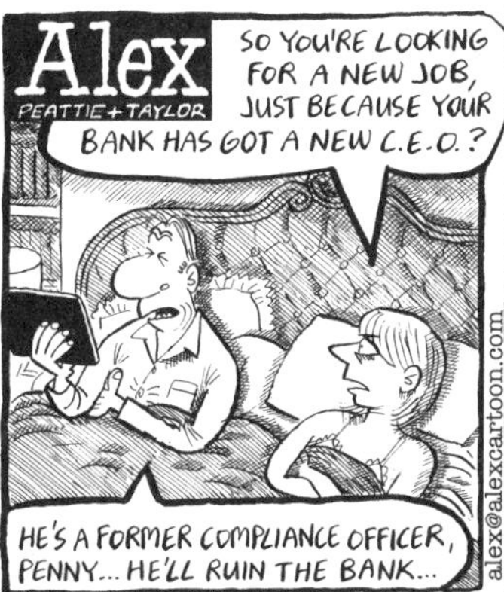
Alex
PEATTIE + TAYLOR
SO YOU'RE LOOKING FOR A NEW JOB, JUST BECAUSE YOUR BANK HAS GOT A NEW C.E.O.?
HE'S A FORMER COMPLIANCE OFFICER, PENNY... HE'LL RUIN THE BANK...
alex@alexcartoon.com

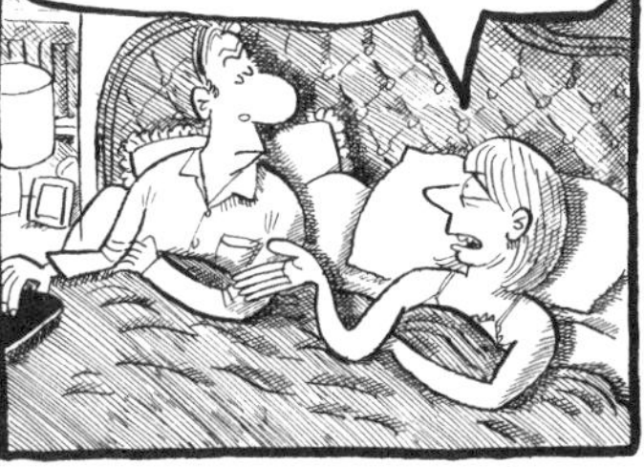
TYPICAL OF YOU, ALEX... THIS NEW BOSS HAS BEEN BROUGHT IN TO MAKE SOME LONG-OVERDUE CHANGES TO HOW THE BANK IS RUN, AND YOUR RESPONSE IS TO THINK OF YOUR OWN INTERESTS AND PLAN TO JUMP SHIP...

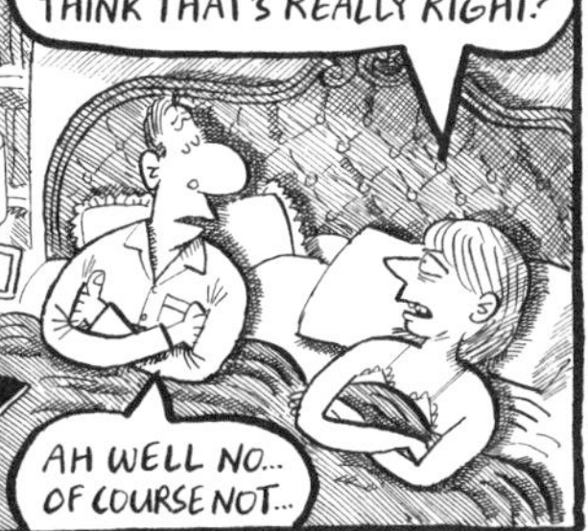
CONSIDERING THAT YOU WERE ONE OF THE BANKERS WHO HELPED TARNISH THE BANK'S REPUTATION IN THE FINANCIAL CRISIS, DO YOU THINK THAT'S REALLY RIGHT?
AH WELL NO... OF COURSE NOT...
THERE MUST BE A GOOD CHANCE THEY'LL MAKE ME REDUNDANT... I'LL HANG AROUND AND SEE IF I GET A PAY-OFF...
THANKS FOR THE TIP, PENNY.

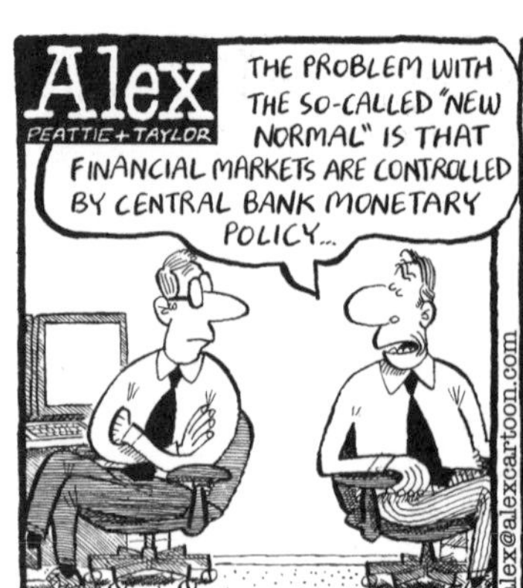
Alex
PEATTIE + TAYLOR
THE PROBLEM WITH THE SO-CALLED "NEW NORMAL" IS THAT FINANCIAL MARKETS ARE CONTROLLED BY CENTRAL BANK MONETARY POLICY...
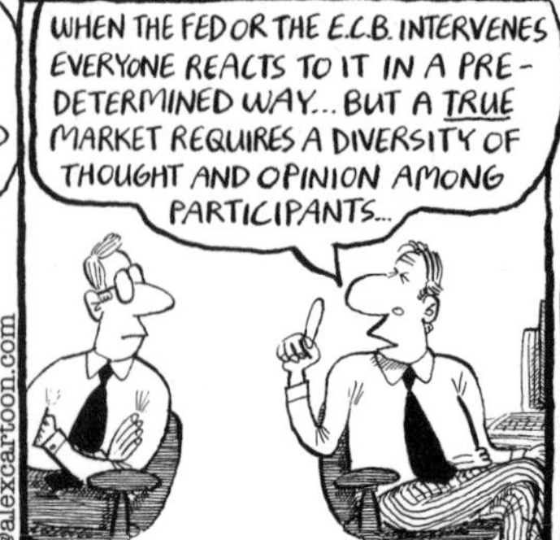
WHEN THE FED OR THE E.C.B. INTERVENES EVERYONE REACTS TO IT IN A PRE-DETERMINED WAY... BUT A TRUE MARKET REQUIRES A DIVERSITY OF THOUGHT AND OPINION AMONG PARTICIPANTS...
alex@alexcartoon.com
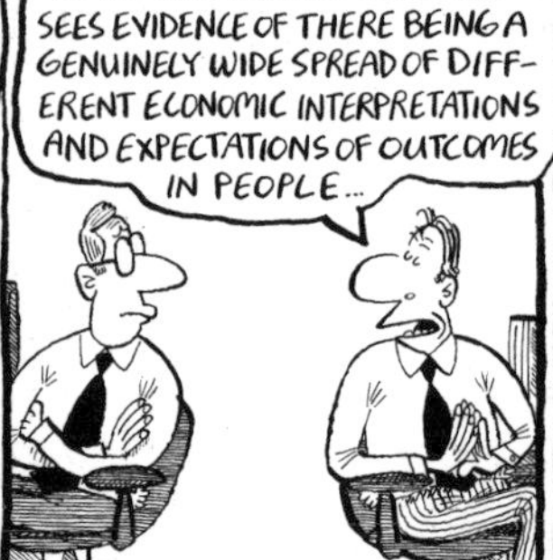
SO IT'S A REVELATION WHEN ONE SEES EVIDENCE OF THERE BEING A GENUINELY WIDE SPREAD OF DIFFERENT ECONOMIC INTERPRETATIONS AND EXPECTATIONS OF OUTCOMES IN PEOPLE...
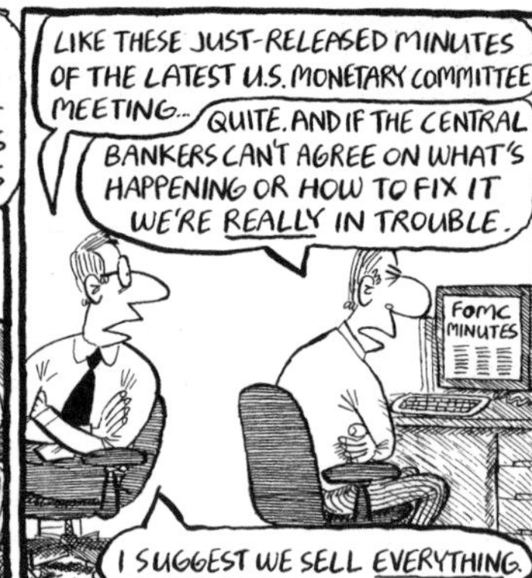
LIKE THESE JUST-RELEASED MINUTES OF THE LATEST U.S. MONETARY COMMITTEE MEETING...
QUITE. AND IF THE CENTRAL BANKERS CAN'T AGREE ON WHAT'S HAPPENING OR HOW TO FIX IT WE'RE REALLY IN TROUBLE.
FOMC MINUTES
I SUGGEST WE SELL EVERYTHING.

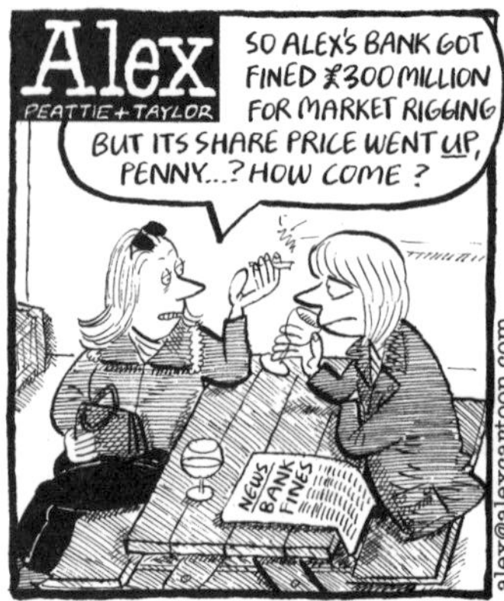
Alex
PEATTIE + TAYLOR
SO ALEX'S BANK GOT FINED ₮300 MILLION FOR MARKET RIGGING BUT ITS SHARE PRICE WENT UP, PENNY...? HOW COME?
NEWS BANK FINES
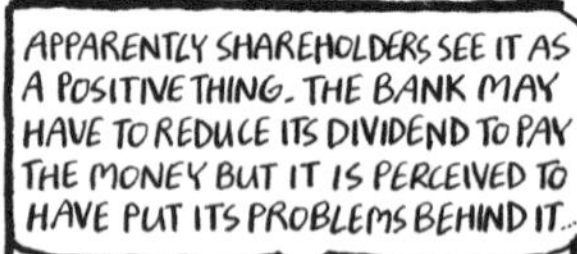
APPARENTLY SHAREHOLDERS SEE IT AS A POSITIVE THING. THE BANK MAY HAVE TO REDUCE ITS DIVIDEND TO PAY THE MONEY BUT IT IS PERCEIVED TO HAVE PUT ITS PROBLEMS BEHIND IT...
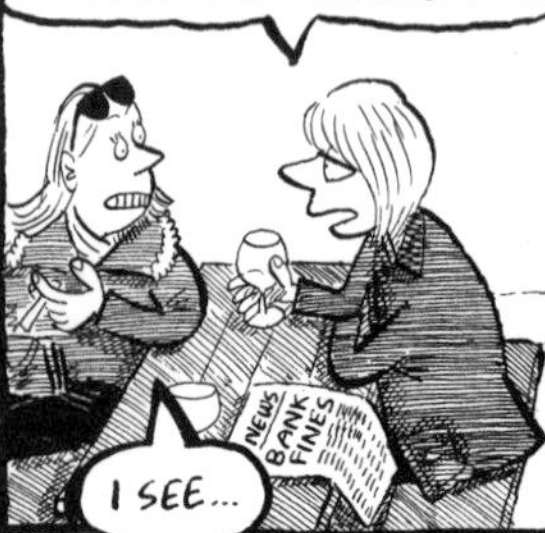
NEWS BANK FINES
I SEE...
alex@alexcartoon.com
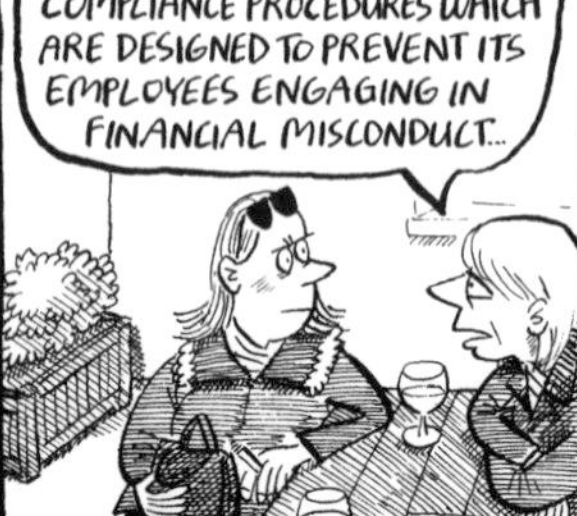
ALSO IT HAS BROUGHT IN TIGHTER COMPLIANCE PROCEDURES WHICH ARE DESIGNED TO PREVENT ITS EMPLOYEES ENGAGING IN FINANCIAL MISCONDUCT...
NEWS BANK FINES
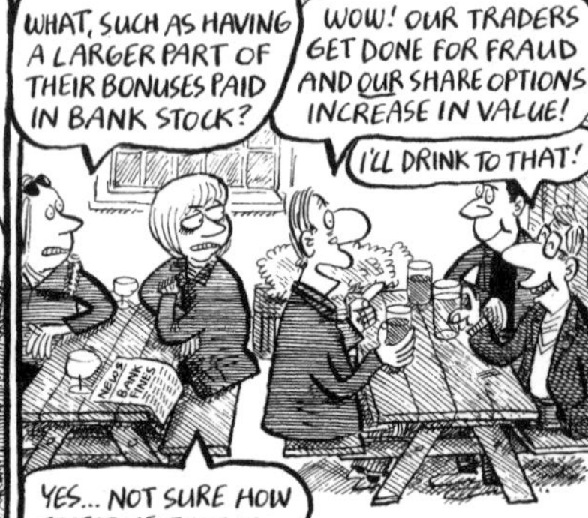
WHAT, SUCH AS HAVING A LARGER PART OF THEIR BONUSES PAID IN BANK STOCK?
WOW! OUR TRADERS GET DONE FOR FRAUD AND OUR SHARE OPTIONS INCREASE IN VALUE!
I'LL DRINK TO THAT!
YES... NOT SURE HOW EFFECTIVE THAT IS...

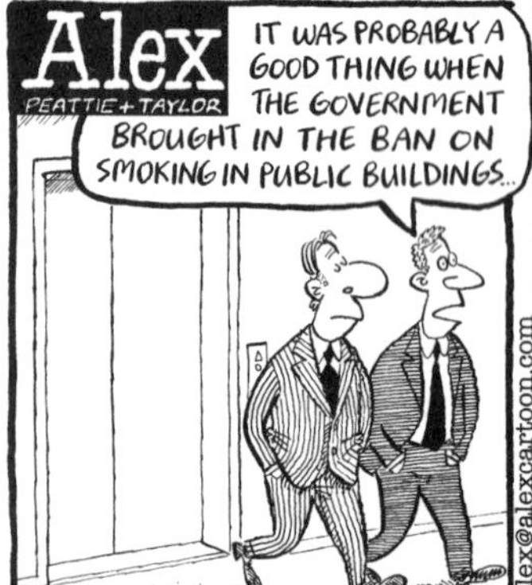
Alex
PEATTIE + TAYLOR
IT WAS PROBABLY A GOOD THING WHEN THE GOVERNMENT BROUGHT IN THE BAN ON SMOKING IN PUBLIC BUILDINGS...
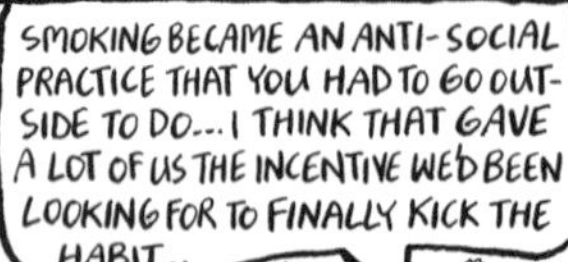
SMOKING BECAME AN ANTI-SOCIAL PRACTICE THAT YOU HAD TO GO OUTSIDE TO DO... I THINK THAT GAVE A LOT OF US THE INCENTIVE WE'D BEEN LOOKING FOR TO FINALLY KICK THE HABIT...
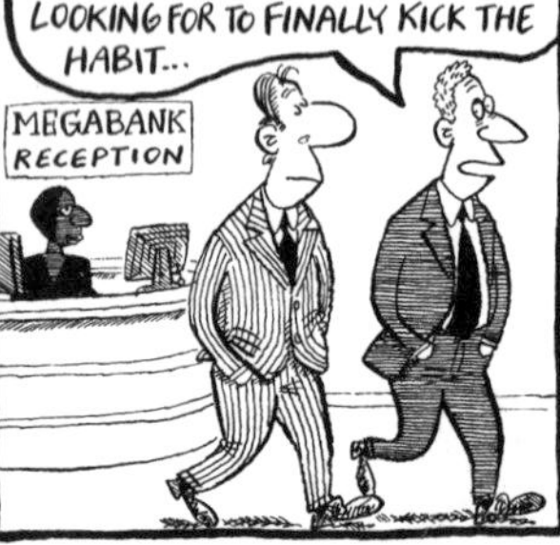
MEGABANK RECEPTION
alex@alexcartoon.com
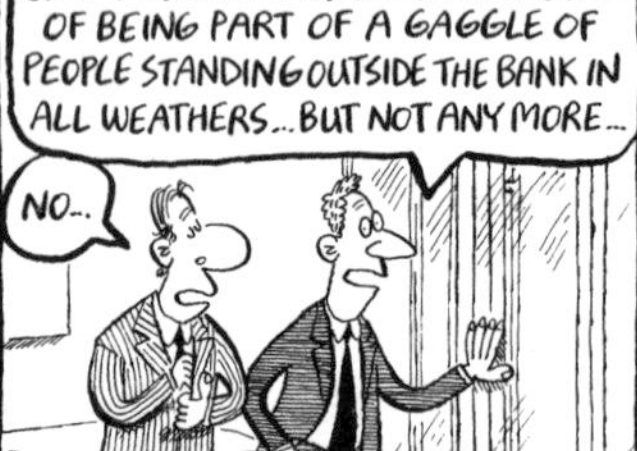
I MUST ADMIT FOR A WHILE AFTER I QUIT I USED TO MISS THE CAMARADERIE OF BEING PART OF A GAGGLE OF PEOPLE STANDING OUTSIDE THE BANK IN ALL WEATHERS... BUT NOT ANY MORE...
NO...
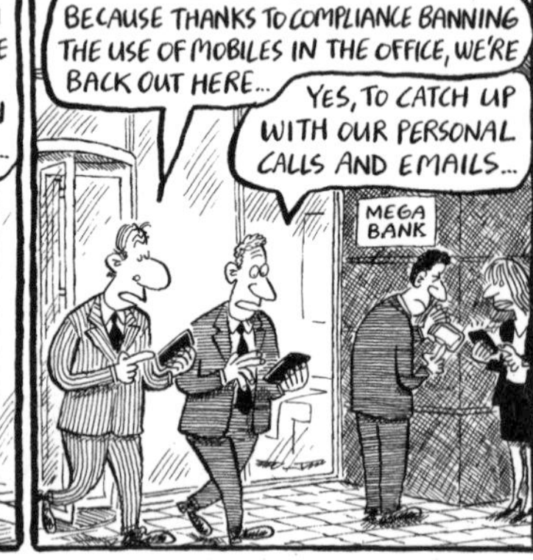
BECAUSE THANKS TO COMPLIANCE BANNING THE USE OF MOBILES IN THE OFFICE, WE'RE BACK OUT HERE...
YES, TO CATCH UP WITH OUR PERSONAL CALLS AND EMAILS...
MEGA BANK

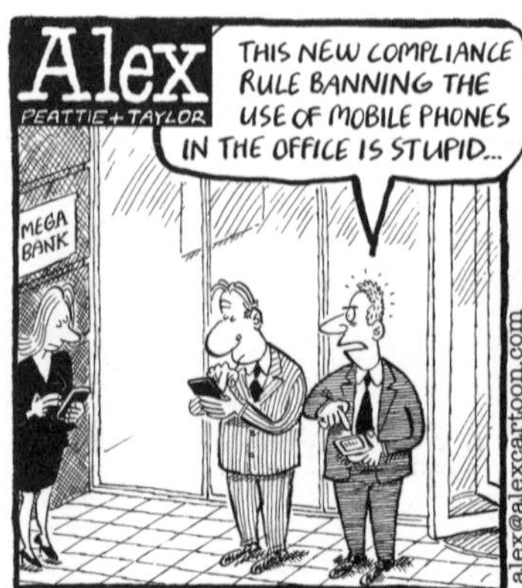
Alex
PEATTIE + TAYLOR
THIS NEW COMPLIANCE RULE BANNING THE USE OF MOBILE PHONES IN THE OFFICE IS STUPID...
MEGA BANK
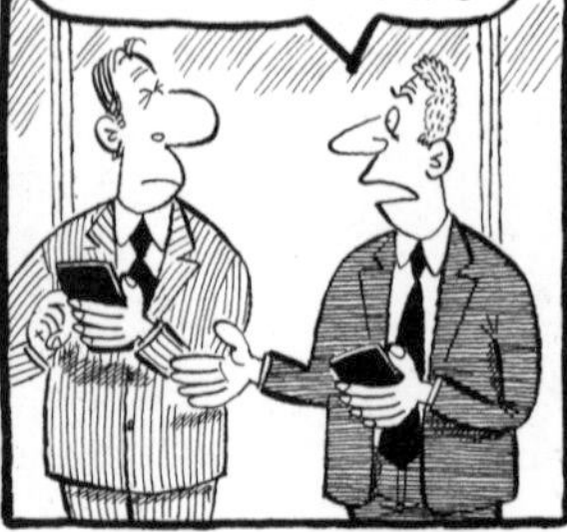
OKAY, SO WE ALL USED TO SLIP THE ODD PERSONAL PHONE CALL OR EMAIL INTO OUR WORKING TIME AT OUR DESKS, BUT WAS THAT REALLY SO BAD?
alex@alexcartoon.com
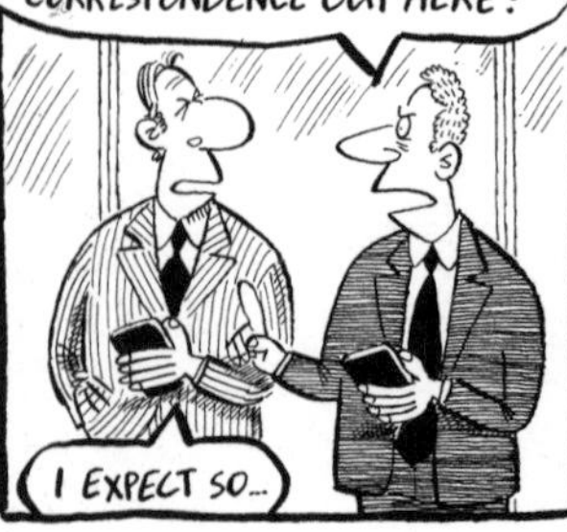
DOES COMPLIANCE THINK IT'S SOMEHOW MORE EFFICIENT THAT WE'VE TAKEN TO TROOPING OUT OF OUR OFFICE AND DEALING WITH OUR PERSONAL CORRESPONDENCE OUT HERE?
I EXPECT SO...
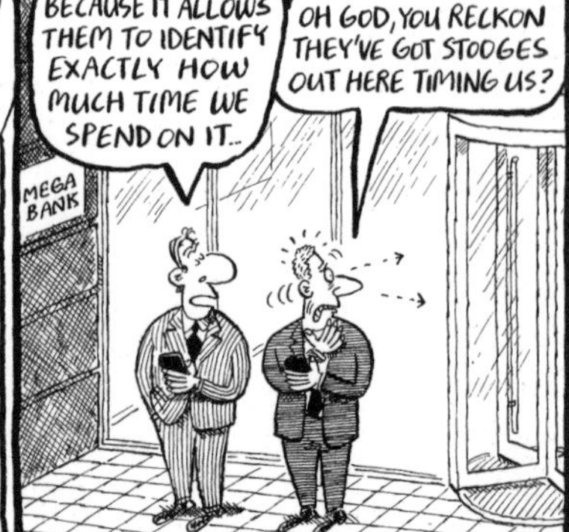
BECAUSE IT ALLOWS THEM TO IDENTIFY EXACTLY HOW MUCH TIME WE SPEND ON IT...
OH GOD, YOU RECKON THEY'VE GOT STOOGES OUT HERE TIMING US?
MEGA BANK

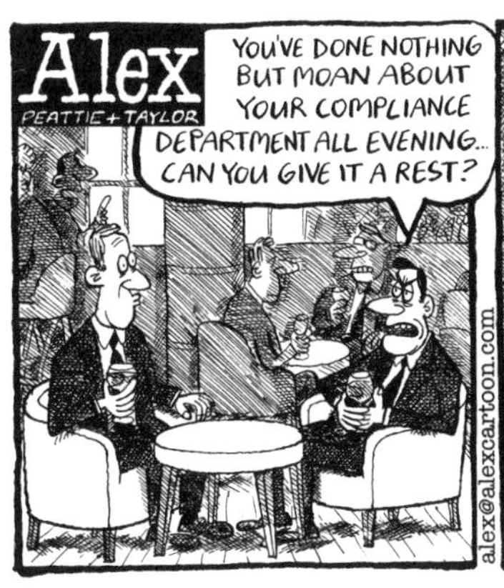
Alex
PEATTIE + TAYLOR
YOU'VE DONE NOTHING BUT MOAN ABOUT YOUR COMPLIANCE DEPARTMENT ALL EVENING... CAN YOU GIVE IT A REST?
alex@alexcartoon.com

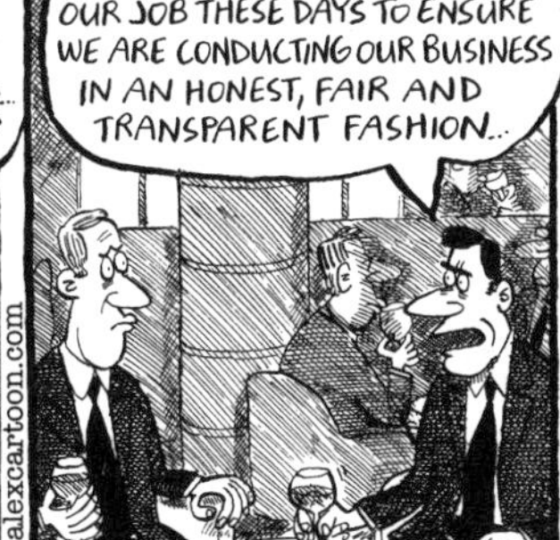
AS FUND MANAGERS IT'S PART OF OUR JOB THESE DAYS TO ENSURE WE ARE CONDUCTING OUR BUSINESS IN AN HONEST, FAIR AND TRANSPARENT FASHION...

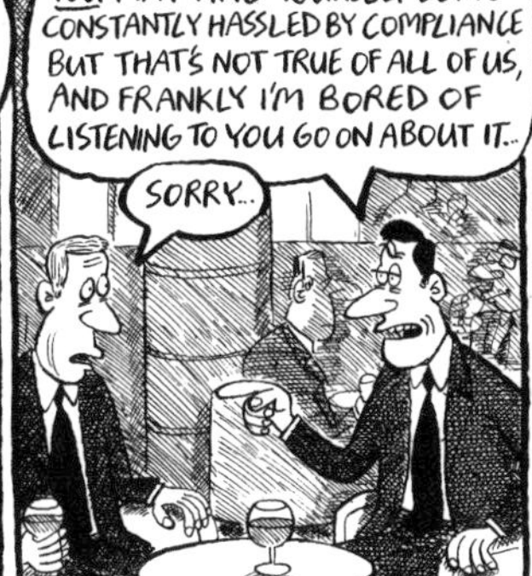
YOU MAY FIND YOURSELF BEING CONSTANTLY HASSLED BY COMPLIANCE BUT THAT'S NOT TRUE OF ALL OF US, AND FRANKLY I'M BORED OF LISTENING TO YOU GO ON ABOUT IT...
SORRY...

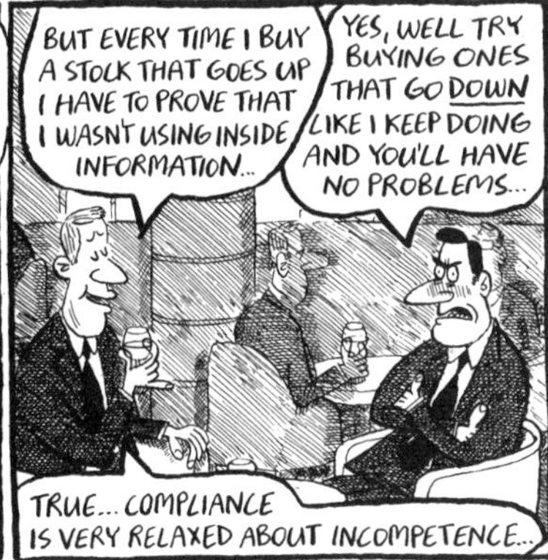
BUT EVERY TIME I BUY A STOCK THAT GOES UP I HAVE TO PROVE THAT I WASN'T USING INSIDE INFORMATION...
YES, WELL TRY BUYING ONES THAT GO DOWN LIKE I KEEP DOING AND YOU'LL HAVE NO PROBLEMS...
TRUE... COMPLIANCE IS VERY RELAXED ABOUT INCOMPETENCE...

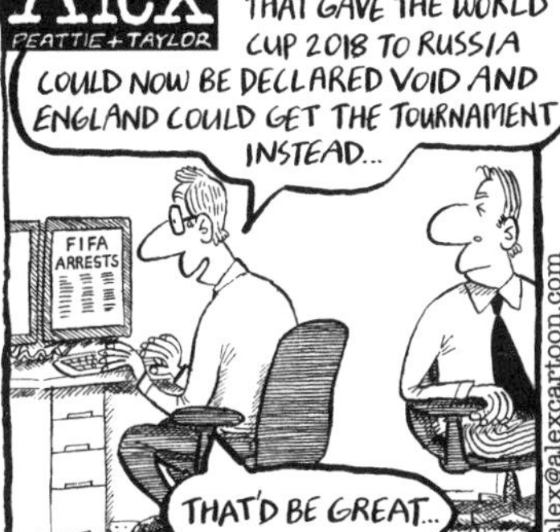
Alex
PEATTIE + TAYLOR
IT SEEMS THE FIFA VOTE THAT GAVE THE WORLD CUP 2018 TO RUSSIA COULD NOW BE DECLARED VOID AND ENGLAND COULD GET THE TOURNAMENT INSTEAD...
FIFA ARRESTS
THAT'D BE GREAT...
alex@alexcartoon.com

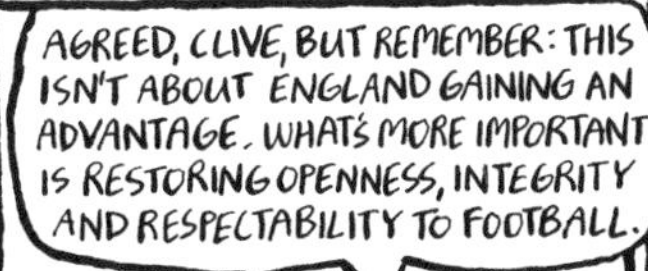
AGREED, CLIVE, BUT REMEMBER: THIS ISN'T ABOUT ENGLAND GAINING AN ADVANTAGE. WHAT'S MORE IMPORTANT IS RESTORING OPENNESS, INTEGRITY AND RESPECTABILITY TO FOOTBALL.

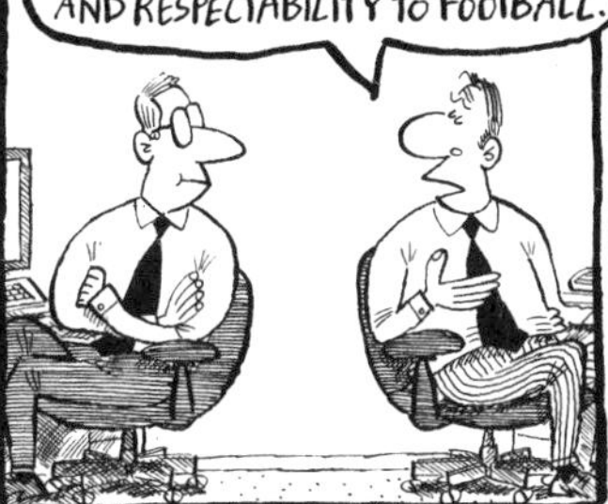

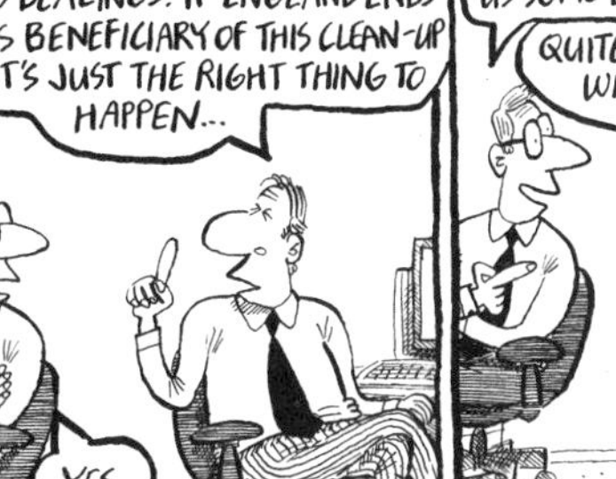
IT'S ABOUT RIDDING THE BEAUTIFUL GAME OF ASSOCIATIONS WITH BRIBERY, CORRUPTION AND UNDER-HAND DEALINGS. IF ENGLAND ENDS UP AS BENEFICIARY OF THIS CLEAN-UP THAT'S JUST THE RIGHT THING TO HAPPEN...
YES...

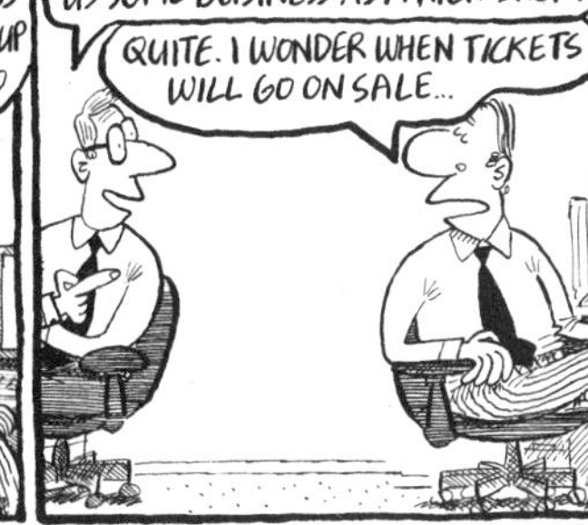
'COS WE'LL BE ABLE TO ENTERTAIN OUR CLIENTS AT THE TOURNAMENT AND HOPEFULLY INDUCE THEM TO GIVE US SOME BUSINESS AS A KICK-BACK.
QUITE. I WONDER WHEN TICKETS WILL GO ON SALE...

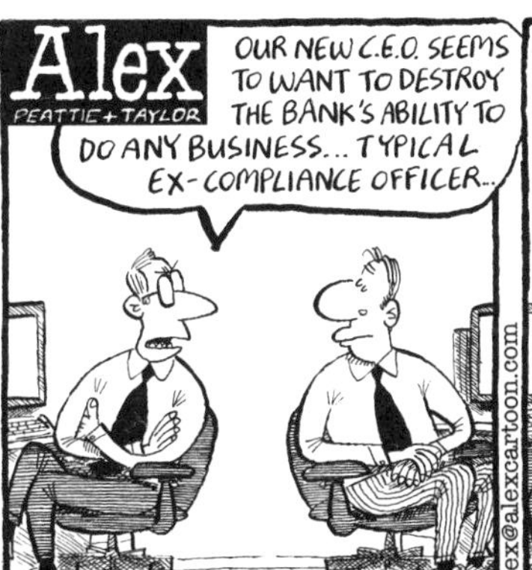
Alex
PEATTIE + TAYLOR
OUR NEW C.E.O. SEEMS TO WANT TO DESTROY THE BANK'S ABILITY TO DO ANY BUSINESS... TYPICAL EX-COMPLIANCE OFFICER...
alex@alexcartoon.com

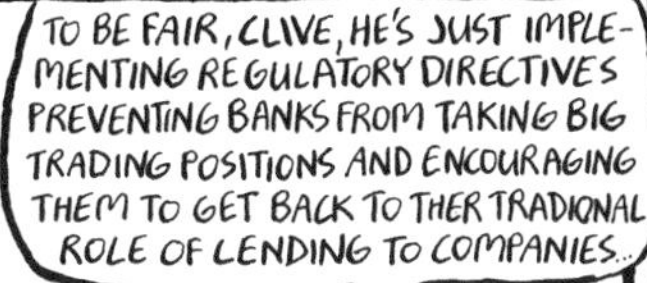
TO BE FAIR, CLIVE, HE'S JUST IMPLE-MENTING REGULATORY DIRECTIVES PREVENTING BANKS FROM TAKING BIG TRADING POSITIONS AND ENCOURAGING THEM TO GET BACK TO THER TRADIONAL ROLE OF LENDING TO COMPANIES...

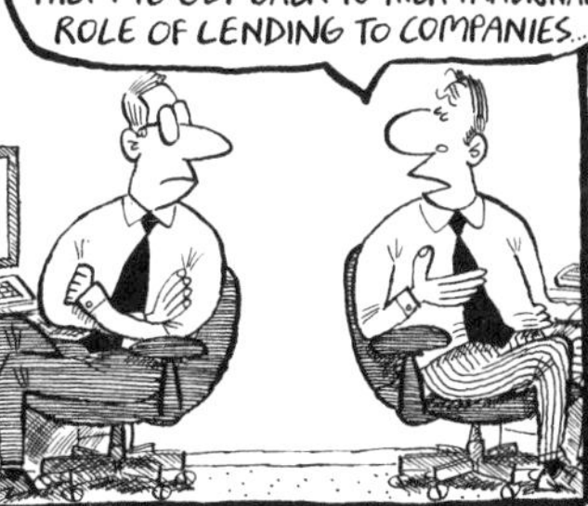

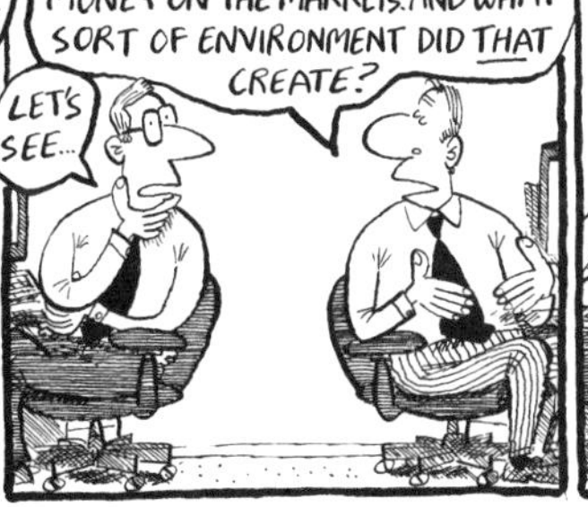
BANKS WERE PERCEIVED TO HAVE LOST THEIR WAY IN THE EARLY 2000s, BECOMING GLORIFIED HEDGE FUNDS PUNTING THEIR OWN MONEY ON THE MARKETS. AND WHAT SORT OF ENVIRONMENT DID THAT CREATE?
LET'S SEE...

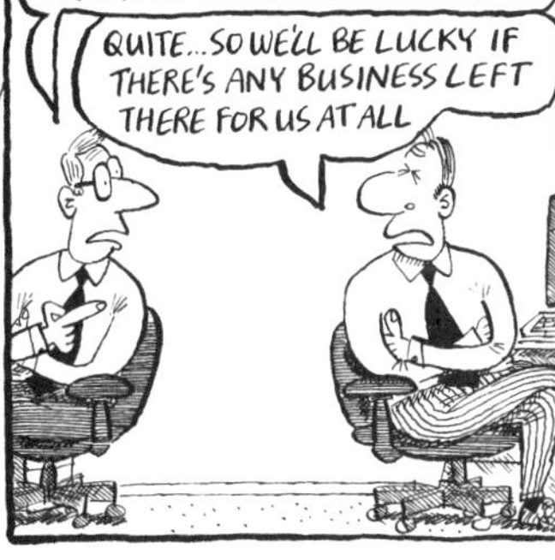
ONE WHERE LOTS OF SMALL START-UPS BEGAN INTERNET-BASED PEER-TO-PEER LENDING AND CORNERED THE MARKET.
QUITE... SO WE'LL BE LUCKY IF THERE'S ANY BUSINESS LEFT THERE FOR US AT ALL

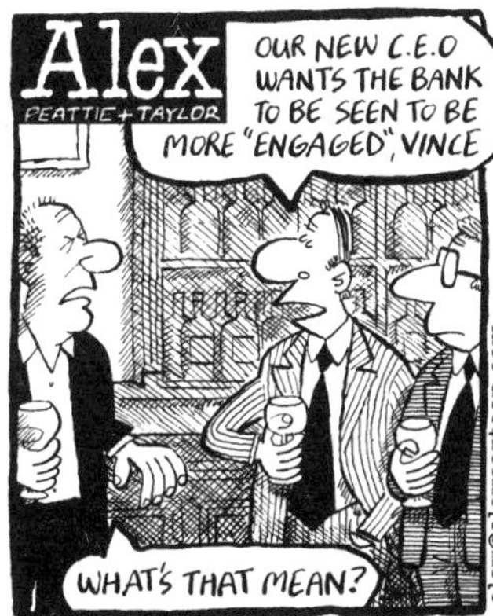
Alex
PEATTIE + TAYLOR
OUR NEW C.E.O WANTS THE BANK TO BE SEEN TO BE MORE "ENGAGED", VINCE
WHAT'S THAT MEAN?

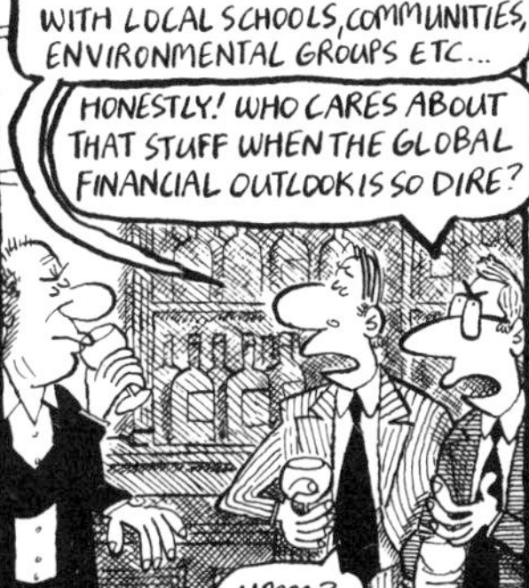
IT'S ALL ABOUT FORGING LINKS WITH LOCAL SCHOOLS, COMMUNITIES, ENVIRONMENTAL GROUPS ETC...
HONESTLY! WHO CARES ABOUT THAT STUFF WHEN THE GLOBAL FINANCIAL OUTLOOK IS SO DIRE?
HMM?
alex@alexcartoon.com

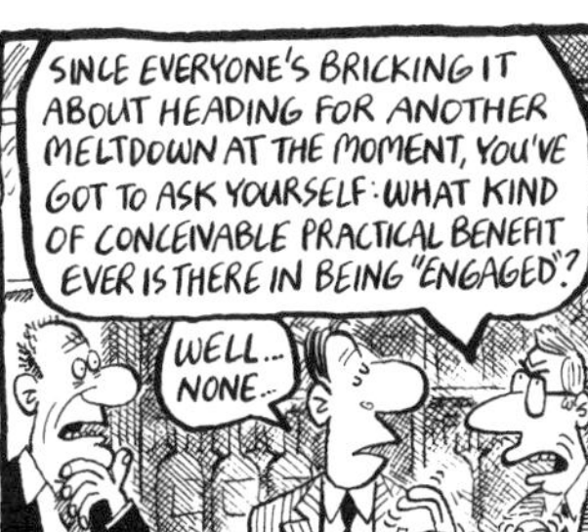
SINCE EVERYONE'S BRICKING IT ABOUT HEADING FOR ANOTHER MELTDOWN AT THE MOMENT, YOU'VE GOT TO ASK YOURSELF: WHAT KIND OF CONCEIVABLE PRACTICAL BENEFIT EVER IS THERE IN BEING "ENGAGED"?
WELL... NONE...
ER...

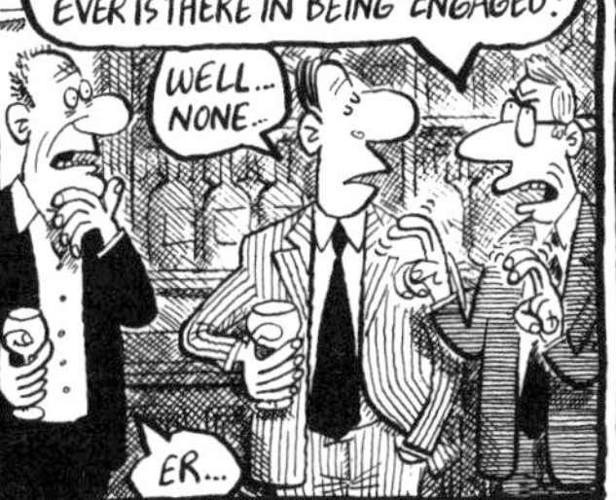

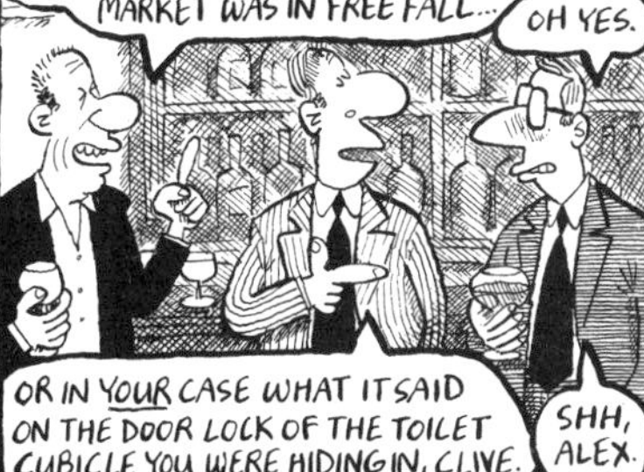
UNLESS YOU'RE TALKING ABOUT OUR PHONES, LIKE IN THE 1987 CRASH WHEN WE ALL TOOK THEM OFF THE HOOK ON OUR TRADING DESK, SO WE WOULDN'T HAVE TO MAKE PRICES WHILE THE MARKET WAS IN FREE FALL...
OH YES.
OR IN YOUR CASE WHAT IT SAID ON THE DOOR LOCK OF THE TOILET CUBICLE YOU WERE HIDING IN, CLIVE.
SHH, ALEX.

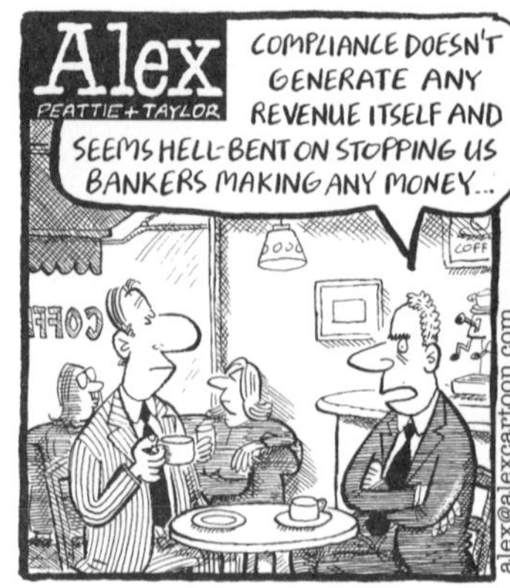
Alex
PEATTIE + TAYLOR
COMPLIANCE DOESN'T GENERATE ANY REVENUE ITSELF AND SEEMS HELL-BENT ON STOPPING US BANKERS MAKING ANY MONEY...
alex@alexcartoon.com

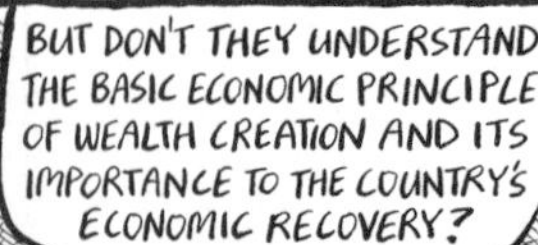
BUT DON'T THEY UNDERSTAND THE BASIC ECONOMIC PRINCIPLE OF WEALTH CREATION AND ITS IMPORTANCE TO THE COUNTRY'S ECONOMIC RECOVERY?

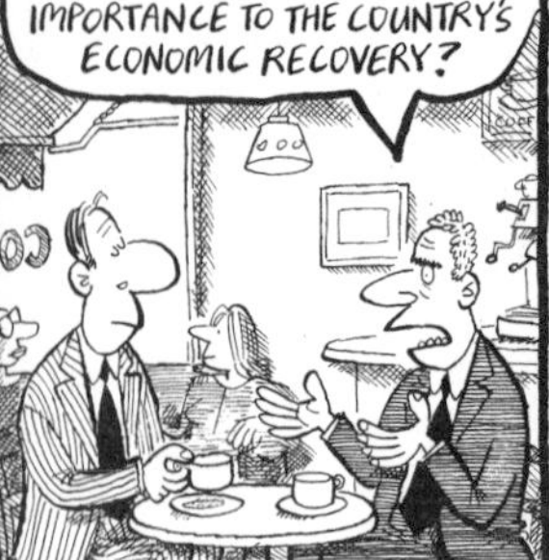

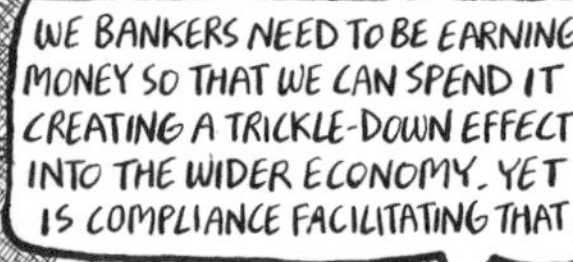
WE BANKERS NEED TO BE EARNING MONEY SO THAT WE CAN SPEND IT CREATING A TRICKLE-DOWN EFFECT INTO THE WIDER ECONOMY. YET IS COMPLIANCE FACILITATING THAT?

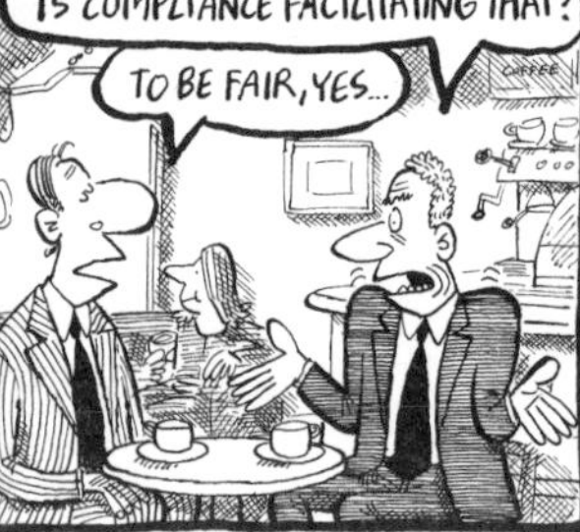
TO BE FAIR, YES...

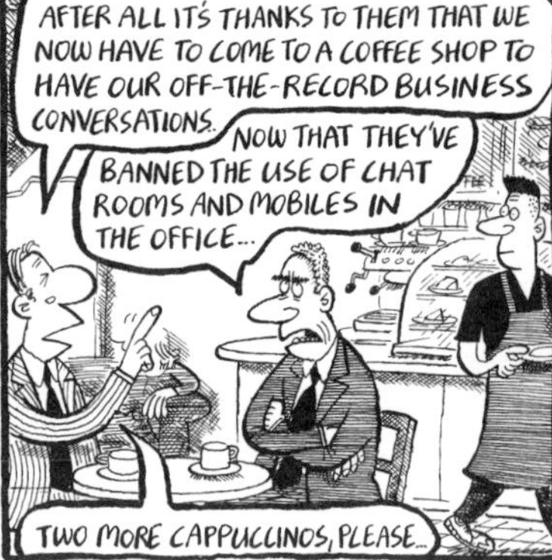
AFTER ALL IT'S THANKS TO THEM THAT WE NOW HAVE TO COME TO A COFFEE SHOP TO HAVE OUR OFF-THE-RECORD BUSINESS CONVERSATIONS...
NOW THAT THEY'VE BANNED THE USE OF CHAT ROOMS AND MOBILES IN THE OFFICE...
TWO MORE CAPPUCCINOS, PLEASE...

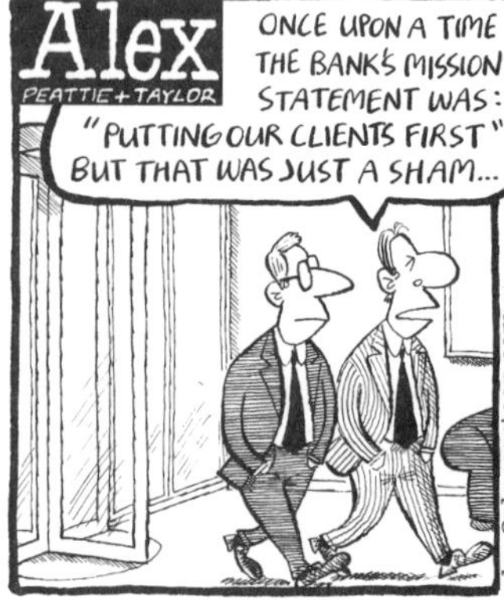
Alex
PEATTIE + TAYLOR
ONCE UPON A TIME THE BANK'S MISSION STATEMENT WAS: "PUTTING OUR CLIENTS FIRST" BUT THAT WAS JUST A SHAM...
alex@alexcartoon.com

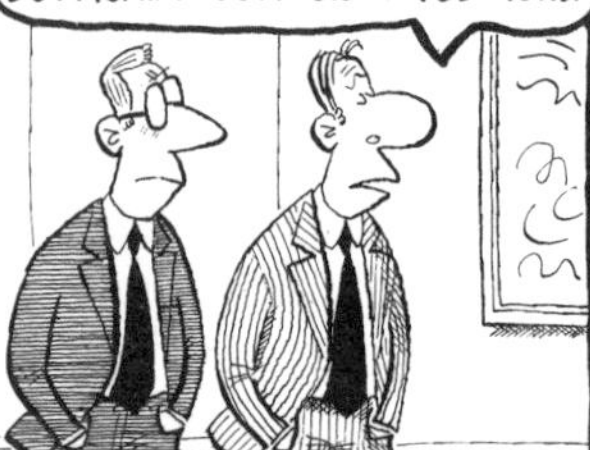
THE REALITY WAS WE'D REGULARLY SHAFT OUR CLIENTS, KEEPING ALL THE BEST DEALS FOR OURSELVES AND PUTTING THEM INTO THE RUBBISH ONES. THE BANK'S TRADERS WOULD EVEN BET AGAINST OUR CLIENTS' POSITIONS...

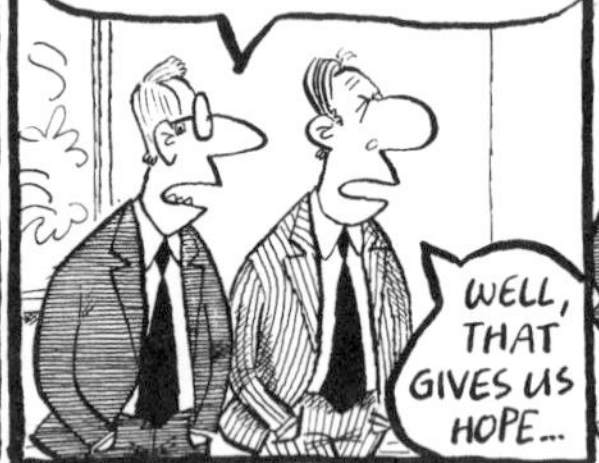
WELL, ALEX, WE'VE NOW GOT A C.E.O. WHO'S AN EX-COMPLIANCE OFFICER AND WHO HAS INTRODUCED A NEW CULTURE BASED AROUND FULL IMPLEMENTATION OF ALL THE LATEST REGULATORY DIRECTIVES...
WELL, THAT GIVES US HOPE...

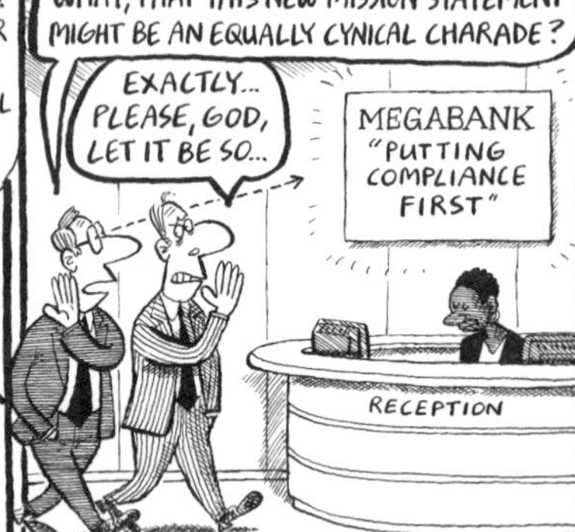
WHAT, THAT THIS NEW MISSION STATEMENT MIGHT BE AN EQUALLY CYNICAL CHARADE?
EXACTLY... PLEASE, GOD, LET IT BE SO...
MEGABANK "PUTTING COMPLIANCE FIRST"
RECEPTION

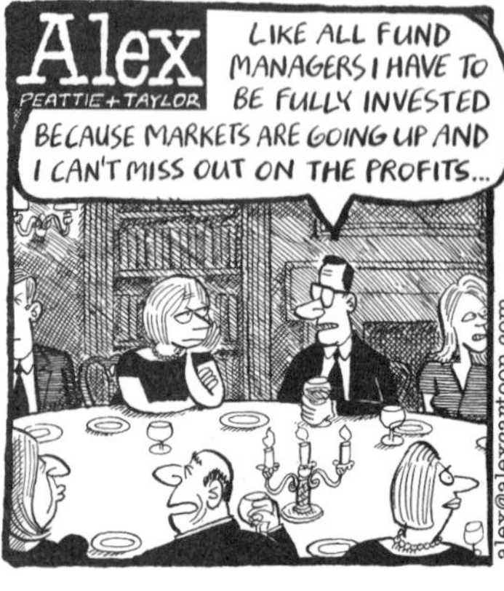
Alex
PEATTIE + TAYLOR
LIKE ALL FUND MANAGERS I HAVE TO BE FULLY INVESTED BECAUSE MARKETS ARE GOING UP AND I CAN'T MISS OUT ON THE PROFITS...
alex@alexcartoon.com

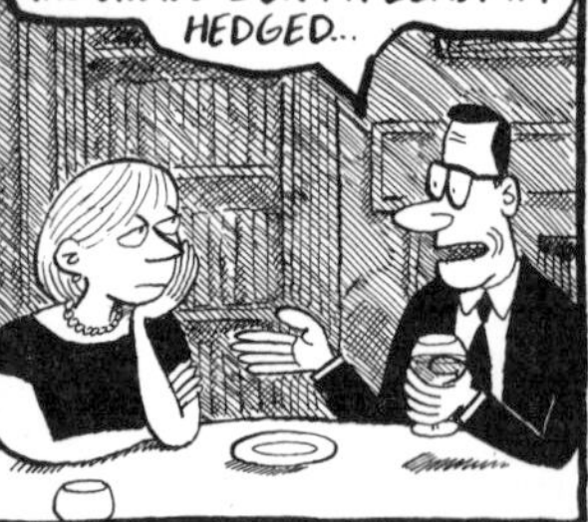
BUT I'M FEARFUL OF A MARKET CRASH, SO I KEEP 10% OF MY INVESTORS' MONEY IN GOLD AND CASH, I MAY MISS OUT A BIT ON THE UPSIDE BUT AT LEAST I'M HEDGED...

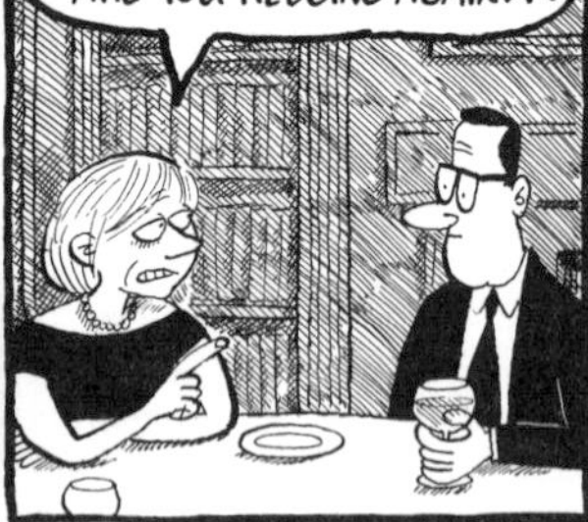
10%? BUT IS THAT REALLY GOING TO MAKE ANY DIFFERENCE IF MARKETS CRASH AND YOUR FUND'S VALUE COLLAPSES? WHAT ARE YOU HEDGING AGAINST?

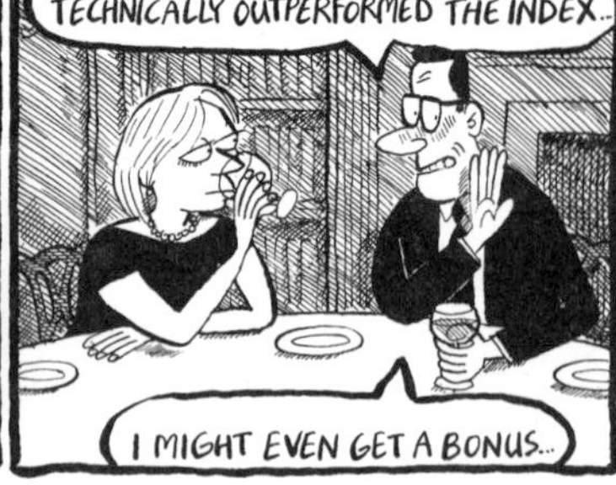
ER, ME GETTING FIRED... OUR BOSSES WILL BE LOOKING FOR SCAPEGOATS AND IF MY FUND LOST SLIGHTLY LESS THAN EVERYONE ELSE'S, THEN I'LL HAVE TECHNICALLY OUTPERFORMED THE INDEX...
I MIGHT EVEN GET A BONUS...

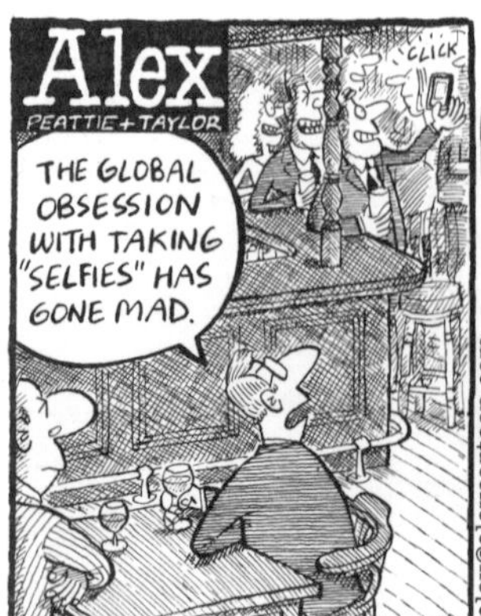
Alex
PEATTIE + TAYLOR
CLICK
THE GLOBAL OBSESSION WITH TAKING "SELFIES" HAS GONE MAD.
alex@alexcartoon.com

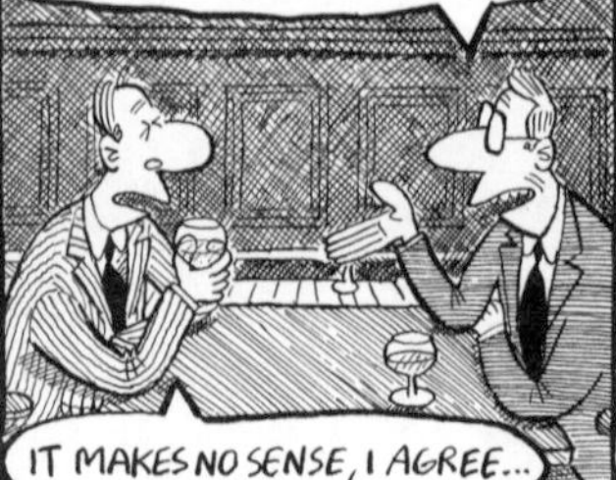
APPARENTLY YOU CAN NOW BUY REMOTE CONTROLLED MINI DRONES WHICH HOVER IN THE AIR AND TAKE PHOTOS OF YOU WHICH YOU CAN THEN POST ON SOCIAL MEDIA SITES...
IT MAKES NO SENSE, I AGREE...

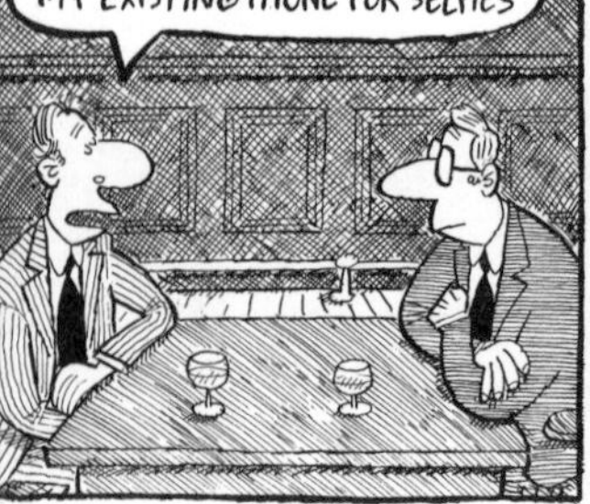
I MEAN IF ONE'S TALKING ABOUT HAVING TO BLOW A LOAD OF MONEY ON AN OVERPRICED, GLORIFIED AIR-BORNE CAMERA I PREFER TO USE MY EXISTING PHONE FOR SELFIES

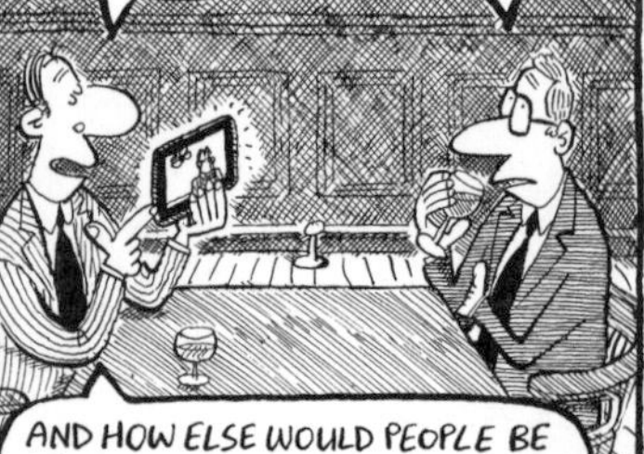
LOOK... I TOOK THESE ONES OF ME WITH MY DRONE IN THE BACKGROUND...
I MIGHT HAVE GUESSED YOU'D BE AN EARLY ADOPTER, ALEX...
AND HOW ELSE WOULD PEOPLE BE ABLE TO SEE THAT I OWNED ONE?

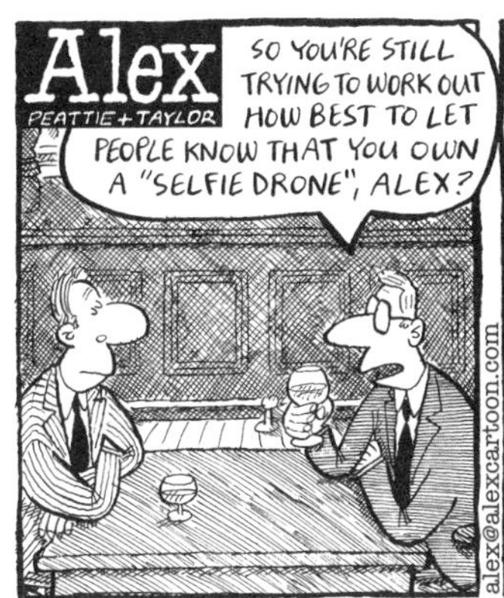
Alex
PEATTIE+TAYLOR
SO YOU'RE STILL TRYING TO WORK OUT HOW BEST TO LET PEOPLE KNOW THAT YOU OWN A "SELFIE DRONE", ALEX?
alex@alexcartoon.com

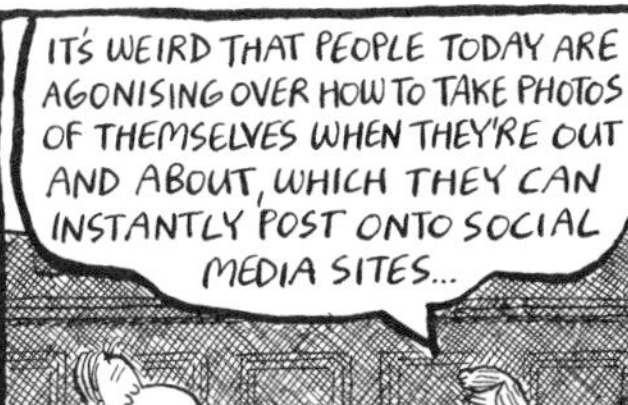
IT'S WEIRD THAT PEOPLE TODAY ARE AGONISING OVER HOW TO TAKE PHOTOS OF THEMSELVES WHEN THEY'RE OUT AND ABOUT, WHICH THEY CAN INSTANTLY POST ONTO SOCIAL MEDIA SITES...

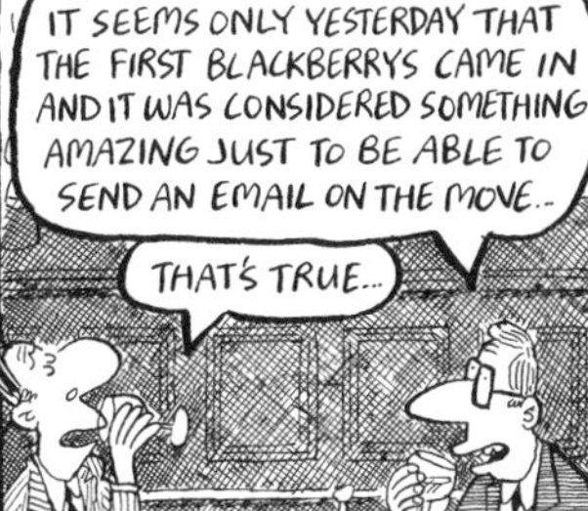
IT SEEMS ONLY YESTERDAY THAT THE FIRST BLACKBERRYS CAME IN AND IT WAS CONSIDERED SOMETHING AMAZING JUST TO BE ABLE TO SEND AN EMAIL ON THE MOVE..
THAT'S TRUE...

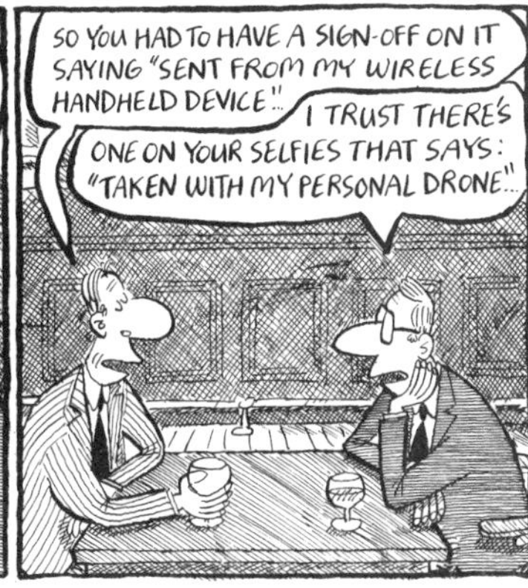
SO YOU HAD TO HAVE A SIGN-OFF ON IT SAYING "SENT FROM MY WIRELESS HANDHELD DEVICE"..
I TRUST THERE'S ONE ON YOUR SELFIES THAT SAYS: "TAKEN WITH MY PERSONAL DRONE"..

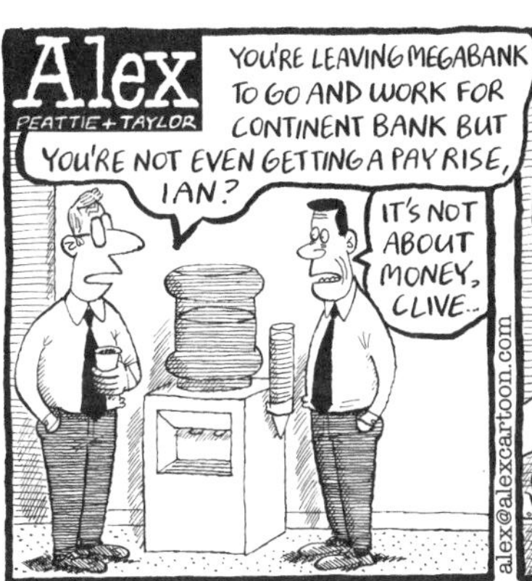
Alex
PEATTIE+TAYLOR
YOU'RE LEAVING MEGABANK TO GO AND WORK FOR CONTINENT BANK BUT YOU'RE NOT EVEN GETTING A PAY RISE, IAN?
IT'S NOT ABOUT MONEY, CLIVE..
alex@alexcartoon.com

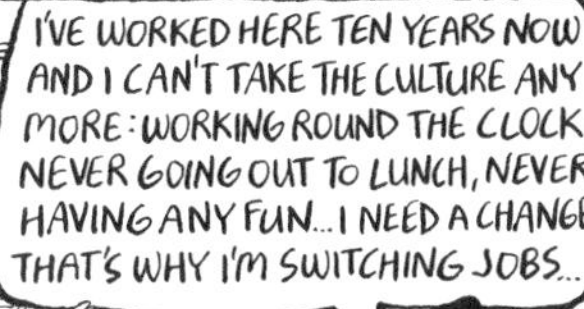
I'VE WORKED HERE TEN YEARS NOW AND I CAN'T TAKE THE CULTURE ANY MORE: WORKING ROUND THE CLOCK, NEVER GOING OUT TO LUNCH, NEVER HAVING ANY FUN...I NEED A CHANGE. THAT'S WHY I'M SWITCHING JOBS...

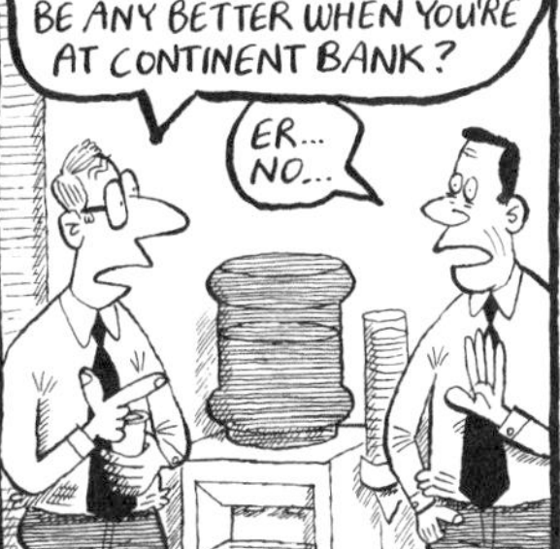
BUT ALL THE BANKS ARE THE SAME THESE DAYS... DO YOU REALLY THINK YOUR LIFE WILL BE ANY BETTER WHEN YOU'RE AT CONTINENT BANK?
ER... NO...

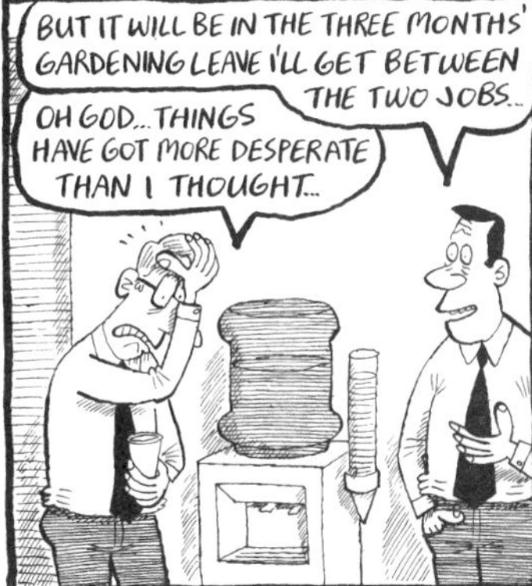
BUT IT WILL BE IN THE THREE MONTHS' GARDENING LEAVE I'LL GET BETWEEN THE TWO JOBS...
OH GOD... THINGS HAVE GOT MORE DESPERATE THAN I THOUGHT...

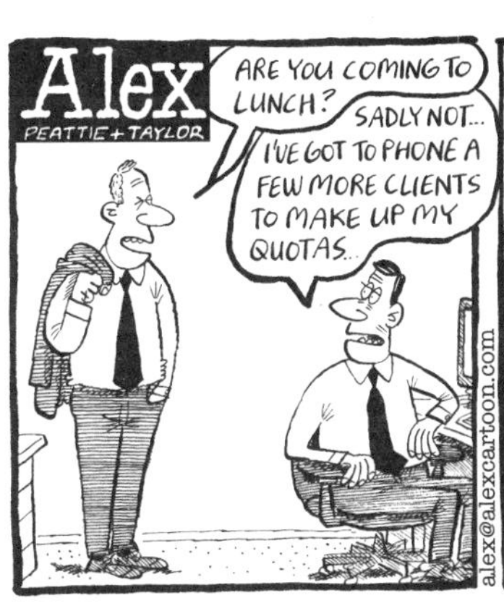
Alex
PEATTIE+TAYLOR
ARE YOU COMING TO LUNCH?
SADLY NOT... I'VE GOT TO PHONE A FEW MORE CLIENTS TO MAKE UP MY QUOTAS..
alex@alexcartoon.com

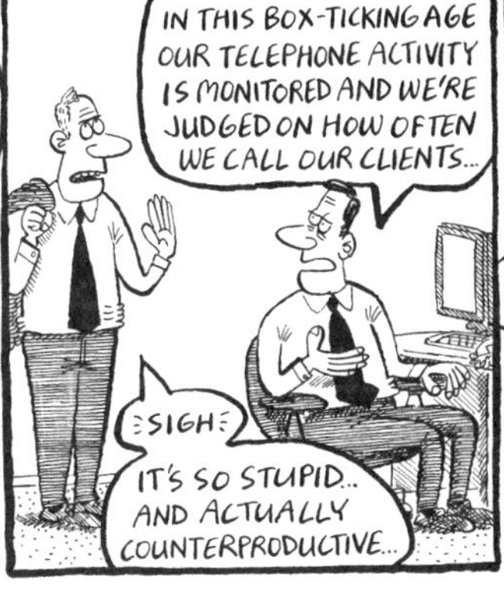
IN THIS BOX-TICKING AGE OUR TELEPHONE ACTIVITY IS MONITORED AND WE'RE JUDGED ON HOW OFTEN WE CALL OUR CLIENTS...
SIGH
IT'S SO STUPID... AND ACTUALLY COUNTERPRODUCTIVE...

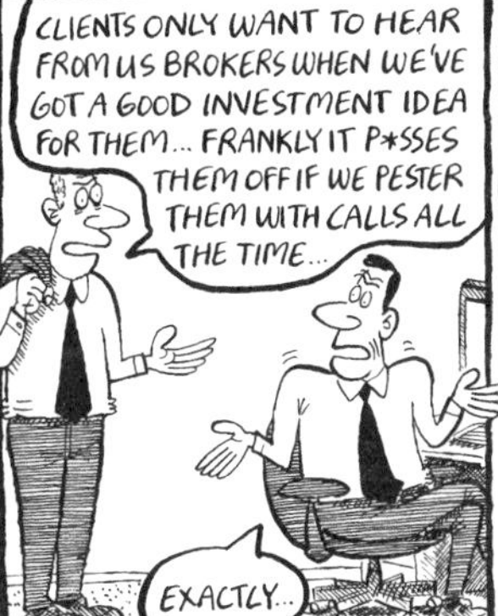
CLIENTS ONLY WANT TO HEAR FROM US BROKERS WHEN WE'VE GOT A GOOD INVESTMENT IDEA FOR THEM... FRANKLY IT P*SSES THEM OFF IF WE PESTER THEM WITH CALLS ALL THE TIME...
EXACTLY...

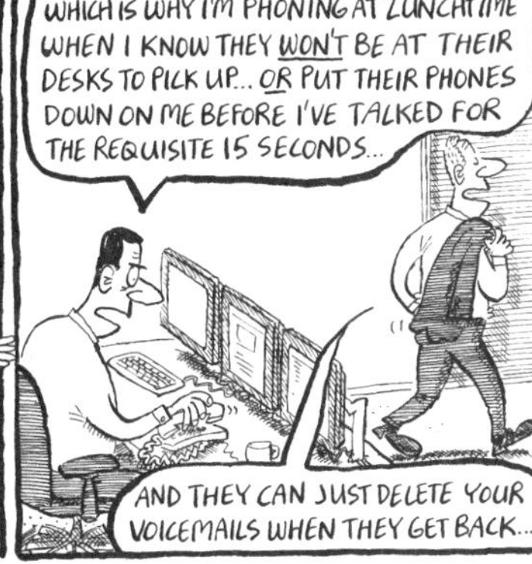
WHICH IS WHY I'M PHONING AT LUNCHTIME WHEN I KNOW THEY WON'T BE AT THEIR DESKS TO PICK UP... OR PUT THEIR PHONES DOWN ON ME BEFORE I'VE TALKED FOR THE REQUISITE 15 SECONDS...
AND THEY CAN JUST DELETE YOUR VOICEMAILS WHEN THEY GET BACK...

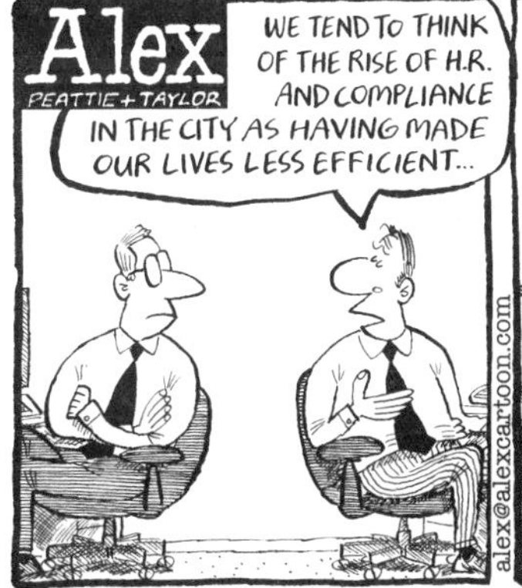
Alex
PEATTIE+TAYLOR
WE TEND TO THINK OF THE RISE OF H.R. AND COMPLIANCE IN THE CITY AS HAVING MADE OUR LIVES LESS EFFICIENT...
alex@alexcartoon.com

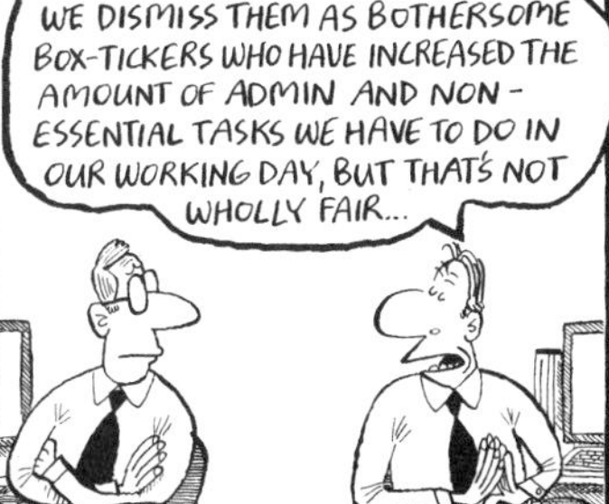
WE DISMISS THEM AS BOTHERSOME BOX-TICKERS WHO HAVE INCREASED THE AMOUNT OF ADMIN AND NON-ESSENTIAL TASKS WE HAVE TO DO IN OUR WORKING DAY, BUT THAT'S NOT WHOLLY FAIR...

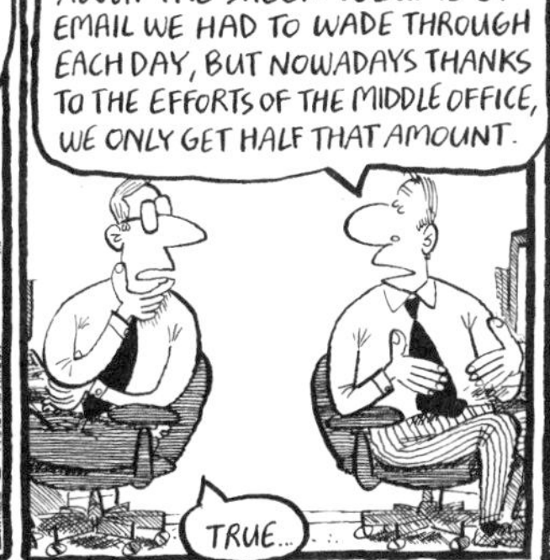
FOR EXAMPLE WE USED TO GRUMBLE ABOUT THE SHEER VOLUME OF EMAIL WE HAD TO WADE THROUGH EACH DAY, BUT NOWADAYS THANKS TO THE EFFORTS OF THE MIDDLE OFFICE, WE ONLY GET HALF THAT AMOUNT.
TRUE...

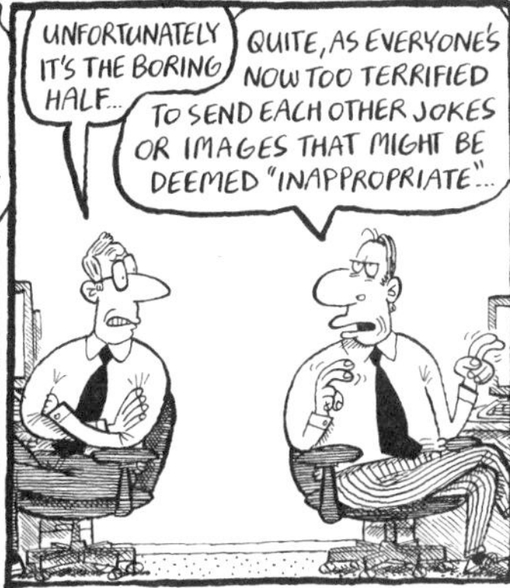
UNFORTUNATELY IT'S THE BORING HALF...
QUITE, AS EVERYONE'S NOW TOO TERRIFIED TO SEND EACH OTHER JOKES OR IMAGES THAT MIGHT BE DEEMED "INAPPROPRIATE"...

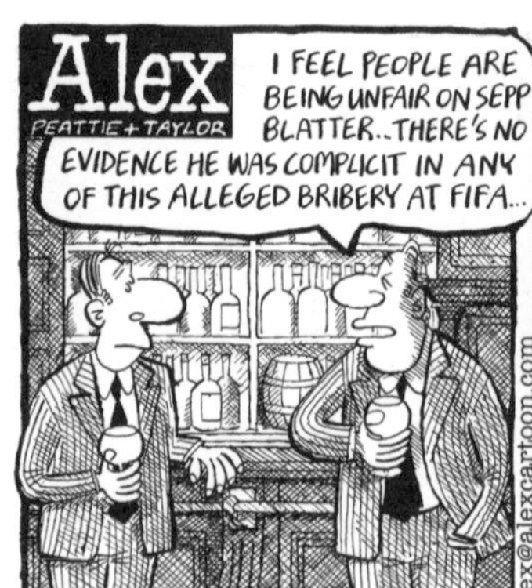
Alex
PEATTIE + TAYLOR
I FEEL PEOPLE ARE BEING UNFAIR ON SEPP BLATTER.. THERE'S NO EVIDENCE HE WAS COMPLICIT IN ANY OF THIS ALLEGED BRIBERY AT FIFA...
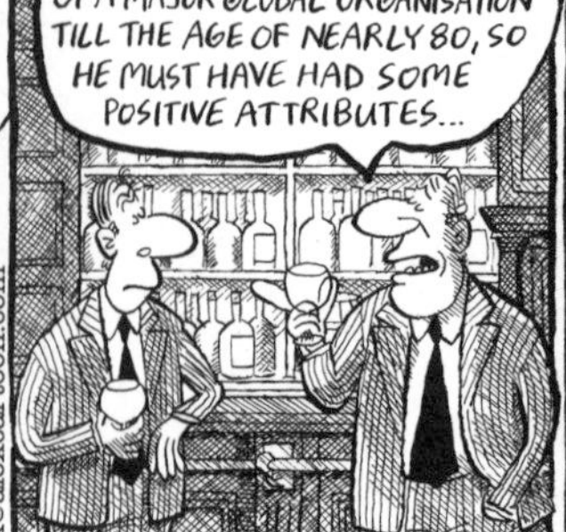
HE MANAGED TO REMAIN AT THE HELM OF A MAJOR GLOBAL ORGANISATION TILL THE AGE OF NEARLY 80, SO HE MUST HAVE HAD SOME POSITIVE ATTRIBUTES...
alex@alexcartoon.com
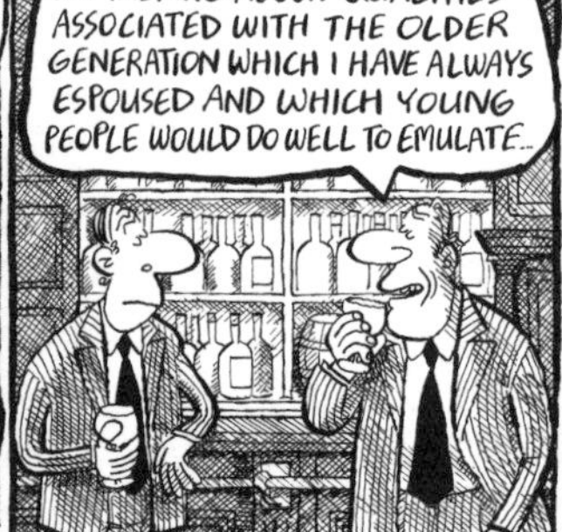
I'M TALKING ABOUT QUALITIES ASSOCIATED WITH THE OLDER GENERATION WHICH I HAVE ALWAYS ESPOUSED AND WHICH YOUNG PEOPLE WOULD DO WELL TO EMULATE...
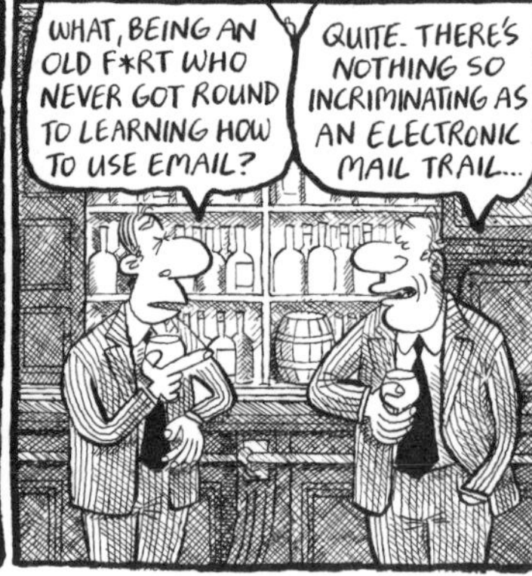
WHAT, BEING AN OLD F*RT WHO NEVER GOT ROUND TO LEARNING HOW TO USE EMAIL?
QUITE. THERE'S NOTHING SO INCRIMINATING AS AN ELECTRONIC MAIL TRAIL...

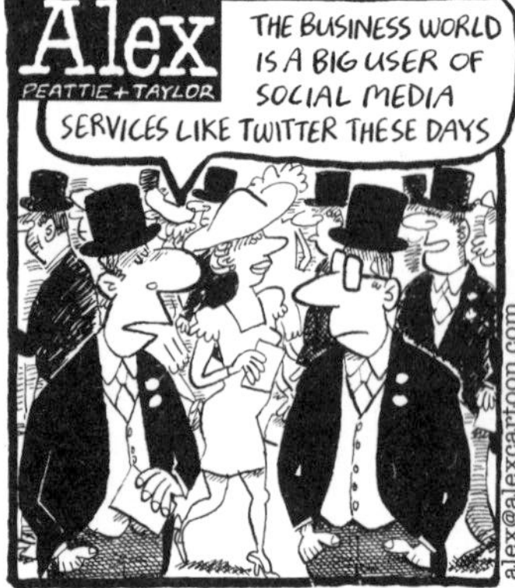
Alex
PEATTIE + TAYLOR
THE BUSINESS WORLD IS A BIG USER OF SOCIAL MEDIA SERVICES LIKE TWITTER THESE DAYS
alex@alexcartoon.com
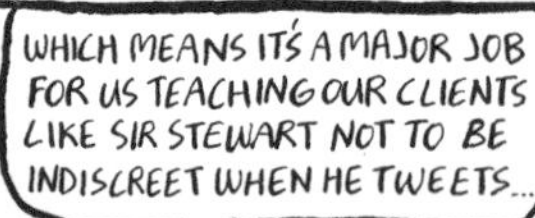
WHICH MEANS IT'S A MAJOR JOB FOR US TEACHING OUR CLIENTS LIKE SIR STEWART NOT TO BE INDISCREET WHEN HE TWEETS...
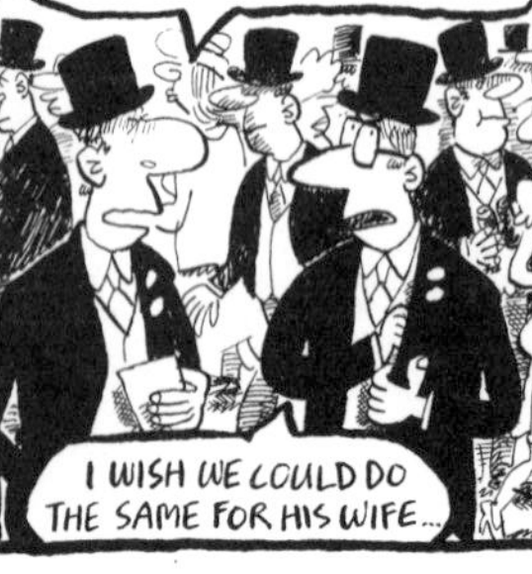
I WISH WE COULD DO THE SAME FOR HIS WIFE...
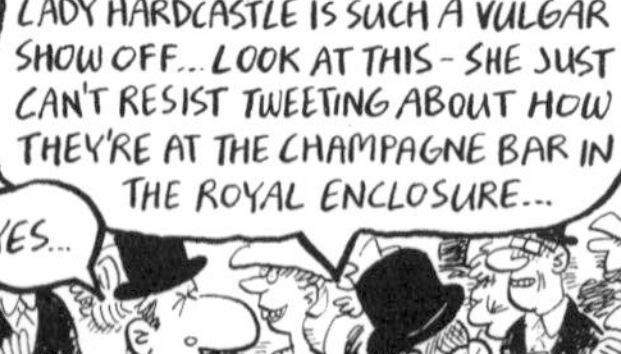
LADY HARDCASTLE IS SUCH A VULGAR SHOW OFF... LOOK AT THIS - SHE JUST CAN'T RESIST TWEETING ABOUT HOW THEY'RE AT THE CHAMPAGNE BAR IN THE ROYAL ENCLOSURE...
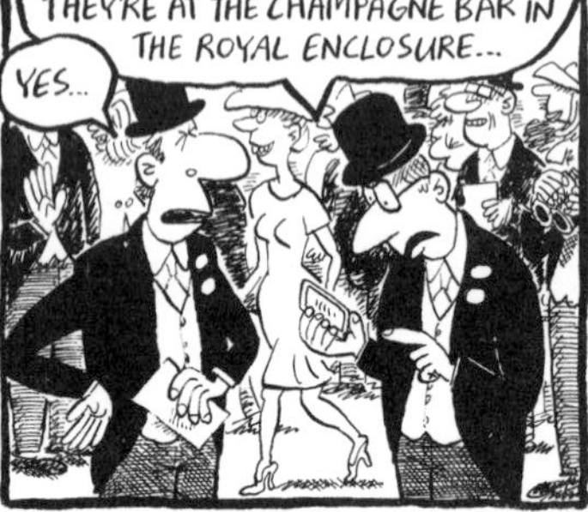
YES...
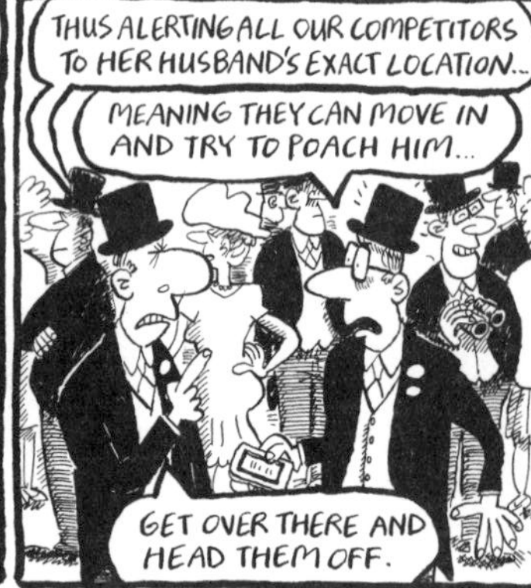
THUS ALERTING ALL OUR COMPETITORS TO HER HUSBAND'S EXACT LOCATION...
MEANING THEY CAN MOVE IN AND TRY TO POACH HIM...
GET OVER THERE AND HEAD THEM OFF.

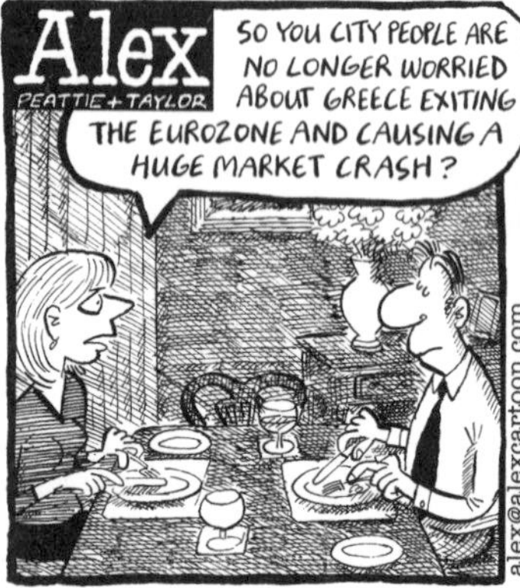
Alex
PEATTIE + TAYLOR
SO YOU CITY PEOPLE ARE NO LONGER WORRIED ABOUT GREECE EXITING THE EUROZONE AND CAUSING A HUGE MARKET CRASH?
alex@alexcartoon.com
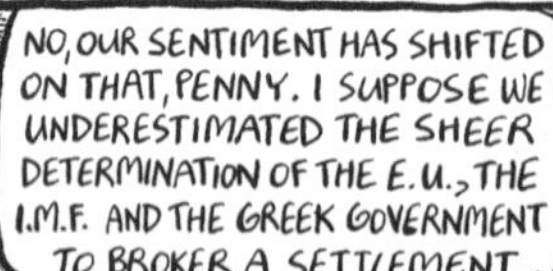
NO, OUR SENTIMENT HAS SHIFTED ON THAT, PENNY. I SUPPOSE WE UNDERESTIMATED THE SHEER DETERMINATION OF THE E.U., THE I.M.F. AND THE GREEK GOVERNMENT TO BROKER A SETTLEMENT...
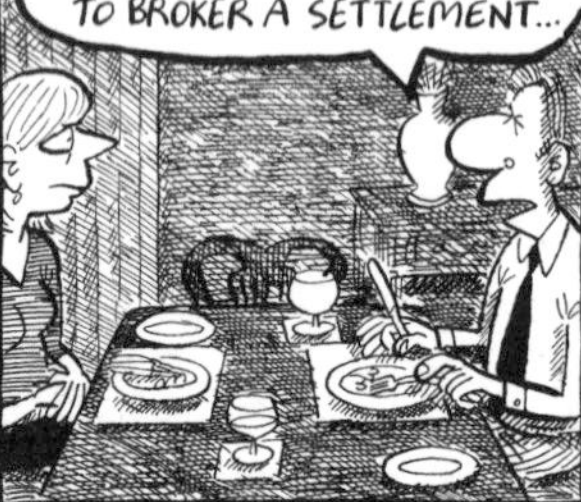
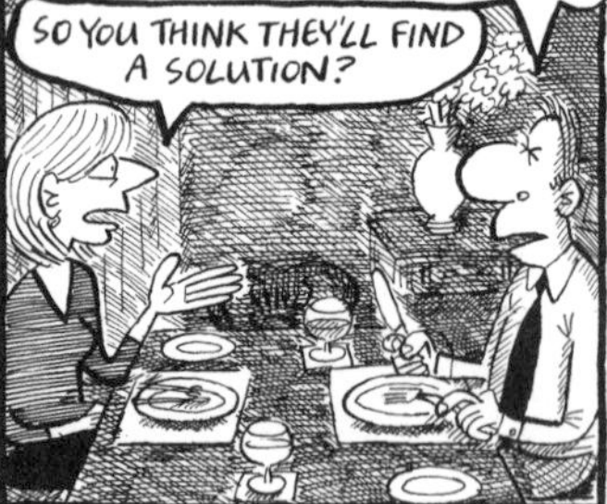
I BELIEVE THE TENACITY AND WILLINGNESS OF ALL PARTIES TO KEEP NEGOTIATING HAS BEEN A VERY IMPORTANT FACTOR IN OFFSETTING OUR NEGATIVE OUTLOOK...
SO YOU THINK THEY'LL FIND A SOLUTION?
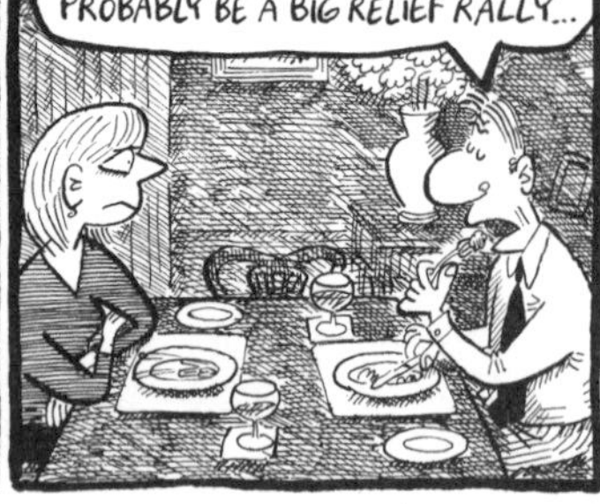
NOT A CHANCE, BUT WE'RE NOW ALL SO UTTERLY SICK AND TIRED OF THE WHOLE BUSINESS THAT WHEN GREECE DOES FINALLY GET BOOTED OUT THERE'LL PROBABLY BE A BIG RELIEF RALLY...

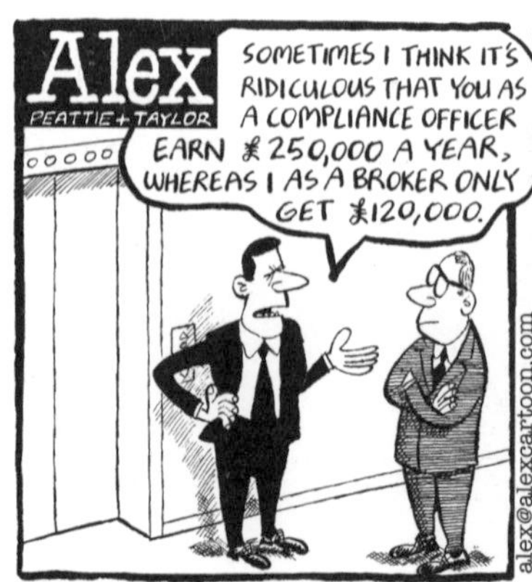
Alex
PEATTIE + TAYLOR
SOMETIMES I THINK IT'S RIDICULOUS THAT YOU AS A COMPLIANCE OFFICER EARN £250,000 A YEAR, WHEREAS I AS A BROKER ONLY GET £120,000.
alex@alexcartoon.com
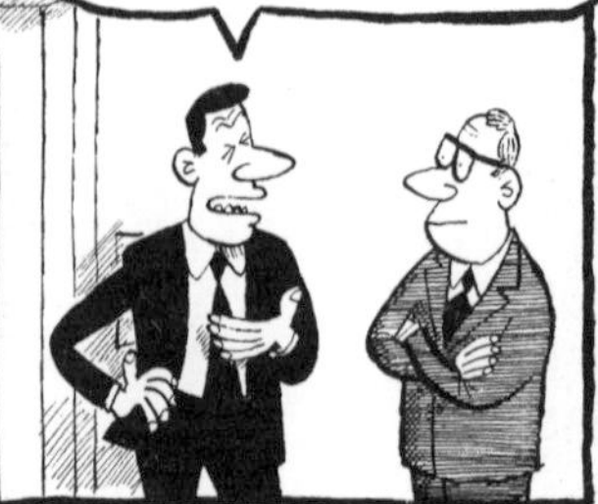
BUT FOR ME AT LEAST THAT'S JUST MY BASIC SALARY. IF I DO MY JOB WELL I'LL EARN COMMISSION AND BONUSES ON TOP OF THAT, WHICH WILL BOOST MY TOTAL REMUNERATION...
SO IT GIVES ME A FINANCIAL MOTIVATION TO PERFORM... IT'S GOOD TO BE INCENTIVISED...
YES...
AND IF I DO MY JOB WELL I'LL PREVENT YOU FROM DOING ANY BUSINESS AND STOP YOU MAKING UP THE GAP BETWEEN US...
I AGREE... IT'S GOOD TO BE INCENTIVISED...

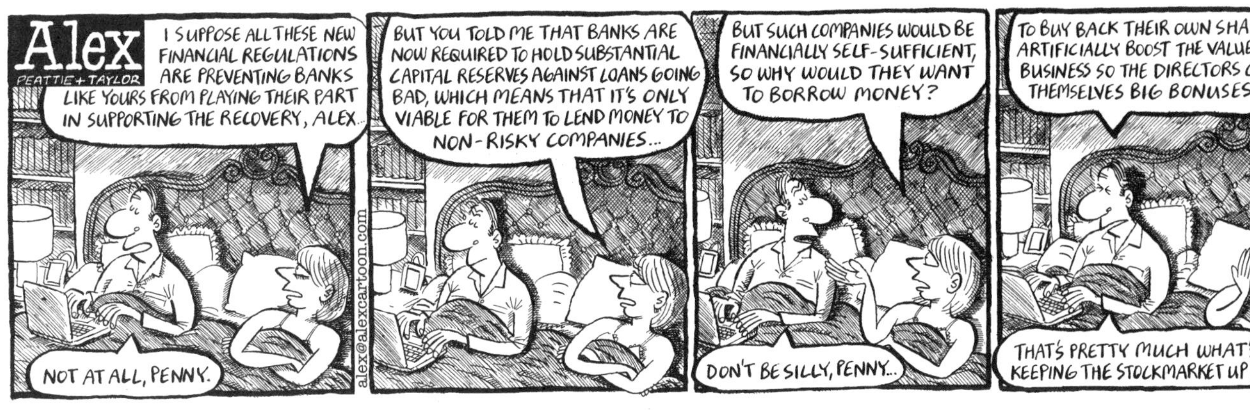
Alex
PEATTIE + TAYLOR
I SUPPOSE ALL THESE NEW FINANCIAL REGULATIONS ARE PREVENTING BANKS LIKE YOURS FROM PLAYING THEIR PART IN SUPPORTING THE RECOVERY, ALEX...
NOT AT ALL, PENNY.
BUT YOU TOLD ME THAT BANKS ARE NOW REQUIRED TO HOLD SUBSTANTIAL CAPITAL RESERVES AGAINST LOANS GOING BAD, WHICH MEANS THAT IT'S ONLY VIABLE FOR THEM TO LEND MONEY TO NON-RISKY COMPANIES...
alex@alexcartoon.com
BUT SUCH COMPANIES WOULD BE FINANCIALLY SELF-SUFFICIENT, SO WHY WOULD THEY WANT TO BORROW MONEY?
DON'T BE SILLY, PENNY...
TO BUY BACK THEIR OWN SHARES AND ARTIFICIALLY BOOST THE VALUE OF THEIR BUSINESS SO THE DIRECTORS CAN PAY THEMSELVES BIG BONUSES...
THAT'S PRETTY MUCH WHAT'S KEEPING THE STOCKMARKET UP ANYWAY...

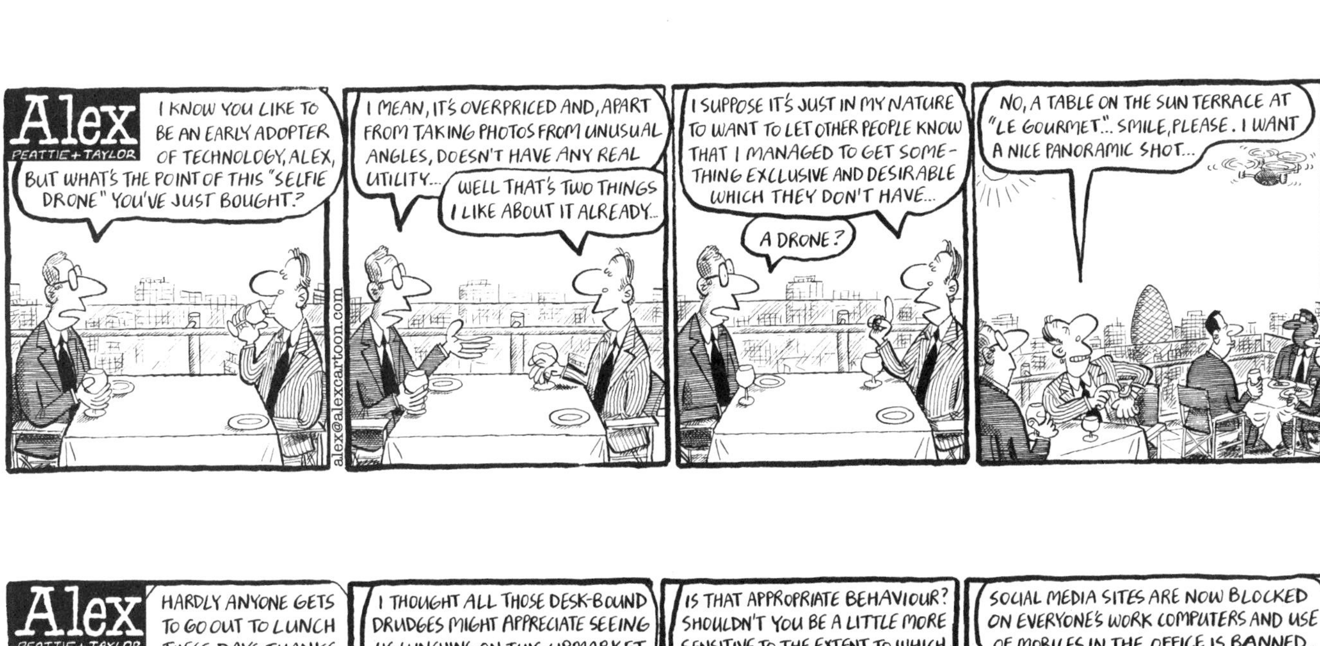
Alex
PEATTIE + TAYLOR
I KNOW YOU LIKE TO BE AN EARLY ADOPTER OF TECHNOLOGY, ALEX, BUT WHAT'S THE POINT OF THIS "SELFIE DRONE" YOU'VE JUST BOUGHT?
I MEAN, IT'S OVERPRICED AND, APART FROM TAKING PHOTOS FROM UNUSUAL ANGLES, DOESN'T HAVE ANY REAL UTILITY...
WELL THAT'S TWO THINGS I LIKE ABOUT IT ALREADY...
alex@alexcartoon.com
I SUPPOSE IT'S JUST IN MY NATURE TO WANT TO LET OTHER PEOPLE KNOW THAT I MANAGED TO GET SOMETHING EXCLUSIVE AND DESIRABLE WHICH THEY DON'T HAVE...
A DRONE?
NO, A TABLE ON THE SUN TERRACE AT "LE GOURMET"... SMILE, PLEASE. I WANT A NICE PANORAMIC SHOT...

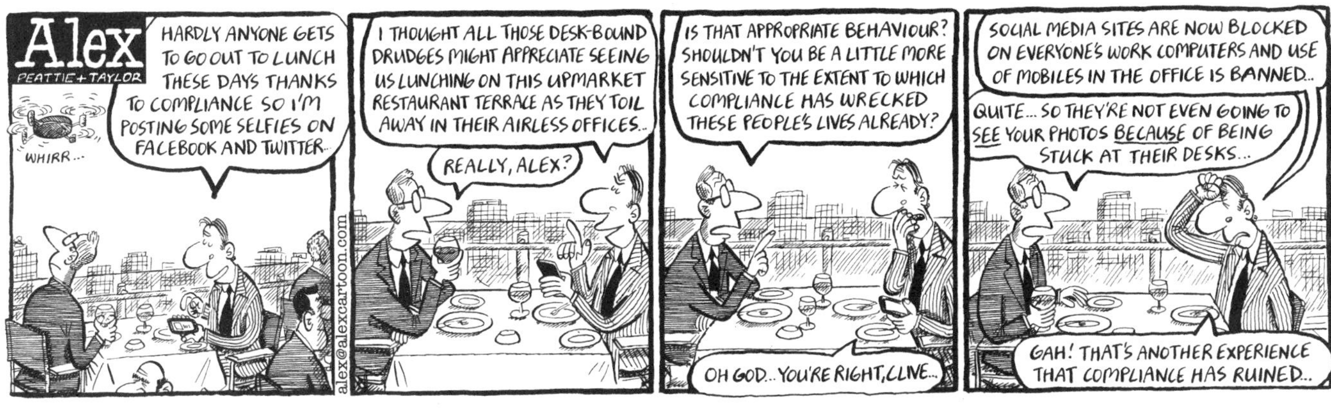
Alex
PEATTIE + TAYLOR
HARDLY ANYONE GETS TO GO OUT TO LUNCH THESE DAYS THANKS TO COMPLIANCE SO I'M POSTING SOME SELFIES ON FACEBOOK AND TWITTER...
WHIRR...
alex@alexcartoon.com
I THOUGHT ALL THOSE DESK-BOUND DRUDGES MIGHT APPRECIATE SEEING US LUNCHING ON THIS UPMARKET RESTAURANT TERRACE AS THEY TOIL AWAY IN THEIR AIRLESS OFFICES...
REALLY, ALEX?
IS THAT APPROPRIATE BEHAVIOUR? SHOULDN'T YOU BE A LITTLE MORE SENSITIVE TO THE EXTENT TO WHICH COMPLIANCE HAS WRECKED THESE PEOPLE'S LIVES ALREADY?
OH GOD... YOU'RE RIGHT, CLIVE...
SOCIAL MEDIA SITES ARE NOW BLOCKED ON EVERYONE'S WORK COMPUTERS AND USE OF MOBILES IN THE OFFICE IS BANNED...
QUITE... SO THEY'RE NOT EVEN GOING TO SEE YOUR PHOTOS BECAUSE OF BEING STUCK AT THEIR DESKS...
GAH! THAT'S ANOTHER EXPERIENCE THAT COMPLIANCE HAS RUINED...

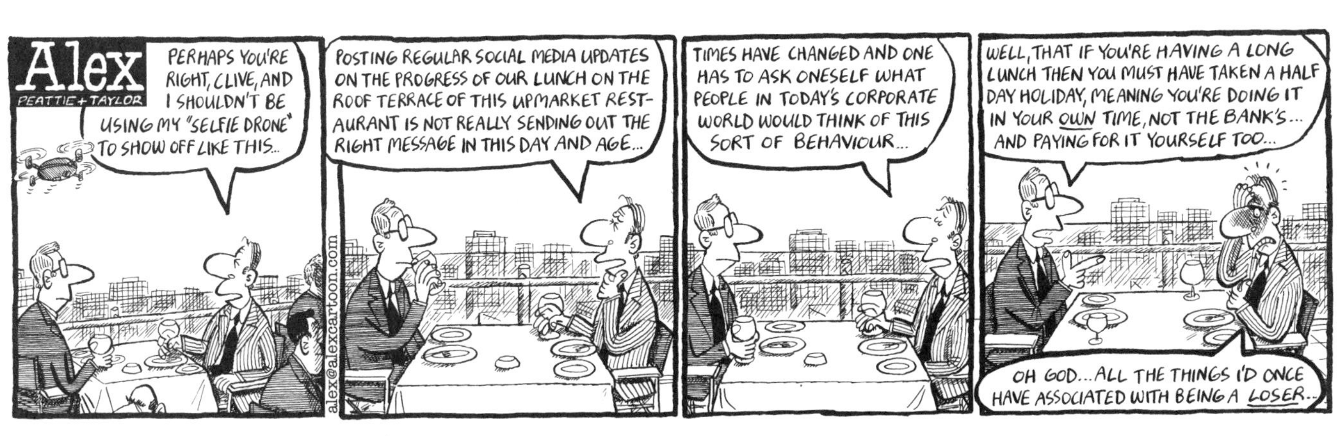
Alex
PEATTIE + TAYLOR
PERHAPS YOU'RE RIGHT, CLIVE, AND I SHOULDN'T BE USING MY "SELFIE DRONE" TO SHOW OFF LIKE THIS...
alex@alexcartoon.com
POSTING REGULAR SOCIAL MEDIA UPDATES ON THE PROGRESS OF OUR LUNCH ON THE ROOF TERRACE OF THIS UPMARKET RESTAURANT IS NOT REALLY SENDING OUT THE RIGHT MESSAGE IN THIS DAY AND AGE...
TIMES HAVE CHANGED AND ONE HAS TO ASK ONESELF WHAT PEOPLE IN TODAY'S CORPORATE WORLD WOULD THINK OF THIS SORT OF BEHAVIOUR...
WELL, THAT IF YOU'RE HAVING A LONG LUNCH THEN YOU MUST HAVE TAKEN A HALF DAY HOLIDAY, MEANING YOU'RE DOING IT IN YOUR OWN TIME, NOT THE BANK'S... AND PAYING FOR IT YOURSELF TOO...
OH GOD... ALL THE THINGS I'D ONCE HAVE ASSOCIATED WITH BEING A LOSER...

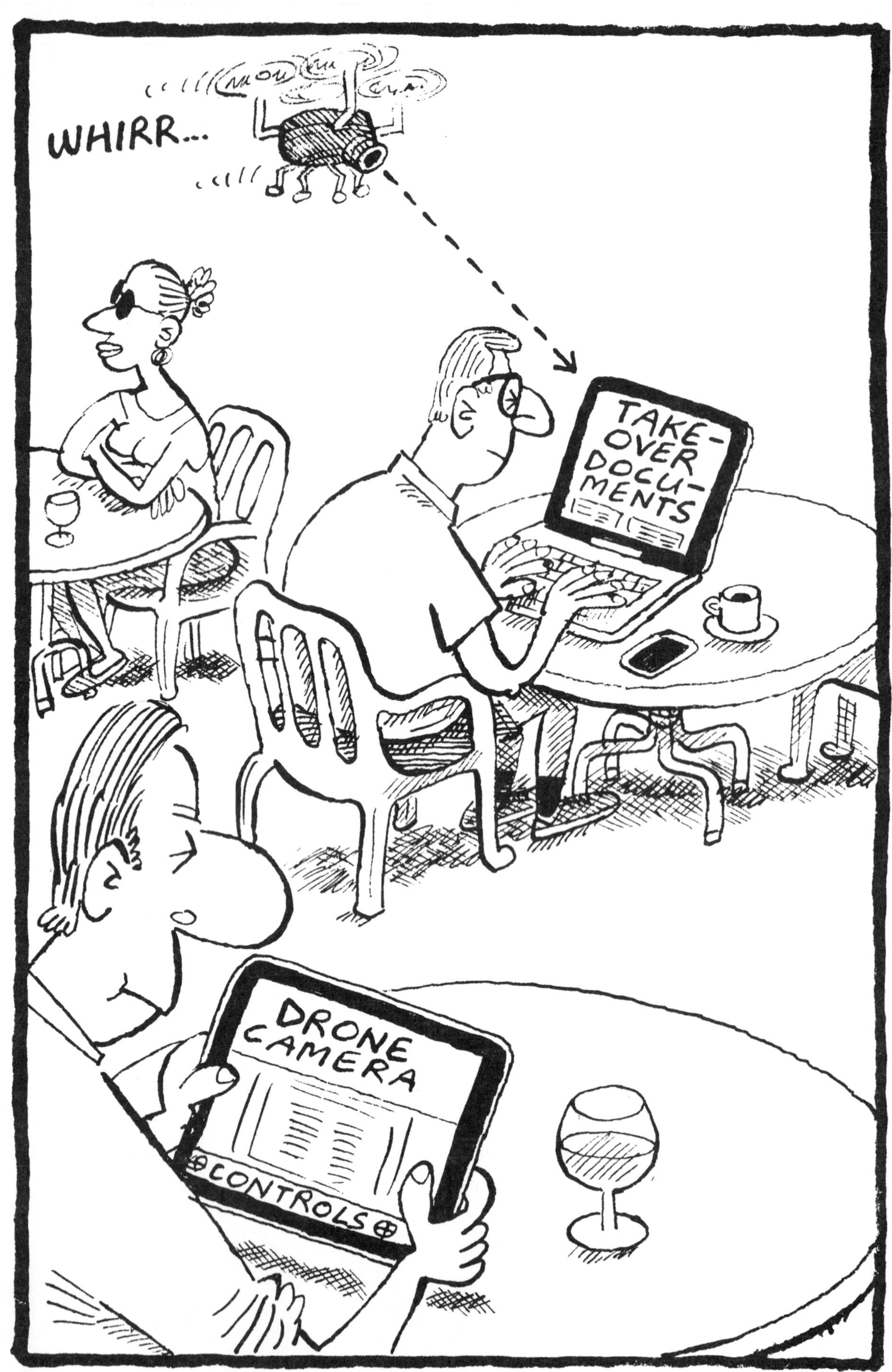
WHIRR...
TAKE-OVER DOCU-MENTS
DRONE CAMERA
CONTROLS

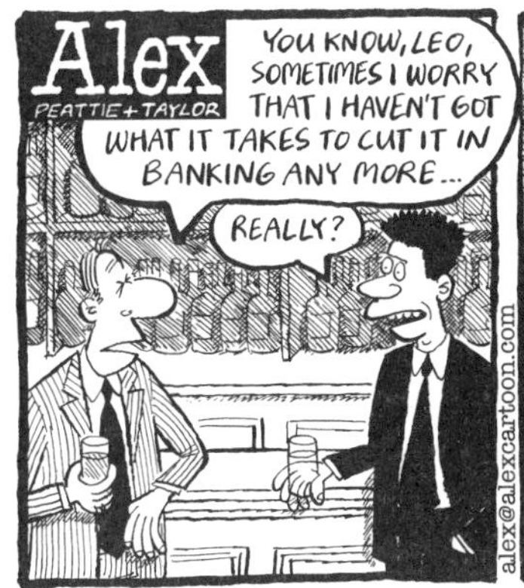
Alex
PEATTIE + TAYLOR
YOU KNOW, LEO, SOMETIMES I WORRY THAT I HAVEN'T GOT WHAT IT TAKES TO CUT IT IN BANKING ANY MORE...
REALLY?
alex@alexcartoon.com

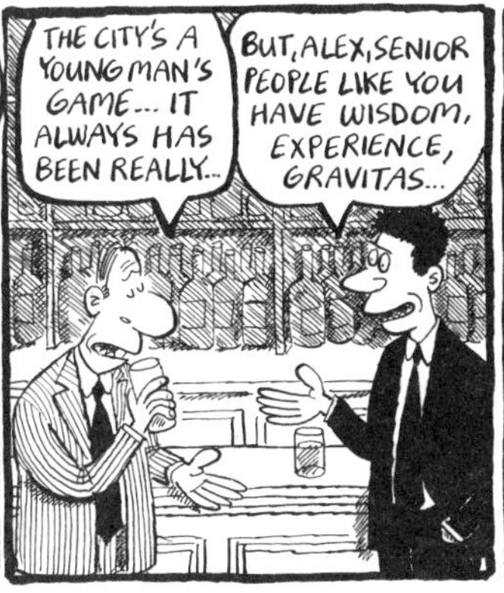
THE CITY'S A YOUNG MAN'S GAME... IT ALWAYS HAS BEEN REALLY...
BUT, ALEX, SENIOR PEOPLE LIKE YOU HAVE WISDOM, EXPERIENCE, GRAVITAS...

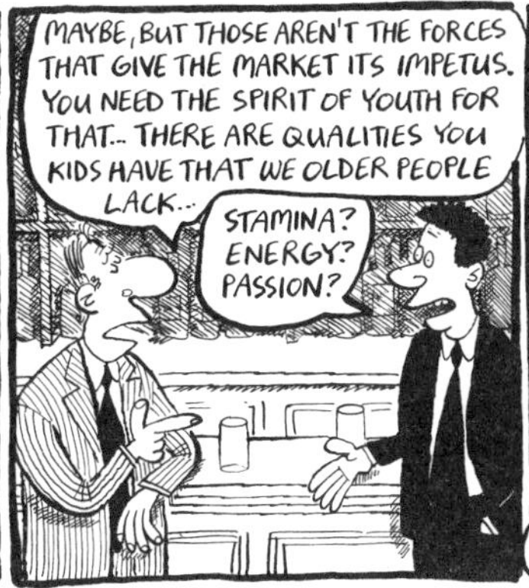
MAYBE, BUT THOSE AREN'T THE FORCES THAT GIVE THE MARKET ITS IMPETUS. YOU NEED THE SPIRIT OF YOUTH FOR THAT... THERE ARE QUALITIES YOU KIDS HAVE THAT WE OLDER PEOPLE LACK...
STAMINA? ENERGY? PASSION?

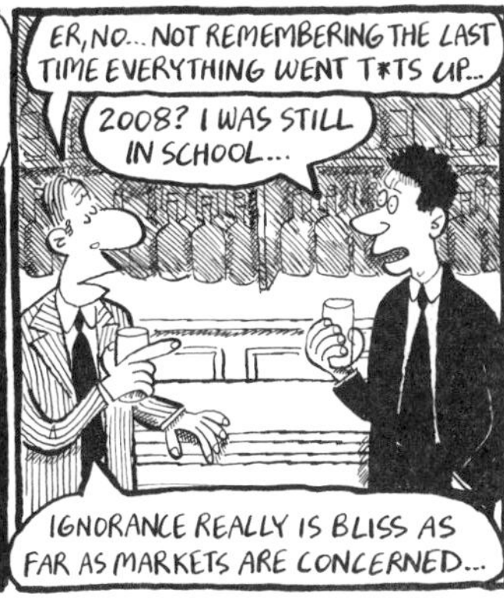
ER, NO... NOT REMEMBERING THE LAST TIME EVERYTHING WENT T*TS UP...
2008? I WAS STILL IN SCHOOL...
IGNORANCE REALLY IS BLISS AS FAR AS MARKETS ARE CONCERNED...

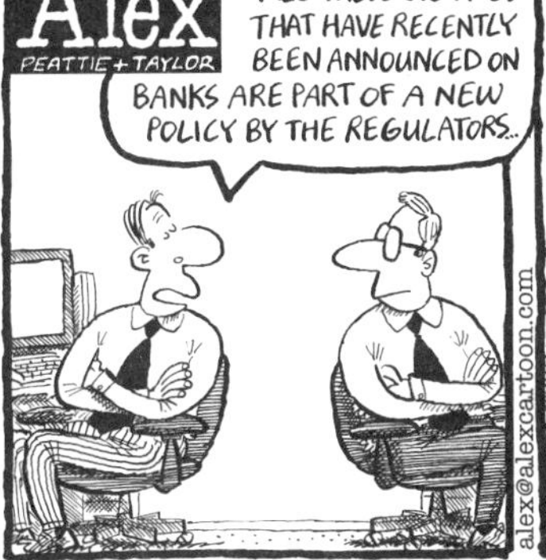
Alex
PEATTIE + TAYLOR
ALL THESE BIG FINES THAT HAVE RECENTLY BEEN ANNOUNCED ON BANKS ARE PART OF A NEW POLICY BY THE REGULATORS...
alex@alexcartoon.com

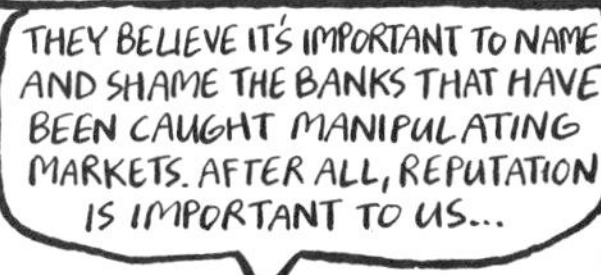
THEY BELIEVE IT'S IMPORTANT TO NAME AND SHAME THE BANKS THAT HAVE BEEN CAUGHT MANIPULATING MARKETS. AFTER ALL, REPUTATION IS IMPORTANT TO US...

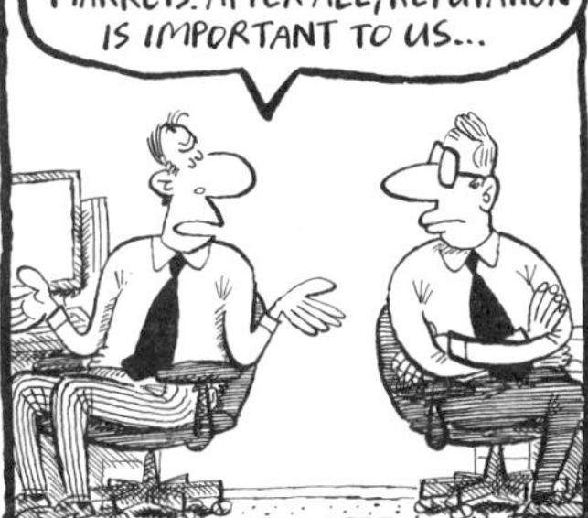

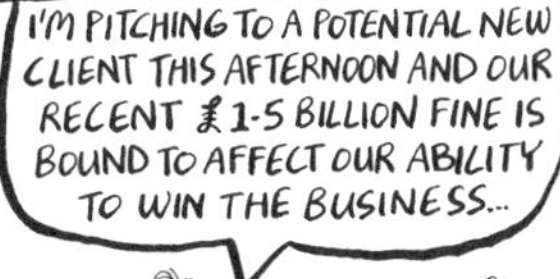
I'M PITCHING TO A POTENTIAL NEW CLIENT THIS AFTERNOON AND OUR RECENT £1.5 BILLION FINE IS BOUND TO AFFECT OUR ABILITY TO WIN THE BUSINESS...

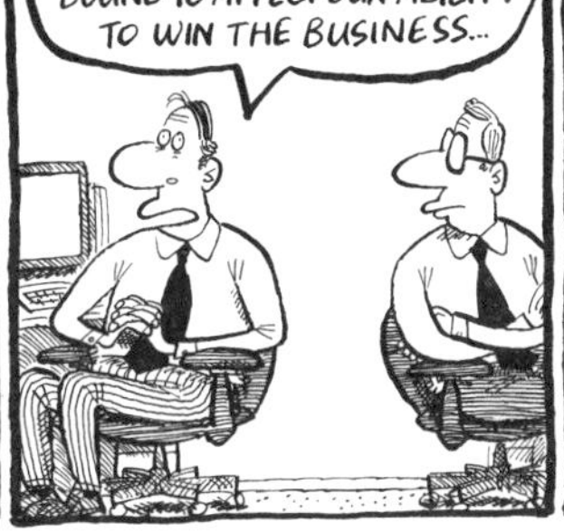

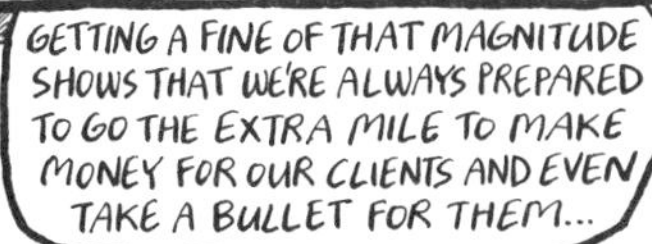
GETTING A FINE OF THAT MAGNITUDE SHOWS THAT WE'RE ALWAYS PREPARED TO GO THE EXTRA MILE TO MAKE MONEY FOR OUR CLIENTS AND EVEN TAKE A BULLET FOR THEM...

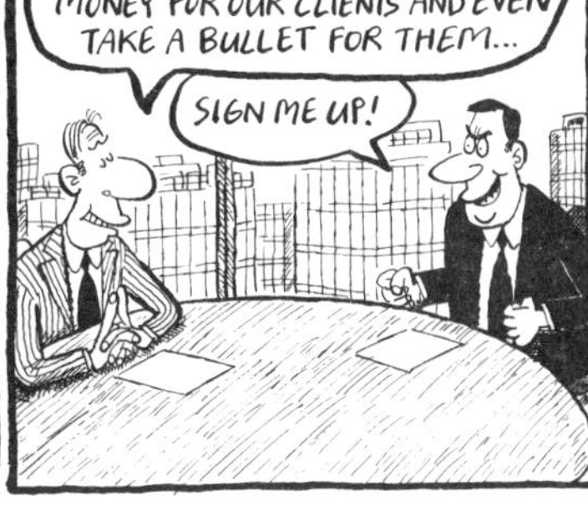
SIGN ME UP!

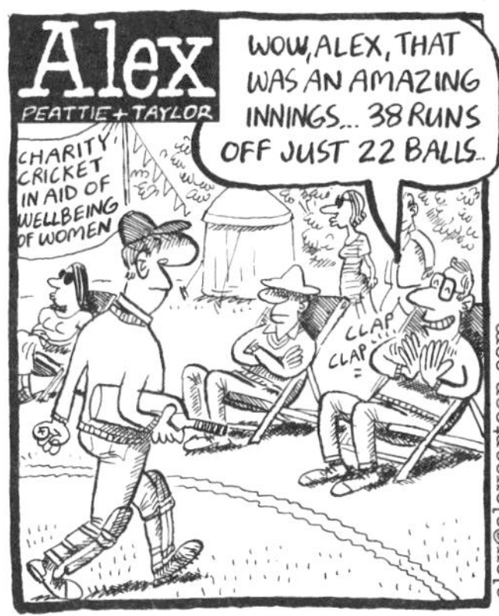
Alex
PEATTIE + TAYLOR
WOW, ALEX, THAT WAS AN AMAZING INNINGS... 38 RUNS OFF JUST 22 BALLS...
CHARITY CRICKET IN AID OF WELLBEING OF WOMEN
CLAP CLAP
alex@alexcartoon.com

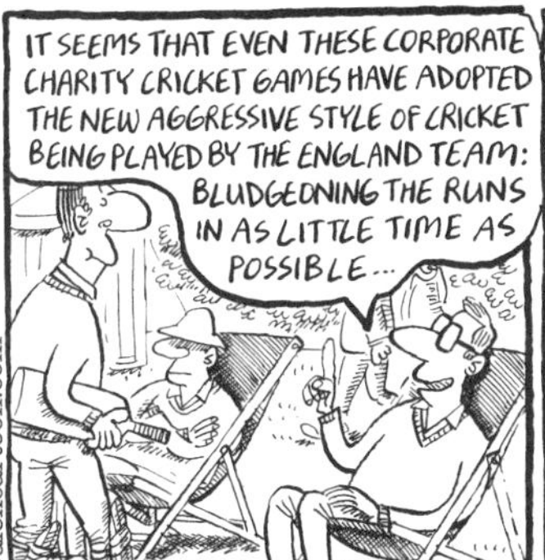
IT SEEMS THAT EVEN THESE CORPORATE CHARITY CRICKET GAMES HAVE ADOPTED THE NEW AGGRESSIVE STYLE OF CRICKET BEING PLAYED BY THE ENGLAND TEAM: BLUDGEONING THE RUNS IN AS LITTLE TIME AS POSSIBLE...

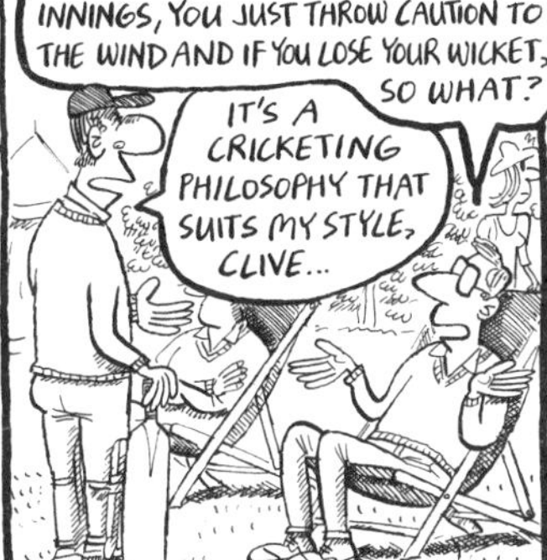
INSTEAD OF PAINSTAKINGLY CRAFTING AN INNINGS, YOU JUST THROW CAUTION TO THE WIND AND IF YOU LOSE YOUR WICKET, SO WHAT?
IT'S A CRICKETING PHILOSOPHY THAT SUITS MY STYLE, CLIVE...

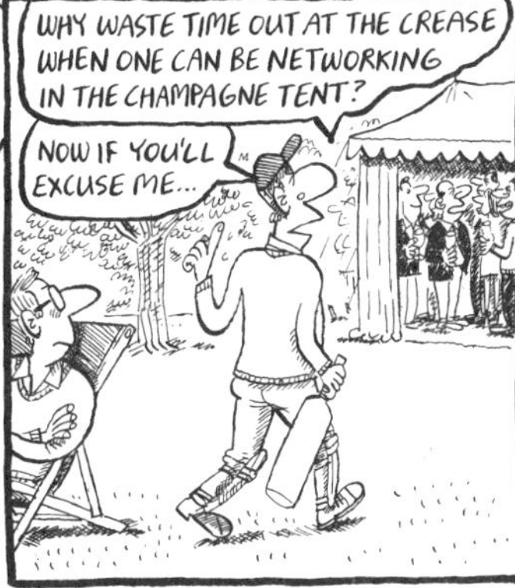
WHY WASTE TIME OUT AT THE CREASE WHEN ONE CAN BE NETWORKING IN THE CHAMPAGNE TENT?
NOW IF YOU'LL EXCUSE ME...

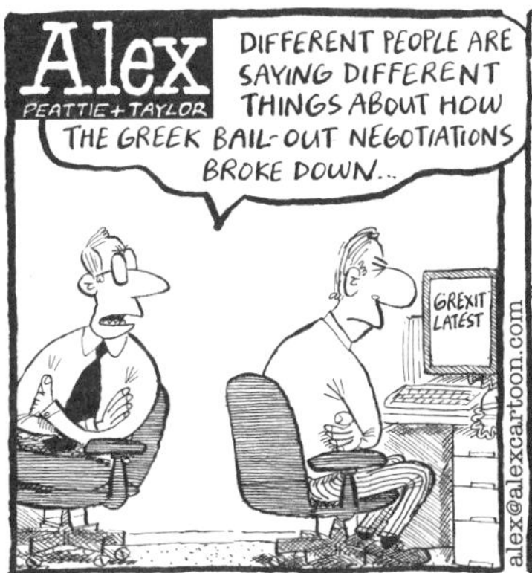
Alex
PEATTIE + TAYLOR
DIFFERENT PEOPLE ARE SAYING DIFFERENT THINGS ABOUT HOW THE GREEK BAIL-OUT NEGOTIATIONS BROKE DOWN...
GREXIT LATEST
alex@alexcartoon.com

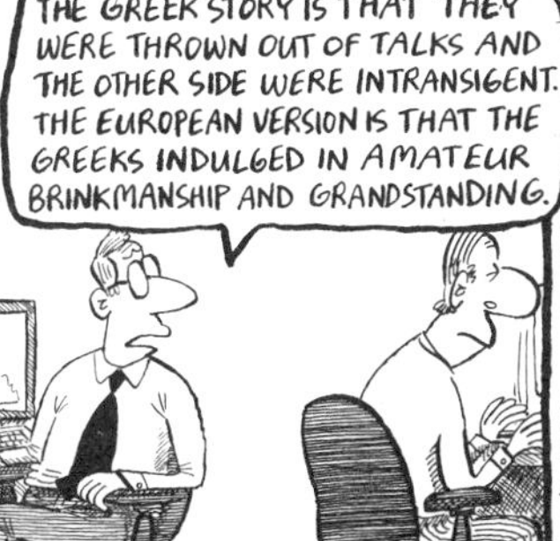
THE GREEK STORY IS THAT THEY WERE THROWN OUT OF TALKS AND THE OTHER SIDE WERE INTRANSIGENT. THE EUROPEAN VERSION IS THAT THE GREEKS INDULGED IN AMATEUR BRINKMANSHIP AND GRANDSTANDING.

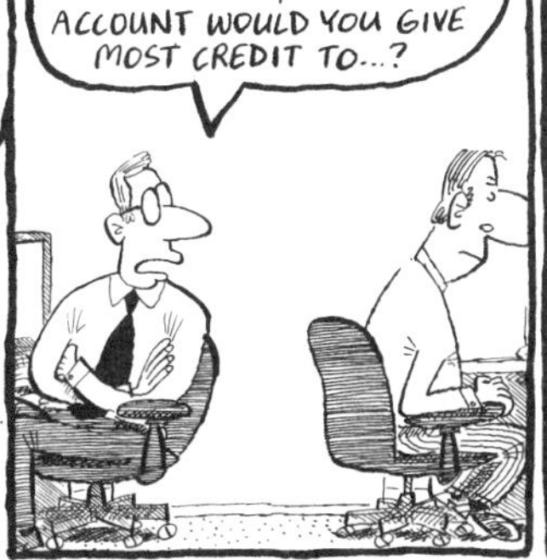
IF YOU WERE A GREEK PERSON AT THE MOMENT, ALEX: WHICH ACCOUNT WOULD YOU GIVE MOST CREDIT TO...?

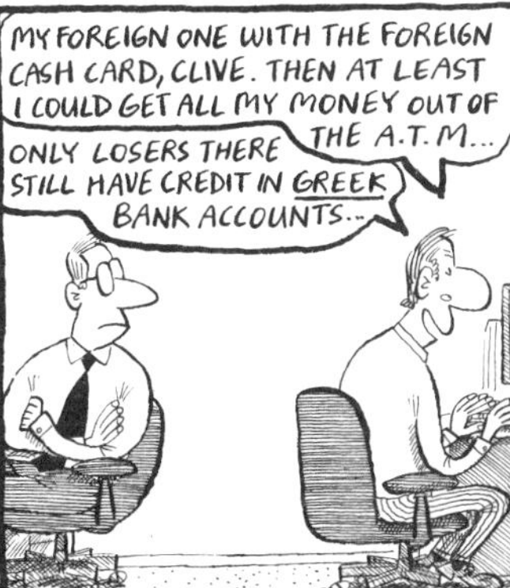
MY FOREIGN ONE WITH THE FOREIGN CASH CARD, CLIVE. THEN AT LEAST I COULD GET ALL MY MONEY OUT OF THE A.T.M...
ONLY LOSERS THERE STILL HAVE CREDIT IN GREEK BANK ACCOUNTS...

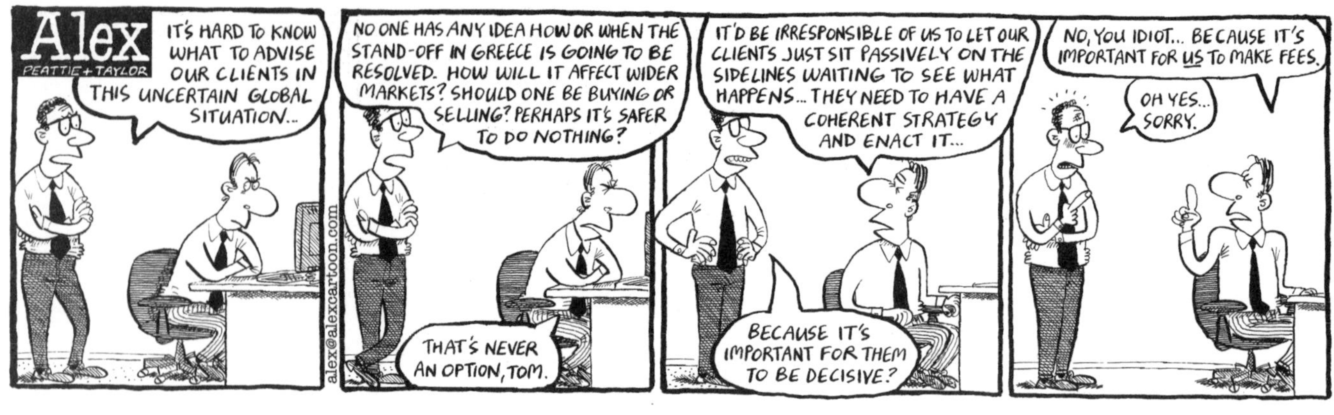
Alex
PEATTIE + TAYLOR
IT'S HARD TO KNOW WHAT TO ADVISE OUR CLIENTS IN THIS UNCERTAIN GLOBAL SITUATION...
NO ONE HAS ANY IDEA HOW OR WHEN THE STAND-OFF IN GREECE IS GOING TO BE RESOLVED. HOW WILL IT AFFECT WIDER MARKETS? SHOULD ONE BE BUYING OR SELLING? PERHAPS IT'S SAFER TO DO NOTHING?
THAT'S NEVER AN OPTION, TOM.
alex@alexcartoon.com
IT'D BE IRRESPONSIBLE OF US TO LET OUR CLIENTS JUST SIT PASSIVELY ON THE SIDELINES WAITING TO SEE WHAT HAPPENS... THEY NEED TO HAVE A COHERENT STRATEGY AND ENACT IT...
BECAUSE IT'S IMPORTANT FOR THEM TO BE DECISIVE?
NO, YOU IDIOT... BECAUSE IT'S IMPORTANT FOR US TO MAKE FEES.
OH YES... SORRY.

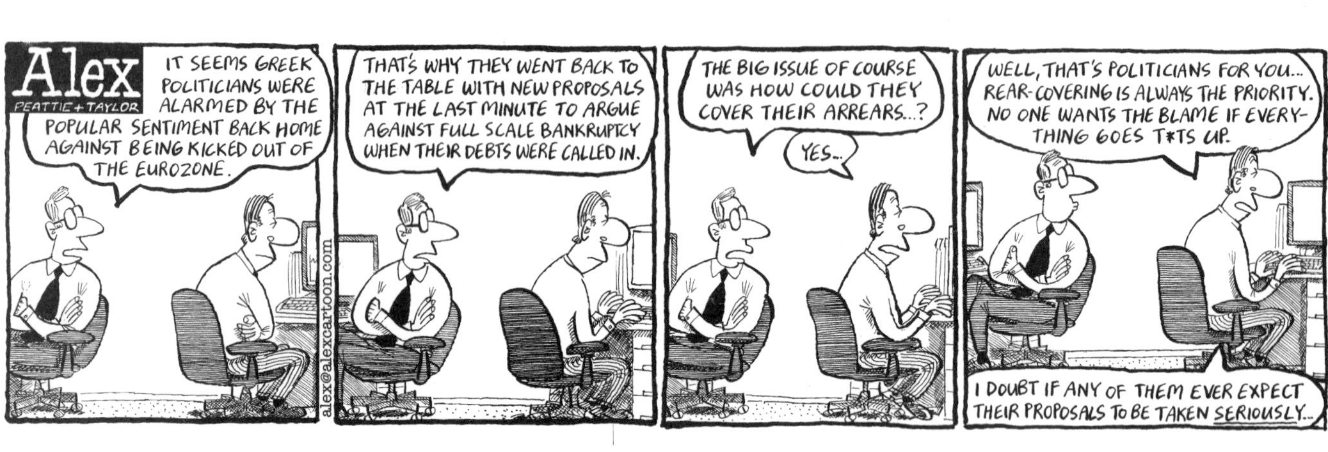
Alex
PEATTIE + TAYLOR
IT SEEMS GREEK POLITICIANS WERE ALARMED BY THE POPULAR SENTIMENT BACK HOME AGAINST BEING KICKED OUT OF THE EUROZONE.
alex@alexcartoon.com
THAT'S WHY THEY WENT BACK TO THE TABLE WITH NEW PROPOSALS AT THE LAST MINUTE TO ARGUE AGAINST FULL SCALE BANKRUPTCY WHEN THEIR DEBTS WERE CALLED IN.
THE BIG ISSUE OF COURSE WAS HOW COULD THEY COVER THEIR ARREARS...?
YES...
WELL, THAT'S POLITICIANS FOR YOU... REAR-COVERING IS ALWAYS THE PRIORITY. NO ONE WANTS THE BLAME IF EVERYTHING GOES T*TS UP.
I DOUBT IF ANY OF THEM EVER EXPECT THEIR PROPOSALS TO BE TAKEN SERIOUSLY...

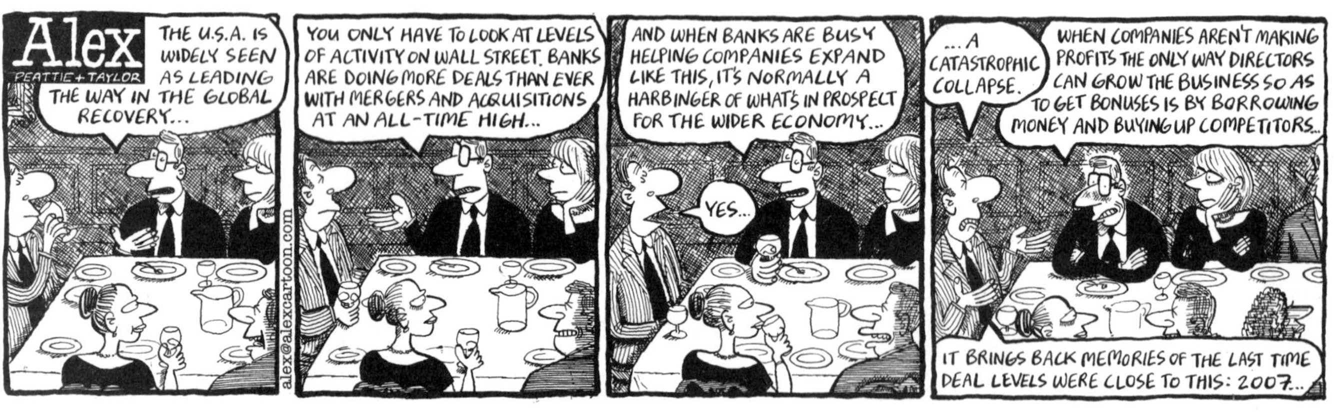
Alex
PEATTIE + TAYLOR
THE U.S.A. IS WIDELY SEEN AS LEADING THE WAY IN THE GLOBAL RECOVERY...
alex@alexcartoon.com
YOU ONLY HAVE TO LOOK AT LEVELS OF ACTIVITY ON WALL STREET. BANKS ARE DOING MORE DEALS THAN EVER WITH MERGERS AND ACQUISITIONS AT AN ALL-TIME HIGH...
AND WHEN BANKS ARE BUSY HELPING COMPANIES EXPAND LIKE THIS, IT'S NORMALLY A HARBINGER OF WHAT'S IN PROSPECT FOR THE WIDER ECONOMY...
YES...
WHEN COMPANIES AREN'T MAKING PROFITS THE ONLY WAY DIRECTORS CAN GROW THE BUSINESS SO AS TO GET BONUSES IS BY BORROWING MONEY AND BUYING UP COMPETITORS...
...A CATASTROPHIC COLLAPSE.
IT BRINGS BACK MEMORIES OF THE LAST TIME DEAL LEVELS WERE CLOSE TO THIS: 2007...

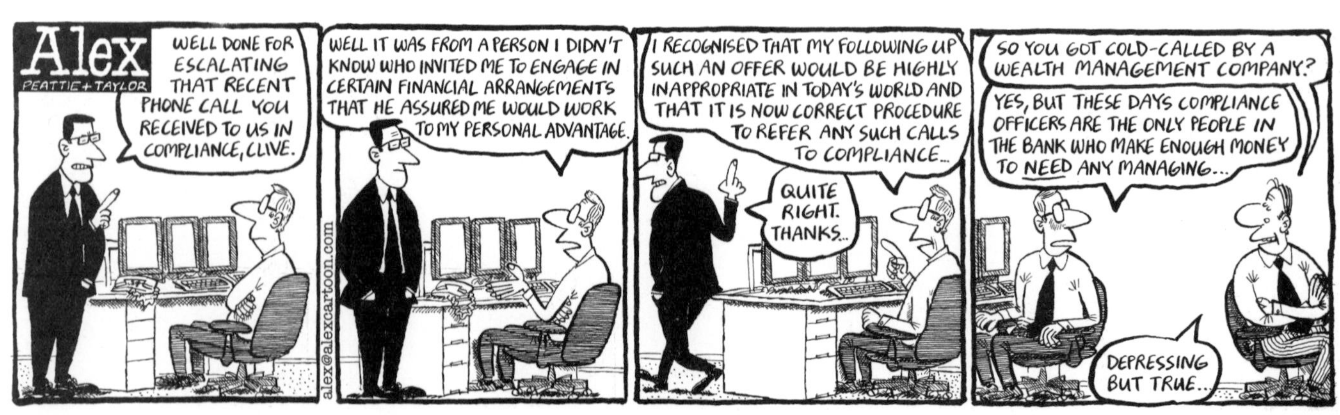
Alex
PEATTIE + TAYLOR
WELL DONE FOR ESCALATING THAT RECENT PHONE CALL YOU RECEIVED TO US IN COMPLIANCE, CLIVE.
alex@alexcartoon.com
WELL IT WAS FROM A PERSON I DIDN'T KNOW WHO INVITED ME TO ENGAGE IN CERTAIN FINANCIAL ARRANGEMENTS THAT HE ASSURED ME WOULD WORK TO MY PERSONAL ADVANTAGE.
I RECOGNISED THAT MY FOLLOWING UP SUCH AN OFFER WOULD BE HIGHLY INAPPROPRIATE IN TODAY'S WORLD AND THAT IT IS NOW CORRECT PROCEDURE TO REFER ANY SUCH CALLS TO COMPLIANCE...
QUITE RIGHT. THANKS...
SO YOU GOT COLD-CALLED BY A WEALTH MANAGEMENT COMPANY?
YES, BUT THESE DAYS COMPLIANCE OFFICERS ARE THE ONLY PEOPLE IN THE BANK WHO MAKE ENOUGH MONEY TO NEED ANY MANAGING...
DEPRESSING BUT TRUE...

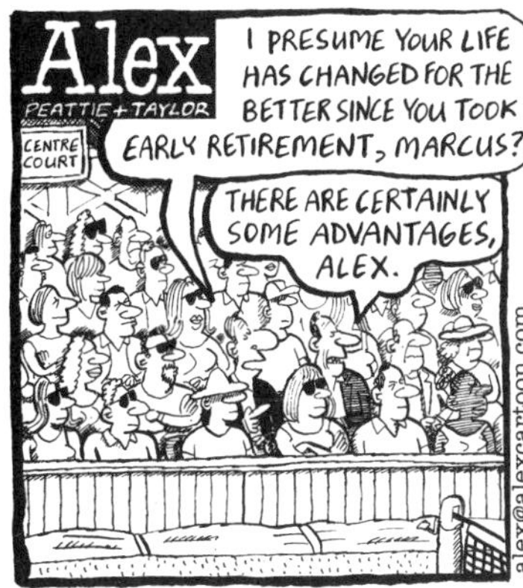
Alex
PEATTIE + TAYLOR
CENTRE COURT
I PRESUME YOUR LIFE HAS CHANGED FOR THE BETTER SINCE YOU TOOK EARLY RETIREMENT, MARCUS?
THERE ARE CERTAINLY SOME ADVANTAGES, ALEX.
alex@alexcartoon.com

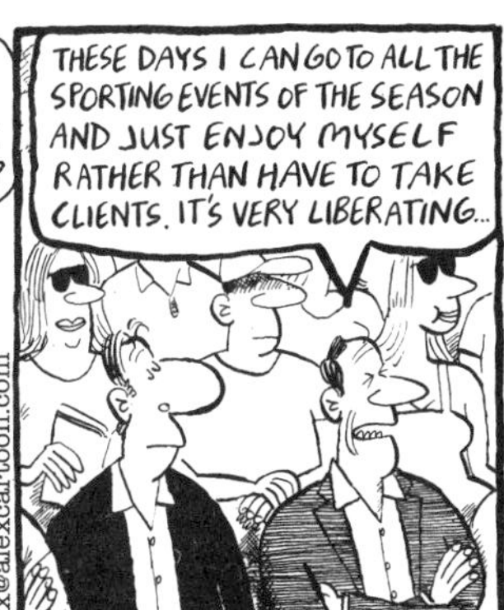
THESE DAYS I CAN GO TO ALL THE SPORTING EVENTS OF THE SEASON AND JUST ENJOY MYSELF RATHER THAN HAVE TO TAKE CLIENTS. IT'S VERY LIBERATING...

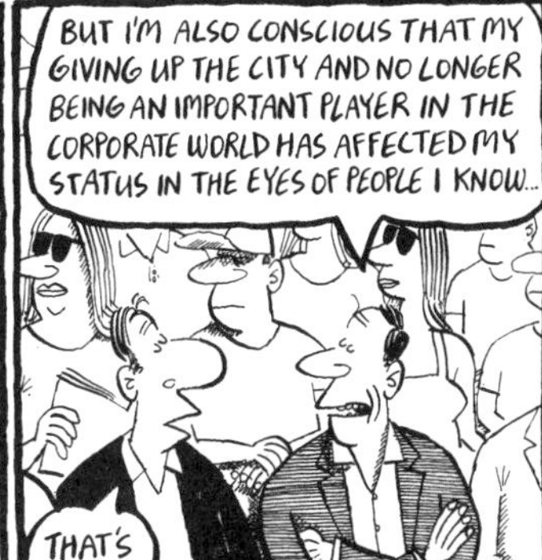
BUT I'M ALSO CONSCIOUS THAT MY GIVING UP THE CITY AND NO LONGER BEING AN IMPORTANT PLAYER IN THE CORPORATE WORLD HAS AFFECTED MY STATUS IN THE EYES OF PEOPLE I KNOW...
THAT'S TRUE...

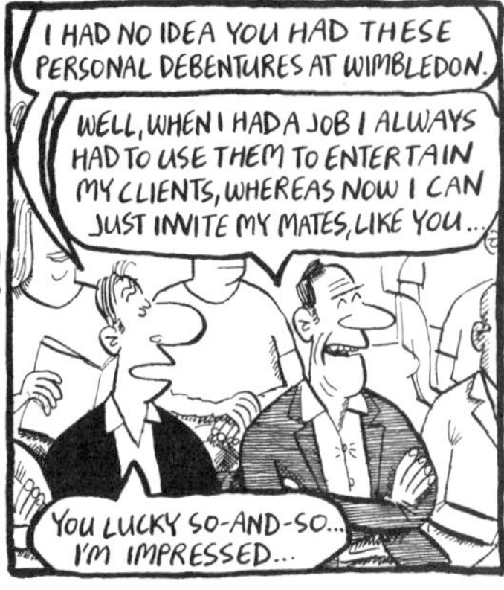
I HAD NO IDEA YOU HAD THESE PERSONAL DEBENTURES AT WIMBLEDON.
WELL, WHEN I HAD A JOB I ALWAYS HAD TO USE THEM TO ENTERTAIN MY CLIENTS, WHEREAS NOW I CAN JUST INVITE MY MATES, LIKE YOU...
YOU LUCKY SO-AND-SO... I'M IMPRESSED...

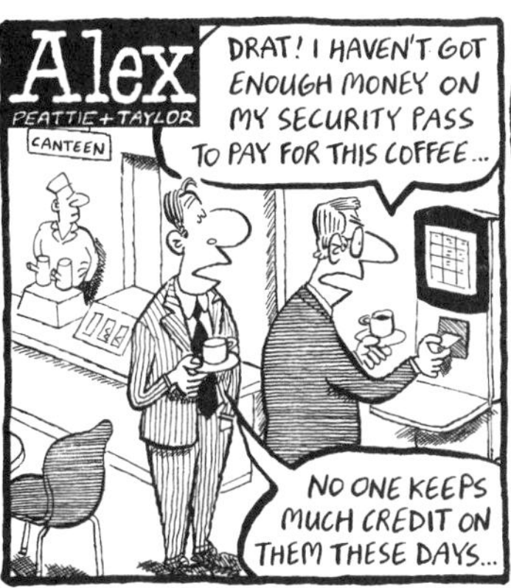
Alex
PEATTIE + TAYLOR
CANTEEN
DRAT! I HAVEN'T GOT ENOUGH MONEY ON MY SECURITY PASS TO PAY FOR THIS COFFEE...
NO ONE KEEPS MUCH CREDIT ON THEM THESE DAYS...
alex@alexcartoon.com

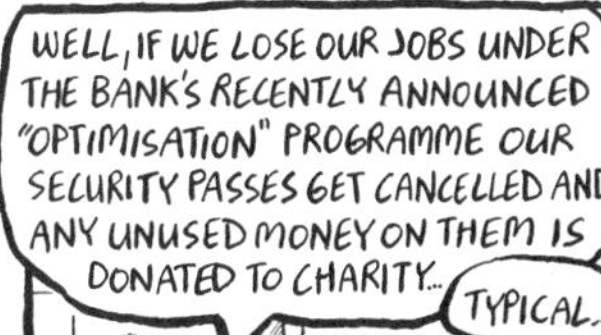
WELL, IF WE LOSE OUR JOBS UNDER THE BANK'S RECENTLY ANNOUNCED "OPTIMISATION" PROGRAMME OUR SECURITY PASSES GET CANCELLED AND ANY UNUSED MONEY ON THEM IS DONATED TO CHARITY...

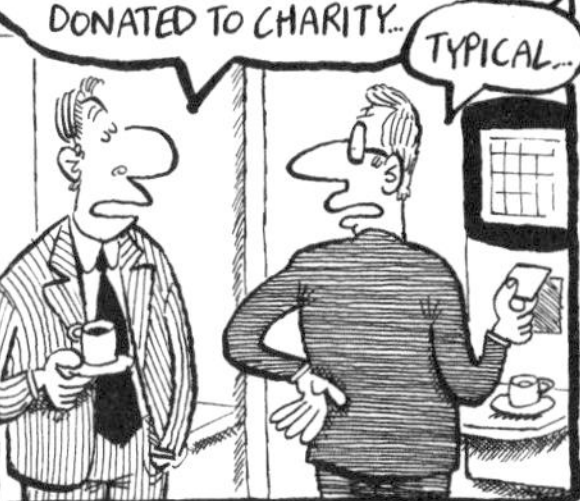
TYPICAL...

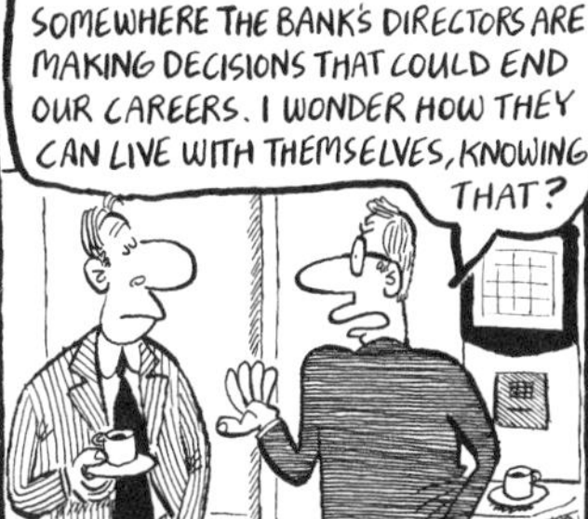
SO WE ALL EXIST IN A CLIMATE OF FEAR AND PARANOIA, KNOWING THAT SOMEWHERE THE BANK'S DIRECTORS ARE MAKING DECISIONS THAT COULD END OUR CAREERS. I WONDER HOW THEY CAN LIVE WITH THEMSELVES, KNOWING THAT?

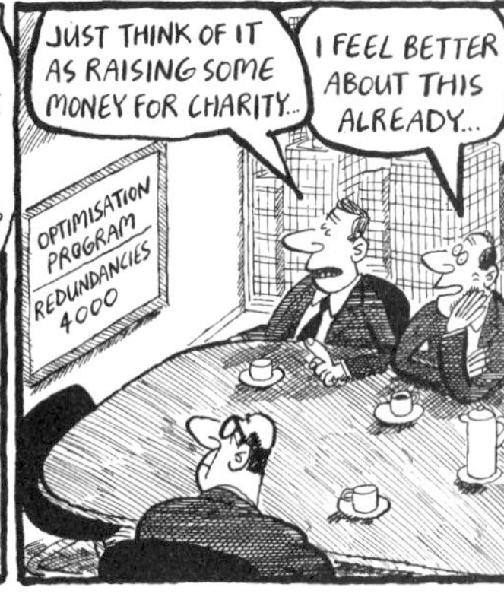
JUST THINK OF IT AS RAISING SOME MONEY FOR CHARITY...
I FEEL BETTER ABOUT THIS ALREADY...
OPTIMISATION PROGRAM
REDUNDANCIES 4000

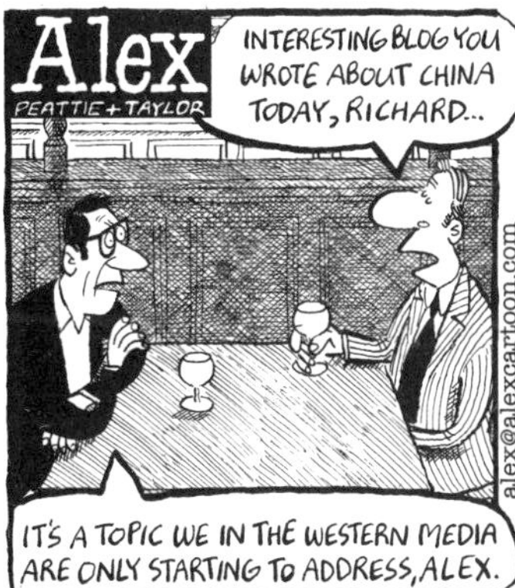
Alex
PEATTIE + TAYLOR
INTERESTING BLOG YOU WROTE ABOUT CHINA TODAY, RICHARD...
IT'S A TOPIC WE IN THE WESTERN MEDIA ARE ONLY STARTING TO ADDRESS, ALEX.
alex@alexcartoon.com

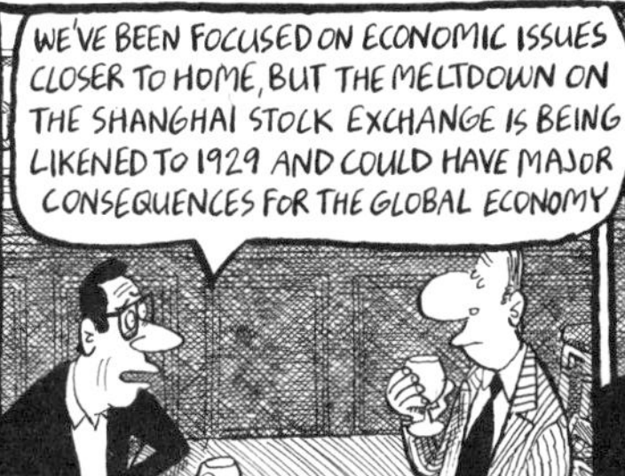
WE'VE BEEN FOCUSED ON ECONOMIC ISSUES CLOSER TO HOME, BUT THE MELTDOWN ON THE SHANGHAI STOCK EXCHANGE IS BEING LIKENED TO 1929 AND COULD HAVE MAJOR CONSEQUENCES FOR THE GLOBAL ECONOMY

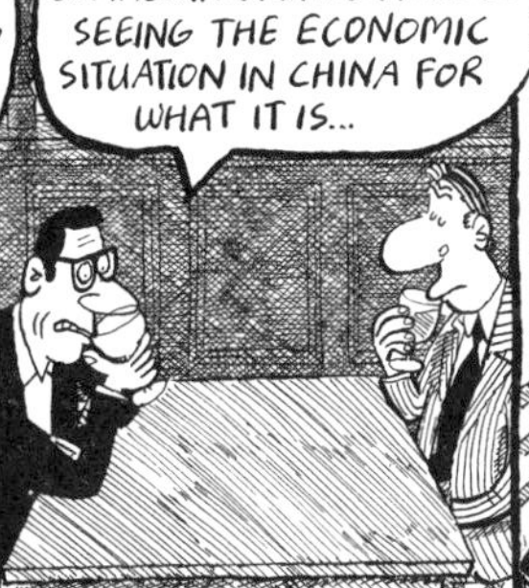
I THINK A LOT OF US FINANCIAL COMMENTATORS ARE FINALLY SEEING THE ECONOMIC SITUATION IN CHINA FOR WHAT IT IS...

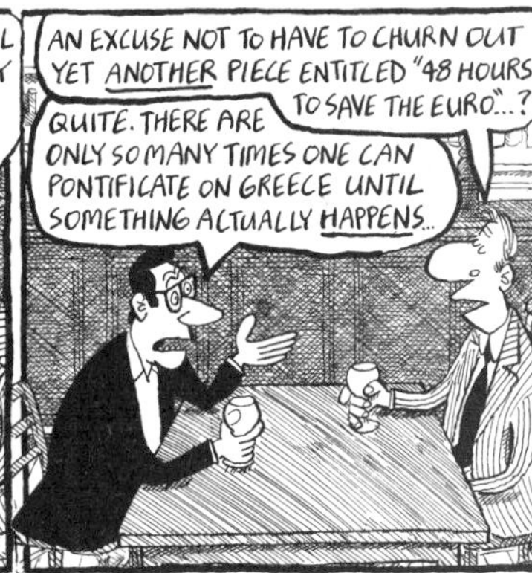
AN EXCUSE NOT TO HAVE TO CHURN OUT YET ANOTHER PIECE ENTITLED "48 HOURS TO SAVE THE EURO"...?
QUITE. THERE ARE ONLY SO MANY TIMES ONE CAN PONTIFICATE ON GREECE UNTIL SOMETHING ACTUALLY HAPPENS...

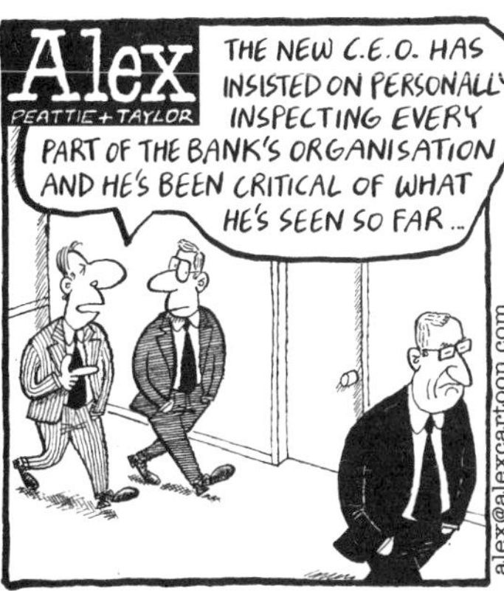
Alex
PEATTIE + TAYLOR
THE NEW C.E.O. HAS INSISTED ON PERSONALLY INSPECTING EVERY PART OF THE BANK'S ORGANISATION AND HE'S BEEN CRITICAL OF WHAT HE'S SEEN SO FAR...

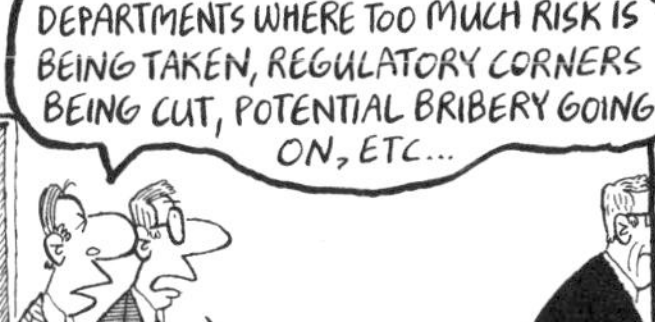
DEPARTMENTS WHERE TOO MUCH RISK IS BEING TAKEN, REGULATORY CORNERS BEING CUT, POTENTIAL BRIBERY GOING ON, ETC...

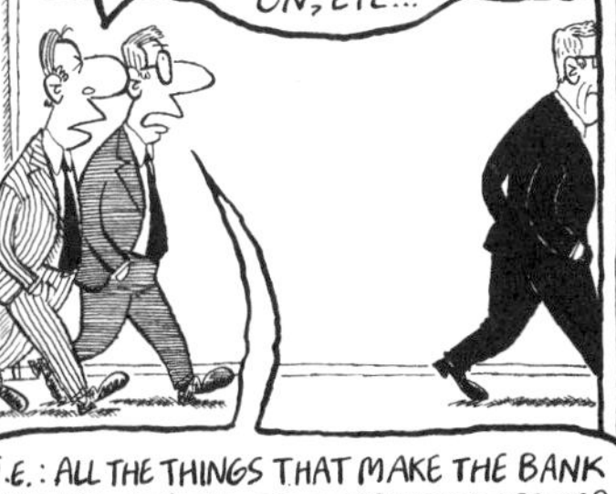
alex@alexcartoon.com

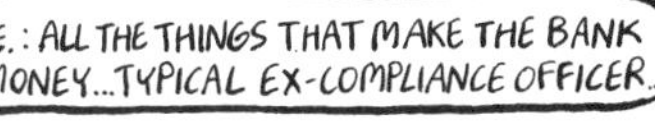
I.E.: ALL THE THINGS THAT MAKE THE BANK MONEY... TYPICAL EX-COMPLIANCE OFFICER...

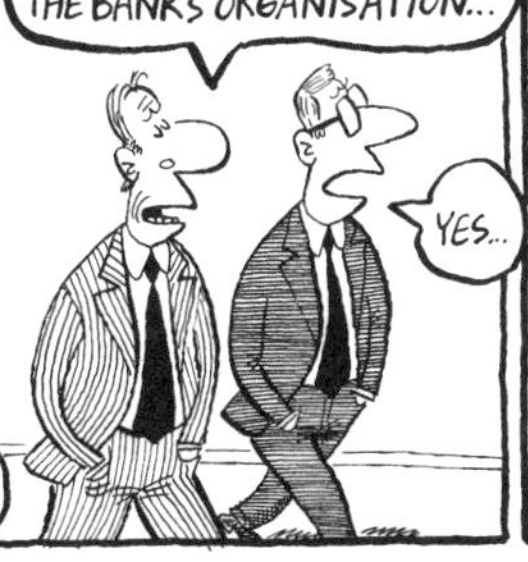
WELL, CLIVE, AT LEAST HE'S FINALLY FOUND A DEPARTMENT WHICH HE FEELS SHOULD SERVE AS A MODEL FOR THE REST OF THE BANK'S ORGANISATION...
YES...

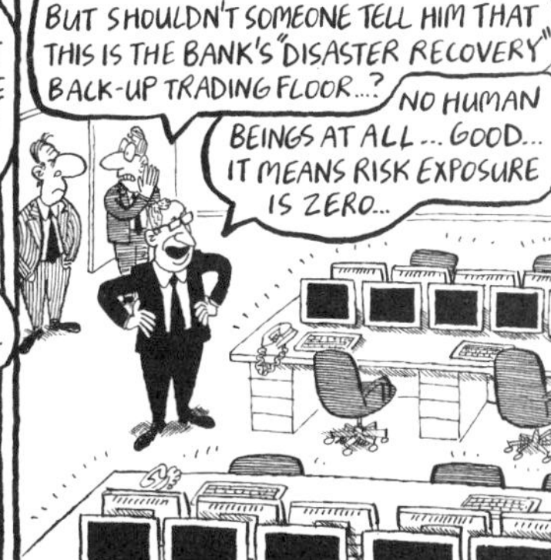
BUT SHOULDN'T SOMEONE TELL HIM THAT THIS IS THE BANK'S "DISASTER RECOVERY" BACK-UP TRADING FLOOR...?
NO HUMAN BEINGS AT ALL... GOOD... IT MEANS RISK EXPOSURE IS ZERO...

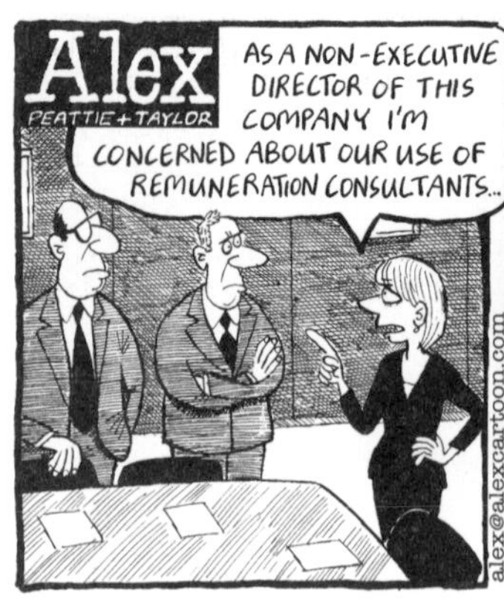
Alex
PEATTIE + TAYLOR
AS A NON-EXECUTIVE DIRECTOR OF THIS COMPANY I'M CONCERNED ABOUT OUR USE OF REMUNERATION CONSULTANTS...

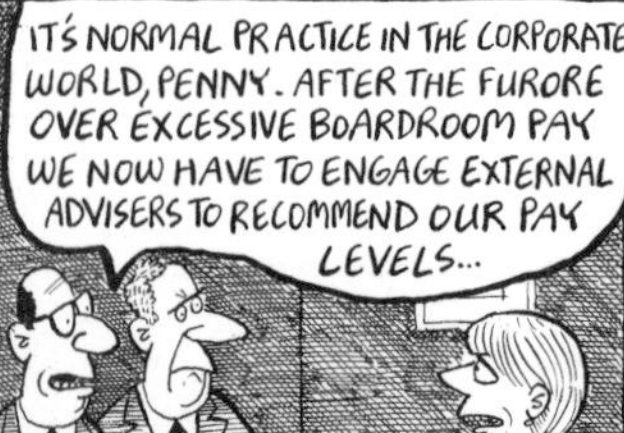
IT'S NORMAL PRACTICE IN THE CORPORATE WORLD, PENNY. AFTER THE FURORE OVER EXCESSIVE BOARDROOM PAY WE NOW HAVE TO ENGAGE EXTERNAL ADVISERS TO RECOMMEND OUR PAY LEVELS...
BUT THEY COULD BE YOUR CRONIES...
alex@alexcartoon.com

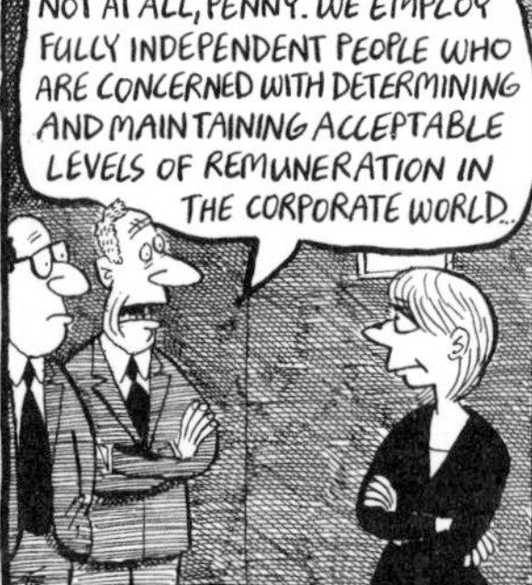
NOT AT ALL, PENNY. WE EMPLOY FULLY INDEPENDENT PEOPLE WHO ARE CONCERNED WITH DETERMINING AND MAINTAINING ACCEPTABLE LEVELS OF REMUNERATION IN THE CORPORATE WORLD...

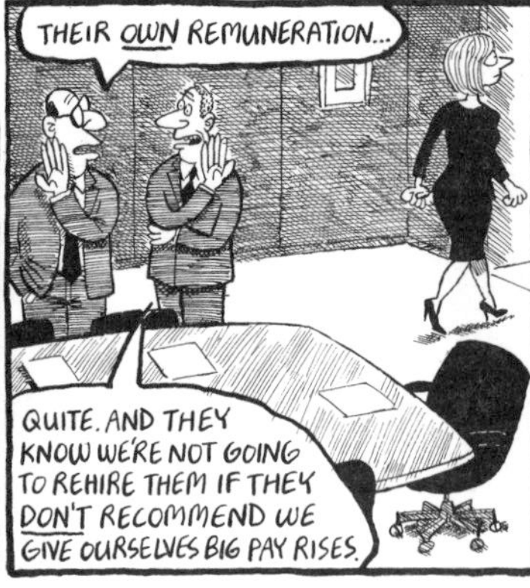
THEIR OWN REMUNERATION...
QUITE. AND THEY KNOW WE'RE NOT GOING TO REHIRE THEM IF THEY DON'T RECOMMEND WE GIVE OURSELVES BIG PAY RISES.

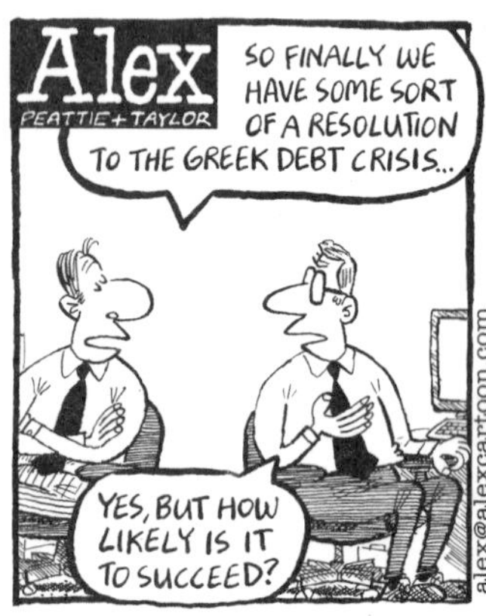
Alex
PEATTIE + TAYLOR
SO FINALLY WE HAVE SOME SORT OF A RESOLUTION TO THE GREEK DEBT CRISIS...
YES, BUT HOW LIKELY IS IT TO SUCCEED?

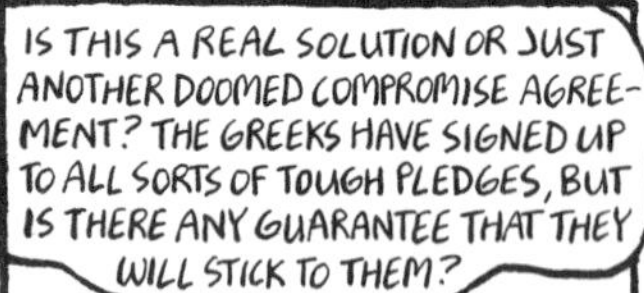
IS THIS A REAL SOLUTION OR JUST ANOTHER DOOMED COMPROMISE AGREEMENT? THE GREEKS HAVE SIGNED UP TO ALL SORTS OF TOUGH PLEDGES, BUT IS THERE ANY GUARANTEE THAT THEY WILL STICK TO THEM?

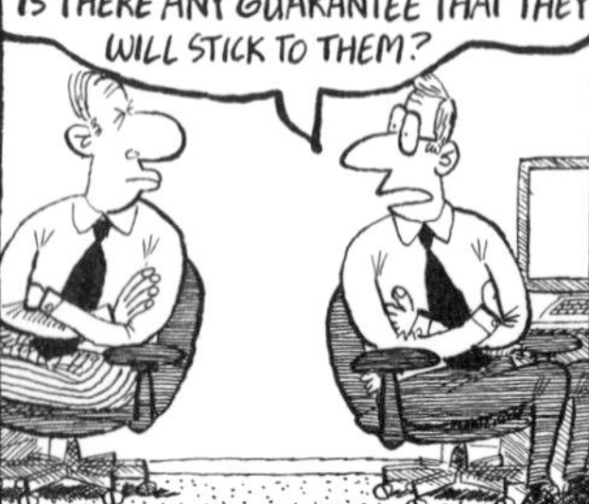
alex@alexcartoon.com

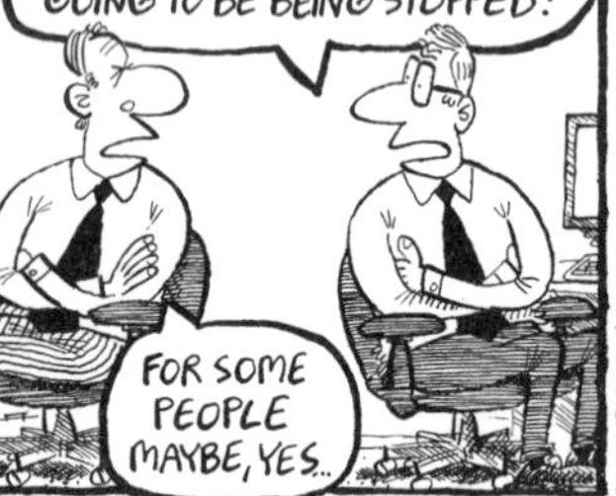
ISN'T THERE A POSSIBILITY THAT THIS IS A TEMPORARY FUDGE THAT WILL MERELY ALLOW THE QUIET RESUMPTION OF THE EVASIONS AND WORK-SHY PRACTICES THAT WERE GOING TO BE BEING STOPPED?
FOR SOME PEOPLE MAYBE, YES...

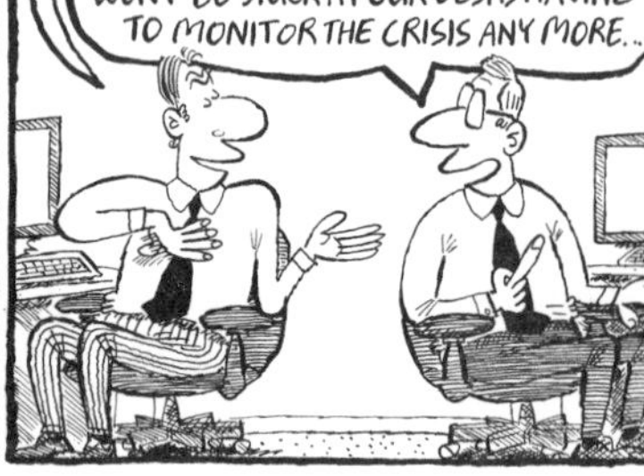
SUCH AS MYSELF, BECAUSE I NOW INTEND TO SKIVE OFF AND WATCH THE CRICKET AS ORIGINALLY PLANNED THIS WEEK.
I'LL JOIN YOU... THANK GOODNESS WE WON'T BE STUCK AT OUR DESKS HAVING TO MONITOR THE CRISIS ANY MORE...

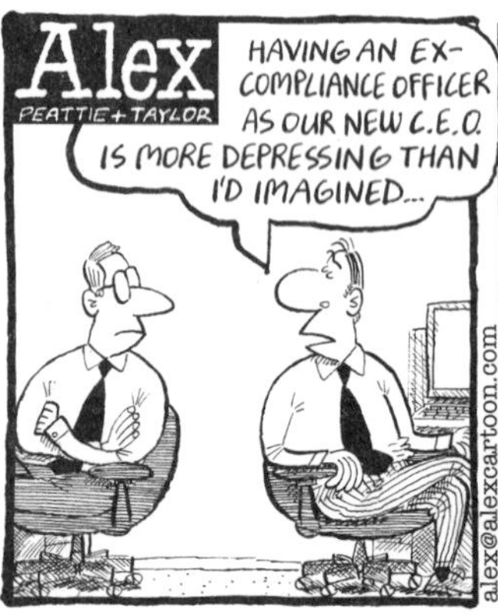
Alex
PEATTIE + TAYLOR
HAVING AN EX-COMPLIANCE OFFICER AS OUR NEW C.E.O. IS MORE DEPRESSING THAN I'D IMAGINED...

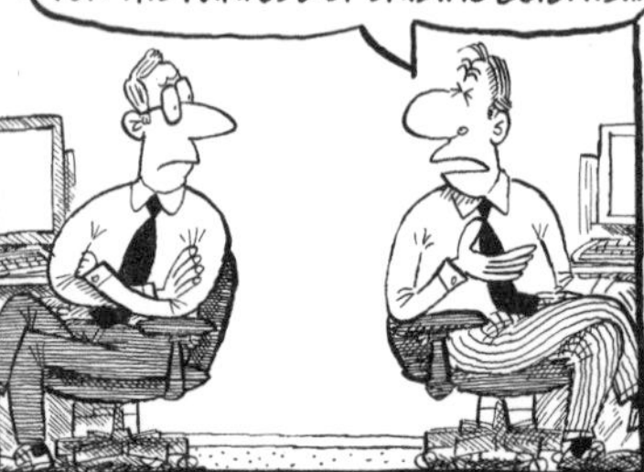
ONE OF HIS FIRST ACTS HAS BEEN TO END THE BANK'S SPONSORSHIP OF THE RUGBY. IN HIS OPINION IT'S AN UNNECESSARY EXPENSE, WHICH IS ONLY BEING USED FOR THE PURPOSE OF BRIBING CLIENTS...
alex@alexcartoon.com

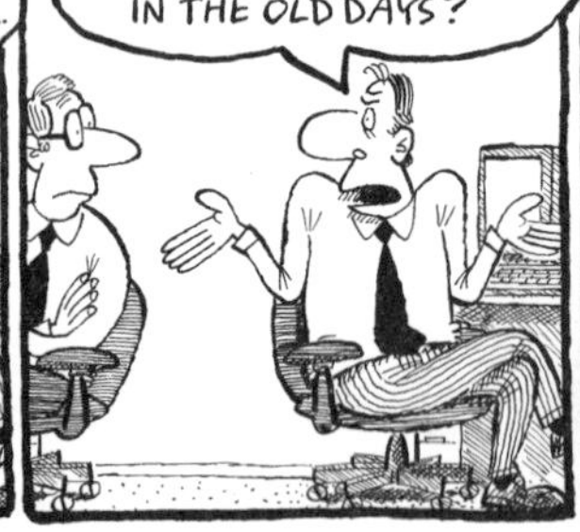
WHAT'S HAPPENED TO C.E.O.s? ARBITRARILY CANCELLING THE BANK'S SPORTING DEBENTURES? WOULD THAT HAVE HAPPENED IN THE OLD DAYS?

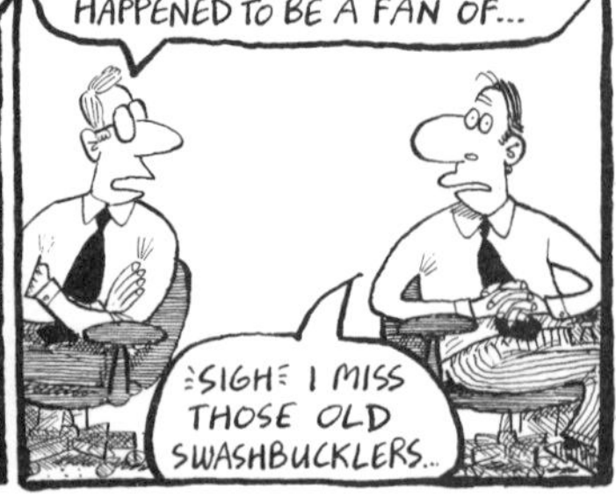
WELL, YES, OF COURSE... HE'D HAVE DITCHED THE RUGBY AND SIGNED US UP TO SPONSOR THE MOTOR RACING OR WHATEVER SPORT HE HAPPENED TO BE A FAN OF...
SIGH I MISS THOSE OLD SWASHBUCKLERS...

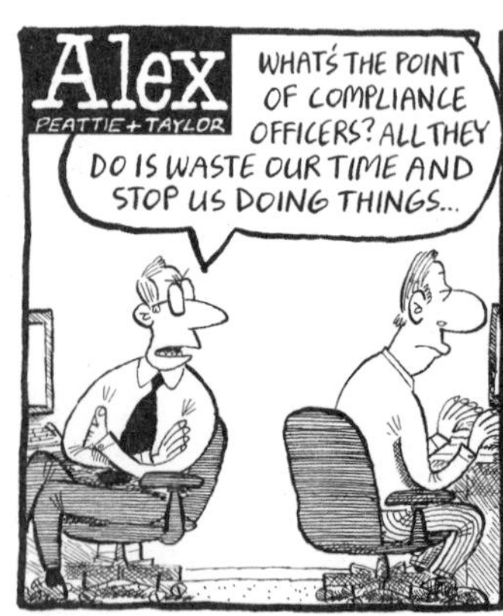
Alex
PEATTIE + TAYLOR
WHAT'S THE POINT OF COMPLIANCE OFFICERS? ALL THEY DO IS WASTE OUR TIME AND STOP US DOING THINGS...

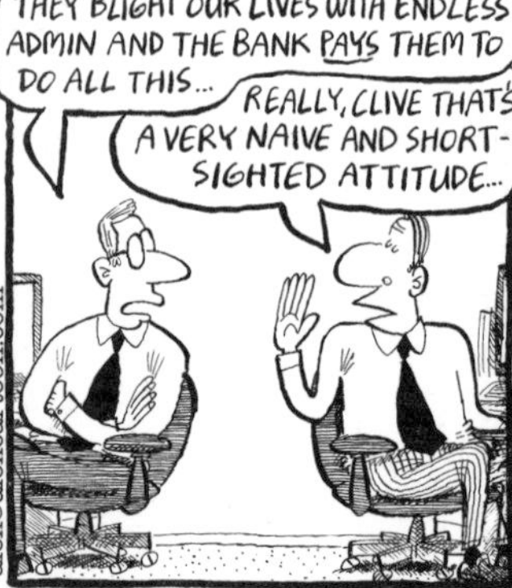
THEY BLIGHT OUR LIVES WITH ENDLESS ADMIN AND THE BANK PAYS THEM TO DO ALL THIS...
REALLY, CLIVE THAT'S A VERY NAIVE AND SHORT-SIGHTED ATTITUDE...
alex@alexcartoon.com

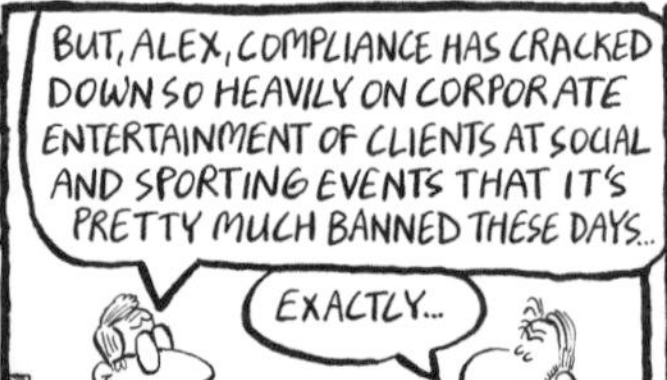
BUT, ALEX, COMPLIANCE HAS CRACKED DOWN SO HEAVILY ON CORPORATE ENTERTAINMENT OF CLIENTS AT SOCIAL AND SPORTING EVENTS THAT IT'S PRETTY MUCH BANNED THESE DAYS...

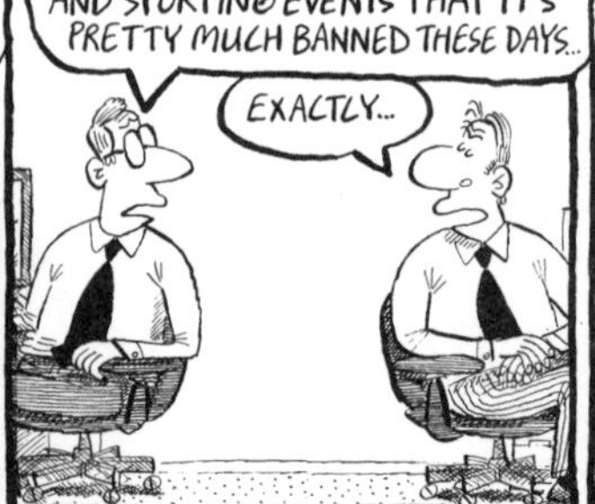
EXACTLY...

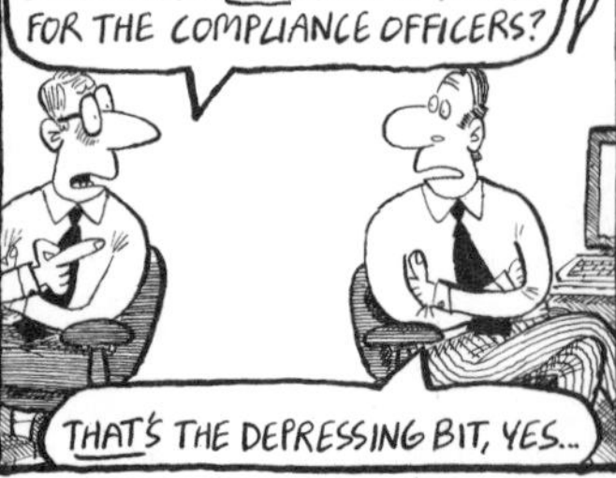
SO WE END UP PAYING FOR IT OUT OF OUR OWN POCKETS, MEANING THE BANK IS ACTUALLY SAVING MONEY...
HOLD ON... SO THAT MEANS EFFECTIVELY WE'RE SORT OF PAYING FOR THE COMPLIANCE OFFICERS?
THAT'S THE DEPRESSING BIT, YES...

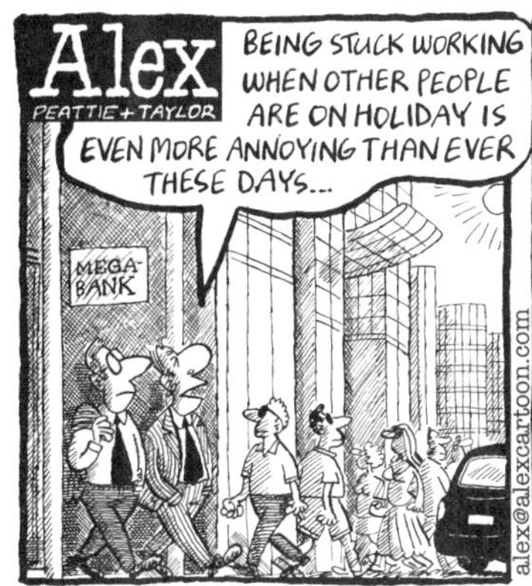

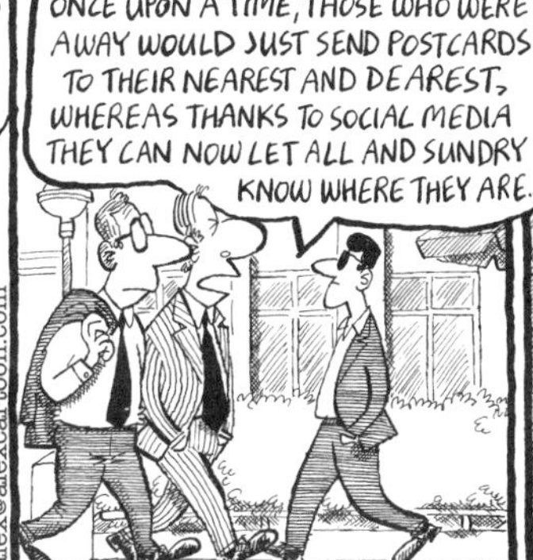

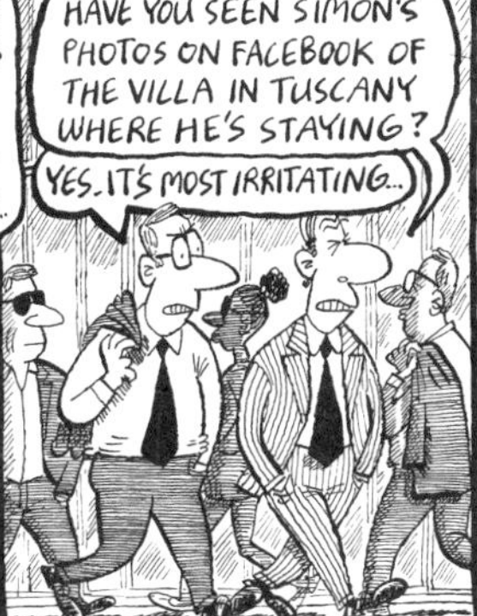

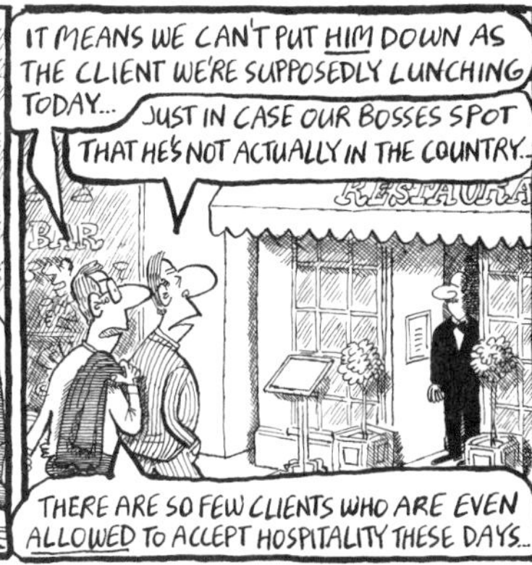

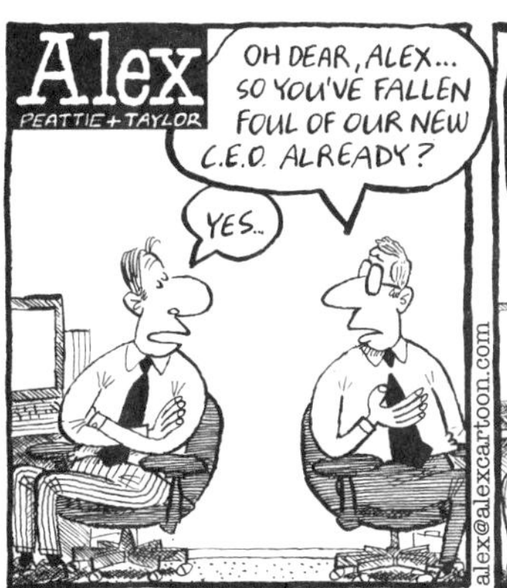

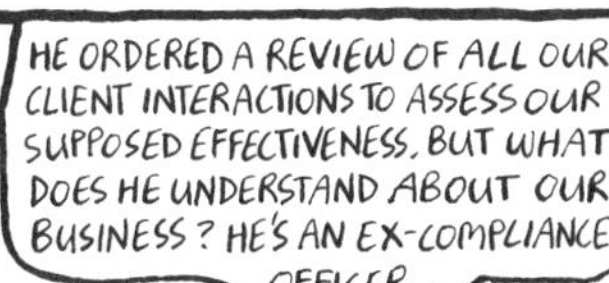

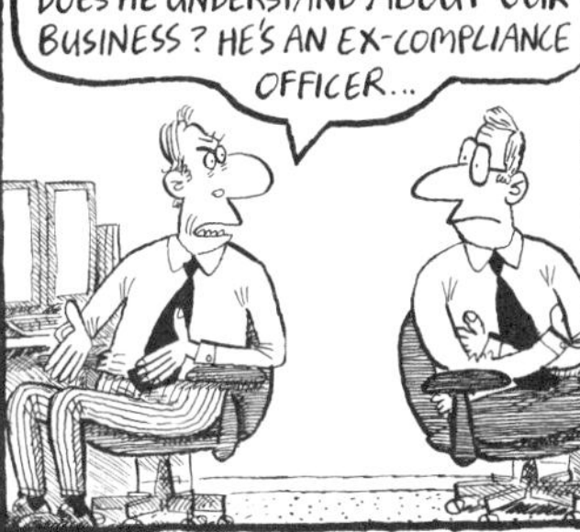

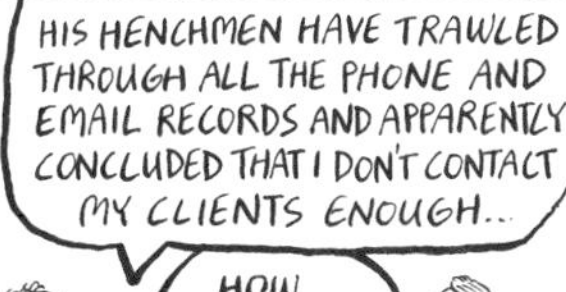

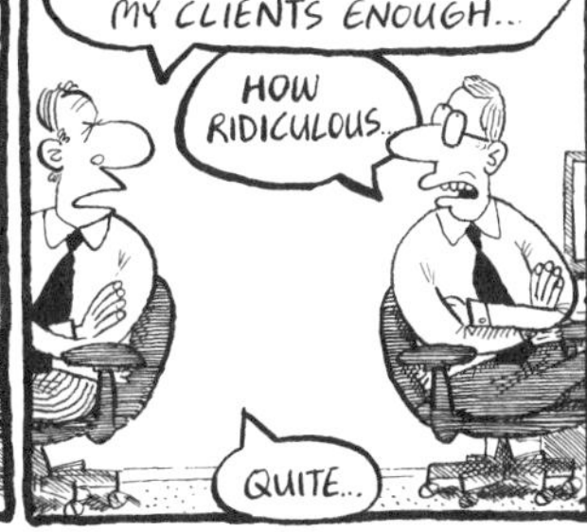

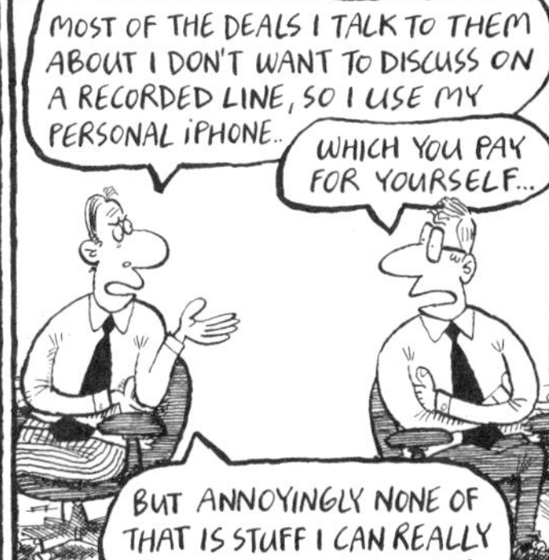

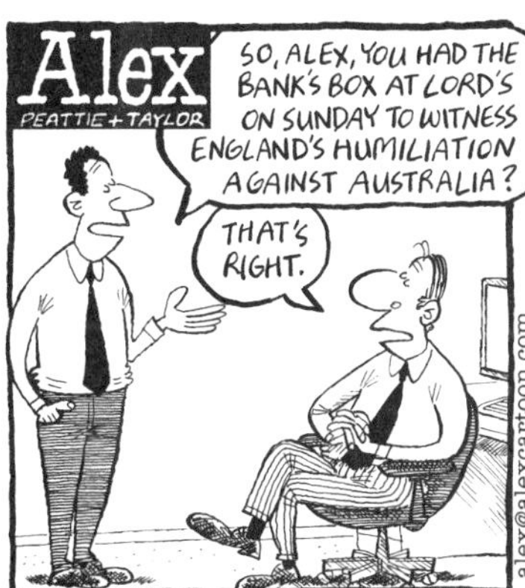

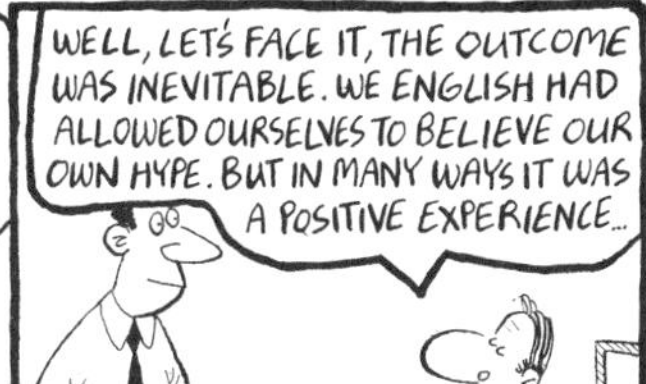

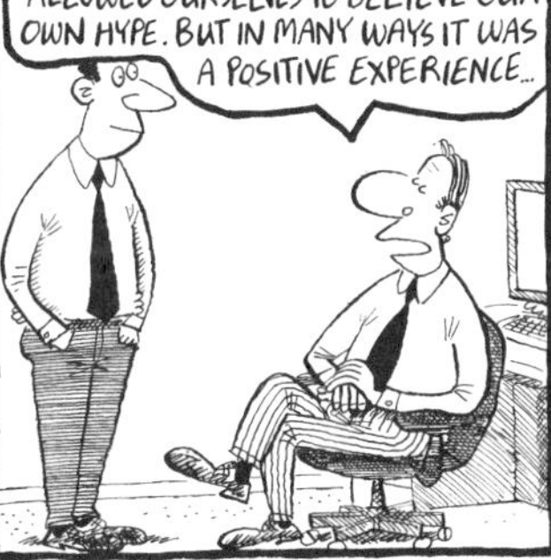

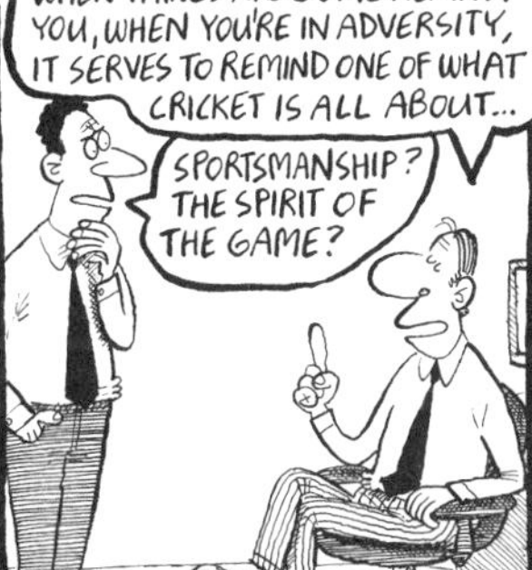

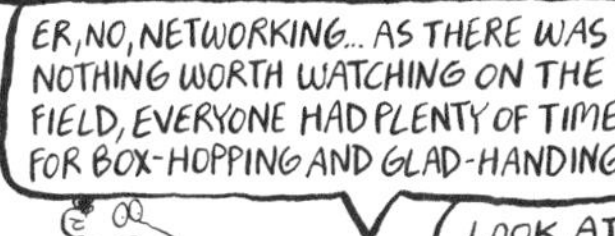

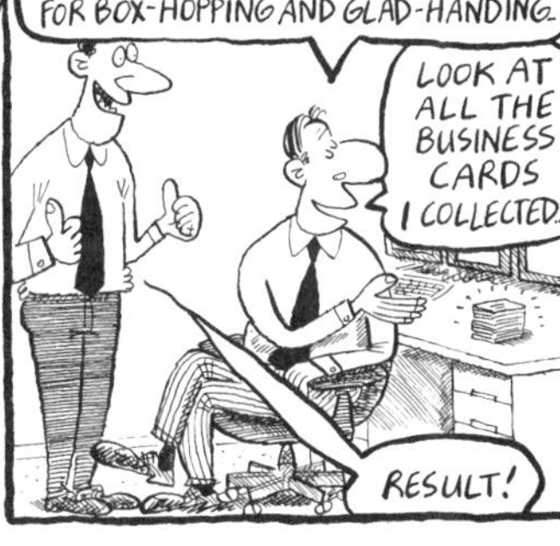

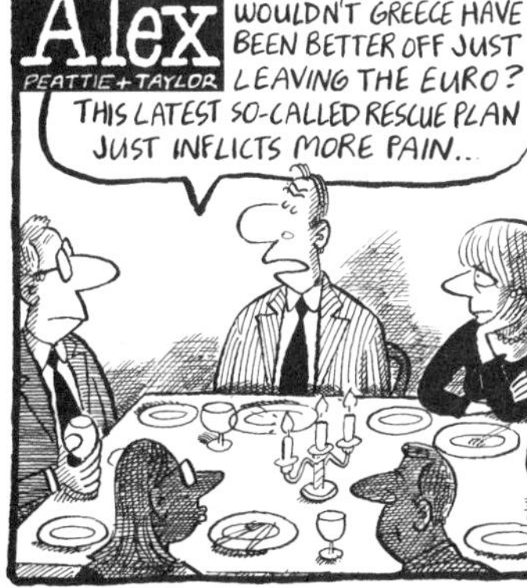

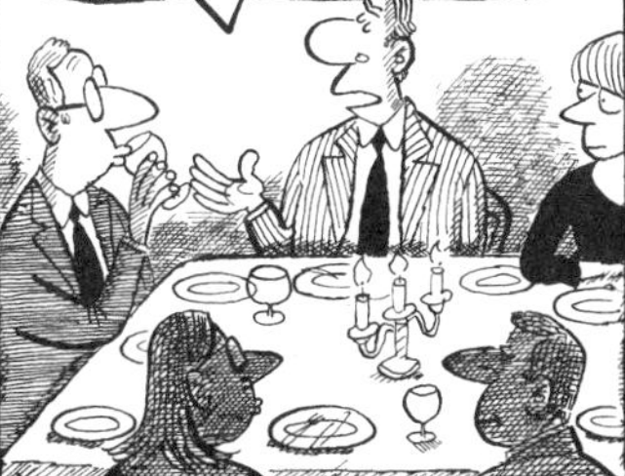

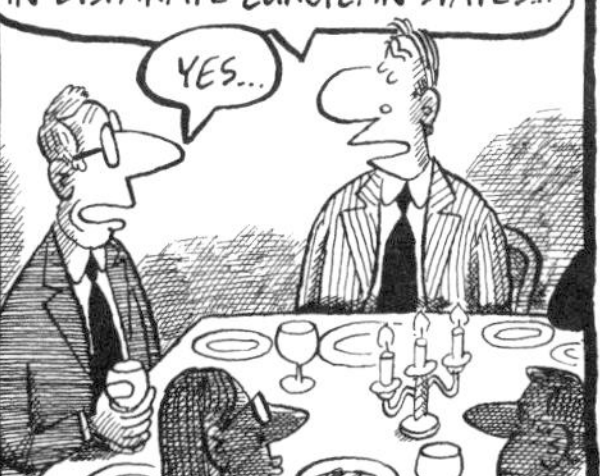

IT BRINGS DOWN THE COST OF OUR ANNUAL STAYS IN TUSCANY AND PROVENCE..
AND UNLIKE ANYONE GOING TO GREECE WE DON'T HAVE TO WORRY ABOUT CIVIL UNREST OR GETTING MUGGED FOR OUR CASH...

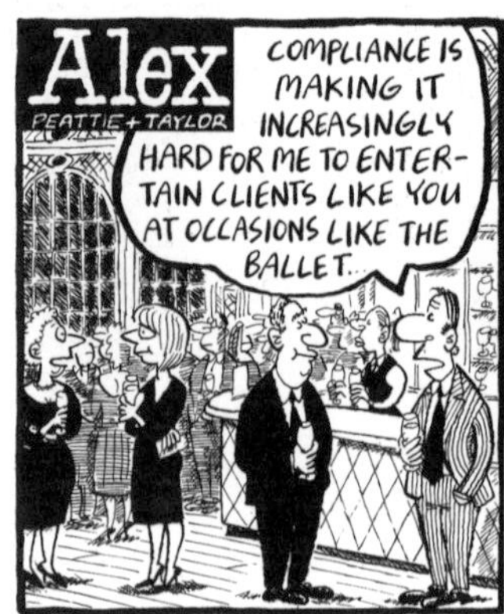
Alex
PEATTIE + TAYLOR
COMPLIANCE IS MAKING IT INCREASINGLY HARD FOR ME TO ENTERTAIN CLIENTS LIKE YOU AT OCCASIONS LIKE THE BALLET...

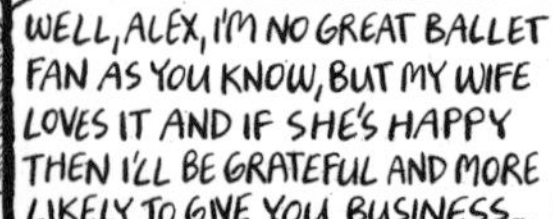
WELL, ALEX, I'M NO GREAT BALLET FAN AS YOU KNOW, BUT MY WIFE LOVES IT AND IF SHE'S HAPPY THEN I'LL BE GRATEFUL AND MORE LIKELY TO GIVE YOU BUSINESS...

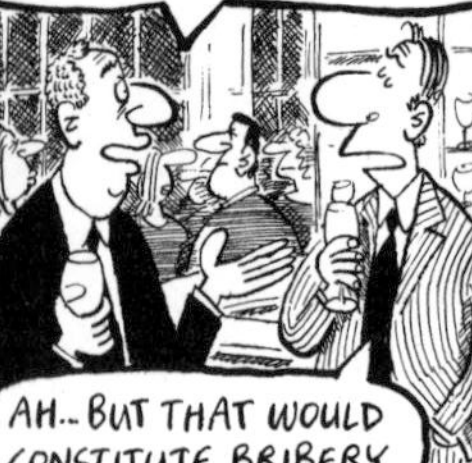
AH.. BUT THAT WOULD CONSTITUTE BRIBERY...
alex@alexcartoon.com

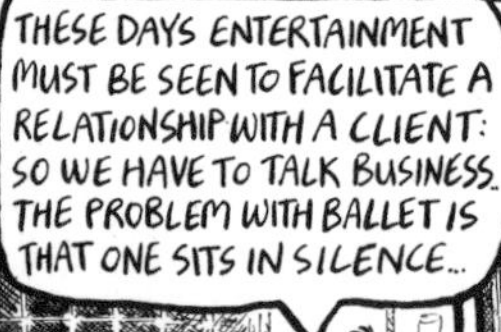
THESE DAYS ENTERTAINMENT MUST BE SEEN TO FACILITATE A RELATIONSHIP WITH A CLIENT: SO WE HAVE TO TALK BUSINESS. THE PROBLEM WITH BALLET IS THAT ONE SITS IN SILENCE...
AH...

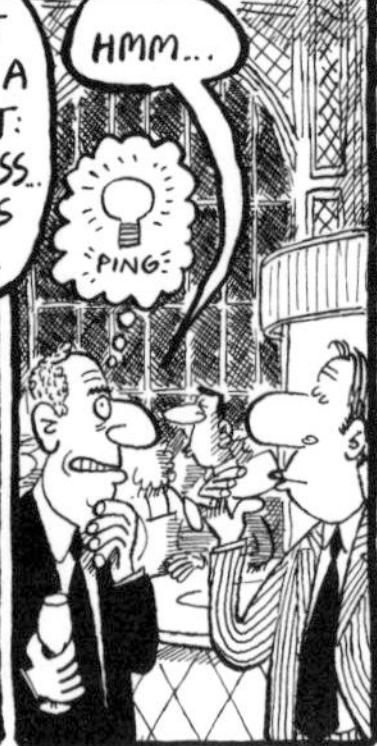
HMM...
PING!

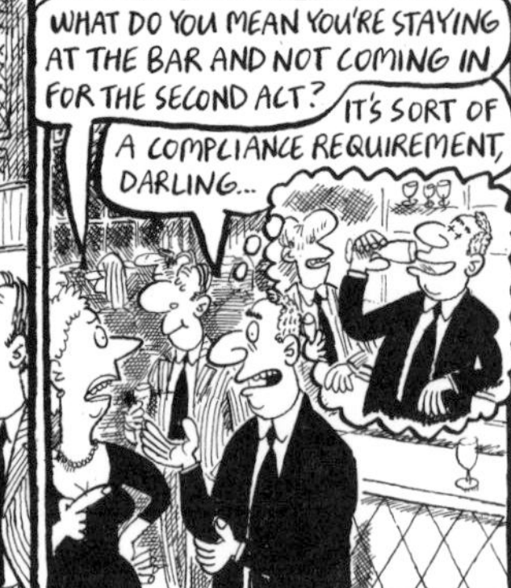
WHAT DO YOU MEAN YOU'RE STAYING AT THE BAR AND NOT COMING IN FOR THE SECOND ACT?
IT'S SORT OF A COMPLIANCE REQUIREMENT, DARLING...

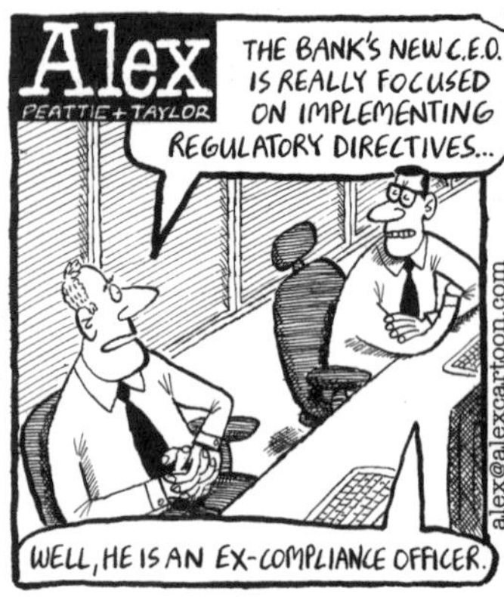
Alex
PEATTIE + TAYLOR
THE BANK'S NEW C.E.O. IS REALLY FOCUSED ON IMPLEMENTING REGULATORY DIRECTIVES...
WELL, HE IS AN EX-COMPLIANCE OFFICER.

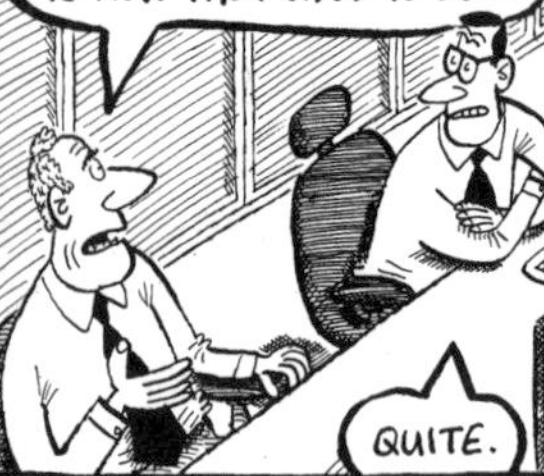
HIS OBSESSION WITH PROCEDURE HAS SERIOUSLY IMPACTED ON THE ABILITY OF ANALYSTS LIKE YOU AND ME TO DO OUR JOBS. ONE ONLY HAS TO COMPARE THINGS NOW TO HOW THEY USED TO BE...
QUITE.
alex@alexcartoon.com

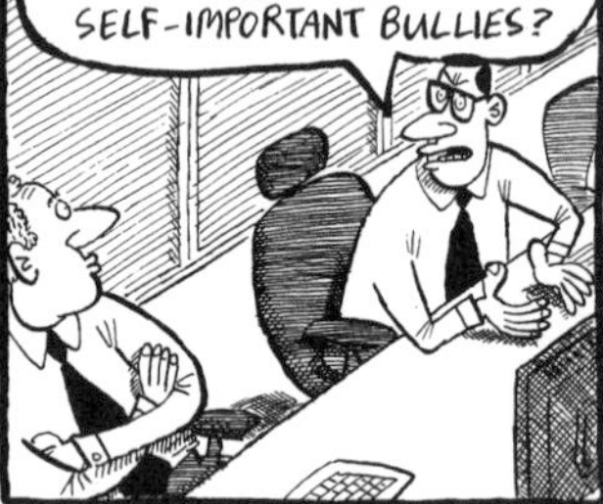
DO WE REALLY WANT TO SLAVE UNDER A REGIME WHERE OUR HANDS ARE TIED AND OUR ROLE MADE IMPOSSIBLE DUE TO PETTY RESTRICTIONS FOISTED ON US BY JUMPED-UP SELF-IMPORTANT BULLIES?

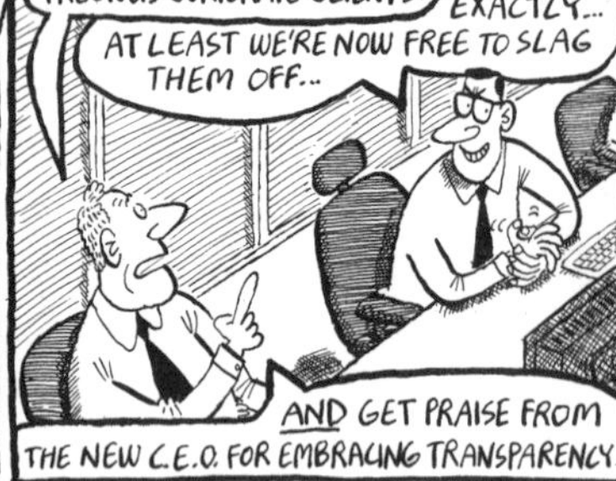
WHAT, LIKE IN THE OLD DAYS WHEN ALEX MASTERLEY WOULDN'T LET US WRITE ANY RESEARCH WHICH MIGHT UPSET ANY OF HIS PRECIOUS CORPORATE CLIENTS?
EXACTLY... AT LEAST WE'RE NOW FREE TO SLAG THEM OFF...
AND GET PRAISE FROM THE NEW C.E.O. FOR EMBRACING TRANSPARENCY.

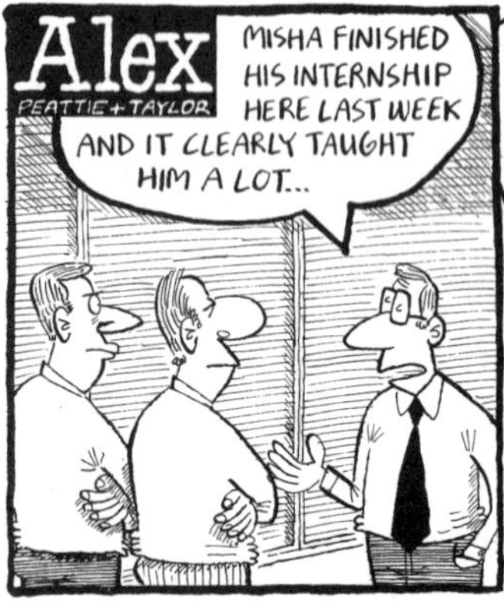
Alex
PEATTIE + TAYLOR
MISHA FINISHED HIS INTERNSHIP HERE LAST WEEK AND IT CLEARLY TAUGHT HIM A LOT...

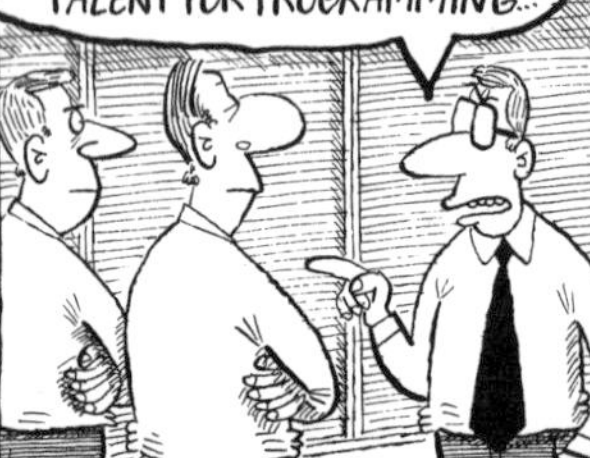
UNLIKE YOU, ALEX, I DON'T JUST GIVE INTERNS GRUNT JOBS LIKE FETCHING THE COFFEE. I PREFER TO ASSIGN THEM TO PRACTICAL TASKS, FOR EXAMPLE MISHA IS BRIGHT AND HAS A TALENT FOR PROGRAMMING...
alex@alexcartoon.com

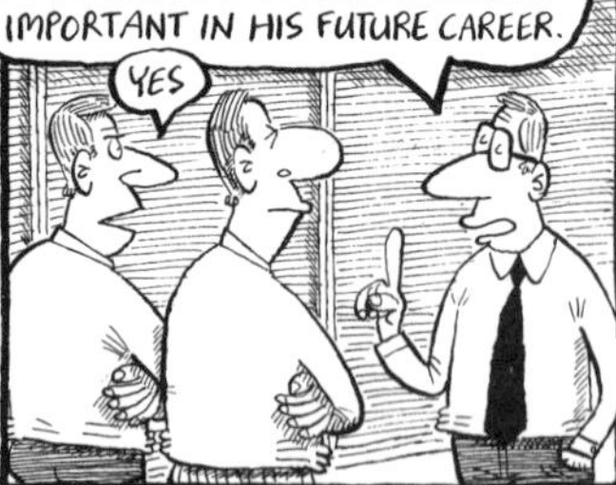
SO I GOT HIM TO DESIGN A NEW RISK MANAGEMENT SYSTEM FOR OUR DESK. THIS ENABLED HIM TO UTILISE HIS EXISTING ABILITIES AND DEVELOP AND HONE NEW SKILLS THAT'LL BE IMPORTANT IN HIS FUTURE CAREER.
YES

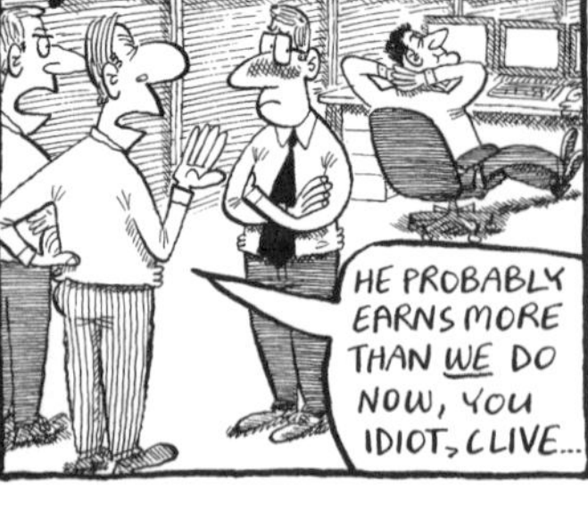
SUCH AS MAKING HIMSELF INDISPENSABLE.. NONE OF US UNDERSTANDS HOW HIS SYSTEM WORKS SO WE'VE HAD TO REHIRE HIM AS A CONSULTANT ON A DAILY RATE...
HE PROBABLY EARNS MORE THAN WE DO NOW, YOU IDIOT, CLIVE...

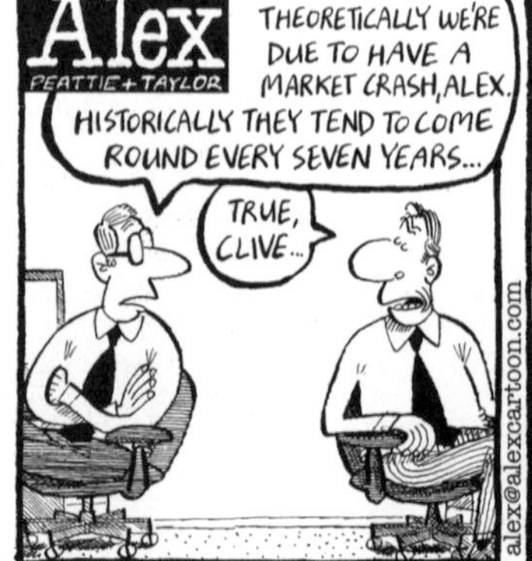
Alex
PEATTIE + TAYLOR
THEORETICALLY WE'RE DUE TO HAVE A MARKET CRASH, ALEX. HISTORICALLY THEY TEND TO COME ROUND EVERY SEVEN YEARS...
TRUE, CLIVE...

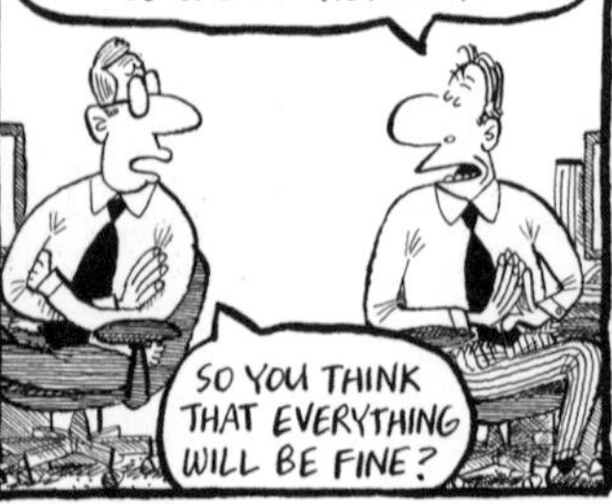
OF COURSE THINGS ARE DIFFERENT THESE DAYS... SINCE 2008 CENTRAL BANKS HAVE PLAYED A MUCH MORE ACTIVE ROLE IN DEALING WITH CRISES AND MANAGING THE GLOBAL FINANCIAL SYSTEM...
SO YOU THINK THAT EVERYTHING WILL BE FINE?
alex@alexcartoon.com

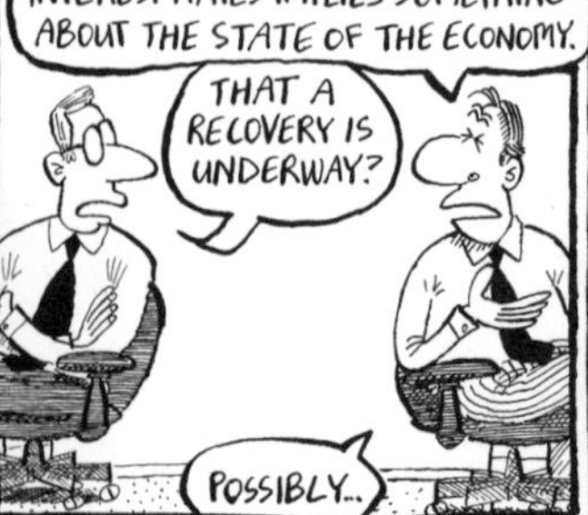
WELL, INTEREST RATES FINALLY LOOK SET TO RISE, HAVING BEEN HELD AT ZERO FOR YEARS... AND BRINGING IN HIGHER INTEREST RATES IMPLIES SOMETHING ABOUT THE STATE OF THE ECONOMY.
THAT A RECOVERY IS UNDERWAY?
POSSIBLY..

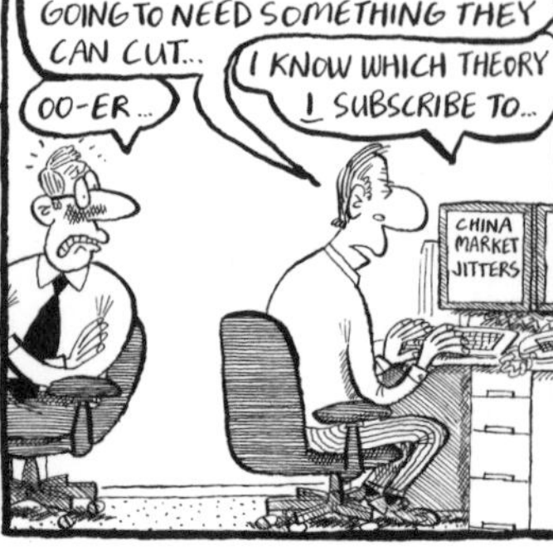
OR THAT WE'RE HEADED FOR ANOTHER CRISIS AND THE CENTRAL BANKS ARE GOING TO NEED SOMETHING THEY CAN CUT...
OO-ER...
I KNOW WHICH THEORY I SUBSCRIBE TO...
CHINA MARKET JITTERS

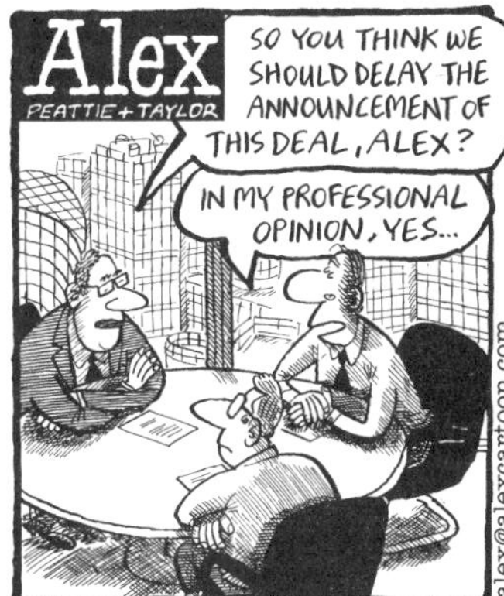
Alex
PEATTIE + TAYLOR
SO YOU THINK WE SHOULD DELAY THE ANNOUNCEMENT OF THIS DEAL, ALEX?
IN MY PROFESSIONAL OPINION, YES...
alex@alexcartoon.com

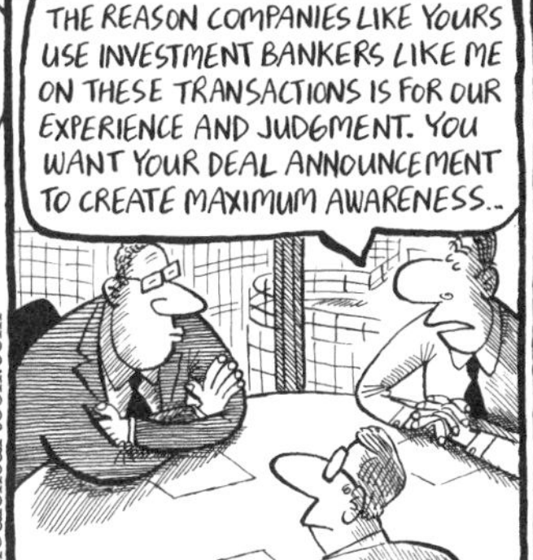
THE REASON COMPANIES LIKE YOURS USE INVESTMENT BANKERS LIKE ME ON THESE TRANSACTIONS IS FOR OUR EXPERIENCE AND JUDGMENT. YOU WANT YOUR DEAL ANNOUNCEMENT TO CREATE MAXIMUM AWARENESS...

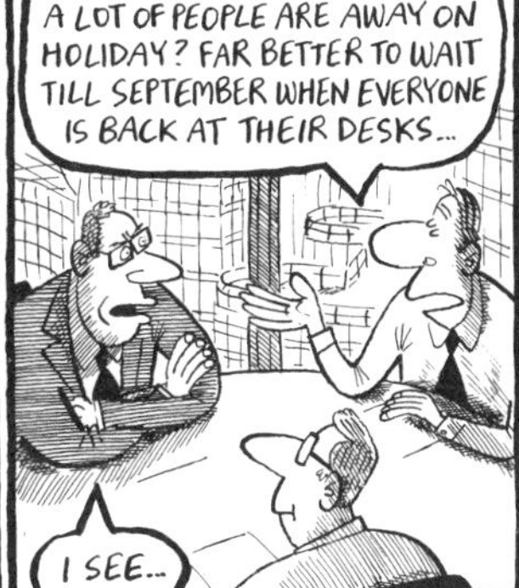
WHY PUT IT OUT NOW WHEN A LOT OF PEOPLE ARE AWAY ON HOLIDAY? FAR BETTER TO WAIT TILL SEPTEMBER WHEN EVERYONE IS BACK AT THEIR DESKS...
I SEE...

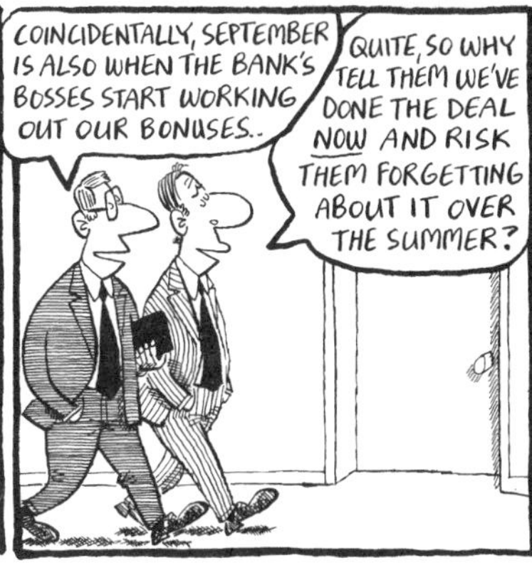
COINCIDENTALLY, SEPTEMBER IS ALSO WHEN THE BANK'S BOSSES START WORKING OUT OUR BONUSES...
QUITE, SO WHY TELL THEM WE'VE DONE THE DEAL NOW AND RISK THEM FORGETTING ABOUT IT OVER THE SUMMER?

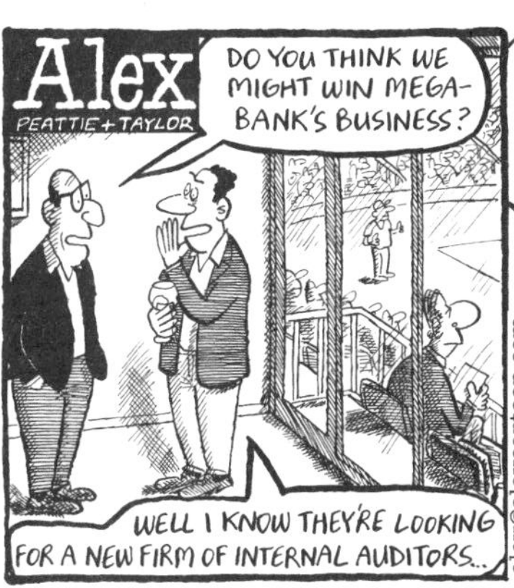
Alex
PEATTIE + TAYLOR
DO YOU THINK WE MIGHT WIN MEGA-BANK'S BUSINESS?
WELL I KNOW THEY'RE LOOKING FOR A NEW FIRM OF INTERNAL AUDITORS...
alex@alexcartoon.com

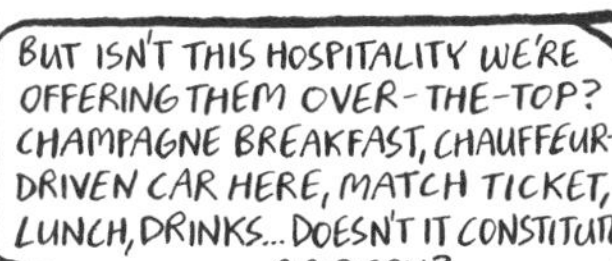
BUT ISN'T THIS HOSPITALITY WE'RE OFFERING THEM OVER-THE-TOP? CHAMPAGNE BREAKFAST, CHAUFFEUR-DRIVEN CAR HERE, MATCH TICKET, LUNCH, DRINKS... DOESN'T IT CONSTITUTE BRIBERY?

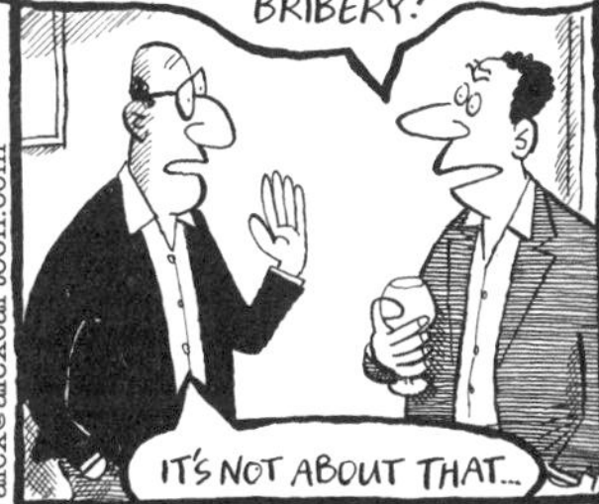
IT'S NOT ABOUT THAT...

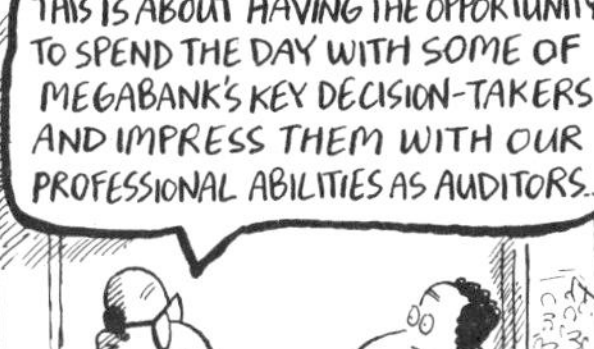
THIS IS ABOUT HAVING THE OPPORTUNITY TO SPEND THE DAY WITH SOME OF MEGABANK'S KEY DECISION-TAKERS AND IMPRESS THEM WITH OUR PROFESSIONAL ABILITIES AS AUDITORS...

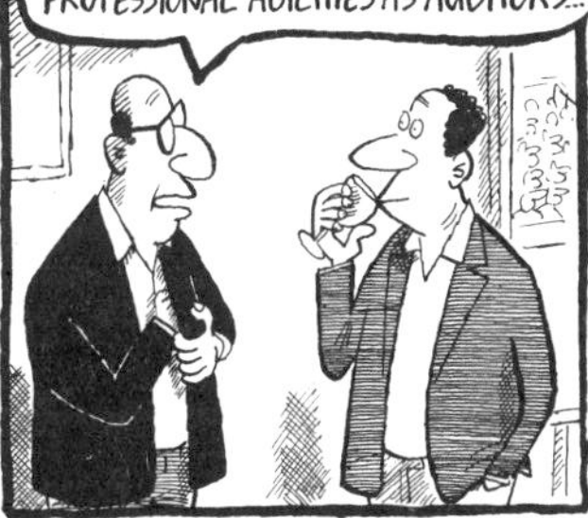

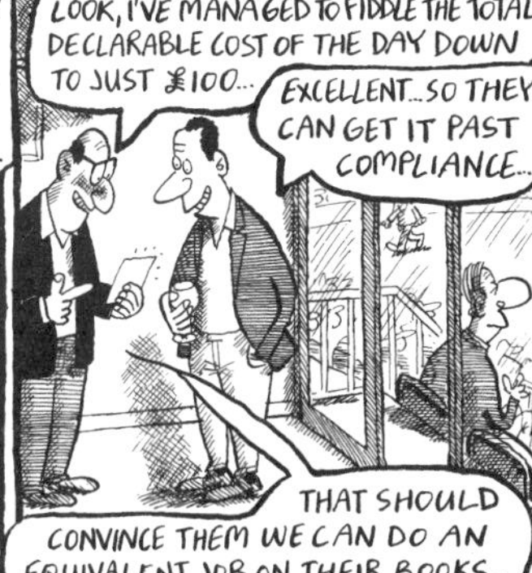
LOOK, I'VE MANAGED TO FIDDLE THE TOTAL DECLARABLE COST OF THE DAY DOWN TO JUST £100...
EXCELLENT... SO THEY CAN GET IT PAST COMPLIANCE...
THAT SHOULD CONVINCE THEM WE CAN DO AN EQUIVALENT JOB ON THEIR BOOKS...

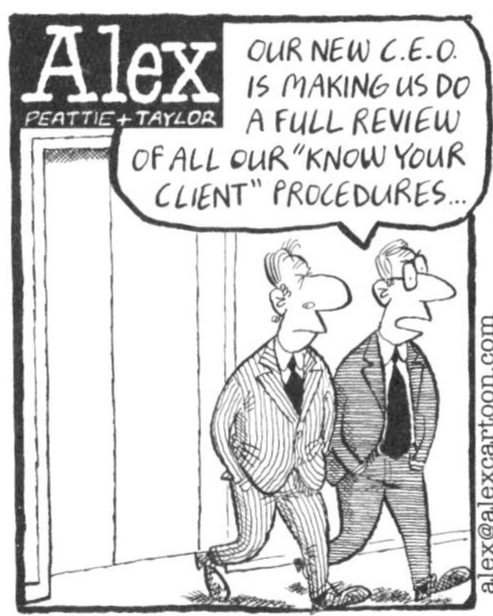
Alex
PEATTIE + TAYLOR
OUR NEW C.E.O. IS MAKING US DO A FULL REVIEW OF ALL OUR "KNOW YOUR CLIENT" PROCEDURES...
alex@alexcartoon.com

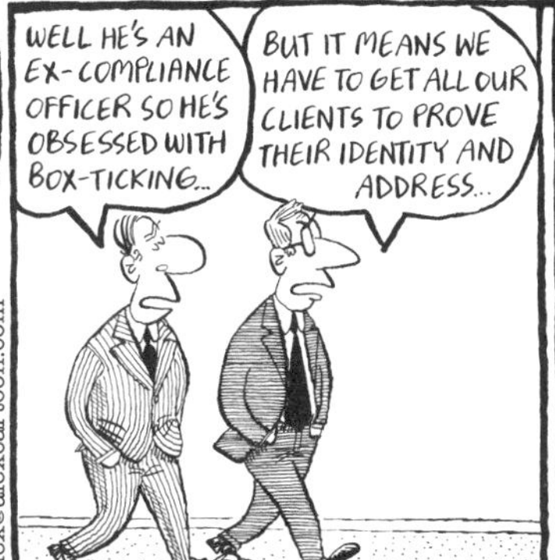
WELL HE'S AN EX-COMPLIANCE OFFICER SO HE'S OBSESSED WITH BOX-TICKING...
BUT IT MEANS WE HAVE TO GET ALL OUR CLIENTS TO PROVE THEIR IDENTITY AND ADDRESS...

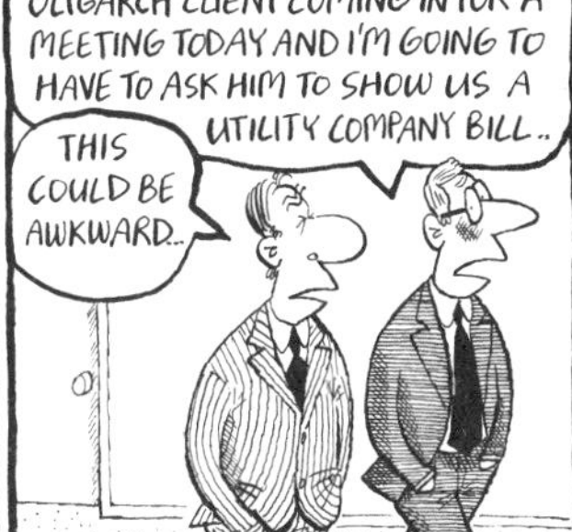
WE'VE GOT OUR BILLIONAIRE RUSSIAN OLIGARCH CLIENT COMING IN FOR A MEETING TODAY AND I'M GOING TO HAVE TO ASK HIM TO SHOW US A UTILITY COMPANY BILL...
THIS COULD BE AWKWARD...

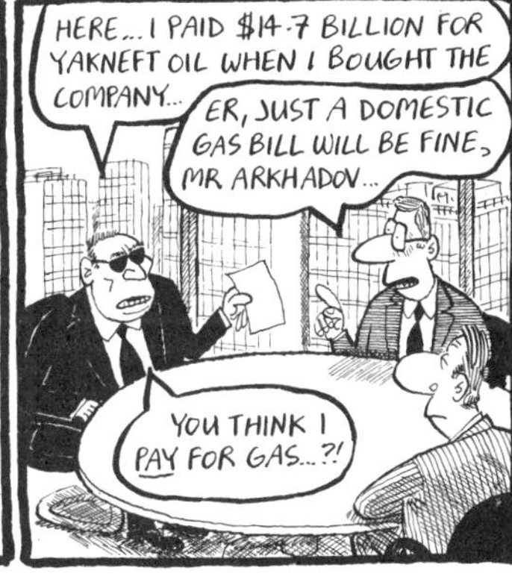
HERE... I PAID $14.7 BILLION FOR YAKNEFT OIL WHEN I BOUGHT THE COMPANY...
ER, JUST A DOMESTIC GAS BILL WILL BE FINE, MR ARKHADOV...
YOU THINK I PAY FOR GAS...?!

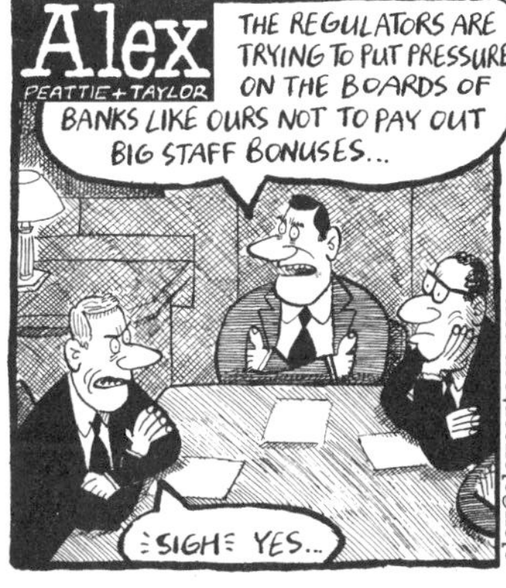
Alex
PEATTIE + TAYLOR
THE REGULATORS ARE TRYING TO PUT PRESSURE ON THE BOARDS OF BANKS LIKE OURS NOT TO PAY OUT BIG STAFF BONUSES...
≡SIGH≡ YES...
alex@alexcartoon.com

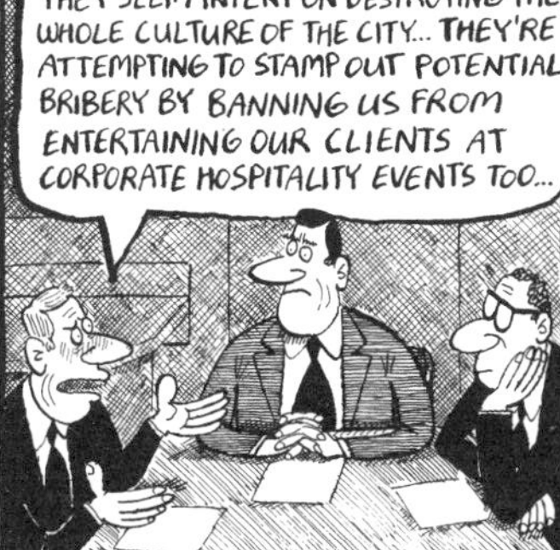
THEY SEEM INTENT ON DESTROYING THE WHOLE CULTURE OF THE CITY... THEY'RE ATTEMPTING TO STAMP OUT POTENTIAL BRIBERY BY BANNING US FROM ENTERTAINING OUR CLIENTS AT CORPORATE HOSPITALITY EVENTS TOO...

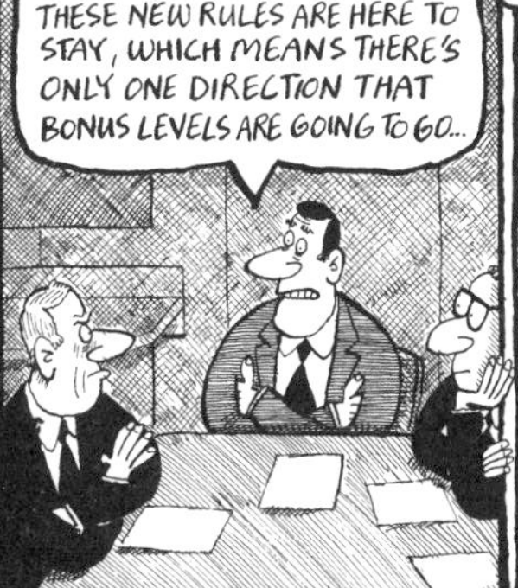
WELL, WE HAVE TO ACCEPT THAT THESE NEW RULES ARE HERE TO STAY, WHICH MEANS THERE'S ONLY ONE DIRECTION THAT BONUS LEVELS ARE GOING TO GO...

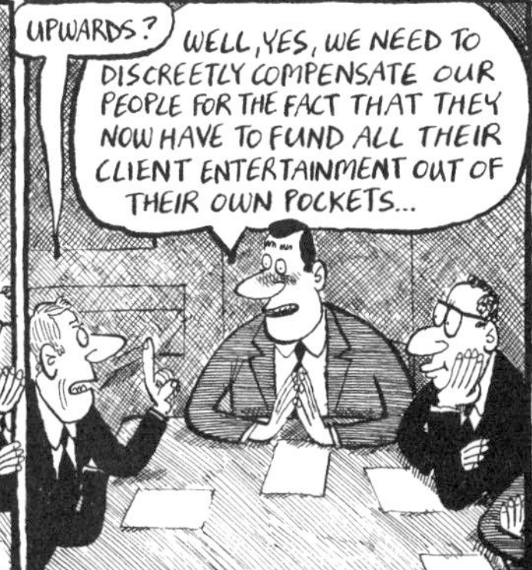
UPWARDS?
WELL, YES, WE NEED TO DISCREETLY COMPENSATE OUR PEOPLE FOR THE FACT THAT THEY NOW HAVE TO FUND ALL THEIR CLIENT ENTERTAINMENT OUT OF THEIR OWN POCKETS...

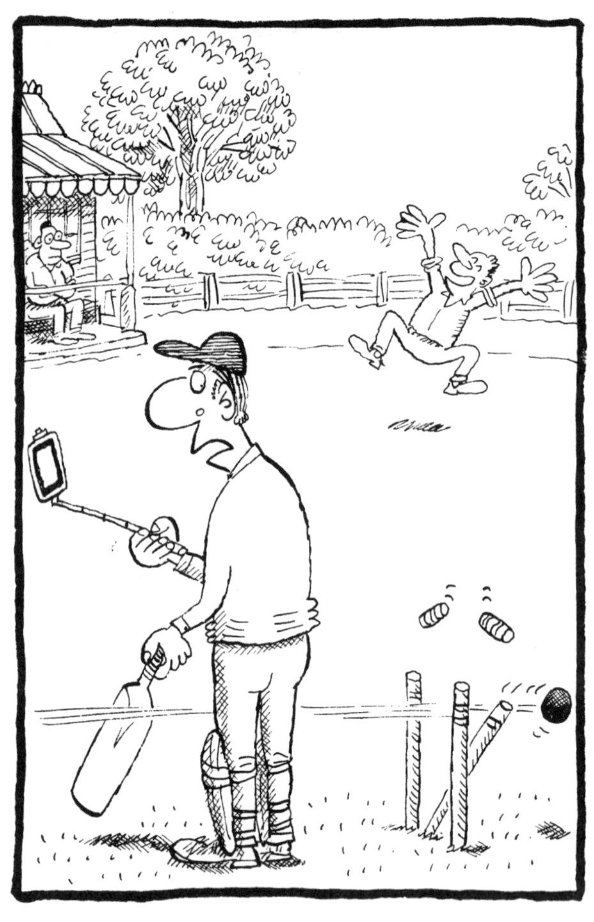

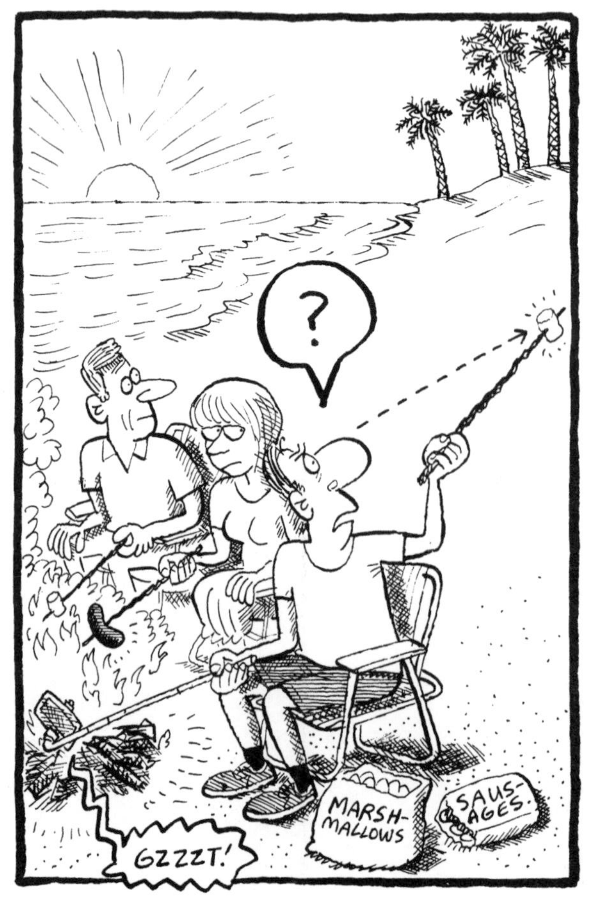
?
MARSH-
MALLOWS
SAUS-
AGES.
GZZZT!

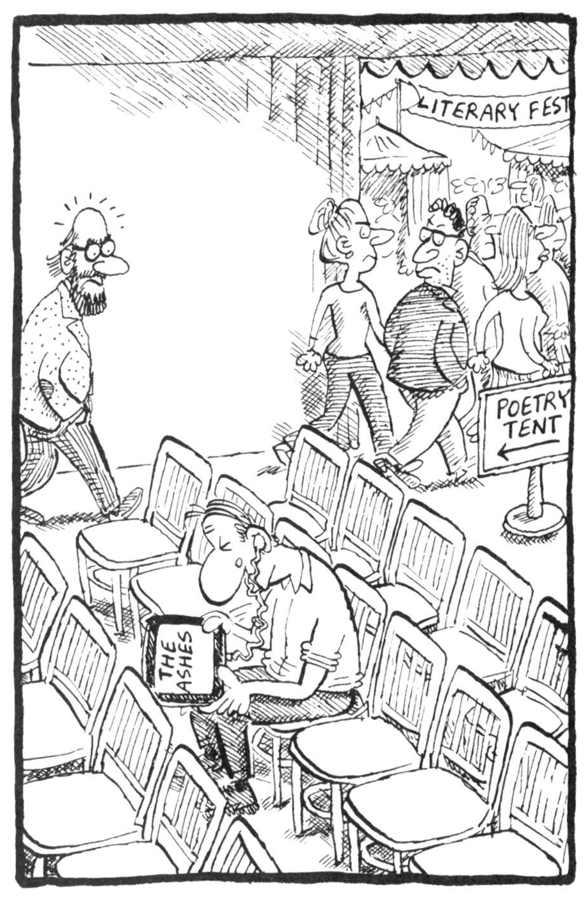
LITERARY FEST
POETRY TENT
THE ASHES

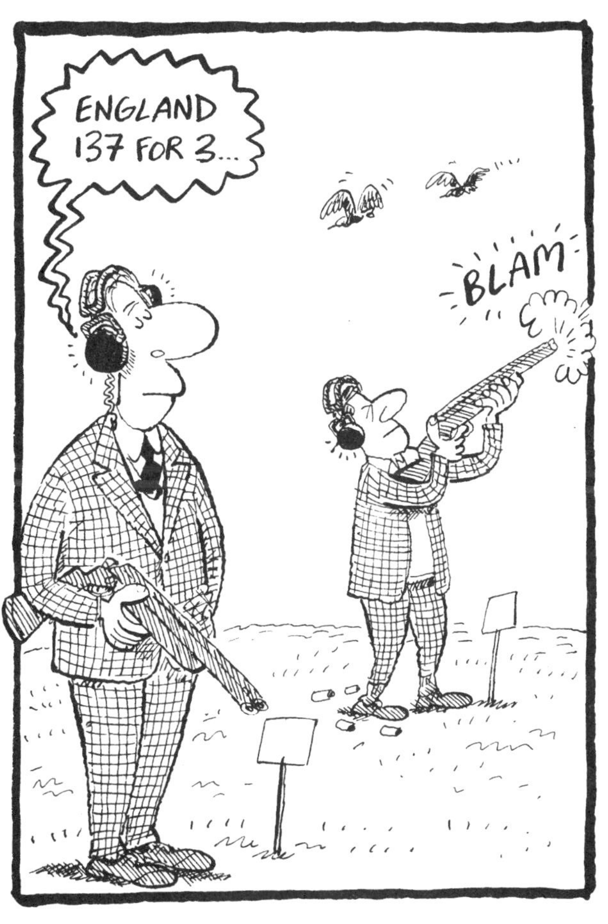
ENGLAND 137 FOR 3...
BLAM

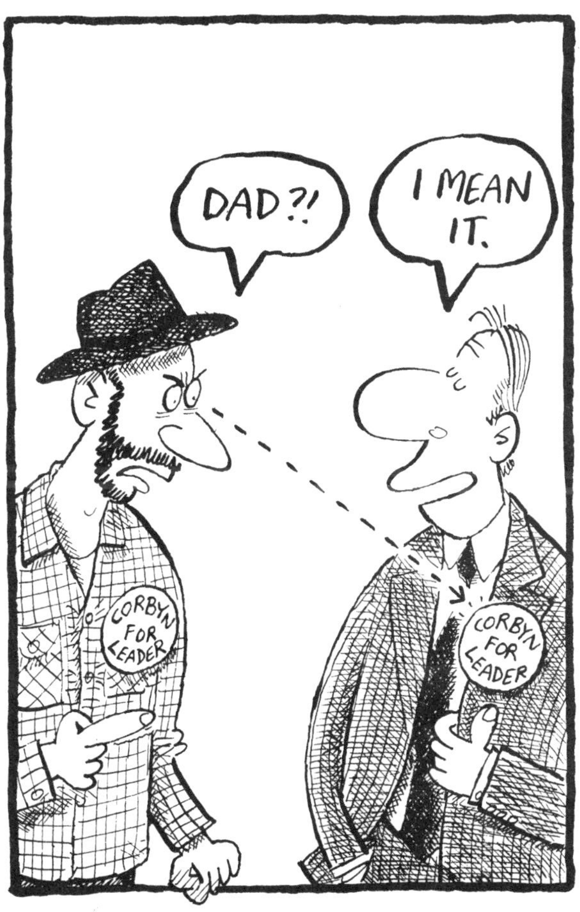
DAD?!
I MEAN IT.
CORBYN FOR LEADER
CORBYN FOR LEADER

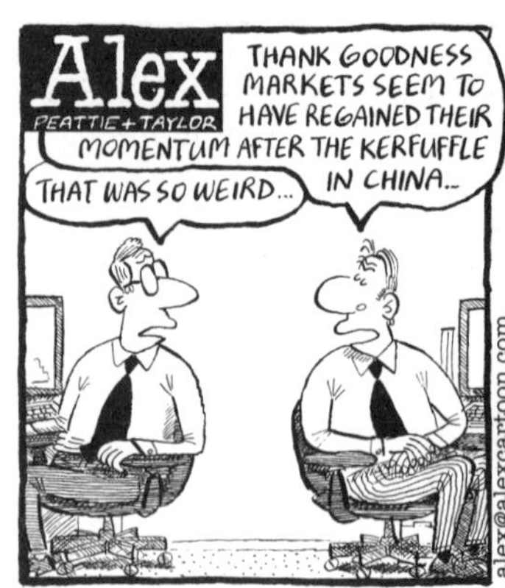
Alex
PEATTIE + TAYLOR
THANK GOODNESS MARKETS SEEM TO HAVE REGAINED THEIR MOMENTUM AFTER THE KERFUFFLE IN CHINA...
THAT WAS SO WEIRD...

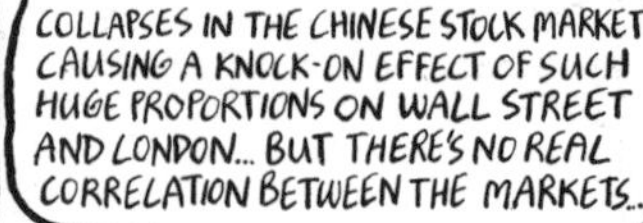
COLLAPSES IN THE CHINESE STOCK MARKET CAUSING A KNOCK-ON EFFECT OF SUCH HUGE PROPORTIONS ON WALL STREET AND LONDON... BUT THERE'S NO REAL CORRELATION BETWEEN THE MARKETS...

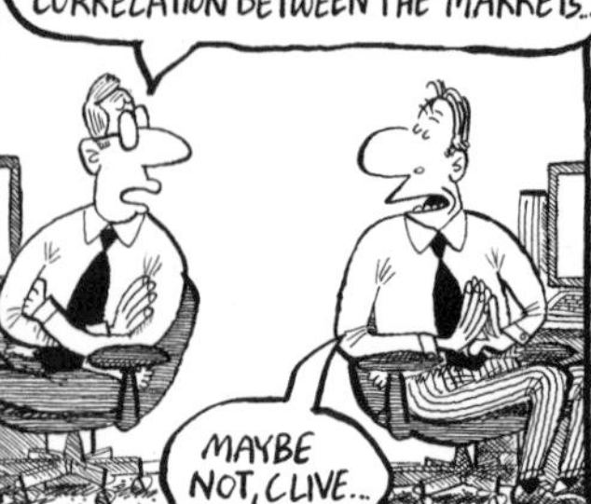
MAYBE NOT, CLIVE...

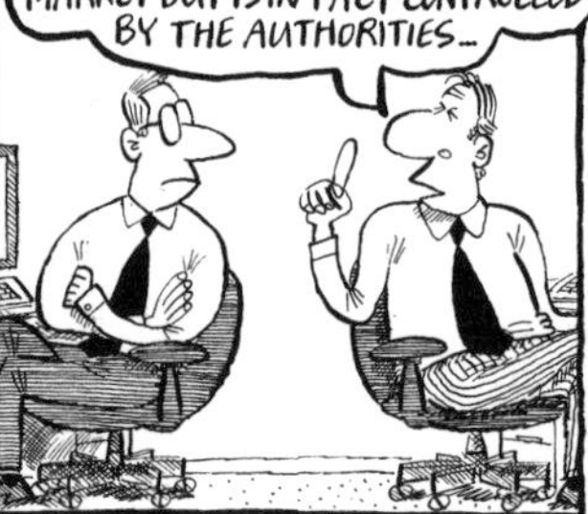
BUT THIS IS WHAT HAPPENS WHEN YOU HAVE A SUDDEN COLLAPSE IN CONFIDENCE IN AN ECONOMY WHICH PAYS LIP SERVICE TO THE NOTION OF THE FREE MARKET BUT IS IN FACT CONTROLLED BY THE AUTHORITIES...

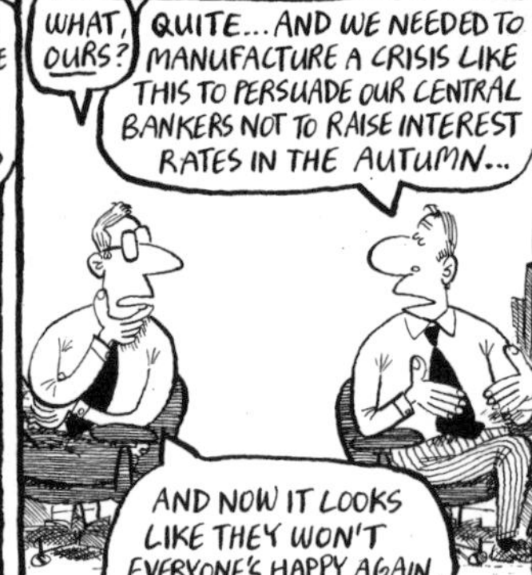
WHAT, OURS?
QUITE... AND WE NEEDED TO MANUFACTURE A CRISIS LIKE THIS TO PERSUADE OUR CENTRAL BANKERS NOT TO RAISE INTEREST RATES IN THE AUTUMN...
AND NOW IT LOOKS LIKE THEY WON'T
EVERYONE'S HAPPY AGAIN...

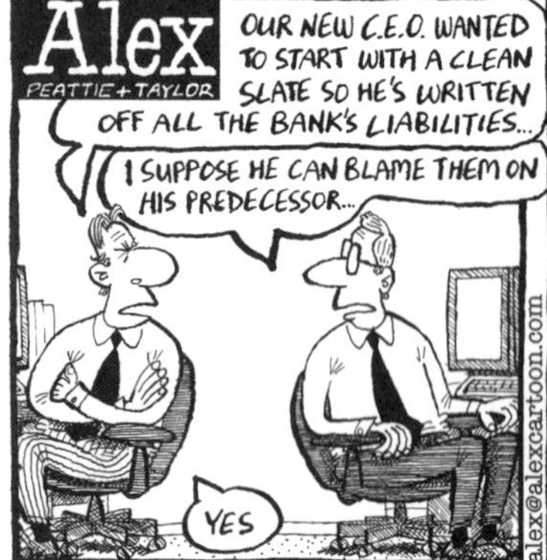
Alex
PEATTIE + TAYLOR
OUR NEW C.E.O. WANTED TO START WITH A CLEAN SLATE SO HE'S WRITTEN OFF ALL THE BANK'S LIABILITIES...
I SUPPOSE HE CAN BLAME THEM ON HIS PREDECESSOR...
YES

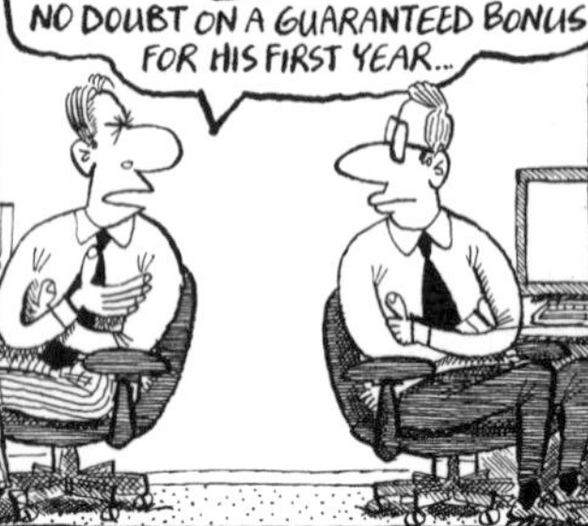
BUT IT MEANS THE BANK WILL SHOW A BIG LOSS THIS YEAR, WHICH WILL HAVE TO BE ABSORBED BY OUR BONUSES BEING CUT... BUT HE'S OKAY BECAUSE HE'S NO DOUBT ON A GUARANTEED BONUS FOR HIS FIRST YEAR...

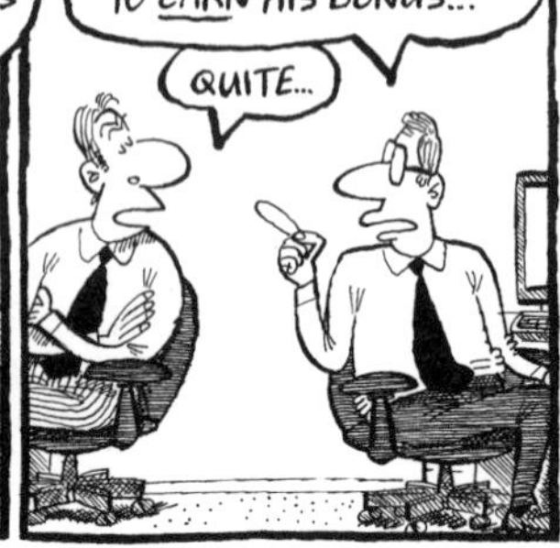
IT'S ANNOYING, ALEX, I AGREE, BUT REMEMBER: NEXT YEAR HE'S ACTUALLY GOING TO HAVE TO EARN HIS BONUS...
QUITE...

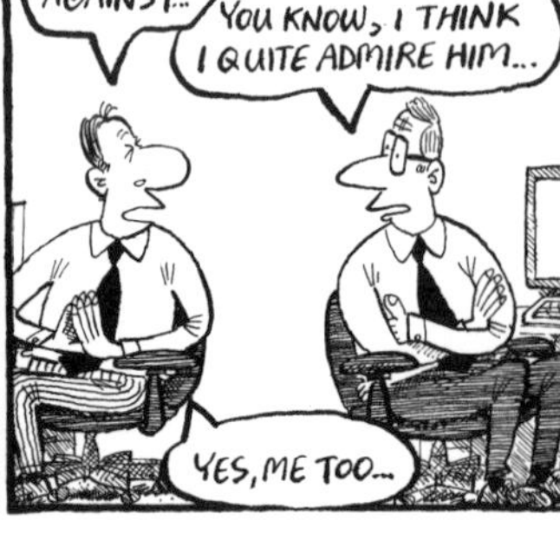
AND HE'S SET HIMSELF A CONVENIENTLY LOW BENCHMARK FOR HIS PERFORMANCE TO BE MEASURED AGAINST...
YOU KNOW, I THINK I QUITE ADMIRE HIM...
YES, ME TOO...

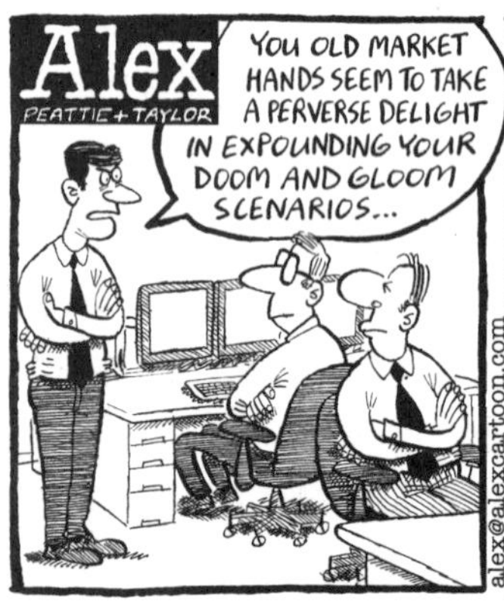
Alex
PEATTIE + TAYLOR
YOU OLD MARKET HANDS SEEM TO TAKE A PERVERSE DELIGHT IN EXPOUNDING YOUR DOOM AND GLOOM SCENARIOS...

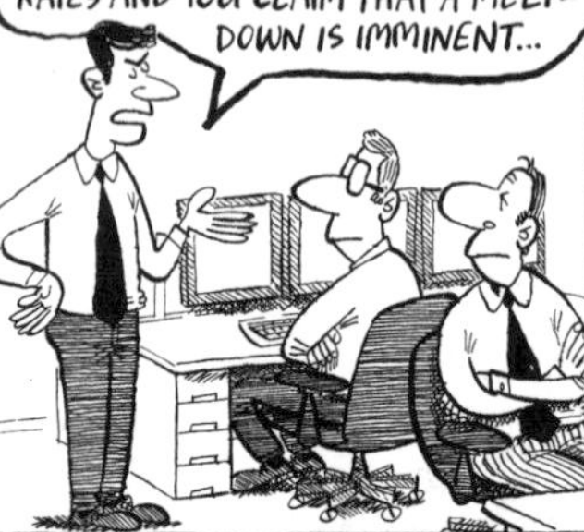
YOU BANG ON ABOUT HOW CENTRAL BANKS HAVE DISTORTED MARKETS WITH MONEY PRINTING AND ARTIFICIALLY LOW INTEREST RATES AND YOU CLAIM THAT A MELT-DOWN IS IMMINENT...

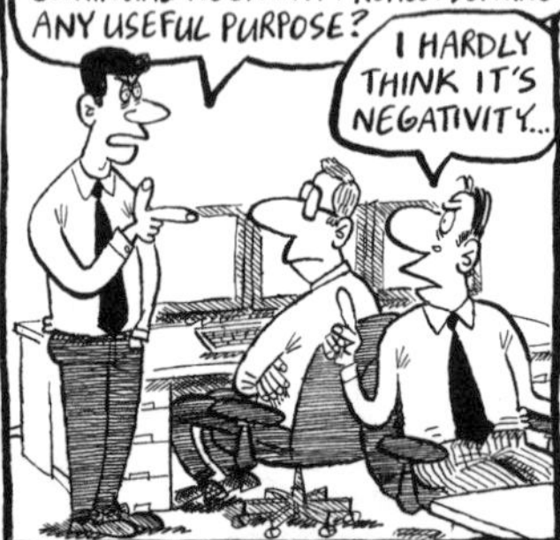
WELL, WITH ALL DUE RESPECT YOU'VE BEEN WRONG FOR YEARS NOW... IS YOUR CONTINUAL NEGATIVITY REALLY SERVING ANY USEFUL PURPOSE?
I HARDLY THINK IT'S NEGATIVITY...

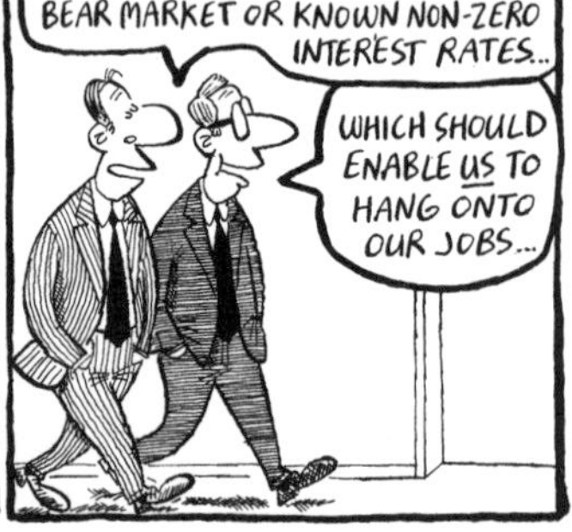
THE LONGER THINGS GO ON LIKE THIS THE FEWER PEOPLE THERE WILL BE IN THE BANK WHO'VE EVER SEEN A BEAR MARKET OR KNOWN NON-ZERO INTEREST RATES...
WHICH SHOULD ENABLE US TO HANG ONTO OUR JOBS...

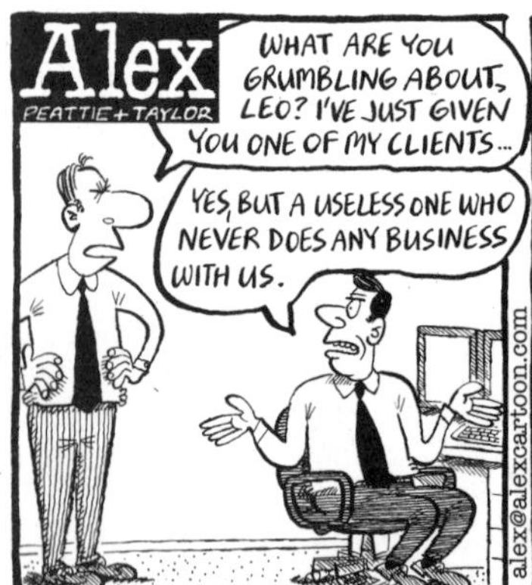
Alex
PEATTIE + TAYLOR
WHAT ARE YOU GRUMBLING ABOUT, LEO? I'VE JUST GIVEN YOU ONE OF MY CLIENTS...
YES, BUT A USELESS ONE WHO NEVER DOES ANY BUSINESS WITH US.

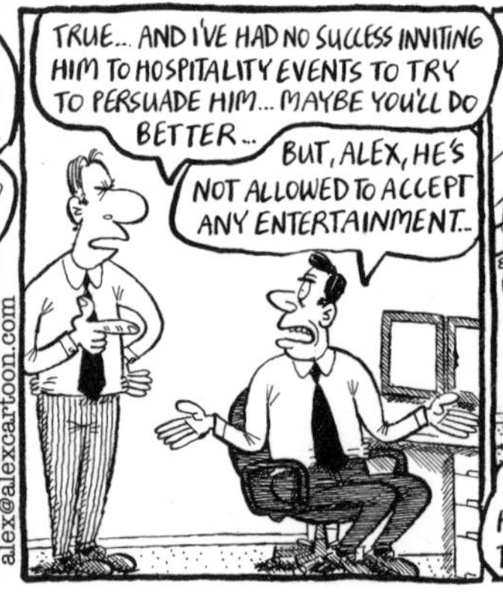
TRUE... AND I'VE HAD NO SUCCESS INVITING HIM TO HOSPITALITY EVENTS TO TRY TO PERSUADE HIM... MAYBE YOU'LL DO BETTER...
BUT, ALEX, HE'S NOT ALLOWED TO ACCEPT ANY ENTERTAINMENT...

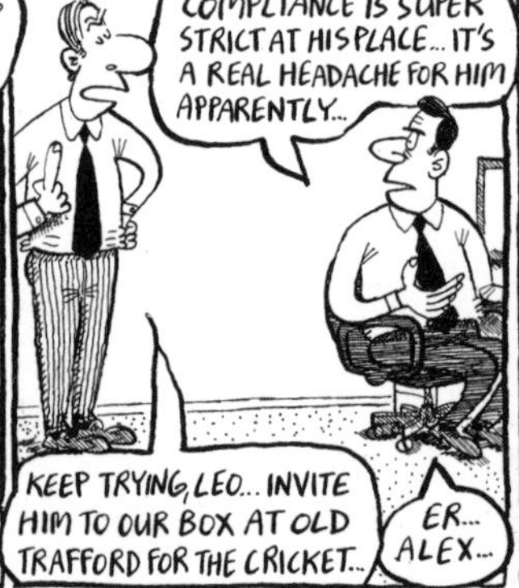
COMPLIANCE IS SUPER STRICT AT HIS PLACE... IT'S A REAL HEADACHE FOR HIM APPARENTLY...
KEEP TRYING, LEO... INVITE HIM TO OUR BOX AT OLD TRAFFORD FOR THE CRICKET...
ER... ALEX...

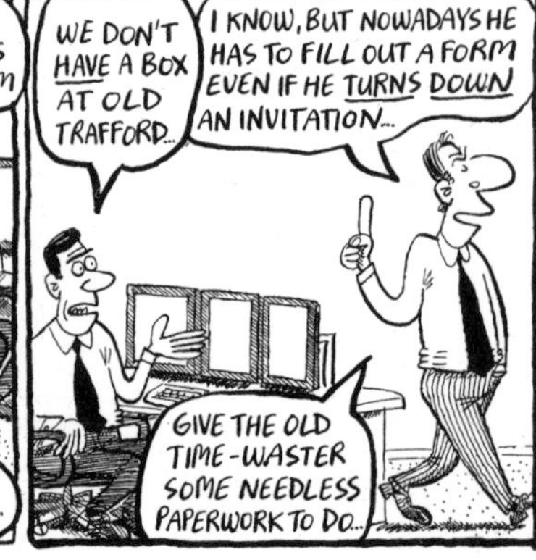
WE DON'T HAVE A BOX AT OLD TRAFFORD...
I KNOW, BUT NOWADAYS HE HAS TO FILL OUT A FORM EVEN IF HE TURNS DOWN AN INVITATION...
GIVE THE OLD TIME-WASTER SOME NEEDLESS PAPERWORK TO DO...

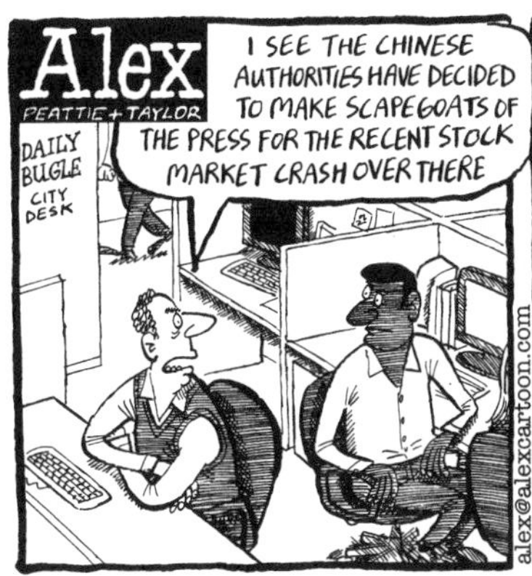
Alex
PEATTIE + TAYLOR
DAILY BUGLE
CITY DESK
I SEE THE CHINESE AUTHORITIES HAVE DECIDED TO MAKE SCAPEGOATS OF THE PRESS FOR THE RECENT STOCK MARKET CRASH OVER THERE

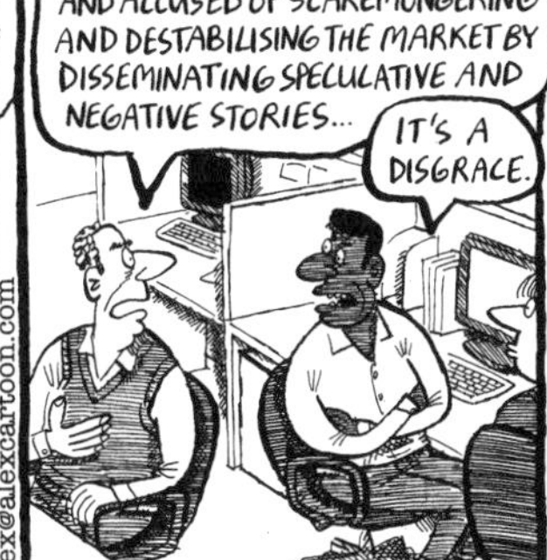
JOURNALISTS HAVE BEEN ARRESTED AND ACCUSED OF SCAREMONGERING AND DESTABILISING THE MARKET BY DISSEMINATING SPECULATIVE AND NEGATIVE STORIES...
IT'S A DISGRACE.

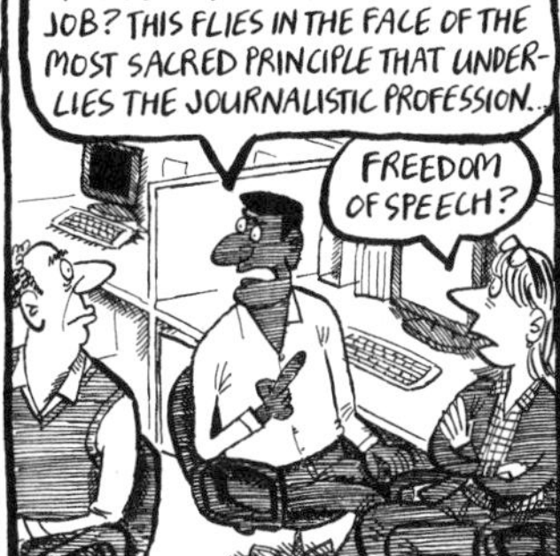
REPORTERS FACING CRIMINAL CHARGES FOR SIMPLY DOING THEIR JOB? THIS FLIES IN THE FACE OF THE MOST SACRED PRINCIPLE THAT UNDERLIES THE JOURNALISTIC PROFESSION...
FREEDOM OF SPEECH?

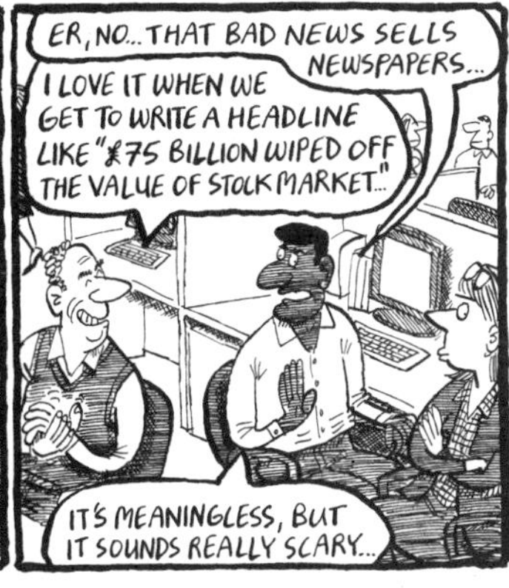
ER, NO... THAT BAD NEWS SELLS NEWSPAPERS...
I LOVE IT WHEN WE GET TO WRITE A HEADLINE LIKE "£75 BILLION WIPED OFF THE VALUE OF STOCK MARKET..."
IT'S MEANINGLESS, BUT IT SOUNDS REALLY SCARY...

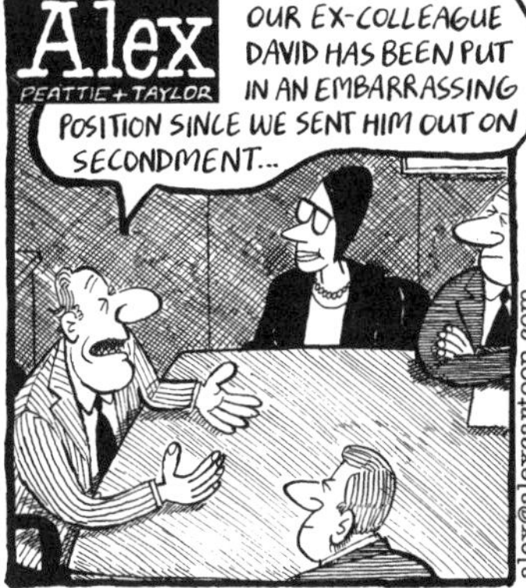
Alex
PEATTIE + TAYLOR
OUR EX-COLLEAGUE DAVID HAS BEEN PUT IN AN EMBARRASSING POSITION SINCE WE SENT HIM OUT ON SECONDMENT...

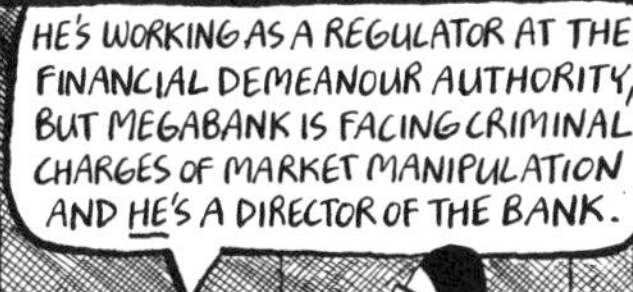
HE'S WORKING AS A REGULATOR AT THE FINANCIAL DEMEANOUR AUTHORITY, BUT MEGABANK IS FACING CRIMINAL CHARGES OF MARKET MANIPULATION AND HE'S A DIRECTOR OF THE BANK.

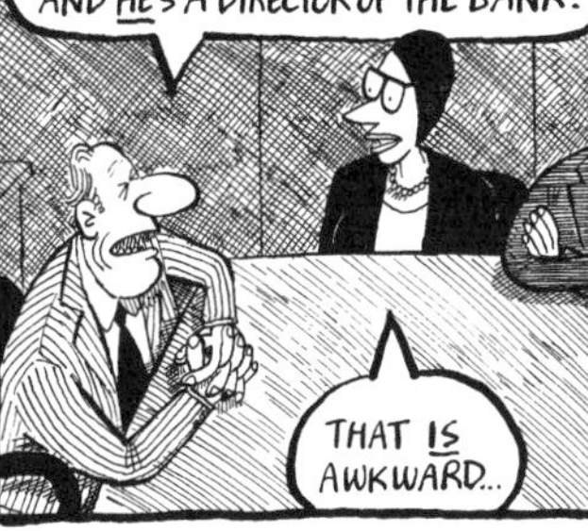
THAT IS AWKWARD...

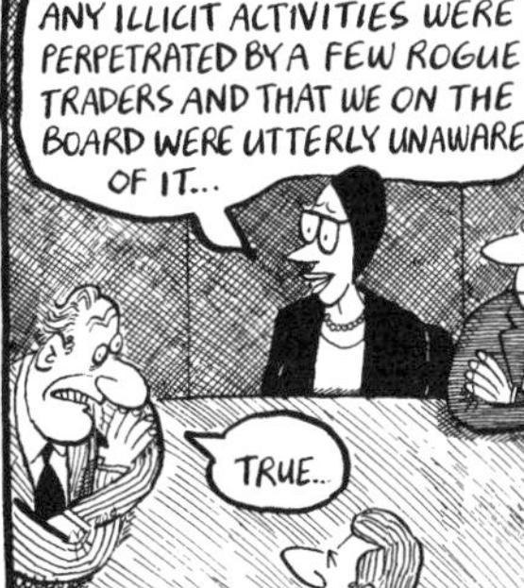
BUT OUR OFFICIAL LINE IS THAT ANY ILLICIT ACTIVITIES WERE PERPETRATED BY A FEW ROGUE TRADERS AND THAT WE ON THE BOARD WERE UTTERLY UNAWARE OF IT...
TRUE...

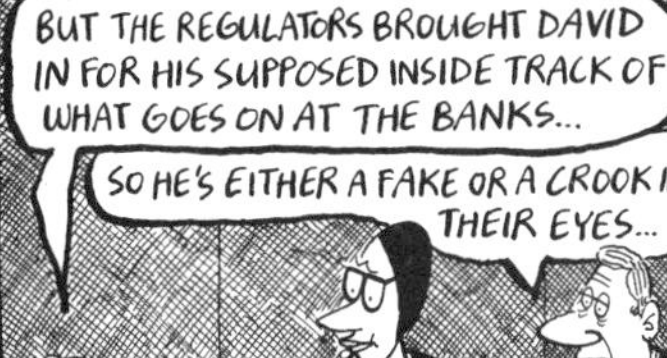
BUT THE REGULATORS BROUGHT DAVID IN FOR HIS SUPPOSED INSIDE TRACK OF WHAT GOES ON AT THE BANKS...
SO HE'S EITHER A FAKE OR A CROOK IN THEIR EYES...

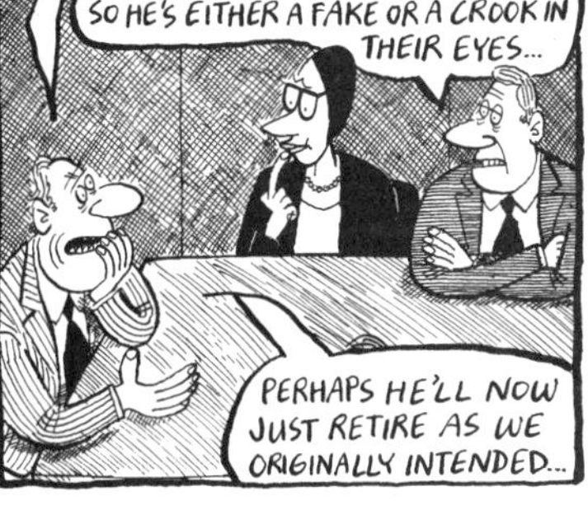
PERHAPS HE'LL NOW JUST RETIRE AS WE ORIGINALLY INTENDED...

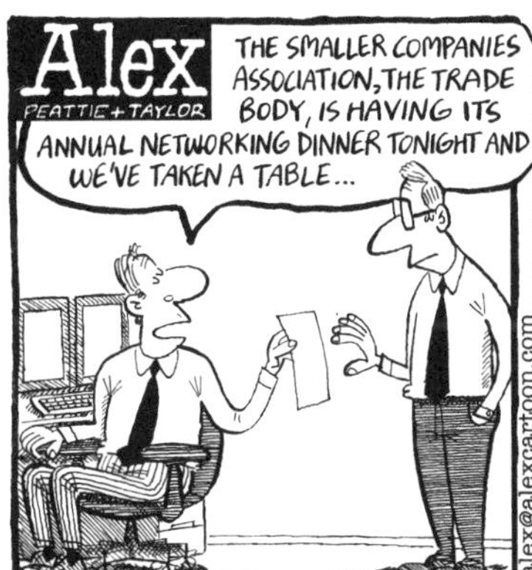
Alex
PEATTIE + TAYLOR
THE SMALLER COMPANIES ASSOCIATION, THE TRADE BODY, IS HAVING ITS ANNUAL NETWORKING DINNER TONIGHT AND WE'VE TAKEN A TABLE...

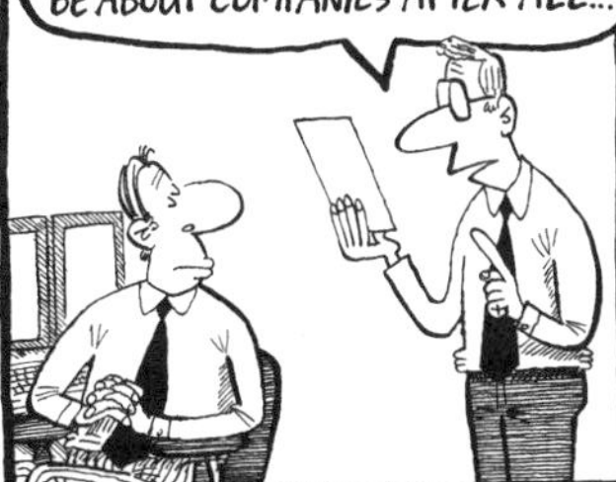
BUT, ALEX, YOU'VE ONLY INVITED PEOPLE FROM THE BANK... ISN'T THE IDEA THAT WE'RE SUPPOSED TO BRING SOME OF OUR CLIENTS ALONG? IT'S AN EVENING THAT'S SUPPOSED TO BE ABOUT COMPANIES AFTER ALL...

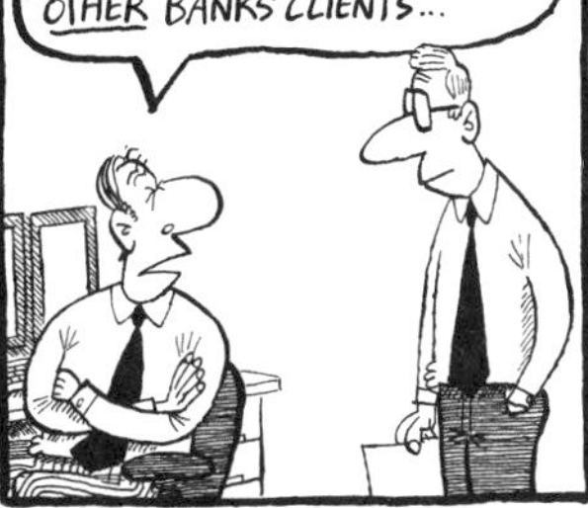
DON'T BE SILLY, CLIVE. IF WE TAKE OUR CLIENTS THEN OUR COMPETITORS MIGHT POACH THEM... BESIDES WE NEED A FULL COMPLEMENT OF OUR PEOPLE TO SCHMOOZE ALL THE OTHER BANKS' CLIENTS...

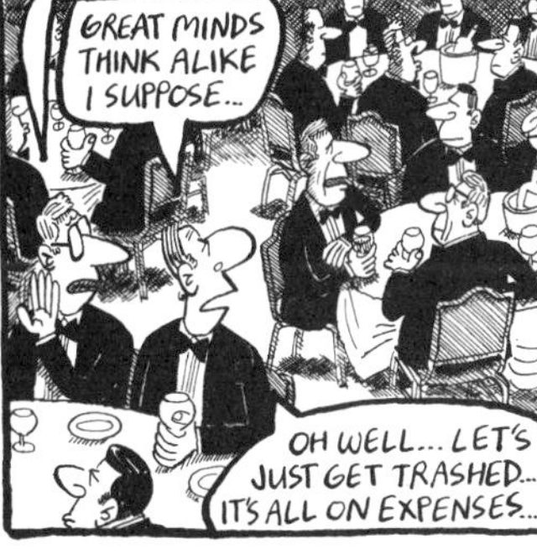
ER, ALEX, IT'S ALL BANKERS AND BROKERS. NO ONE HAS BROUGHT ANY CLIENTS...
GREAT MINDS THINK ALIKE I SUPPOSE...
OH WELL... LET'S JUST GET TRASHED... IT'S ALL ON EXPENSES...

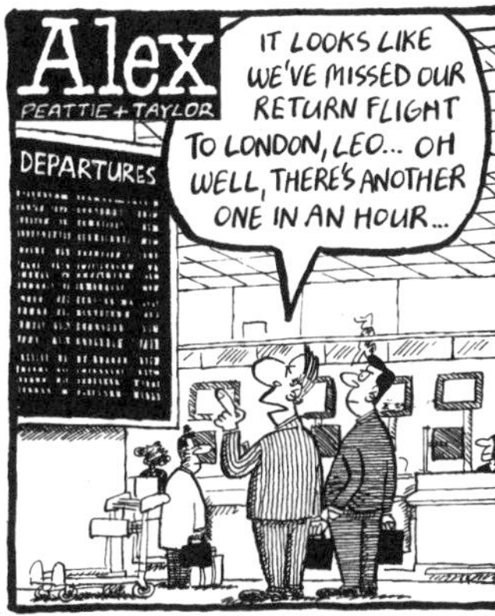
Alex
PEATTIE + TAYLOR
DEPARTURES
IT LOOKS LIKE WE'VE MISSED OUR RETURN FLIGHT TO LONDON, LEO... OH WELL, THERE'S ANOTHER ONE IN AN HOUR...

I'LL CALL THE OFFICE AND EXPLAIN THAT OUR CLIENT MEETING OVERRAN...
BUT, ALEX, THE MEETING FINISHED ON TIME. YOU JUST STARTED MAKING SMALL TALK WITH THE CLIENT AFTERWARDS...

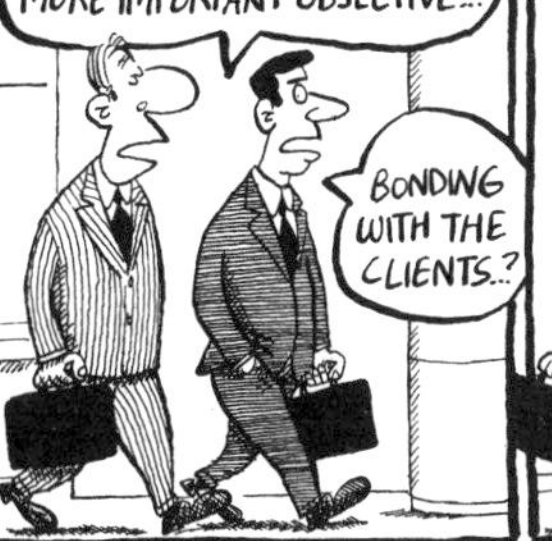
THERE WAS A GOOD REASON FOR THAT, LEO. AND SOMETIMES ONE NEEDS TO MISS THE OCCASIONAL FLIGHT IN ORDER TO ATTAIN A MORE IMPORTANT OBJECTIVE...
BONDING WITH THE CLIENTS..?

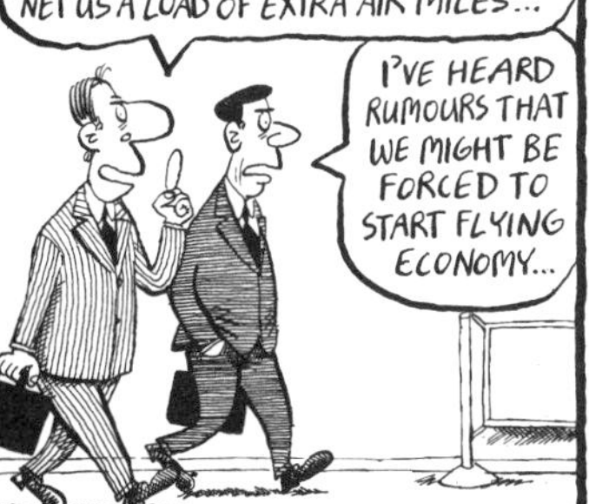
NO, ENSURING THAT THE BANK CONTINUES TO BUY US BUSINESS CLASS TICKETS WHICH ARE FULLY FLEXIBLE, AND, MORE CRUCIALLY, NET US A LOAD OF EXTRA AIR MILES...
I'VE HEARD RUMOURS THAT WE MIGHT BE FORCED TO START FLYING ECONOMY...

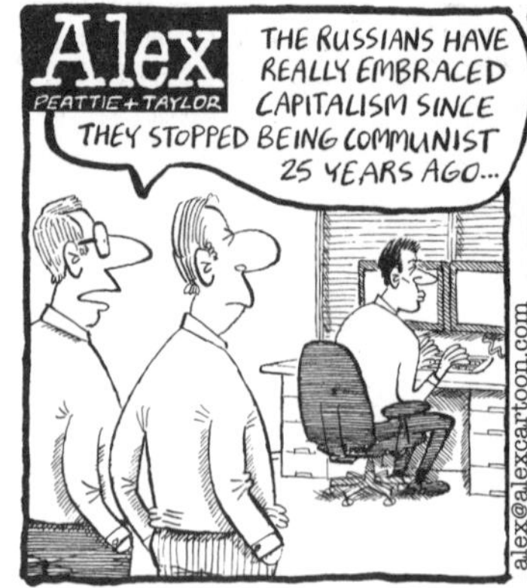
Alex
PEATTIE + TAYLOR
THE RUSSIANS HAVE REALLY EMBRACED CAPITALISM SINCE THEY STOPPED BEING COMMUNIST 25 YEARS AGO...
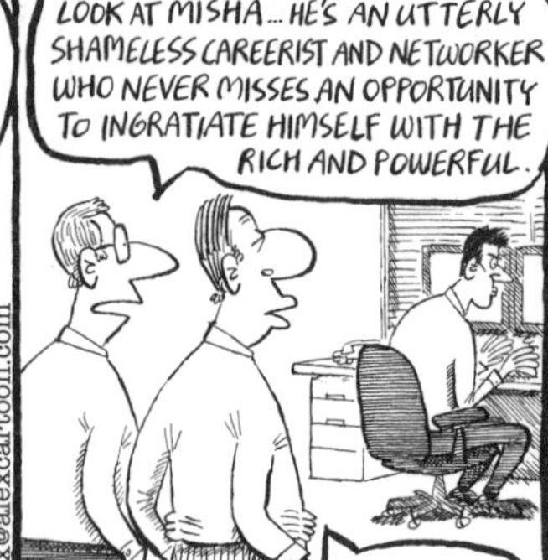
LOOK AT MISHA... HE'S AN UTTERLY SHAMELESS CAREERIST AND NETWORKER WHO NEVER MISSES AN OPPORTUNITY TO INGRATIATE HIMSELF WITH THE RICH AND POWERFUL..
TRUE, CLIVE...
alex@alexcartoon.com
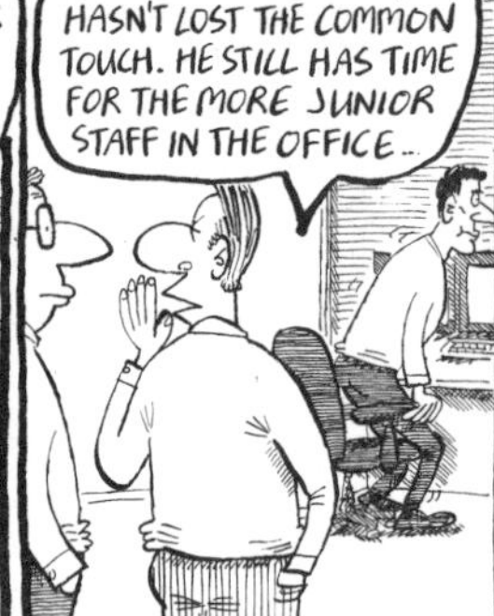
BUT TO BE FAIR ON HIM, HE HASN'T LOST THE COMMON TOUCH. HE STILL HAS TIME FOR THE MORE JUNIOR STAFF IN THE OFFICE..
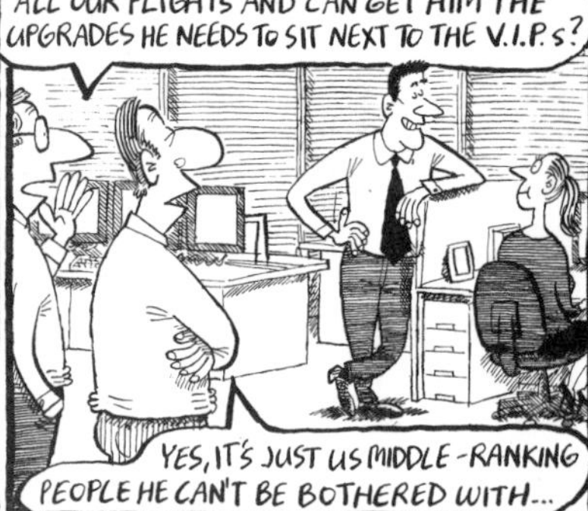
WHAT, LIKE THE DESK ASSISTANT WHO BOOKS ALL OUR FLIGHTS AND CAN GET HIM THE UPGRADES HE NEEDS TO SIT NEXT TO THE V.I.P.s?
YES, IT'S JUST US MIDDLE-RANKING PEOPLE HE CAN'T BE BOTHERED WITH...
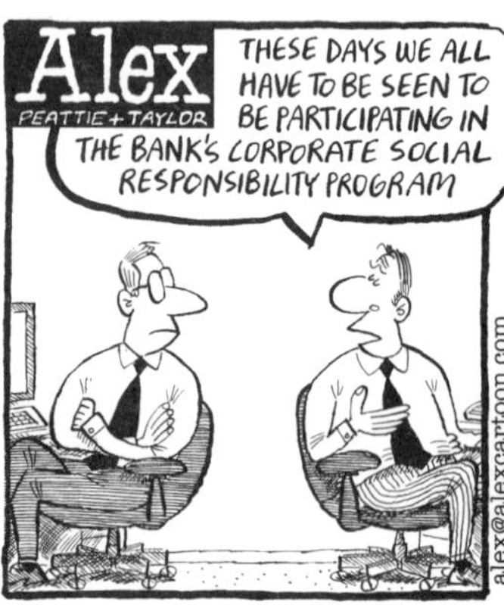
Alex
PEATTIE + TAYLOR
THESE DAYS WE ALL HAVE TO BE SEEN TO BE PARTICIPATING IN THE BANK'S CORPORATE SOCIAL RESPONSIBILITY PROGRAM
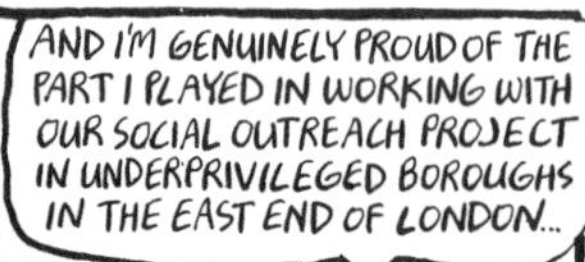
AND I'M GENUINELY PROUD OF THE PART I PLAYED IN WORKING WITH OUR SOCIAL OUTREACH PROJECT IN UNDERPRIVILEGED BOROUGHS IN THE EAST END OF LONDON...
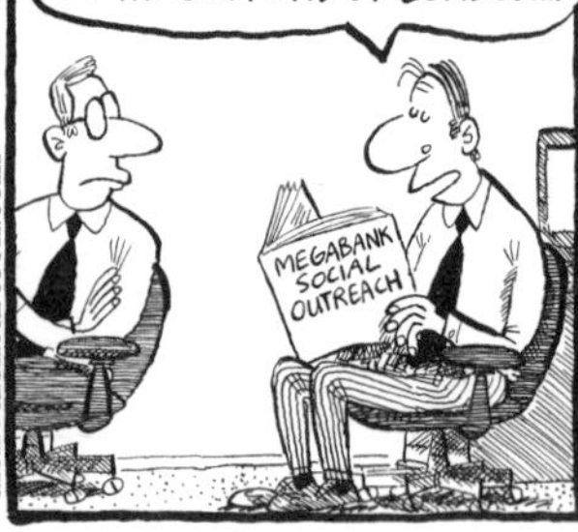
MEGABANK SOCIAL OUTREACH
alex@alexcartoon.com
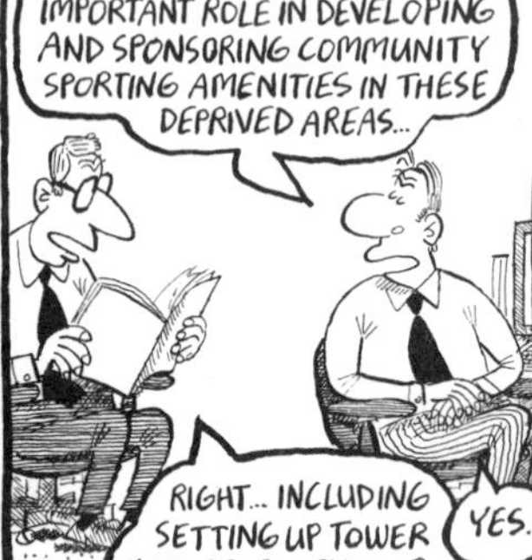
THE BANK HAS FULFILLED AN IMPORTANT ROLE IN DEVELOPING AND SPONSORING COMMUNITY SPORTING AMENITIES IN THESE DEPRIVED AREAS...
RIGHT... INCLUDING SETTING UP TOWER HAMLETS RUGBY CLUB..
YES...
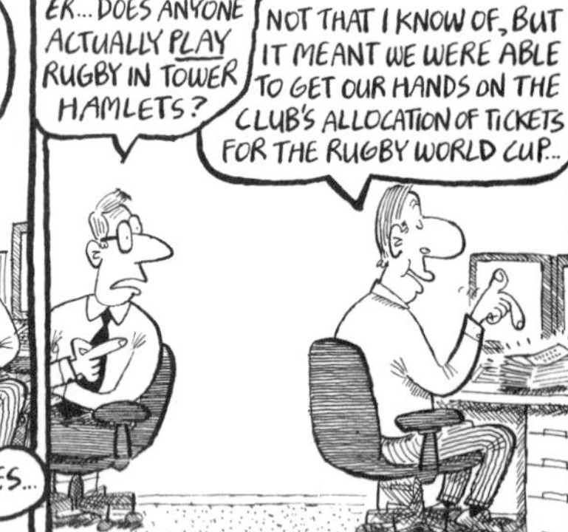
ER... DOES ANYONE ACTUALLY PLAY RUGBY IN TOWER HAMLETS?
NOT THAT I KNOW OF, BUT IT MEANT WE WERE ABLE TO GET OUR HANDS ON THE CLUB'S ALLOCATION OF TICKETS FOR THE RUGBY WORLD CUP...
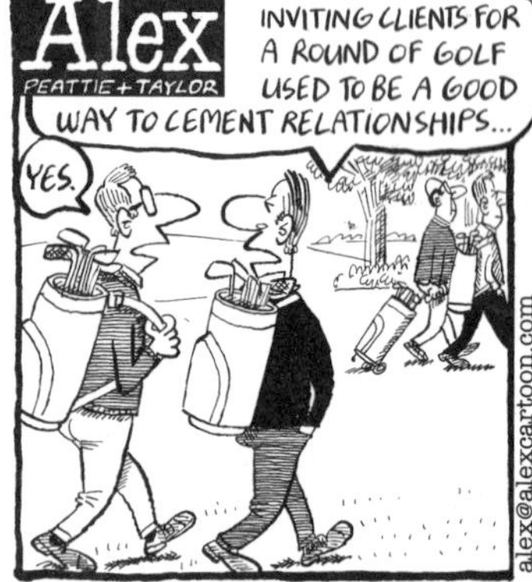
Alex
PEATTIE + TAYLOR
INVITING CLIENTS FOR A ROUND OF GOLF USED TO BE A GOOD WAY TO CEMENT RELATIONSHIPS...
YES.
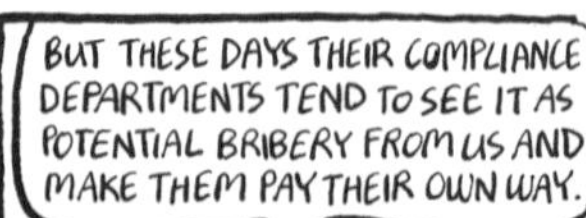
BUT THESE DAYS THEIR COMPLIANCE DEPARTMENTS TEND TO SEE IT AS POTENTIAL BRIBERY FROM US AND MAKE THEM PAY THEIR OWN WAY.
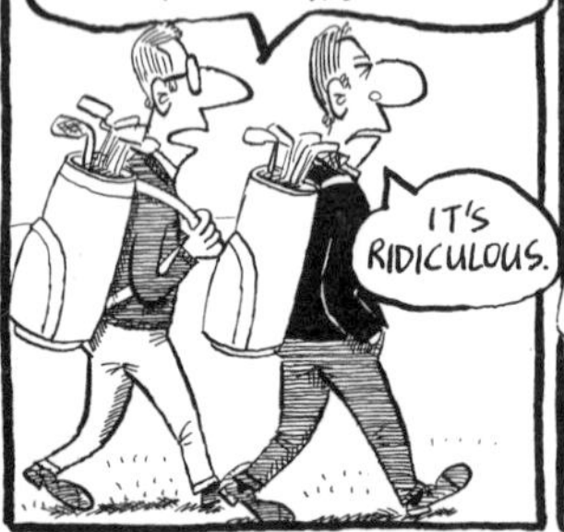
IT'S RIDICULOUS.
alex@alexcartoon.com
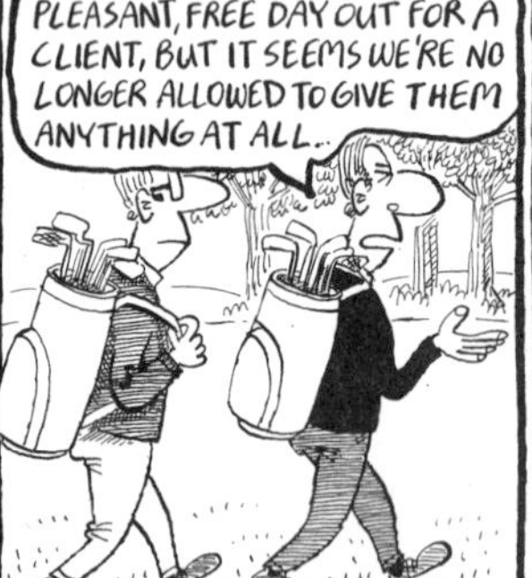
A GAME OF GOLF SHOULD BE A PLEASANT, FREE DAY OUT FOR A CLIENT, BUT IT SEEMS WE'RE NO LONGER ALLOWED TO GIVE THEM ANYTHING AT ALL..
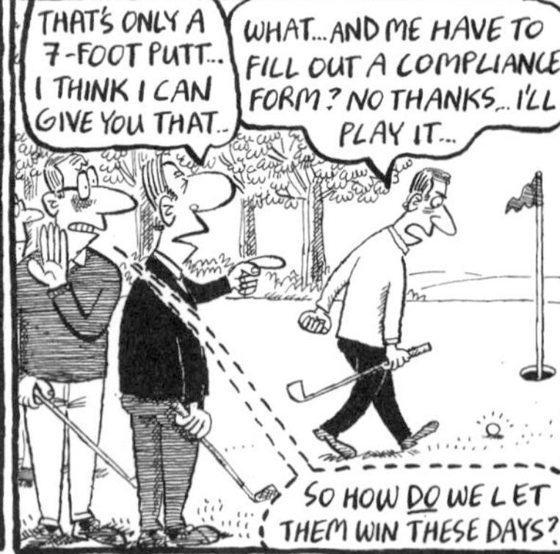
THAT'S ONLY A 7-FOOT PUTT.. I THINK I CAN GIVE YOU THAT..
WHAT... AND ME HAVE TO FILL OUT A COMPLIANCE FORM? NO THANKS... I'LL PLAY IT...
SO HOW DO WE LET THEM WIN THESE DAYS?
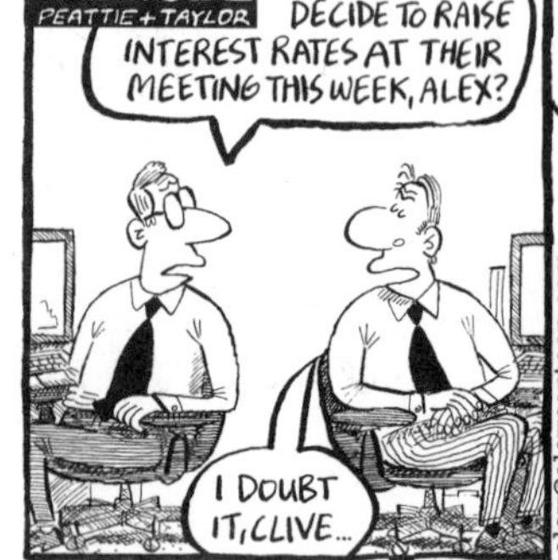
Alex
PEATTIE + TAYLOR
DO YOU THINK THE FED WILL DECIDE TO RAISE INTEREST RATES AT THEIR MEETING THIS WEEK, ALEX?
I DOUBT IT, CLIVE...
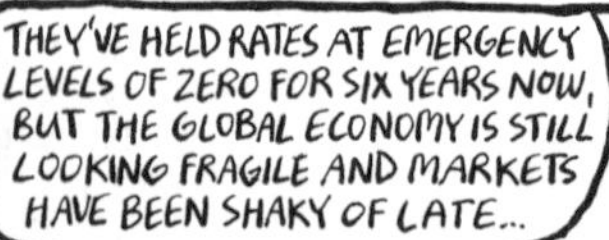
THEY'VE HELD RATES AT EMERGENCY LEVELS OF ZERO FOR SIX YEARS NOW, BUT THE GLOBAL ECONOMY IS STILL LOOKING FRAGILE AND MARKETS HAVE BEEN SHAKY OF LATE...
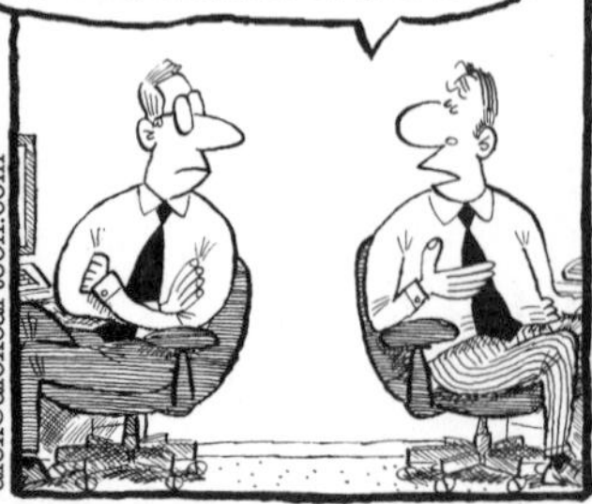
alex@alexcartoon.com
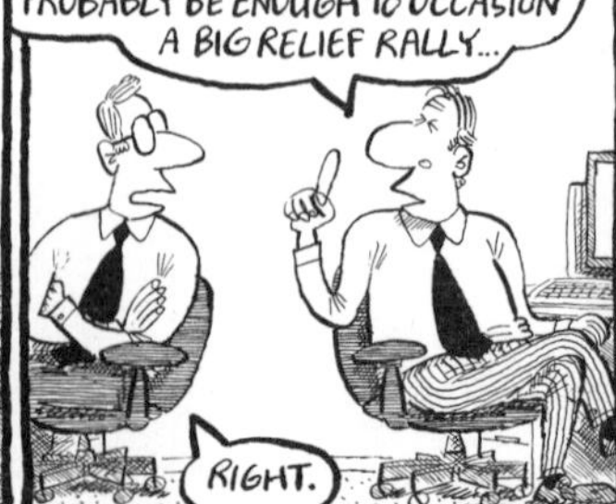
ANY MOVE TOWARDS A TIGHTENING OF MONETARY POLICY WOULD RISK CAUSING A PANICKY SELL-OFF WHEREAS KEEPING RATES ON HOLD WOULD PROBABLY BE ENOUGH TO OCCASION A BIG RELIEF RALLY...
RIGHT.
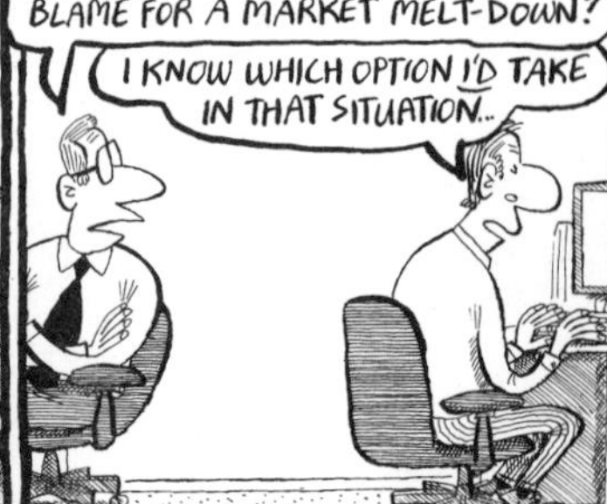
SO THE AUTHORITIES COULD JUST KEEP ON DOING NOTHING AND BE HEROES... OR DO SOMETHING AND POTENTIALLY GET THE BLAME FOR A MARKET MELT-DOWN?
I KNOW WHICH OPTION I'D TAKE IN THAT SITUATION..

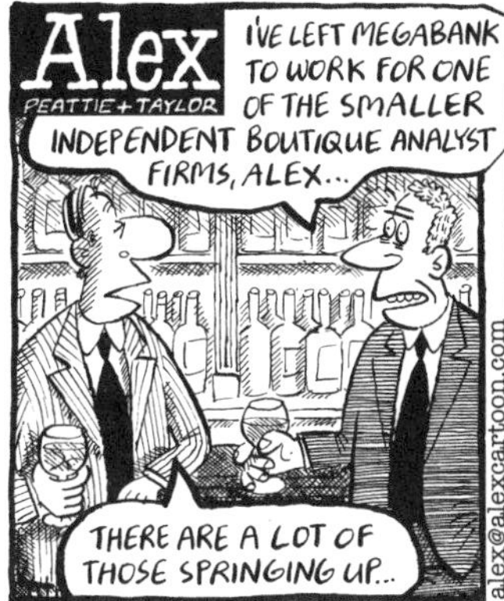
Alex
PEATTIE + TAYLOR
I'VE LEFT MEGABANK TO WORK FOR ONE OF THE SMALLER INDEPENDENT BOUTIQUE ANALYST FIRMS, ALEX...
THERE ARE A LOT OF THOSE SPRINGING UP...
alex@alexcartoon.com
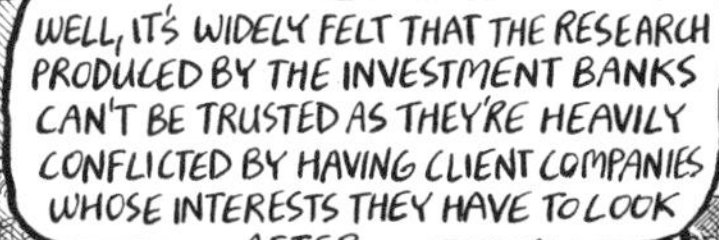
WELL, IT'S WIDELY FELT THAT THE RESEARCH PRODUCED BY THE INVESTMENT BANKS CAN'T BE TRUSTED AS THEY'RE HEAVILY CONFLICTED BY HAVING CLIENT COMPANIES WHOSE INTERESTS THEY HAVE TO LOOK AFTER...
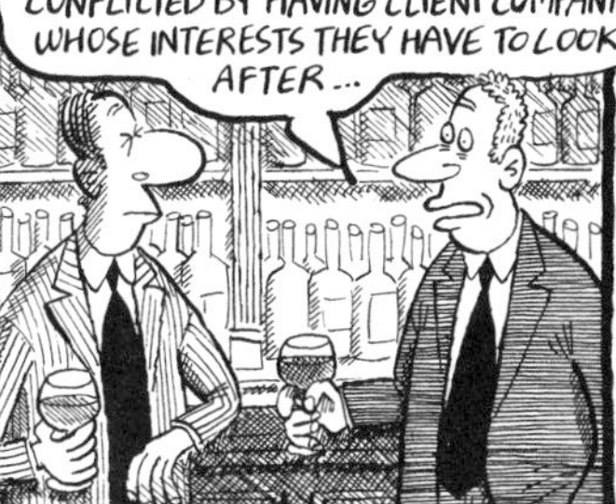
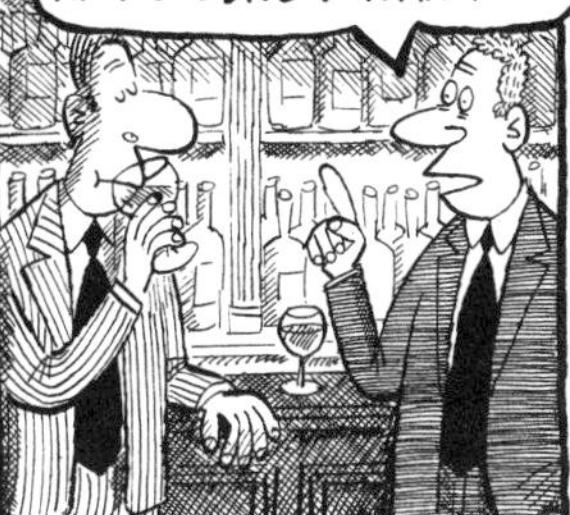
THAT MORE ANALYSTS LIKE ME ARE BECOMING FREE TO PRODUCE INDEPENDENT, BALANCED AND OBJECTIVE RESEARCH CAN ONLY HAVE ONE EFFECT ON MARKETS...
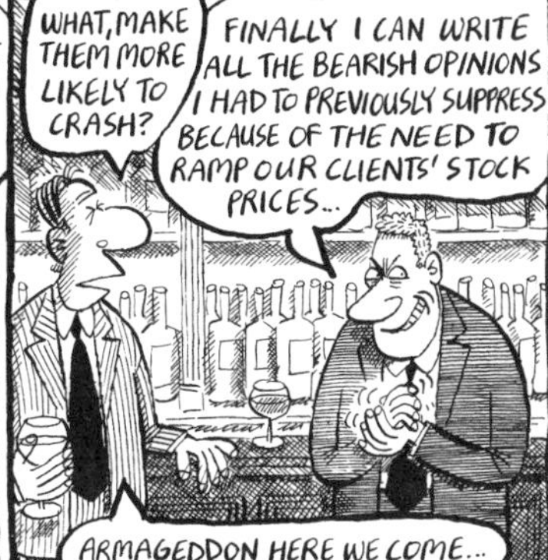
WHAT, MAKE THEM MORE LIKELY TO CRASH?
FINALLY I CAN WRITE ALL THE BEARISH OPINIONS I HAD TO PREVIOUSLY SUPPRESS BECAUSE OF THE NEED TO RAMP OUR CLIENTS' STOCK PRICES...
ARMAGEDDON HERE WE COME...

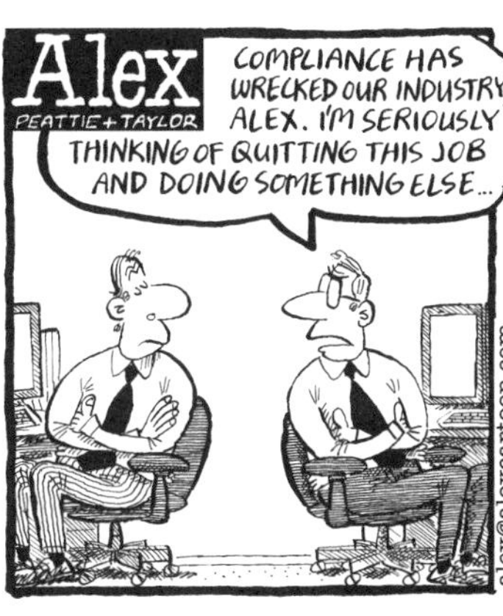
Alex
PEATTIE + TAYLOR
COMPLIANCE HAS WRECKED OUR INDUSTRY, ALEX. I'M SERIOUSLY THINKING OF QUITTING THIS JOB AND DOING SOMETHING ELSE...
alex@alexcartoon.com
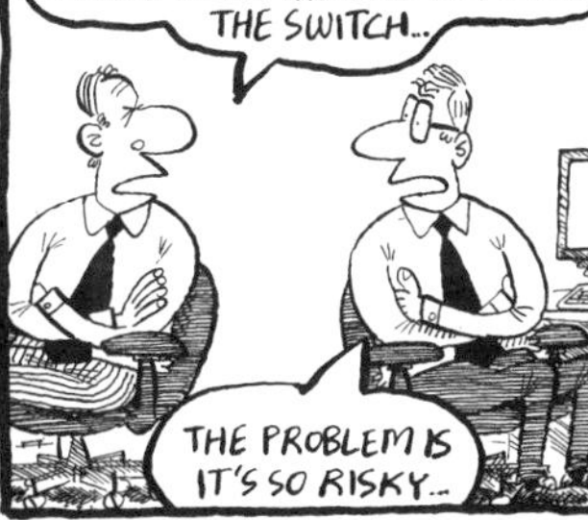
WELL, IT WOULDN'T BE THE FIRST TIME WE'VE DECIDED THE CITY IS FINISHED AND CONTEMPLATED A CAREER CHANGE. WE'VE RESISTED IT IN THE PAST, BUT MAYBE NOW'S THE TIME TO MAKE THE SWITCH...
THE PROBLEM IS IT'S SO RISKY...
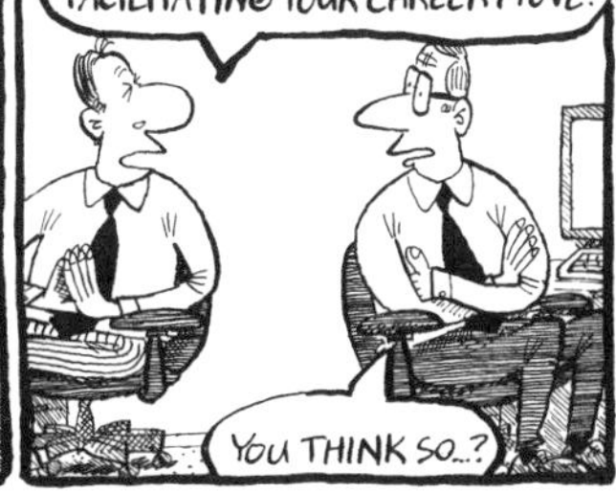
THINK POSITIVELY, CLIVE. YOUR SKILLS ARE PORTABLE. YOU COULD GET A JOB AS A COMPANY FINANCE DIRECTOR. YOU MIGHT EVEN END UP BEING GRATEFUL TO COMPLIANCE FOR FACILITATING YOUR CAREER MOVE.
YOU THINK SO..?
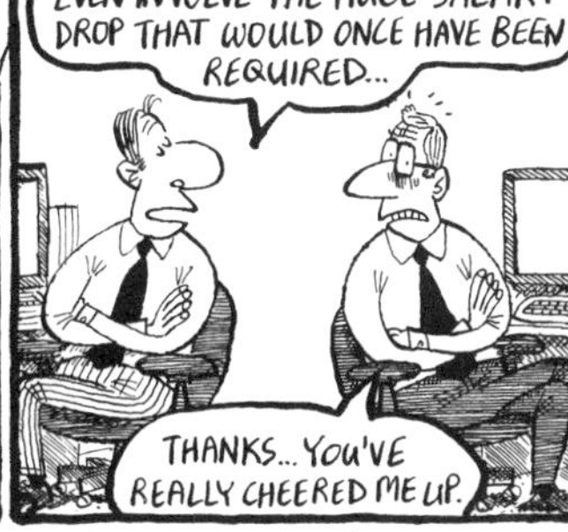
WELL, THEY'VE DRIVEN DOWN OUR BONUSES TO SUCH PITIFUL LEVELS THAT WORKING IN INDUSTRY WOULDN'T EVEN INVOLVE THE HUGE SALARY DROP THAT WOULD ONCE HAVE BEEN REQUIRED...
THANKS... YOU'VE REALLY CHEERED ME UP.

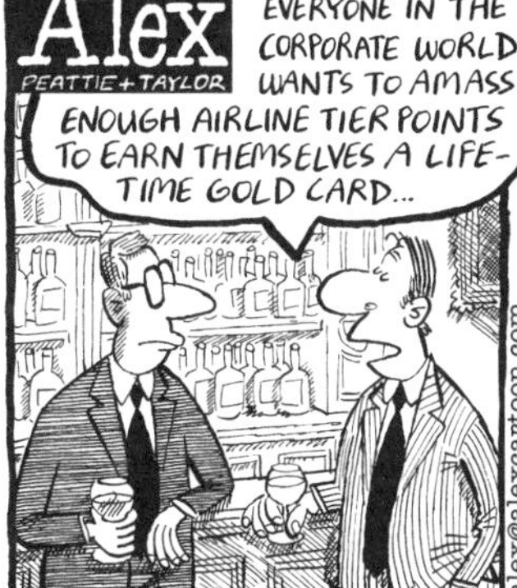
Alex
PEATTIE + TAYLOR
EVERYONE IN THE CORPORATE WORLD WANTS TO AMASS ENOUGH AIRLINE TIER POINTS TO EARN THEMSELVES A LIFE-TIME GOLD CARD...
alex@alexcartoon.com
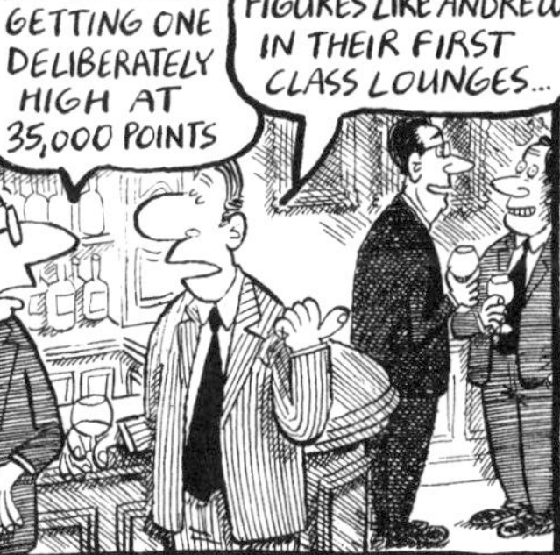
BUT B.A. HAS SET THE BAR TO GETTING ONE DELIBERATELY HIGH AT 35,000 POINTS
WELL THEY ONLY WANT SENIOR BUSINESS FIGURES LIKE ANDREW IN THEIR FIRST CLASS LOUNGES...
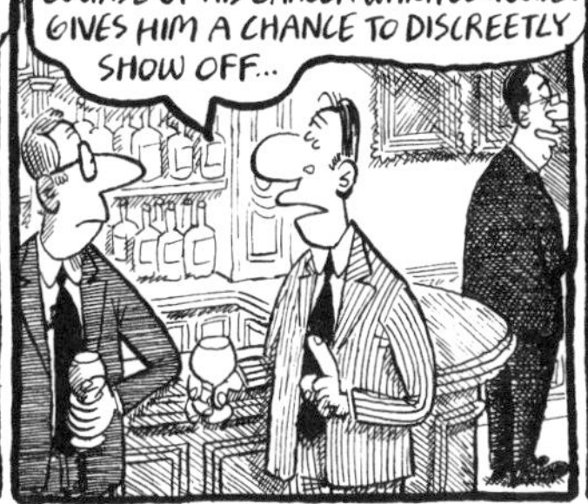
HE FLIES REGULARLY ON BUSINESS AND COULD EXPECT TO ATTAIN THE REQUIRED POINTS TOTAL OVER THE COURSE OF HIS CAREER WHICH OBVIOUSLY GIVES HIM A CHANCE TO DISCREETLY SHOW OFF...
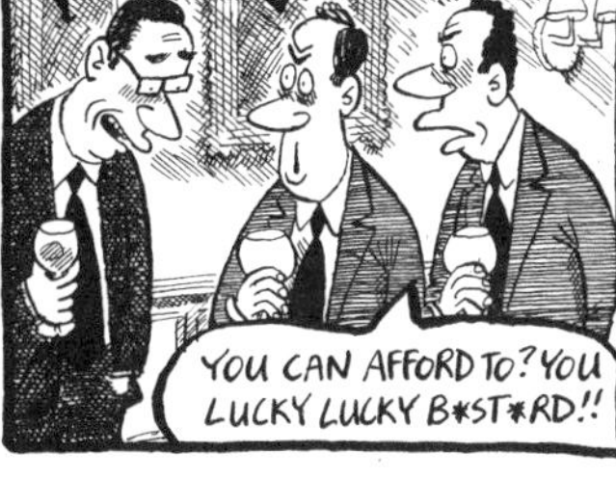
SIGH I DON'T THINK I'M EVER GOING TO MAKE IT TO 35,000 POINTS...
WHAT? BUT YOU'RE ONLY 50... THAT MUST MEAN YOU'RE PLANNING TO RETIRE SOON...
YOU CAN AFFORD TO? YOU LUCKY LUCKY B*ST*RD!!

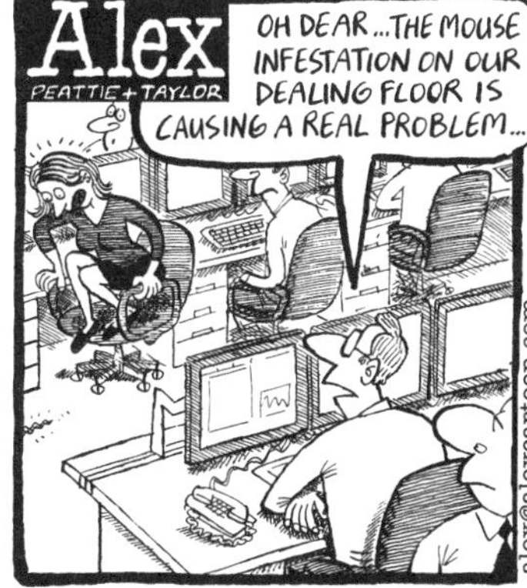
Alex
PEATTIE + TAYLOR
OH DEAR... THE MOUSE INFESTATION ON OUR DEALING FLOOR IS CAUSING A REAL PROBLEM...
alex@alexcartoon.com
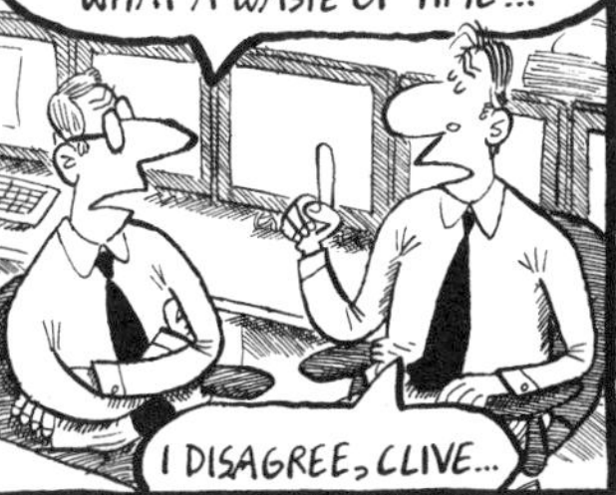
NOT LEAST OF WHICH IS THAT IT'S GIVEN THE MIDDLE OFFICE BOSSYBOOTS WHO RUN OUR LIVES THE CHANCE TO MAKE US FILL OUT THESE WORK-STATION HYGIENE ASSESSMENT FORMS. WHAT A WASTE OF TIME...
I DISAGREE, CLIVE...
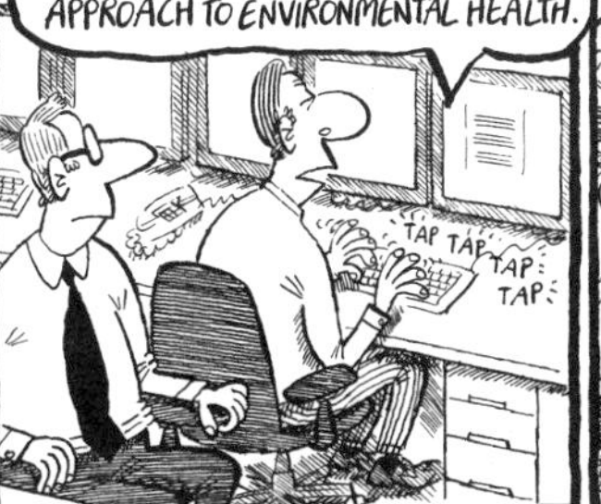
THE BANK HAS A RODENT PROBLEM AND I THINK IT'S IMPORTANT TO SHOW THAT ONE IS A RESPONSIBLE EMPLOYEE WHO IS TAKING A CONSTRUCTIVE APPROACH TO ENVIRONMENTAL HEALTH.
TAP TAP TAP TAP
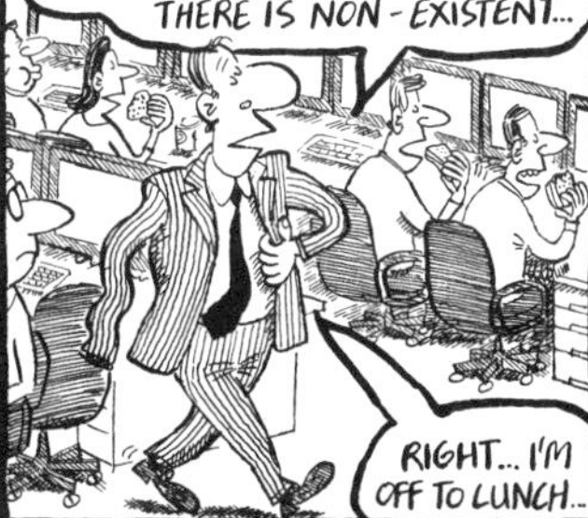
SO I'VE JUST CONFIRMED THAT I NEVER, AS A MATTER OF PRINCIPLE, EAT SAND-WICHES AT MY DESK AND THEREFORE THE RISK OF CRUMBS BEING FOUND THERE IS NON-EXISTENT...
RIGHT... I'M OFF TO LUNCH...

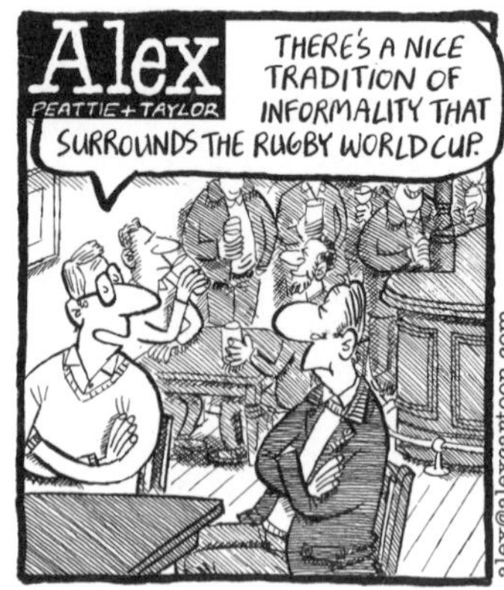
Alex
PEATTIE+TAYLOR
THERE'S A NICE TRADITION OF INFORMALITY THAT SURROUNDS THE RUGBY WORLD CUP.
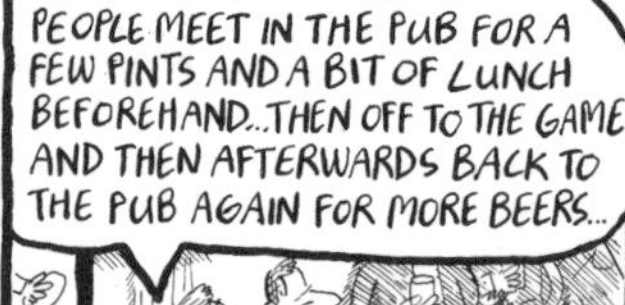
PEOPLE MEET IN THE PUB FOR A FEW PINTS AND A BIT OF LUNCH BEFOREHAND...THEN OFF TO THE GAME. AND THEN AFTERWARDS BACK TO THE PUB AGAIN FOR MORE BEERS...
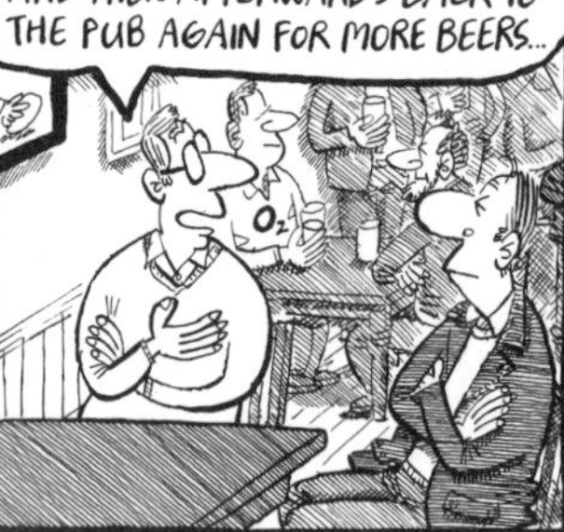
alex@alexcartoon.com
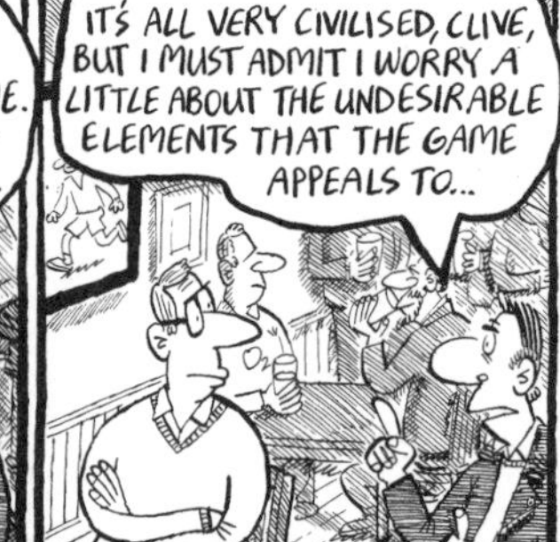
IT'S ALL VERY CIVILISED, CLIVE, BUT I MUST ADMIT I WORRY A LITTLE ABOUT THE UNDESIRABLE ELEMENTS THAT THE GAME APPEALS TO...
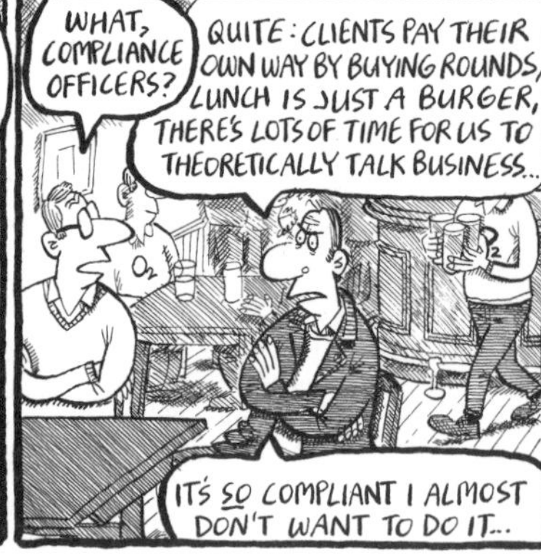
WHAT, COMPLIANCE OFFICERS?
QUITE: CLIENTS PAY THEIR OWN WAY BY BUYING ROUNDS, LUNCH IS JUST A BURGER, THERE'S LOTS OF TIME FOR US TO THEORETICALLY TALK BUSINESS...
IT'S SO COMPLIANT I ALMOST DON'T WANT TO DO IT...

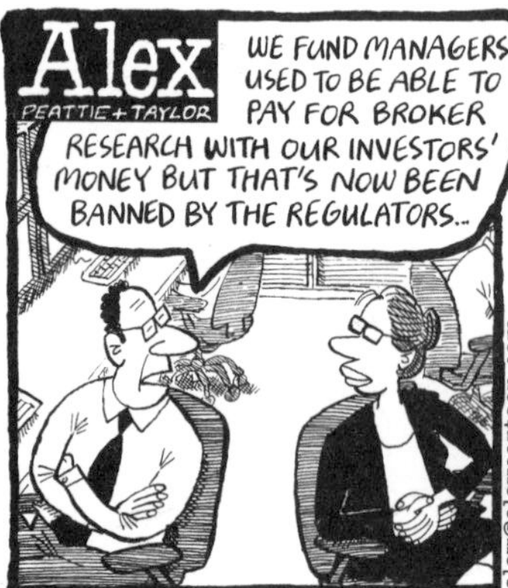
Alex
PEATTIE+TAYLOR
WE FUND MANAGERS USED TO BE ABLE TO PAY FOR BROKER RESEARCH WITH OUR INVESTORS' MONEY BUT THAT'S NOW BEEN BANNED BY THE REGULATORS...
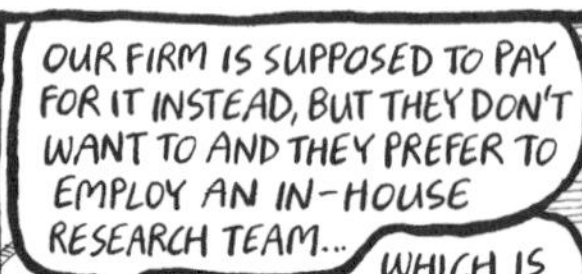
OUR FIRM IS SUPPOSED TO PAY FOR IT INSTEAD, BUT THEY DON'T WANT TO AND THEY PREFER TO EMPLOY AN IN-HOUSE RESEARCH TEAM...
WHICH IS ACTUALLY BAD FOR US...
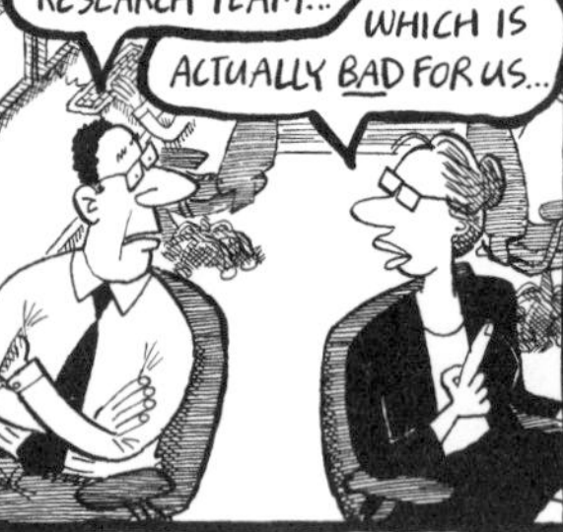
alex@alexcartoon.com
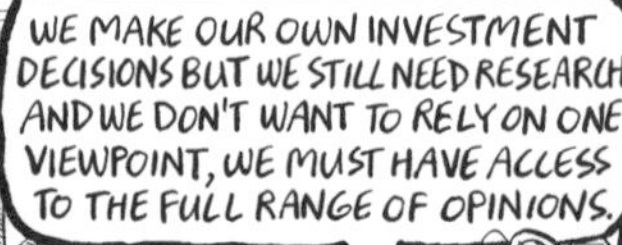
WE MAKE OUR OWN INVESTMENT DECISIONS BUT WE STILL NEED RESEARCH. AND WE DON'T WANT TO RELY ON ONE VIEWPOINT, WE MUST HAVE ACCESS TO THE FULL RANGE OF OPINIONS.
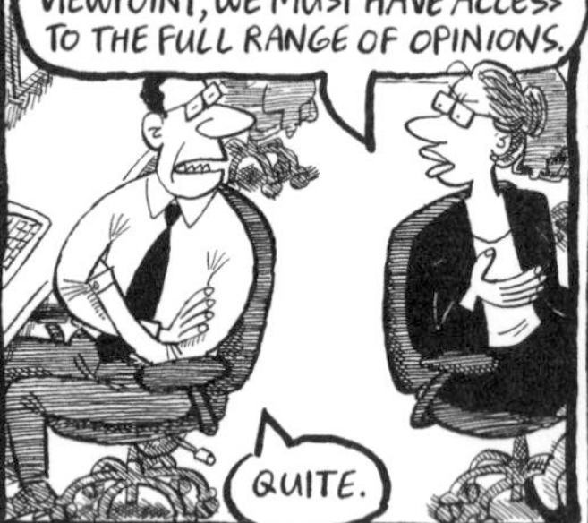
QUITE.
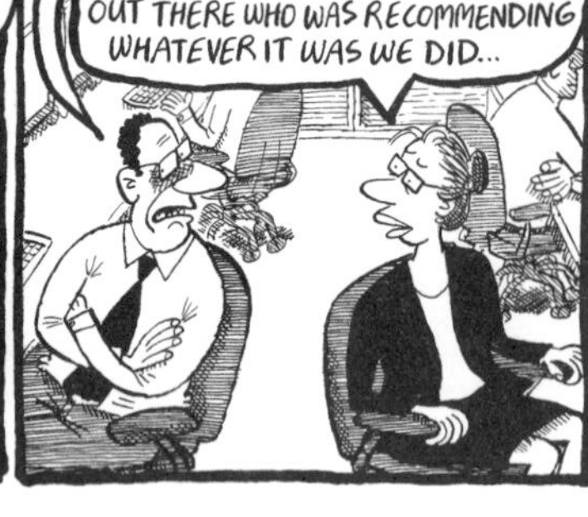
SO WHEN WE COCK UP WE CAN ALWAYS FIND A SCAPEGOAT TO BLAME IT ON...
WELL THERE'S BOUND TO BE SOMEONE OUT THERE WHO WAS RECOMMENDING WHATEVER IT WAS WE DID...

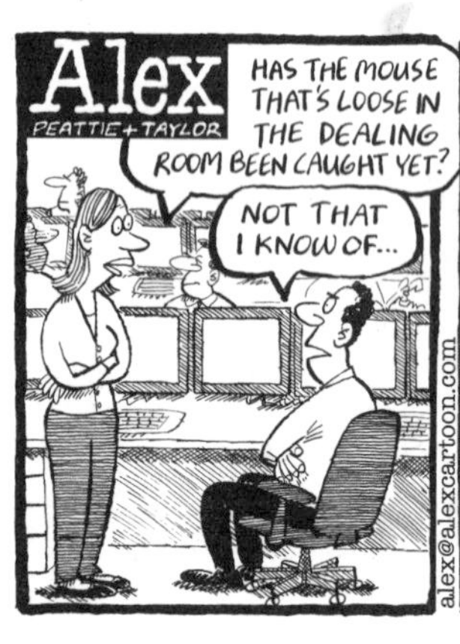
Alex
PEATTIE+TAYLOR
HAS THE MOUSE THAT'S LOOSE IN THE DEALING ROOM BEEN CAUGHT YET?
NOT THAT I KNOW OF...
alex@alexcartoon.com
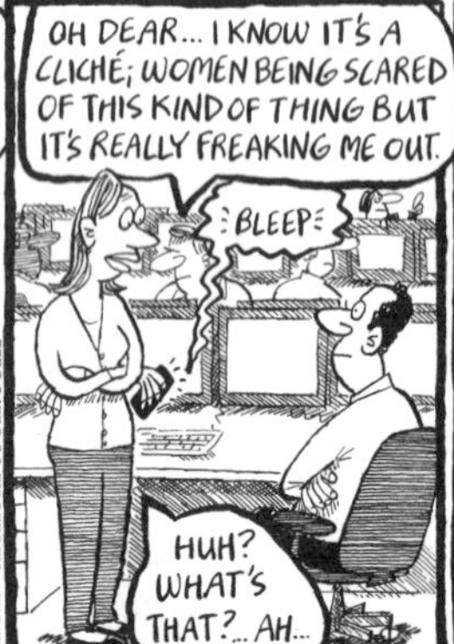
OH DEAR... I KNOW IT'S A CLICHÉ; WOMEN BEING SCARED OF THIS KIND OF THING BUT IT'S REALLY FREAKING ME OUT.
BLEEP
HUH? WHAT'S THAT?... AH...
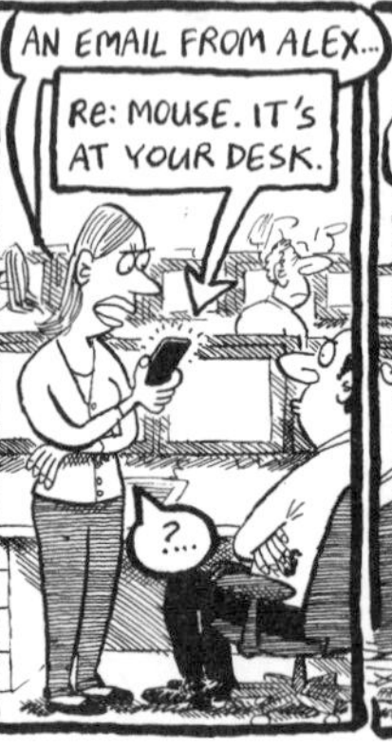
AN EMAIL FROM ALEX...
Re: MOUSE. IT'S AT YOUR DESK.
?...
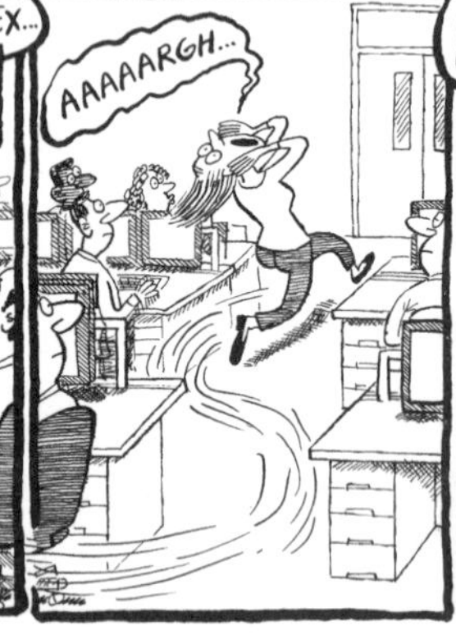
AAAAARGH...
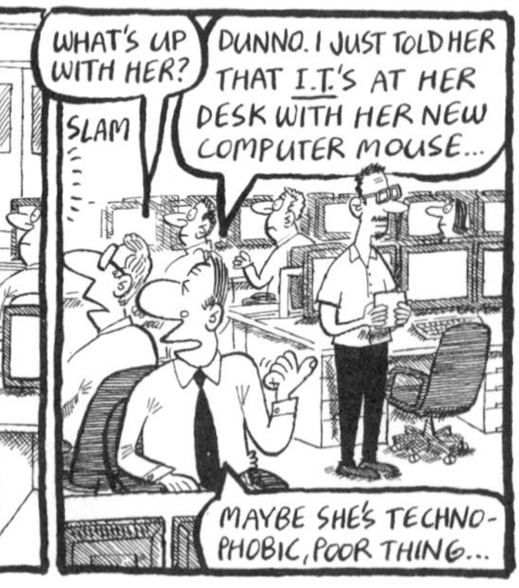
WHAT'S UP WITH HER?
SLAM
DUNNO. I JUST TOLD HER THAT I.T.'S AT HER DESK WITH HER NEW COMPUTER MOUSE...
MAYBE SHE'S TECHNO-PHOBIC, POOR THING...

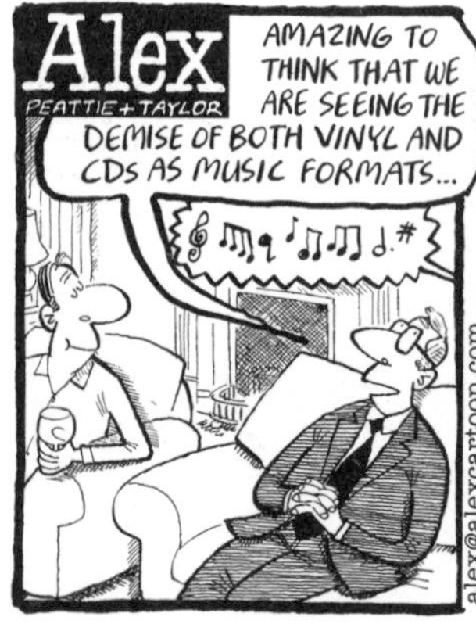
Alex
PEATTIE+TAYLOR
AMAZING TO THINK THAT WE ARE SEEING THE DEMISE OF BOTH VINYL AND CDs AS MUSIC FORMATS...
alex@alexcartoon.com
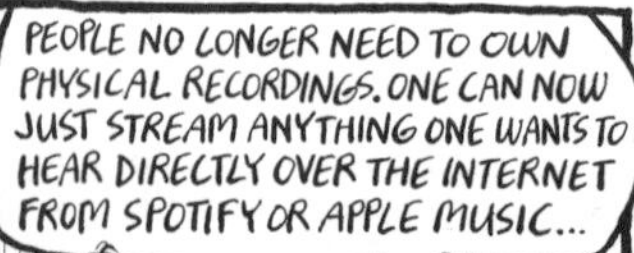
PEOPLE NO LONGER NEED TO OWN PHYSICAL RECORDINGS. ONE CAN NOW JUST STREAM ANYTHING ONE WANTS TO HEAR DIRECTLY OVER THE INTERNET FROM SPOTIFY OR APPLE MUSIC...
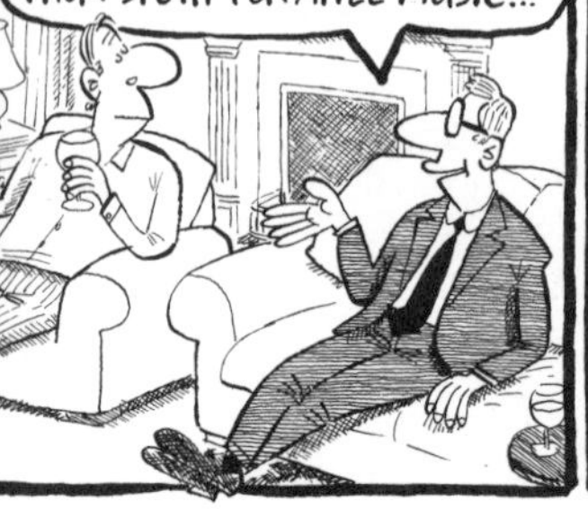
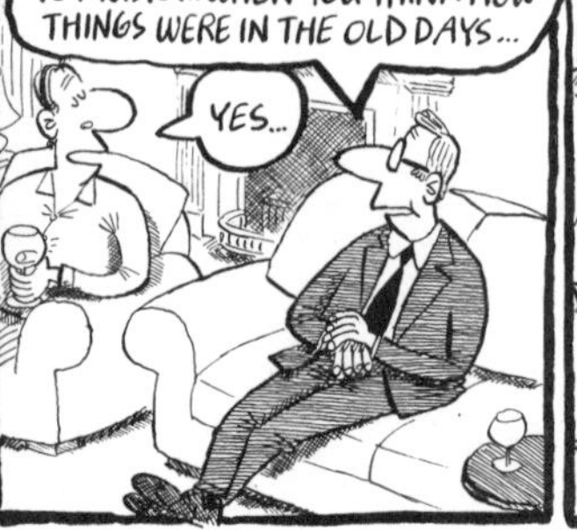
IT'S SO MUCH SIMPLER AND MORE PRACTICAL. IT'S REALLY LIBERATED THE WHOLE EXPERIENCE OF LISTENING TO MUSIC... WHEN YOU THINK HOW THINGS WERE IN THE OLD DAYS...
YES...
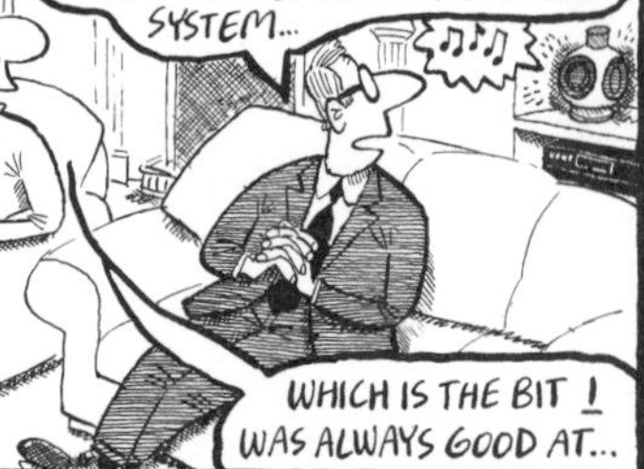
WHEN ONE WAS OBLIGED TO HAVE A COOL, ECLECTIC RECORD COLLECTION TO IMPRESS VISITORS TO ONE'S HOME WITH...
WHEREAS NOW YOU JUST NEED AN OSTENTATIOUSLY EXPENSIVE SOUND SYSTEM...
WHICH IS THE BIT I WAS ALWAYS GOOD AT...

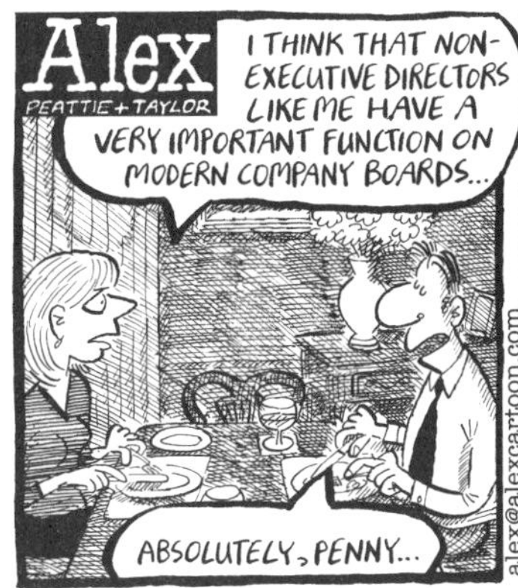
Alex
PEATTIE + TAYLOR
I THINK THAT NON-EXECUTIVE DIRECTORS LIKE ME HAVE A VERY IMPORTANT FUNCTION ON MODERN COMPANY BOARDS...
ABSOLUTELY, PENNY...
alex@alexcartoon.com
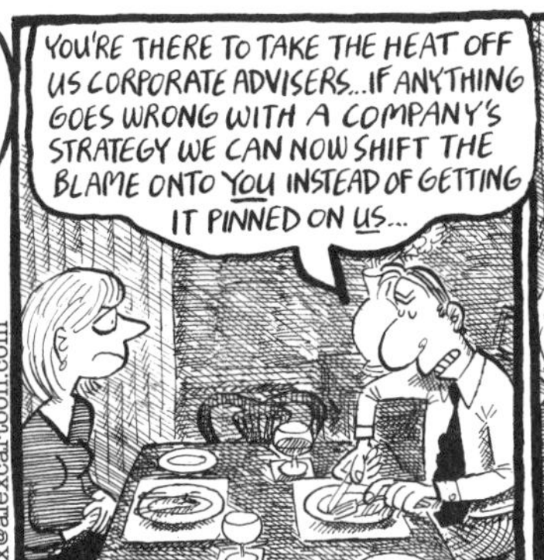
YOU'RE THERE TO TAKE THE HEAT OFF US CORPORATE ADVISERS...IF ANYTHING GOES WRONG WITH A COMPANY'S STRATEGY WE CAN NOW SHIFT THE BLAME ONTO YOU INSTEAD OF GETTING IT PINNED ON US...
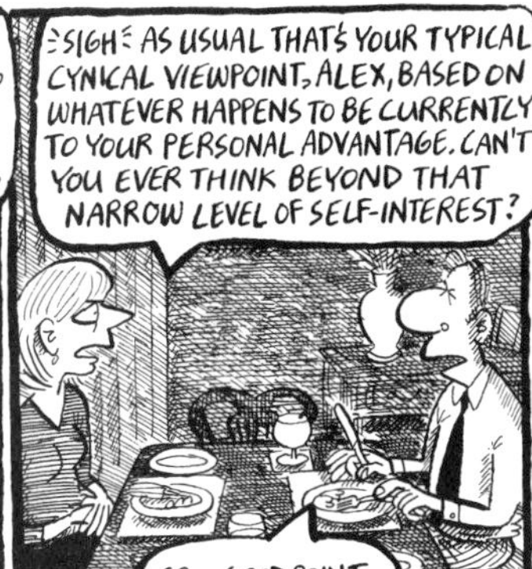
:SIGH: AS USUAL THAT'S YOUR TYPICAL CYNICAL VIEWPOINT, ALEX, BASED ON WHATEVER HAPPENS TO BE CURRENTLY TO YOUR PERSONAL ADVANTAGE. CAN'T YOU EVER THINK BEYOND THAT NARROW LEVEL OF SELF-INTEREST?
ER... GOOD POINT...
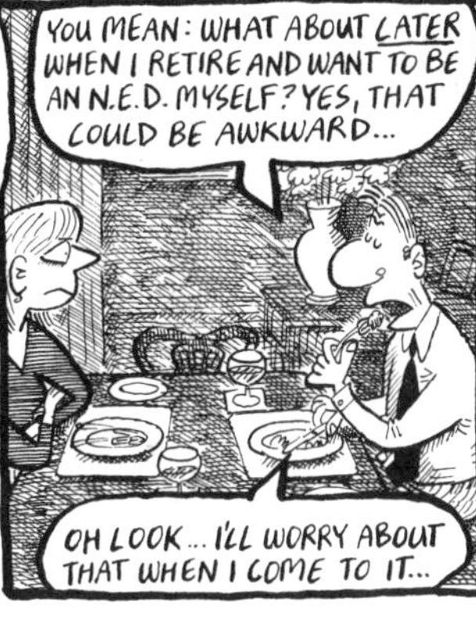
YOU MEAN: WHAT ABOUT LATER WHEN I RETIRE AND WANT TO BE AN N.E.D. MYSELF? YES, THAT COULD BE AWKWARD...
OH LOOK... I'LL WORRY ABOUT THAT WHEN I COME TO IT...

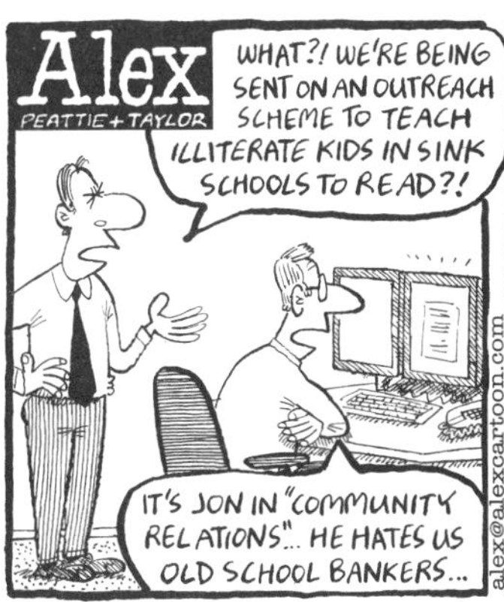
Alex
PEATTIE + TAYLOR
WHAT?! WE'RE BEING SENT ON AN OUTREACH SCHEME TO TEACH ILLITERATE KIDS IN SINK SCHOOLS TO READ?!
IT'S JON IN "COMMUNITY RELATIONS"... HE HATES US OLD SCHOOL BANKERS...
alex@alexcartoon.com
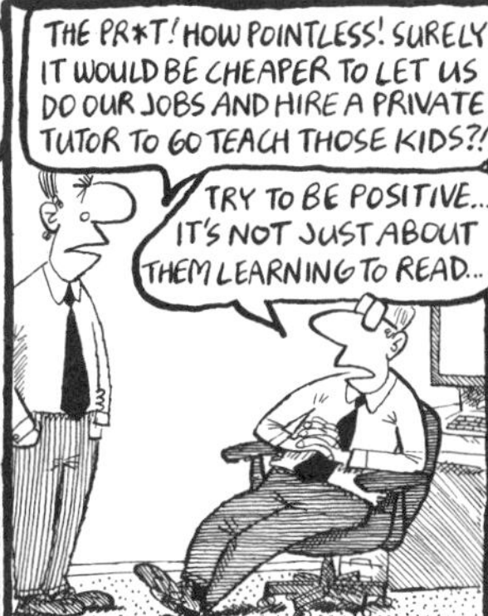
THE PR*T! HOW POINTLESS! SURELY IT WOULD BE CHEAPER TO LET US DO OUR JOBS AND HIRE A PRIVATE TUTOR TO GO TEACH THOSE KIDS?!
TRY TO BE POSITIVE... IT'S NOT JUST ABOUT THEM LEARNING TO READ...
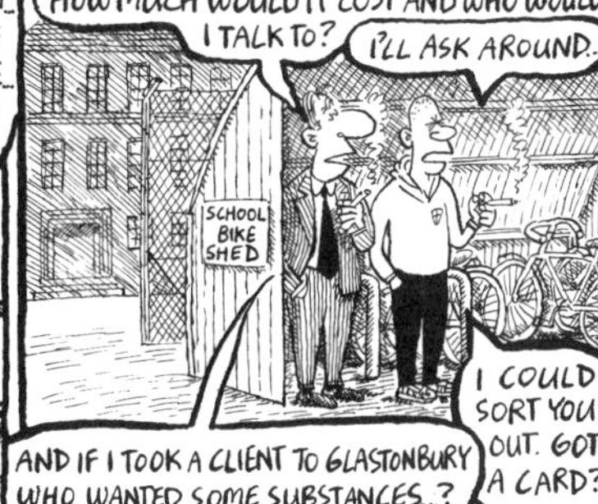
IT'S ABOUT CREATING LINKS BETWEEN DIFFERENT SECTORS OF SOCIETY AND FACILITATING OPPORTUNITIES FOR THEM... MANY OF THESE KIDS HAVE NO ROLE MODELS OTHER THAN GANG CULTURE... IT'S ABOUT ALLOWING THE RIGHT SORT OF CONTACTS TO BE MADE...
?
ER, IF I WANTED SOMEONE - A BANK COMMUNITY RELATIONS OFFICER, SAY - TO BE GIVEN A KICKING... HOW MUCH WOULD IT COST AND WHO WOULD I TALK TO?
I'LL ASK AROUND...
SCHOOL BIKE SHED
AND IF I TOOK A CLIENT TO GLASTONBURY WHO WANTED SOME SUBSTANCES...?
I COULD SORT YOU OUT. GOT A CARD?

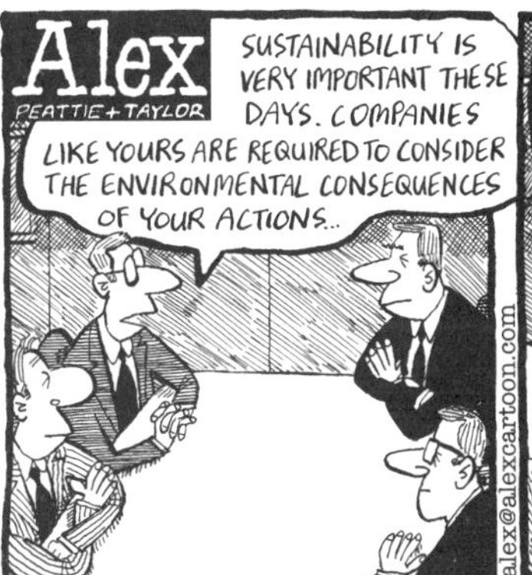
Alex
PEATTIE + TAYLOR
SUSTAINABILITY IS VERY IMPORTANT THESE DAYS. COMPANIES LIKE YOURS ARE REQUIRED TO CONSIDER THE ENVIRONMENTAL CONSEQUENCES OF YOUR ACTIONS...
alex@alexcartoon.com
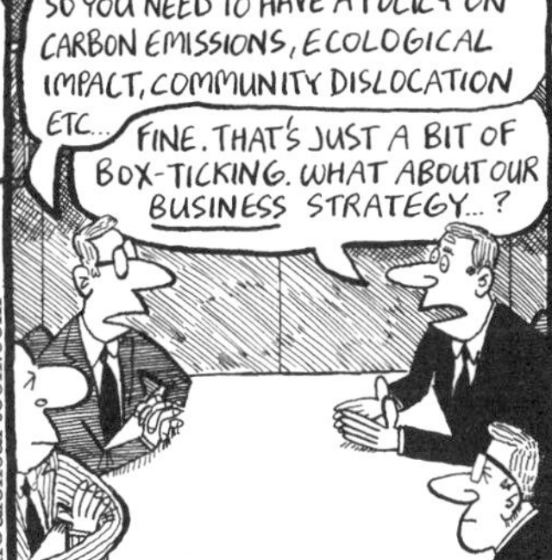
SO YOU NEED TO HAVE A POLICY ON CARBON EMISSIONS, ECOLOGICAL IMPACT, COMMUNITY DISLOCATION ETC...
FINE. THAT'S JUST A BIT OF BOX-TICKING. WHAT ABOUT OUR BUSINESS STRATEGY...?
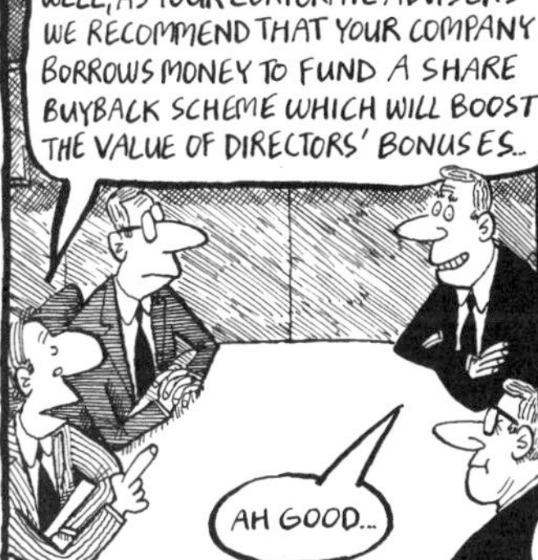
WELL, AS YOUR CORPORATE ADVISERS WE RECOMMEND THAT YOUR COMPANY BORROWS MONEY TO FUND A SHARE BUYBACK SCHEME WHICH WILL BOOST THE VALUE OF DIRECTORS' BONUSES...
AH GOOD...
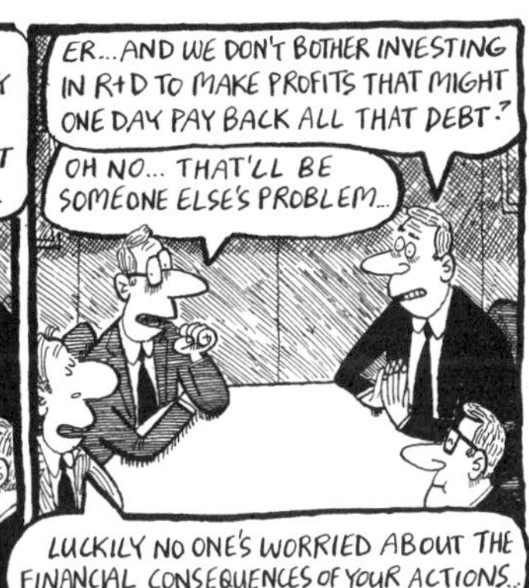
ER... AND WE DON'T BOTHER INVESTING IN R+D TO MAKE PROFITS THAT MIGHT ONE DAY PAY BACK ALL THAT DEBT?
OH NO... THAT'LL BE SOMEONE ELSE'S PROBLEM...
LUCKILY NO ONE'S WORRIED ABOUT THE FINANCIAL CONSEQUENCES OF YOUR ACTIONS...

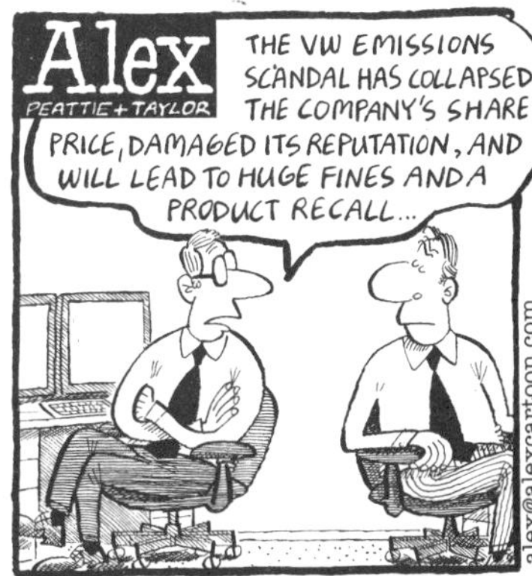
Alex
PEATTIE + TAYLOR
THE VW EMISSIONS SCANDAL HAS COLLAPSED THE COMPANY'S SHARE PRICE, DAMAGED ITS REPUTATION, AND WILL LEAD TO HUGE FINES AND A PRODUCT RECALL...
alex@alexcartoon.com
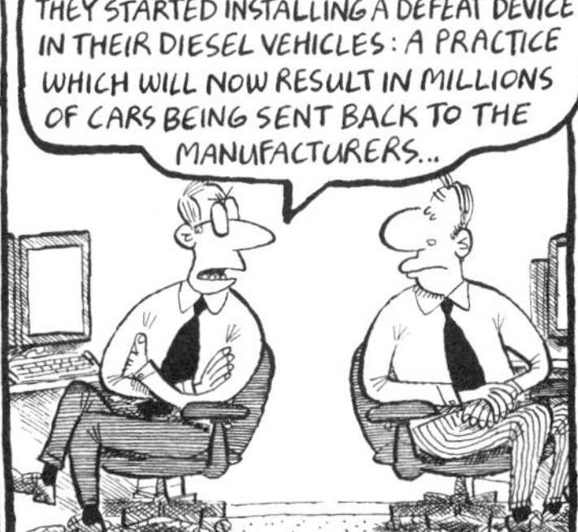
THEY REALLY MESSED UP BIG TIME WHEN THEY STARTED INSTALLING A "DEFEAT DEVICE" IN THEIR DIESEL VEHICLES: A PRACTICE WHICH WILL NOW RESULT IN MILLIONS OF CARS BEING SENT BACK TO THE MANUFACTURERS...
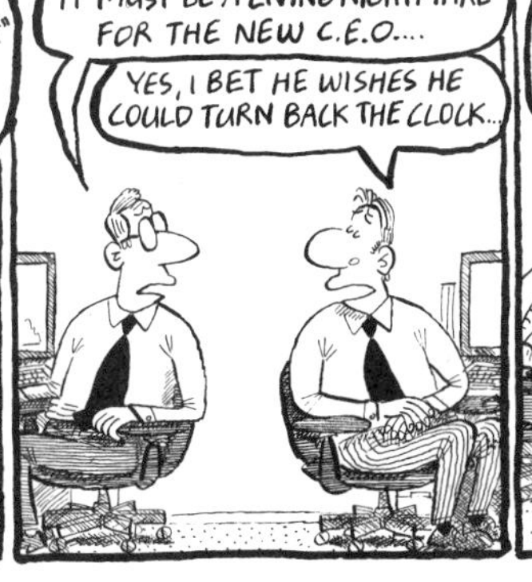
IT MUST BE A LIVING NIGHTMARE FOR THE NEW C.E.O....
YES, I BET HE WISHES HE COULD TURN BACK THE CLOCK...
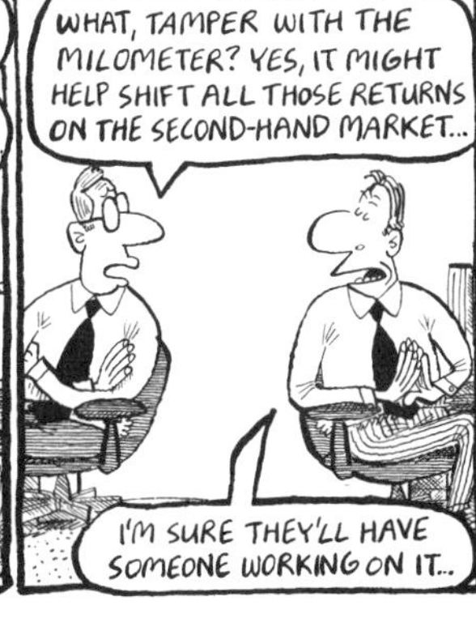
WHAT, TAMPER WITH THE MILOMETER? YES, IT MIGHT HELP SHIFT ALL THOSE RETURNS ON THE SECOND-HAND MARKET...
I'M SURE THEY'LL HAVE SOMEONE WORKING ON IT...

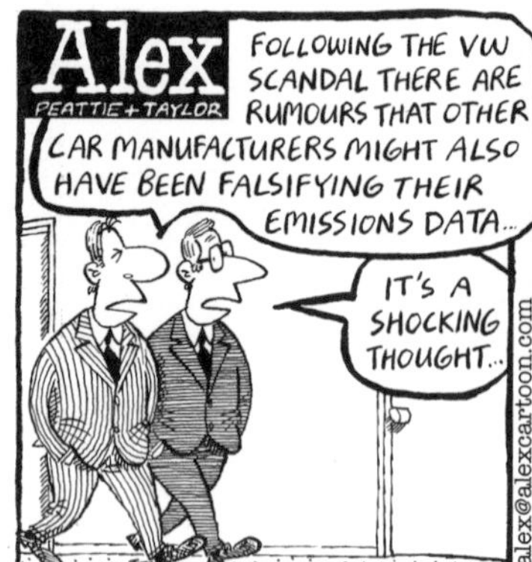

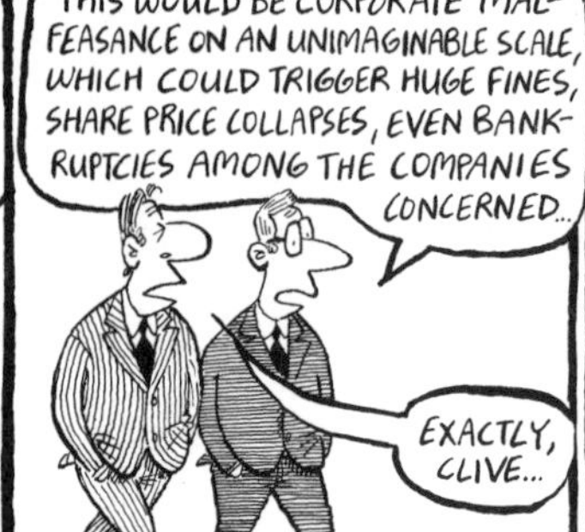

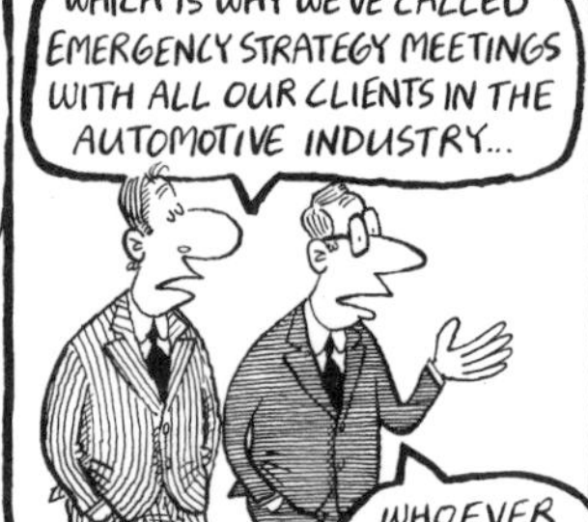

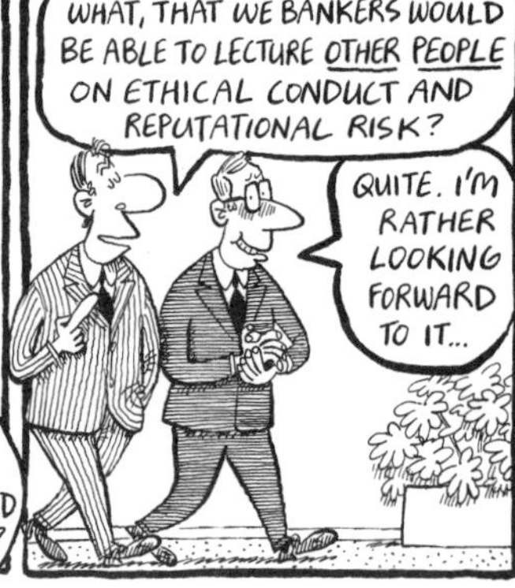

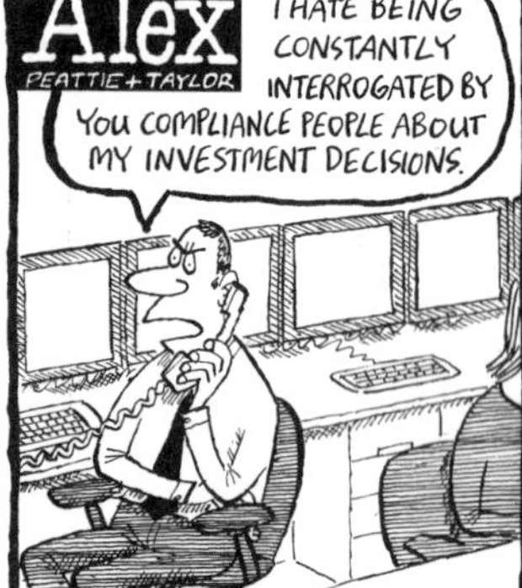

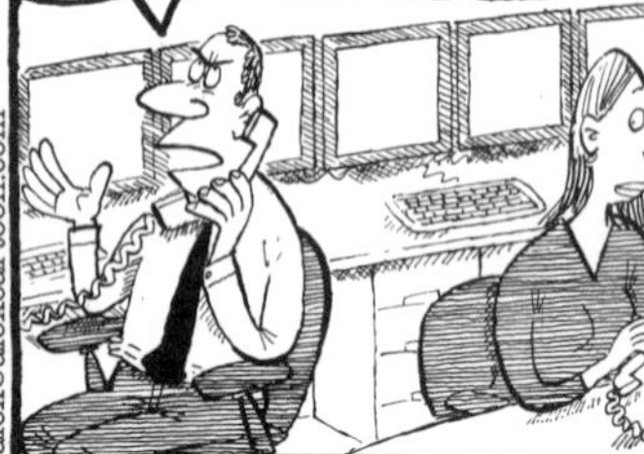

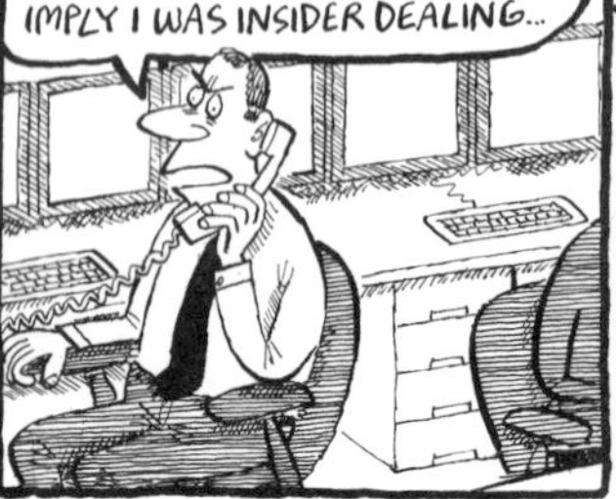

I SOLD THE STOCK... I ACTUALLY LOST MONEY
DO THEY DO THIS BECAUSE THEY'RE STUPID OR BECAUSE THEY LIKE THE EXCUSE TO POINT OUT WHEN WE'VE BEEN STUPID?
WHO CAN SAY?

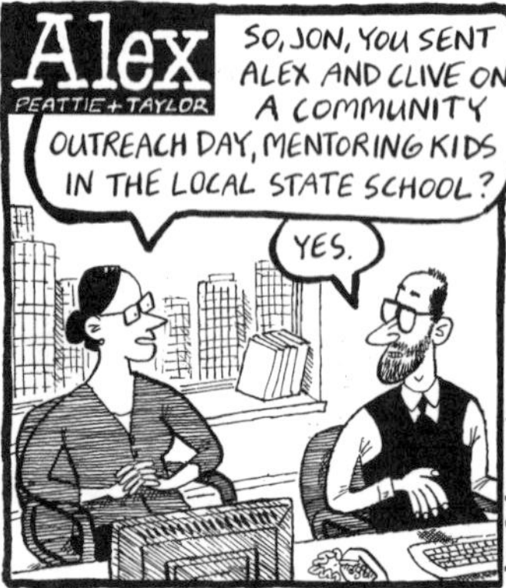

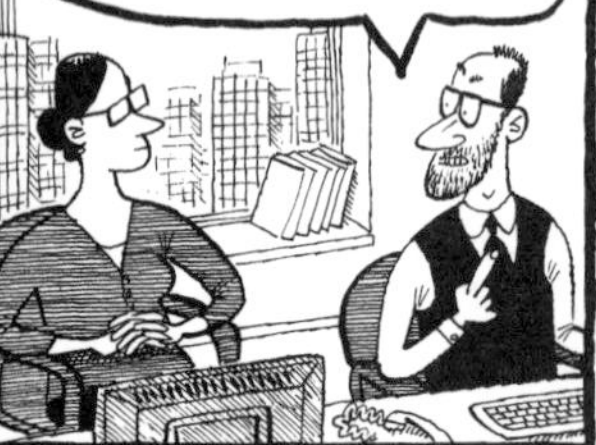

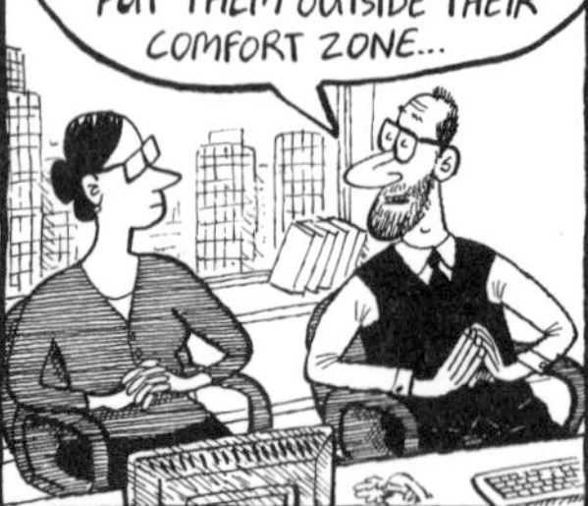

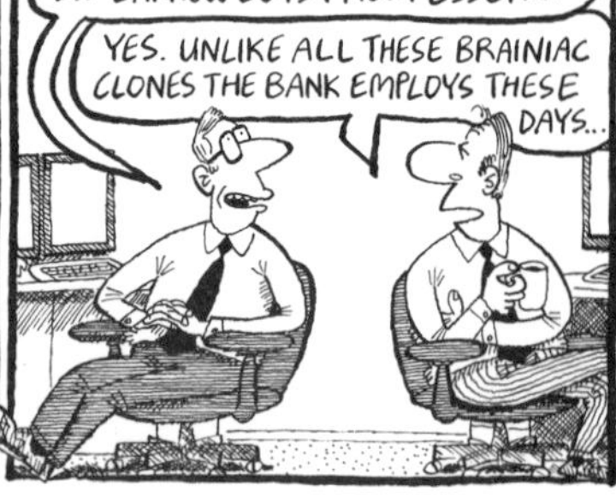

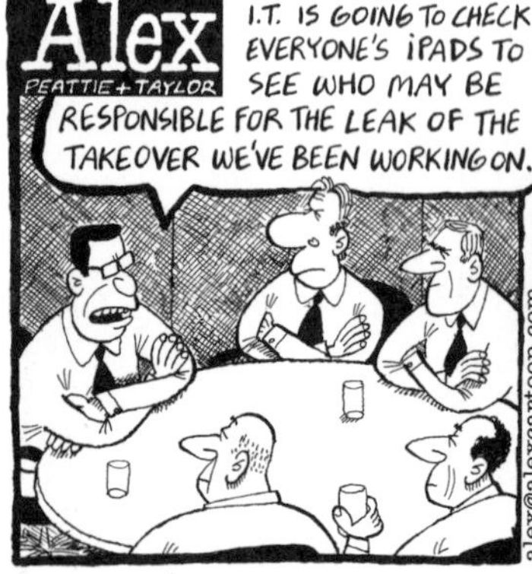

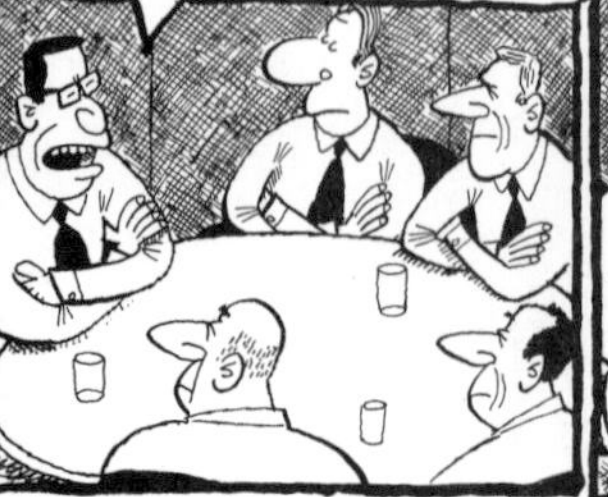

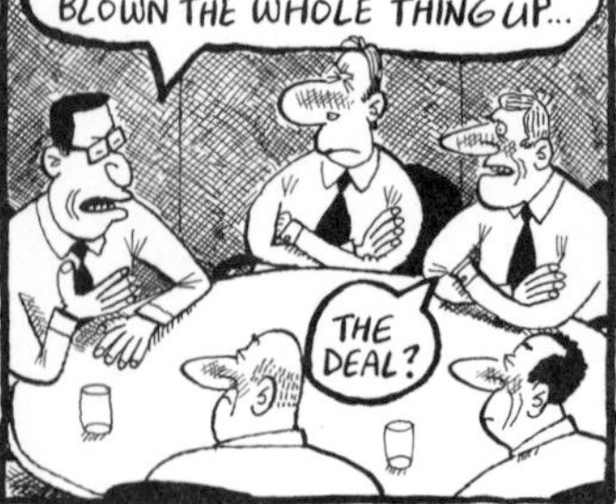

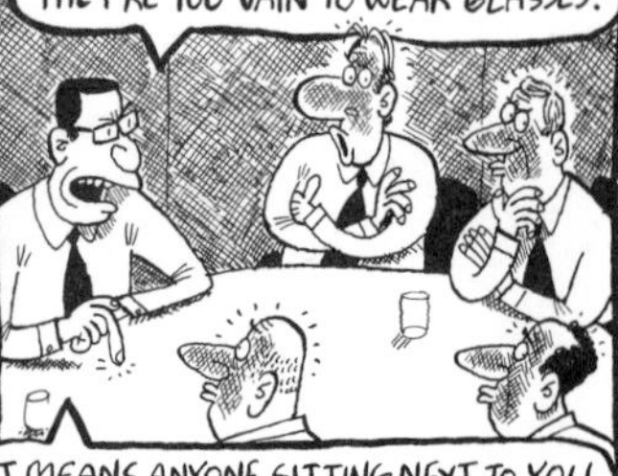

NEXT PAGE: READ ON TO LOOK BACK TO THE 1980s - THE EARLY DAYS OF CHARLES' AND RUSSELL'S CAREER AND A PIVOTAL MOMENT IN THEIR CREATIVE PARTNERSHIP...

1987 RUSSELL AND I HAD STARTED PRODUCING 'ALEX' CARTOONS FOR THE LONDON DAILY NEWS (DEFUNCT). WE'D HEARD OF THE GROUCHO CLUB BUT WE BOTH DESPISED ALL THOSE TRENDY MEDIA TYPES...

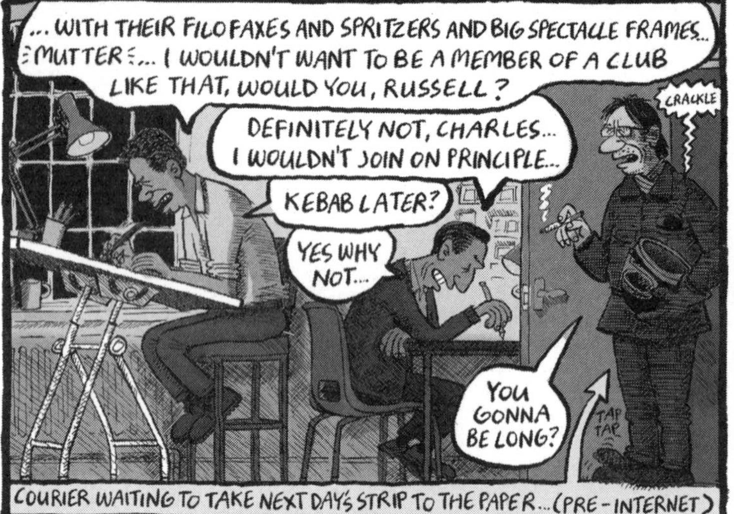

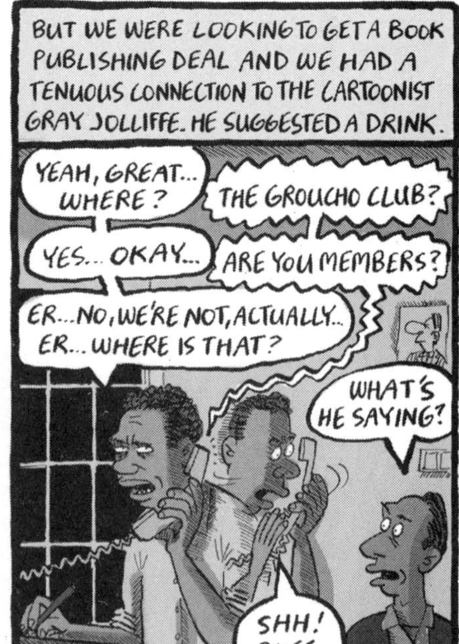

THE FOLLOWING WEEK WE WERE WITH GRAY IN THE GROUCHO CLUB: BEAUTIFUL WOMEN, FAMOUS PEOPLE STROLLING PAST AS IF THEY WERE NORMAL (WELL, FAIRLY NORMAL) AND IN THOSE DAYS – (WHICH IS TO SAY: LONG BEFORE PEOPLE STARTED SAYING "BACK IN THE DAY" WHICH CAME IN WITH "THE WIRE") THERE WERE FREE PEANUTS AND OLIVES ON THE TABLES FOR EVERYONE - REPLENISHED REGULARLY.*...

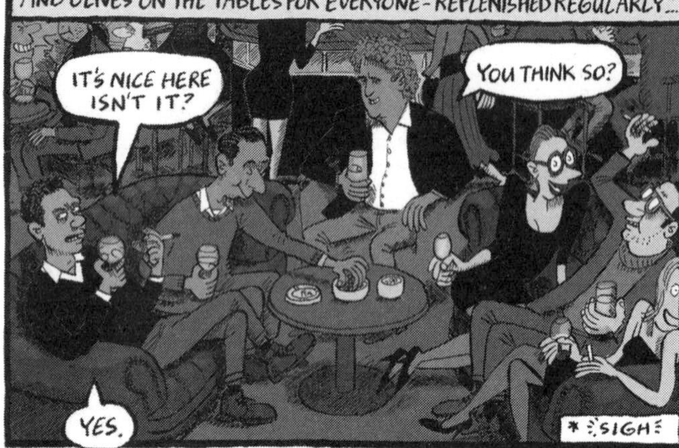

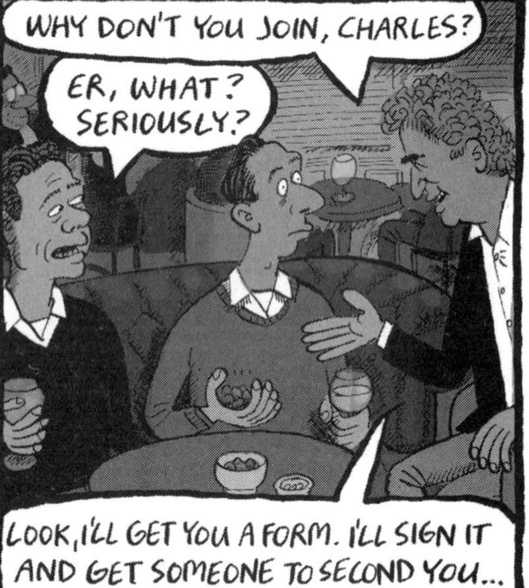

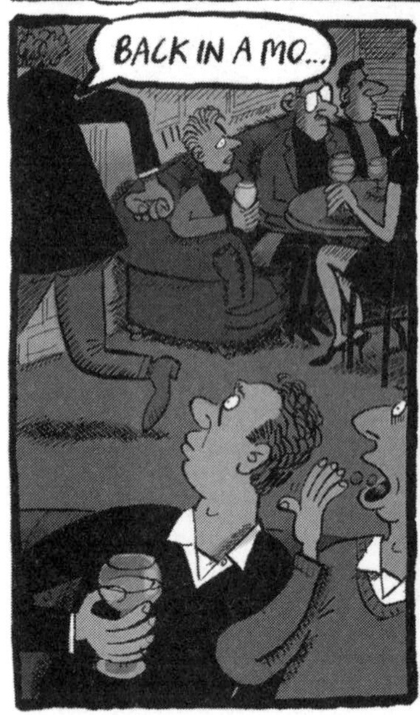

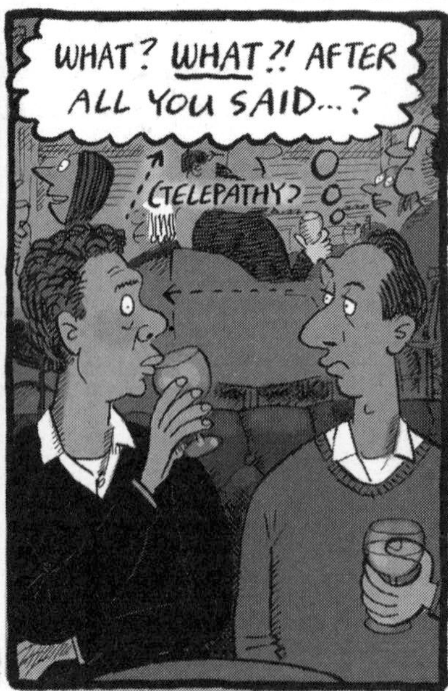

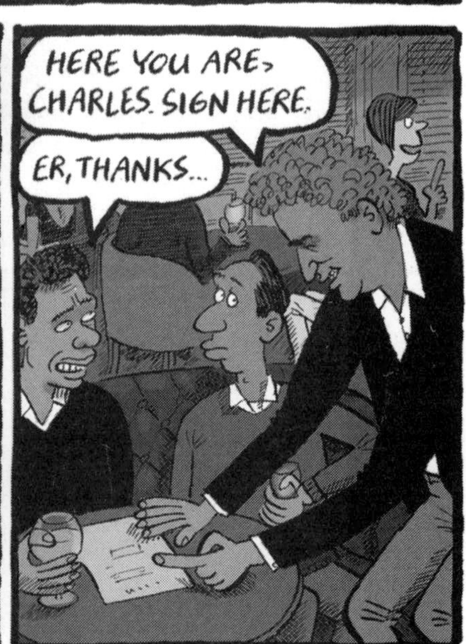

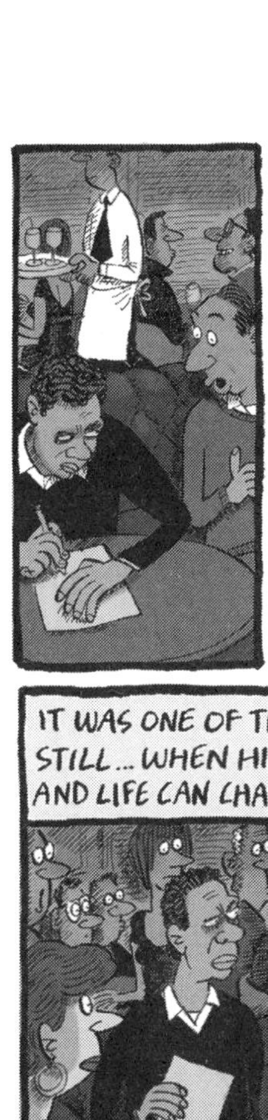
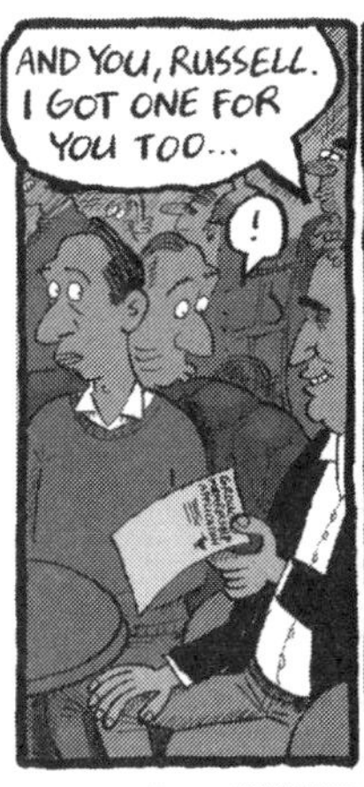
AND YOU, RUSSELL. I GOT ONE FOR YOU TOO...
!
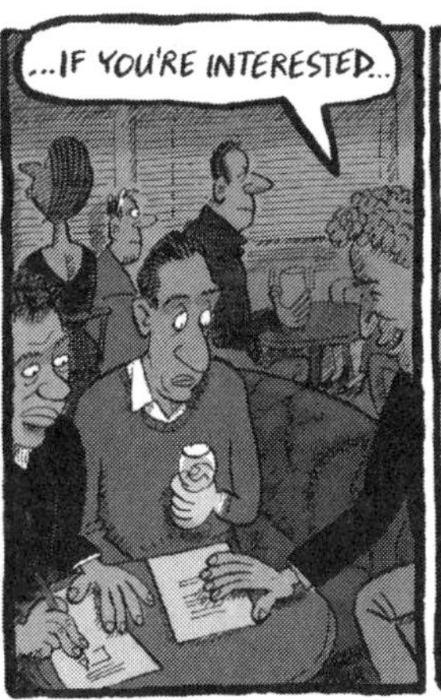
...IF YOU'RE INTERESTED...
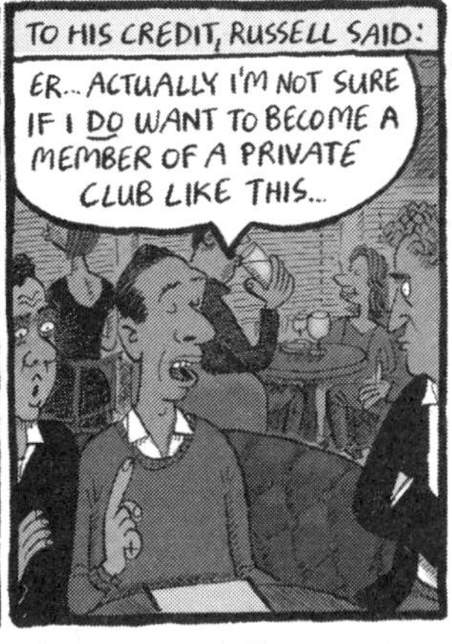
TO HIS CREDIT, RUSSELL SAID:
ER... ACTUALLY I'M NOT SURE IF I DO WANT TO BECOME A MEMBER OF A PRIVATE CLUB LIKE THIS...
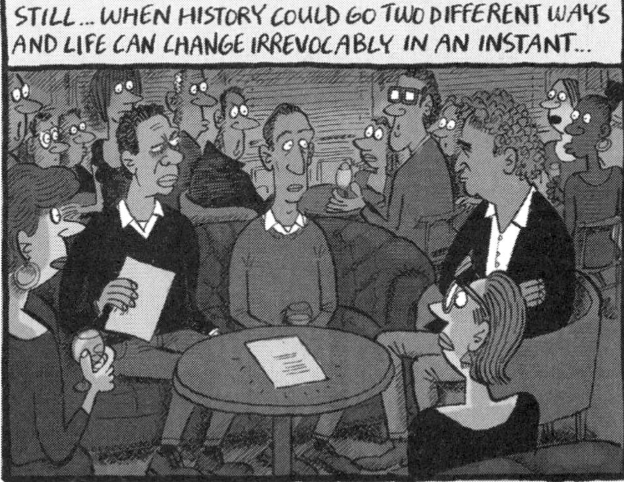
IT WAS ONE OF THOSE MOMENTS WHEN TIME STOOD STILL... WHEN HISTORY COULD GO TWO DIFFERENT WAYS AND LIFE CAN CHANGE IRREVOCABLY IN AN INSTANT...
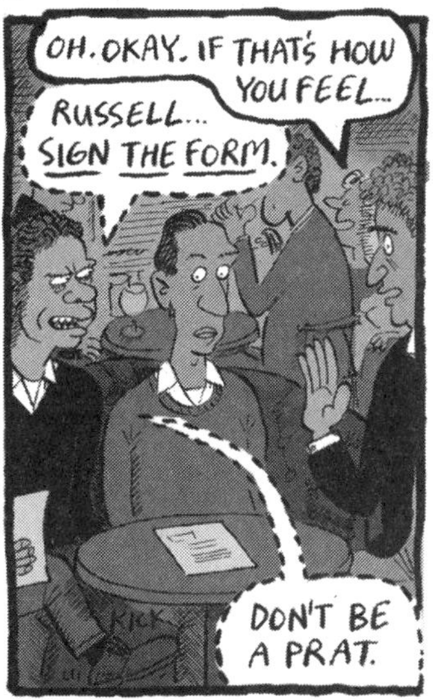
OH. OKAY. IF THAT'S HOW YOU FEEL...
RUSSELL... SIGN THE FORM.
KICK
DON'T BE A PRAT.
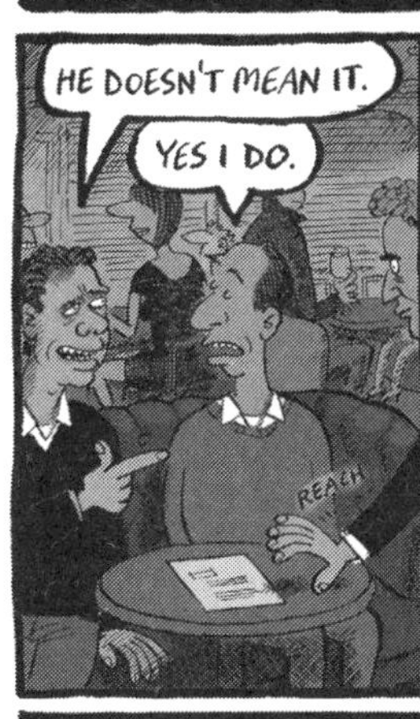
HE DOESN'T MEAN IT.
YES I DO.
REACH
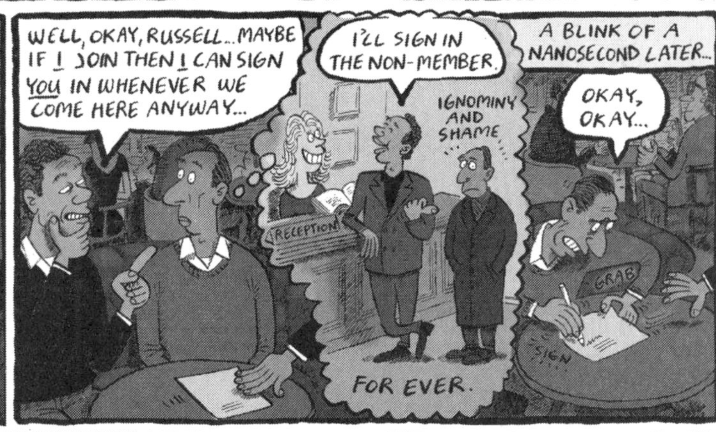
WELL, OKAY, RUSSELL... MAYBE IF I JOIN THEN I CAN SIGN YOU IN WHENEVER WE COME HERE ANYWAY...
I'LL SIGN IN THE NON-MEMBER.
RECEPTION
IGNOMINY AND SHAME
FOR EVER.
A BLINK OF A NANOSECOND LATER...
OKAY, OKAY...
GRAB
SIGN
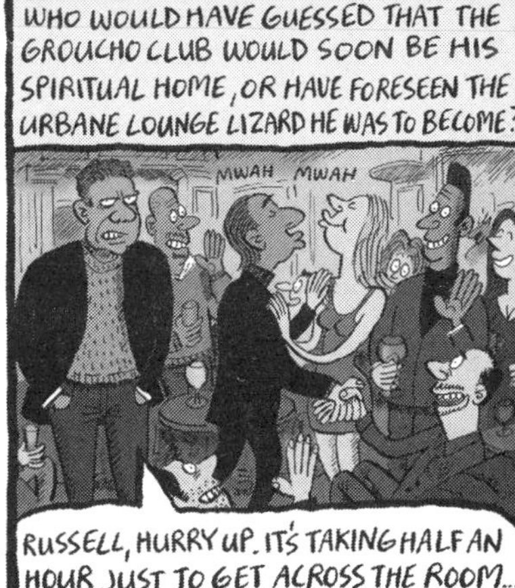
WHO WOULD HAVE GUESSED THAT THE GROUCHO CLUB WOULD SOON BE HIS SPIRITUAL HOME, OR HAVE FORESEEN THE URBANE LOUNGE LIZARD HE WAS TO BECOME?
MWAH MWAH
RUSSELL, HURRY UP. IT'S TAKING HALF AN HOUR JUST TO GET ACROSS THE ROOM...
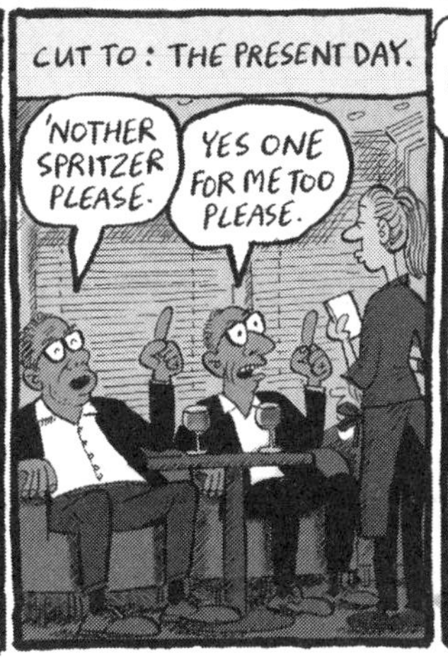
CUT TO: THE PRESENT DAY.
'NOTHER SPRITZER PLEASE.
YES ONE FOR ME TOO PLEASE.
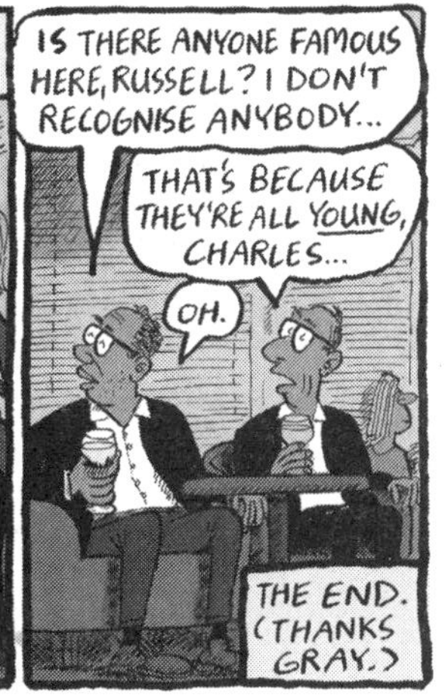
IS THERE ANYONE FAMOUS HERE, RUSSELL? I DON'T RECOGNISE ANYBODY...
THAT'S BECAUSE THEY'RE ALL YOUNG, CHARLES...
OH.
THE END. (THANKS GRAY.)

Also available from Masterley Publishing

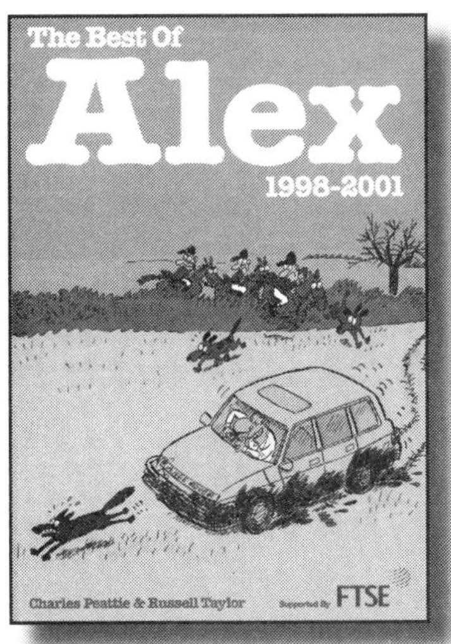

The Best of Alex 1998 - 2001
Boom to bust via the dotcom bubble.

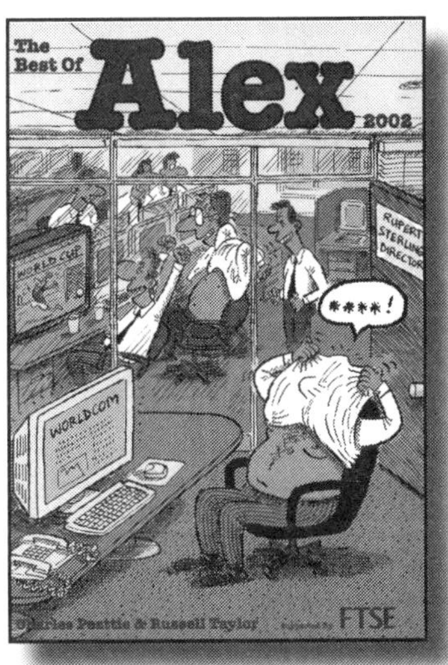

The Best of Alex 2002
Scandals rock the corporate world.

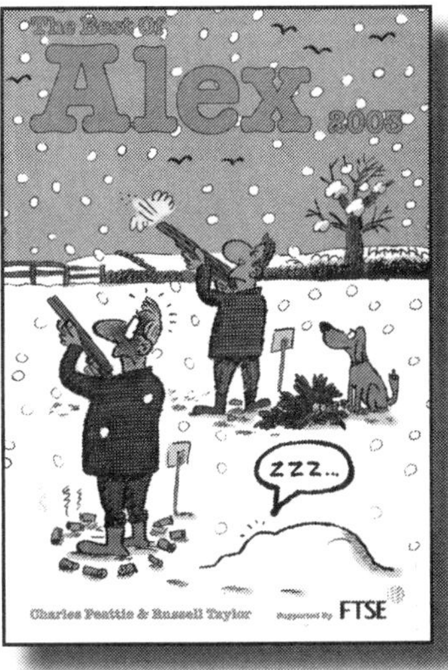

The Best of Alex 2003
Alex gets made redundant.

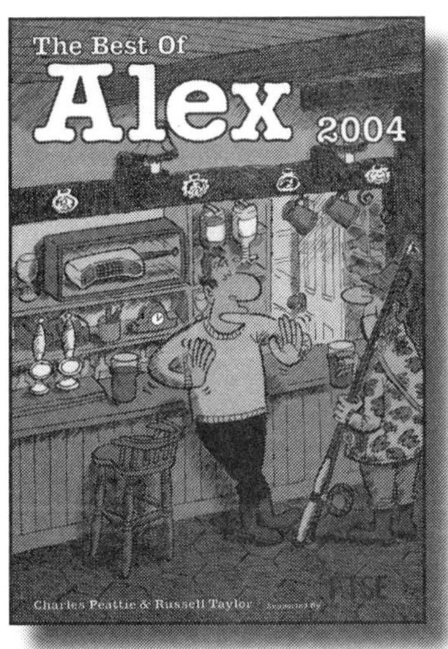

The Best of Alex 2004
And gets his job back.

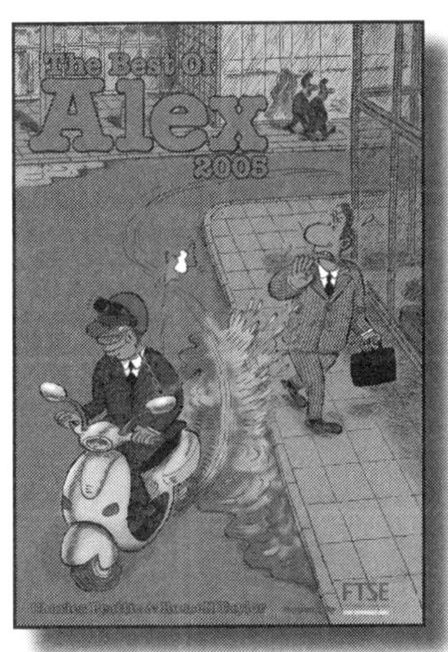

The Best of Alex 2005
Alex has problems with the French.

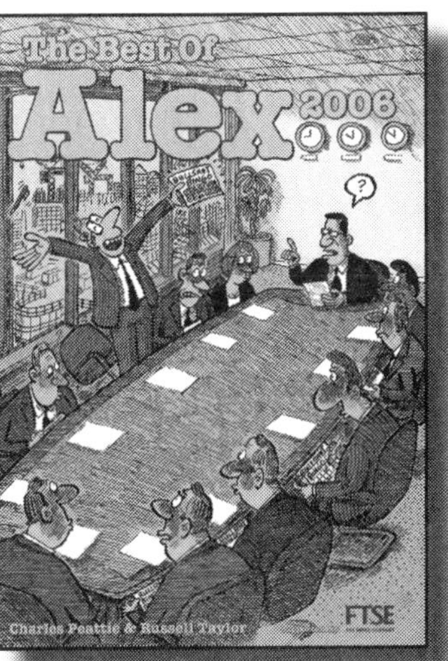

The Best of Alex 2006
Alex gets a new American boss.

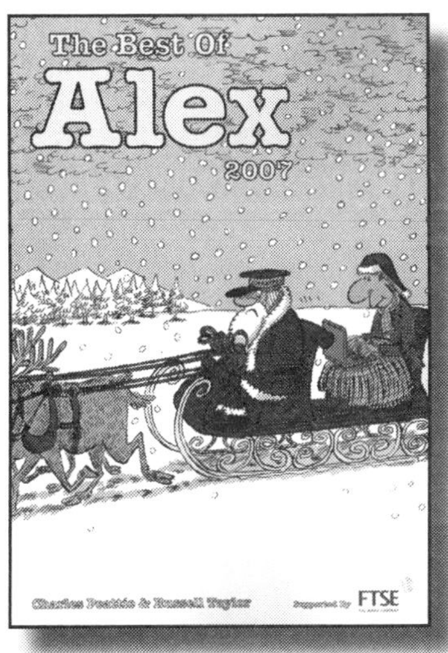

The Best of Alex 2007
Alex restructures Christmas.

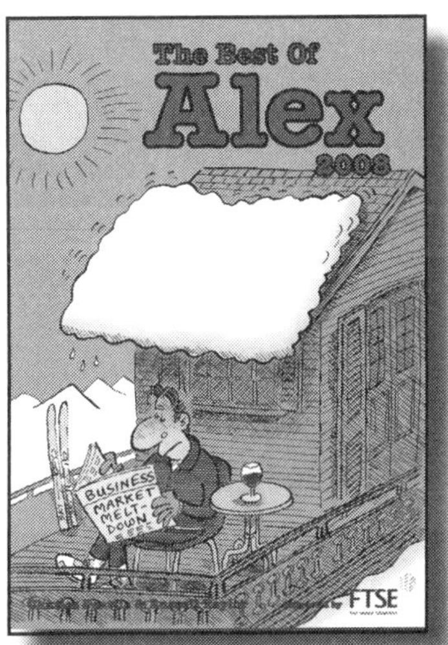

The Best of Alex 2008
The credit crunch bites

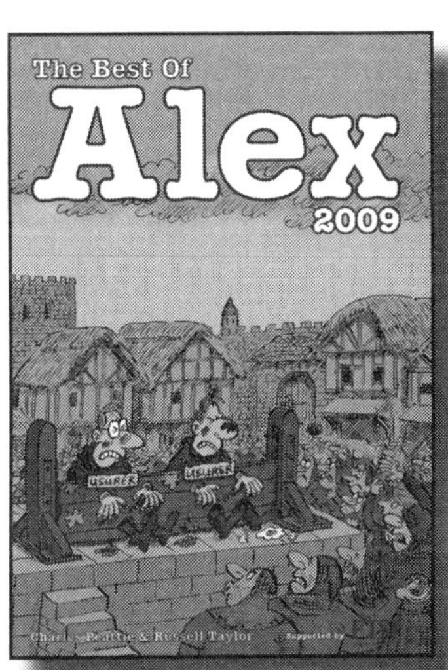

The Best of Alex 2009
Global capitalism self-destructs.

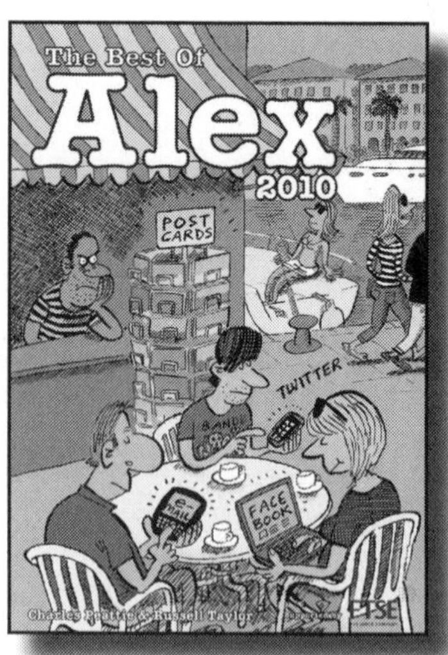

The Best of Alex 2010
Somehow the City lurches on.

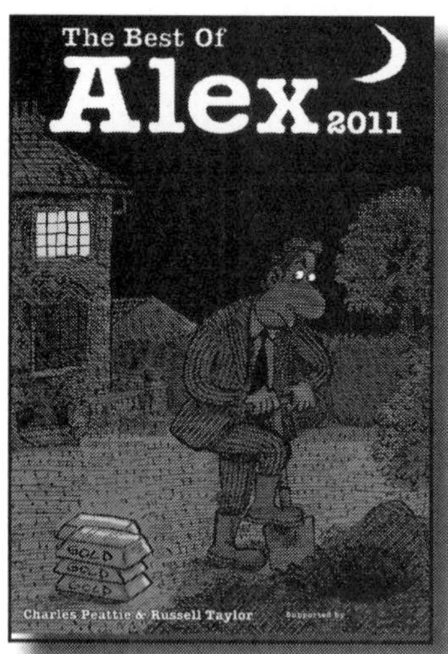

The Best of Alex 2011
The financial crisis continues.

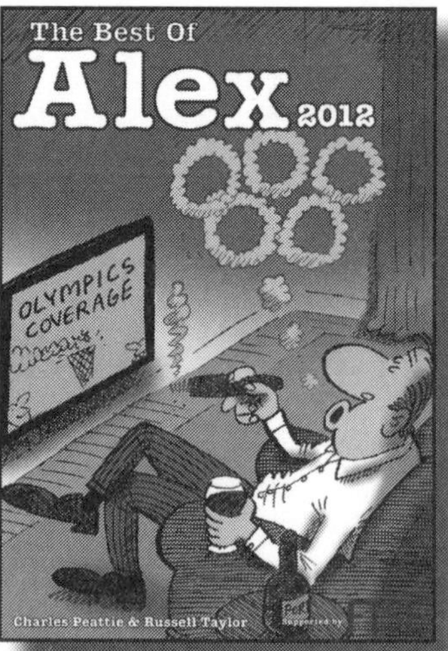

The Best of Alex 2012
The Olympics come to London.

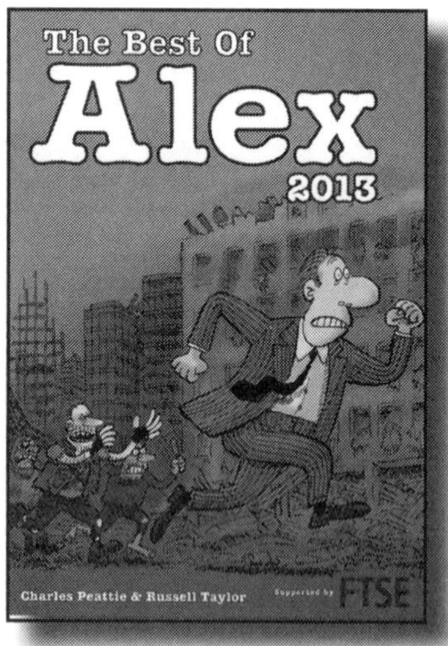

The Best of Alex 2013
It's a wonderful crisis.

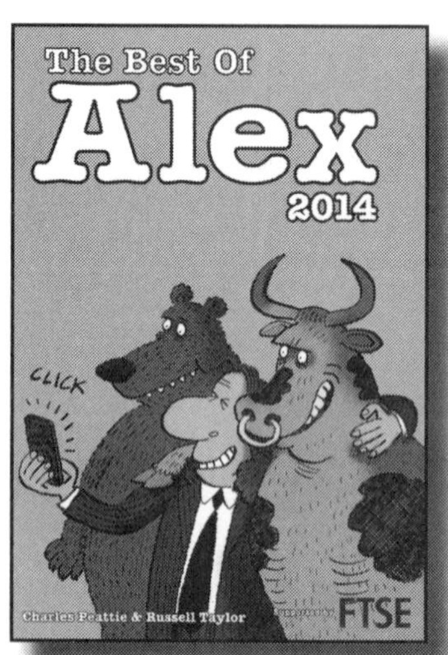

The Best of Alex 2014
The 'New Normal' takes hold.

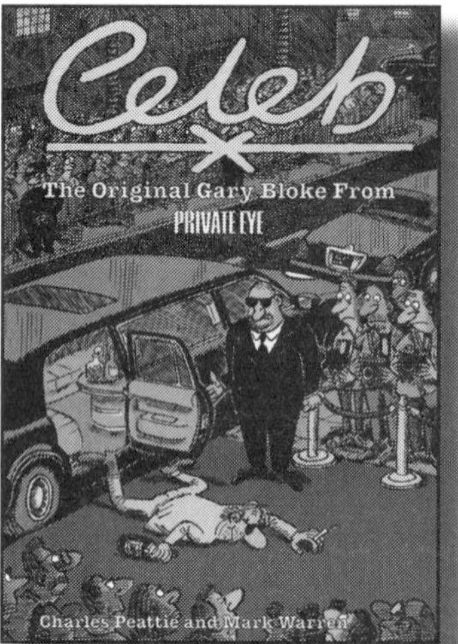

Celeb
Wrinkly rock star Gary Bloke.

Cartoon originals and prints
All our cartoon originals are for sale. They measure 4 x 14 inches. Prints are also available.
All originals and prints are signed by the creators.

For further details on prices and delivery charges for books,
cartoons or merchandise:
Tel: 020 8374 1225
Email: alex@alexcartoon.com
Web: www.alexcartoon.com
Twitter: @alexmasterley